Digital Signal Processing Using MATLAB®

A PROBLEM SOLVING COMPANION

Fourth Edition

Digital Signal Processing Using MATLAB®

A PROBLEM SOLVING COMPANION

Fourth Edition

Vinay K. Ingle
John G. Proakis

Northeastern University

Australia • Brazil • India • Mexico • Singapore • United Kingdom • United States

 CENGAGE

Digital Signal Processing Using MATLAB®: A Problem Solving Companion, Fourth Edition

Vinay K. Ingle and John G. Proakis

ISBN-13: 978-93-86668-11-0
ISBN-10: 93-86668-11-4

Cengage Learning India Pvt. Ltd.
418, F.I.E., Patparganj
Delhi 110092
Tel: 91-11-43641111
Fax: 91-11-43641100
Email: asia.infoindia@cengage.com

Cengage Learning is a leading provider of customized learning solutions with office locations around the globe, including Andover, Melbourne, Mexico City, Stamford (CT), Toronto, Hong Kong, New Delhi, Seoul, Singapore, and Tokyo. Locate your local office at: www.cengage.com/global

Cengage Learning Products are represented in Canada by Nelson Education, Ltd.

For product information, visit our website at **www.cengage.co.in**

Printed in India
First Indian Reprint 2018

Disclaimer:
This book contains link to resources which are a part of the US edition. The same may not be available with the Indian edition. The buyer needs to purchase a copy of the US edition to have full access to those resources. In no event the publisher shall be liable for any limitation or performance due to unavailability of these resources.

Contents

3 THE DISCRETE-TIME FOURIER ANALYSIS 59

4 THE z-TRANSFORM 103

5 THE DISCRETE FOURIER TRANSFORM 141

6 IMPLEMENTATION OF DISCRETE-TIME FILTERS 212

7 FIR FILTER DESIGN 291

8 IIR FILTER DESIGN 370

9 SAMPLING RATE CONVERSION 458

10 ROUND-OFF EFFECTS IN DIGITAL FILTERS 518

11 APPLICATIONS IN ADAPTIVE FILTERING 573

12 APPLICATIONS IN COMMUNICATIONS 586

13 RANDOM PROCESSES* 614

14 LINEAR PREDICTION AND OPTIMUM LINEAR FILTERS* 686

*Chapters 13–15 are available for download from the Instructor's Companion Website at www.cengage.com/login.

15   ADAPTIVE FILTERS*   769

*Chapters 13–15 are available for download from the Instructor's Companion Website at www.cengage.com/login.

Preface

Since the beginning of the 1980s, we have witnessed a revolution in computer technology and an explosion in user-friendly applications. This revolution is still continuing today, with low-cost laptop systems that rival the performance of expensive workstations. This technological prowess should be brought to bear on the educational process and, in particular, on effective teaching that can result in enhanced learning. This problem-solving companion book on digital signal processing (DSP) makes a contribution toward reaching that goal. The fourth edition continues our innovative approach of blending MATLAB®-based learning with traditional teaching to advanced DSP topics such as optimal and adaptive filters.

The teaching methods in signal processing have changed over the years from the simple "lecture-only" format to a more integrated "lecture-laboratory" environment in which practical hands-on issues are taught using DSP hardware. However, for effective teaching of DSP, the lecture component must also make extensive use of computer-based explanations, examples, and exercises. For the past three decades, the MATLAB software developed by *The MathWorks, Inc.* has established itself as the de facto standard for numerical computation in the signal-processing community and as a platform of choice for algorithm development. There are several reasons for this development, but the most important reason is that MATLAB is available on practically all computing platforms. In this book, we have made an attempt at integrating MATLAB with traditional topics in DSP so that it can be used to explore difficult topics and solve problems to gain insight. Many problems or design algorithms in DSP require considerable amount of computation. It is for these that MATLAB provides a convenient tool so that multiple scenarios can be tried with ease. Such an approach can enhance the learning process.

SCOPE OF THE BOOK

This book is primarily intended for use as a problem-solving companion book in senior-level undergraduate or first-year graduate courses on DSP. Although we assume that the student (or user) is familiar with the fundamentals of MATLAB, we have provided a brief introduction to MATLAB in Chapter 1. This book is not written as a textbook in DSP, because of the ready availability of excellent textbooks. What we have tried to do is to provide enough depth to the material augmented by MATLAB functions and examples so that the presentation is consistent, logical, and enjoyable. Therefore, this book can also be used as a self-study guide by anyone interested in DSP.

WHAT IS NEW IN THE FOURTH EDITION

- A new Chapter 13 provides a review on random variables and random processes, including bandpass processes. Extensive use of MATLAB examples makes these topics easier to understand.
- A new Chapter 14 discusses linear prediction and optimal (or Wiener) filters, preparing students for graduate studies.
- A new Chapter 15 deals with theory and applications of adaptive filters. This chapter contains easy-to-understand LMS and RLS algorithms with an extensive set of practical applications, including system identification, echo and noise cancellation, and adaptive arrays. All algorithms and applications are explained and analyzed using MATLAB.
- The coverage of lattice/ladder filters has moved from Chapter 6 to Chapter 14 for a more logical presentation of information.
- All MATLAB functions and scripts have been tested and updated so that they can execute on MATLAB-2014b version and later. Similarly, all MATLAB plots have been recreated with superior graphic elements.
- We have trimmed many included MATLAB scripts from their plotting commands to streamline their appearance and to reduce unnecessary printing. However, all scripts and functions will be made available in their entirety on the book website.

ORGANIZATION OF THE BOOK

The first ten chapters of this book discuss traditional material typically covered in an introductory course on DSP. The next two chapters are presented as applications in DSP, with emphasis on MATLAB-based projects. The last three chapters deal with advanced material in DSP and are intended for graduate studies. In order to keep the size and the cost of the book down, we have provided these last three chapters through our book's instructor website. Information on how to obtain these chapters is provided in the next section. The following is a list of chapters and a brief description of their contents.

Chapter 1, Introduction: This chapter introduces readers to the discipline of signal processing and presents several applications of digital signal processing, including musical sound processing, echo generation, echo removal, and digital reverberation. A brief introduction to MATLAB is also provided.

Chapter 2, Discrete-Time Signals and Systems: This chapter provides a brief review of discrete-time signals and systems in the time domain. Appropriate use of MATLAB functions is demonstrated.

Chapter 3, The Discrete-Time Fourier Analysis: This chapter discusses discrete-time signal and system representation in the frequency domain. Sampling and reconstruction of analog signals are also presented.

Chapter 4, The z-Transform: This chapter provides signal and system description in the complex frequency domain. MATLAB techniques are introduced to analyze z-transforms and to compute inverse z-transforms. Solutions of difference equations using the z-transform and MATLAB are provided.

Chapter 5, The Discrete Fourier Transform: This chapter is devoted to the computation of the Fourier transform and its efficient implementation. The discrete Fourier series is used to introduce the discrete Fourier transform, and several of its properties are demonstrated using MATLAB. Topics such as fast convolution and fast Fourier transform are thoroughly discussed.

Chapter 6, Implementation of Discrete-Time Filters: This chapter discusses several structures for the implementation of digital filters. Several useful MATLAB functions are developed for the determination and implementation of these structures. In addition to considering various filter structures, we also treat quantization effects when finite-precision arithmetic is used in the implementation of IIR and FIR filters.

Chapter 7, FIR Filter Design: This chapter and the next introduce the important topic of digital filter design. Three important design techniques for FIR filters—namely, window design, frequency sampling design, and the equiripple filter design—are discussed. Several design examples are provided using MATLAB.

Chapter 8, IIR Filter Design: Included in this chapter are techniques used in IIR filter design. The chapter begins with the treatment of some basic filter types—namely, digital resonators, notch filters, comb filters, allpass filters, and digital sinusoidal oscillators. This is followed by a brief description of the characteristics of three widely used analog filters. Transformations are described for converting these prototype analog filters into different frequency-selective digital filters. The chapter concludes with several IIR filter designs using MATLAB.

Chapter 9, Sampling Rate Conversion: This chapter treats the important problem of sampling rate conversion in digital signal processing. Topics treated include decimation and interpolation by integer factors, sampling rate conversion by a rational factor, and polyphase filter structures for sampling rate conversion.

Chapter 10, Round-Off Effects in Digital Filters: The focus of this chapter is on the effects of finite-precision arithmetic to the filtering aspects in signal processing. Quantization noise introduced in analog-to-digital conversion is characterized statistically, and the quantization effects in finite-precision multiplication and additions are also modeled statistically. The effects of these errors in the filter output are characterized as correlated errors, called limit cycles, and as uncorrelated errors, called round-off noise.

Chapter 11, Applications in Adaptive Filtering: This chapter is the first of two chapters on projects using MATLAB. Included is an introduction to the theory and implementation of adaptive FIR filters with projects in system identification, interference suppression, narrowband frequency enhancement, and adaptive equalization.

Chapter 12, Applications in Communications: This chapter focuses on several projects dealing with waveform representation and coding and with digital communications. Included is a description of pulse-code modulation (PCM), differential PCM (DPCM) and adaptive DPCM (ADPCM), delta modulation (DM) and adaptive DM (ADM), linear predictive coding (LPC), generation and detection of dual-tone multifrequency (DTMF) signals, and a description of signal detection applications in binary communications and spread-spectrum communications.

Chapter 13, Random Processes: This is the first of the last three chapters that are available online through the website for the book. In this chapter, we provide a brief review of analytical concepts in random signals that model waveform variations and provide sound techniques to calculate the response of linear filters to random signals. We begin by defining probability functions and statistical averages, and continue with pairs of random variables. These concepts are extended to random signals, in terms of second-order statistics, and then delve into stationary and ergodic processes, correlation functions, and power spectra. We apply this theory to processing of random signals through LTI systems using both the time and frequency domains. Finally, we discuss a few representative random processes, including Gaussian, Markov, white noise, and filtered noise processes.

Chapter 14, Linear Prediction and Optimum Linear Filters: In this chapter, we treat the problem of optimum filter design from a statistical viewpoint. The filters are constrained to be linear, and the optimization criterion is based on the minimization of the mean square error. We discuss the design of optimum filters for linear prediction, which has applications in speech signal processing, image processing, and noise suppression in communication systems. This design technique requires the solution of a set of linear equations with special symmetry. We describe two algorithms, Levinson–Durbin and Schur, which provide the solution to the equations through computationally efficient procedures that exploit the symmetry properties. The last section of this chapter treats an important class of optimum filters called Wiener filters, which are widely used in many applications involving the estimation of signals corrupted with additive noise.

Chapter 15, Adaptive Filters: The focus of this chapter is on *adaptive filters*, which have adjustable coefficients for use in applications in which the filter coefficients cannot be designed a priori due to unknown or changing statistics. We begin with several practical applications in which adaptive filters have been successfully used in the estimation of signals corrupted by noise and other interference. Adaptive filters incorporate algorithms that allow the filter coefficients to adapt to changes in the signal statistics. We describe two basic algorithms: the least-mean-square (LMS) algorithm, which is based on gradient optimization for determining the coefficients, and the class of recursive least-squares (RLS) algorithms.

ACKNOWLEDGMENTS

We are indebted to numerous students in our undergraduate DSP course at Northeastern University who provided us a forum to test teaching ideas using MATLAB and who endured our constant emphasis on MATLAB. Many efficient MATLAB functions used in this book were developed by some of these students. We are also indebted to reviewers of the original edition, whose constructive criticism resulted in a better presentation of the material: Abeer A. H. Alwan, University of California, Los Angeles; Steven Chin, Catholic University; Prof. Huaichen, Xidian University, P. R. China; and Joel Trussel, North Carolina State University. The following reviewers provided additional encouragement, numerous refinements, and useful comments for the second edition: Jyotsna Bapat, Fairleigh Dickinson University; David Clark, California State Polytechnic University; Artyom Grigoryan, University of Texas, San Antonio; Tao Li, University of Florida; and Zixiang Xiong, Texas A & M University. Based on their use of the second edition, the following reviewers provided several suggestions, changes, and modifications that led to the third edition: Kalyan Mondal, Fairleigh Dickinson University; Artyom M. Grigoryan, University of Texas at San Antonio; A. David Salvia, Pennsylvania State University; Matthew Valenti, West Virginia University; and Christopher J. James, University of Southampton, UK. Finally, the fourth edition was motivated by the constructive feedback and comments provided by Wasfy B. Mikhael, University of Central Florida; Hongbin Li, Stevens Institute of Technology; Robert Paz, New Mexico State University; and Ramakrishnan Sundaram, Gannon University. We sincerely thank all of them.

We would also like to take this opportunity to acknowledge several people at Cengage Learning without whom this project would not have been possible. We thank the Product Director, Timothy Anderson, who oversees the Global Engineering publishing program at Cengage, for encouraging the fourth edition. Media Assistant Ashley Kaupert worked on the revisions and helped see the fourth edition through development to production. This project could not have been completed within time limits without their constant push. Senior Content Project Manager Jennifer Risden oversaw the book's production process. We thank them all for their professional help. Finally, we express our sincere gratitude to Richard Camp for his diligent copy editing and everyone at Cengage Learning who aided in the development of this edition.

Vinay K. Ingle
John G. Proakis
Boston, Massachusetts

CHAPTER 1

Introduction

During the past several decades, the field of digital signal processing (DSP) has grown to be important, both theoretically and technologically. A major reason for its success in industry is the development and use of low-cost software and hardware. New technologies and applications in various fields are now taking advantage of DSP algorithms. This will lead to a greater demand for electrical and computer engineers with a background in DSP. Therefore, it is necessary to make DSP an integral part of any electrical engineering curriculum.

Three decades ago an introductory course on DSP was given mainly at the graduate level. It was supplemented by computer exercises on filter design, spectrum estimation, and related topics using mainframe (or mini) computers. However, considerable advances in personal computers and software during the past three decades have made it necessary to introduce a DSP course to undergraduates. Since DSP applications are primarily algorithms that are implemented either on a DSP processor [36] or in software, a fair amount of programming is required. Using interactive software, such as MATLAB, it is now possible to place more emphasis on learning new and difficult concepts than on programming algorithms. Interesting practical examples can be discussed, and useful problems can be explored.

With this philosophy in mind, we have developed this book as a *companion book* (to traditional textbooks like [71, 79]) in which MATLAB is an integral part in the discussion of topics and concepts. We have chosen MATLAB as the programming tool primarily because of its wide availability on computing platforms in many universities across the world. Furthermore, a low-cost student version of MATLAB has been available for several years, placing it among the least expensive software products for educational purposes. We have treated MATLAB as a computational and programming toolbox containing several tools (sort of a super calculator with several keys) that can be used to explore and solve problems and, thereby, enhance the learning process.

This book is written at an introductory level in order to introduce undergraduate students to the exciting and practical field of DSP. We emphasize that this is not a textbook in the traditional sense but a companion book in which more attention is given to problem solving and hands-on experience with MATLAB. Similarly, it is not a tutorial book in MATLAB. We assume that the student is familiar with MATLAB and is currently taking a course in DSP. The book provides basic analytical tools needed to process real-world signals (a.k.a. analog signals) using digital techniques. We deal mostly with discrete-time signals and systems, which are analyzed in both the time and the frequency domains. The analysis and design of processing structures called *filters* and *spectrum analyzers* are among some of the most important aspects of DSP and are treated in great detail in this book. Similarly, the topics of finite word-length effects on filter performance as well as on filter output and the sampling-rate conversion between two DSP systems are of practical significance. These are also treated extensively in this book. To further our philosophy of MATLAB-based learning to advanced topics taught in graduate courses, we have also included some material from statistical and adaptive signal processing areas such as random signals, linear prediction, optimal filters, and adaptive filters.

In this chapter, we provide a brief overview of DSP and an introduction to MATLAB.

1.1 OVERVIEW OF DIGITAL SIGNAL PROCESSING

In this modern world, we are surrounded by all kinds of signals in various forms. Some of the signals are natural, but most of the signals are man-made. Some signals are necessary (speech), some are pleasant (music), while many are unwanted or unnecessary in a given situation. In an engineering context, signals are carriers of information, both useful and unwanted. Therefore, extracting or enhancing the useful information from a mix of conflicting information is the simplest form of signal processing. More generally, signal processing is an operation designed for extracting, enhancing, storing, and transmitting useful information. The distinction between useful and unwanted information is often subjective as well as objective. Hence signal processing tends to be application dependent.

1.1.1 HOW ARE SIGNALS PROCESSED?

The signals that we encounter in practice are mostly analog signals. These signals, which vary continuously in time and amplitude, are processed using electrical networks containing active and passive circuit elements. This approach is known as analog signal processing (ASP)—for example, radio and television receivers.

$$\text{Analog signal: } x_a(t) \longrightarrow \boxed{\text{Analog signal processor}} \longrightarrow y_a(t) \text{ :Analog signal}$$

They can also be processed using digital hardware containing adders, multipliers, and logic elements or using special-purpose microprocessors. However, one needs to convert analog signals into a form suitable for digital hardware. This form of the signal is called a digital signal. It takes one of the finite number of values at specific instances in time, and hence it can be represented by binary numbers, or bits. The processing of digital signals is called DSP; in block diagram form it is represented by

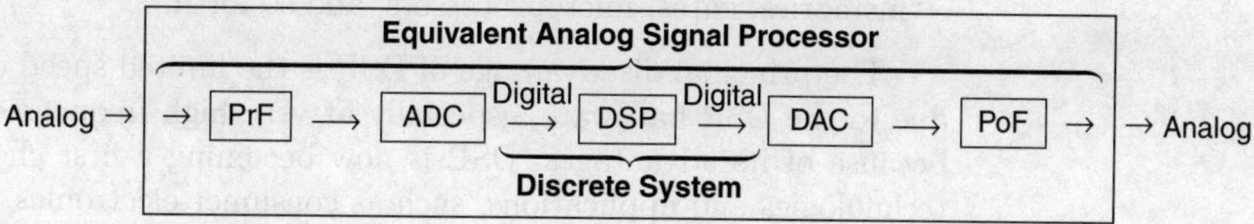

The various block elements are discussed as follows.

PrF: This is a prefilter or an antialiasing filter, which conditions the analog signal to prevent aliasing.

ADC: This is an analog-to-digital converter, which produces a stream of binary numbers from analog signals.

Digital Signal Processor: This is the heart of DSP and can represent a general-purpose computer or a special-purpose processor, or digital hardware, and so on.

DAC: This is the inverse operation to the ADC, called a digital-to-analog converter, which produces a staircase waveform from a sequence of binary numbers, a first step toward producing an analog signal.

PoF: This is a postfilter to smooth out staircase waveform into the desired analog signal.

It appears from the above two approaches to signal processing, analog and digital, that the DSP approach is the more complicated, containing more components than the "simpler looking" ASP. Therefore, one might ask, Why process signals digitally? The answer lies in the many advantages offered by DSP.

1.1.2 ADVANTAGES OF DSP OVER ASP

A major drawback of ASP is its limited scope for performing complicated signal-processing applications. This translates into nonflexibility in processing and complexity in system designs. All of these generally lead to expensive products. On the other hand, using a DSP approach, it is possible to convert an inexpensive personal computer into a powerful signal processor. Some important advantages of DSP are these:

1. Systems using the DSP approach can be developed using software running on a general-purpose computer. Therefore, DSP is relatively convenient to develop and test, and the software is portable.
2. DSP operations are based solely on additions and multiplications, leading to extremely stable processing capability—for example, stability independent of temperature.
3. DSP operations can easily be modified in real time, often by simple programming changes or by reloading of registers.
4. DSP has lower cost due to VLSI technology, which reduces costs of memories, gates, microprocessors, and so forth.

The principal disadvantage of DSP is the limited speed of operations due to the DSP hardware, especially at very high frequencies. Primarily because of its advantages, DSP is now becoming a first choice in many technologies and applications, such as consumer electronics, communications, wireless telephones, and medical imaging.

1.1.3 TWO IMPORTANT CATEGORIES OF DSP

Most DSP operations can be categorized as being either signal *analysis* tasks or signal *filtering* tasks:

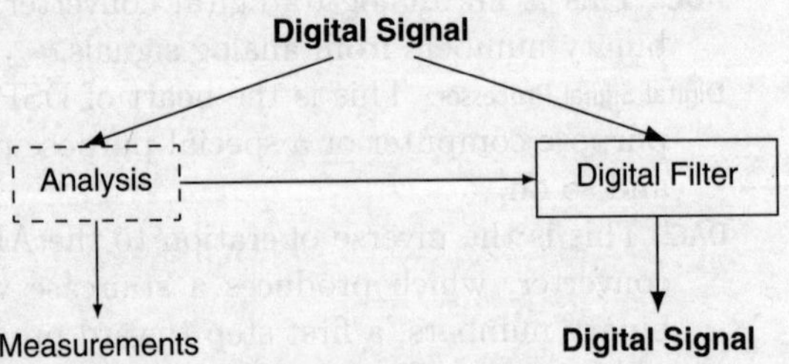

Signal analysis This task deals with the measurement of signal properties. It is generally a frequency-domain operation. Some of its applications are

- spectrum (frequency and/or phase) analysis,
- speech recognition,
- speaker verification, and
- target detection.

Signal filtering   This task is characterized by the signal-in signal-out situation. The systems that perform this task are generally called *filters*. It is usually (but not always) a time-domain operation. Some of the applications are

- removal of unwanted background noise,
- removal of interference,
- separation of frequency bands, and
- shaping of the signal spectrum.

In some applications, such as voice synthesis, a signal is first analyzed to study its characteristics, which are then used in digital filtering to generate a synthetic voice.

1.2 A BRIEF INTRODUCTION TO MATLAB

MATLAB is an interactive, matrix-based system for scientific and engineering numeric computation and visualization. Its strength lies in the fact that complex numerical problems can be solved easily and in a fraction of the time required by a programming language such as Fortran or C. It is also powerful in the sense that, with its relatively simple programming capability, MATLAB can be easily extended to create new commands and functions.

MATLAB is available in a number of computing environments: PCs running all flavors of Windows, Apple Macs running OS-X, UNIX/Linux workstations, and parallel computers. The basic MATLAB program is further enhanced by the availability of numerous toolboxes (collections of specialized functions in specific topics) over the years. The information in this book generally applies to all these environments. In addition to the basic MATLAB product, the Signal Processing toolbox (SP toolbox) is required for this book. The original development of the book was done using the professional version 3.5 running under DOS. The MATLAB scripts and functions described in the book were later extended and made compatible with the present version of MATLAB. Furthermore, through the services of www.cengagebrain.com, every effort will be made to preserve this compatibility under future versions of MATLAB.

In this section, we will undertake a brief review of MATLAB. The scope and power of MATLAB go far beyond the few topics discussed in this section. For more detailed tutorial-based discussion, students and readers new to MATLAB should also consult several excellent reference books available in the literature, including [29], [35], and [76]. The information given in all these references, along with the online MATLAB's `help` facility, usually is sufficient to enable readers to use this book.

The best approach to become familiar with MATLAB is to open a MATLAB session and experiment with various operators, functions, and commands until their use and capabilities are understood. Then one can progress to writing simple MATLAB scripts and functions to execute a sequence of instructions to accomplish an analytical goal.

1.2.1 GETTING STARTED

The interaction with MATLAB is through the command window of its graphical user interface (GUI). In the command window, the user types MATLAB instructions, which are executed instantaneously, and the results are displayed in the window. In the MATLAB command window, the characters ">>" indicate the prompt that is waiting for the user to type a command to be executed. For example,

```
>> command;
```

means an instruction `command` has been issued at the MATLAB prompt. If a semicolon (;) is placed at the end of a command, then all output from that command is suppressed. Multiple commands can be placed on the same line, separated by semicolons. Comments are marked by the percent sign (%), in which case MATLAB ignores anything to the right of the sign. The comments allow the reader to follow code more easily. The integrated help manual provides help for every command through the fragment

```
>> help command;
```

which will provide information on the inputs, outputs, usage, and functionality of the command. A complete listing of commands sorted by functionality can be obtained by typing `help` at the prompt.

There are three basic elements in MATLAB: numbers, variables, and operators. In addition, punctuation marks (,, ;, :, etc.) have special meanings.

Numbers   MATLAB is a high-precision numerical engine and can handle all types of numbers—that is, integers, real numbers, complex numbers, among others—with relative ease. For example, the real number 1.23 is represented as simply `1.23`, while the real number 4.56×10^7 can be written as `4.56e7`. The imaginary number $\sqrt{-1}$ is denoted either by `1i` or `1j`, although in this book we will use the symbol `1j`. Hence the complex number whose real part is 5 and whose imaginary part is 3 will be written as `5+1j*3`. Other constants preassigned by MATLAB are `pi` for π, `inf` for ∞, and `NaN` for not a number (e.g., 0/0). These preassigned constants are very important and, to avoid confusion, should not be redefined by users.

Variables In MATLAB, which stands for MATrix LABoratory, the basic variable is a matrix, or an array. Hence, when MATLAB operates on this variable, it operates on all its elements. This is what makes it a powerful and an efficient engine. MATLAB now supports multidimensional arrays; we will discuss only up to two-dimensional arrays of numbers.

1. **Matrix:** A matrix is a two-dimensional set of numbers arranged in rows and columns. Numbers can be real- or complex-valued.
2. **Array:** This is another name for matrix. However, operations on arrays are treated differently from those on matrices. This difference is very important in implementation.

The following are four types of matrices (or arrays).

- **Scalar:** This is a 1×1 matrix or a single number that is denoted by the *variable* symbol, that is, lowercase italic typeface like

$$a = a_{11}$$

- **Column vector:** This is an $(N \times 1)$ matrix or a vertical arrangement of numbers. It is denoted by the *vector* symbol, that is, lowercase bold typeface like

$$\mathbf{x} = [x_{i1}]_{i:1,\ldots,N} = \begin{bmatrix} x_{11} \\ x_{21} \\ \vdots \\ x_{N1} \end{bmatrix}$$

A typical vector in linear algebra is denoted by the column vector.
- **Row vector:** This is a $(1 \times M)$ matrix or a horizontal arrangement of numbers. It is also denoted by the vector symbol, that is,

$$\mathbf{y} = [y_{1j}]_{j=1,\ldots,M} = \begin{bmatrix} y_{11} & y_{12} & \cdots & y_{1M} \end{bmatrix}$$

A one-dimensional discrete-time signal is typically represented by an array as a row vector.
- **General matrix:** This is the most general case of an $(N \times M)$ matrix and is denoted by the matrix symbol, that is, uppercase bold typeface like

$$\mathbf{A} = [a_{ij}]_{i=1,\ldots,N;j=1,\ldots,m} = \begin{bmatrix} a_{11} & a_{12} & \cdots & a_{1M} \\ a_{21} & a_{22} & \cdots & a_{2M} \\ \vdots & \vdots & \ddots & \vdots \\ a_{N1} & a_{N2} & \cdots & a_{NM} \end{bmatrix}$$

This arrangement is typically used for two-dimensional discrete-time signals or images.

MATLAB does not distinguish between an array and a matrix except for operations. The following assignments denote indicated matrix types in MATLAB:

```
a = [3] is a scalar,
x = [1,2,3] is a row vector,
y = [1;2;3] is a column vector, and
A = [1,2,3;4,5,6] is a matrix.
```

MATLAB provides many useful functions to create special matrices. These include `zeros(M,N)` for creating a matrix of all zeros, `ones(M,N)` for creating matrix of all ones, `eye(N)` for creating an $N \times N$ identity matrix, and so on. Consult MATLAB's help manual for a complete list.

Operators   MATLAB provides several arithmetic and logical operators, some of which follow. For a complete list, MATLAB's help manual should be consulted.

= assignment	== equality
+ addition	- subtraction or minus
* multiplication	.* array multiplication
^ power	.^ array power
/ division	./ array division
<> relational operators	& logical AND
| logical OR	~ logical NOT
' transpose	.' array transpose

We now provide a more detailed explanation on some of these operators.

1.2.2 MATRIX OPERATIONS

Following are the most useful and important operations on matrices.

- **Matrix addition and subtraction:** These are straightforward operations that are also used for array addition and subtraction. Care must be taken that the two matrix operands be *exactly* the same size.
- **Matrix conjugation:** This operation is meaningful only for complex-valued matrices. It produces a matrix in which all imaginary parts are negated. It is denoted by $\mathbf{A}^*$ in analysis and by `conj(A)` in MATLAB.
- **Matrix transposition:** This is an operation in which every row (column) is turned into column (row). Let $\mathbf{X}$ be an $(N \times M)$ matrix. Then

$$\mathbf{X}' = [x_{ji}]; \quad j = 1, \ldots, M,\ i = 1, \ldots, N$$

is an $(M \times N)$ matrix. In MATLAB, this operation has one additional feature. If the matrix is real-valued, then the operation produces the usual transposition. However, if the matrix is complex-valued, then the operation produces a complex-conjugate transposition. To obtain just the transposition, we use the array operation of conjugation, that is, `A.'` will do just the transposition.

- **Multiplication by a scalar:** This is a simple straightforward operation in which each element of a matrix is scaled by a constant, that is,

$$ab \Rightarrow \texttt{a*b} \ (\text{scalar})$$

$$a\mathbf{x} \Rightarrow \texttt{a*x} \ (\text{vector or array})$$

$$a\mathbf{X} \Rightarrow \texttt{a*X} \ (\text{matrix})$$

This operation is also valid for an array scaling by a constant.

- **Vector-vector multiplication:** In this operation, one has to be careful about matrix dimensions to avoid invalid results. The operation produces either a scalar or a matrix. Let $\mathbf{x}$ be an $(N \times 1)$ vector and $\mathbf{y}$ be a $(1 \times M)$ vector. Then

$$\mathbf{x} * \mathbf{y} \Rightarrow \mathbf{xy} = \begin{bmatrix} x_1 \\ \vdots \\ x_N \end{bmatrix} \begin{bmatrix} y_1 & \cdots & y_M \end{bmatrix} = \begin{bmatrix} x_1 y_1 & \cdots & x_1 y_M \\ \vdots & \ddots & \vdots \\ x_N y_1 & \cdots & x_N y_M \end{bmatrix}$$

produces a matrix. If $M = N$, then

$$\mathbf{y} * \mathbf{x} \Rightarrow \mathbf{yx} = \begin{bmatrix} y_1 & \cdots & y_M \end{bmatrix} \begin{bmatrix} x_1 \\ \vdots \\ x_M \end{bmatrix} = x_1 y_1 + \cdots + x_M y_M$$

- **Matrix-vector multiplication:** If the matrix and the vector are compatible (i.e., the number of matrix-columns is equal to the vector-rows), then this operation produces a column vector:

$$\mathbf{y} = \texttt{A*x} \Rightarrow \mathbf{y} = \mathbf{Ax} = \begin{bmatrix} a_{11} & \cdots & a_{1M} \\ \vdots & \ddots & \vdots \\ a_{N1} & \cdots & a_{NM} \end{bmatrix} \begin{bmatrix} x_1 \\ \vdots \\ x_M \end{bmatrix} = \begin{bmatrix} y_1 \\ \vdots \\ y_N \end{bmatrix}$$

- **Matrix-matrix multiplication:** Finally, if two matrices are compatible, then their product is well defined. The result is also a matrix with the number of rows equal to that of the first matrix and the number of columns equal to that of the second matrix. Note that the order in matrix multiplication is very important.

Array Operations   These operations treat matrices as arrays. They are also known as *dot operations* because the arithmetic operators are prefixed by a dot (.), that is, `.*`, `./`, or `.^`.

- **Array multiplication:** This is an element by element multiplication operation. For it to be a valid operation, both arrays must be the same size. Thus we have

$$\texttt{x.*y} \rightarrow \text{1D array}$$

$$\texttt{X.*Y} \rightarrow \text{2D array}$$

- **Array exponentiation:** In this operation, a scalar (real- or complex-valued) is raised to the power equal to every element in an array, that is,

$$\texttt{a.\^{}x} \equiv \begin{bmatrix} a^{x_1} \\ a^{x_2} \\ \vdots \\ a^{x_N} \end{bmatrix}$$

is an $(N \times 1)$ array, whereas

$$\texttt{a.\^{}X} \equiv \begin{bmatrix} a^{x_{11}} & a^{x_{12}} & \cdots & a^{x_{1M}} \\ a^{x_{21}} & a^{x_{22}} & \cdots & a^{x_{2M}} \\ \vdots & \vdots & \ddots & \vdots \\ a^{x_{N1}} & a^{x_{N2}} & \cdots & a^{x_{NM}} \end{bmatrix}$$

is an $(N \times M)$ array.

- **Array transposition:** As explained, the operation `A.'` produces transposition of real- or complex-valued array `A`.

Indexing Operations   MATLAB provides very useful and powerful array-indexing operations using operator `:`. It can be used to generate sequences of numbers as well as to access certain row/column elements of a matrix. Using the fragment `x = [a:b:c]`, we can generate numbers from `a` to `c` in `b` increments. If `b` is positive (negative), then we get increasing (decreasing) values in the sequence `x`.

The fragment `x(a:b:c)` accesses elements of `x` beginning with index `a` in steps of `b` and ending at `c`. Care must be taken to use integer values for indexing elements. Similarly, the `:` operator can be used to extract a submatrix from a matrix. For example, `B = A(2:4,3:6)` extracts a 3×4 submatrix starting at row 2 and column 3.

Another use of the `:` operator is in forming column vectors from row vectors or matrices. When used on the right-hand side of the equality (`=`) operator, the fragment `x=A(:)` forms a long column vector `x` of elements of `A` by concatenating its columns. Similarly, `x=A(:,3)` forms a vector `x` from the third column of `A`. However, when used on the right-hand side of the `=` operator, the fragment `A(:)=x` reformats elements in `x` into a predefined size of `A`.

Control-Flow MATLAB provides a variety of commands that allow us to control the flow of commands in a program. The most common construct is the `if-elseif-else` structure. With these commands, we can allow different blocks of code to be executed depending on some condition. The format of this construct is

```
    if condition1
        command1
    elseif condition2
        command2
    else
        command3
    end
```

which executes statements in `command1` if `condition-1` is satisfied; otherwise, it executes statements in `command2` if `condition-2` is satisfied, or, finally, statements in `command3`.

Another common control flow construct is the `for..end` loop. It is simply an iteration loop that tells the computer to repeat some task a given number of times. The format of a `for..end` loop is

```
    for index = values
        program statements
            :
    end
```

Although `for..end` loops are useful for processing data inside of arrays by using the iteration variable as an index into the array, whenever possible the user should try to use MATLAB's whole array mathematics. This will result in shorter programs and more efficient code. In some situations, the use of the `for..end` loop is unavoidable. The following example illustrates these concepts.

☐   **EXAMPLE 1.1**   Consider the following sum of sinusoidal functions:

$$x(t) = \sin(2\pi t) + \tfrac{1}{3}\sin(6\pi t) + \tfrac{1}{5}\sin(10\pi t) = \sum_{k=1,3,5} \frac{1}{k}\sin(2\pi k t), \qquad 0 \le t \le 1$$

Using MATLAB, we want to generate samples of $x(t)$ at time instances `0:0.01:1`. We will discuss three approaches.

Approach 1

Here we will consider a typical C or Fortran approach, that is, we will use two `for..end` loops, one each on `t` and `k`. This is the most inefficient approach in MATLAB, but possible.

```
>> t = 0:0.01:1; N = length(t); xt = zeros(1,N);
>> for n = 1:N
>>     temp = 0;
>>     for k = 1:2:5
>>         temp = temp + (1/k)*sin(2*pi*k*t(n));
>>     end
>>     xt(n) = temp;
>> end
```

Approach 2

In this approach, we will compute each sinusoidal component in one step as a vector, using the time vector `t = 0:0.01:1`, and then add all components using one `for..end` loop.

```
>> t = 0:0.01:1; xt = zeros(1,length(t));
>> for k = 1:2:5
>>     xt = xt + (1/k)*sin(2*pi*k*t);
>> end
```

Clearly, this is a better approach with fewer lines of code than the first one.

Approach 3

In this approach, we will use matrix-vector multiplication, in which MATLAB is very efficient. For the purpose of demonstration, consider only four values for $t = [t_1, t_2, t_3, t_4]$. Then

$$x(t_1) = \sin(2\pi t_1) + \tfrac{1}{3}\sin(2\pi 3 t_1) + \tfrac{1}{5}\sin(2\pi 5 t_1)$$

$$x(t_2) = \sin(2\pi t_2) + \tfrac{1}{3}\sin(2\pi 3 t_2) + \tfrac{1}{5}\sin(2\pi 5 t_2)$$

$$x(t_3) = \sin(2\pi t_3) + \tfrac{1}{3}\sin(2\pi 3 t_3) + \tfrac{1}{5}\sin(2\pi 5 t_3)$$

$$x(t_4) = \sin(2\pi t_4) + \tfrac{1}{3}\sin(2\pi 3 t_4) + \tfrac{1}{5}\sin(2\pi 5 t_4)$$

which can be written in matrix form as

$$\begin{bmatrix} x(t_1) \\ x(t_2) \\ x(t_3) \\ x(t_4) \end{bmatrix} = \begin{bmatrix} \sin(2\pi t_1) & \sin(2\pi 3 t_1) & \sin(2\pi 5 t_1) \\ \sin(2\pi t_2) & \sin(2\pi 3 t_2) & \sin(2\pi 5 t_2) \\ \sin(2\pi t_3) & \sin(2\pi 3 t_3) & \sin(2\pi 5 t_3) \\ \sin(2\pi t_4) & \sin(2\pi 3 t_4) & \sin(2\pi 5 t_4) \end{bmatrix} \begin{bmatrix} 1 \\ \tfrac{1}{3} \\ \tfrac{1}{5} \end{bmatrix}$$

$$= \sin\left(2\pi \begin{bmatrix} t_1 \\ t_2 \\ t_3 \\ t_4 \end{bmatrix} \begin{bmatrix} 1 & 3 & 5 \end{bmatrix} \right) \begin{bmatrix} 1 \\ \tfrac{1}{3} \\ \tfrac{1}{5} \end{bmatrix}$$

or, after taking transposition,

$$\begin{bmatrix} x(t_1) & x(t_2) & x(t_3) & x(t_4) \end{bmatrix} = \begin{bmatrix} 1 & \frac{1}{3} & \frac{1}{5} \end{bmatrix} \sin\left(2\pi \begin{bmatrix} 1 \\ 3 \\ 5 \end{bmatrix} \begin{bmatrix} t_1 & t_2 & t_3 & t_4 \end{bmatrix} \right)$$

Thus the MATLAB code is

```
>> t = 0:0.01:1; k = 1:2:5;
>> xt = (1./k)*sin(2*pi*k'*t);
```

Note the use of the array division (`1./k`) to generate a row vector and matrix multiplications to implement all other operations. This is the most compact code and the most efficient execution in MATLAB, especially when the number of sinusoidal terms is very large.

1.2.3 SCRIPTS AND FUNCTIONS

MATLAB is convenient in the interactive command mode if we want to execute few lines of code. But it is not efficient if we want to write code of several lines that we want to run repeatedly or if we want to use the code in several programs with different variable values. MATLAB provides two constructs for this purpose.

Scripts   The first construct can be accomplished by using the so-called block mode of operation. In MATLAB, this mode is implemented using a *script* file called an m-file (with an extension .m), which is only a text file that contains each line of the file as though you typed them at the command prompt. These scripts are created using MATLAB's built-in editor, which also provides for context-sensitive colors and indents for making fewer mistakes and for easy reading. The script is executed by typing the name of the script at the command prompt. The script file must be in the current directory or in the directory of the **path** environment. As an example, consider the sinusoidal function in Example 1.1. A general form of this function is

$$x(t) = \sum_{k=1}^{K} c_k \sin(2\pi kt) \tag{1.1}$$

If we want to experiment with different values of the coefficients c_k and/or the number of terms K, then we should create a script file. To implement the third approach in Example 1.1, we can write a script file

```
% Script file to implement (1.1)
t = 0:0.01:1; k = 1:2:5; ck = 1./k;
xt = ck * sin(2*pi*k'*t);
```

Now we can experiment with different values.

Functions   The second construct of creating a block of code is through subroutines. These are called *functions*, which also allow us to extend the capabilities of MATLAB. In fact, a major portion of MATLAB is assembled using function files in several categories and using special collections called *toolboxes*. Functions are also m-files (with extension .m). A major difference between script and function files is that the first executable line in a function file begins with the keyword `function` followed by an output-input variable declaration. As an example, consider the computation of the $x(t)$ function in Example 1.1 with an arbitrary number of sinusoidal terms, which we will implement as a function stored as m-file `sinsum.m`.

```
function xt = sinsum(t,ck)
% Computes sum of sinusoidal terms of the form in (1.1)
% x = sinsum(t,ck)
%
K = length(ck); k = 1:K;
ck = ck(:)'; t = t(:)';
xt = ck * sin(2*pi*k'*t);
```

The vectors `t` and `ck` should be assigned prior to using the `sinsum` function. Note that `ck(:)'` and `t(:)'` use indexing and transposition operations to force them to be row vectors. Also note the comments immediately following the `function` declaration, which are used by the `help sinsum` command. Sufficient information should be given there for the user to understand what the function is supposed to do.

1.2.4 PLOTTING

One of the most powerful features of MATLAB for signal and data analysis is its graphical data plotting. MATLAB provides several types of plots, starting with simple two-dimensional (2D) graphs and progressing to complex, higher-dimensional full-color plots. We will examine only the 2D plotting, which is the plotting of one array versus another in a 2D coordinate system. The basic plotting command is the `plot(t,x)` command, which generates a plot of `x` values versus `t` values in a separate figure window. The arrays `t` and `x` should be the same length and orientation. Optionally, some additional formatting keywords can also be provided in the `plot` function. The commands `xlabel` and `ylabel` are used to add text to the axes, and the command `title` is used to provide a title on the top of the graph. When plotting data, one should get into the habit of always labeling the axes and providing a title. Almost all aspects of a plot (style, size, color, etc.) can be changed by appropriate commands embedded in the program or directly through the GUI.

The following set of commands creates a list of sample points, evaluates the sine function at those points, and then generates a plot of a simple sinusoidal wave, putting axis labels and title on the plot.

```
>> t = 0:0.01:2; % sample points from 0 to 2 in steps of 0.01
>> xt = sin(2*pi*t); % Evaluate sin(2 pi t)
>> plot(t,xt,'b'); % Create plot with blue line
>> xlabel('t in sec'); ylabel('x(t)'); % Label axis
>> title('Plot of sin(2\pi t)'); % Title plot
```

The resulting plot is shown in Figure 1.1.

For plotting a set of discrete numbers (or discrete-time signals), we will use the **stem** command, which displays data values as a stem, that is, a small circle at the end of a line connecting it to the horizontal axis. The circle can be open (default) or filled (using the option `'filled'`). Using Handle Graphics (MATLAB's extensive manipulation of graphics primitives), we can resize circle markers. The following set of commands displays a discrete-time sine function using these constructs.

```
>> n = 0:1:40; % sample index from 0 to 40
>> xn = sin(0.1*pi*n); % Evaluate sin(0.1 pi n)
>> stem(n,xn,'b','filled','marker size',4); % Stem-plot
>> xlabel('n'); ylabel('x(n)'); % Label axis
>> title('Stem Plot of sin(0.1\pi n)'); % Title plot
```

The resulting plot is shown in Figure 1.2.

MATLAB provides an ability to display more than one graph in the same figure window. By means of the **hold on** command, several graphs

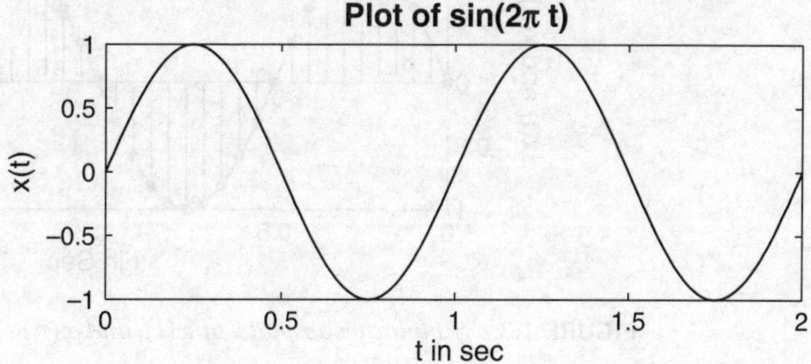

FIGURE 1.1   *Plot of the* $\sin(2\pi t)$ *function*

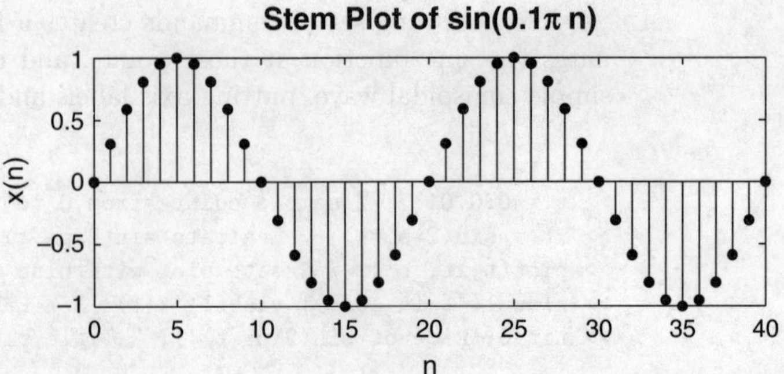

FIGURE 1.2   *Plot of the* $\sin(0.1\pi n)$ *sequence*

can be plotted on the same set of axes. The `hold off` command stops the simultaneous plotting. The following MATLAB fragment (Figure 1.3) displays graphs in Figures 1.1 and 1.2 as one plot, depicting a "sampling" operation that we will study later.

```
>> plot(t,xt,'b'); hold on; % Create plot with blue line
>> Hs = stem(n*0.05,xn,'b','filled'); % Stem-plot with handle Hs
>> set(Hs,'markersize',4); hold off; % Change circle size
```

Another approach is to use the `subplot` command, which displays several graphs in each individual set of axes arranged in a grid, using the parameters in the `subplot` command. The following fragment (Figure 1.4) displays graphs in Figure 1.1 and 1.2 as two separate plots in two rows.

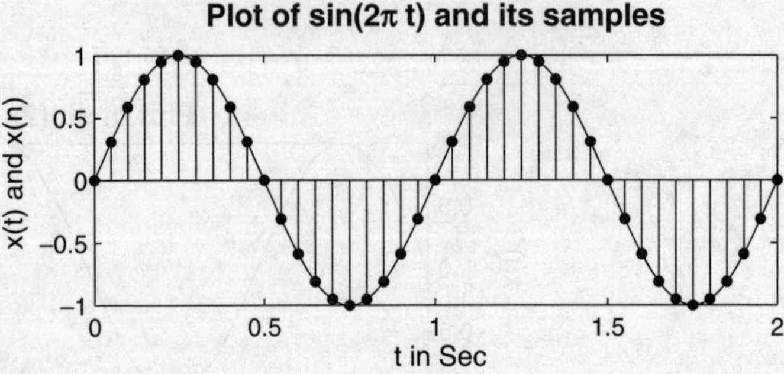

FIGURE 1.3   *Simultaneous plots of* $x(t)$ *and* $x(n)$

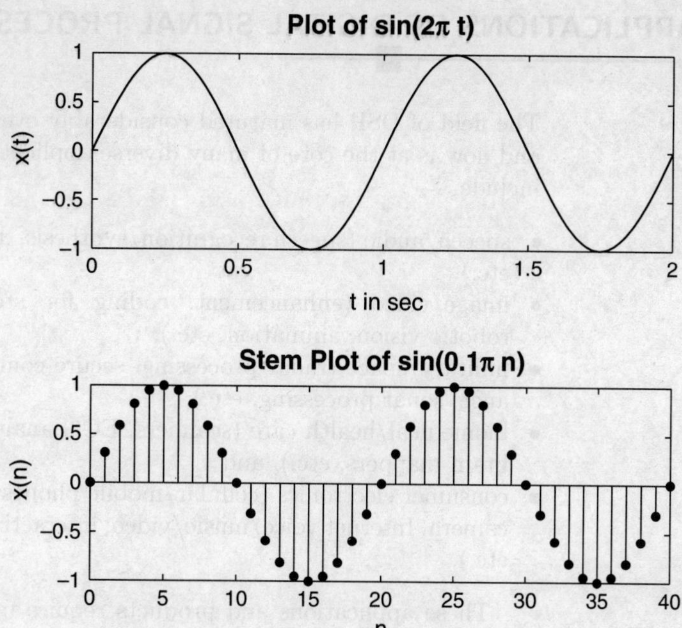

FIGURE 1.4 *Plots of $x(t)$ and $x(n)$ in two rows*

```
>> subplot(2,1,1); % Two rows, one column, first plot
>> plot(t,xt,'b'); % Create plot with blue line
. . .
>> subplot(2,1,2); % Two rows, one column, second plot
>> Hs = stem(n,xn,'b','filled','marker size',4); % Stem-plot
. . .
```

The plotting environment provided by MATLAB is very rich in its complexity and usefulness. It is made even richer using the Handle Graphics constructs. Therefore, readers are strongly recommended to consult MATLAB's manuals on plotting. Many of these constructs will be used throughout this book.

In this brief review, we have barely made a dent in the enormous capabilities and functionalities in MATLAB. Using its basic integrated help system, detailed help browser, and tutorials, it is possible to acquire sufficient skills in MATLAB in a reasonable amount of time.

1.3 APPLICATIONS OF DIGITAL SIGNAL PROCESSING

The field of DSP has matured considerably over the last several decades and now is at the core of many diverse applications and products. These include

- speech/audio (speech recognition/synthesis, digital audio, equalization, etc.),
- image/video (enhancement, coding for storage and transmission, robotic vision, animation, etc.),
- military/space (radar processing, secure communication, missile guidance, sonar processing, etc.),
- biomedical/health care (scanners, ECG analysis, X-ray analysis, EEG brain mappers, etc.), and
- consumer electronics (cellular/mobile phones, digital television, digital camera, Internet voice/music/video, interactive entertainment systems, etc.).

These applications and products require many interconnected complex steps, such as collection, processing, transmission, analysis, audio/display of real-world information in near real time. DSP technology has made it possible to incorporate these steps into devices that are innovative, affordable, and of high quality (e.g., the iPhone from Apple). A typical application to music is now considered as a motivation for the study of DSP.

Musical sound processing   In the music industry, almost all musical products (songs, albums, etc.) are produced in basically two stages. First, the sound from an individual instrument or performer is recorded in an acoustically inert studio on a single track of a multitrack recording device. Then, stored signals from each track are digitally processed by the sound engineer by adding special effects and combined into a stereo recording, which is then made available either on a CD or as an audio file.

The audio effects are artificially generated using various signal-processing techniques. These effects include echo generation, reverberation (concert hall effect), flanging (in which audio playback is slowed down by placing the DJ's thumb on the *flange* of the feed reel), chorus effect (when several musicians play the same instrument with small changes in amplitudes and delays), and phasing (a.k.a. phase shifting, in which an audio effect takes advantage of how sound waves interact with each other when they are out of phase). We now discuss a few of these sound effects in some detail.

Echo Generation   The most basic of all audio effects is that of *time delay*, or echoes. It is used as the building block of more complicated effects such as reverb or flanging. In a listening space such as a room, sound waves arriving at our ears consist of *direct* sound from the source as well as *reflected* off the walls, arriving with different amounts of attenuation and delays.

Echoes are delayed signals, and as such they are generated using delay units. For example, the combination of the direct sound represented by discrete signal $y[n]$ and a single echo appearing D samples later (which is related to delay in seconds) can be generated by an equation (called a difference equation) of the form

$$x[n] = y[n] + \alpha y[n - D], \qquad |\alpha| < 1 \qquad (1.2)$$

where $x[n]$ is the resulting signal and α models attenuation of the direct sound. Difference equations are implemented in MATLAB using the `filter` function. Available in MATLAB is a short snippet of Handel's "Hallelujah Chorus," which is a digital sound about 9 seconds long, sampled at 8192 sam/sec. To experience the sound with echo in (1.2), execute the following fragment at the command window. The echo is delayed by $D = 4196$ samples, which amount to 0.5 sec of delay.

```
load handel; % The signal is in y and sampling freq in Fs
sound(y,Fs); pause(10); % Play the original sound
alpha = 0.9; D = 4196; % Echo parameters
b = [1,zeros(1,D),alpha]; % Filter parameters
x = filter(b,1,y); % Generate sound plus its echo
sound(x,Fs); % Play sound with echo
```

You should be able to hear the distinct echo of the chorus in about a half second.

Echo Removal   After executing this simulation, you may experience that the echo is an objectionable interference while listening. Again DSP can be used effectively to reduce (almost eliminate) echoes. Such an echo-removal system is given by the difference equation

$$w[n] + \alpha w[n - D] = x[n] \qquad (1.3)$$

where $x[n]$ is the echo-corrupted sound signal and $w[n]$ is the output sound signal, which has the echo (hopefully) removed. Note again that this system is very simple to implement in software or hardware. Now try the following MATLAB script on the signal $x[n]$.

```
w = filter(1,b,x);
sound(w,Fs)
```

The echo should no longer be audible.

Digital Reverberation Multiple close-spaced echoes eventually lead to reverberation, which can be created digitally using a somewhat more involved difference equation

$$x[n] = \sum_{k=0}^{N-1} \alpha^k y[n - kD] \tag{1.4}$$

which generates multiple echoes spaced D samples apart with exponentially decaying amplitudes. Another natural-sounding reverberation is given by

$$x[n] = \alpha y[n] + y[n - D] + \alpha x[n - D], \quad |\alpha| < 1 \tag{1.5}$$

which simulates a higher echo density.

These simple applications are examples of DSP. Using techniques, concepts, and MATLAB functions learned in this book, you should be able to simulate these and other interesting sound effects.

1.4 BRIEF OVERVIEW OF THE BOOK

The book is organized roughly in four parts. The first three parts are included in the printed copy, as was done in the previous editions of the book, while the last part on advanced topics is available only through the book's website (see the Preface for instructions on accessing the book's website).

The first part of this book, which comprises Chapters 2 through 5, deals with the signal-analysis aspect of DSP. Chapter 2 begins with basic descriptions of discrete-time signals and systems. These signals and systems are analyzed in the frequency domain in Chapter 3. A generalization of the frequency-domain description, called the z-transform, is introduced in Chapter 4. The practical algorithms for computing the Fourier transform are discussed in Chapter 5 in the form of the discrete Fourier transform and the fast Fourier transform.

Chapters 6 through 8 constitute the second part of this book, which is devoted to the signal-filtering aspect of DSP. Chapter 6 describes various implementations and structures of digital filters. It also introduces finite-precision number representation and filter coefficient quantization and their effect on filter performance. Chapter 7 introduces design techniques and algorithms for designing one type of digital filter called *finite-duration impulse response (FIR) filters*, and Chapter 8 provides a similar treatment for another type of filter called *infinite-duration impulse response (IIR) filters*. In both chapters, only the simpler but practically useful techniques of filter design are discussed. More advanced techniques are not covered.

The third part, which consists of Chapters 9 through 12, provides important topics and applications in DSP. Chapter 9 deals with the useful topic of sampling-rate conversion and applies FIR filter designs from Chapter 7 to implement practical sample-rate converters. Chapter 10 extends the treatment of finite-precision numerical representation to signal quantization and the effect of finite-precision arithmetic on filter performance. The last two chapters provide some practical applications in the form of projects that can be done using material presented in the first 10 chapters. In Chapter 11, concepts in adaptive filtering are introduced, and simple projects in system identification, interference suppression, adaptive line enhancement, and so forth, are discussed. In Chapter 12, a brief introduction to digital communications is presented, with projects involving such topics as PCM, DPCM, and LPC being outlined.

Finally, Chapters 13 through 15 round out the last part of the book and it is intended as topics in advanced undergraduate or graduate courses. In Chapter 13, we treat signals as stochastic entities, called *random processes* (or *signals*), and provide their probabilistic as well as statistical descriptions through the concept of random variables. We also discuss a few representative random processes. In Chapter 14, we develop theory for *optimum filters* for processing random signals. For this treatment, we consider filters for linear prediction and Wiener filters for estimating signals corrupted by additive noise. In Chapter 15, we present *adaptive filters*, which are stochastic systems for applications in which statistics is not known a priori. We provide descriptions of LMS and RLS, two basic yet important adaptive algorithms.

In all these chapters, the central theme is the generous use and adequate demonstration of MATLAB, which can be used as an effective teaching as well as learning tool. Most of the existing MATLAB functions for DSP are described in detail, and their correct use is demonstrated in many examples. Furthermore, many new MATLAB functions are developed to provide insights into the working of many algorithms. The authors believe that this hand-holding approach enables students to dispel fears about DSP and provides an enriching learning experience.

CHAPTER 2

Discrete-Time Signals and Systems

We begin with the concepts of signals and systems in discrete time. A number of important types of signals and their operations are introduced. Linear and shift-invariant systems are discussed mostly because they are easier to analyze and implement. The convolution and the difference equation representations are given special attention because of their importance in digital signal processing and in MATLAB. The emphasis in this chapter is on the representations and implementation of signals and systems using MATLAB.

2.1 DISCRETE-TIME SIGNALS

Signals are broadly classified into analog and discrete signals. An analog signal will be denoted by $x_a(t)$, in which the variable t can represent any physical quantity but we will assume that it represents time in seconds. A discrete signal will be denoted by $x(n)$, in which the variable n is integer-valued and represents discrete instances in time. Therefore, it is also called a discrete-time signal, which is a *number sequence* and will be denoted by one of the following notations:

$$x(n) = \{x(n)\} = \{\ldots, x(-1), x(0), x(1), \ldots\}$$
$$\uparrow$$

where the *up-arrow* indicates the sample at $n = 0$.

In MATLAB, we can represent a *finite-duration* sequence by a *row vector* of appropriate values. However, such a vector does not have any information about sample position n. Therefore, a correct representation of $x(n)$ would require two vectors, one each for x and n. For example, a sequence $x(n) = \{2, 1, -1, 0, 1, 4, 3, 7\}$ can be represented in MATLAB by

```
>> n=[-3,-2,-1,0,1,2,3,4];   x=[2,1,-1,0,1,4,3,7];
```

Generally, we will use the x-vector representation alone when the sample position information is not required or when such information is trivial (e.g., when the sequence begins at $n = 0$). An arbitrary *infinite-duration* sequence cannot be represented in MATLAB, due to the finite memory limitations.

2.1.1 TYPES OF SEQUENCES

We use several elementary sequences in digital signal processing for analysis purposes. Their definitions and MATLAB representations follow.

1. **Unit sample sequence:**

$$\delta(n) = \begin{cases} 1, & n = 0 \\ 0, & n \neq 0 \end{cases} = \left\{ \ldots, 0, 0, \underset{\uparrow}{1}, 0, 0, \ldots \right\}$$

In MATLAB, the function `zeros(1,N)` generates a row vector of N zeros, which can be used to implement $\delta(n)$ over a finite interval. However, the logical relation `n==0` is an elegant way of implementing $\delta(n)$. For example, to implement

$$\delta(n - n_0) = \begin{cases} 1, & n = n_0 \\ 0, & n \neq n_0 \end{cases}$$

over the $n_1 \leq n_0 \leq n_2$ interval, we will use the following MATLAB function.

```
function [x,n] = impseq(n0,n1,n2)
% Generates x(n) = delta(n-n0); n1 <= n <= n2
% ---------------------------------------------------
% [x,n] = impseq(n0,n1,n2)
%
n = [n1:n2]; x = [(n-n0) == 0];
```

2. **Unit step sequence:**

$$u(n) = \begin{cases} 1, & n \geq 0 \\ 0, & n < 0 \end{cases} = \left\{ \ldots, 0, 0, \underset{\uparrow}{1}, 1, 1, \ldots \right\}$$

In MATLAB, the function `ones(1,N)` generates a row vector of N ones. It can be used to generate $u(n)$ over a finite interval. Once again, an elegant approach is to use the logical relation `n>=0`. To implement

$$u(n - n_0) = \begin{cases} 1, & n \geq n_0 \\ 0, & n < n_0 \end{cases}$$

over the $n_1 \leq n_0 \leq n_2$ interval, we will use the following MATLAB function.

```
function [x,n] = stepseq(n0,n1,n2)
% Generates x(n) = u(n-n0); n1 <= n <= n2
% ------------------------------------------
% [x,n] = stepseq(n0,n1,n2)
%
n = [n1:n2]; x = [(n-n0) >= 0];
```

3. **Real-valued exponential sequence**:

$$x(n) = a^n, \forall n; \; a \in \mathbb{R}$$

In MATLAB, an array operator ".^" is required to implement a real exponential sequence. For example, to generate $x(n) = (0.9)^n$, $0 \leq n \leq 10$, we will need the following MATLAB script.

```
>> n = [0:10]; x = (0.9).^n;
```

4. **Complex-valued exponential sequence**:

$$x(n) = e^{(\sigma + j\omega_0)n}, \forall n$$

where σ produces an attenuation (if <0) or amplification (if >0) and ω_0 is the frequency in radians. A MATLAB function `exp` is used to generate exponential sequences. For example, to generate $x(n) = \exp[(2 + j3)n], 0 \leq n \leq 10$, we will need the following MATLAB script.

```
>> n = [0:10]; x = exp((2+3j)*n);
```

5. **Sinusoidal sequence**:

$$x(n) = A\cos(\omega_0 n + \theta_0), \forall n$$

where A is an amplitude and θ_0 is the phase in radians. A MATLAB function `cos` (or `sin`) is used to generate sinusoidal sequences.

For example, to generate $x(n) = 3\cos(0.1\pi n + \pi/3) + 2\sin(0.5\pi n)$, $0 \le n \le 10$, we will need the following MATLAB script.

```
>> n = [0:10]; x = 3*cos(0.1*pi*n+pi/3) + 2*sin(0.5*pi*n);
```

6. **Random sequences**: Many practical sequences cannot be described by mathematical expressions like those above. These sequences are called random (or stochastic) sequences and are characterized by parameters of the associated probability density functions. In MATLAB, two types of (pseudo-) random sequences are available. The `rand(1,N)` generates a length N random sequence whose elements are uniformly distributed between $[0, 1]$. The `randn(1,N)` generates a length N Gaussian random sequence with mean 0 and variance 1. Other random sequences can be generated using transformations of the above functions.

7. **Periodic sequence**: A sequence $x(n)$ is periodic if $x(n) = x(n + N)$, $\forall n$. The smallest integer N that satisfies this relation is called the *fundamental* period. We will use $\tilde{x}(n)$ to denote a periodic sequence. To generate P periods of $\tilde{x}(n)$ from one period $\{x(n), \quad 0 \le n \le N-1\}$, we can copy $x(n)$ P times:

```
>> xtilde = [x,x,...,x];
```

But an elegant approach is to use MATLAB's powerful indexing capabilities. First we generate a matrix containing P rows of $x(n)$ values. Then we can concatenate P rows into a long row vector using the construct (:). However, this construct works only on columns. Hence we will have to use the matrix transposition operator ' to provide the same effect on rows.

```
>> xtilde = x' * ones(1,P);    % P columns of x; x is a row vector
>> xtilde = xtilde(:);         % Long column vector
>> xtilde = xtilde';           % Long row vector
```

Note that the last two lines can be combined into one for compact coding. This is shown in Example 2.1.

2.1.2 OPERATIONS ON SEQUENCES

Here we briefly describe basic sequence operations and their MATLAB equivalents.

1. **Signal addition**: This is a sample-by-sample addition given by

$$\{x_1(n)\} + \{x_2(n)\} = \{x_1(n) + x_2(n)\}$$

It is implemented in MATLAB by the arithmetic operator "+". However, the lengths of $x_1(n)$ and $x_2(n)$ must be the same. If sequences are of unequal lengths, or if the sample positions are different for equal-length sequences, then we cannot directly use the operator +. We have to first augment $x_1(n)$ and $x_2(n)$ so that they have the same position vector n (and hence the same length). This requires careful attention to MATLAB's indexing operations. In particular, logical operation of intersection "&", relational operations like "<=" and "==", and the find function are required to make $x_1(n)$ and $x_2(n)$ of equal length. The following function, called the sigadd function, demonstrates these operations.

```
function [y,n] = sigadd(x1,n1,x2,n2)
% Implements y(n) = x1(n)+x2(n)
% -----------------------------
% [y,n] = sigadd(x1,n1,x2,n2)
%   y = sum sequence over n, which includes n1 and n2
%   x1 = first sequence over n1
%   x2 = second sequence over n2 (n2 can be different from n1)
%
n = min(min(n1),min(n2)):max(max(n1),max(n2));  % Duration of y(n)
y1 = zeros(1,length(n)); y2 = y1;               % Initialization
y1(find((n>=min(n1))&(n<=max(n1))==1))=x1;      % x1 with duration of y
y2(find((n>=min(n2))&(n<=max(n2))==1))=x2;      % x2 with duration of y
y = y1+y2;                                       % Sequence addition
```

Its use is illustrated in Example 2.2.

2. **Signal multiplication**: This is a sample-by-sample (or "dot") multiplication given by

$$\{x_1(n)\} \cdot \{x_2(n)\} = \{x_1(n)x_2(n)\}$$

It is implemented in MATLAB by the array operator .*. Once again, the similar restrictions apply for the .* operator as for the + operator. Therefore, we have developed the sigmult function, which is similar to the sigadd function.

```
function [y,n] = sigmult(x1,n1,x2,n2)
% Implements y(n) = x1(n)*x2(n)
% -----------------------------
% [y,n] = sigmult(x1,n1,x2,n2)
%   y = product sequence over n, which includes n1 and n2
%   x1 = first sequence over n1
%   x2 = second sequence over n2 (n2 can be different from n1)
%
```

```
n = min(min(n1),min(n2)):max(max(n1),max(n2));   % Duration of y(n)
y1 = zeros(1,length(n)); y2 = y1;                 %
y1(find((n>=min(n1))&(n<=max(n1))==1))=x1;        % x1 with duration of y
y2(find((n>=min(n2))&(n<=max(n2))==1))=x2;        % x2 with duration of y
y = y1 .* y2;                                     % Sequence multiplication
```

Its use is also given in Example 2.2.

3. **Scaling**: In this operation, each sample is multiplied by a scalar α.

$$\alpha \left\{ x(n) \right\} = \left\{ \alpha x(n) \right\}$$

An arithmetic operator (*) is used to implement the scaling operation in MATLAB.

4. **Shifting**: In this operation, each sample of $x(n)$ is shifted by an amount k to obtain a shifted sequence $y(n)$.

$$y(n) = \left\{ x(n - k) \right\}$$

If we let $m = n - k$, then $n = m + k$ and the above operation is given by

$$y(m + k) = \left\{ x(m) \right\}$$

Hence this operation has no effect on the vector x, but the vector n is changed by adding k to each element. This is shown in the function `sigshift`.

```
function [y,n] = sigshift(x,m,k)
% Implements y(n) = x(n-k)
% -------------------------
% [y,n] = sigshift(x,m,k)
%
n = m+k; y = x;
```

Its use is given in Example 2.2.

5. **Folding**: In this operation, each sample of $x(n)$ is flipped around $n = 0$ to obtain a folded sequence $y(n)$.

$$y(n) = \left\{ x(-n) \right\}$$

In MATLAB, this operation is implemented by `fliplr(x)` function for sample values and by `-fliplr(n)` function for sample positions, as shown in the `sigfold` function.

```
function [y,n] = sigfold(x,n)
% Implements y(n) = x(-n)
% -----------------------
% [y,n] = sigfold(x,n)
%
y = fliplr(x); n = -fliplr(n);
```

6. **Sample summation**: This operation differs from the signal addition operation. It adds all sample values of $x(n)$ between n_1 and n_2.

$$\sum_{n=n_1}^{n_2} x(n) = x(n_1) + \cdots + x(n_2)$$

It is implemented by the `sum(x(n1:n2))` function.

7. **Sample products**: This operation also differs from the signal multiplication operation. It multiplies all sample values of $x(n)$ between n_1 and n_2.

$$\prod_{n_1}^{n_2} x(n) = x(n_1) \times \cdots \times x(n_2)$$

It is implemented by the `prod(x(n1:n2))` function.

8. **Signal energy**: The energy of a sequence $x(n)$ is given by

$$\mathcal{E}_x = \sum_{-\infty}^{\infty} x(n)x^*(n) = \sum_{-\infty}^{\infty} |x(n)|^2$$

where superscript * denotes the operation of complex conjugation.[1] The energy of a finite-duration sequence $x(n)$ can be computed in MATLAB using

```
>> Ex = sum(x .* conj(x)); % One approach
>> Ex = sum(abs(x) .^ 2); % Another approach
```

9. **Signal power**: The average power of a periodic sequence $\tilde{x}(n)$ with fundamental period N is given by

$$\mathcal{P}_x = \frac{1}{N} \sum_{0}^{N-1} |\tilde{x}(n)|^2$$

☐   **EXAMPLE 2.1**   Generate and plot each of the following sequences over the indicated interval.

     a. $x(n) = 2\delta(n+2) - \delta(n-4)$, $-5 \le n \le 5$.

     b. $x(n) = n[u(n) - u(n-10)] + 10e^{-0.3(n-10)}[u(n-10) - u(n-20)], 0 \le n \le 20$.

     c. $x(n) = \cos(0.04\pi n) + 0.2w(n)$, $0 \le n \le 50$, where $w(n)$ is a Gaussian random sequence with zero mean and unit variance.

     d. $\tilde{x}(n) = \{..., 5, 4, 3, 2, 1, 5, 4, 3, 2, 1, 5, 4, 3, 2, 1, ...\}$; $-10 \le n \le 9$.

---

[1]The symbol * denotes many operations in digital signal processing. Its font (roman or computer) and its position (normal or superscript) will distinguish each operation.

Solution   **a.** $x(n) = 2\delta(n+2) - \delta(n-4), \quad -5 \leq n \leq 5.$

```
>> n = [-5:5];
>> x = 2*impseq(-2,-5,5) - impseq(4,-5,5);
>> stem(n,x); title('Sequence in Problem 2.1a')
>> xlabel('n'); ylabel('x(n)');
```

The plot of the sequence is shown in Figure 2.1.

b. $x(n) = n\left[u(n) - u(n-10)\right] + 10e^{-0.3(n-10)}\left[u(n-10) - u(n-20)\right], 0 \leq n \leq 20.$

```
>> n = [0:20]; x1 = n.*(stepseq(0,0,20)-stepseq(10,0,20));
>> x2 = 10*exp(-0.3*(n-10)).*(stepseq(10,0,20)-stepseq(20,0,20));
>> x = x1+x2;
>> subplot(2,2,3); stem(n,x); title('Sequence in Problem 2.1b')
>> xlabel('n'); ylabel('x(n)');
```

The plot of the sequence is shown in Figure 2.1.

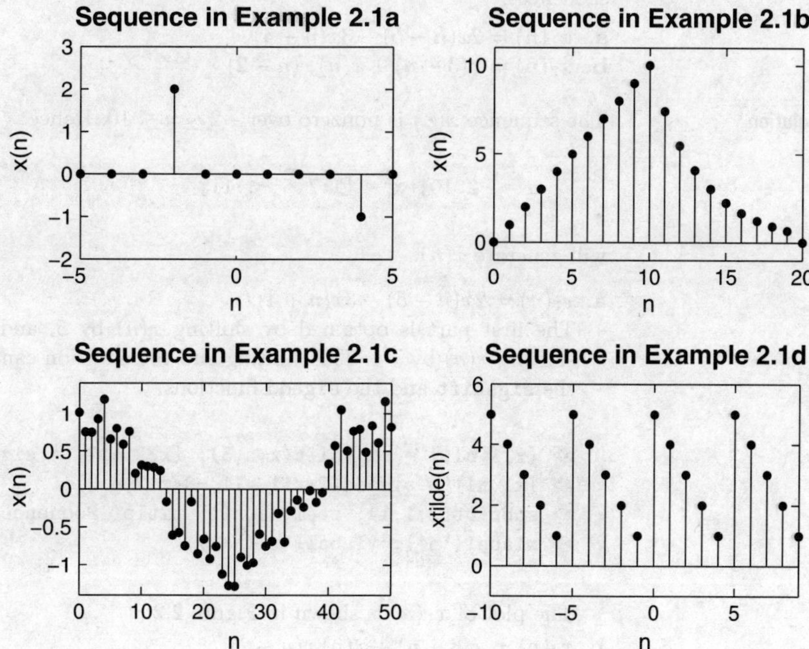

FIGURE 2.1   *Sequences in Example 2.1*

c. $x(n) = \cos(0.04\pi n) + 0.2w(n), \quad 0 \le n \le 50$.

```
>> n = [0:50]; x = cos(0.04*pi*n)+0.2*randn(size(n));
>> subplot(2,2,2); stem(n,x); title('Sequence in Problem 2.1c')
>> xlabel('n'); ylabel('x(n)');
```

The plot of the sequence is shown in Figure 2.1.

d. $\tilde{x}(n) = \{...,5,4,3,2,1,5,4,3,2,1,5,4,3,2,1,...\}; \quad -10 \le n \le 9$.

Note that over the given interval, the sequence $\tilde{x}(n)$ has four periods.

```
>> n = [-10:9]; x = [5,4,3,2,1];
>> xtilde = x' * ones(1,4);    xtilde = (xtilde(:))';
>> subplot(2,2,4); stem(n,xtilde); title('Sequence in Problem 2.1d')
>> xlabel('n'); ylabel('xtilde(n)');
```

The plot of the sequence is shown in Figure 2.1.   □

□ **EXAMPLE 2.2**   Let $x(n) = \{1,2,3,4,5,6,7,6,5,4,3,2,1\}$. Determine and plot the following sequences.

a. $x_1(n) = 2x(n-5) - 3x(n+4)$
b. $x_2(n) = x(3-n) + x(n)\,x(n-2)$

Solution   The sequence $x(n)$ is nonzero over $-2 \le n \le 10$. Hence

```
>> n = -2:10; x = [1:7,6:-1:1];
```

will generate $x(n)$.

a. $x_1(n) = 2x(n-5) - 3x(n+4)$.
The first part is obtained by shifting $x(n)$ by 5, and the second part by shifting $x(n)$ by -4. This shifting and the addition can be easily done using the `sigshift` and the `sigadd` functions.

```
>> [x11,n11] = sigshift(x,n,5); [x12,n12] = sigshift(x,n,-4);
>> [x1,n1] = sigadd(2*x11,n11,-3*x12,n12);
>> subplot(2,1,1); stem(n1,x1); title('Sequence in Example 2.2a')
>> xlabel('n'); ylabel('x1(n)');
```

The plot of $x_1(n)$ is shown in Figure 2.2.

b. $x_2(n) = x(3-n) + x(n)\,x(n-2)$.
The first term can be written as $x(-(n-3))$. Hence it is obtained by first folding $x(n)$ and then shifting the result by 3. The second part is a multiplication of $x(n)$ and $x(n-2)$, both of which have the same length but different

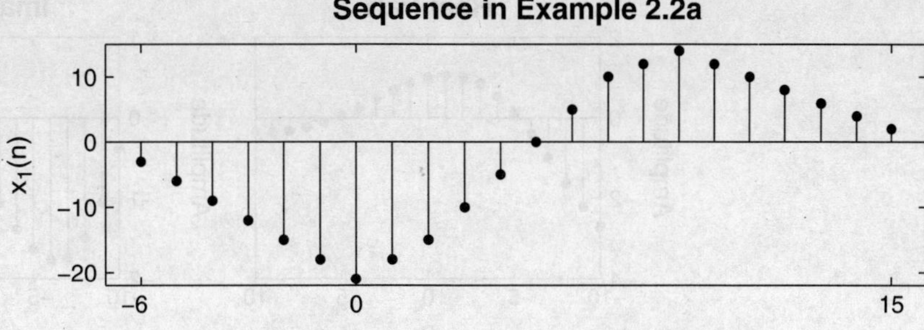

Sequence in Example 2.2a

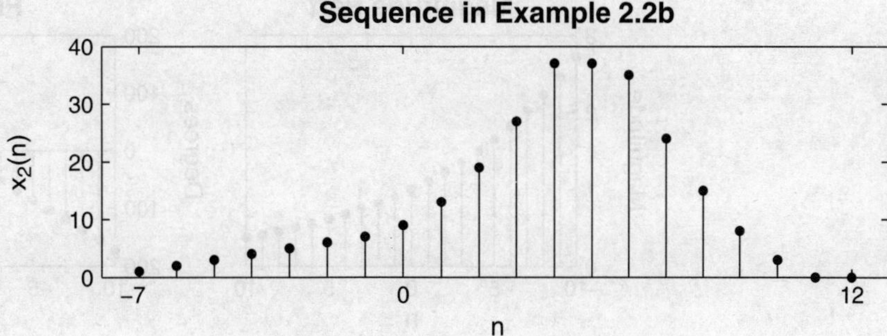

Sequence in Example 2.2b

FIGURE 2.2   *Sequences in Example 2.2*

support (or sample positions). These operations can be easily done using the `sigfold` and the `sigmult` functions.

```
>> [x21,n21] = sigfold(x,n); [x21,n21] = sigshift(x21,n21,3);
>> [x22,n22] = sigshift(x,n,2); [x22,n22] = sigmult(x,n,x22,n22);
>> [x2,n2] = sigadd(x21,n21,x22,n22);
>> subplot(2,1,2); stem(n2,x2); title('Sequence in Example 2.2b')
>> xlabel('n'); ylabel('x2(n)');
```

The plot of $x_2(n)$ is shown in Figure 2.2.   □

Example 2.2 shows that the four `sig*` functions developed in this section provide a convenient approach for sequence manipulations.

□ **EXAMPLE 2.3**   Generate the complex-valued signal

$$x(n) = e^{(-0.1+j0.3)n}, \quad -10 \le n \le 10$$

and plot its magnitude, its phase, its real part, and its imaginary part in four separate subplots.

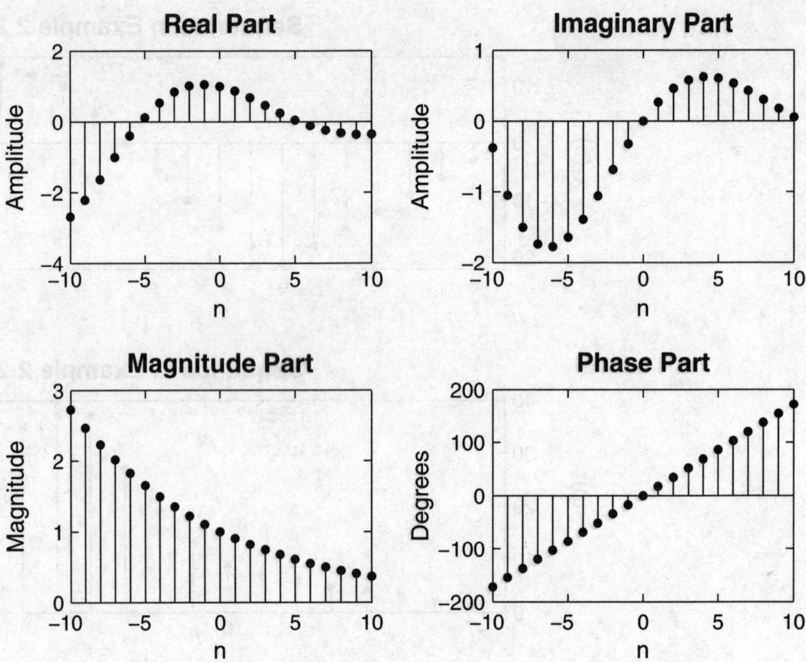

FIGURE 2.3 *Complex-valued sequence plots in Example 2.3*

Solution

MATLAB script:

```
>> n = [-10:1:10]; alpha = -0.1+0.3j;
>> x = exp(alpha*n);
>> subplot(2,2,1); stem(n,real(x));title('Real Part');xlabel('n')
>> subplot(2,2,2); stem(n,imag(x));title('Imaginary Part');xlabel('n')
>> subplot(2,2,3); stem(n,abs(x));title('Magnitude Part');xlabel('n')
>> subplot(2,2,4); stem(n,(180/pi)*angle(x));title('Phase Part');xlabel('n')
```

The plot of the sequence is shown in Figure 2.3.   □

2.1.3 DISCRETE-TIME SINUSOIDS

In the last section, we introduced the discrete-time sinusoidal sequence $x(n) = A\cos(\omega_0 n + \theta_0)$, for all n, as one of the basic signals. This signal is very important in signal theory as a basis for Fourier transform and in system theory as a basis for steady-state analysis. It can be conveniently related to the continuous-time sinusoid $x_a(t) = A\cos(\Omega_0 t + \theta_0)$ using an operation called *sampling* (Chapter 3), in which continuous-time sinusoidal values at equally spaced points $t = nT_s$ are assigned to $x(n)$.

The quantity T_s is called the sampling interval, and $\Omega_0 = \omega_0/T_s$ is called the analog frequency, measured in radians per second.

The fact that n is a discrete variable, whereas t is a continuous variable, leads to some important differences between discrete-time and continuous-time sinusoidal signals.

Periodicity in time   From our definition of periodicity, the sinusoidal sequence is periodic if

$$x[n + N] = A\cos(\omega_0 n + \omega_0 N + \theta) = A\cos(\omega_0 n + \theta_0) = x[n] \qquad (2.1)$$

This is possible if and only if $\omega_0 N = 2\pi k$, where k is an integer. This leads to the following important result (see Problem P2.5):

> The sequence $x(n) = A\cos(\omega_0 n + \theta_0)$ is periodic if and only if $f_0 \triangleq \omega_0/2\pi = k/N$, that is, f_0 is a rational number. If k and N are a pair of prime numbers, then N is the fundamental period of $x(n)$ and k represents an integer number of periods kT_s of the corresponding continuous-time sinusoid.

Periodicity in frequency   From the definition of the discrete-time sinusoid, we can easily see that

$$A\cos[(\omega_0 + k2\pi)n + \theta_0] = A\cos(\omega_0 n + kn2\pi + \theta_0)$$
$$= A\cos(\omega_0 n + \theta_0)$$

since $(kn)2\pi$ is always an integer multiple of 2π. Therefore, we have the following property:

> The sequence $x(n) = A\cos(\omega_0 n + \theta)$ is periodic in ω_0 with fundamental period 2π and periodic in f_0 with fundamental period 1.

This property has a number of very important implications:

1. Sinusoidal sequences with radian frequencies separated by integer multiples of 2π are identical.
2. All distinct sinusoidal sequences have frequencies within an interval of 2π radians. We shall use the so-called *fundamental* frequency ranges

$$-\pi < \omega \leq \pi \quad \text{or} \quad 0 \leq \omega < 2\pi \qquad (2.2)$$

Therefore, if $0 \leq \omega_0 < 2\pi$, the frequencies ω_0 and $\omega_0 + m2\pi$ are indistinguishable from the observation of the corresponding sequences.
3. Since $A\cos[\omega_0(n + n_0) + \theta] = A\cos[\omega_0 n + (\omega_0 n_0 + \theta)]$, a time shift is equivalent to a phase change.
4. The rate of oscillation of a discrete-time sinusoid increases as ω_0 increases from $\omega_0 = 0$ to $\omega_0 = \pi$. However, as ω_0 increases from $\omega_0 = \pi$ to $\omega_0 = 2\pi$, the oscillations become slower. Therefore, low frequencies (slow oscillations) are at the vicinity of $\omega_0 = k2\pi$, and high frequencies (rapid oscillations) are at the vicinity of $\omega_0 = \pi + k2\pi$.

2.1.4 SOME USEFUL RESULTS

There are several important results in discrete-time signal theory. We will discuss some that are useful in digital signal processing.

Unit sample synthesis   Any arbitrary sequence $x(n)$ can be synthesized as a weighted sum of delayed and scaled unit sample sequences, such as

$$x(n) = \sum_{k=-\infty}^{\infty} x(k)\delta(n-k) \tag{2.3}$$

We will use this result in the next section.

Even and odd synthesis   A real-valued sequence $x_e(n)$ is called even (symmetric) if

$$x_e(-n) = x_e(n)$$

Similarly, a real-valued sequence $x_o(n)$ is called odd (antisymmetric) if

$$x_o(-n) = -x_o(n)$$

Then any arbitrary real-valued sequence $x(n)$ can be decomposed into its even and odd components

$$x(n) = x_e(n) + x_o(n) \tag{2.4}$$

where the even and odd parts are given by

$$x_e(n) = \frac{1}{2}\left[x(n) + x(-n)\right] \quad \text{and} \quad x_o(n) = \frac{1}{2}\left[x(n) - x(-n)\right] \tag{2.5}$$

respectively. We will use this decomposition in studying properties of the Fourier transform. Therefore, it is a good exercise to develop a simple MATLAB function to decompose a given sequence into its even and odd components. Using MATLAB operations discussed so far, we can obtain the following `evenodd` function.

```
function [xe, xo, m] = evenodd(x,n)
% Real signal decomposition into even and odd parts
% ---------------------------------------------------
% [xe, xo, m] = evenodd(x,n)
%
if any(imag(x) ~= 0)
      error('x is not a real sequence')
end
m = -fliplr(n);
m1 = min([m,n]); m2 = max([m,n]); m = m1:m2;
nm = n(1)-m(1); n1 = 1:length(n);
x1 = zeros(1,length(m));    x1(n1+nm) = x; x = x1;
xe = 0.5*(x + fliplr(x));   xo = 0.5*(x - fliplr(x));
```

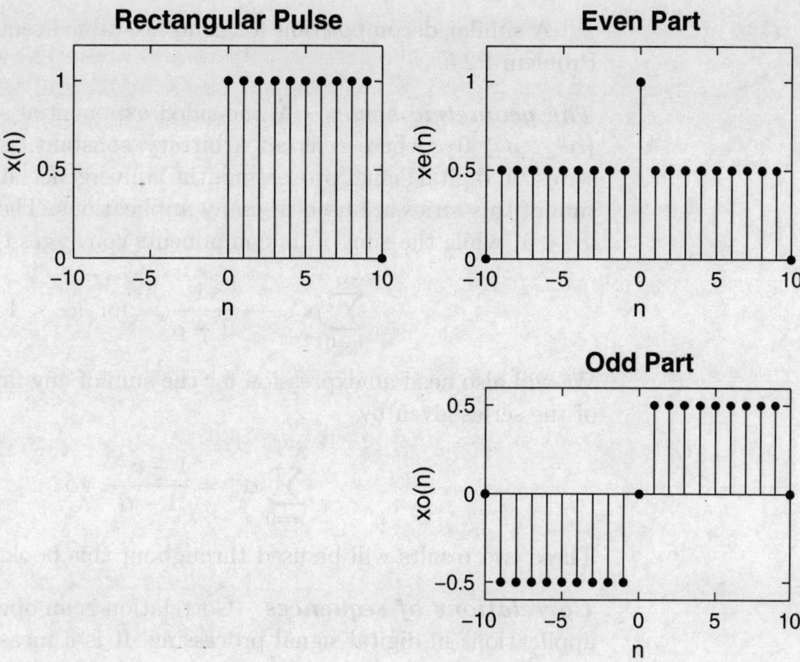

FIGURE 2.4 *Even-odd decomposition in Example 2.4*

The sequence and its support are supplied in x and n arrays, respectively. It first checks if the given sequence is real and determines the support of the even and odd components in m array. It then implements (2.5) with special attention to the MATLAB indexing operation. The resulting components are stored in xe and xo arrays.

☐ **EXAMPLE 2.4**   Let $x(n) = u(n) - u(n - 10)$. Decompose $x(n)$ into even and odd components.

Solution   The sequence $x(n)$, which is nonzero over $0 \leq n \leq 9$, is called a *rectangular pulse*. We will use MATLAB to determine and plot its even and odd parts.

```
>> n = [0:10]; x = stepseq(0,0,10)-stepseq(10,0,10);
>> [xe,xo,m] = evenodd(x,n);
>> subplot(2,2,1); stem(n,x); title('Rectangular Pulse')
>> xlabel('n'); ylabel('x(n)'); axis([-10,10,0,1.2])
>> subplot(2,2,2); stem(m,xe); title('Even Part')
>> xlabel('n'); ylabel('xe(n)'); axis([-10,10,0,1.2])
>> subplot(2,2,4); stem(m,xo); title('Odd Part')
>> xlabel('n'); ylabel('xo(n)'); axis([-10,10,-0.6,0.6])
```

The plots shown in Figure 2.4 clearly demonstrate the decomposition. ☐

A similar decomposition for complex-valued sequences is explored in Problem P2.5.

The geometric series   A one-sided exponential sequence of the form $\{\alpha^n, \ n \geq 0\}$, where α is an arbitrary constant, .is called a geometric series. In digital signal processing, the convergence and expression for the sum of this series are used in many applications. The series converges for $|\alpha| < 1$, while the sum of its components converges to

$$\sum_{n=0}^{\infty} \alpha^n \longrightarrow \frac{1}{1-\alpha}, \quad \text{for } |\alpha| < 1 \tag{2.6}$$

We will also need an expression for the sum of any finite number of terms of the series given by

$$\sum_{n=0}^{N-1} \alpha^n = \frac{1-\alpha^N}{1-\alpha}, \forall \alpha \tag{2.7}$$

These two results will be used throughout this book.

Correlations of sequences   Correlation is an operation used in many applications in digital signal processing. It is a measure of the degree to which two sequences are similar. Given two real-valued sequences $x(n)$ and $y(n)$ of finite energy, the *cross-correlation* of $x(n)$ and $y(n)$ is a sequence $r_{xy}(\ell)$ defined as

$$r_{xy}(\ell) = \sum_{n=-\infty}^{\infty} x(n)y(n-\ell) \tag{2.8}$$

The index ℓ is called the shift or lag parameter. The special case of (2.8) when $y(n) = x(n)$ is called *autocorrelation* and is defined by

$$r_{xx}(\ell) = \sum_{n=-\infty}^{\infty} x(n)x(n-\ell) \tag{2.9}$$

It provides a measure of self-similarity between different alignments of the sequence. MATLAB functions to compute auto- and cross-correlations are discussed later in the chapter.

2.2 DISCRETE SYSTEMS

■

Mathematically, a discrete-time system (or *discrete system* for short) is described as an operator $T[\cdot]$ that takes a sequence $x(n)$ (called *excitation*) and transforms it into another sequence $y(n)$ (called *response*). That is,

$$y(n) = T[x(n)]$$

In DSP, we will say that the system processes an *input* signal into an *output* signal. Discrete systems are broadly classified into *linear* and *nonlinear* systems. We will deal mostly with linear systems.

2.2.1 LINEAR SYSTEMS

A discrete system $T[\cdot]$ is a linear operator $L[\cdot]$ if and only if $L[\cdot]$ satisfies the principle of superposition, namely,

$$L[a_1 x_1(n) + a_2 x_2(n)] = a_1 L[x_1(n)] + a_2 L[x_2(n)], \forall a_1, a_2, x_1(n), x_2(n) \tag{2.10}$$

Using (2.3) and (2.10), the output $y(n)$ of a linear system to an arbitrary input $x(n)$ is given by

$$y(n) = L[x(n)] = L\left[\sum_{n=-\infty}^{\infty} x(k)\,\delta(n-k)\right] = \sum_{n=-\infty}^{\infty} x(k)L[\delta(n-k)]$$

The response $L[\delta(n-k)]$ can be interpreted as the response of a linear system at time n due to a unit sample (a well-known sequence) at time k. It is called an *impulse response* and is denoted by $h(n,k)$. The output then is given by the *superposition summation*

$$y(n) = \sum_{n=-\infty}^{\infty} x(k)h(n,k) \tag{2.11}$$

The computation of (2.11) requires the *time-varying* impulse response $h(n,k)$, which in practice is not very convenient. Therefore, time-invariant systems are widely used in DSP.

☐ **EXAMPLE 2.5**   Determine whether the following systems are linear.

1. $y(n) = T[x(n)] = 3x^2(n)$
2. $y(n) = 2x(n-2) + 5$
3. $y(n) = x(n+1) - x(n-1)$

Solution   Let $y_1(n) = T\big[x_1(n)\big]$ and $y_2(n) = T\big[x_2(n)\big]$. We will determine the response of each system to the linear combination $a_1 x_1(n) + a_2 x_2(n)$ and check whether it is equal to the linear combination $a_1 x_1(n) + a_2 x_2(n)$ where a_1 and a_2 are arbitrary constants.

1. $y(n) = T[x(n)] = 3x^2(n)$: Consider

$$T\big[a_1 x_1(n) + a_2 x_2(n)\big] = 3\big[a_1 x_1(n) + a_2 x_2(n)\big]^2$$

$$= 3a_1^2 x_1^2(n) + 3a_2^2 x_2^2(n) + 6a_1 a_2 x_1(n)x_2(n)$$

which is not equal to

$$a_1 y_1(n) + a_2 y_2(n) = 3a_1^2 x_1^2(n) + 3a_2^2 x_2^2(n)$$

Hence the given system is nonlinear.

2. $y(n) = 2x(n-2) + 5$: Consider

$$T\big[a_1 x_1(n) + a_2 x_2(n)\big] = 2\big[a_1 x_1(n-2) + a_2 x_2(n-2)\big] + 5$$

$$= a_1 y_1(n) + a_2 y_2(n) - 5$$

Clearly, the given system is nonlinear even though the input-output relation is a straight-line function.

3. $y(n) = x(n+1) - x(1-n)$: Consider

$$T[a_1 x_1(n) + a_2 x_2(n)] = a_1 x_1(n+1) + a_2 x_2(n+1) + a_1 x_1(1-n)$$

$$+ a_2 x_2(1-n)$$

$$= a_1[x_1(n+1) - x_1(1-n)]$$

$$+ a_2[x_2(n+1) - x_2(1-n)]$$

$$= a_1 y_1(n) + a_2 y_2(n)$$

Hence the given system is linear.   □

Linear time-invariant (LTI) system   A linear system in which an input-output pair, $x(n)$ and $y(n)$, is invariant to a shift k in time is called a linear time-invariant system, that is,

$$y(n) = L[x(n)] \Rightarrow L[x(n-k)] = y(n-k) \tag{2.12}$$

For an LTI system, the $L[\cdot]$ and the shifting operators are reversible as shown here.

$$x(n) \longrightarrow \boxed{L\,[\cdot]} \longrightarrow y(n) \longrightarrow \boxed{\text{Shift by } k} \longrightarrow y(n-k)$$

$$x(n) \longrightarrow \boxed{\text{Shift by } k} \longrightarrow x(n-k) \longrightarrow \boxed{L\,[\cdot]} \longrightarrow y(n-k)$$

□ **EXAMPLE 2.6**   Determine whether the following linear systems are time-invariant.

1. $y(n) = L[x(n)] = 10\sin(0.1\pi n)x(n)$
2. $y(n) = L[x(n)] = x(n+1) - x(1-n)$
3. $y(n) = L[x(n)] = \frac{1}{4}x(n) + \frac{1}{2}x(n-1) + \frac{1}{4}x(n-2)$

Solution   First we will compute the response $y_k(n) \triangleq L[x(n-k)]$ to the shifted input sequence. This is obtained by subtracting k from the arguments of every input sequence term on the right-hand side of the linear transformation. To determine time-invariance, we will then compare it to the shifted output sequence $y(n-k)$, obtained after replacing every n by $(n-k)$ on the right-hand side of the linear transformation.

1. $y(n) = L[x(n)] = 10\sin(0.1\pi n)x(n)$: The response due to shifted input is

$$y_k(n) = L[x(n-k)] = 10\sin(0.1\pi n)x(n-k)$$

while the shifted output is

$$y(n-k) = 10\sin[0.1\pi(n-k)]x(n-k) \neq y_k(n)$$

Hence the given system is not time-invariant.

2. $y(n) = L[x(n)] = x(n+1) - x(1-n)$: The response due to shifted input is

$$y_k(n) = L[x(n-k)] = x(n-k+1) - x(1-n-k)$$

while the shifted output is

$$y(n-k) = x(n-k) - x(1-[n-k]) = x(n-k+1) - x(1-n+k) \neq y_k(n).$$

Hence the given system is not time-invariant.

3. $y(n) = L[x(n)] = \frac{1}{4}x(n) + \frac{1}{2}x(n-1) + \frac{1}{4}x(n-2)$: The response due to shifted input is

$$y_k(n) = L[x(n-k)] = \frac{1}{4}x(n-k) + \frac{1}{2}x(n-1-k) + \frac{1}{4}x(n-2-k)$$

while the shifted output is

$$y(n-k) = \frac{1}{4}x(n-k) + \frac{1}{2}x(n-k-1) + \frac{1}{4}x(n-k-2) = y_k(n)$$

Hence the given system is time-invariant. $\square$

We will denote an LTI system by the operator $LTI\,[\cdot]$. Let $x(n)$ and $y(n)$ be the input-output pair of an LTI system. Then the time-varying function $h(n,k)$ becomes a time-invariant function $h(n-k)$, and the output from (2.11) is given by

$$y(n) = LTI\,[x(n)] = \sum_{k=-\infty}^{\infty} x(k)h(n-k) \qquad (2.13)$$

The impulse response of an LTI system is given by $h(n)$. The mathematical operation in (2.13) is called a *linear convolution sum* and is denoted by

$$y(n) \triangleq x(n) * h(n) \qquad (2.14)$$

Hence an LTI system is completely characterized in the time domain by the impulse response $h(n)$.

$$x(n) \longrightarrow \boxed{h(n)} \longrightarrow y(n) = x(n) * h(n)$$

We will explore several properties of the convolution in Problem P2.14.

Stability This is a very important concept in linear system theory. The primary reason for considering stability is to avoid building harmful systems or to avoid burnout or saturation in the system operation. A system is said to be *bounded-input bounded-output (BIBO) stable* if every bounded input produces a bounded output.

$$|x(n)| < \infty \Rightarrow |y(n)| < \infty, \forall x, y$$

An LTI system is BIBO stable if and only if its impulse response is *absolutely summable*.

$$\text{BIBO Stability} \Longleftrightarrow \sum_{-\infty}^{\infty} |h(n)| < \infty \qquad (2.15)$$

Causality This important concept is necessary to make sure that systems can be built. A system is said to be causal if the output at index n_0 depends only on the input up to and including the index n_0; that is, the output does not depend on the future values of the input. An LTI system is causal if and only if the impulse response

$$h(n) = 0, \quad n < 0 \qquad (2.16)$$

Such a sequence is termed a *causal sequence*. In signal processing, unless otherwise stated, we will always assume that the system is causal.

2.3 CONVOLUTION

We introduced the convolution operation (2.14) to describe the response of an LTI system. In DSP, it is an important operation and has many other uses that we will see throughout this book. Convolution can be evaluated in many different ways. If the sequences are mathematical functions (of finite or infinite duration), then we can analytically evaluate (2.14) for all n to obtain a functional form of $y(n)$.

□ **EXAMPLE 2.7** Let the rectangular pulse $x(n) = u(n) - u(n-10)$ of Example 2.4 be an input to an LTI system with impulse response

$$h(n) = (0.9)^n u(n)$$

Determine the output $y(n)$.

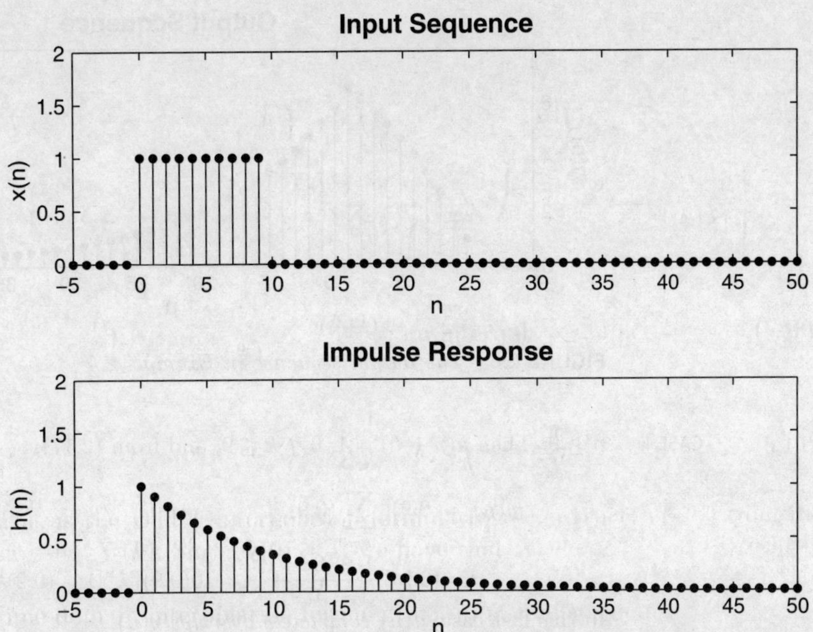

FIGURE 2.5 *The input sequence and the impulse response in Example 2.7*

Solution

The input $x(n)$ and the impulse response $h(n)$ are shown in Figure 2.5. From (2.14),

$$y(n) = \sum_{k=0}^{9} (1)\,(0.9)^{(n-k)}\,u(n-k) = (0.9)^n \sum_{k=0}^{9} (0.9)^{-k}\,u(n-k) \qquad (2.17)$$

The sum in (2.17) is almost a geometric series sum except that the term $u(n-k)$ takes different values depending on n and k. There are three possible conditions under which $u(n-k)$ can be evaluated.

CASE i $n < 0$: Then $u(n-k) = 0$, $\quad 0 \le k \le 9$. Hence, from (2.17),

$$y(n) = 0 \qquad (2.18)$$

In this case, the nonzero values of $x(n)$ and $h(n)$ *do not overlap*.

CASE ii $0 \le n < 9$: Then $u(n-k) = 1$, $0 \le k \le n$. Hence, from (2.17),

$$y(n) = (0.9)^n \sum_{k=0}^{n} (0.9)^{-k} = (0.9)^n \sum_{k=0}^{n} [(0.9)^{-1}]^k$$

$$= (0.9)^n \frac{1 - (0.9)^{-(n+1)}}{1 - (0.9)^{-1}} = 10[1 - (0.9)^{n+1}], \quad 0 \le n < 9 \qquad (2.19)$$

In this case, the impulse response $h(n)$ *partially overlaps* the input $x(n)$.

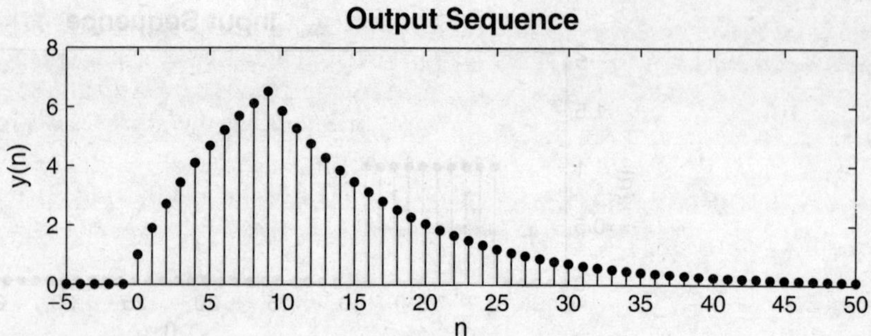

FIGURE 2.6   *The output sequence in Example 2.7*

CASE iii $n \geq 9$: Then $u(n - k) = 1$, $0 \leq k \leq 9$, and from (2.17),

$$y(n) = (0.9)^n \sum_{k=0}^{9} (0.9)^{-k}$$

$$= (0.9)^n \frac{1 - (0.9)^{-10}}{1 - (0.9)^{-1}} = 10(0.9)^{n-9}[1 - (0.9)^{10}], \quad n \geq 9 \qquad (2.20)$$

In this last case, $h(n)$ *completely overlaps* $x(n)$.

The complete response is given by (2.18), (2.19), and (2.20). It is shown in Figure 2.6, which depicts the distortion of the input pulse.   □

This example can also be done using a method called graphical convolution, in which (2.14) is given a graphical interpretation. In this method, $h(n - k)$ is interpreted as a *folded-and-shifted* version of $h(k)$. The output $y(n)$ is obtained as a sample sum under the overlap of $x(k)$ and $h(n - k)$. We use an example to illustrate this.

□ **EXAMPLE 2.8**   Given the two sequences

$$x(n) = [3, 11, 7, 0, -1, 4, 2], \quad -3 \leq n \leq 3; \qquad h(n) = [2, 3, 0, -5, 2, 1], \quad -1 \leq n \leq 4$$

determine the convolution $y(n) = x(n) * h(n)$.

Solution   In Figure 2.7, we show four plots. The top-left plot shows $x(k)$ and $h(k)$, the original sequences. The top-right plot shows $x(k)$ and $h(-k)$, the folded version of $h(k)$. The bottom-left plot shows $x(k)$ and $h(-1-k)$, the "folded and shifted by -1" version of $h(k)$. Then

$$\sum_k x(k)h(-1-k) = 3 \times (-5) + 11 \times 0 + 7 \times 3 + 0 \times 2 = 6 = y(-1)$$

The bottom-right plot shows $x(k)$ and $h(2-k)$, the "folded and shifted by 2" version of $h(k)$, which gives

$$\sum_k x(k)h(2-k) = 11 \times 1 + 7 \times 2 + 0 \times (-5) + (-1) \times 0 + 4 \times 3 + 2 \times 2 = 41 = y(2)$$

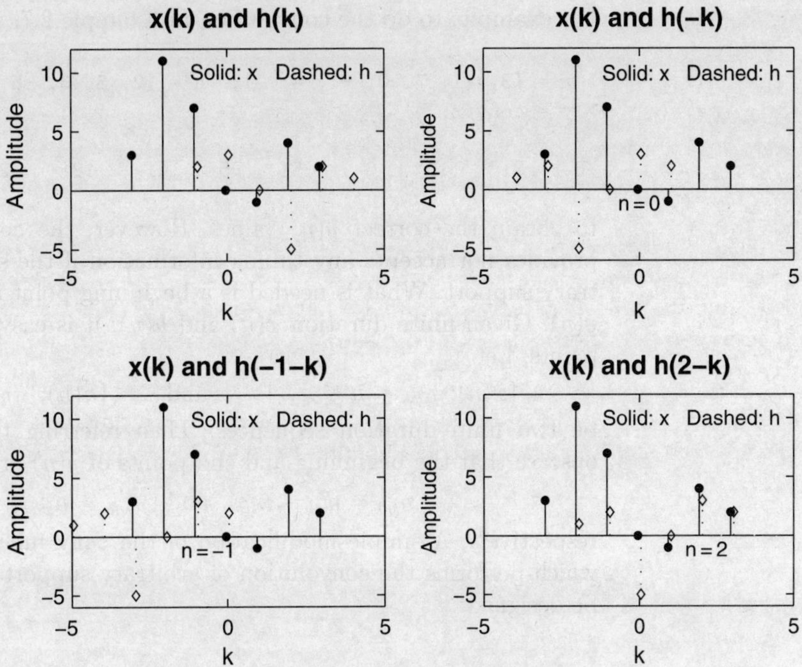

FIGURE 2.7 *Graphical convolution in Example 2.8*

Thus we have obtained two values of $y(n)$. Similar graphical calculations can be done for other remaining values of $y(n)$. Note that the beginning point (first nonzero sample) of $y(n)$ is given by $n = -3 + (-1) = -4$, while the end point (the last nonzero sample) is given by $n = 3 + 4 = 7$. The complete output is given by

$$y(n) = \{6, 31, 47, 6, -51, -5, 41, 18, -22, -3, 8, 2\}$$
$$\uparrow$$

Students are strongly encouraged to verify the above result. Note that the resulting sequence $y(n)$ has a *longer length* than both the $x(n)$ and $h(n)$ sequences.
□

2.3.1 MATLAB IMPLEMENTATION

If arbitrary sequences are of infinite duration, then MATLAB cannot be used *directly* to compute the convolution. MATLAB does provide a built-in function called `conv` that computes the convolution between two finite-duration sequences. The `conv` function assumes that the two sequences begin at $n = 0$ and is invoked by

```
>> y = conv(x,h);
```

For example, to do the convolution in Example 2.7, we could use

```
>> x = [3, 11, 7, 0, -1, 4, 2];  h = [2, 3, 0, -5, 2, 1];
>> y = conv(x, h)
y =
    6    31    47    6    -51    -5    41    18    -22    -3    8    2
```

to obtain the correct $y(n)$ values. However, the conv function neither provides nor accepts any timing information if the sequences have arbitrary support. What is needed is a beginning point and an end point of $y(n)$. Given finite duration $x(n)$ and $h(n)$, it is easy to determine these points. Let

$$\{x(n);\ n_{xb} \leq n \leq n_{xe}\} \qquad \text{and} \qquad \{h(n);\ n_{hb} \leq n \leq n_{he}\}$$

be two finite-duration sequences. Then referring to Example 2.8, we observe that the beginning and end points of $y(n)$ are

$$n_{yb} = n_{xb} + n_{hb} \quad \text{and} \quad n_{ye} = n_{xe} + n_{he}$$

respectively. A simple modification of the conv function, called conv_m, which performs the convolution of arbitrary support sequences, can now be designed.

```
function [y,ny] = conv_m(x,nx,h,nh)
% Modified convolution routine for signal processing
% ---------------------------------------------------
%  [y,ny] = conv_m(x,nx,h,nh)
%  [y,ny] = convolution result
%  [x,nx] = first signal
%  [h,nh] = second signal
%
nyb = nx(1)+nh(1); nye = nx(length(x)) + nh(length(h));
ny = [nyb:nye];    y = conv(x,h);
```

☐   **EXAMPLE 2.9**   Perform the convolution in Example 2.8 using the conv_m function.

Solution   MATLAB script:

```
>> x = [3, 11, 7, 0, -1, 4, 2]; nx = [-3:3];
>> h = [2, 3, 0, -5, 2, 1]; nh = [-1:4];
```

```
>> [y,ny] = conv_m(x,nx,h,nh)
y =
    6    31    47    6    -51    -5    41    18    -22    -3    8    2
ny =
   -4    -3    -2    -1     0     1     2     3     4     5    6    7
```

Hence

$$y(n) = \{6, 31, 47, 6, -51, -5, 41, 18, -22, -3, 8, 2\}$$
$$\uparrow$$

as in Example 2.8. $\qquad\qquad\square$

An alternate method in MATLAB can be used to perform the convolution. This method uses a matrix-vector multiplication approach, which we will explore in Problem P2.17.

2.3.2 SEQUENCE CORRELATIONS REVISITED

If we compare the convolution operation (2.14) with that of the cross-correlation of two sequences defined in (2.8), we observe a close resemblance. The cross-correlation $r_{yx}(\ell)$ can be put in the form

$$r_{yx}(\ell) = y(\ell) * x(-\ell)$$

with the autocorrelation $r_{xx}(\ell)$ in the form

$$r_{xx}(\ell) = x(\ell) * x(-\ell)$$

Therefore, these correlations can be computed using the `conv_m` function if sequences are of finite duration.

☐ **EXAMPLE 2.10**   In this example, we will demonstrate one application of the cross-correlation sequence. Let

$$x(n) = [3, 11, 7, 0, -1, 4, 2]$$
$$\uparrow$$

be a prototype sequence, and let $y(n)$ be its noise-corrupted-and-shifted version

$$y(n) = x(n-2) + w(n)$$

where $w(n)$ is a Gaussian sequence with mean 0 and variance 1. Compute the cross-correlation between $y(n)$ and $x(n)$.

Solution   From the construction of $y(n)$, it follows that $y(n)$ is "similar" to $x(n-2)$ and hence their cross-correlation would show the strongest similarity at $\ell = 2$. To test this out using MATLAB, let us compute the cross-correlation using two different noise sequences.

```
% Noise sequence 1
>> x = [3, 11, 7, 0, -1, 4, 2]; nx=[-3:3]; % Given signal x(n)
>> [y,ny] = sigshift(x,nx,2);              % Obtain x(n-2)
>> w = randn(1,length(y)); nw = ny;        % Generate w(n)
>> [y,ny] = sigadd(y,ny,w,nw);             % Obtain y(n) = x(n-2) + w(n)
>> [x,nx] = sigfold(x,nx);                 % Obtain x(-n)
```

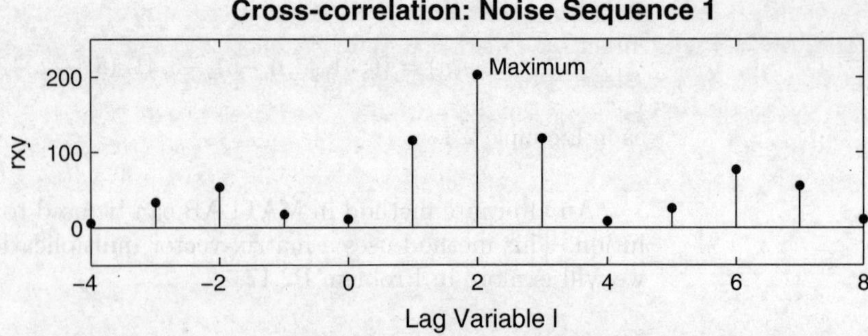

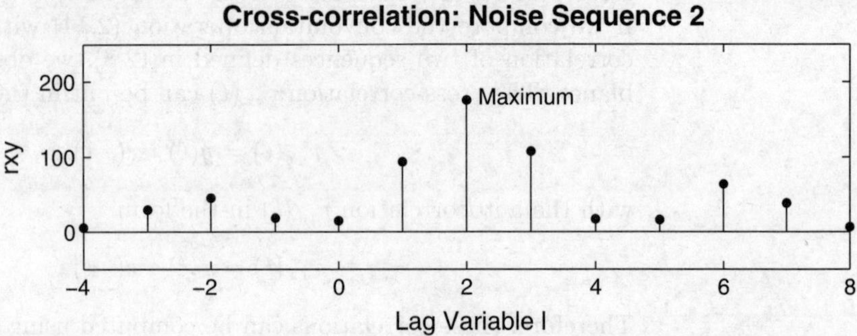

FIGURE 2.8   *Cross-correlation sequence with two different noise realizations*

```
>> [rxy,nrxy] = conv_m(y,ny,x,nx);          % Cross-correlation
>> subplot(1,1,1), subplot(2,1,1);stem(nrxy,rxy)
>> axis([-5,10,-50,250]);xlabel('Lag Variable l')
>> ylabel('rxy');title('Cross-correlation: Noise Sequence 1')
%
% Noise sequence 2
>> x = [3, 11, 7, 0, -1, 4, 2]; nx=[-3:3]; % Given signal x(n)
>> [y,ny] = sigshift(x,nx,2);               % Obtain x(n-2)
>> w = randn(1,length(y)); nw = ny;         % Generate w(n)
>> [y,ny] = sigadd(y,ny,w,nw);              % Obtain y(n) = x(n-2) + w(n)
>> [x,nx] = sigfold(x,nx);                  % Obtain x(-n)
>> [rxy,nrxy] = conv_m(y,ny,x,nx);          % Cross-correlation
>> subplot(2,1,2);stem(nrxy,rxy)
>> axis([-5,10,-50,250]);xlabel('Lag Variable l')
>> ylabel('rxy');title('Cross-correlation: Noise sequence 2')
```

From Figure 2.8, we observe that the cross-correlation indeed peaks at $\ell = 2$, which implies that $y(n)$ is similar to $x(n)$ shifted by 2. This approach can be used in applications like radar signal processing in identifying and localizing targets.   □

Note that the signal-processing toolbox in MATLAB also provides a function called `xcorr` for sequence correlation computations. In its simplest form,

```
>> xcorr(x,y)
```

computes the cross-correlation between vectors `x` and `y`, while

```
>> xcorr(x)
```

computes the autocorrelation of vector `x`. It generates results that are identical to the one obtained from the proper use of the `conv_m` function. However, the `xcorr` function cannot provide the timing (or lag) information (as done by the `conv_m` function), which then must be obtained by some other means.

2.4 DIFFERENCE EQUATIONS

An LTI discrete system can also be described by a linear constant coefficient difference equation of the form

$$\sum_{k=0}^{N} a_k y(n-k) = \sum_{m=0}^{M} b_m x(n-m), \quad \forall n \tag{2.21}$$

If $a_N \neq 0$, then the difference equation is of order N. This equation describes a recursive approach for computing the current output, given the input values and previously computed output values. In practice, this equation is computed forward in time, from $n = -\infty$ to $n = \infty$. Therefore, another form of this equation is

$$y(n) = \sum_{m=0}^{M} b_m x(n-m) - \sum_{k=1}^{N} a_k y(n-k) \tag{2.22}$$

A solution to this equation can be obtained in the form

$$y(n) = y_{\mathrm{H}}(n) + y_{\mathrm{P}}(n)$$

The *homogeneous part* of the solution, $y_{\mathrm{H}}(n)$, is given by

$$y_{\mathrm{H}}(n) = \sum_{k=1}^{N} c_k z_k^n$$

where $z_k, k = 1, \ldots, N$ are N roots (also called *natural frequencies*) of the characteristic equation

$$\sum_0^N a_k z^{N-k} = 0$$

This characteristic equation is important in determining the stability of systems. If the roots z_k satisfy the condition

$$|z_k| < 1, \ k = 1, \ldots, N \tag{2.23}$$

then a causal system described by (2.22) is stable. The *particular part* of the solution, $y_P(n)$, is determined from the right-hand side of (2.21). In Chapter 4, we will discuss the analytical approach of solving difference equations using the z-transform.

2.4.1 MATLAB IMPLEMENTATION

A function called `filter` is available to solve difference equations numerically, given the input and the difference equation coefficients. In its simplest form, this function is invoked by

```
y = filter(b,a,x)
```

where

```
b = [b0, b1, ..., bM]; a = [a0, a1, ..., aN];
```

are the coefficient arrays from the equation given in (2.21) and `x` is the input sequence array. The output `y` has the same length as input `x`. One must ensure that the coefficient `a0` not be zero.

To compute and plot impulse response, MATLAB provides the function `impz`. When invoked by

```
h = impz(b,a,n);
```

it computes samples of the impulse response of the filter at the sample indices given in `n` with numerator coefficients in `b` and denominator coefficients in `a`. When no output arguments are given, the `impz` function plots the response in the current figure window using the `stem` function. We will illustrate the use of these functions in the following example.

☐ **EXAMPLE 2.11**   Consider the following difference equation:

$$y(n) - y(n-1) + 0.9y(n-2) = x(n); \quad \forall n$$

a.   Calculate and plot the impulse response $h(n)$ at $n = -20, \ldots, 100$.
b.   Calculate and plot the unit step response $s(n)$ at $n = -20, \ldots, 100$.
c.   Is the system specified by $h(n)$ stable?

Solution   From the given difference equation, the coefficient arrays are

```
b = [1]; a=[1, -1, 0.9];
```

a. MATLAB script:

```
>> b = [1]; a = [1, -1, 0.9];  n = [-20:120];
>> h = impz(b,a,n);
>> subplot(2,1,1); stem(n,h);
>> title('Impulse Response'); xlabel('n'); ylabel('h(n)')
```

The plot of the impulse response is shown in Figure 2.9.

b. MATLAB script:

```
>> x = stepseq(0,-20,120);   s = filter(b,a,x);
>> subplot(2,1,2); stem(n,s)
>> title('Step Response'); xlabel('n'); ylabel('s(n)')
```

The plot of the unit step response is shown in Figure 2.9.

c. To determine the stability of the system, we have to determine $h(n)$ for all n. Although we have not described a method to solve the difference equation,

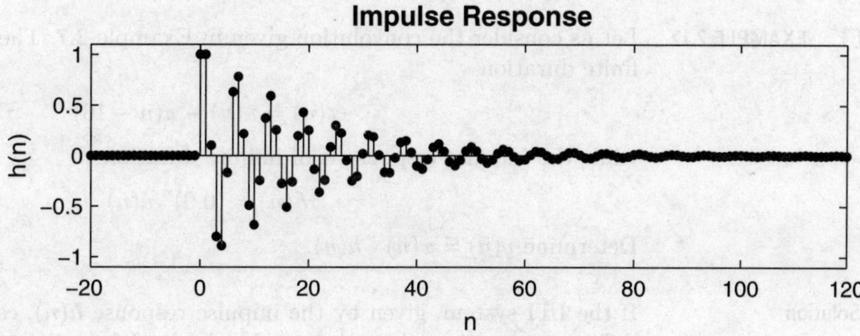

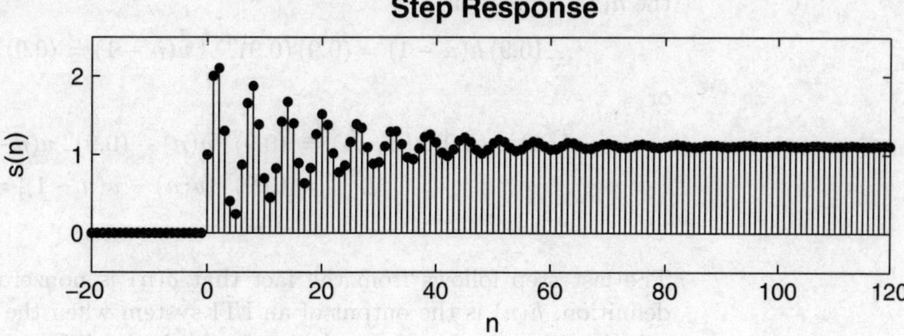

FIGURE 2.9   *Impulse response and step response plots in Example 2.11*

we can use the plot of the impulse response to observe that $h(n)$ is practically zero for $n > 120$. Hence the sum $\sum |h(n)|$ can be determined from MATLAB using

```
>> sum(abs(h))
ans = 14.8785
```

which implies that the system is stable. An alternate approach is to use the stability condition (2.23) using MATLAB's `roots` function.

```
>>z = roots(a);    magz = abs(z)
magz =    0.9487
          0.9487
```

Since the magnitudes of both roots are less than 1, the system is stable.

☐

In the previous section, we noted that if one or both sequences in the convolution are of infinite length, then the `conv` function cannot be used. If one of the sequences is of infinite length, then it is possible to use MATLAB for numerical evaluation of the convolution. This is done using the `filter` function, as we will see in the following example.

☐ **EXAMPLE 2.12**   Let us consider the convolution given in Example 2.7. The input sequence is of finite duration

$$x(n) = u(n) - u(n - 10)$$

while the impulse response is of infinite duration

$$h(n) = (0.9)^n u(n)$$

Determine $y(n) = x(n) * h(n)$.

Solution   If the LTI system, given by the impulse response $h(n)$, can be described by a difference equation, then $y(n)$ can be obtained from the `filter` function. From the $h(n)$ expression,

$$(0.9)\,h(n-1) = (0.9)\,(0.9)^{n-1}\,u(n-1) = (0.9)^n\,u(n-1)$$

or

$$h(n) - (0.9)\,h(n-1) = (0.9)^n\,u(n) - (0.9)^n\,u(n-1)$$
$$= (0.9)^n\,[u(n) - u(n-1)] = (0.9)^n\,\delta(n)$$
$$= \delta(n)$$

The last step follows from the fact that $\delta(n)$ is nonzero only at $n = 0$. By definition, $h(n)$ is the output of an LTI system when the input is $\delta(n)$. Hence substituting $x(n)$ for $\delta(n)$ and $y(n)$ for $h(n)$, the difference equation is

$$y(n) - 0.9y(n-1) = x(n)$$

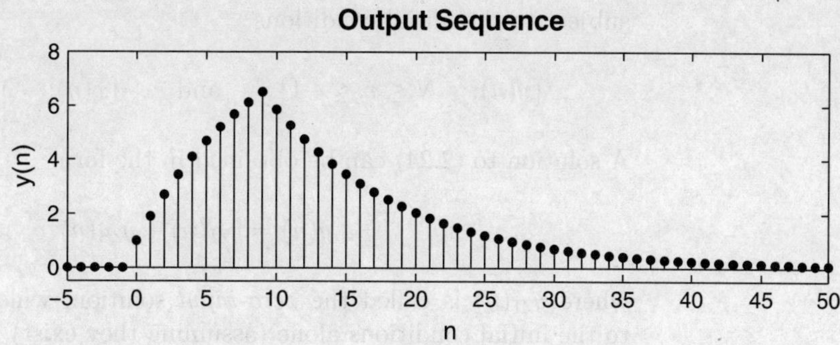

FIGURE 2.10   *Output sequence in Example 2.12*

Now MATLAB's `filter` function can be used to compute the convolution indirectly.

```
>> b = [1]; a = [1,-0.9];
>> n = -5:50; x = stepseq(0,-5,50) - stepseq(10,-5,50);
>> y = filter(b,a,x);
>> subplot(2,1,2); stem(n,y); title('Output Sequence')
>> xlabel('n'); ylabel('y(n)'); axis([-5,50,-0.5,8])
```

The plot of the output is shown in Figure 2.10, which is exactly the same as that in Figure 2.6.   □

In Example 2.12, the impulse response was a one-sided exponential sequence for which we could determine a difference equation representation. This means that not all infinite-length impulse responses can be converted into difference equations. The above analysis, however, can be extended to a linear combination of one-sided exponential sequences, which results in higher-order difference equations. We will discuss this topic of conversion from one representation to another one in Chapter 4.

2.4.2 ZERO-INPUT AND ZERO-STATE RESPONSES

In DSP, the difference equation is generally solved forward in time from $n = 0$. Therefore, initial conditions on $x(n)$ and $y(n)$ are necessary to determine the output for $n \geq 0$. The difference equation is then given by

$$y(n) = \sum_{m=0}^{M} b_m x(n-m) - \sum_{k=1}^{N} a_k y(n-k); \; n \geq 0 \qquad \textbf{(2.24)}$$

subject to the initial conditions

$$\{y(n);\ -N \le n \le -1\} \quad \text{and} \quad \{x(n);\ -M \le n \le -1\}$$

A solution to (2.24) can be obtained in the form

$$y(n) = y_{\mathrm{ZI}}(n) + y_{\mathrm{ZS}}(n)$$

where $y_{\mathrm{ZI}}(n)$ is called the *zero-input* solution, which is a solution due to the initial conditions alone (assuming they exist), while the *zero-state* solution, $y_{\mathrm{ZS}}(n)$, is a solution due to input $x(n)$ alone (or assuming that the initial conditions are zero). In MATLAB, another form of the function `filter` can be used to solve for the difference equation, given its initial conditions. We will illustrate the use of this form in Chapter 4.

2.4.3 DIGITAL FILTERS

Filter is a generic name that means a linear time-invariant system designed for a specific job of frequency selection or frequency discrimination. Hence discrete-time LTI systems are also called digital filters. There are two types of digital filters.

FIR filter   If the unit impulse response of an LTI system is of finite duration, then the system is called a *finite-duration impulse response* (or FIR) filter. Hence, for an FIR filter, $h(n) = 0$ for $n < n_1$ and for $n > n_2$. The following part of the difference equation (2.21) describes a *causal* FIR filter:

$$y(n) = \sum_{m=0}^{M} b_m x(n - m) \tag{2.25}$$

Furthermore, $h(0) = b_0$, $h(1) = b_1, \ldots, h(M) = b_M$, while all other $h(n)$'s are 0. FIR filters are also called *nonrecursive* or *moving average* (MA) filters. In MATLAB, FIR filters are represented either as impulse response values $\{h(n)\}$ or as difference equation coefficients $\{b_m\}$ and $\{a_0 = 1\}$. Therefore, to implement FIR filters, we can use either the `conv(x,h)` function (and its modification that we discussed) or the `filter(b,1,x)` function. There is a difference in the outputs of these two implementations that should be noted. The output sequence from the `conv(x,h)` function has a *longer length* than both the $x(n)$ and $h(n)$ sequences. On the other hand, the output sequence from the `filter(b,1,x)` function has exactly the *same length* as the input $x(n)$ sequence. In practice (and especially for processing signals), the use of the `filter` function is encouraged.

IIR filter   If the impulse response of an LTI system is of infinite duration, then the system is called an *infinite-duration impulse response* (or IIR) filter. The part of difference equation (2.21)

$$\sum_{k=0}^{N} a_k y(n-k) = x(n) \tag{2.26}$$

describes a *recursive* filter in which the output $y(n)$ is recursively computed from its previously computed values and is called an *autoregressive* (AR) filter. The impulse response of such a filter is of infinite duration, and hence it represents an IIR filter. The general equation (2.21) also describes an IIR filter. It has two parts: an AR part and an MA part. Such an IIR filter is called an *autoregressive moving average*, or an ARMA, filter. In MATLAB, IIR filters are described by the difference equation coefficients $\{b_m\}$ and $\{a_k\}$ and are implemented by the `filter(b,a,x)` function.

2.5 PROBLEMS

P2.1   Generate the following sequences using the basic MATLAB signal functions and the basic MATLAB signal operations discussed in this chapter. Plot signal samples using the `stem` function.

1. $x_1(n) = 3\delta(n+2) + 2\delta(n) - \delta(n-3) + 5\delta(n-7)$, $-5 \le n \le 15$.
2. $x_2(n) = \sum_{k=-5}^{5} e^{-|k|}\delta(n-2k)$, $-10 \le n \le 10$.
3. $x_3(n) = 10u(n) - 5u(n-5) - 10u(n-10) + 5u(n-15)$.
4. $x_4(n) = e^{0.1n}[u(n+20) - u(n-10)]$.
5. $x_5(n) = 5[\cos(0.49\pi n) + \cos(0.51\pi n)]$, $-200 \le n \le 200$. Comment on the waveform shape.
6. $x_6(n) = 2\sin(0.01\pi n)\cos(0.5\pi n)$, $-200 \le n \le 200$. Comment on the waveform shape.
7. $x_7(n) = e^{-0.05n}\sin(0.1\pi n + \pi/3)$, $0 \le n \le 100$. Comment on the waveform shape.
8. $x_8(n) = e^{0.01n}\sin(0.1\pi n)$, $0 \le n \le 100$. Comment on the waveform shape.

P2.2   Generate the following random sequences and obtain their histogram using the `hist` function with 100 bins. Use the `bar` function to plot each histogram.

1. $x_1(n)$ is a random sequence whose samples are independent and uniformly distributed over $[0, 2]$ interval. Generate 100,000 samples.
2. $x_2(n)$ is a Gaussian random sequence whose samples are independent with mean 10 and variance 10. Generate 10,000 samples.
3. $x_3(n) = x_1(n) + x_1(n-1)$ where $x_1(n)$ is the random sequence given in part 1 above. Comment on the shape of this histogram and explain the shape.
4. $x_4(n) = \sum_{k=1}^{4} y_k(n)$ where each random sequence $y_k(n)$ is independent of others with samples uniformly distributed over $[-0.5, 0.5]$. Comment on the shape of this histogram.

P2.3 Generate the following periodic sequences and plot their samples (using the **stem** function) over the indicated number of periods.

1. $\tilde{x}_1(n) = \{\ldots, -2, -1, 0, 1, 2, \ldots\}_{\text{periodic}}$. Plot five periods.

2. $\tilde{x}_2(n) = e^{0.1n}[u(n) - u(n - 20)]_{\text{periodic}}$. Plot three periods.
3. $\tilde{x}_3(n) = \sin(0.1\pi n)[u(n) - u(n - 10)]$. Plot four periods.
4. $\tilde{x}_4(n) = \{\ldots, 1, 2, 3, \ldots\}_{\text{periodic}} + \{\ldots, 1, 2, 3, 4, \ldots\}_{\text{periodic}}, \ 0 \leq n \leq 24$. What is the period of $\tilde{x}_4(n)$?

P2.4 Let $x(n) = \{2, 4, -3, 1, -5, 4, 7\}$. Generate and plot the samples (use the **stem** function) of the following sequences.

1. $x_1(n) = 2x(n - 3) + 3x(n + 4) - x(n)$
2. $x_2(n) = 4x(4 + n) + 5x(n + 5) + 2x(n)$
3. $x_3(n) = x(n + 3)x(n - 2) + x(1 - n)x(n + 1)$
4. $x_4(n) = 2e^{0.5n}x(n) + \cos(0.1\pi n)\, x(n + 2), \ -10 \leq n \leq 10$

P2.5 The complex exponential sequence $e^{j\omega_0 n}$ or the sinusoidal sequence $\cos(\omega_0 n)$ are periodic if the *normalized* frequency $f_0 \triangleq \dfrac{\omega_0}{2\pi}$ is a rational number; that is, $f_0 = \dfrac{K}{N}$, where K and N are integers.

1. Prove the above result.
2. Generate $\exp(j0.1\pi n)$, $-100 \leq n \leq 100$. Plot its real and imaginary parts using the **stem** function. Is this sequence periodic? If it is, what is its fundamental period? From the examination of the plot, what interpretation can you give to the integers K and N above?
3. Generate and plot $\cos(0.1n)$, $-20 \leq n \leq 20$. Is this sequence periodic? What do you conclude from the plot? If necessary, examine the values of the sequence in MATLAB to arrive at your answer.

P2.6 Using the **evenodd** function, decompose the following sequences into their even and odd components. Plot these components using the **stem** function.

1. $x_1(n) = \{0, 1, 2, 3, 4, 5, 6, 7, 8, 9\}$
2. $x_2(n) = e^{0.1n}[u(n + 5) - u(n - 10)]$
3. $x_3(n) = \cos(0.2\pi n + \pi/4), \ -20 \leq n \leq 20$
4. $x_4(n) = e^{-0.05n}\sin(0.1\pi n + \pi/3), \ 0 \leq n \leq 100$

P2.7 A complex-valued sequence $x_e(n)$ is called *conjugate-symmetric* if $x_e(n) = x_e^*(-n)$, and a complex-valued sequence $x_o(n)$ is called *conjugate-antisymmetric* if $x_o(n) = -x_o^*(-n)$. Then any arbitrary complex-valued sequence $x(n)$ can be decomposed into $x(n) = x_e(n) + x_o(n)$, where $x_e(n)$ and $x_o(n)$ are given by

$$x_e(n) = \frac{1}{2}\left[x(n) + x^*(-n)\right] \quad \text{and} \quad x_o(n) = \frac{1}{2}\left[x(n) - x^*(-n)\right] \tag{2.27}$$

respectively.

1. Modify the **evenodd** function discussed in the text so that it accepts an arbitrary sequence and decomposes it into its conjugate-symmetric and conjugate-antisymmetric components by implementing (2.27).
2. Decompose the sequence

$$x(n) = 10\exp([-0.1 + j0.2\pi]n), \quad 0 \le n \le 10$$

into its conjugate-symmetric and conjugate-antisymmetric components. Plot their real and imaginary parts to verify the decomposition. (Use the **subplot** function.)

P2.8 The operation of *signal dilation* (or *decimation* or *down-sampling*) is defined by

$$y(n) = x(nM)$$

in which the sequence $x(n)$ is down-sampled by an integer factor M. For example, if

$$x(n) = \{\dots, -2, 4, 3, -6, 5, -1, 8, \dots\}$$
$$\uparrow$$

then the down-sampled sequences by a factor 2 are given by

$$y(n) = \{\dots, -2, 3, 5, 8, \dots\}$$
$$\uparrow$$

1. Develop a MATLAB function **dnsample** that has the form

```
function [y,m] = dnsample(x,n,M)
% Downsample sequence x(n) by a factor M to obtain y(m)
```

to implement the above operation. Use the indexing mechanism of MATLAB with careful attention to the origin of the time axis $n = 0$.
2. Generate $x(n) = \sin(0.125\pi n), -50 \le n \le 50$. Decimate $x(n)$ by a factor of 4 to generate $y(n)$. Plot both $x(n)$ and $y(n)$ using **subplot**, and comment on the results.
3. Repeat the above using $x(n) = \sin(0.5\pi n), -50 \le n \le 50$. Qualitatively discuss the effect of down-sampling on signals.

P2.9 Using the **conv_m** function, determine the autocorrelation sequence $r_{xx}(\ell)$ and the cross-correlation sequence $r_{xy}(\ell)$ for the following sequences:

$$x(n) = (0.9)^n, \quad 0 \le n \le 20; \qquad y(n) = (0.8)^{-n}, \quad -20 \le n \le 0$$

Describe your observations of these results.

P2.10 In a certain concert hall, echoes of the original audio signal $x(n)$ are generated due to the reflections at the walls and ceiling. The audio signal experienced by the listener $y(n)$ is a combination of $x(n)$ and its echoes. Let

$$y(n) = x(n) + \alpha x(n - k)$$

where k is the amount of delay in samples and α is its relative strength. We want to estimate the delay using the correlation analysis.

1. Determine analytically the cross-correlation $r_{yx}(\ell)$ in terms of the autocorrelation $r_{xx}(\ell)$.
2. Let $x(n) = \cos(0.2\pi n) + 0.5\cos(0.6\pi n)$, $\alpha = 0.1$, and $k = 50$. Generate 200 samples of $y(n)$ and determine its cross-correlation. Can you obtain α and k by observing $r_{yx}(\ell)$?

P2.11 Consider the following discrete-time systems:

$$T_1[x(n)] = x(n)u(n) \qquad\qquad T_2[x(n)] = x(n) + n\,x(n+1)$$

$$T_3[x(n)] = x(n) + \frac{1}{2}x(n-2) - \frac{1}{3}x(n-3)x(2n) \qquad T_4[x(n)] = \sum_{k=-\infty}^{n+5} 2x(k)$$

$$T_5[x(n)] = x(2n) \qquad\qquad T_6[x(n)] = \text{round}[x(n)]$$

where round[·] denotes rounding to the nearest integer.

1. Use (2.10) to determine analytically whether these systems are linear.
2. Let $x_1(n)$ be a uniformly distributed random sequence between $[0, 1]$ over $0 \le n \le 100$, and let $x_2(n)$ be a Gaussian random sequence with mean 0 and variance 10 over $0 \le n \le 100$. Using these sequences, verify the linearity of these systems. Choose any values for constants a_1 and a_2 in (2.10). You should use several realizations of the above sequences to arrive at your answers.

P2.12 Consider the discrete-time systems given in Problem P2.11.

1. Use (2.12) to determine analytically whether these systems are time-invariant.
2. Let $x(n)$ be a Gaussian random sequence with mean 0 and variance 10 over $0 \le n \le 100$. Using this sequence, verify the time invariance of the above systems. Choose any values for sample shift k in (2.12). You should use several realizations of the above sequence to arrive at your answers.

P2.13 For the systems given in Problem P2.11, determine analytically their stability and causality.

P2.14 The linear convolution defined in (2.14) has several properties:

$$\begin{array}{ll}
x_1(n) * x_2(n) = x_1(n) * x_2(n) & : \text{Commutation} \\[4pt]
[x_1(n) * x_2(n)] * x_3(n) = x_1(n) * [x_2(n) * x_3(n)] & : \text{Association} \\[4pt]
x_1(n) * [x_2(n) + x_3(n)] = x_1(n) * x_2(n) + x_1(n) * x_3(n) & : \text{Distribution} \\[4pt]
x(n) * \delta(n - n_0) = x(n - n_0) & : \text{Identity}
\end{array} \qquad (2.28)$$

1. Analytically prove these properties.
2. Using the following three sequences, verify the above properties:

$$x_1(n) = \cos(\pi n/4)[u(n+5) - u(n-25)]$$

$$x_2(n) = (0.9)^{-n}[u(n) - u(n-20)]$$

$$x_3(n) = \text{round}[5w(n)], \quad -10 \le n \le 10, \text{ where } w(n) \text{ is uniform over } [-1, 1]$$

Use the `conv_m` function.

P2.15 Determine analytically the convolution $y(n) = x(n) * h(n)$ of the following sequences, and verify your answers using the `conv_m` function.

1. $x(n) = \{2, -4, 5, 3, -1, -2, 6\}$, $h(n) = \{1, -1, 1, -1, 1\}$
$\qquad\qquad\qquad\quad\uparrow \qquad\qquad\qquad\qquad\qquad\qquad\uparrow$

2. $x(n) = \{1, 1, 0, 1, 1\}$, $h(n) = \{1, -2, -3, 4\}$
   $\qquad\quad\uparrow \qquad\qquad\qquad\quad\uparrow$

3. $x(n) = (1/4)^{-n}[u(n+1) - u(n-4)]$, $h(n) = u(n) - u(n-5)$

4. $x(n) = n/4[u(n) - u(n-6)]$, $h(n) = 2[u(n+2) - u(n-3)]$

P2.16 Let $x(n) = (0.8)^n u(n)$, $h(n) = (-0.9)^n u(n)$, and $y(n) = h(n) * x(n)$. Use three columns and one row of subplots for the following parts.

1. Determine $y(n)$ analytically. Plot first 51 samples of $y(n)$ using the **stem** function.
2. Truncate $x(n)$ and $h(n)$ to 26 samples. Use **conv** function to compute $y(n)$. Plot $y(n)$ using the **stem** function. Compare your results with those of part 1.
3. Using the **filter** function, determine the first 51 samples of $x(n) * h(n)$. Plot $y(n)$ using the **stem** function. Compare your results with those of parts 1 and 2.

P2.17 When the sequences $x(n)$ and $h(n)$ are of finite duration N_x and N_h, respectively, then their linear convolution (2.13) can also be implemented using *matrix-vector multiplication*. If elements of $y(n)$ and $x(n)$ are arranged in column vectors $\mathbf{x}$ and $\mathbf{y}$, respectively, then from (2.13) we obtain

$$\mathbf{y} = \mathbf{H}\mathbf{x}$$

where linear shifts in $h(n-k)$ for $n = 0, \ldots, N_h - 1$ are arranged as rows in the matrix $\mathbf{H}$. This matrix has an interesting structure and is called a *Toeplitz* matrix. To investigate this matrix, consider the sequences

$$x(n) = \{1, 2, 3, 4, 5\} \qquad \text{and} \qquad h(n) = \{6, 7, 8, 9\}$$
$$\qquad\qquad\quad\uparrow \qquad\qquad\qquad\qquad\qquad\qquad\quad\uparrow$$

1. Determine the linear convolution $y(n) = h(n) * x(n)$.
2. Express $x(n)$ as a 5×1 column vector $\mathbf{x}$ and $y(n)$ as a 8×1 column vector $\mathbf{y}$. Now determine the 8×5 matrix $\mathbf{H}$ so that $\mathbf{y} = \mathbf{H}\mathbf{x}$.
3. Characterize the matrix $\mathbf{H}$. From this characterization, can you give a definition of a Toeplitz matrix? How does this definition compare with that of time invariance?
4. What can you say about the first column and the first row of $\mathbf{H}$?

P2.18 MATLAB provides a function called **toeplitz** to generate a Toeplitz matrix, given the first row and the first column.

1. Using this function and your answer to Problem P2.17, part 4, develop another MATLAB function to implement linear convolution. The format of the function should be

```
function [y,H]=conv_tp(h,x)
% Linear Convolution using Toeplitz Matrix
% -----------------------------------------------
% [y,H] = conv_tp(h,x)
% y = output sequence in column vector form
% H = Toeplitz matrix corresponding to sequence h so that y = Hx
% h = Impulse response sequence in column vector form
% x = input sequence in column vector form
```

2. Verify your function on the sequences given in Problem P2.17.

P2.19 A linear and time-invariant system is described by the difference equation

$$y(n) - 0.5y(n-1) + 0.25y(n-2) = x(n) + 2x(n-1) + x(n-3)$$

1. Using the `filter` function, compute and plot the impulse response of the system over $0 \le n \le 100$.
2. Determine the stability of the system from this impulse response.
3. If the input to this system is $x(n) = [5 + 3\cos(0.2\pi n) + 4\sin(0.6\pi n)]\, u(n)$, determine the response $y(n)$ over $0 \le n \le 200$ using the `filter` function.

P2.20 A "simple" *digital differentiator* is given by

$$y(n) = x(n) - x(n-1)$$

which computes a backward first-order difference of the input sequence. Implement this differentiator on the following sequences, and plot the results. Comment on the appropriateness of this simple differentiator.

1. $x(n) = 5\,[u(n) - u(n-20)]$: a rectangular pulse
2. $x(n) = n\,[u(n) - u(n-10)] + (20-n)\,[u(n-10) - u(n-20)]$: a triangular pulse
3. $x(n) = \sin\left(\dfrac{\pi n}{25}\right)[u(n) - u(n-100)]$: a sinusoidal pulse

CHAPTER 3

The Discrete-Time Fourier Analysis

We have seen how a linear and time-invariant system can be represented using its response to the unit sample sequence. This response, called the *unit impulse response* $h(n)$, allows us to compute the system response to any arbitrary input $x(n)$ using the linear convolution

$$x(n) \longrightarrow \boxed{h(n)} \longrightarrow y(n) = h(n) * x(n)$$

This convolution representation is based on the fact that any signal can be represented by a linear combination of scaled and delayed unit samples. Similarly, we can also represent any arbitrary discrete signal as a linear combination of basis signals introduced in Chapter 2. Each basis signal set provides a new signal representation. Each representation has some advantages and some disadvantages depending upon the type of system under consideration. However, when the system is linear and time-invariant, only one representation stands out as the most useful. It is based on the complex exponential signal set $\{e^{j\omega n}\}$ and is called the *discrete-time Fourier transform*.

3.1 THE DISCRETE-TIME FOURIER TRANSFORM (DTFT)

If $x(n)$ is absolutely summable, that is, $\sum_{-\infty}^{\infty} |x(n)| < \infty$, then its discrete-time Fourier transform is given by

$$X(e^{j\omega}) \triangleq \mathcal{F}[x(n)] = \sum_{n=-\infty}^{\infty} x(n)e^{-j\omega n} \tag{3.1}$$

The inverse discrete-time Fourier transform (IDTFT) of $X(e^{j\omega})$ is given by

$$x(n) \triangleq \mathcal{F}^{-1}[X(e^{j\omega})] = \frac{1}{2\pi} \int_{-\pi}^{\pi} X(e^{j\omega}) e^{j\omega n} d\omega \tag{3.2}$$

The operator $\mathcal{F}[\cdot]$ transforms a discrete signal $x(n)$ into a complex-valued continuous function $X(e^{j\omega})$ of real variable ω, called a digital frequency, which is measured in radians/sample.

☐ **EXAMPLE 3.1**   Determine the discrete-time Fourier transform of $x(n) = (0.5)^n u(n)$.

Solution   The sequence $x(n)$ is absolutely summable; therefore, its discrete-time Fourier transform exists.

$$X(e^{j\omega}) = \sum_{-\infty}^{\infty} x(n) e^{-j\omega n} = \sum_{0}^{\infty} (0.5)^n e^{-j\omega n}$$

$$= \sum_{0}^{\infty} (0.5 e^{-j\omega})^n = \frac{1}{1 - 0.5e^{-j\omega}} = \frac{e^{j\omega}}{e^{j\omega} - 0.5}$$

☐

☐ **EXAMPLE 3.2**   Determine the discrete-time Fourier transform of the following finite-duration sequence:

$$x(n) = \{1, 2, 3, 4, 5\}$$
$$\uparrow$$

Solution   Using definition (3.1),

$$X(e^{j\omega}) = \sum_{-\infty}^{\infty} x(n) e^{-j\omega n} = e^{j\omega} + 2 + 3e^{-j\omega} + 4e^{-j2\omega} + 5e^{-j3\omega}$$

☐

Since $X(e^{j\omega})$ is a complex-valued function, we will have to plot its magnitude and its angle (or the real part and the imaginary part) with respect to ω separately to visually describe $X(e^{j\omega})$. Now ω is a real variable between $-\infty$ and ∞, which would mean that we can plot only a part of the $X(e^{j\omega})$ function using MATLAB. Using two important properties of the discrete-time Fourier transform, we can reduce this domain to the $[0, \pi]$ interval for real-valued sequences. We will discuss other useful properties of $X(e^{j\omega})$ in the next section.

3.1.1 TWO IMPORTANT PROPERTIES
We will state the following two properties without proof.

1. **Periodicity:** The discrete-time Fourier transform $X(e^{j\omega})$ is periodic in ω with period 2π.

$$X(e^{j\omega}) = X(e^{j[\omega+2\pi]})$$

Implication: We need only one period of $X(e^{j\omega})$ (i.e., $\omega \in [0, 2\pi]$, or $[-\pi, \pi]$, etc.) for analysis and not the whole domain $-\infty < \omega < \infty$.

2. **Symmetry:** For real-valued $x(n)$, $X(e^{j\omega})$ is conjugate symmetric.

$$X(e^{-j\omega}) = X^*(e^{j\omega})$$

or

$$\mathrm{Re}[X(e^{-j\omega})] = \mathrm{Re}[X(e^{j\omega})] \quad \text{(even symmetry)}$$

$$\mathrm{Im}[X(e^{-j\omega})] = -\mathrm{Im}[X(e^{j\omega})] \quad \text{(odd symmetry)}$$

$$|X(e^{-j\omega})| = |X(e^{j\omega})| \quad \text{(even symmetry)}$$

$$\angle X(e^{-j\omega}) = -\angle X(e^{j\omega}) \quad \text{(odd symmetry)}$$

Implication: To plot $X(e^{j\omega})$, we now need to consider only a half-period of $X(e^{j\omega})$. Generally, in practice this period is chosen to be $\omega \in [0, \pi]$.

3.1.2 MATLAB IMPLEMENTATION

If $x(n)$ is of infinite duration, then MATLAB cannot be used directly to compute $X(e^{j\omega})$ from $x(n)$. However, we can use it to evaluate the expression $X(e^{j\omega})$ over $[0, \pi]$ frequencies and then plot its magnitude and angle (or real and imaginary parts).

☐   **EXAMPLE 3.3**   Evaluate $X(e^{j\omega})$ in Example 3.1 at 501 equispaced points between $[0, \pi]$ and plot its magnitude, angle, real part, and imaginary part.

Solution   MATLAB script:

```
>> w = [0:1:500]*pi/500;  % [0, pi]  axis divided into 501 points.
>> X = exp(j*w) ./ (exp(j*w) - 0.5*ones(1,501));
>> magX = abs(X); angX = angle(X);  realX = real(X); imagX = imag(X);
>> subplot(2,2,1); plot(w/pi,magX); grid
>> title('Magnitude Part'); ylabel('Magnitude')
>> subplot(2,2,3); plot(w/pi,angX); grid
>> xlabel('frequency in pi units'); title('Angle Part'); ylabel('Radians')
>> subplot(2,2,2); plot(w/pi,realX); grid
>> title('Real Part'); ylabel('Real')
>> subplot(2,2,4); plot(w/pi,imagX); grid
>> xlabel('frequency in pi units'); title('Imaginary Part'); ylabel('Imaginary')
```

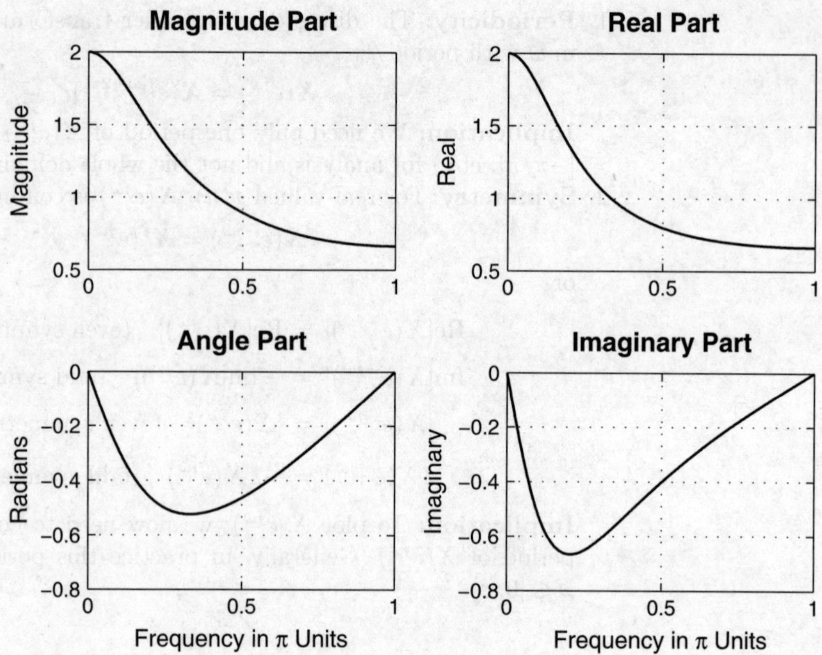

FIGURE 3.1 *Plots in Example 3.3*

The resulting plots are shown in Figure 3.1. Note that we divided the `w` array by `pi` before plotting so that the frequency axes are in the units of π and therefore easier to read. *This practice is strongly recommended.* □

If $x(n)$ is of finite duration, then MATLAB can be used to compute $X(e^{j\omega})$ numerically at any frequency ω. The approach is to implement (3.1) directly. If, in addition, we evaluate $X(e^{j\omega})$ at equispaced frequencies between $[0, \pi]$, then (3.1) can be implemented as a *matrix-vector multiplication* operation. To understand this, let us assume that the sequence $x(n)$ has N samples between $n_1 \leq n \leq n_N$ (i.e., not necessarily between $[0, N-1]$) and that we want to evaluate $X(e^{j\omega})$ at

$$\omega_k \overset{\triangle}{=} \frac{\pi}{M}k, \quad k = 0, 1, \ldots, M$$

which are $(M+1)$ equispaced frequencies between $[0, \pi]$. Then (3.1) can be written as

$$X(e^{j\omega_k}) = \sum_{\ell=1}^{N} e^{-j(\pi/M)kn_\ell} x(n_\ell), \quad k = 0, 1, \ldots, M$$

When $\{x(n_\ell)\}$ and $\{X(e^{j\omega_k})\}$ are arranged as *column* vectors $\mathbf{x}$ and $\mathbf{X}$, respectively, we have

$$\mathbf{X} = \mathbf{W}\mathbf{x} \qquad (3.3)$$

where $\mathbf{W}$ is an $(M+1) \times N$ matrix given by

$$\mathbf{W} \triangleq \left\{ e^{-j(\pi/M)kn_\ell};\ n_1 \leq n \leq n_N, \quad k = 0, 1, \ldots, M \right\}$$

In addition, if we arrange $\{k\}$ and $\{n_\ell\}$ as *row* vectors $\mathbf{k}$ and $\mathbf{n}$, respectively, then

$$\mathbf{W} = \left[\exp\left(-j\frac{\pi}{M}\mathbf{k}^T\mathbf{n}\right) \right]$$

In MATLAB, we represent sequences and indices as row vectors; therefore, taking the transpose of (3.3), we obtain

$$\mathbf{X}^T = \mathbf{x}^T \left[\exp\left(-j\frac{\pi}{M}\mathbf{n}^T\mathbf{k}\right) \right] \qquad (3.4)$$

Note that $\mathbf{n}^T\mathbf{k}$ is an $N \times (M+1)$ matrix. Now (3.4) can be implemented in MATLAB as follows.

```
>> k = [0:M]; n = [n1:n2];
>> X = x * (exp(-j*pi/M)) .^ (n'*k);
```

□ **EXAMPLE 3.4**   Numerically compute the discrete-time Fourier transform of the sequence $x(n)$ given in Example 3.2 at 501 equispaced frequencies between $[0, \pi]$.

Solution   MATLAB script:

```
>> n = -1:3; x = 1:5;  k = 0:500; w = (pi/500)*k;
>> X = x * (exp(-j*pi/500)) .^ (n'*k);
>> magX = abs(X); angX = angle(X);
>> realX = real(X); imagX = imag(X);
>> subplot(2,2,1); plot(k/500,magX);grid
>> title('Magnitude Part')
>> subplot(2,2,3); plot(k/500,angX/pi);grid
>> xlabel('Frequency in \pi Units'); title('Angle Part')
>> subplot(2,2,2); plot(k/500,realX);grid
>> title('Real Part')
>> subplot(2,2,4); plot(k/500,imagX);grid
>> xlabel('Frequency in \pi Units'); title('Imaginary Part')
```

The frequency-domain plots are shown in Figure 3.2. Note that the angle plot is depicted as a discontinuous function between $-\pi$ and π. This is because the **angle** function in MATLAB computes the principal angle.   □

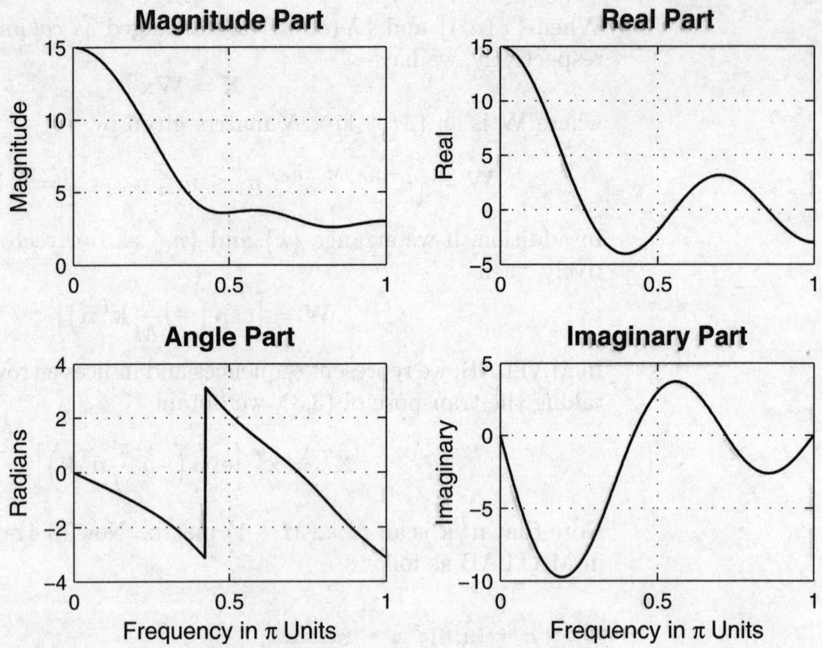

FIGURE 3.2   *Plots in Example 3.4*

The procedure of Example 3.4 can be compiled into a MATLAB function—say, a `dtft` function—for ease of implementation. This is explored in Problem P3.1. This numerical computation is based on definition (3.1). It is not the most elegant way of numerically computing the discrete-time Fourier transform of a finite-duration sequence. In Chapter 5, we will discuss in detail the topic of a computable transform called the discrete Fourier transform (DFT) and its efficient computation, called the fast Fourier transform (FFT). Also, there is an alternate approach based on the z-transform using the MATLAB function `freqz`, which we will discuss in Chapter 4. In this chapter, we will continue to use the approaches discussed so far for calculation as well as for investigation purposes.

In the next two examples, we investigate the periodicity and symmetry properties using complex-valued and real-valued sequences.

☐   **EXAMPLE 3.5**   Let $x(n) = (0.9 \exp{(j\pi/3)})^n$, $0 \le n \le 10$. Determine $X(e^{j\omega})$ and investigate its periodicity.

Solution   Since $x(n)$ is complex-valued, $X(e^{j\omega})$ satisfies only the periodicity property. Therefore, it is uniquely defined over one period of 2π. However, we will evaluate and plot it at 401 frequencies over two periods between $[-2\pi, 2\pi]$ to observe its periodicity.

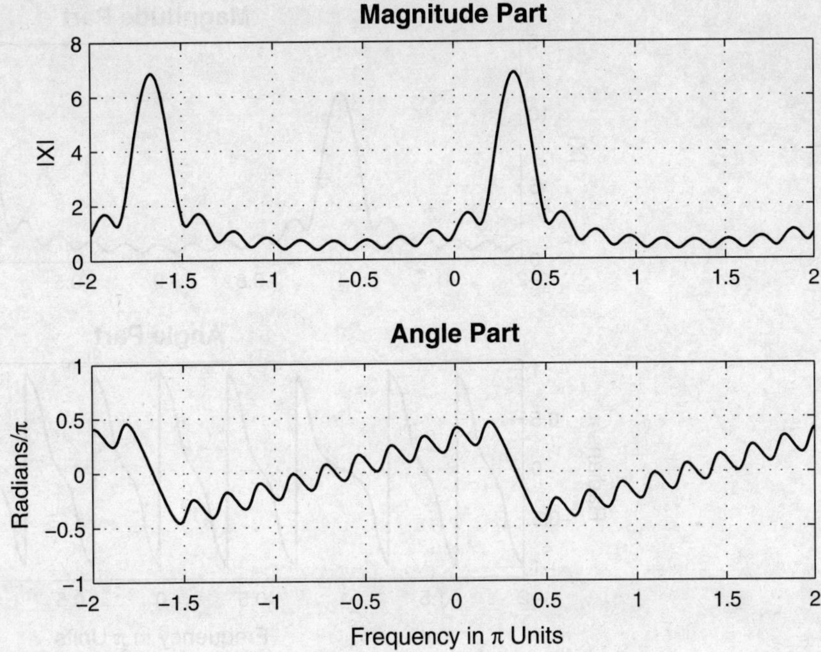

FIGURE 3.3 *Plots in Example 3.5*

MATLAB script:

```
>> n = 0:10; x = (0.9*exp(j*pi/3)).^n;
>> k = -200:200; w = (pi/100)*k;
>> X = x * (exp(-j*pi/100)) .^ (n'*k);
>> magX = abs(X); angX =angle(X);
>> subplot(2,1,1); plot(w/pi,magX);grid
>> ylabel('|X|')
>> title('Magnitude Part')
>> subplot(2,1,2); plot(w/pi,angX/pi);grid
>> xlabel('Frequency in \pi Units'); ylabel('Radians/\pi')
>> title('Angle Part')
```

From the plots in Figure 3.3, we observe that $X(e^{j\omega})$ is periodic in ω but is not conjugate-symmetric. □

□ **EXAMPLE 3.6** Let $x(n) = (-0.9)^n$, $-5 \leq n \leq 5$. Investigate the conjugate-symmetry property of its discrete-time Fourier transform.

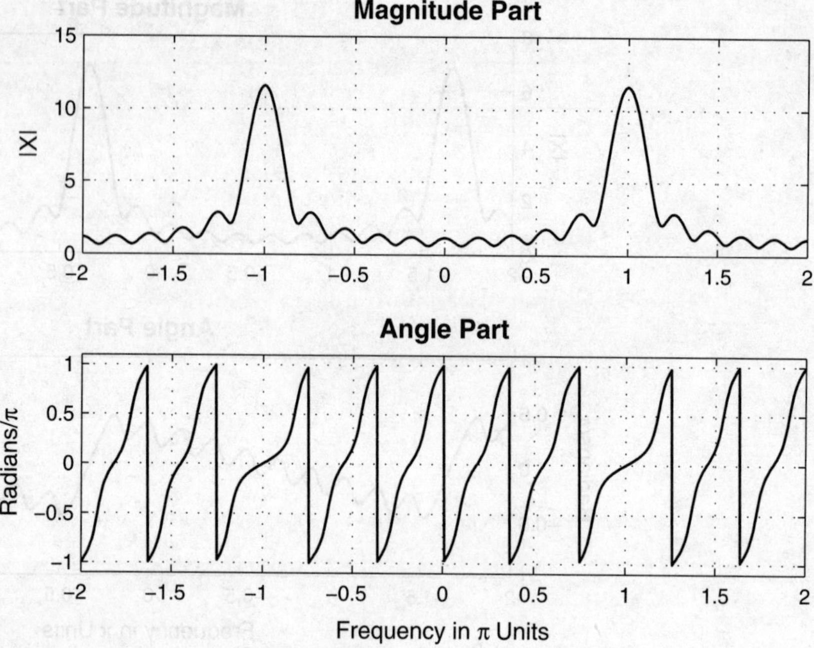

FIGURE 3.4　*Plots in Example 3.6*

Solution

Once again, we will compute and plot $X(e^{j\omega})$ over two periods to study its symmetry property.

MATLAB script:

```
>> n = -5:5; x = (-0.9).^n;
>> k = -200:200; w = (pi/100)*k;  X = x * (exp(-j*pi/100)) .^ (n'*k);
>> magX = abs(X); angX =angle(X);
>> subplot(2,1,1); plot(w/pi,magX);grid;  axis([-2,2,0,15])
>> ylabel('|X|')
>> title('Magnitude Part')
>> subplot(2,1,2); plot(w/pi,angX/pi);grid;  axis([-2,2,-1,1])
>> xlabel('Frequency in \pi Units'); ylabel('Radians/\pi')
>> title('Angle Part')
```

From the plots in Figure 3.4, we observe that $X(e^{j\omega})$ is not only periodic in ω but is also conjugate-symmetric. Therefore, for real sequences we will plot their Fourier transform magnitude and angle graphs from 0 to π.　　　□

3.1.3 SOME COMMON DTFT PAIRS

The discrete-time Fourier transforms of the basic sequences discussed in Chapter 2 are very useful. The discrete-time Fourier transforms of some

TABLE 3.1 *Some common DTFT pairs*

Signal Type	*Sequence* $x(n)$	DTFT $X\left(e^{j\omega}\right)$, $-\pi \le \omega \le \pi$
Unit impulse	$\delta(n)$	1
Constant	1	$2\pi\delta(\omega)$
Unit step	$u(n)$	$\dfrac{1}{1 - e^{-j\omega}} + \pi\delta(\omega)$
Causal exponential	$\alpha^n u(n)$	$\dfrac{1}{1 - \alpha e^{-j\omega}}$
Complex exponential	$e^{j\omega_0 n}$	$2\pi\delta(\omega - \omega_0)$
Cosine	$\cos(\omega_0 n)$	$\pi[\delta(\omega - \omega_0) + \delta(\omega + \omega_0)]$
Sine	$\sin(\omega_0 n)$	$j\pi[\delta(\omega + \omega_0) - \delta(\omega - \omega_0)]$
Double exponential	$\alpha^{|n|}$	$\dfrac{1 - \alpha^2}{1 - 2\alpha\cos(\omega) + \alpha^2}$

Note: Since $X\left(e^{j\omega}\right)$ is periodic with period 2π, expressions over only the primary period of $-\pi \le \omega \le \pi$ are given.

of these sequences can be easily obtained using the basic definitions (3.1) and (3.2). These transform pairs and those of few other pairs are given in Table 3.1. Note that, even if sequences like unit step $u(n)$ are not absolutely summable, their discrete-time Fourier transforms exist in the limiting sense if we allow impulses in the Fourier transform. Such sequences are said to have finite power, that is, $\sum_n |x(n)|^2 < \infty$. Using this table and the properties of the Fourier transform (discussed in Section 3.2), it is possible to obtain discrete-time Fourier transform of many more sequences.

3.2 THE PROPERTIES OF THE DTFT

In the previous section, we discussed two important properties that we needed for plotting purposes. We now discuss the remaining useful properties, which are given below without proof. Let $X(e^{j\omega})$ be the discrete-time Fourier transform of $x(n)$.

1. **Linearity:** The discrete-time Fourier transform is a linear transformation; that is,

$$\mathcal{F}[\alpha x_1(n) + \beta x_2(n)] = \alpha \mathcal{F}[x_1(n)] + \beta \mathcal{F}[x_2(n)] \tag{3.5}$$

for every α, β, $x_1(n)$, and $x_2(n)$.

2. **Time shifting:** A shift in the time domain corresponds to the phase shifting.

$$\mathcal{F}[x(n-k)] = X(e^{j\omega})e^{-j\omega k} \qquad (3.6)$$

3. **Frequency shifting:** Multiplication by a complex exponential corresponds to a shift in the frequency domain.

$$\mathcal{F}\left[x(n)e^{j\omega_0 n}\right] = X(e^{j(\omega-\omega_0)}) \qquad (3.7)$$

4. **Conjugation:** Conjugation in the time domain corresponds to the folding and conjugation in the frequency domain.

$$\mathcal{F}[x^*(n)] = X^*(e^{-j\omega}) \qquad (3.8)$$

5. **Folding:** Folding in the time domain corresponds to the folding in the frequency domain.

$$\mathcal{F}[x(-n)] = X(e^{-j\omega}) \qquad (3.9)$$

6. **Symmetries in real sequences:** We have already studied the conjugate symmetry of real sequences. These real sequences can be decomposed into their even and odd parts, as discussed in Chapter 2.

$$x(n) = x_e(n) + x_o(n)$$

Then

$$\mathcal{F}[x_e(n)] = \mathrm{Re}\left[X(e^{j\omega})\right]$$
$$\qquad (3.10)$$
$$\mathcal{F}[x_o(n)] = j\,\mathrm{Im}\left[X(e^{j\omega})\right]$$

Implication: If the sequence $x(n)$ is real and even, then $X(e^{j\omega})$ is also real and even. Hence only one plot over $[0, \pi]$ is necessary for its complete representation.

A similar property for complex-valued sequences is explored in Problem P3.7.

7. **Convolution:** This is one of the most useful properties that makes system analysis convenient in the frequency domain.

$$\mathcal{F}[x_1(n) * x_2(n)] = \mathcal{F}[x_1(n)]\,\mathcal{F}[x_2(n)] = X_1(e^{j\omega})X_2(e^{j\omega}) \qquad (3.11)$$

8. **Multiplication:** This is a dual of the convolution property.

$$\mathcal{F}[x_1(n)\cdot x_2(n)] = \mathcal{F}[x_1(n)] \circledast \mathcal{F}[x_2(n)] \triangleq \frac{1}{2\pi}\int_{-\pi}^{\pi} X_1(e^{j\theta})X_2(e^{j(\omega-\theta)})d\theta$$

(3.12)

This convolution-like operation is called a *periodic convolution* and hence denoted by $\circledast$. It is discussed (in its discrete form) in Chapter 5.

9. **Energy:** The energy of the sequence $x(n)$ can be written as

$$\mathcal{E}_x = \sum_{-\infty}^{\infty}|x(n)|^2 = \frac{1}{2\pi}\int_{-\pi}^{\pi}|X(e^{j\omega})|^2 d\omega \tag{3.13}$$

$$= \int_{0}^{\pi}\frac{|X(e^{j\omega})|^2}{\pi}d\omega \quad \text{(for real sequences using even symmetry)}$$

This is also known as Parseval's theorem. From (3.13), the *energy density spectrum* of $x(n)$ is defined as

$$\Phi_x(\omega) \triangleq \frac{|X(e^{j\omega})|^2}{\pi} \tag{3.14}$$

Then the energy of $x(n)$ in the $[\omega_1,\omega_2]$ band is given by

$$\int_{\omega_1}^{\omega_2}\Phi_x(\omega)d\omega, \quad 0 \le \omega_1 < \omega_2 \le \pi$$

In the next several examples, we will verify some of these properties using finite-duration sequences. We will follow our numerical procedure to compute discrete-time Fourier transforms in each case. Although this does not analytically prove the validity of each property, it provides us with an experimental tool in practice.

☐   **EXAMPLE 3.7**   In this example, we will verify the linearity property (3.5) using real-valued finite-duration sequences. Let $x_1(n)$ and $x_2(n)$ be two random sequences uniformly distributed between $[0, 1]$ over $0 \le n \le 10$. Then we can use our numerical discrete-time Fourier transform procedure as follows.

MATLAB script:

```
>> x1 = rand(1,11); x2 = rand(1,11); n = 0:10;
>> alpha = 2; beta = 3;  k = 0:500; w = (pi/500)*k;
>> X1 = x1 * (exp(-j*pi/500)).^(n'*k);  % DTFT of x1
>> X2 = x2 * (exp(-j*pi/500)).^(n'*k);  % DTFT of x2
>> x = alpha*x1 + beta*x2;              % Linear combination of x1 & x2
```

```
>> X = x * (exp(-j*pi/500)).^(n'*k);      % DTFT of x
>> % Verification
>> X_check = alpha*X1 + beta*X2;          % Linear combination of X1 & X2
>> error = max(abs(X-X_check))            % Difference
error =
   7.1054e-015
```

Since the maximum absolute error between the two Fourier transform arrays is less than 10^{-14}, the two arrays are identical within the limited numerical precision of MATLAB. □

EXAMPLE 3.8 Let $x(n)$ be a random sequence uniformly distributed between $[0, 1]$ over $0 \leq n \leq 10$, and let $y(n) = x(n-2)$. Then we can verify the sample shift property (3.6) as follows.

```
>> x = rand(1,11); n = 0·10;
>> k = 0:500; w = (pi/500)*k;
>> X = x * (exp(-j*pi/500)).^(n'*k);      % DTFT of x
>> % Signal shifted by two samples
>> y = x; m = n+2;
>> Y = y * (exp(-j*pi/500)).^(m'*k);      % DTFT of y
>> % verification
>> Y_check = (exp(-j*2).^w).*X;           % Multiplication by exp(-j2w)
>> error = max(angle(Y-Y_check))          % Difference
error =
   1.2204e-015
```
□

EXAMPLE 3.9 To verify the frequency shift property (3.7), we will use the graphical approach. Let

$$x(n) = \cos(\pi n/2), \quad 0 \leq n \leq 100 \quad \text{and} \quad y(n) = e^{j\pi n/4} x(n)$$

Then using MATLAB,

```
>> n = 0:100; x = cos(pi*n/2);
>> k = -100:100; w = (pi/100)*k;          % Frequency between -pi and +pi
>> X = x * (exp(-j*pi/100)).^(n'*k);      % DTFT of x
>> y = exp(j*pi*n/4).*x;                  % Signal multiplied by exp(j*pi*n/4)
>> Y = y * (exp(-j*pi/100)).^(n'*k);      % DTFT of y
>> % Graphical verification
>> subplot(2,2,1); plot(w/pi,abs(X)); grid; axis([-1,1,0,60])
>> title('Magnitude of X'); ylabel('|X|')
>> subplot(2,2,2); plot(w/pi,angle(X)/pi); grid; axis([-1,1,-1,1])
>> title('Angle of X'); ylabel('radians/\pi')
>> subplot(2,2,3); plot(w/pi,abs(Y)); grid; axis([-1,1,0,60])
```

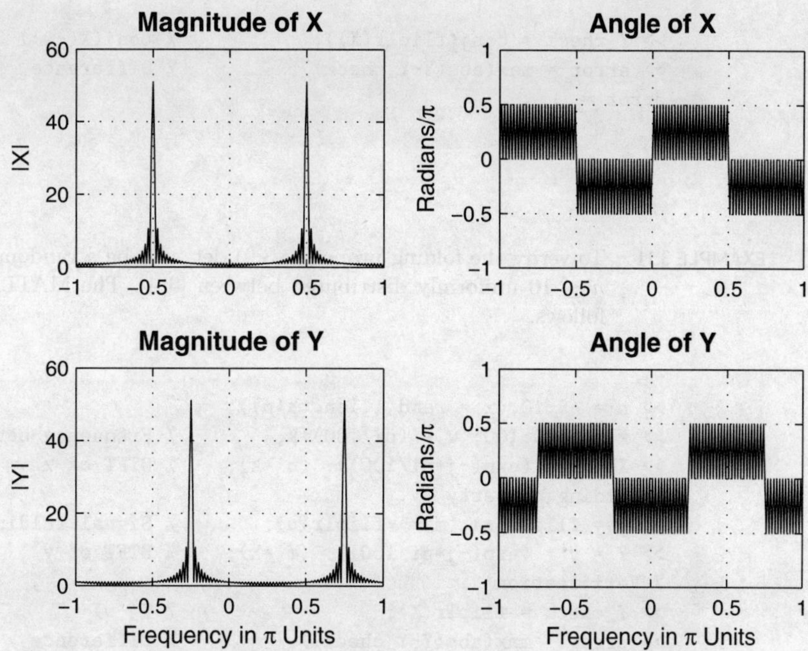

FIGURE 3.5 *Plots in Example 3.9*

```
>> xlabel('Frequency in \pi Units'); ylabel('|Y|')
>> title('Magnitude of Y')
>> subplot(2,2,4); plot(w/pi,angle(Y)/pi); grid; axis([-1,1,-1,1])
>> xlabel('Frequency in \pi Units'); ylabel('radians/\pi')
>> title('Angle of Y')
```

From the plots in Figure 3.5, we observe that $X(e^{j\omega})$ is indeed shifted by $\pi/4$ in both magnitude and angle. $\square$

EXAMPLE 3.10   To verify the conjugation property (3.8), let $x(n)$ be a complex-valued random sequence over $-5 \le n \le 10$ with real and imaginary parts uniformly distributed between $[0, 1]$. The MATLAB verification is as follows.

```
>> n = -5:10; x = rand(1,length(n)) + j*rand(1,length(n));
>> k = -100:100; w = (pi/100)*k;        % Frequency between -pi and +pi
>> X = x * (exp(-j*pi/100)).^(n'*k);    % DTFT of x
% Conjugation property
>> y = conj(x);                         % Signal conjugation
>> Y = y * (exp(-j*pi/100)).^(n'*k);    % DTFT of y
% Verification
```

```
>> Y_check = conj(fliplr(X));          % conj(X(-w))
>> error = max(abs(Y-Y_check))         % Difference
error =
     0
```

□

□ **EXAMPLE 3.11**   To verify the folding property (3.9), let $x(n)$ be a random sequence over $-5 \leq n \leq 10$ uniformly distributed between $[0,1]$. The MATLAB verification is as follows.

```
>> n = -5:10; x = rand(1,length(n));
>> k = -100:100; w = (pi/100)*k;        % Frequency between -pi and +pi
>> X = x * (exp(-j*pi/100)).^(n'*k);    % DTFT of x
% Folding property
>> y = fliplr(x); m = -fliplr(n);       % Signal folding
>> Y = y * (exp(-j*pi/100)).^(m'*k);    % DTFT of y
% Verification
>> Y_check = fliplr(X);                 % X(-w)
>> error = max(abs(Y-Y_check))          % Difference
error =
     0
```
□

□ **EXAMPLE 3.12**   In this problem, we verify the symmetry property (3.10) of real signals. Let

$$x(n) = \sin(\pi n/2), \quad -5 \leq n \leq 10$$

Then, using the `evenodd` function developed in Chapter 2, we can compute the even and odd parts of $x(n)$ and then evaluate their discrete-time Fourier transforms. We will provide the numerical as well as graphical verification.

MATLAB script:

```
>> n = -5:10; x = sin(pi*n/2);
>> k = -100:100; w = (pi/100)*k;        % Frequency between -pi and +pi
>> X = x * (exp(-j*pi/100)).^(n'*k);    % DTFT of x
% Signal decomposition
>> [xe,xo,m] = evenodd(x,n);            % Even and odd parts
>> XE = xe * (exp(-j*pi/100)).^(m'*k);  % DTFT of xe
>> XO = xo * (exp(-j*pi/100)).^(m'*k);  % DTFT of xo
% Verification
>> XR = real(X);                        % Real part of X
>> error1 = max(abs(XE-XR))             % Difference
error1 =
   1.8974e-019
>> XI = imag(X);                        % Imag part of X
```

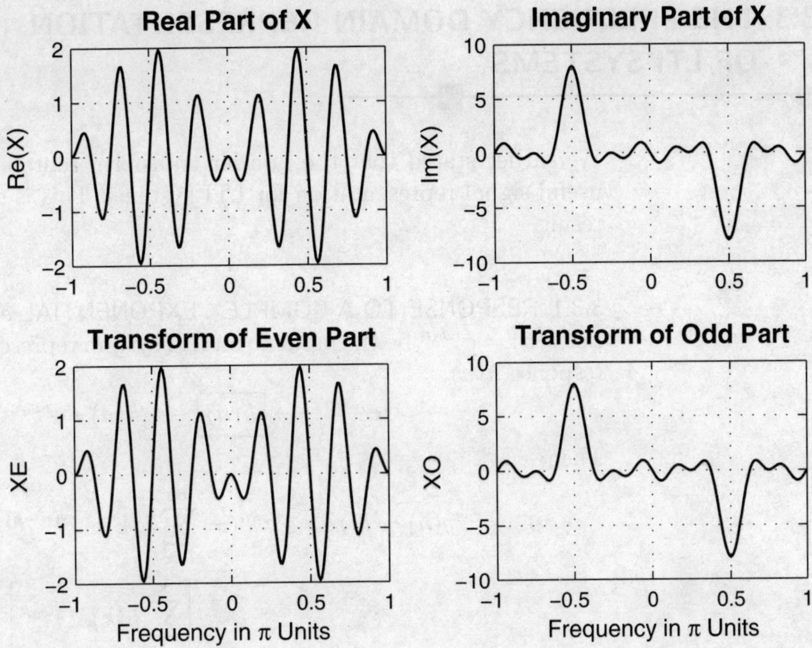

FIGURE 3.6 *Plots in Example 3.12*

```
>> error2 = max(abs(XO-j*XI))           % Difference
error2 =
  1.8033e-019
% Graphical verification
>> subplot(2,2,1); plot(w/pi,XR); grid; axis([-1,1,-2,2])
>> title('Real Part of X'); ylabel('Re(X)');
>> subplot(2,2,2); plot(w/pi,XI); grid; axis([-1,1,-10,10])
>> title('Imaginary Part of X'); ylabel('Im(X)');
>> subplot(2,2,3); plot(w/pi,real(XE)); grid; axis([-1,1,-2,2])
>> xlabel('Frequency in \pi Units'); ylabel('XE');
>> title('Transform of Even Part')
>> subplot(2,2,4); plot(w/pi,imag(XO)); grid; axis([-1,1,-10,10])
>> xlabel('Frequency in \pi Units'); ylabel('XO');
>> title('Transform of Odd Part')
```

From the plots in Figure 3.6, we observe that the real part of $X(e^{j\omega})$ [or the imaginary part of $X(e^{j\omega})$] is equal to the discrete-time Fourier transform of $x_e(n)$ [or $x_o(n)$]. ☐

3.3 THE FREQUENCY DOMAIN REPRESENTATION OF LTI SYSTEMS

We earlier stated that the Fourier transform representation is the most useful signal representation for LTI systems. This is due to the following result.

3.3.1 RESPONSE TO A COMPLEX EXPONENTIAL $e^{j\omega_0 n}$

Let $x(n) = e^{j\omega_0 n}$ be the input to an LTI system represented by the impulse response $h(n)$.

$$e^{j\omega_0 n} \longrightarrow \boxed{h(n)} \longrightarrow h(n) * e^{j\omega_0 n}$$

Then

$$y(n) = h(n) * e^{j\omega_0 n} = \sum_{-\infty}^{\infty} h(k) e^{j\omega_0(n-k)}$$

$$= \left[\sum_{-\infty}^{\infty} h(k) e^{-j\omega_0 k} \right] e^{j\omega_0 n} \tag{3.15}$$

$$= \left[\mathcal{F}[h(n)] \big|_{\omega=\omega_0} \right] e^{j\omega_0 n}$$

DEFINITION 1   *Frequency Response*

The discrete-time Fourier transform of an impulse response is called the frequency response *(or* transfer function) *of an LTI system and is denoted by*

$$H(e^{j\omega}) \triangleq \sum_{n=-\infty}^{\infty} h(n) e^{-j\omega n} \tag{3.16}$$

Then from (3.15) we can represent the system by

$$x(n) = e^{j\omega_0 n} \longrightarrow \boxed{H(e^{j\omega})} \longrightarrow y(n) = H(e^{j\omega_0}) \times e^{j\omega_0 n} \tag{3.17}$$

Hence the output sequence is the input exponential sequence *modified* by the response of the system at frequency ω_0. This justifies the definition of $H(e^{j\omega})$ as a frequency response because it is what the complex exponential is multiplied by to obtain the output $y(n)$. This powerful result can be extended to a linear combination of complex exponentials using the linearity of LTI systems:

$$\sum_k A_k e^{j\omega_k n} \longrightarrow \boxed{h(n)} \longrightarrow \sum_k A_k H(e^{j\omega_k}) e^{j\omega_k n}$$

In general, the frequency response $H(e^{j\omega})$ is a complex function of ω. The magnitude $|H(e^{j\omega})|$ of $H(e^{j\omega})$ is called the *magnitude (or gain) response* function, and the angle $\angle H(e^{j\omega})$ is called the *phase response* function, as we shall see below.

3.3.2 RESPONSE TO SINUSOIDAL SEQUENCES

Let $x(n) = A\cos(\omega_0 n + \theta_0)$ be an input to an LTI system $h(n)$. Then from (3.17) we can show that the response $y(n)$ is another sinusoid of the same frequency ω_0, with amplitude *gained* by $|H(e^{j\omega_0})|$ and phase *shifted* by $\angle H(e^{j\omega_0})$, that is,

$$y(n) = A|H(e^{j\omega_0})|\cos(\omega_0 n + \theta_0 + \angle H(e^{j\omega_0})) \tag{3.18}$$

This response is called the *steady-state response*, denoted by $y_{\mathrm{ss}}(n)$. It can be extended to a linear combination of sinusoidal sequences.

$$\sum_k A_k \cos(\omega_k n + \theta_k) \longrightarrow \boxed{H(e^{j\omega})} \longrightarrow \sum_k A_k |H(e^{j\omega_k})|\cos(\omega_k n + \theta_k + \angle H(e^{j\omega_k}))$$

3.3.3 RESPONSE TO ARBITRARY SEQUENCES

Finally, (3.17) can be generalized to arbitrary *absolutely summable* sequences. Let $X(e^{j\omega}) = \mathcal{F}[x(n)]$, and let $Y(e^{j\omega}) = \mathcal{F}[y(n)]$; then, using the convolution property (3.11), we have

$$Y(e^{j\omega}) = H(e^{j\omega})\, X(e^{j\omega}) \tag{3.19}$$

Therefore, an LTI system can be represented in the frequency domain by

$$X(e^{j\omega}) \longrightarrow \boxed{H(e^{j\omega})} \longrightarrow Y(e^{j\omega}) = H(e^{j\omega})\, X(e^{j\omega})$$

The output $y(n)$ is then computed from $Y(e^{j\omega})$ using the inverse discrete-time Fourier transform (3.2). This requires an integral operation, which is not a convenient operation in MATLAB. As we shall see in Chapter 4, there is an alternate approach to the computation of output to arbitrary inputs using the z-transform and partial fraction expansion. In this chapter, we will concentrate on computing the steady-state response.

☐ **EXAMPLE 3.13** Determine the frequency response $H(e^{j\omega})$ of a system characterized by $h(n) = (0.9)^n u(n)$. Plot the magnitude and the phase responses.

Solution Using (3.16),

$$H(e^{j\omega}) = \sum_{-\infty}^{\infty} h(n)e^{-j\omega n} = \sum_{0}^{\infty} (0.9)^n e^{-j\omega n}$$

$$= \sum_{0}^{\infty} (0.9e^{-j\omega})^n = \frac{1}{1 - 0.9e^{-j\omega}}$$

Hence

$$|H(e^{j\omega})| = \sqrt{\frac{1}{(1 - 0.9\cos\omega)^2 + (0.9\sin\omega)^2}} = \frac{1}{\sqrt{1.81 - 1.8\cos\omega}}$$

and

$$\angle H(e^{j\omega}) = -\arctan\left[\frac{0.9\sin\omega}{1 - 0.9\cos\omega}\right]$$

To plot these responses, we can either implement the $|H(e^{j\omega})|$ and $\angle H(e^{j\omega})$ functions or the frequency response $H(e^{j\omega})$ and then compute its magnitude and phase. The latter approach is more useful from a practical viewpoint [as shown in (3.18)].

```
>> w = [0:1:500]*pi/500;  % [0, pi] axis divided into 501 points.
>> H = exp(j*w) ./ (exp(j*w) - 0.9*ones(1,501));
>> magH = abs(H); angH = angle(H);
>> subplot(2,1,1); plot(w/pi,magH); grid;
>> title('Magnitude Response'); ylabel('|H|');
>> subplot(2,1,2); plot(w/pi,angH/pi); grid
>> xlabel('Frequency in \pi Units'); ylabel('Phase in \pi Radians');
>> title('Phase Response');
```

The plots are shown in Figure 3.7.   □

□ **EXAMPLE 3.14**   Let an input to the system in Example 3.13 be $0.1u(n)$. Determine the steady-state response $y_{ss}(n)$.

Solution   Since the input is not absolutely summable, the discrete-time Fourier transform is not particularly useful in computing the complete response. However, it can be used to compute the steady-state response. In the steady state (i.e., $n \to \infty$), the input is a constant sequence (or a sinusoid with $\omega_0 = \theta_0 = 0$). Then the output is

$$y_{ss}(n) = 0.1 \times H(e^{j0}) = 0.1 \times 10 = 1$$

where the gain of the system at $\omega = 0$ (also called the DC gain) is $H(e^{j0}) = 10$, which is obtained from Figure 3.7.   □

3.3.4 FREQUENCY RESPONSE FUNCTION FROM DIFFERENCE EQUATIONS

When an LTI system is represented by the difference equation

$$y(n) + \sum_{\ell=1}^{N} a_\ell y(n - \ell) = \sum_{m=0}^{M} b_m x(n - m) \tag{3.20}$$

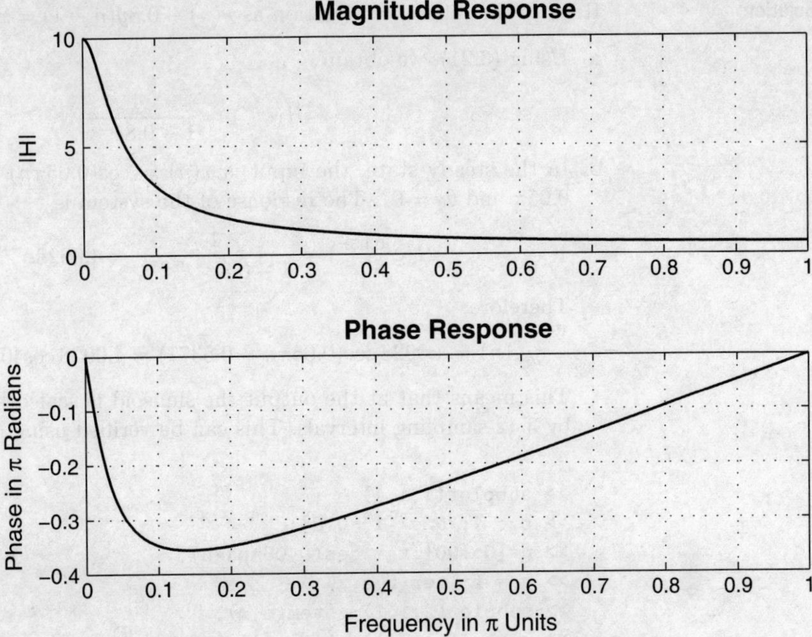

FIGURE 3.7   *Frequency response plots in Example 3.13*

then to evaluate its frequency response from (3.16), we would need the impulse response $h(n)$. However, using (3.17), we can easily obtain $H(e^{j\omega})$. We know that when $x(n) = e^{j\omega n}$, then $y(n)$ must be $H(e^{j\omega})e^{j\omega n}$. Substituting in (3.20), we have

$$H(e^{j\omega})e^{j\omega n} + \sum_{\ell=1}^{N} a_\ell H(e^{j\omega})e^{j\omega(n-\ell)} = \sum_{m=0}^{M} b_m \, e^{j\omega(n-m)}$$

or

$$H(e^{j\omega}) = \frac{\sum_{m=0}^{M} b_m \, e^{-j\omega m}}{1 + \sum_{\ell=1}^{N} a_\ell \, e^{-j\omega\ell}} \tag{3.21}$$

after canceling the common factor $e^{j\omega n}$ term and rearranging. This equation can easily be implemented in MATLAB, given the difference equation parameters.

□   **EXAMPLE 3.15**   An LTI system is specified by the difference equation

$$y(n) = 0.8y(n-1) + x(n)$$

a. Determine $H(e^{j\omega})$.
b. Calculate and plot the steady-state response $y_{\text{ss}}(n)$ to

$$x(n) = \cos(0.05\pi n)u(n)$$

Solution   Rewrite the difference equation as $y(n) - 0.8y(n-1) = x(n)$.

a. Using (3.21), we obtain

$$H(e^{j\omega}) = \frac{1}{1 - 0.8e^{-j\omega}} \tag{3.22}$$

b. In the steady state, the input is $x(n) = \cos(0.05\pi n)$ with frequency $\omega_0 = 0.05\pi$ and $\theta_0 = 0°$. The response of the system is

$$H(e^{j0.05\pi}) = \frac{1}{1 - 0.8e^{-j0.05\pi}} = 4.0928e^{-j0.5377}$$

Therefore,

$$y_{\mathrm{ss}}(n) = 4.0928\cos(0.05\pi n - 0.5377) = 4.0928\cos\left[0.05\pi(n - 3.42)\right]$$

This means that at the output the sinusoid is scaled by 4.0928 and shifted by 3.42 sampling intervals. This can be verified using MATLAB.

```
>> subplot(1,1,1)
>> b = 1; a = [1,-0.8];
>> n=[0:100];x = cos(0.05*pi*n);
>> y = filter(b,a,x);
>> subplot(2,1,1); stem(n,x);
>> ylabel('x(n)'); title('Input Sequence')
>> subplot(2,1,2); stem(n,y);
>> xlabel('n'); ylabel('y(n)'); title('Output Sequence')
```

From the plots in Figure 3.8, we note that the amplitude of $y_{\mathrm{ss}}(n)$ is approximately 4. To determine the shift in the output sinusoid, we can compare zero crossings of the input and the output. This is shown in Figure 3.8, from which the shift is approximately 3.4 samples.   □

In Example 3.15, the system was characterized by a first-order difference equation. It is fairly straightforward to implement (3.22) in MATLAB, as we did in Example 3.13. In practice, the difference equations are of large order, and hence we need a compact procedure to implement the general expression (3.21). This can be done using a simple matrix-vector multiplication. If we evaluate $H(e^{j\omega})$ at $k = 0, 1, \ldots, K$ equispaced frequencies over $[0, \pi]$, then

$$H(e^{j\omega_k}) = \frac{\sum_{m=0}^{M} b_m\, e^{-j\omega_k m}}{1 + \sum_{\ell=1}^{N} a_\ell\, e^{-j\omega_k \ell}}, \quad k = 0, 1, \ldots, K \tag{3.23}$$

If we let $\{b_m\}$, $\{a_\ell\}$ (with $a_0 = 1$), $\{m = 0, \ldots, M\}$, $\{\ell = 0, \ldots, N\}$, and $\{\omega_k\}$ be arrays (or row vectors), then the numerator and the denominator of (3.23) become

$$\underline{b}\exp(-j\underline{m}^T\underline{\omega}); \quad \underline{a}\exp(-j\underline{\ell}^T\underline{\omega})$$

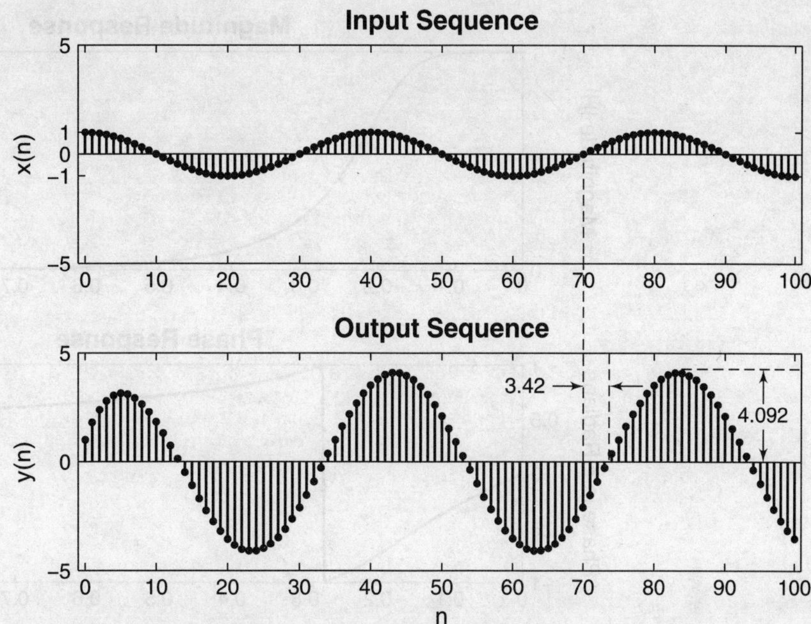

FIGURE 3.8   *Plots in Example 3.15*

respectively. Now the array $H(e^{j\omega_k})$ in (3.23) can be computed using a `./` operation. This procedure can be implemented in a MATLAB function to determine the frequency response function, given $\{b_m\}$ and $\{a_\ell\}$ arrays. We will explore this in Example 3.16 and in Problem P3.16.

☐   **EXAMPLE 3.16**   A 3rd-order lowpass filter is described by the difference equation

$$y(n) = 0.0181x(n) + 0.0543x(n-1) + 0.0543x(n-2) + 0.0181x(n-3)$$
$$+ 1.76y(n-1) - 1.1829y(n-2) + 0.2781y(n-3)$$

Plot the magnitude and the phase response of this filter, and verify that it is a lowpass filter.

Solution   We will implement this procedure in MATLAB and then plot the filter responses.

```
>> b = [0.0181,  0.0543, 0.0543,  0.0181]; % Filter coefficient array b
>> a = [1.0000, -1.7600, 1.1829, -0.2781]; % Filter coefficient array a
>> m = 0:length(b)-1; l = 0:length(a)-1;   % Index arrays m and l
>> K = 500; k = 0:1:K;                      % Index array k for frequencies
>> w = pi*k/K;                              % [0, pi] axis divided into 501 points.
>> num = b * exp(-j*m'*w);                  % Numerator calculations
>> den = a * exp(-j*l'*w);                  % Denominator calculations
>> H = num ./ den;                          % Frequency response
>> magH = abs(H); angH = angle(H);          % Mag and phase responses
```

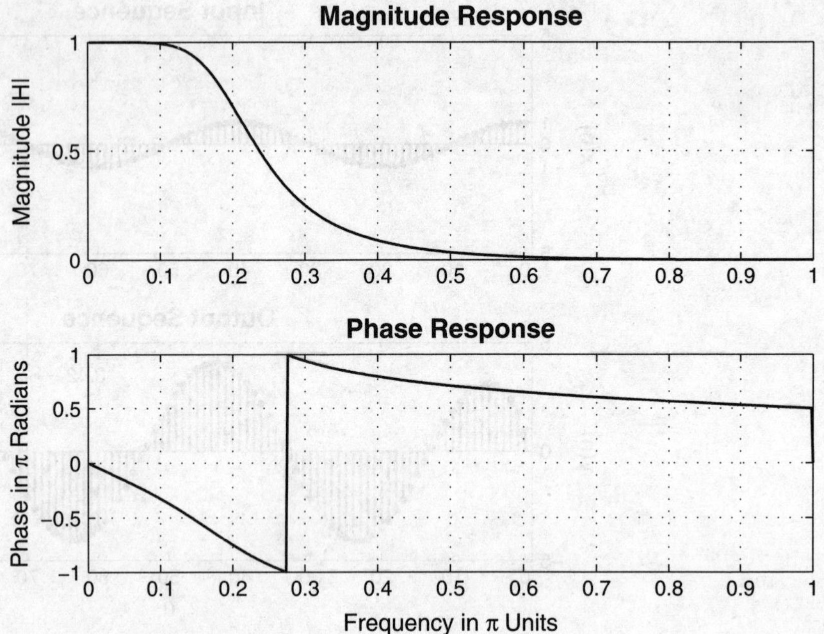

FIGURE 3.9 *Plots for Example 3.16*

```
>> subplot(2,1,1); plot(w/pi,magH); grid; axis([0,1,0,1])
>> ylabel('Magnitude |H|');
>> title('Magnitude Response');
>> subplot(2,1,2); plot(w/pi,angH/pi); grid
>> xlabel('Frequency in \pi Units'); ylabel('Phase in \pi Radians');
>> title('Phase Response');
```

From the plots in Figure 3.9, we see that the filter is indeed a lowpass filter. □

3.4 SAMPLING AND RECONSTRUCTION OF ANALOG SIGNALS

In many applications—for example, in digital communications—real-world analog signals are converted into discrete signals using sampling and quantization operations (collectively called analog-to-digital conversion, or ADC). These discrete signals are processed by digital signal processors, and the processed signals are converted into analog signals using a reconstruction operation (called digital-to-analog conversion, or

DAC). Using Fourier analysis, we can describe the sampling operation from the frequency-domain viewpoint, analyze its effects, and then address the reconstruction operation. We will also assume that the number of quantization levels is sufficiently large that the effect of quantization on discrete signals is negligible. We will study the effects of quantization in Chapter 10.

3.4.1 SAMPLING

Let $x_a(t)$ be an analog (absolutely integrable) signal. Its continuous-time Fourier transform (CTFT) is given by

$$X_a(j\Omega) \triangleq \int_{-\infty}^{\infty} x_a(t)e^{-j\Omega t}dt \qquad (3.24)$$

where Ω is an analog frequency in radians/sec. The inverse continuous-time Fourier transform is given by

$$x_a(t) = \frac{1}{2\pi} \int_{-\infty}^{\infty} X_a(j\Omega)e^{j\Omega t}d\Omega \qquad (3.25)$$

We now sample $x_a(t)$ at *sampling interval* T_s seconds apart to obtain the discrete-time signal $x(n)$:

$$x(n) \triangleq x_a(\,nT_s)$$

Let $X(e^{j\omega})$ be the discrete-time Fourier transform of $x(n)$. Then it can be shown [79] that $X(e^{j\omega})$ is a countable sum of amplitude-scaled, frequency-scaled, and translated versions of the Fourier transform $X_a(j\Omega)$.

$$X(e^{j\omega}) = \frac{1}{T_s} \sum_{\ell=-\infty}^{\infty} X_a\left[j\left(\frac{\omega}{T_s} - \frac{2\pi}{T_s}\ell\right)\right] \qquad (3.26)$$

This relation is known as the *aliasing formula*. The analog and digital frequencies are related through T_s,

$$\omega = \Omega T_s \qquad (3.27)$$

while the sampling frequency F_s is given by

$$F_s \triangleq \frac{1}{T_s}, \quad \text{sam/sec} \qquad (3.28)$$

The graphical illustration of (3.26) is shown in Figure 3.10, from which we observe that, in general, the discrete signal is an *aliased version* of the corresponding analog signal because higher frequencies are aliased into lower frequencies if there is an overlap. However, it is possible to recover the Fourier transform $X_a(j\Omega)$ from $X(e^{j\omega})$ [or equivalently, the analog

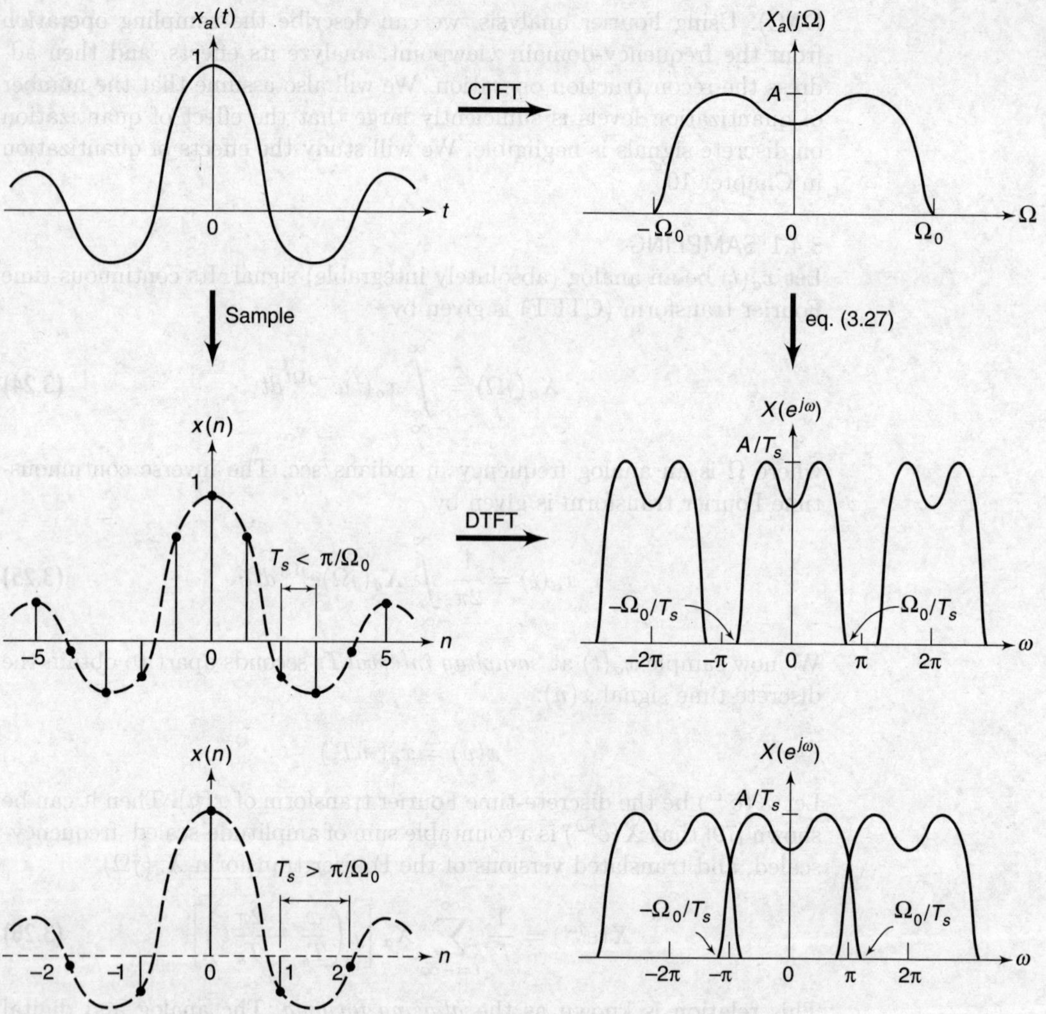

FIGURE 3.10   *Sampling operation in the time and frequency domains*

signal $x_a(t)$ from its samples $x(n)$] if the infinite "replicas" of $X_a(j\Omega)$ do not overlap with each other to form $X(e^{j\omega})$. This is true for band-limited analog signals.

■   **DEFINITION 2**   ***Band-Limited Signal***
A signal is band-limited if there exists a finite radian frequency Ω_0 such that $X_a(j\Omega)$ is zero for $|\Omega| > \Omega_0$. The frequency $F_0 = \Omega_0/2\pi$ is called the signal bandwidth in Hz.

Referring to Figure 3.10, if $\pi > \Omega_0 T_s$—or equivalently, $F_s/2 > F_0$—then

$$X(e^{j\omega}) = \frac{1}{T_s} X\left(j\frac{\omega}{T_s}\right); \quad -\frac{\pi}{T_s} < \frac{\omega}{T_s} \leq \frac{\pi}{T_s} \tag{3.29}$$

which leads to the sampling theorem for band-limited signals.

■ THEOREM 3 **_Sampling Principle_**

A band-limited signal $x_a(t)$ with bandwidth F_0 can be reconstructed from its sample values $x(n) = x_a(nT_s)$ if the sampling frequency $F_s = 1/T_s$ is greater than twice the bandwidth F_0 of $x_a(t)$.

$$F_s > 2F_0$$

Otherwise, aliasing would result in $x(n)$. The sampling rate of $2F_0$ for an analog band-limited signal is called the Nyquist rate.

Note: After $x_a(t)$ is sampled, the highest analog frequency that $x(n)$ represents is $F_s/2$ Hz (or $\omega = \pi$). This agrees with the implication stated in property 2 of the discrete-time Fourier transform in Section 3.1. Before we delve into MATLAB implementation of sampling, we first consider sampling of sinusoidal signals and the resulting Fourier transform in the following example.

□ **EXAMPLE 3.17**   The analog signal $x_a(t) = 4 + 2\cos(150\pi t + \pi/3) + 4\sin(350\pi t)$ is sampled at $F_s = 200$ sam/sec to obtain the discrete-time signal $x(n)$. Determine $x(n)$ and its corresponding DTFT $X(e^{j\omega})$.

Solution   The highest frequency in the given $x_a(t)$ is $F_0 = 175$ Hz. Since $F_s = 200$, which is less than $2F_0$, there will be aliasing in $x(n)$ after sampling. The sampling interval is $T_s = 1/F_s = 0.005$ sec. Hence we have

$$x(n) = x_a(nT_s) = x_a(0.005n)$$

$$= 4 + 2\cos\left(0.75\pi n + \frac{\pi}{3}\right) + 4\sin(1.75\pi n) \tag{3.30}$$

Note that the digital frequency, 1.75π, of the third term in (3.30) is outside the primary interval of $-\pi \leq \omega \leq \pi$, signifying that aliasing has occurred. From the periodicity property of digital sinusoidal sequences in Chapter 2, we know that the period of the digital sinusoid is 2π. Hence we can determine the alias of the frequency 1.75π. From (3.30), we have

$$x(n) = 4 + 2\cos(0.75\pi n + \tfrac{\pi}{3}) + 4\sin(1.75\pi n - 2\pi n)$$

$$= 4 + 2\cos(0.75\pi n + \tfrac{\pi}{3}) - 4\sin(0.25\pi n) \tag{3.31}$$

Using Euler's identity, we can expess $x(n)$ as

$$x(n) = 4 + e^{j\pi/3}e^{j0.75\pi n} + e^{-j\pi/3}e^{-j0.75\pi n} + 2je^{j0.25\pi n} - 2je^{j0.25\pi n} \quad \textbf{(3.32)}$$

From Table 3.1 and the DTFT properties, the DTFT of $x(n)$ is given by

$$X(e^{j\omega}) = 8\pi\delta(\omega) + 2\pi e^{j\pi/3}\delta(\omega - 0.75\pi) + 2\pi e^{-j\pi/3}\delta(\omega + 0.75\pi)$$

$$+ j4\pi\delta(\omega - 0.25\pi) - j4\pi\delta(\omega + 0.25\pi), \ -\pi \le \omega \le \pi \quad \textbf{(3.33)}$$

The plot of $X(e^{j\omega})$ is shown in Figure 3.15.   □

3.4.2 MATLAB IMPLEMENTATION

In a strict sense, it is not possible to analyze analog signals using MATLAB unless we use the Symbolic toolbox. However, if we sample $x_a(t)$ on a fine grid that has a sufficiently small time increment to yield a smooth plot and a large enough maximum time to show all the modes, then we can approximate its analysis. Let Δt be the grid interval such that $\Delta t \ll T_s$. Then

$$x_G(m) \triangleq x_a(m\Delta t) \quad \textbf{(3.34)}$$

can be used as an array to simulate an analog signal. The sampling interval T_s should not be confused with the grid interval Δt, which is used strictly to represent an analog signal in MATLAB. Similarly, the Fourier transform relation (3.24) should also be approximated in light of (3.34) as follows:

$$X_a(j\Omega) \approx \sum_m x_G(m)e^{-j\Omega m\Delta t}\Delta t = \Delta t \sum_m x_G(m)e^{-j\Omega m\Delta t} \quad \textbf{(3.35)}$$

Now if $x_a(t)$ [and hence $x_G(m)$] is of finite duration, then (3.35) is similar to the discrete-time Fourier transform relation (3.3) and hence can be implemented in MATLAB in a similar fashion to analyze the sampling phenomenon.

□ **EXAMPLE 3.18**   Let $x_a(t) = e^{-1000|t|}$. Determine and plot its Fourier transform.

Solution   From (3.24),

$$X_a(j\Omega) = \int_{-\infty}^{\infty} x_a(t)e^{-j\Omega t}dt = \int_{-\infty}^{0} e^{1000t}e^{-j\Omega t}dt + \int_{0}^{\infty} e^{-1000t}e^{-j\Omega t}dt$$

$$= \frac{0.002}{1 + (\frac{\Omega}{1000})^2} \quad \textbf{(3.36)}$$

which is a real-valued function since $x_a(t)$ is a real and even signal. To evaluate $X_a(j\Omega)$ numerically, we have to first approximate $x_a(t)$ by a finite-duration grid sequence $x_G(m)$. Using the approximation $e^{-5} \approx 0$, we note that $x_a(t)$ can be approximated by a finite-duration signal over $-0.005 \le t \le 0.005$ (or equivalently, over $[-5, 5]$ msec). Similarly from (3.36), $X_a(j\Omega) \approx 0$ for $\Omega \ge 2\pi\,(2000)$. Hence choosing

$$\Delta t = 5 \times 10^{-5} \ll \frac{1}{2\,(2000)} = 25 \times 10^{-5}$$

we can obtain $x_G(m)$ and then implement (3.35) in MATLAB.

```
% Analog signal
>> Dt = 0.00005; t = -0.005:Dt:0.005; xa = exp(-1000*abs(t));
% Continuous-time Fourier transform
>>Wmax = 2*pi*2000; K = 500; k = 0:1:K; W = k*Wmax/K;
>>Xa = xa * exp(-j*t'*W) * Dt; Xa = real(Xa);
>>W = [-fliplr(W), W(2:501)]; % Omega from -Wmax to Wmax
>>Xa = [fliplr(Xa), Xa(2:501)]; % Xa over -Wmax to Wmax interval
>>subplot(2,1,1);plot(t*1000,xa);
>>xlabel('t in msec'); ylabel('Amplitude')
>>title('Analog Signal')
>>subplot(2,1,2);plot(W/(2*pi*1000),Xa*1000);
>>xlabel('Frequency in KHz'); ylabel('Amplitude/1000')
>>title('Continuous-Time Fourier Transform')
```

Figure 3.11 shows the plots of $x_a(t)$ and $X_a(j\Omega)$. Note that to reduce the number of computations, we computed $X_a(j\Omega)$ over $[0, 4000\pi]$ rad/sec (or equivalently, over $[0, 2]$ KHz) and then duplicated it over $[-4000\pi, 0]$ for plotting purposes. The displayed plot of $X_a(j\Omega)$ agrees with (3.36). $\qquad\square$

☐ **EXAMPLE 3.19**   To study the effect of sampling on the frequency-domain quantities, we will sample $x_a(t)$ in Example 3.18 at two different sampling frequencies.

    a. Sample $x_a(t)$ at $F_s = 5000$ sam/sec to obtain $x_1(n)$. Determine and plot $X_1(e^{j\omega})$.

    b. Sample $x_a(t)$ at $F_s = 1000$ sam/sec to obtain $x_2(n)$. Determine and plot $X_2(e^{j\omega})$.

Solution   **a.** Since the bandwidth of $x_a(t)$ is 2KHz, the Nyquist rate is 4000 sam/sec, which is less than the given F_s. Therefore, aliasing will be (almost) nonexistent.

Analog Signal

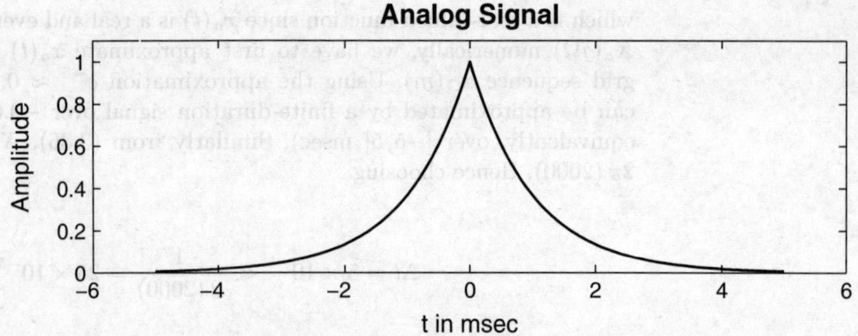

Continuous–Time Fourier Transform

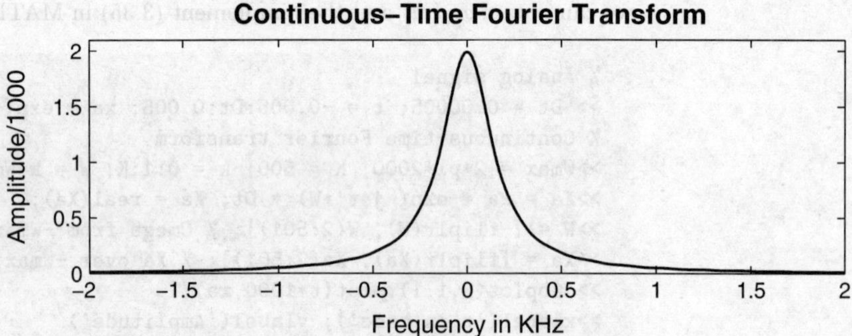

FIGURE 3.11   *Plots in Example 3.18*

MATLAB script:

```
% Analog signal
>> Dt = 0.00005; t = -0.005:Dt:0.005; xa = exp(-1000*abs(t));
% Discrete-time signal
>> Ts = 0.0002; n = -25:1:25; x = exp(-1000*abs(n*Ts));
% Discrete-time Fourier transform
>> K = 500; k = 0:1:K; w = pi*k/K;
>> X = x * exp(-j*n'*w); X = real(X);
>> w = [-fliplr(w), w(2:K+1)];   X = [fliplr(X), X(2:K+1)];
>> subplot(2,1,1);plot(t*1000,xa);
>> xlabel('t in msec'); ylabel('Amplitude')
>> title('Discrete Signal'); hold on
>> stem(n*Ts*1000,x); gtext('Ts=0.2 msec'); hold off
>> subplot(2,1,2);plot(w/pi,X);
>> xlabel('Frequency in \pi Units'); ylabel('Amplitude')
>> title('Discrete-Time Fourier Transform')
```

In the top plot in Figure 3.12, we have superimposed the discrete signal $x_1(n)$ over $x_a(t)$ to emphasize the sampling. The plot of $X_2(e^{j\omega})$ shows that it is a scaled version (scaled by $F_s = 5000$) of $X_a(j\Omega)$. Clearly there is no aliasing.

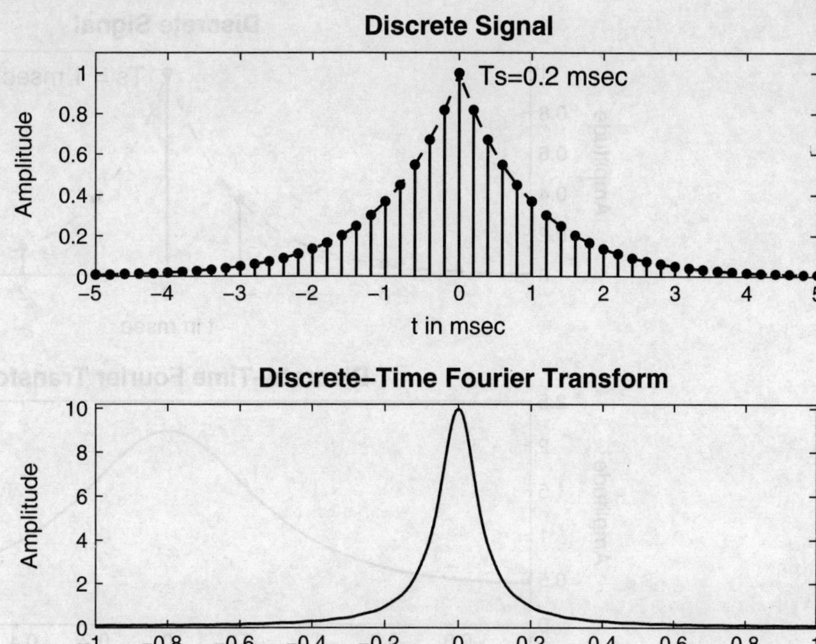

FIGURE 3.12 *Plots in Example 3.19a*

b. Here $F_s = 1000 < 4000$. Hence there will be a considerable amount of aliasing. This is evident from Figure 3.13, in which the shape of $X(e^{j\omega})$ is different from that of $X_a(j\Omega)$ and can be seen to be a result of adding overlapping replicas of $X_a(j\Omega)$. □

3.4.3 RECONSTRUCTION

From the sampling theorem and the preceding examples, it is clear that if we sample band-limited $x_a(t)$ above its Nyquist rate, then we can reconstruct $x_a(t)$ from its samples $x(n)$. This reconstruction can be thought of as a two-step process:

- First, the samples are converted into a weighted impulse train:

$$\sum_{n=-\infty}^{\infty} x(n)\delta(t - nT_s) = \cdots + x(-1)\delta(n + T_s) + x(0)\delta(t) + x(1)\delta(n - T_s) + \cdots$$

- Then, the impulse train is filtered through an ideal analog lowpass filter band-limited to the $[-F_s/2, F_s/2]$ band:

$$x(n) \longrightarrow \boxed{\begin{array}{c}\text{Impulse train}\\\text{conversion}\end{array}} \longrightarrow \boxed{\begin{array}{c}\text{Ideal lowpass}\\\text{filter}\end{array}} \longrightarrow x_a(t)$$

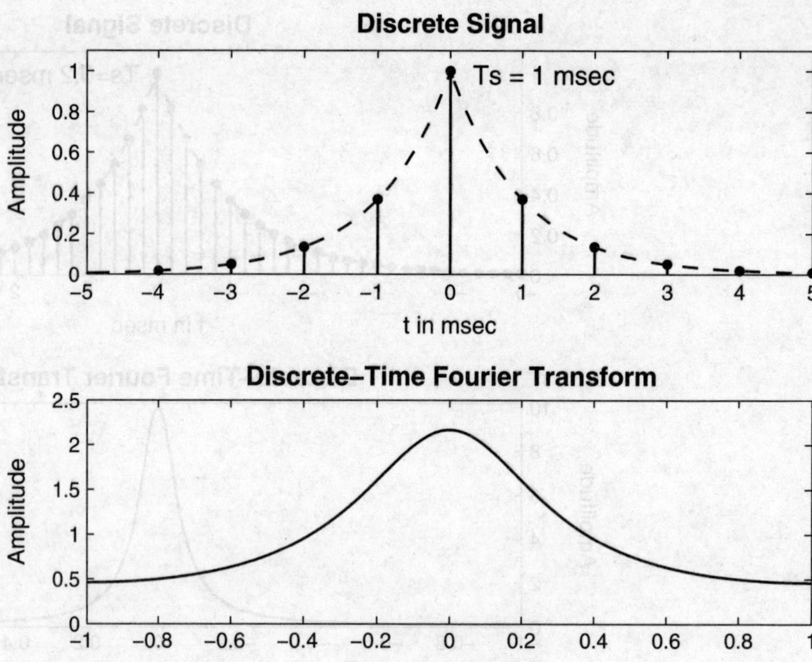

FIGURE 3.13 *Plots in Example 3.19b*

This two-step procedure can be described mathematically using an interpolating formula [79],

$$x_a(t) = \sum_{n=-\infty}^{\infty} x(n)\operatorname{sinc}\left[F_s(t - nT_s)\right] \tag{3.37}$$

where $\operatorname{sinc}(x) = \frac{\sin \pi x}{\pi x}$ is an interpolating function. The physical interpretation of the above reconstruction (3.37) is given in Figure 3.14, from which we observe that this *ideal* interpolation is not practically feasible, because the entire system is noncausal and hence not realizable.

☐ **EXAMPLE 3.20**   Consider the sampled signal $x(n)$ from Example 3.17. It is applied as an input to an ideal D/A converter (i.e., an ideal interpolator) to obtain the analog signal $y_a(t)$. The ideal D/A converter is also operating at $F_s = 200$ sam/sec. Obtain the reconstructed signal $y_a(t)$, and determine whether the sampling/reconstruction operation resulted in any aliasing. Also, plot the Fourier transforms $X_a(j\Omega)$, $X(e^{j\omega})$, and $Y_a(j\Omega)$.

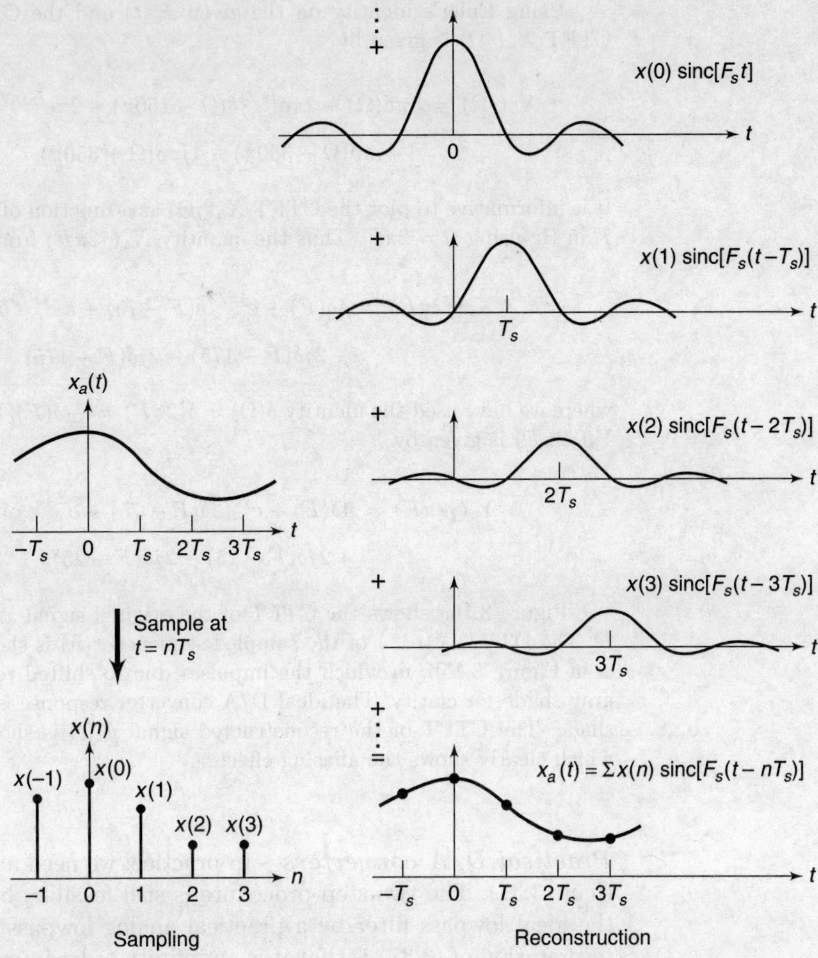

FIGURE 3.14 *Reconstruction of band-limited signal from its samples*

Solution   We can determine $y_a(t)$ using (3.31). However, since all frequencies in the sinusoidal sequence $x(n)$ are between the primary period of $-\pi \le \omega \le \pi$, we can equivalently obtain $y_a(t)$ by substituting n by tF_s. Thus from (3.31), we have

$$y_a(t) = x(n)\Big|_{n=tF_s} = x(n)\Big|_{n=200t}$$

$$= 4 + 2\cos\left(0.75\pi 200t + \frac{\pi}{3}\right) - 4\sin(0.25\pi 200t)$$

$$= 4 + 2\cos\left(150\pi t + \frac{\pi}{3}\right) - 4\sin(50\pi t) \tag{3.38}$$

As expected, the 175 Hz component in $x_a(t)$ is aliased into the 25 Hz component in $y_a(t)$.

Using Euler's identity on the given $x_a(t)$ and the CTFT properties, the CTFT $X_a(j\Omega)$ is given by

$$X_a(j\Omega) = 8\pi\delta(\Omega) + 2\pi e^{j\pi/3}\delta(\Omega - 150\pi) + 2\pi e^{-j\pi/3}\delta(\Omega + 150\pi)$$

$$+ 4j\pi\delta(\Omega - 350\pi) - 4j\pi\delta(\Omega + 350\pi) \tag{3.39}$$

It is informative to plot the CTFT $X_a(j\Omega)$ as a function of the cyclic frequency F in Hz using $\Omega = 2\pi F$. Thus the quantity $X_a(j2\pi F)$ from (3.39) is given by

$$X_a(j2\pi F) = 4\delta(F) + e^{j\pi/3}\delta(F - 75) + e^{-j\pi/3}\delta(F + 75)$$

$$+ 2j\delta(F - 175) - 2j\delta(F + 175) \tag{3.40}$$

where we have used the identity $\delta(\Omega) = \delta(2\pi F) = \frac{1}{2\pi}\delta(F)$. Similarly, the CTFT $Y_a(j2\pi F)$ is given by

$$Y_a(j2\pi F) = 4\delta(F) + e^{j\pi/3}\delta(F - 75) + e^{-j\pi/3}\delta(F + 75)$$

$$+ 2j\delta(F - 25) - 2j\delta(F + 25) \tag{3.41}$$

Figure 3.15a shows the CTFT of the original signal $x_a(t)$ as a function of F. The DTFT $X\left(e^{j\omega}\right)$ of the sampled sequence $x(n)$ is shown as a function of ω in Figure 3.15b, in which the impulses due to shifted replicas are shown in gray shade for clarity. The ideal D/A converter response is also shown in gray shade. The CTFT of the reconstructed signal $y_a(t)$ is shown in Figure 3.15c, which clearly shows the aliasing effect.   □

Practical D/A converters   In practice, we need a different approach than (3.37). The two-step procedure is still feasible, but now we replace the ideal lowpass filter by a practical analog lowpass filter. Another interpretation of (3.37) is that it is an infinite-order interpolation. We want finite-order (and in fact low-order) interpolations. There are several approaches to do this.

- **Zero-order-hold (ZOH) interpolation:** In this interpolation, a given sample value is held for the sample interval until the next sample is received,

$$\hat{x}_a(t) = x(n), \quad nT_s \le n < (n + 1)T_s$$

which can be obtained by filtering the impulse train through an interpolating filter of the form

$$h_0(t) = \begin{cases} 1, & 0 \le t \le T_s \\ 0, & \text{otherwise} \end{cases}$$

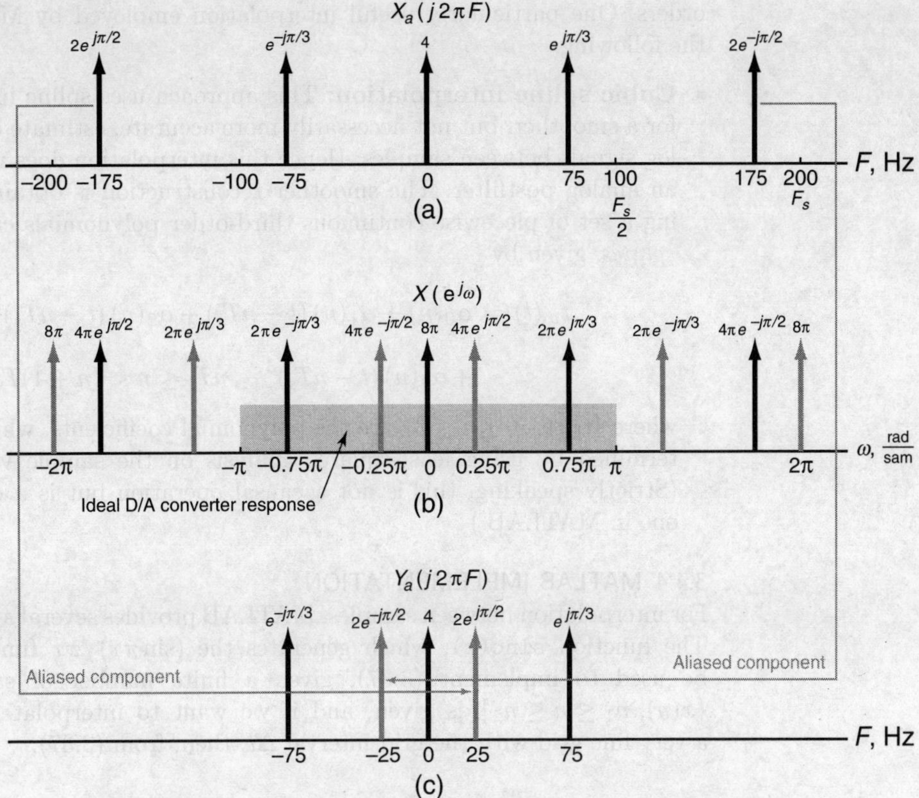

FIGURE 3.15   *Fourier transforms of the sinusoidal signals $x_a(t)$, $x(n)$, and $y_a(t)$*

which is a rectangular pulse. The resulting signal is a piecewise-constant (staircase) waveform that requires an appropriately designed analog postfilter for accurate waveform reconstruction.

$$x(n) \longrightarrow \boxed{\text{ZOH}} \longrightarrow \hat{x}_a(t) \longrightarrow \boxed{\text{Postfilter}} \longrightarrow x_a(t)$$

- **First-order-hold (FOH) interpolation:** In this case, the adjacent samples are joined by straight lines. This can be obtained by filtering the impulse train through

$$h_1(t) = \begin{cases} 1 + \dfrac{t}{T_s}, & 0 \le t \le T_s \\[2mm] 1 - \dfrac{t}{T_s}, & T_s \le t \le 2T_s \\[2mm] 0, & \text{otherwise} \end{cases}$$

Once again, an appropriately designed analog postfilter is required for accurate reconstruction. These interpolations can be extended to higher orders. One particularly useful interpolation employed by MATLAB is the following.

- **Cubic spline interpolation:** This approach uses spline interpolants for a smoother, but not necessarily more accurate, estimate of the analog signals between samples. Hence this interpolation does not require an analog postfilter. The smoother reconstruction is obtained by using a set of piecewise continuous third-order polynomials called *cubic splines*, given by

$$x_a(t) = \alpha_0(n) + \alpha_1(n)(t - nT_s) + \alpha_2(n)(t - nT_s)^2$$

$$+ \alpha_3(n)(t - nT_s)^3, \quad nT_s \leq n < (n+1)T_s \tag{3.42}$$

where $\{\alpha_i(n), 0 \leq i \leq 3\}$ are the polynomial coefficients, which are determined by using least-squares analysis on the sample values [10]. (Strictly speaking, this is not a causal operation but is a convenient one in MATLAB.)

3.4.4 MATLAB IMPLEMENTATION

For interpolation between samples, MATLAB provides several approaches. The function `sinc(x)`, which generates the $(\sin \pi x)/\pi x$ function, can be used to implement (3.37), given a finite number of samples. If $\{x(n),\, n_1 \leq n \leq n_2\}$ is given, and if we want to interpolate $x_a(t)$ on a very fine grid with the grid interval Δt, then, from (3.37),

$$x_a(m\Delta t) \approx \sum_{n=n_1}^{n_2} x(n) \operatorname{sinc}\left[F_s(m\Delta t - nT_s)\right], \quad t_1 \leq m\Delta t \leq t_2 \tag{3.43}$$

which can be implemented as a matrix-vector multiplication operation as shown below.

```
>> n = n1:n2; t = t1:t2; Fs = 1/Ts; nTs = n*Ts;  % Ts is the sampling interval
>> xa = x * sinc(Fs*(ones(length(n),1)*t-nTs'*ones(1,length(t))));
```

Note that it is not possible to obtain an *exact* analog $x_a(t)$ in light of the fact that we have assumed a finite number of samples. We now demonstrate the use of the `sinc` function in the following two examples and also study the aliasing problem in the time domain.

☐ **EXAMPLE 3.21**   From the samples $x_1(n)$ in Example 3.19a, reconstruct $x_a(t)$ and comment on the results.

Solution   Note that $x_1(n)$ was obtained by sampling $x_a(t)$ at $T_s = 1/F_s = 0.0002$ sec. We will use the grid spacing of 0.00005 sec over $-0.005 \leq t \leq 0.005$, which gives $x(n)$ over $-25 \leq n \leq 25$.

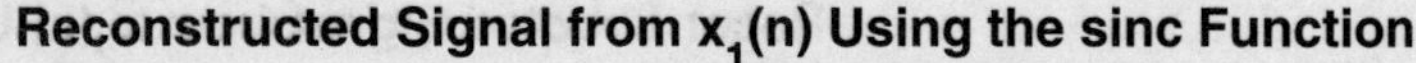

Reconstructed Signal from x₁(n) Using the sinc Function

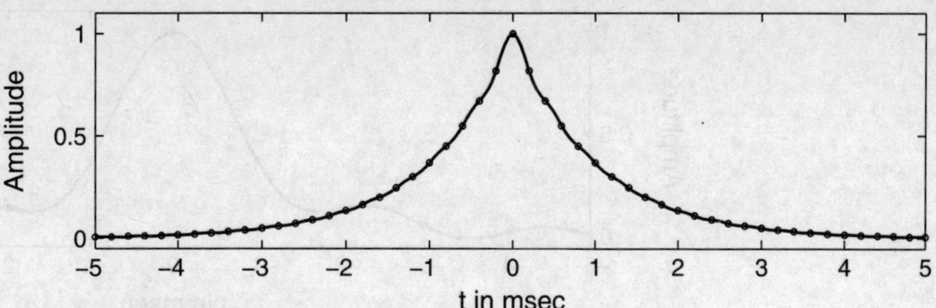

FIGURE 3.16 *Reconstructed signal in Example 3.21*

MATLAB script:

```
% Discrete-time signal x1(n)
>> Ts = 0.0002; n = -25:1:25; nTs = n*Ts;   x = exp(-1000*abs(nTs));
% Analog signal reconstruction
>> Dt = 0.00005; t = -0.005:Dt:0.005;
>> xa = x * sinc(Fs*(ones(length(n),1)*t-nTs'*ones(1,length(t))));
% Check
>> error = max(abs(xa - exp(-1000*abs(t))))
error =
    0.0363
```

The maximum error between the reconstructed and the actual analog signal is 0.0363, which is due to the fact that $x_a(t)$ is not strictly band-limited (and also we have a finite number of samples). From Figure 3.16, we note that visually the reconstruction is excellent. □

☐ **EXAMPLE 3.22** From the samples $x_2(n)$ in Example 3.17b, reconstruct $x_a(t)$ and comment on the results.

Solution In this case, $x_2(n)$ was obtained by sampling $x_a(t)$ at $T_s = 1/F_s = 0.001$ sec. We will again use the grid spacing of 0.00005 sec over $-0.005 \leq t \leq 0.005$, which gives $x(n)$ over $-5 \leq n \leq 5$.

```
% Discrete-time signal x2(n)
>> Ts = 0.001; n = -5:1:5; nTs = n*Ts;   x = exp(-1000*abs(nTs));
% Analog signal reconstruction
>> Dt = 0.00005; t = -0.005:Dt:0.005;
>> xa = x * sinc(Fs*(ones(length(n),1)*t-nTs'*ones(1,length(t))));
% Check
>> error = max(abs(xa - exp(-1000*abs(t))))
error =
    0.1852
```

Reconstructed Signal from $x_2(n)$ Using the sinc Function

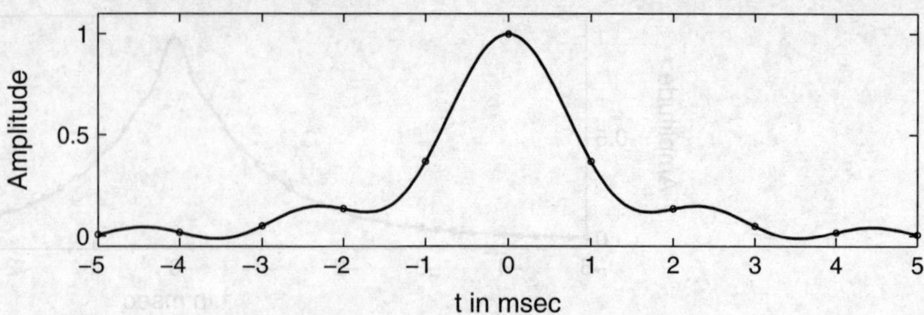

FIGURE 3.17 *Reconstructed signal in Example 3.22*

The maximum error between the reconstructed and the actual analog signals is 0.1852, which is significant and cannot be attributed to the nonband-limitedness of $x_a(t)$ alone. From Figure 3.17, observe that the reconstructed signal differs from the actual one in many places over the interpolated regions. This is the visual demonstration of aliasing in the time domain. □

The second MATLAB approach for signal reconstruction is a plotting approach. The `stairs` function plots a staircase (ZOH) rendition of the analog signal, given its samples, while the `plot` function depicts a linear (FOH) interpolation between samples.

□ **EXAMPLE 3.23**   Plot the reconstructed signal from the samples $x_1(n)$ in Example 3.19 using the ZOH and the FOH interpolations. Comment on the plots.

Solution   Note that in this reconstruction, we do not compute $x_a(t)$ but merely plot it using its samples.

```
% Discrete-time signal x1(n) : Ts = 0.0002
>> Ts = 0.0002; n = -25:1:25; nTs = n*Ts;  x = exp(-1000*abs(nTs));
% Plots
>> subplot(2,1,1); stairs(nTs*1000,x);
>> xlabel('t in msec'); ylabel('Amplitude')
>> title('Reconstructed Signal from x_1(n) Using ZOH'); hold on
>> stem(n*Ts*1000,x); hold off
%
% Discrete-time signal x1(n) : Ts = 0.001
>> Ts = 0.001; n = -5:1:5; nTs = n*Ts;  x = exp(-1000*abs(nTs));
% Plots
>> subplot(2,1,2); plot(nTs*1000,x);
>> xlabel('t in msec'); ylabel('Amplitude')
>> title('Reconstructed Signal from x_1(n) Using FOH'); hold on
>> stem(n*Ts*1000,x); hold off
```

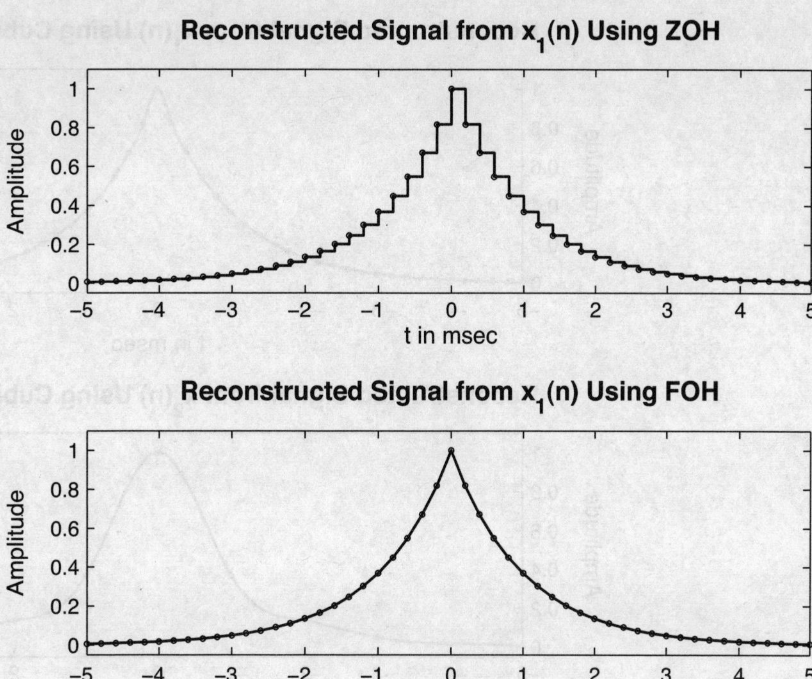

FIGURE 3.18 *Signal reconstruction in Example 3.23*

The plots are shown in Figure 3.18, from which we observe that the ZOH reconstruction is a crude one and that the further processing of analog signal is necessary. The FOH reconstruction appears to be a good one, but a careful observation near $t = 0$ reveals that the peak of the signal is not correctly reproduced. In general, if the sampling frequency is much higher than the Nyquist rate, then the FOH interpolation provides an acceptable reconstruction. □

The third approach of reconstruction in MATLAB involves the use of cubic spline functions. The `spline` function implements interpolation between sample points. It is invoked by `xa = spline(nTs,x,t)`, in which `x` and `nTs` are arrays containing samples $x(n)$ at nT_s instances, respectively, and `t` array contains a fine grid at which $x_a(t)$ values are desired. Note once again that it is not possible to obtain an *exact* analog $x_a(t)$.

□ **EXAMPLE 3.24**   From the samples $x_1(n)$ and $x_2(n)$ in Example 3.19, reconstruct $x_a(t)$ using the `spline` function. Comment on the results.

Solution   This example is similar to Examples 3.21 and 3.22. Hence sampling parameters are the same as before.

Reconstructed Signal from $x_1(n)$ Using Cubic Spline Function

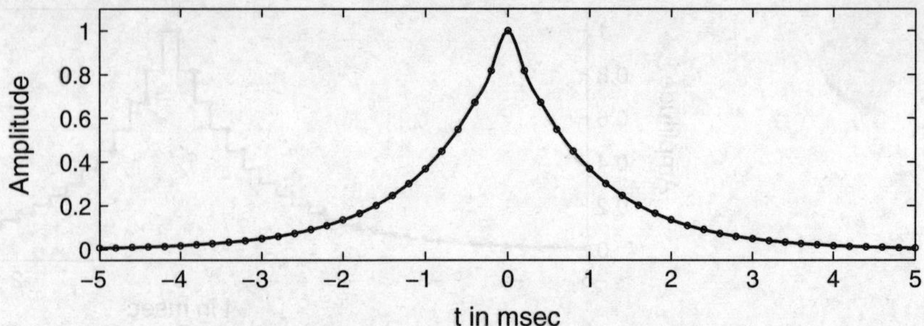

Reconstructed Signal from $x_2(n)$ Using Cubic Spline Function

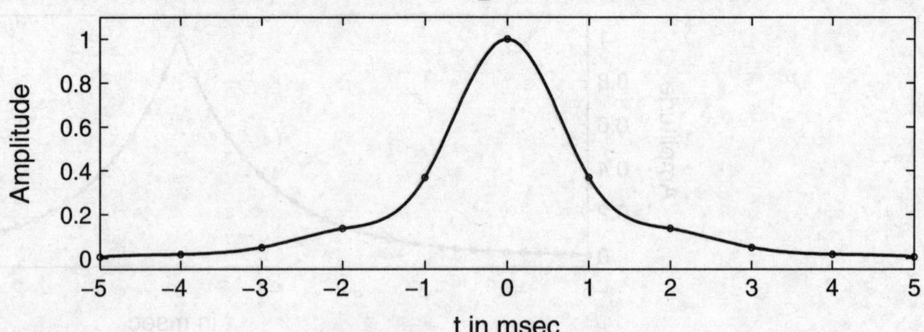

FIGURE 3.19　*Reconstructed signal in Example 3.24*

MATLAB script:

```
% a) Discrete-time signal x1(n): Ts = 0.0002
>> Ts = 0.0002; n = -25:1:25; nTs = n*Ts;   x = exp(-1000*abs(nTs));
% Analog signal reconstruction
>> Dt = 0.00005; t = -0.005:Dt:0.005;   xa = spline(nTs,x,t);
% Check
>> error = max(abs(xa - exp(-1000*abs(t))))
error = 0.0317
```

The maximum error between the reconstructed and the actual analog signal is 0.0317, which is due to the nonideal interpolation and the fact that $x_a(t)$ is nonband-limited. Comparing this error with that from the sinc (or ideal) interpolation, we note that this error is lower. The ideal interpolation generally suffers more from time-limitedness (or from a finite number of samples). From the top plot in Figure 3.19, we observe that visually the reconstruction is excellent.

MATLAB script:

```
% Discrete-time signal x2(n): Ts = 0.001
>> Ts = 0.001; n = -5:1:5; nTs = n*Ts;   x = exp(-1000*abs(nTs));
% Analog signal reconstruction
>> Dt = 0.00005; t = -0.005:Dt:0.005;   xa = spline(nTs,x,t);
```

```
% Check
>> error = max(abs(xa - exp(-1000*abs(t))))
error = 0.1679
```

The maximum error in this case is 0.1679, which is significant and cannot be attributed to the nonideal interpolation or nonband-limitedness of $x_a(t)$. From the bottom plot in Figure 3.19, observe that the reconstructed signal again differs from the actual one in many places over the interpolated regions. $\square$

From these examples, it is clear that for practical purposes the `spline` interpolation provides the best results.

3.5 PROBLEMS

P3.1   Using the matrix-vector multiplication approach discussed in this chapter, write a MATLAB function to compute the DTFT of a finite-duration sequence. The format of the function should be

```
function [X] = dtft(x,n,w)
% Computes discrete-time Fourier transform
% [X] = dtft(x,n,w)
%    X = DTFT values computed at w frequencies
%    x = finite duration sequence over n
%    n = sample position vector
%    w = frequency location vector
```

Use this function to compute the DTFT $X(e^{j\omega})$ of the following finite-duration sequences over $-\pi \leq \omega \leq \pi$. Plot DTFT magnitude and angle graphs in one figure window.

1. $x(n) = (0.6)^{|n|} [u(n+10) - u(n-11)]$. Comment on the angle plot.
2. $x(n) = n(0.9)^n [u(n) - u(n-21)]$.
3. $x(n) = [\cos(0.5\pi n) + j\sin(0.5\pi n)][u(n) - u(n-51)]$. Comment on the magnitude plot.
4. $x(n) = \{4, 3, 2, 1, 1, 2, 3, 4\}$. Comment on the angle plot.
5. $x(n) = \{\overset{\uparrow}{4}, 3, 2, 1, -1, -2, -3, -4\}$. Comment on the angle plot.

P3.2   Let $x_1(n) = \{1, 2, 2, 1\}$. A new sequence $x_2(n)$ is formed using

$$x_2(n) = \begin{cases} x_1(n), & 0 \leq n \leq 3 \\ x_1(n-4), & 4 \leq n \leq 7 \\ 0, & \text{otherwise} \end{cases} \tag{3.44}$$

1. Express $X_2(e^{j\omega})$ in terms of $X_1(e^{j\omega})$ without explicitly computing $X_1(e^{j\omega})$.
2. Verify your result using MATLAB by computing and plotting magnitudes of the respective DTFTs.

P3.3   Determine analytically the DTFT of each of the following sequences. Plot the magnitude and angle of $X(e^{j\omega})$ over $0 \leq \omega \leq \pi$.

1. $x(n) = 2\,(0.5)^n\,u(n+2)$
2. $x(n) = (0.6)^{|n|}\,[u(n+10) - u(n-11)]$
3. $x(n) = n\,(0.9)^n\,u(n+3)$
4. $x(n) = (n+3)\,(0.8)^{n-1}\,u(n-2)$
5. $x(n) = 4\,(-0.7)^n\,\cos(0.25\pi n)u(n)$

P3.4   The following finite-duration sequences are called *windows* and are very useful in DSP:

$$\text{Rectangular: } \mathcal{R}_M(n) = \begin{cases} 1,\ 0 \leq n < M \\ 0,\ \text{otherwise} \end{cases}$$

$$\text{Hanning: } \mathcal{C}_M(n) = 0.5 \left[1 - \cos\frac{2\pi n}{M-1}\right] \mathcal{R}_M(n)$$

$$\text{Triangular: } \mathcal{T}_M(n) = \left[1 - \frac{|M-1-2n|}{M-1}\right] \mathcal{R}_M(n)$$

$$\text{Hamming: } \mathcal{H}_M(n) = \left[0.54 - 0.46\cos\frac{2\pi n}{M-1}\right] \mathcal{R}_M(n)$$

For each of these windows, determine their DTFTs for $M = 10, 25, 50, 101$. Scale transform values so that the maximum value is equal to 1. Plot the magnitude of the normalized DTFT over $-\pi \leq \omega \leq \pi$. Study these plots and comment on their behavior as a function of M.

P3.5   Using the definition of the DTFT in (3.1), determine the sequences corresponding to the following DTFTs.

1. $X(e^{j\omega}) = 3 + 2\cos(\omega) + 4\cos(2\omega)$
2. $X(e^{j\omega}) = [1 - 6\cos(3\omega) + 8\cos(5\omega)]\,e^{-j3\omega}$
3. $X(e^{j\omega}) = 2 + j4\sin(2\omega) - 5\cos(4\omega)$
4. $X(e^{j\omega}) = [1 + 2\cos(\omega) + 3\cos(2\omega)]\cos(\omega/2)e^{-j5\omega/2}$
5. $X(e^{j\omega}) = j\,[3 + 2\cos(\omega) + 4\cos(2\omega)]\sin(\omega)e^{-j3\omega}$

P3.6   Using the definition of the inverse DTFT in (3.2), determine the sequences corresponding to the following DTFTs.

1. $X(e^{j\omega}) = \begin{cases} 1, & 0 \leq |\omega| \leq \pi/3 \\ 0, & \pi/3 < |\omega| \leq \pi \end{cases}$

2. $X(e^{j\omega}) = \begin{cases} 0, & 0 \leq |\omega| \leq 3\pi/4 \\ 1, & 3\pi/4 < |\omega| \leq \pi \end{cases}$

3. $X(e^{j\omega}) = \begin{cases} 2, & 0 \leq |\omega| \leq \pi/8 \\ 1, & \pi/8 < |\omega| \leq 3\pi/4 \\ 0, & 3\pi/4 < |\omega| \leq \pi \end{cases}$

4. $X(e^{j\omega}) = \begin{cases} 0, & -\pi \leq |\omega| < \pi/4 \\ 1, & \pi/4 \leq |\omega| \leq 3\pi/4 \\ 0, & 3\pi/4 < |\omega| \leq \pi \end{cases}$

5. $X(e^{j\omega}) = \omega\,e^{j(\pi/2 - 10\omega)}$

Remember that the above transforms are periodic in ω with period equal to 2π. Hence functions are given only over the primary period of $-\pi \leq \omega \leq \pi$.

P3.7 A complex-valued sequence $x(n)$ can be decomposed into a conjugate symmetric part $x_e(n)$ and a conjugate antisymmetric part $x_o(n)$ as discussed in Chapter 2. Show that

$$\mathcal{F}[x_e(n)] = X_R(e^{j\omega}) \quad \text{and} \quad \mathcal{F}[x_o(n)] = jX_I(e^{j\omega})$$

where $X_R(e^{j\omega})$ and $X_I(e^{j\omega})$ are the real and imaginary parts of the DTFT $X(e^{j\omega})$, respectively. Verify this property on

$$x(n) = 2(0.9)^{-n} \left[\cos(0.1\pi n) + j\sin(0.9\pi n)\right] \left[u(n) - u(n-10)\right]$$

using the MATLAB functions developed in Chapter 2.

P3.8 A complex-valued DTFT $X(e^{j\omega})$ can also be decomposed into its conjugate symmetric part $X_e(e^{j\omega})$ and conjugate antisymmetric part $X_o(e^{j\omega})$, that is,

$$X(e^{j\omega}) = X_e(e^{j\omega}) + X_o(e^{j\omega})$$

where

$$X_e(e^{j\omega}) = \frac{1}{2}[X(e^{j\omega}) + X^*(e^{-j\omega})] \quad \text{and} \quad X_o(e^{j\omega}) = \frac{1}{2}[X(e^{j\omega}) - X^*(e^{-j\omega})]$$

Show that

$$\mathcal{F}^{-1}[X_e(e^{j\omega})] = x_R(n) \quad \text{and} \quad \mathcal{F}^{-1}[X_o(e^{j\omega})] = jx_I(n)$$

where $x_R(n)$ and $x_I(n)$ are the real and imaginary parts of $x(n)$. Verify this property on

$$x(n) = e^{j0.1\pi n} \left[u(n) - u(n-20)\right]$$

using the MATLAB functions developed in Chapter 2.

P3.9 Using the frequency-shifting property of the DTFT, show that the real part of $X(e^{j\omega})$ of a sinusoidal pulse

$$x(n) = (\cos\omega_o n)\mathcal{R}_M(n)$$

where $\mathcal{R}_M(n)$ is the rectangular pulse given in Problem P3.4 is given by

$$X_R(e^{j\omega}) = \frac{1}{2}\cos\left\{\frac{(\omega - \omega_0)(M-1)}{2}\right\} \frac{\sin\left\{(\omega - \omega_0)M/2\right\}}{\sin\left\{(\omega - \omega_0)/2\right\}}$$

$$+ \frac{1}{2}\cos\left\{\frac{(\omega + \omega_0)(M-1)}{2}\right\} \frac{\sin\left\{[\omega - (2\pi - \omega_0)]M/2\right\}}{\sin\left\{[\omega - (2\pi - \omega_0)]/2\right\}}$$

Compute and plot $X_R(e^{j\omega})$ for $\omega_o = \pi/2$ and $M = 5, 15, 25, 100$. Use the plotting interval $[-\pi, \pi]$. Comment on your results.

P3.10 Let $x(n) = \mathcal{T}_{10}(n)$ be a triangular pulse given in Problem P3.4. Using properties of the DTFT, determine and plot the DTFT of the following sequences.

1. $x(n) = \mathcal{T}_{10}(-n)$
2. $x(n) = \mathcal{T}_{10}(n) - \mathcal{T}_{10}(n-10)$
3. $x(n) = \mathcal{T}_{10}(n) * \mathcal{T}_{10}(-n)$
4. $x(n) = \mathcal{T}_{10}(n)e^{j\pi n}$
5. $x(n) = \cos(0.1\pi n)\mathcal{T}_{10}(n)$

P3.11   For each of the linear, shift-invariant systems described by the impulse response, determine the frequency response function $H(e^{j\omega})$. Plot the magnitude response $|H(e^{j\omega})|$ and the phase response $\angle H(e^{j\omega})$ over the interval $[-\pi, \pi]$.

1. $h(n) = (0.9)^{|n|}$
2. $h(n) = \text{sinc}(0.2n)[u(n+20) - u(n-20)]$, where $\text{sinc}(0) = 1$
3. $h(n) = \text{sinc}(0.2n)[u(n) - u(n-40)]$
4. $h(n) = [(0.5)^n + (0.4)^n]u(n)$
5. $h(n) = (0.5)^{|n|}\cos(0.1\pi n)$

P3.12   Let $x(n) = A\cos(\omega_0 n + \theta_0)$ be an input sequence to an LTI system described by the impulse response $h(n)$. Show that the output sequence $y(n)$ is given by

$$y(n) = A|H(e^{j\omega_0})|\cos[\omega_0 n + \theta_0 + \angle H(e^{j\omega_0})]$$

P3.13   Let $x(n) = 3\cos(0.5\pi n + 60°) + 2\sin(0.3\pi n)$ be the input to each of the systems described in Problem P3.11. In each case, determine the output sequence $y(n)$.

P3.14   An ideal lowpass filter is described in the frequency domain by

$$H_d(e^{j\omega}) = \begin{cases} 1 \cdot e^{-j\alpha\omega}, & |\omega| \leq \omega_c \\ 0, & \omega_c < |\omega| \leq \pi \end{cases}$$

where ω_c is called the cutoff frequency and α is called the phase delay.

1. Determine the ideal impulse response $h_d(n)$ using the IDTFT relation (3.2).
2. Determine and plot the truncated impulse response

$$h(n) = \begin{cases} h_d(n), & 0 \leq n \leq N - 1 \\ 0, & \text{otherwise} \end{cases}$$

for $N = 41$, $\alpha = 20$, and $\omega_c = 0.5\pi$.
3. Determine and plot the frequency response function $H(e^{j\omega})$, and compare it with the ideal lowpass filter response $H_d(e^{j\omega})$. Comment on your observations.

P3.15   An ideal highpass filter is described in the frequency-domain by

$$H_d(e^{j\omega}) = \begin{cases} 1 \cdot e^{-j\alpha\omega}, & \omega_c < |\omega| \leq \pi \\ 0, & |\omega| \leq \omega_c \end{cases}$$

where ω_c is called the cutoff frequency and α is called the phase delay.

1. Determine the ideal impulse response $h_d(n)$ using the IDTFT relation (3.2).
2. Determine and plot the truncated impulse response

$$h(n) = \begin{cases} h_d(n), & 0 \leq n \leq N - 1 \\ 0, & \text{otherwise} \end{cases}$$

for $N = 31$, $\alpha = 15$, and $\omega_c = 0.5\pi$.
3. Determine and plot the frequency response function $H(e^{j\omega})$, and compare it with the ideal highpass filter response $H_d(e^{j\omega})$. Comment on your observations.

P3.16 For a linear, shift-invariant system described by the difference equation

$$y(n) = \sum_{m=0}^{M} b_m x(n-m) - \sum_{\ell=1}^{N} a_\ell y(n-\ell)$$

the frequency-response function is given by

$$H(e^{j\omega}) = \frac{\sum_{m=0}^{M} b_m e^{-j\omega m}}{1 + \sum_{\ell=1}^{N} a_\ell e^{-j\omega \ell}}$$

Write a MATLAB function `freqresp` to implement this relation. The format of this function should be

```
function [H] = freqresp(b,a,w)
% Frequency response function from difference equation
%   [H] = freqresp(b,a,w)
% H = frequency response array evaluated at w frequencies
% b = numerator coefficient array
% a = denominator coefficient array (a(1)=1)
% w = frequency location array
```

P3.17 Determine $H(e^{j\omega})$, and plot its magnitude and phase for each of the following systems.

1. $y(n) = \frac{1}{5} \sum_{m=0}^{4} x(n-m)$
2. $y(n) = x(n) - x(n-2) + 0.95y(n-1) - 0.9025y(n-2)$
3. $y(n) = x(n) - x(n-1) + x(n-2) + 0.95y(n-1) - 0.9025y(n-2)$
4. $y(n) = x(n) - 1.7678x(n-1) + 1.5625x(n-2) + 1.1314y(n-1) - 0.64y(n-2)$
5. $y(n) = x(n) - \sum_{\ell=1}^{5} (0.5)^\ell y(n-\ell)$

P3.18 A linear, shift-invariant system is described by the difference equation

$$y(n) = \sum_{m=0}^{3} x(n-2m) - \sum_{\ell=1}^{3} (0.81)^\ell y(n-2\ell)$$

Determine the steady-state response of the system to the following inputs.

1. $x(n) = 5 + 10(-1)^n$
2. $x(n) = 1 + \cos(0.5\pi n + \pi/2)$
3. $x(n) = 2\sin(\pi n/4) + 3\cos(3\pi n/4)$
4. $x(n) = \sum_{k=0}^{5} (k+1)\cos(\pi k n/4)$
5. $x(n) = \cos(\pi n)$

In each case, generate $x(n)$, $0 \le n \le 200$, and process it through the `filter` function to obtain $y(n)$. Compare your $y(n)$ with the steady-state responses in each case.

P3.19 An analog signal $x_a(t) = \sin(1000\pi t)$ is sampled using the following sampling intervals. In each case, plot the spectrum of the resulting discrete-time signal.

1. $T_s = 0.1$ msec
2. $T_s = 1$ msec
3. $T_s = 0.01$ sec

P3.20 We implement the following analog filter using a discrete filter:

$$x_a\left(t\right) \longrightarrow \boxed{\text{A/D}} \overset{x(n)}{\longrightarrow} \boxed{h(n)} \overset{y(n)}{\longrightarrow} \boxed{\text{D/A}} \longrightarrow y_a\left(t\right)$$

The sampling rate in the A/D and D/A is 8000 sam/sec, and the impulse response is $h(n) = (-0.9)^n\, u(n)$.

1. What is the digital frequency in $x(n)$ if $x_a\left(t\right) = 10\cos\left(10{,}000\pi t\right)$?
2. Determine the steady-state output $y_a\left(t\right)$ if $x_a\left(t\right) = 10\cos\left(10{,}000\pi t\right)$.
3. Determine the steady-state output $y_a\left(t\right)$ if $x_a\left(t\right) = 5\sin(8{,}000\pi t)$.
4. Find two other analog signals $x_a\left(t\right)$, with different analog frequencies, that will give the same steady-state output $y_a(t)$ when $x_a(t) = 10\cos(10{,}000\pi t)$ is applied.
5. To prevent aliasing, a prefilter would be required to process $x_a\left(t\right)$ before it passes to the A/D converter. What type of filter should be used, and what should be the largest cutoff frequency that would work for the given configuration?

P3.21 Consider an analog signal $x_a\left(t\right) = \cos(20\pi t)$, $0 \leq t \leq 1$. It is sampled at $T_s = 0.01$, 0.05, and 0.1 sec intervals to obtain $x(n)$.

1. For each T_s, plot $x(n)$.
2. Reconstruct the analog signal $y_a\left(t\right)$ from the samples $x(n)$ using the sinc interpolation (use $\Delta t = 0.001$) and determine the frequency in $y_a\left(t\right)$ from your plot. (Ignore the end effects.)
3. Reconstruct the analog signal $y_a\left(t\right)$ from the samples $x(n)$ using the cubic spline interpolation, and determine the frequency in $y_a\left(t\right)$ from your plot. (Again, ignore the end effects.)
4. Comment on your results.

P3.22 Consider the analog signal $x_a\left(t\right) = \cos\left(20\pi t + \theta\right)$, $0 \leq t \leq 1$. It is sampled at $T_s = 0.05$ sec intervals to obtain $x(n)$. Let $\theta = 0,\ \pi/6,\ \pi/4,\ \pi/3,\ \pi/2$. For each of these θ values, perform the following.

1. Plot $x_a\left(t\right)$ and superimpose $x(n)$ on it using the `plot(n,x,'o')` function.
2. Reconstruct the analog signal $y_a\left(t\right)$ from the samples $x(n)$ using the sinc interpolation (Use $\Delta t = 0.001$) and superimpose $x(n)$ on it.
3. Reconstruct the analog signal $y_a\left(t\right)$ from the samples $x(n)$ using the cubic spline interpolation and superimpose $x(n)$ on it.
4. You should observe that the resultant reconstruction in each case has the correct frequency but a different amplitude. Explain this observation. Comment on the role of phase of $x_a\left(t\right)$ on the sampling and reconstruction of signals.

CHAPTER 4

The z-Transform

In Chapter 3, we studied the discrete-time Fourier transform approach for representing discrete signals using complex exponential sequences. This representation clearly has advantages for LTI systems because it describes systems in the frequency domain using the frequency response function $H(e^{j\omega})$. The computation of the sinusoidal steady-state response is greatly facilitated by the use of $H(e^{j\omega})$. Furthermore, response to any arbitrary absolutely summable sequence $x(n)$ can easily be computed in the frequency domain by multiplying the transform $X(e^{j\omega})$ and the frequency response $H(e^{j\omega})$. However, there are *two* shortcomings to the Fourier transform approach. First, there are many useful signals in practice—such as $u(n)$ and $nu(n)$—for which the discrete-time Fourier transform does not exist. Second, the transient response of a system due to initial conditions or due to changing inputs cannot be computed using the discrete-time Fourier transform approach.

Therefore, we now consider an extension of the discrete-time Fourier transform to address these two problems. This extension is called the *z-transform*. Its bilateral (or two-sided) version provides another domain in which a larger class of sequences and systems can be analyzed, and its unilateral (or one-sided) version can be used to obtain system responses with initial conditions or changing inputs.

4.1 THE BILATERAL z-TRANSFORM

The z-transform of a sequence $x(n)$ is given by

$$X(z) \triangleq \mathcal{Z}[x(n)] = \sum_{n=-\infty}^{\infty} x(n)z^{-n} \tag{4.1}$$

where z is a complex variable. The set of z values for which $X(z)$ exists is called the *region of convergence* (*ROC*) and is given by

$$R_{x-} < |z| < R_{x+} \tag{4.2}$$

for some nonnegative numbers R_{x-} and R_{x+}.

The inverse z-transform of a complex function $X(z)$ is given by

$$x(n) \triangleq \mathcal{Z}^{-1}[X(z)] = \frac{1}{2\pi j} \oint_C X(z) z^{n-1} dz \tag{4.3}$$

where C is a **counterclockwise contour** encircling the origin and lying in the ROC.

Comments:

1. The complex variable z is called the *complex frequency* given by $z = |z|e^{j\omega}$, where $|z|$ is the magnitude and ω is the real frequency.
2. Since the ROC (4.2) is defined in terms of the magnitude $|z|$, the shape of the ROC is an open ring, as shown in Figure 4.1. Note that R_{x-} may be equal to zero and/or R_{x+} could possibly be ∞.
3. If $R_{x+} < R_{x-}$, then the ROC is a *null space* and the z-transform *does not exist*.
4. The function $|z| = 1$ (or $z = e^{j\omega}$) is a circle of unit radius in the z-plane and is called the *unit circle*. If the ROC contains the unit circle, then we can evaluate $X(z)$ on the unit circle:

$$X(z)\big|_{z=e^{j\omega}} = X(e^{j\omega}) = \sum_{n=-\infty}^{\infty} x(n)e^{-j\omega n} = \mathcal{F}[x(n)]$$

Therefore, the discrete-time Fourier transform $X(e^{j\omega})$ may be viewed as a special case of the z-transform $X(z)$.

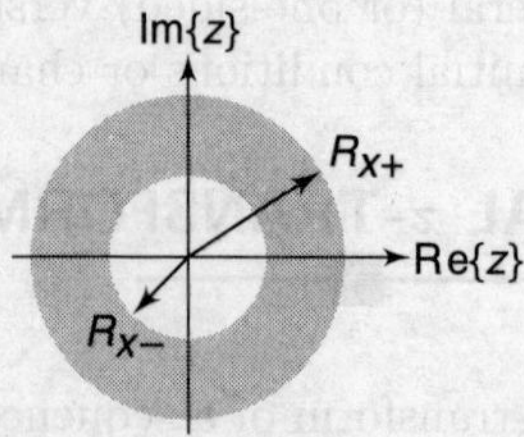

FIGURE 4.1 *A general region of convergence*

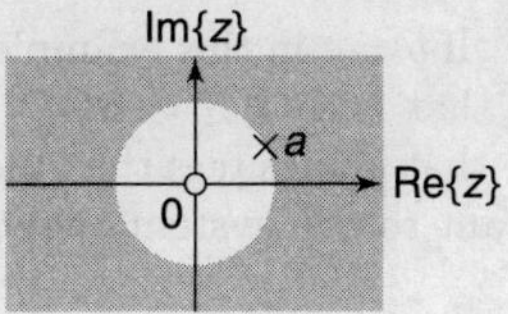

FIGURE 4.2 *The ROC in Example 4.1*

☐ **EXAMPLE 4.1** Let $x_1(n) = a^n u(n)$, $0 < |a| < \infty$. (This sequence is called a *positive-time sequence*.) Then

$$X_1(z) = \sum_0^\infty a^n z^{-n} = \sum_0^\infty \left(\frac{a}{z}\right)^n = \frac{1}{1 - az^{-1}}; \quad \text{if } \left|\frac{a}{z}\right| < 1$$

$$= \frac{z}{z - a}, \quad |z| > |a| \Rightarrow \text{ROC}_1: \underbrace{|a|}_{R_{x-}} < |z| < \underbrace{\infty}_{R_{x+}}$$

Note: $X_1(z)$ in this example is a rational function; that is,

$$X_1(z) \triangleq \frac{B(z)}{A(z)} = \frac{z}{z - a}$$

where $B(z) = z$ is the *numerator polynomial* and $A(z) = z-a$ is the *denominator polynomial*. The roots of $B(z)$ are called the *zeros* of $X(z)$, whereas the roots of $A(z)$ are called the *poles* of $X(z)$. In this example, $X_1(z)$ has a zero at the origin $z = 0$ and a pole at $z = a$. Hence $x_1(n)$ can also be represented by a *pole-zero diagram* in the z-plane in which zeros are denoted by ○ and poles by ×, as shown in Figure 4.2. ☐

☐ **EXAMPLE 4.2** Let $x_2(n) = -b^n u(-n-1), 0 < |b| < \infty$. (This sequence is called a *negative-time sequence*.) Then

$$X_2(z) = -\sum_{-\infty}^{-1} b^n z^{-n} = -\sum_{-\infty}^{-1} \left(\frac{b}{z}\right)^n = -\sum_1^\infty \left(\frac{z}{b}\right)^n = 1 - \sum_0^\infty \left(\frac{z}{b}\right)^n$$

$$= 1 - \frac{1}{1 - z/b} = \frac{z}{z - b}, \quad \text{ROC}_2: \underbrace{0}_{R_{x-}} < |z| < \underbrace{|b|}_{R_{x+}}$$

The ROC$_2$ and the pole-zero plot for this $x_2(n)$ are shown in Figure 4.3.

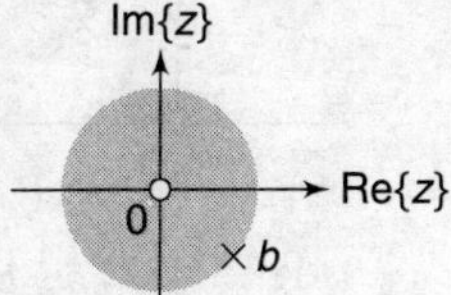

FIGURE 4.3 *The ROC in Example 4.2*

Note: If $b = a$ in this example, then $X_2(z) = X_1(z)$ except for their respective ROCs; that is, $\text{ROC}_1 \neq \text{ROC}_2$. This implies that the ROC is a distinguishing feature that guarantees the uniqueness of the z-transform. Hence it plays a very important role in system analysis.   □

□   **EXAMPLE 4.3**   Let $x_3(n) = x_1(n) + x_2(n) = a^n u(n) - b^n u(-n-1)$ (This sequence is called a *two-sided sequence*.) Then, using the preceding two examples,

$$
X_3(z) = \sum_{n=0}^{\infty} a^n z^{-n} - \sum_{-\infty}^{-1} b^n z^{-n}
$$

$$
= \left\{ \frac{z}{z-a}, \text{ROC}_1\colon |z| > |a| \right\} + \left\{ \frac{z}{z-b}, \text{ROC}_2\colon |z| < |b| \right\}
$$

$$
= \frac{z}{z-a} + \frac{z}{z-b}; \quad \text{ROC}_3\colon \text{ROC}_1 \cap \text{ROC}_2
$$

If $|b| < |a|$, then ROC_3 is a null space, and $X_3(z)$ does not exist. If $|a| < |b|$, then the ROC_3 is $|a| < |z| < |b|$, and $X_3(z)$ exists in this region as shown in Figure 4.4.   □

4.1.1 PROPERTIES OF THE ROC

From the observation of the ROCs in the preceding three examples, we state the following properties.

1. The ROC is **always bounded by a circle** since the convergence condition is on the magnitude $|z|$.
2. The sequence $x_1(n) = a^n u(n)$ in Example 4.1 is a special case of a *right-sided sequence*, defined as a sequence $x(n)$ that is zero for some $n < n_0$. From Example 4.1, the ROC for right-sided sequences is **always outside of a circle of radius R_{x-}**. If $n_0 \geq 0$, then the right-sided sequence is also called a *causal* sequence.
3. The sequence $x_2(n) = -b^n u(-n-1)$ in Example 4.2 is a special case of a *left-sided* sequence, defined as a sequence $x(n)$ that is zero for some $n > n_0$. If $n_0 \leq 0$, the resulting sequence is called an *anticausal* sequence. From Example 4.2, the ROC for left-sided sequences is **always inside of a circle of radius R_{x+}**.

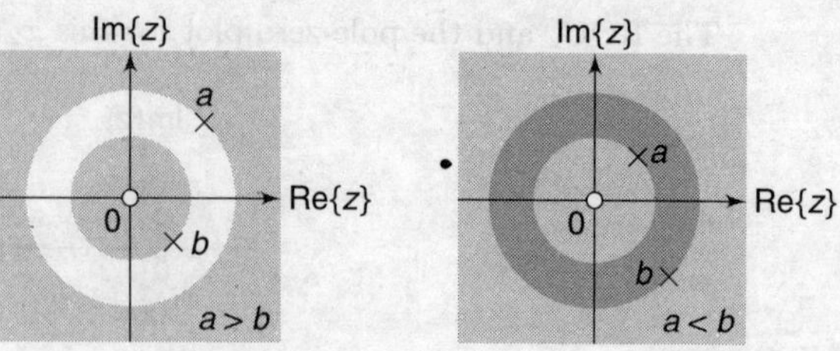

FIGURE 4.4   *The ROC in Example 4.3*

4. The sequence $x_3(n)$ in Example 4.3 is a two-sided sequence. The ROC for two-sided sequences is **always an open ring $R_{x-} < |z| < R_{x+}$,** if it exists.

5. The sequences that are zero for $n < n_1$ and $n > n_2$ are called *finite-duration sequences*. The ROC for such sequences is **the entire z-plane**. If $n_1 < 0$, then $z = \infty$ is not in the ROC. If $n_2 > 0$, then $z = 0$ is not in the ROC.

6. The ROC cannot include a pole, since $X(z)$ converges uniformly in there.

7. There is at least one pole on the boundary of a ROC of a rational $X(z)$.

8. The ROC is one contiguous region; that is, the ROC does not come in pieces.

In digital signal processing, signals are assumed to be causal since almost every digital data is acquired in real time. Therefore, the only ROC of interest to us is the one given in statement 2.

4.2 IMPORTANT PROPERTIES OF THE z-TRANSFORM

The properties of the z-transform are generalizations of the properties of the discrete-time Fourier transform that we studied in Chapter 3. We state the following important properties of the z-transform without proof.

1. **Linearity:**

$$\mathcal{Z}\left[a_1 x_1(n) + a_2 x_2(n)\right] = a_1 X_1(z) + a_2 X_2(z); \quad \text{ROC: ROC}_{x_1} \cap \text{ROC}_{x_2}$$

$$(4.4)$$

2. **Sample shifting:**

$$\mathcal{Z}\left[x\left(n - n_0\right)\right] = z^{-n_0} X(z); \quad \text{ROC: ROC}_x \tag{4.5}$$

3. **Frequency shifting:**

$$\mathcal{Z}\left[a^n x(n)\right] = X\left(\frac{z}{a}\right); \quad \text{ROC: ROC}_x \text{ scaled by } |a| \tag{4.6}$$

4. **Folding:**

$$\mathcal{Z}\left[x\left(-n\right)\right] = X\left(1/z\right); \quad \text{ROC: Inverted ROC}_x \tag{4.7}$$

5. **Complex conjugation:**

$$\mathcal{Z}\left[x^*(n)\right] = X^*(z^*); \quad \text{ROC: ROC}_x \tag{4.8}$$

6. **Differentiation in the z-domain:**

$$\mathcal{Z}[nx(n)] = -z\frac{dX(z)}{dz}; \quad \text{ROC: ROC}_x \qquad (4.9)$$

This property is also called the *multiplication-by-a-ramp property*.

7. **Multiplication:**

$$\mathcal{Z}[x_1(n)x_2(n)] = \frac{1}{2\pi j}\oint_C X_1(\nu)X_2(z/\nu)\nu^{-1}d\nu; \qquad (4.10)$$
$$\text{ROC: ROC}_{x_1} \cap \text{Inverted ROC}_{x_2}$$

where C is a closed contour that encloses the origin and lies in the common ROC.

8. **Convolution:**

$$\mathcal{Z}[x_1(n) * x_2(n)] = X_1(z)X_2(z); \quad \text{ROC: ROC}_{x_1} \cap \text{ROC}_{x_2} \qquad (4.11)$$

This last property transforms the time-domain convolution operation into a multiplication between two functions. It is a significant property in many ways. First, if $X_1(z)$ and $X_2(z)$ are two polynomials, then their product can be implemented using the **conv** function in MATLAB.

☐ **EXAMPLE 4.4**   Let $X_1(z) = 2+3z^{-1}+4z^{-2}$, and let $X_2(z) = 3+4z^{-1}+5z^{-2}+6z^{-3}$. Determine $X_3(z) = X_1(z)X_2(z)$.

Solution   From the definition of the z-transform, we observe that

$$x_1(n) = \{2,3,4\} \qquad \text{and} \qquad x_2(n) = \{3,4,5,6\}$$
$$\quad\uparrow \qquad\qquad\qquad\qquad\qquad \uparrow$$

Then the convolution of these two sequences will give the coefficients of the required polynomial product.

MATLAB script:

```
>> x1 = [2,3,4]; x2 = [3,4,5,6]; x3 = conv(x1,x2)
x3 =
        6      17      34      43      38      24
```

Hence

$$X_3(z) = 6 + 17z^{-1} + 34z^{-2} + 43z^{-3} + 38z^{-4} + 24z^{-5}$$

Using the **conv_m** function developed in Chapter 2, we can also multiply two z-domain polynomials corresponding to noncausal sequences.   ☐

☐ **EXAMPLE 4.5**   Let $X_1(z) = z + 2 + 3z^{-1}$, and let $X_2(z) = 2z^2 + 4z + 3 + 5z^{-1}$. Determine $X_3(z) = X_1(z)X_2(z)$.

Solution   Note that

$$x_1(n) = \{1, 2, 3\} \qquad \text{and} \qquad x_2(n) = \{2, 4, 3, 5\}$$
$$\qquad\quad\uparrow \qquad\qquad\qquad\qquad\qquad\quad \uparrow$$

Using the MATLAB script

```
>> x1 = [1,2,3]; n1 = [-1:1];   x2 = [2,4,3,5]; n2 = [-2:1];
>> [x3,n3] = conv_m(x1,n1,x2,n2)
x3 =
      2     8    17    23    19    15
n3 =
     -3    -2    -1     0     1     2
```

we have

$$X_3(z) = 2z^3 + 8z^2 + 17z + 23 + 19z^{-1} + 15z^{-2} \qquad\qquad \square$$

In passing, we note that to divide one polynomial by another one, we would require an inverse operation called *deconvolution* [79, Chapter 6]. In MATLAB, `[p,r] = deconv(b,a)` computes the result of dividing **b** by **a** in a polynomial part **p** and a remainder **r**. For example, if we divide the polynomial $X_3(z)$ in Example 4.4 by $X_1(z)$, as follows,

```
>> x3 = [6,17,34,43,38,24]; x1 = [2,3,4]; [x2,r] = deconv(x3,x1)
x2 =
      3     4     5     6
r =
      0     0     0     0     0     0
```

then we obtain the coefficients of the polynomial $X_2(z)$ as expected. To obtain the sample index, we will have to modify the **deconv** function as we did in the **conv_m** function. This is explored in Problem P4.10. This operation is useful in obtaining a *proper* rational part from an *improper* rational function.

The second important use of the convolution property is in system output computations, as we shall see in a later section. This interpretation is particularly useful for verifying the z-transform expression $X(z)$ of a causal sequence using MATLAB. Note that since MATLAB is a numerical processor (unless the Symbolic toolbox is used), it cannot be used for symbolic z-transform calculations. We will now elaborate on this. Let $x(n)$ be a sequence with a rational transform

$$X(z) = \frac{B(z)}{A(z)}$$

where $B(z)$ and $A(z)$ are polynomials in z^{-1}. If we use the coefficients of $B(z)$ and $A(z)$ as the **b** and **a** arrays in the **filter** routine and excite this filter by the impulse sequence $\delta(n)$, then from (4.11) and using $\mathcal{Z}[\delta(n)] = 1$, the output of the filter will be $x(n)$. (This is a numerical approach of computing the inverse z-transform; we will discuss the analytical approach in the next section.) We can compare this output with the given $x(n)$ to verify that $X(z)$ is indeed the transform of $x(n)$. This is illustrated in Example 4.6. An equivalent approach is to use the `impz` function discussed in Chapter 2.

4.2.1 SOME COMMON z-TRANSFORM PAIRS

Using the definition of z-transform and its properties, one can determine z-transforms of common sequences. A list of some of these sequences is given in Table 4.1.

TABLE 4.1 *Some common z-transform pairs*

Sequence	Transform	ROC
$\delta(n)$	1	$\forall z$
$u(n)$	$\dfrac{1}{1 - z^{-1}}$	$\|z\| > 1$
$-u(-n - 1)$	$\dfrac{1}{1 - z^{-1}}$	$\|z\| < 1$
$a^n u(n)$	$\dfrac{1}{1 - az^{-1}}$	$\|z\| > \|a\|$
$-b^n u(-n - 1)$	$\dfrac{1}{1 - bz^{-1}}$	$\|z\| < \|b\|$
$[a^n \sin \omega_0 n]\, u(n)$	$\dfrac{(a \sin \omega_0) z^{-1}}{1 - (2a \cos \omega_0) z^{-1} + a^2 z^{-2}}$	$\|z\| > \|a\|$
$[a^n \cos \omega_0 n]\, u(n)$	$\dfrac{1 - (a \cos \omega_0) z^{-1}}{1 - (2a \cos \omega_0) z^{-1} + a^2 z^{-2}}$	$\|z\| > \|a\|$
$na^n u(n)$	$\dfrac{az^{-1}}{(1 - az^{-1})^2}$	$\|z\| > \|a\|$
$-nb^n u(-n - 1)$	$\dfrac{bz^{-1}}{(1 - bz^{-1})^2}$	$\|z\| < \|b\|$

☐ **EXAMPLE 4.6** Using z-transform properties and the z-transform table, determine the z-transform of

$$x(n) = (n - 2)(0.5)^{(n-2)} \cos\left[\frac{\pi}{3}(n - 2)\right] u(n - 2)$$

Solution Applying the sample-shift property,

$$X(z) = \mathcal{Z}[x(n)] = z^{-2} \mathcal{Z}\left[n(0.5)^n \cos\left(\frac{\pi n}{3}\right) u(n)\right]$$

with no change in the ROC. Applying the multiplication by a ramp property,

$$X(z) = z^{-2} \left\{ -z \frac{d\mathcal{Z}[(0.5)^n \cos(\frac{\pi}{3}n)u(n)]}{dz} \cdot \right\}$$

with no change in the ROC. Now the z-transform of $(0.5)^n \cos(\frac{\pi}{3}n)u(n)$ from Table 4.1 is

$$\mathcal{Z}\left[(0.5)^n \cos\left(\frac{\pi n}{3}\right)u(n)\right] = \frac{1 - (0.5\cos\frac{\pi}{3})z^{-1}}{1 - 2(0.5\cos\frac{\pi}{3})z^{-1} + 0.25z^{-2}}; \quad |z| > 0.5$$

$$= \frac{1 - 0.25z^{-1}}{1 - 0.5z^{-1} + 0.25z^{-2}}; \quad |z| > 0.5$$

Hence

$$X(z) = -z^{-1} \frac{d}{dz} \left\{ \frac{1 - 0.25z^{-1}}{1 - 0.5z^{-1} + 0.25z^{-2}} \right\}, \qquad |z| > 0.5$$

$$= -z^{-1} \left\{ \frac{-0.25z^{-2} + 0.5z^{-3} - 0.0625z^{-4}}{1 - z^{-1} + 0.75z^{-2} - 0.25z^{-3} + 0.0625z^{-4}} \right\}, \qquad |z| > 0.5$$

$$= \frac{0.25z^{-3} - 0.5z^{-4} + 0.0625z^{-5}}{1 - z^{-1} + 0.75z^{-2} - 0.25z^{-3} + 0.0625z^{-4}}, \qquad |z| > 0.5$$

MATLAB verification: To check that this $X(z)$ is indeed the correct expression, let us compute the first eight samples of the sequence $x(n)$ corresponding to $X(z)$, as discussed before.

```
>> b = [0,0,0,0.25,-0.5,0.0625]; a = [1,-1,0.75,-0.25,0.0625];
>> [delta,n]=impseq(0,0,7)
delta =
     1    0    0    0    0    0    0    0
n =
     0    1    2    3    4    5    6    7
>> x = filter(b,a,delta) % check sequence
x =
  Columns 1 through 4
                   0                  0                  0   0.25000000000000
  Columns 5 through 8
 -0.25000000000000  -0.37500000000000  -0.12500000000000   0.07812500000000
>> x = [(n-2).*(1/2).^(n-2).*cos(pi*(n-2)/3)].*stepseq(2,0,7) % original sequence
x =
  Columns 1 through 4
                   0                  0                  0   0.25000000000000
  Columns 5 through 8
 -0.25000000000000  -0.37500000000000  -0.12500000000000   0.07812500000000
```

This approach can be used to verify the z-transform computations. $\square$

4.3 INVERSION OF THE z-TRANSFORM

From equation (4.3), the inverse z-transform computation requires an evaluation of a complex contour integral that, in general, is a complicated procedure. The most practical approach is to use the partial fraction expansion method. It makes use of the z-transform Table 4.1 (or similar tables available in many textbooks). The z-transform, however, must be a rational function. This requirement is generally satisfied in digital signal processing.

Central Idea   When $X(z)$ is a rational function of z^{-1}, it can be expressed as a sum of simple factors using the partial fraction expansion. The individual sequences corresponding to these factors can then be written down using the z-transform table.

The inverse z-transform procedure can be summarized using the following steps:

1. Consider the rational function

$$X(z) = \frac{b_0 + b_1 z^{-1} + \cdots + b_M z^{-M}}{1 + a_1 z^{-1} + \cdots + a_N z^{-N}}, \; R_{x-} < |z| < R_{x+} \qquad \textbf{(4.12)}$$

2. Express (4.12) as

$$X(z) = \underbrace{\frac{\tilde{b}_0 + \tilde{b}_1 z^{-1} + \cdots + \tilde{b}_{N-1} z^{-(N-1)}}{1 + a_1 z^{-1} + \cdots + a_N z^{-N}}}_{\text{Proper rational part}} + \underbrace{\sum_{k=0}^{M-N} C_k z^{-k}}_{\text{Polynomial part if } M \geq N}$$

where the first term on the right-hand side is the proper rational part and the second term is the polynomial (finite-length) part. This can be obtained by performing polynomial division if $M \geq N$ using the **deconv** function.

3. Perform a partial fraction expansion on the proper rational part of $X(z)$ to obtain

$$X(z) = \sum_{k=1}^{N} \frac{R_k}{1 - p_k z^{-1}} + \underbrace{\sum_{k=0}^{M-N} C_k z^{-k}}_{M \geq N} \qquad \textbf{(4.13)}$$

where p_k is the kth pole of $X(z)$ and R_k is the residue at p_k. It is assumed that the poles are distinct, for which the residues are given by

$$R_k = \left. \frac{\tilde{b}_0 + \tilde{b}_1 z^{-1} + \cdots + \tilde{b}_{N-1} z^{-(N-1)}}{1 + a_1 z^{-1} + \cdots + a_N z^{-N}} (1 - p_k z^{-1}) \right|_{z=p_k}$$

For repeated poles, the expansion (4.13) has a more general form. If a pole p_k has multiplicity r, then its expansion is given by

$$\sum_{\ell=1}^{r} \frac{R_{k,\ell} z^{-(\ell-1)}}{(1 - p_k z^{-1})^{\ell}} = \frac{R_{k,1}}{1 - p_k z^{-1}} + \frac{R_{k,2} z^{-1}}{(1 - p_k z^{-1})^2} + \cdots + \frac{R_{k,r} z^{-(r-1)}}{(1 - p_k z^{-1})^r}$$

$$(4.14)$$

where the residues $R_{k,\ell}$ are computed using a more general formula, which is available in reference [79].

4. Assuming distinct poles as in (4.13), write $x(n)$ as

$$x(n) = \sum_{k=1}^{N} R_k \mathcal{Z}^{-1} \left[\frac{1}{1 - p_k z^{-1}} \right] + \underbrace{\sum_{k=0}^{M-N} C_k \delta(n - k)}_{M \geq N}$$

5. Finally, use the relation from Table 4.1

$$\mathcal{Z}^{-1} \left[\frac{1}{1 - p_k z^{-1}} \right] = \begin{cases} p_k^n u(n) & |z_k| \leq R_{x-} \\ -p_k^n u(-n - 1) & |z_k| \geq R_{x+} \end{cases} \qquad (4.15)$$

to complete $x(n)$.

A similar procedure is used for repeated poles.

☐   **EXAMPLE 4.7**   Find the inverse z-transform of $x(z) = \dfrac{z}{3z^2 - 4z + 1}$.

Solution   Write

$$X(z) = \frac{z}{3(z^2 - \frac{4}{3}z + \frac{1}{3})} = \frac{\frac{1}{3} z^{-1}}{1 - \frac{4}{3} z^{-1} + \frac{1}{3} z^{-2}}$$

$$= \frac{\frac{1}{3} z^{-1}}{(1 - z^{-1})(1 - \frac{1}{3} z^{-1})} = \frac{\frac{1}{2}}{1 - z^{-1}} - \frac{\frac{1}{2}}{1 - \frac{1}{3} z^{-1}}$$

or

$$X(z) = \frac{1}{2} \left(\frac{1}{1 - z^{-1}} \right) - \frac{1}{2} \left(\frac{1}{1 - \frac{1}{3} z^{-1}} \right)$$

Now, $X(z)$ has two poles: $z_1 = 1$ and $z_2 = \frac{1}{3}$, and since the ROC is not specified, there are *three* possible ROCs, as shown in Figure 4.5.

a. ROC_1: $1 < |z| < \infty$. Here both poles are on the interior side of the ROC_1; that is, $|z_1| \leq R_{x-} = 1$ and $|z_2| \leq 1$. Hence from (4.15),

$$x_1(n) = \frac{1}{2} u(n) - \frac{1}{2} \left(\frac{1}{3} \right)^n u(n)$$

which is a right-sided sequence.

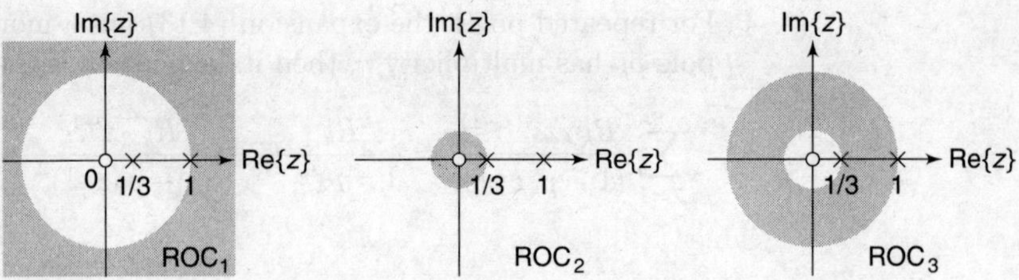

FIGURE 4.5   *The ROCs in Example 4.7*

b. ROC_2: $0 < |z| < \frac{1}{3}$. Here both poles are on the exterior side of the ROC_2; that is, $|z_1| \geq R_{x+} = \frac{1}{3}$ and $|z_2| \geq \frac{1}{3}$. Hence from (4.15),

$$x_2(n) = \frac{1}{2}\left\{-u(-n-1)\right\} - \frac{1}{2}\left\{-\left(\tfrac{1}{3}\right)^n u(-n-1)\right\}$$

$$= \frac{1}{2}\left(\frac{1}{3}\right)^n u(-n-1) - \frac{1}{2}u(-n-1)$$

which is a left-sided sequence.

c. ROC_3: $\frac{1}{3} < |z| < 1$. Here pole z_1 is on the exterior side of the ROC_3, that is, $|z_1| \geq R_{x+} = 1$ and pole z_2 is on the interior side, that is, $|z_2| \leq \frac{1}{3}$. Hence from (4.15),

$$x_3(n) = -\frac{1}{2}u(-n-1) - \frac{1}{2}\left(\frac{1}{3}\right)^n u(n)$$

which is a two-sided sequence.   □

4.3.1 MATLAB IMPLEMENTATION

A MATLAB function `residuez` is available to compute the residue part and the direct (or polynomial) terms of a rational function in z^{-1}. Let

$$X(z) = \frac{b_0 + b_1 z^{-1} + \cdots + b_M z^{-M}}{a_0 + a_1 z^{-1} + \cdots + a_N z^{-N}} = \frac{B(z)}{A(z)}$$

$$= \sum_{k=1}^{N} \frac{R_k}{1 - p_k z^{-1}} + \underbrace{\sum_{k=0}^{M-N} C_k z^{-k}}_{M \geq N}$$

be a rational function in which the numerator and the denominator polynomials are in *ascending* powers of z^{-1}. Then `[R,p,C]=residuez(b,a)` computes the residues, poles, and direct terms of $X(z)$ in which two polynomials $B(z)$ and $A(z)$ are given in two vectors `b` and `a`, respectively. The returned column vector `R` contains the residues, column vector `p` contains the pole locations, and row vector `C` contains the direct terms.

If $\texttt{p(k)}=\ldots=\texttt{p(k+r-1)}$ is a pole of multiplicity $\texttt{r}$, then the expansion includes the term of the form

$$\frac{R_k}{1 - p_k z^{-1}} + \frac{R_{k+1}}{\left(1 - p_k z^{-1}\right)^2} + \cdots + \frac{R_{k+r-1}}{\left(1 - p_k z^{-1}\right)^r} \qquad (4.16)$$

which is different from (4.14).

Similarly, $\texttt{[b,a]=residuez(R,p,C)}$, with three input arguments and two output arguments, converts the partial fraction expansion back to polynomials with coefficients in row vectors $\mathbf{b}$ and $\mathbf{a}$.

☐   **EXAMPLE 4.8**   To verify our residue calculations, let us consider the rational function

$$X(z) = \frac{z}{3z^2 - 4z + 1}$$

given in Example 4.7.

Solution   First, rearrange $X(z)$ so that it is a function in ascending powers of z^{-1}:

$$X(z) = \frac{z^{-1}}{3 - 4z^{-1} + z^{-2}} = \frac{0 + z^{-1}}{3 - 4z^{-1} + z^{-2}}$$

Now, using the MATLAB script

```
>> b = [0,1]; a = [3,-4,1]; [R,p,C] = residuez(b,a)
R =
      0.5000
     -0.5000
p =
      1.0000
      0.3333
C =
     []
```

we obtain

$$X(z) = \frac{\frac{1}{2}}{1 - z^{-1}} - \frac{\frac{1}{2}}{1 - \frac{1}{3}z^{-1}}$$

as before. Similarly, to convert back to the rational function form,

```
>> [b,a] = residuez(R,p,C)
b =
      0.0000
      0.3333
```

```
a =
     1.0000
    -1.3333
     0.3333
```

so that

$$X(z) = \frac{0 + \frac{1}{3}z^{-1}}{1 - \frac{4}{3}z^{-1} + \frac{1}{3}z^{-2}} = \frac{z^{-1}}{3 - 4z^{-1} + z^{-2}} = \frac{z}{3z^2 - 4z + 1}$$

as before.   □

□ **EXAMPLE 4.9** Compute the inverse z-transform of

$$X(z) = \frac{1}{\left(1 - 0.9z^{-1}\right)^2 \left(1 + 0.9z^{-1}\right)}, \quad |z| > 0.9$$

Solution We will evaluate the denominator polynomial as well as the residues using the following MATLAB script:

```
>> b = 1; a = poly([0.9,0.9,-0.9])
a =
     1.0000     -0.9000     -0.8100      0.7290
>> [R,p,C]=residuez(b,a)
R =
     0.2500
     0.5000
     0.2500
p =
     0.9000
     0.9000
    -0.9000
c =
     []
```

Note that the denominator polynomial is computed using MATLAB's polynomial function **poly**, which computes the polynomial coefficients, given its roots. We could have used the **conv** function, but the use of the **poly** function is more convenient for this purpose. From the residue calculations and using the order of residues given in (4.16), we have

$$X(z) = \frac{0.25}{1 - 0.9z^{-1}} + \frac{0.5}{\left(1 - 0.9z^{-1}\right)^2} + \frac{0.25}{1 + 0.9z^{-1}}, \qquad |z| > 0.9$$

$$= \frac{0.25}{1 - 0.9z^{-1}} + \frac{0.5}{0.9}z\frac{\left(0.9z^{-1}\right)}{\left(1 - 0.9z^{-1}\right)^2} + \frac{0.25}{1 + 0.9z^{-1}}, \quad |z| > 0.9$$

Hence from Table 4.1 and using the z-transform property of time-shift,

$$x(n) = 0.25(0.9)^n u(n) + \frac{5}{9}(n+1)(0.9)^{n+1}u(n+1) + 0.25\,(-0.9)^n\,u(n)$$

which, upon simplification, becomes

$$x(n) = 0.75(0.9)^n u(n) + 0.5n(0.9)^n u(n) + 0.25\,(-0.9)^n\,u(n)$$

MATLAB verification:

```
>> [delta,n] = impseq(0,0,7);  x = filter(b,a,delta) % Check sequence
x =
  Columns 1 through 4
    1.00000000000000    0.90000000000000    1.62000000000000    1.45800000000000
  Columns 5 through 8
    1.96830000000000    1.77147000000000    2.12576400000000    1.91318760000000
>> x = (0.75)*(0.9).^n + (0.5)*n.*(0.9).^n + (0.25)*(-0.9).^n % answer sequence
x =
  Columns 1 through 4
    1.00000000000000    0.90000000000000    1.62000000000000    1.45800000000000
  Columns 5 through 8
    1.96830000000000    1.77147000000000    2.12576400000000    1.91318760000000
```

☐   **EXAMPLE 4.10**   Determine the inverse z-transform of

$$X(z) = \frac{1 + 0.4\sqrt{2}z^{-1}}{1 - 0.8\sqrt{2}z^{-1} + 0.64z^{-2}}$$

so that the resulting sequence is causal and contains no complex numbers.

Solution   We will have to find the poles of $X(z)$ in the polar form to determine the ROC of the causal sequence.

MATLAB script:

```
>> b = [1,0.4*sqrt(2)]; a=[1,-0.8*sqrt(2),0.64];
>> [R,p,C] = residuez(b,a)
R =
    0.5000 - 1.0000i
    0.5000 + 1.0000i
p =
    0.5657 + 0.5657i
    0.5657 - 0.5657i
C =
     []
>> Mp=(abs(p))'   % Pole magnitudes
Mp =
    0.8000    0.8000
>> Ap=(angle(p))'/pi   % Pole angles in pi units
Ap =
    0.2500    -0.2500
```

From these calculations,

$$X(z) = \frac{0.5 - j}{1 - 0.8 e^{+j\frac{\pi}{4}} z^{-1}} + \frac{0.5 + j}{1 - 0.8 e^{-j\frac{\pi}{4}} z^{-1}}, \quad |z| > 0.8$$

and from Table 4.1, we have

$$x(n) = (0.5 - j)\, 0.8^n e^{+j\frac{\pi}{4} n} u(n) + (0.5 + j)\, 0.8^n e^{-j\frac{\pi}{4} n} u(n)$$

$$= 0.8^n [0.5\{e^{+j\frac{\pi}{4} n} + e^{-j\frac{\pi}{4} n}\} - j\{e^{+j\frac{\pi}{4} n} - e^{-j\frac{\pi}{4} n}\}] u(n)$$

$$= 0.8^n \left[\cos\left(\frac{\pi n}{4}\right) + 2\sin\left(\frac{\pi n}{4}\right) \right] u(n)$$

MATLAB verification:

```
>> [delta, n] = impseq(0,0,6);
 x = filter(b,a,delta) % Check sequence
x =
  Columns 1 through 4
   1.00000000000000    1.69705627484771    1.28000000000000    0.36203867196751
  Columns 5 through 8
  -0.40960000000000   -0.69511425017762   -0.52428800000000   -0.14829104003789
>> x = ((0.8).^n).*(cos(pi*n/4)+2*sin(pi*n/4))
x =
  Columns 1 through 4
   1.00000000000000    1.69705627484771    1.28000000000000    0.36203867196751
  Columns 5 through 8
  -0.40960000000000   -0.69511425017762   -0.52428800000000   -0.14829104003789
```

4.4 SYSTEM REPRESENTATION IN THE z-DOMAIN

Similar to the frequency response function $H(e^{j\omega})$, we can define the z-domain function, $H(z)$, called the *system function*. However, unlike $H(e^{j\omega})$, $H(z)$ exists for systems that may not be BIBO stable.

■ **DEFINITION 1**   ***The System Function***
   The system function $H(z)$ is given by

$$H(z) \triangleq \mathcal{Z}[h(n)] = \sum_{-\infty}^{\infty} h(n) z^{-n}; \quad R_{h-} < |z| < R_{h+} \qquad (4.17)$$

Using the convolution property (4.11) of the z-transform, the output transform $Y(z)$ is given by

$$Y(z) = H(z)\, X(z) \quad : \mathrm{ROC}_y = \mathrm{ROC}_h \cap \mathrm{ROC}_x \qquad (4.18)$$

provided ROC_x overlaps with ROC_h. Therefore, a linear and time-invariant system can be represented in the z-domain by

$$X(z) \longrightarrow \boxed{H(z)} \longrightarrow Y(z) = H(z)\,X(z)$$

4.4.1 SYSTEM FUNCTION FROM THE DIFFERENCE EQUATION REPRESENTATION

When LTI systems are described by a difference equation

$$y(n) + \sum_{k=1}^{N} a_k y(n-k) = \sum_{\ell=0}^{M} b_\ell x(n-\ell) \tag{4.19}$$

the system function $H(z)$ can easily be computed. Taking the z-transform of both sides, and using properties of the z-transform,

$$Y(z) + \sum_{k=1}^{N} a_k z^{-k} Y(z) = \sum_{\ell=0}^{M} b_\ell z^{-\ell} X(z)$$

or

$$H(z) \triangleq \frac{Y(z)}{X(z)} = \frac{\sum_{\ell=0}^{M} b_\ell z^{-\ell}}{1 + \sum_{k=1}^{N} a_k z^{-k}} = \frac{B(z)}{A(z)}$$

$$= \frac{b_0 z^{-M} \left(z^M + \cdots + \frac{b_M}{b_0} \right)}{z^{-N} \left(z^N + \cdots + a_N \right)} \tag{4.20}$$

After factorization, we obtain

$$H(z) = b_0 \, z^{N-M} \, \frac{\prod_{\ell=1}^{N}(z - z_\ell)}{\prod_{k=1}^{N}(z - p_k)} \tag{4.21}$$

where z_ℓ's are the system zeros and p_k's are the system poles. Thus $H(z)$ (and hence an LTI system) can also be represented in the z-domain using a pole-zero plot. This fact is useful in designing simple filters by proper placement of poles and zeros.

To determine zeros and poles of a rational $H(z)$, we can use the MATLAB function `roots` on both the numerator and the denominator polynomials. (Its inverse function `poly` determines polynomial coefficients from its roots, as discussed in the previous section.) It is also possible to use MATLAB to plot these roots for a visual display of a pole-zero plot. The function `zplane(b,a)` plots poles and zeros, given the numerator *row* vector **b** and the denominator *row* vector **a**. As before, the symbol o represents a zero and the symbol x represents a pole. The plot includes the unit circle for reference. Similarly, `zplane(z,p)` plots the zeros in *column* vector **z** and the poles in *column* vector **p**. Note very carefully the form of the input arguments for the proper use of this function.

4.4.2 TRANSFER FUNCTION REPRESENTATION

If the ROC of $H(z)$ includes a unit circle $(z = e^{j\omega})$, then we can evaluate $H(z)$ on the unit circle, resulting in a frequency response function or transfer function $H(e^{j\omega})$. Then from (4.21),

$$H(e^{j\omega}) = b_0 \, e^{j(N-M)\omega} \, \frac{\prod_1^M (e^{j\omega} - z_\ell)}{\prod_1^N (e^{j\omega} - p_k)} \tag{4.22}$$

The factor $(e^{j\omega} - z_\ell)$ can be interpreted as a *vector* in the complex z-plane from a zero z_ℓ to the unit circle at $z = e^{j\omega}$, while the factor $(e^{j\omega} - p_k)$ can be interpreted as a vector from a pole p_k to the unit circle at $z = e^{j\omega}$. This is shown in Figure 4.6. Hence the magnitude response function

$$|H(e^{j\omega})| = |b_0| \frac{|e^{j\omega} - z_1| \cdots |e^{j\omega} - z_M|}{|e^{j\omega} - p_1| \cdots |e^{j\omega} - p_N|} \tag{4.23}$$

can be interpreted as a product of the lengths of vectors from the zeros to the unit circle *divided* by the lengths of vectors from the poles to the unit circle and *scaled* by $|b_0|$. Similarly, the phase response function

$$\angle H(e^{j\omega}) = \underbrace{[0 \text{ or } \pi]}_{\text{Constant}} + \underbrace{[(N-M)\,\omega]}_{\text{Linear}} + \underbrace{\sum_1^M \angle(e^{j\omega} - z_k) - \sum_1^N \angle(e^{j\omega} - p_k)}_{\text{Nonlinear}}$$

$$\tag{4.24}$$

can be interpreted as a sum of a constant factor, a linear-phase factor, and a nonlinear-phase factor (angles from the "zero vectors" *minus* the sum of angles from the "pole vectors").

4.4.3 MATLAB IMPLEMENTATION

In Chapter 3, we plotted magnitude and phase responses in MATLAB by directly implementing their functional forms. MATLAB also provides

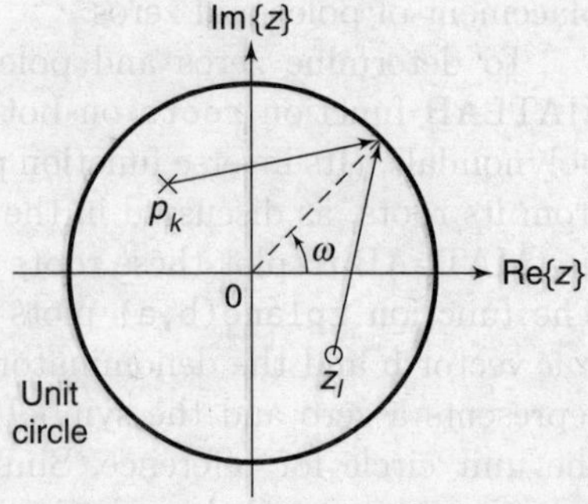

FIGURE 4.6 *Pole and zero vectors*

a function called `freqz` for this computation, which uses the preceding interpretation. In its simplest form, this function is invoked by

```
[H,w] = freqz(b,a,N)
```

which returns the N-point frequency vector `w` and the N-point complex frequency response vector `H` of the system, given its numerator and denominator coefficients in vectors `b` and `a`. The frequency response is evaluated at N points equally spaced around the upper half of the unit circle. Note that the `b` and `a` vectors are the same vectors we use in the `filter` function or derived from the difference equation representation (4.19).

The second form

```
[H,w] = freqz(b,a,N,'whole')
```

uses N points around the whole unit circle for computation.

In yet another form,

```
H = freqz(b,a,w)
```

it returns the frequency response at frequencies designated in vector `w`, normally between 0 and π. It should be noted that the `freqz` function can also be used for numerical computation of the DTFT of a *finite-duration, causal* sequence $x(n)$. In this approach, `b = x` and `a = 1`.

☐ **EXAMPLE 4.11**   Consider a causal system

$$y(n) = 0.9y(n-1) + x(n)$$

a. Determine $H(z)$ and sketch its pole-zero plot.
b. Plot $|H(e^{j\omega})|$ and $\angle H(e^{j\omega})$.
c. Determine the impulse response $h(n)$.

Solution   The difference equation can be put in the form

$$y(n) - 0.9y(n-1) = x(n)$$

a. From (4.21),

$$H(z) = \frac{1}{1 - 0.9z^{-1}}; \quad |z| > 0.9$$

since the system is causal. There is one pole at 0.9 and one zero at the origin. We will use MATLAB to illustrate the use of the `zplane` function.

```
>> b = [1, 0]; a = [1, -0.9]; zplane(b,a)
```

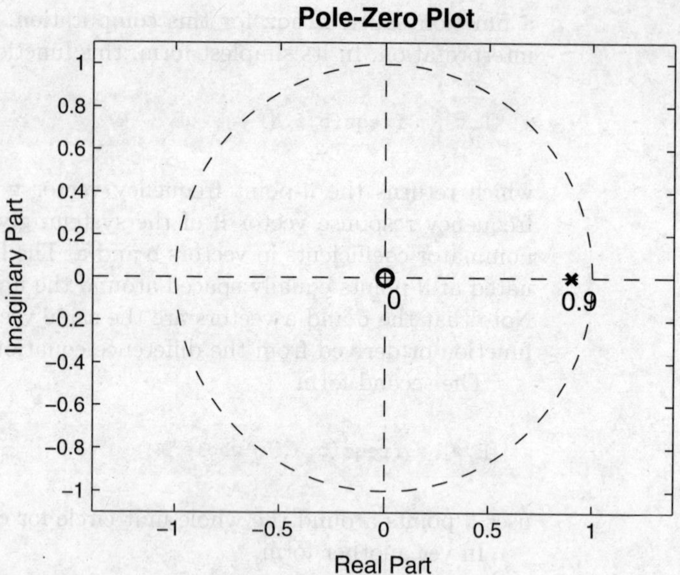

FIGURE 4.7   *Pole-zero plot of Example 4.11a*

Note that we specified b=[1,0] instead of b=1 because the `zplane` function assumes that scalars are zeros or poles. The resulting pole-zero plot is shown in Figure 4.7.

b. Using (4.23) and (4.24), we can determine the magnitude and phase of $H(e^{j\omega})$. Once again, we will use MATLAB to illustrate the use of the `freqz` function. Using its first form, we will take 100 points along the upper half of the unit circle.

MATLAB script:

```
>> [H,w] = freqz(b,a,100);  magH = abs(H); phaH = angle(H);
>> subplot(2,1,1);plot(w/pi,magH);grid
>> title('Magnitude Response'); ylabel('Magnitude');
>> subplot(2,1,2);plot(w/pi,phaH/pi);grid
>> xlabel('Frequency in \pi Units'); ylabel('Phase in \pi Units');
>> title('Phase Response')
```

The response plots are shown in Figure 4.8. If you study these plots carefully, you will observe that the plots are computed between $0 \leq \omega \leq 0.99\pi$ and fall short at $\omega = \pi$. This is due to the fact that in MATLAB the lower half

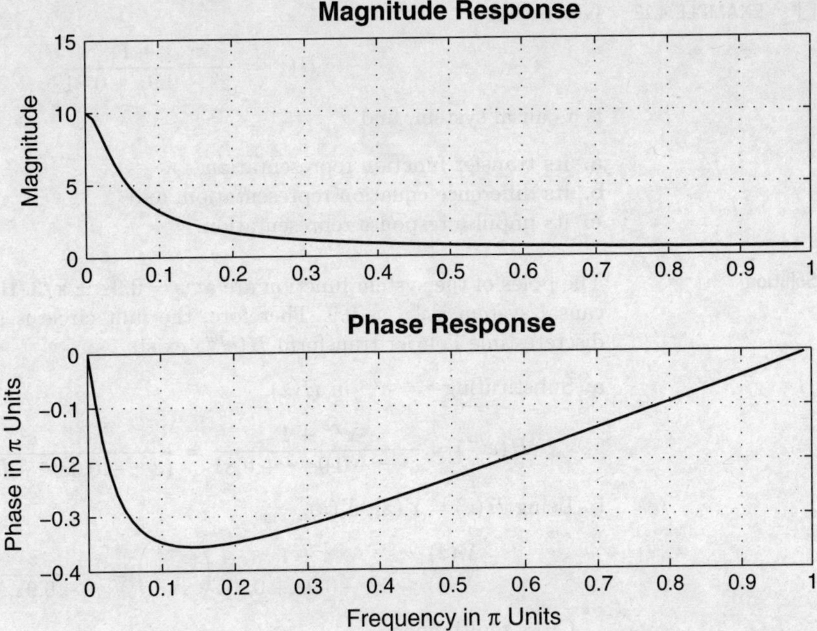

FIGURE 4.8   *Frequency response plots in Example 4.11*

of the unit circle begins at $\omega = \pi$. To overcome this problem, we will use the second form of the **freqz** function as follows.

```
>> [H,w] = freqz(b,a,200,'whole');
>> magH = abs(H(1:101)); phaH = angle(H(1:101));
```

Now the 101st element of the array H will correspond to $\omega = \pi$. A similar result can be obtained using the third form of the **freqz** function.

```
>> w = [0:1:100]*pi/100;  H = freqz(b,a,w);
>> magH = abs(H); phaH = angle(H);
```

In the future, we will use any one of these forms, depending on our convenience. Also note that in the plots we divided the **w** and **phaH** arrays by **pi** so that the plot axes are in the units of π and easier to read. *This practice is strongly recommended.*

c. From the z-transform in Table 4.1,

$$h(n) = \mathcal{Z}^{-1}\left[\frac{1}{1 - 0.9z^{-1}},\ |z| > 0.9\right] = (0.9)^n u(n) \qquad \square$$

☐ **EXAMPLE 4.12**   Given that

$$H(z) = \frac{z+1}{z^2 - 0.9z + 0.81}$$

is a causal system, find

a. its transfer function representation,
b. its difference equation representation, and
c. its impulse response representation.

Solution   The poles of the system function are at $z = 0.9\angle \pm \pi/3$. Hence the ROC of this causal system is $|z| > 0.9$. Therefore, the unit circle is in the ROC, and the discrete-time Fourier transform $H(e^{j\omega})$ exists.

a. Substituting $z = e^{j\omega}$ in $H(z)$,

$$H(e^{j\omega}) = \frac{e^{j\omega}+1}{e^{j2\omega} - 0.9e^{j\omega} + 0.81} = \frac{e^{j\omega}+1}{(e^{j\omega} - 0.9e^{j\pi/3})(e^{j\omega} - 0.9e^{-j\pi/3})}$$

b. Using $H(z) = Y(z)/X(z)$,

$$\frac{Y(z)}{X(z)} = \frac{z+1}{z^2 - 0.9z + 0.81}\left(\frac{z^{-2}}{z^{-2}}\right) = \frac{z^{-1} + z^{-2}}{1 - 0.9z^{-1} + 0.81z^{-2}}$$

Cross multiplying,

$$Y(z) - 0.9z^{-1}Y(z) + 0.81z^{-2}Y(z) = z^{-1}X(z) + z^{-2}X(z)$$

Now taking the inverse z-transform,

$$y(n) - 0.9y(n-1) + 0.81y(n-2) = x(n-1) + x(n-2)$$

or

$$y(n) = 0.9y(n-1) - 0.81y(n-2) + x(n-1) + x(n-2)$$

c. Using the MATLAB script

```
>> b = [0,1,1]; a = [1,-0.9,0.81];   [R,p,C] = residuez(b,a)
R =
  -0.6173 - 0.9979i
  -0.6173 + 0.9979i
p =
   0.4500 + 0.7794i
   0.4500 - 0.7794i
C =
    1.2346
>> Mp = (abs(p))'
Mp =
    0.9000     0.9000
>> Ap = (angle(p))'/pi
Ap =
    0.3333    -0.3333
```

we have

$$H(z) = 1.2346 + \frac{-0.6173 + j0.9979}{1 - 0.9e^{-j\pi/3}z^{-1}} + \frac{-0.6173 - j0.9979}{1 - 0.9e^{j\pi/3}z^{-1}}, \quad |z| > 0.9$$

Hence from Table 4.1,

$$\begin{aligned}
h(n) &= 1.2346\delta(n) + [(-0.6173 + j0.9979)0.9^n e^{-j\pi n/3} \\
&\quad + (-0.6173 - j0.9979)0.9^n e^{j\pi n/3}]u(n) \\
&= 1.2346\delta(n) + 0.9^n[-1.2346\cos(\pi n/3) + 1.9958\sin(\pi n/3)]u(n) \\
&= 0.9^n[-1.2346\cos(\pi n/3) + 1.9958\sin(\pi n/3)]u(n-1)
\end{aligned}$$

The last step results from the fact that $h(0) = 0$. $\qquad\square$

4.4.4 RELATIONSHIPS BETWEEN SYSTEM REPRESENTATIONS

In this and the previous two chapters, we developed several system representations. Figure 4.9 depicts the relationships among these representations in a graphical form.

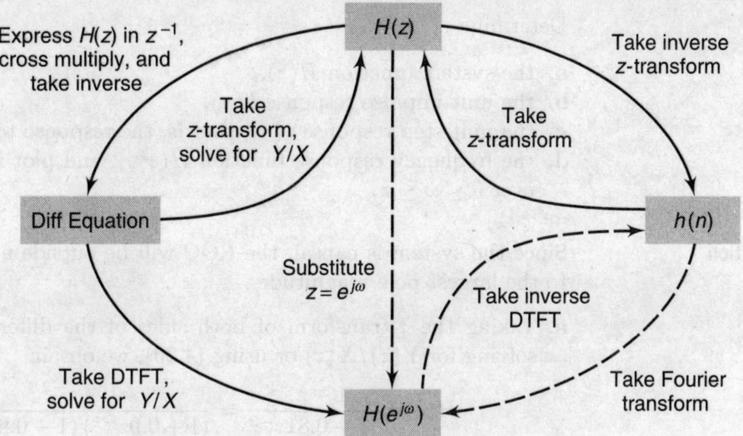

FIGURE 4.9 *System representations in pictorial form*

4.4.5 STABILITY AND CAUSALITY

For LTI systems, the BIBO stability is equivalent to $\sum_{-\infty}^{\infty} |h(k)| < \infty$. From the existence of the discrete-time Fourier transform, this stability implies that $H(e^{j\omega})$ exists, which further implies that the unit circle $|z| = 1$ must be in the ROC of $H(z)$. This result is called the *z-domain stability theorem*; therefore, the dashed paths in Figure 4.9 exist only if the system is stable.

■ THEOREM 2   ***z-Domain LTI Stability***

An LTI system is stable if and only if the unit circle is in the ROC of $H(z)$.

For LTI causality, we require that $h(n) = 0$, for $n < 0$ (i.e., a right-sided sequence). This implies that the ROC of $H(z)$ must be outside some circle of radius R_{h-}. This is not a sufficient condition, since any right-sided sequence has a similar ROC. However, when the system is stable, then its causality is easy to check.

■ THEOREM 3   ***z-Domain Causal LTI Stability***

A causal LTI system is stable if and only if the system function $H(z)$ has all its poles inside the unit circle.

□ EXAMPLE 4.13   A causal LTI system is described by the following difference equation:

$$y(n) = 0.81y(n-2) + x(n) - x(n-2)$$

Determine

a. the system function $H(z)$,
b. the unit impulse response $h(n)$,
c. the unit step response $v(n)$, that is, the response to the unit step $u(n)$, and
d. the frequency response function $H(e^{j\omega})$, and plot its magnitude and phase over $0 \leq \omega \leq \pi$.

Solution   Since the system is causal, the ROC will be outside a circle with radius equal to the largest pole magnitude.

a. Taking the z-transform of both sides of the difference equation and then solving for $Y(z)/X(z)$ or using (4.20), we obtain

$$H(z) = \frac{1 - z^{-2}}{1 - 0.81z^{-2}} = \frac{1 - z^{-2}}{(1 + 0.9z^{-1})(1 - 0.9z^{-1})}, \quad |z| > 0.9$$

b. Using the MATLAB script for the partial fraction expansion,

```
>> b = [1,0,-1]; a = [1,0,-0.81]; [R,p,C] = residuez(b,a);
R =
   -0.1173
   -0.1173
p =
   -0.9000
    0.9000
C =
    1.2346
```

we have

$$H(z) = 1.2346 - 0.1173\frac{1}{1 + 0.9z^{-1}} - 0.1173\frac{1}{1 - 0.9z^{-1}}, \quad |z| > 0.9$$

or from Table 4.1,

$$h(n) = 1.2346\delta(n) - 0.1173\left\{1 + (-1)^n\right\}(0.9)^n u(n)$$

c. From Table 4.1, $\mathcal{Z}[u(n)] = U(z) = \dfrac{1}{1 - z^{-1}}$, $|z| > 1$. Hence

$$V(z) = H(z)U(z)$$

$$= \left[\frac{(1 + z^{-1})(1 - z^{-1})}{(1 + 0.9z^{-1})(1 - 0.9z^{-1})}\right]\left[\frac{1}{1 - z^{-1}}\right], \quad |z| > 0.9 \cap |z| > 1$$

$$= \frac{1 + z^{-1}}{(1 + 0.9z^{-1})(1 - 0.9z^{-1})}, \quad |z| > 0.9$$

or

$$V(z) = 1.0556\frac{1}{1 - 0.9z^{-1}} - 0.0556\frac{1}{1 + 0.9z^{-1}}, \quad |z| > 0.9$$

Finally,

$$v(n) = \left[1.0556(0.9)^n - 0.0556\,(-0.9)^n\right]u(n)$$

Note that in the calculation of $V(z)$ there is a pole-zero cancellation at $z = 1$. This has two implications. First, the ROC of $V(z)$ is still $\{|z| > 0.9\}$ and not $\{|z| > 0.9 \cap |z| > 1 = |z| > 1\}$. Second, the step response $v(n)$ contains no steady-state term $u(n)$.

d. Substituting $z = e^{j\omega}$ in $H(z)$,

$$H(e^{j\omega}) = \frac{1 - e^{-j2\omega}}{1 - 0.81e^{-j2\omega}}$$

We will use the MATLAB script to compute and plot responses.

```
>> w = [0:1:500]*pi/500; H = freqz(b,a,w);
>> magH = abs(H); phaH = angle(H);
>> subplot(2,1,1); plot(w/pi,magH); grid
>> title('Magnitude Response'); ylabel('Magnitude')
>> subplot(2,1,2); plot(w/pi,phaH/pi); grid
>> xlabel('Frequency in \pi Units'); ylabel('Phase in \pi Units')
>> title('Phase Response')
```

The frequency response plots are shown in Figure 4.10. □

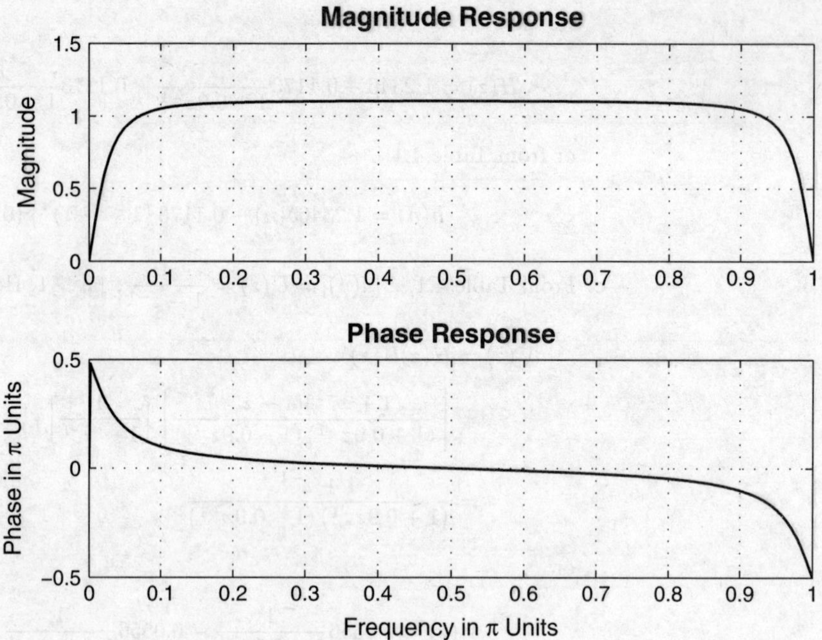

FIGURE 4.10   *Frequency response plots for Example 4.13*

4.5 SOLUTIONS OF THE DIFFERENCE EQUATIONS

In Chapter 2, we mentioned two forms for the solution of linear constant coefficient difference equations. One form involved finding the particular and the homogeneous solutions, while the other form involved finding the zero-input (initial condition) and the zero-state responses. Using z-transforms, we now provide a method for obtaining these forms. In addition, we will also discuss the *transient* and the *steady-state* responses. In digital signal processing, difference equations generally evolve in the positive n direction. Therefore, our time frame for these solutions will be $n \geq 0$. For this purpose, we define a version of the bilateral z-transform called the *one-sided z-transform*.

■ **DEFINITION 4**   ***The One-Sided z-Transform***

The one-sided z-transform of a sequence $x(n)$ is given by

$$\mathcal{Z}^{+}[x(n)] \triangleq \mathcal{Z}\left[x(n)u(n)\right] \triangleq X^{+}(z) = \sum_{n=0}^{\infty} x(n)z^{-n} \qquad \textbf{(4.25)}$$

Then the sample shifting property is given by

$$\mathcal{Z}^{+}\left[x(n-k)\right] = \mathcal{Z}\left[x(n-k)u(n)\right]$$

$$= \sum_{n=0}^{\infty} x(n-k)z^{-n} = \sum_{m=-k}^{\infty} x(m)z^{-(m+k)}$$

$$= \sum_{m=-k}^{-1} x(m)z^{-(m+k)} + \left[\sum_{m=0}^{\infty} x(m)z^{-m}\right] z^{-k}$$

or

$$\mathcal{Z}^{+}\left[x(n-k)\right] = x(-1)z^{1-k} + x(-2)z^{2-k} + \cdots + x(-k) + z^{-k}X^{+}(z) \quad \textbf{(4.26)}$$

This result can now be used to solve difference equations with nonzero initial conditions or with changing inputs. We want to solve the difference equation

$$y(n) + \sum_{k=1}^{N} a_k y(n-k) = \sum_{m=0}^{M} b_m x(n-m), \; n \geq 0$$

subject to these initial conditions:

$$\{y(i), i = -1, \ldots, -N\} \quad \text{and} \quad \{x(i), i = -1, \ldots, -M\}$$

We now demonstrate its solution using an example.

☐ **EXAMPLE 4.14** Solve

$$y(n) - \frac{3}{2}y(n-1) + \frac{1}{2}y(n-2) = x(n), \quad n \geq 0$$

where

$$x(n) = \left(\frac{1}{4}\right)^n u(n)$$

subject to $y(-1) = 4$ and $y(-2) = 10$.

Solution Taking the one-sided z-transform of both sides of the difference equation, we obtain

$$Y^{+}(z) - \frac{3}{2}[y(-1) + z^{-1}Y^{+}(z)] + \frac{1}{2}[y(-2) + z^{-1}y(-1) + z^{-2}Y^{+}(z)] = \frac{1}{1 - \frac{1}{4}z^{-1}}$$

Substituting the initial conditions and rearranging,

$$Y^{+}(z)\left[1 - \frac{3}{2}z^{-1} + \frac{1}{2}z^{-2}\right] = \frac{1}{1 - \frac{1}{4}z^{-1}} + (1 - 2z^{-1})$$

or

$$Y^+(z) = \frac{\dfrac{1}{1 - \frac{1}{4}z^{-1}}}{1 - \frac{3}{2}z^{-1} + \frac{1}{2}z^{-2}} + \frac{1 - 2z^{-1}}{1 - \frac{3}{2}z^{-1} + \frac{1}{2}z^{-2}} \tag{4.27}$$

Finally,

$$Y^+(z) = \frac{2 - \frac{9}{4}z^{-1} + \frac{1}{2}z^{-2}}{(1 - \frac{1}{2}z^{-1})(1 - z^{-1})(1 - \frac{1}{4}z^{-1})}$$

Using the partial fraction expansion, we obtain

$$Y^+(z) = \frac{1}{1 - \frac{1}{2}z^{-1}} + \frac{\frac{2}{3}}{1 - z^{-1}} + \frac{\frac{1}{3}}{1 - \frac{1}{4}z^{-1}} \tag{4.28}$$

After inverse transformation, the solution is

$$y(n) = \left[\left(\frac{1}{2}\right)^n + \frac{2}{3} + \frac{1}{3}\left(\frac{1}{4}\right)^n\right] u(n) \tag{4.29}$$

$\square$

Forms of the solutions   The preceding solution is the *complete response* of the difference equation. It can be expressed in several forms.

- Homogeneous and particular parts:

$$y(n) = \underbrace{\left[\left(\frac{1}{2}\right)^n + \frac{2}{3}\right] u(n)}_{\text{Homogeneous part}} + \underbrace{\frac{1}{3}\left(\frac{1}{4}\right)^n u(n)}_{\text{Particular part}}$$

The homogeneous part is due to the *system poles*, and the particular part is due to the *input poles*.

- Transient and steady-state responses:

$$y(n) = \underbrace{\left[\frac{1}{3}\left(\frac{1}{4}\right)^n + \left(\frac{1}{2}\right)^n\right] u(n)}_{\text{Transient response}} + \underbrace{\frac{2}{3}u(n)}_{\text{Steady-state response}}$$

The transient response is due to poles that are *inside* the unit circle, whereas the steady-state response is due to poles that are *on* the unit circle. Note that when the poles are *outside* the unit circle, the response is termed an *unbounded* response.

- Zero-input (or initial condition) and zero-state responses:
  In equation (4.27), $Y^+(z)$ has two parts. The first part can be interpreted as

$$Y_{\text{ZS}}(z) = H(z)X(z)$$

while the second part as

$$Y_{ZI}(z) = H(z)X_{IC}(z)$$

where $X_{IC}(z)$ can be thought of as an equivalent *initial-condition input* that generates the same output $Y_{ZI}(z)$ as generated by the initial conditions. In this example, $x_{IC}(n)$ is

$$x_{IC}(n) = \{1, -2\}$$
$$\uparrow$$

Now taking the inverse z-transform of each part of (4.27), we write the complete response as

$$y(n) = \underbrace{\left[\frac{1}{3}\left(\frac{1}{4}\right)^n - 2\left(\frac{1}{2}\right)^n + \frac{8}{3}\right]u(n)}_{\text{Zero-state response}} + \underbrace{\left[3\left(\frac{1}{2}\right)^n - 2\right]u(n)}_{\text{Zero-input response}}$$

From this example, it is clear that each part of the complete solution is, in general, a different function and emphasizes a different aspect of system analysis.

4.5.1 MATLAB IMPLEMENTATION

In Chapter 2, we used the `filter` function to solve the difference equation, given its coefficients and an input. This function can also be used to find the complete response when initial conditions are given. In this form, the `filter` function is invoked by

```
y = filter(b,a,x,xic)
```

where `xic` is an equivalent initial-condition input array. To find the complete response in Example 4.14, we will use the MATLAB script

```
>>  n = [0:7]; x = (1/4).^n; xic = [1, -2];
>> format long;   y1 = filter(b,a,x,xic)
y1 =
  Columns 1 through 4
    2.00000000000000    1.25000000000000    0.93750000000000    0.79687500000000
  Columns 5 through 8
    0.73046875000000    0.69824218750000    0.68237304687500    0.67449951171875
>> y2 = (1/3)*(1/4).^n+(1/2).^n+(2/3)*ones(1,8) % MATLAB check
y2 =
  Columns 1 through 4
    2.00000000000000    1.25000000000000    0.93750000000000    0.79687500000000
  Columns 5 through 8
    0.73046875000000    0.69824218750000    0.68237304687500    0.67449951171875
```

which agrees with the response given in (4.29). In Example 4.14, we computed $x_{\text{IC}}(n)$ analytically. However, in practice, and especially for large-order difference equations, it is tedious to determine $x_{\text{IC}}(n)$ analytically. MATLAB provides a function called `filtic`, which is available only in the Signal Processing toolbox. It is invoked by

```
xic = filtic(b,a,Y,X)
```

in which `b` and `a` are the filter coefficient arrays and `Y` and `X` are the initial-condition arrays from the initial conditions on $y(n)$ and $x(n)$, respectively, in the form

$$Y = [y(-1),\ y(-2),\ldots,\ y(-N)]$$
$$X = [x(-1),\ x(-2),\ldots,\ x(-M)]$$

If $x(n) = 0,\quad n \leq -1$, then X need not be specified in the `filtic` function. In Example 4.14, we could have used

```
>> Y = [4, 10];   xic = filtic(b,a,Y)
xic =
     1      -2
```

to determine $x_{\text{IC}}(n)$.

◻ **EXAMPLE 4.15**   Solve the difference equation

$$y(n) = \frac{1}{3}\left[x(n) + x(n-1) + x(n-2)\right] + 0.95y(n-1) - 0.9025y(n-2), \quad n \geq 0$$

where $x(n) = \cos(\pi n/3)u(n)$ and

$$y(-1) = -2,\ y(-2) = -3;\quad x(-1) = 1,\ x(-2) = 1$$

First determine the solution analytically and then by using MATLAB.

Solution   Taking a one-sided z-transform of the difference equation

$$Y^+(z) = \frac{1}{3}[X^+(z) + x(-1) + z^{-1}X^+(z) + x(-2) + z^{-1}x(-1) + z^{-2}X^+(z)]$$
$$+ 0.95[y(-1) + z^{-1}Y^+(z)] - 0.9025[y(-2) + z^{-1}y(-1) + z^{-2}Y^+(z)]$$

and substituting the initial conditions, we obtain

$$Y^+(z) = \frac{\frac{1}{3} + \frac{1}{3}z^{-1} + \frac{1}{3}z^{-2}}{1 - 0.95z^{-1} + 0.9025z^{-2}}X^+(z) + \frac{1.4742 + 2.1383z^{-1}}{1 - 0.95z^{-1} + 0.9025z^{-2}}$$

Clearly, $x_{\text{IC}}(n) = [1.4742, 2.1383]$. Now substituting $X^+(z) = \dfrac{1 - 0.5z^{-1}}{1 - z^{-1} + z^{-2}}$ and simplifying, we will obtain $Y^+(z)$ as a rational function. This simplification and further partial fraction expansion can be done using MATLAB.

MATLAB script:

```
>> b = [1,1,1]/3; a = [1,-0.95,0.9025];
>> Y = [-2,-3]; X = [1,1];  xic=filtic(b,a,Y,X)
xic =
     1.4742    2.1383
>> bxplus = [1,-0.5]; axplus = [1,-1,1]; % X(z) transform coeff.
>> ayplus = conv(a,axplus) % Denominator of Yplus(z)
ayplus =
    1.0000   -1.9500    2.8525   -1.8525    0.9025
>> byplus = conv(b,bxplus)+conv(xic,axplus)  % Numerator of Yplus(z)
byplus =
    1.8075    0.8308   -0.4975    1.9717
>> [R,p,C] = residuez(byplus,ayplus)
R =
  0.0584 + 3.9468i   0.0584 - 3.9468i   0.8453 + 2.0311i   0.8453 - 2.0311i
p =
  0.5000 - 0.8660i   0.5000 + 0.8660i   0.4750 + 0.8227i   0.4750 - 0.8227i
C =
     []
>> Mp = abs(p), Ap = angle(p)/pi % Polar form
Mp =
    1.0000    1.0000    0.9500    0.9500
Ap =
   -0.3333    0.3333    0.3333   -0.3333
```

Hence

$$Y^+(z) = \frac{1.8075 + 0.8308z^{-1} - 0.4975z^{-2} + 1.9717z^{-3}}{1 - 1.95z^{-1} + 2.8525z^{-2} - 1.8525z^{-3} + 0.9025z^{-4}}$$

$$= \frac{0.0584 + j3.9468}{1 - e^{-j\pi/3}z^{-1}} + \frac{0.0584 - j3.9468}{1 - e^{j\pi/3}z^{-1}}$$

$$+ \frac{0.8453 + j2.0311}{1 - 0.95e^{j\pi/3}z^{-1}} + \frac{0.8453 - j2.0311}{1 - 0.95e^{-j\pi/3}z^{-1}}$$

Now from Table 4.1,

$$y(n) = (0.0584 + j3.9468)\, e^{-j\pi n/3} + (0.0584 - j3.9468)\, e^{j\pi n/3}$$

$$+ (0.8453 + j2.031)\,(0.95)^n\, e^{j\pi n/3} + (0.8453 - j2.031)\,(0.95)^n\, e^{-j\pi n/3}$$

$$= 0.1169\cos(\pi n/3) + 7.8937\sin(\pi n/3)$$

$$+ (0.95)^n\,[1.6906\cos(\pi n/3) - 4.0623\sin(\pi n/3)], \quad n \geq 0$$

The first two terms of $y(n)$ correspond to the steady-state response, as well as to the particular response, while the last two terms are the transient response (and homogeneous response) terms.

To solve this example using MATLAB, we will need the `filtic` function, which we have already used to determine the $x_{IC}(n)$ sequence. The solution will be a numerical one. Let us determine the first eight samples of $y(n)$.

MATLAB script:

```
>> n = [0:7]; x = cos(pi*n/3);  y = filter(b,a,x,xic)
y =
  Columns 1 through 4
    1.80750000000000    4.35545833333333    2.83975000000000   -1.56637197916667
  Columns 5 through 8
   -4.71759442187500   -3.40139732291667    1.35963484230469    5.02808085078841
% MATLAB verification
>> A=real(2*R(1)); B=imag(2*R(1)); C=real(2*R(3)); D=imag(2*R(4));
>> y=A*cos(pi*n/3)+B*sin(pi*n/3)+((0.95).^n).*(C*cos(pi*n/3)+D*sin(pi*n/3))
y =
  Columns 1 through 4
    1.80750000000048    4.35545833333359    2.83974999999978   -1.56637197916714
  Columns 5 through 8
   -4.71759442187528   -3.40139732291648    1.35963484230515    5.02808085078871
```

4.6 PROBLEMS

P4.1 Determine the z-transform of the following sequences using the definition (4.1). Indicate the region of convergence for each sequence and verify the z-transform expression using MATLAB.

1. $x(n) = \{3, 2, 1, -2, -3\}$.
   $\uparrow$

2. $x(n) = (0.8)^n u(n-2)$. Verify the z-transform expression using MATLAB.

3. $x(n) = [(0.5)^n + (-0.8)^n]u(n)$. Verify the z-transform expression using MATLAB.

4. $x(n) = 2^n \cos(0.4\pi n)u(-n)$.

5. $x(n) = (n+1)(3)^n u(n)$. Verify the z-transform expression using MATLAB.

P4.2 Consider the sequence $x(n) = (0.9)^n \cos(\pi n/4)u(n)$. Let

$$y(n) = \begin{cases} x(n/2), & n = 0, \pm 2, \pm 4, \cdots \\ 0, & \text{otherwise} \end{cases}$$

1. Show that the z-transform $Y(z)$ of $y(n)$ can be expressed in terms of the z-transform $X(z)$ of $x(n)$ as $Y(z) = X(z^2)$.
2. Determine $Y(z)$.
3. Using MATLAB, verify that the sequence $y(n)$ has the z-transform $Y(z)$.

P4.3 Determine the z-transform of the following sequences using the z-transform table and the z-transform properties. Express $X(z)$ as a rational function in z^{-1}. Verify your results using MATLAB. Indicate the region of convergence in each case, and provide a pole-zero plot.

1. $x(n) = 2\delta(n-2) + 3u(n-3)$
2. $x(n) = 3(0.75)^n \cos(0.3\pi n)u(n) + 4(0.75)^n \sin(0.3\pi n)u(n)$
3. $x(n) = n\sin(\frac{\pi n}{3})u(n) + (0.9)^n u(n-2)$

    4. $x(n) = n^2 (2/3)^{n-2} u(n-1)$

    5. $x(n) = (n-3)(\frac{1}{4})^{n-2} \cos\{\frac{\pi}{2}(n-1)\} u(n)$

P4.4 Let $x(n)$ be a complex-valued sequence with the real part $x_R(n)$ and the imaginary part $x_I(n)$.

    1. Prove the following z-transform relations:

$$X_R(z) \triangleq \mathcal{Z}\left[x_R(n)\right] = \frac{X(z) + X^*(z^*)}{2} \quad \text{and} \quad X_I(z) \triangleq \mathcal{Z}\left[x_I(n)\right] = \frac{X(z) - X^*(z^*)}{2}$$

    2. Verify these relations for $x(n) = \exp\left\{(-1 + j0.2\pi)n\right\} u(n)$.

P4.5 The z-transform of $x(n)$ is $X(z) = 1/(1 + 0.5z^{-1})$, $|z| > 0.5$. Determine the z-transforms of the following sequences and indicate their region of convergence.

    1. $x_1(n) = x(3 - n) + x(n - 3)$

    2. $x_2(n) = (1 + n + n^2)x(n)$

    3. $x_3(n) = (\frac{1}{2})^n x(n - 2)$

    4. $x_4(n) = x(n + 2) * x(n - 2)$

    5. $x_5(n) = \cos(\pi n/2) x^*(n)$

P4.6 Repeat Problem P4.5 if

$$X(z) = \frac{1 + z^{-1}}{1 + \frac{5}{6}z^{-1} + \frac{1}{6}z^{-2}};\ |z| > \frac{1}{2}$$

P4.7 The inverse z-transform of $X(z)$ is $x(n) = (1/2)^n u(n)$. Using the z-transform properties, determine the sequences in each of the following cases.

    1. $X_1(z) = \frac{z-1}{z} X(z)$

    2. $X_2(z) = zX(z^{-1})$

    3. $X_3(z) = 2X(3z) + 3X(z/3)$

    4. $X_4(z) = X(z)X(z^{-1})$

    5. $X_5(z) = z^2 \frac{dX(z)}{dz}$

P4.8 If sequences $x_1(n)$, $x_2(n)$, and $x_3(n)$ are related by $x_3(n) = x_1(n) * x_2(n)$, then

$$\sum_{n=-\infty}^{\infty} x_3(n) = \left(\sum_{n=-\infty}^{\infty} x_1(n)\right)\left(\sum_{n=-\infty}^{\infty} x_2(n)\right)$$

    1. Prove this result by substituting the definition of convolution in the left-hand side.

    2. Prove this result using the convolution property.

    3. Verify this result using MATLAB and choosing any two random sequences $x_1(n)$ and $x_2(n)$.

P4.9 Determine the results of the following polynomial operations using MATLAB.

    1. $X_1(z) = (1 - 2z^{-1} + 3z^{-2} - 4z^{-3})(4 + 3z^{-1} - 2z^{-2} + z^{-3})$

    2. $X_2(z) = (z^2 - 2z + 3 + 2z^{-1} + z^{-2})(z^3 - z^{-3})$

    3. $X_3(z) = (1 + z^{-1} + z^{-2})^3$

    4. $X_4(z) = X_1(z)X_2(z) + X_3(z)$

    5. $X_5(z) = (z^{-1} - 3z^{-3} + 2z^{-5} + 5z^{-7} - z^{-9})(z + 3z^2 + 2z^3 + 4z^4)$

P4.10 The `deconv` function is useful in dividing two causal sequences. Write a MATLAB function `deconv_m` to divide two noncausal sequences (similar to the `conv` function). The format of this function should be

```
function [p,np,r,nr] = deconv_m(b,nb,a,na)
% Modified deconvolution routine for noncausal sequences
% function [p,np,r,nr] = deconv_m(b,nb,a,na)
%
%  p = polynomial part of support np1 <= n <= np2
% np = [np1, np2]
%  r = remainder part of support nr1 <= n <= nr2
% nr = [nr1, nr2]
%  b = numerator polynomial of support nb1 <= n <= nb2
% nb = [nb1, nb2]
%  a = denominator polynomial of support na1 <= n <= na2
% na = [na1, na2]
%
```

Check your function on the following operation:

$$\frac{z^2 + z + 1 + z^{-1} + z^{-2} + z^{-3}}{z + 2 + z^{-1}} = (z - 1 + 2z^{-1} - 2z^{-2}) + \frac{3z^{-2} + 3z^{-3}}{z + 2 + z^{-1}}$$

P4.11 Determine the following inverse z-transforms using the partial fraction expansion method.

1. $X_1(z) = (1 - z^{-1} - 4z^{-2} + 4z^{-3})/(1 - \frac{11}{4}z^{-1} + \frac{13}{8}z^{-2} - \frac{1}{4}z^{-3})$. The sequence is right-sided.

2. $X_2(z) = (1 + z^{-1} - 4z^{-2} + 4z^{-3})/(1 - \frac{11}{4}z^{-1} + \frac{13}{8}z^{-2} - \frac{1}{4}z^{-3})$. The sequence is absolutely summable.

3. $X_3(z) = (z^3 - 3z^2 + 4z + 1)/(z^3 - 4z^2 + z - 0.16)$. The sequence is left-sided.

4. $X_4(z) = z/(z^3 + 2z^2 + 1.25z + 0.25)$, $|z| > 1$.

5. $X_5(z) = z/(z^2 - 0.25)^2$, $|z| < 0.5$.

P4.12 Consider the sequence

$$x(n) = A_c(r)^n \cos(\pi v_0 n)u(n) + A_s(r)^n \sin(\pi v_0 n)u(n) \tag{4.30}$$

The z-transform of this sequence is a second-order (proper) rational function that contains a complex-conjugate pole pair. The objective of this problem is to develop a MATLAB function that can be used to obtain the inverse z-transform of such a rational function so that the inverse does not contain any complex numbers.

1. Show that the z-transform of $x(n)$ in (4.30) is given by

$$X(z) = \frac{b_0 + b_1 z^{-1}}{1 + a_1 z^{-1} + a_2 z^{-2}}; \quad |z| > |r| \tag{4.31}$$

where

$$b_0 = A_c; \; b_1 = r[A_s \sin(\pi v_0) - A_c \cos(\pi v_0)]; \; a_1 = -2r\cos(\pi v_0); \; a_2 = r^2 \tag{4.32}$$

2. Using (4.32), determine the signal parameters A_c, A_s, r, and v_0 in terms of the rational function parameters b_0, b_1, a_1, and a_2.

3. Using your results in part b above, design a MATLAB function, `invCCPP`, that computes signal parameters using the rational function parameters. The format of this function should be

```
function [As,Ac,r,v0] = invCCPP(b0,b1,a1,a2)
```

P4.13 Suppose $X(z)$ is given as follows:

$$X(z) = \frac{2 + 3z^{-1}}{1 - z^{-1} + 0.81z^{-2}}, \quad |z| > 0.9$$

1. Using the MATLAB function `invCCPP` given in Problem P4.12, determine $x(n)$ in a form that contains no complex numbers.

2. Using MATLAB, compute the first 20 samples of $x(n)$, and compare them with your answer in the above part.

P4.14 The z-transform of a causal sequence is given as

$$X(z) = \frac{-2 + 5.65z^{-1} - 2.88z^{-2}}{1 - 0.1z^{-1} + 0.09z^{-2} + 0.648z^{-3}} \tag{4.33}$$

which contains a complex-conjugate pole pair as well as a real-valued pole.

1. Using the `residuez` function, express (4.33) as

$$X(z) = \frac{(\ \ ) + (\ \ )z^{-1}}{1 + (\ \ )z^{-1} + (\ \ )z^{-2}} + \frac{(\ \ )}{1 + (\ \ )z^{-1}} \tag{4.34}$$

Note that you will have to use the `residuez` function in both directions.

2. Now using your function `invCCPP` and the inverse of the real-valued pole factor, determine the causal sequence $x(n)$ from the $X(z)$ in (4.34) so that it contains no complex numbers.

P4.15 For the linear and time-invariant systems described by the following impulse responses, determine (i) the system function representation, (ii) the difference equation representation, (iii) the pole-zero plot, and (iv) the output $y(n)$ if the input is $x(n) = \left(\frac{1}{4}\right)^n u(n)$.

1. $h(n) = 5(1/4)^n u(n)$

2. $h(n) = n(1/3)^n u(n) + (-1/4)^n u(n)$

3. $h(n) = 3(0.9)^n \cos(\pi n/4 + \pi/3)u(n + 1)$

4. $h(n) = \dfrac{(0.5)^n \sin[(n + 1)\pi/3]}{\sin(\pi/3)} u(n)$

5. $h(n) = [2 - \sin(\pi n)]u(n)$

P4.16 Consider the system shown in Figure P4.1.

1. Using the z-transform approach, show that the impulse response, $h(n)$, of the overall system is given by

$$h(n) = \delta(n) - \frac{1}{2}\delta(n - 1)$$

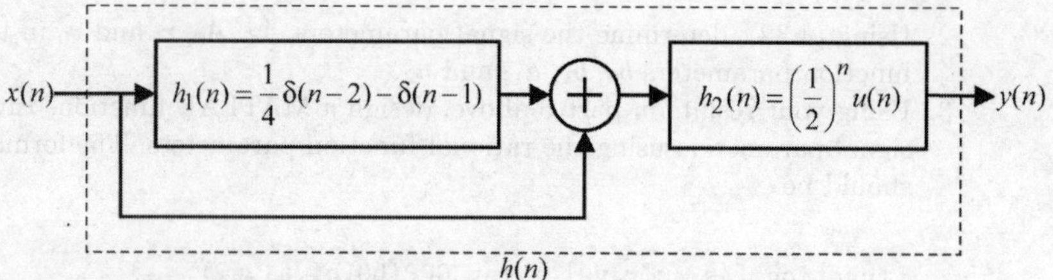

FIGURE P4.1   *System for Problem 4.16*

2. Determine the difference equation representation of the overall system that relates the output $y(n)$ to the input $x(n)$.
3. Is this system causal? BIBO stable? Explain clearly to receive full credit.
4. Determine the frequency response $H(e^{j\omega})$ of the overall system.
5. Using MATLAB, provide a plot of this frequency response over $0 \leq \omega \leq \pi$.

P4.17 For the linear and time-invariant systems described by the following system functions, determine (i) the impulse response representation, (ii) the difference equation representation, (iii) the pole-zero plot, and (iv) the output $y(n)$ if the input is $x(n) = 3\cos(\pi n/3)u(n)$.

1. $H(z) = (z + 1)/(z - 0.5)$, causal system
2. $H(z) = (1 + z^{-1} + z^{-2})/(1 + 0.5z^{-1} - 0.25z^{-2})$, stable system
3. $H(z) = (z^2 - 1)/(z - 3)^2$, anticausal system
4. $H(z) = \dfrac{z}{z - 0.25} + \dfrac{1 - 0.5z^{-1}}{1 + 2z^{-1}}$, stable system
5. $H(z) = (1 + z^{-1} + z^{-2})^2$

P4.18 For the linear, causal, and time-invariant systems described by the following difference equations, determine (i) the impulse response representation, (ii) the system function representation, (iii) the pole-zero plot, and (iv) the output $y(n)$ if the input is $x(n) = 2(0.9)^n u(n)$.

1. $y(n) = [x(n) + 2x(n - 1) + x(n - 3)]/4$
2. $y(n) = x(n) + 0.5x(n - 1) - 0.5y(n - 1) + 0.25y(n - 2)$
3. $y(n) = 2x(n) + 0.9y(n - 1)$
4. $y(n) = -0.45x(n) - 0.4x(n - 1) + x(n - 2) + 0.4y(n - 1) + 0.45y(n - 2)$
5. $y(n) = \sum_{m=0}^{4}(0.8)^m x(n - m) - \sum_{\ell=1}^{4}(0.9)^\ell y(n - \ell)$

P4.19 The output sequence $y(n)$ in Problem P4.18 is the total response. For each of the systems given in Problem P4.18, separate $y(n)$ into (i) the homogeneous part, (ii) the particular part, (iii) the transient response, and (iv) the steady-state response.

P4.20 A stable system has four zeros and four poles as given below.

$$\text{zeros:}\ \pm 1,\ \pm j1 \qquad \text{Poles:}\ \pm 0.9,\ \pm j0.9$$

It is also known that the frequency response function $H(e^{j\omega})$ evaluated at $\omega = \pi/4$ is equal to 1, that is,

$$H(e^{j\pi/4}) = 1$$

1. Determine the system function $H(z)$, and indicate its region of convergence.
2. Determine the difference equation representation.
3. Determine the steady-state response $y_{ss}(n)$ if the input is $x(n) = \cos(\pi n/4)u(n)$.
4. Determine the transient response $y_{tr}(n)$ if the input is $x(n) = \cos(\pi n/4)u(n)$.

P4.21 A digital filter is described by the frequency response function

$$H(e^{j\omega}) = [1 + 2\cos(\omega) + 3\cos(2\omega)]\cos\left(\frac{\omega}{2}\right) e^{-j5\omega/2}$$

1. Determine the difference equation representation.
2. Using the `freqz` function, plot the magnitude and phase of the frequency response of the filter. Note the magnitude and phase at $\omega = \pi/2$ and at $\omega = \pi$.
3. Generate 200 samples of the signal $x(n) = \sin(\pi n/2) + 5\cos(\pi n)$, and process through the filter to obtain $y(n)$. Compare the steady-state portion of $y(n)$ to $x(n)$. How are the amplitudes and phases of two sinusoids affected by the filter?

P4.22 Repeat Problem 4.21 for the following filter:

$$H(e^{j\omega}) = \frac{1 + e^{-j4\omega}}{1 - 0.8145e^{-j4\omega}}$$

P4.23 Solve the following difference equation for $y(n)$ using the one-sided z-transform approach:

$$y(n) = 0.81y(n-2) + x(n) - x(n-1), \ n \ge 0; \quad y(-1) = 2, \ y(-2) = 2$$
$$x(n) = (0.7)^n u(n+1)$$

Generate the first 20 samples of $y(n)$ using MATLAB, and compare them with your answer.

P4.24 Solve the difference equation for $y(n)$, $n \ge 0$,

$$y(n) - 0.4y(n-1) - 0.45y(n-2) = 0.45x(n) + 0.4x(n-1) - x(n-2)$$

driven by the input $x(n) = \left[2 + \left(\frac{1}{2}\right)^n\right]u(n)$ and subject to

$$y(-1) = 0, \ y(-2) = 3; \ x(-1) = x(-2) = 2$$

Decompose the solution $y(n)$ into (i) transient response, (ii) steady-state response, (iii) zero-input response, and (iv) zero-state response.

P4.25 A stable, linear, and time-invariant system is given by the system function

$$H(z) = \frac{4z^2 - 2\sqrt{2}z + 1}{z^2 - 2\sqrt{2}z + 4}$$

1. Determine the difference equation representation for this system.
2. Plot the poles and zeros of $H(z)$, and indicate the ROC.
3. Determine the unit sample response $h(n)$ of this system.
4. Is this system causal? If the answer is yes, justify it. If the answer is no, find a causal unit sample response that satisfies the system function.

P4.26 Determine the zero-input, zero-state, and steady-state responses of the system

$$y(n) = 0.9801y(n-2) + x(n) + 2x(n-1) + x(n-2), \; n \geq 0; \quad y(-2) = 1, \; y(-1) = 0$$

to the input $x(n) = 5(-1)^n u(n)$.

The Discrete Fourier Transform

In Chapters 3 and 4, we studied transform-domain representations of discrete signals. The discrete-time Fourier transform provided the frequency-domain (ω) representation for absolutely summable sequences. The z-transform provided a generalized frequency-domain (z) representation for arbitrary sequences. These transforms have two features in common. First, the transforms are defined for infinite-length sequences. Second, and the most important, they are functions of continuous variables (ω or z). From the numerical computation viewpoint (or from MATLAB's viewpoint), these two features are troublesome because one has to evaluate *infinite sums* at *uncountably infinite* frequencies. To use MATLAB, we have to truncate sequences and then evaluate the expressions at finitely many points. This is what we did in many examples in the two previous chapters. The evaluations were obviously approximations to the exact calculations. In other words, the discrete-time Fourier transform and the z-transform are not *numerically computable* transforms.

Therefore, we turn our attention to a numerically computable transform. It is obtained by sampling the discrete-time Fourier transform in the frequency domain (or the z-transform on the unit circle). We develop this transform by first analyzing periodic sequences. From Fourier analysis, we know that a periodic function (or sequence) can always be represented by a linear combination of harmonically related complex exponentials (which is a form of sampling). This gives us the *discrete Fourier series* (DFS) representation. Since the sampling is in the frequency domain, we study the effects of sampling in the time domain and the issue of reconstruction in the z-domain. We then extend the DFS to *finite-duration sequences*, which leads to a new transform, called the *discrete Fourier transform* (DFT). The DFT avoids the two problems mentioned and is a numerically computable transform that is suitable for computer implementation. We study its properties and its use in system analysis in detail. The numerical computation of the DFT for long sequences is prohibitively time-consuming. Therefore, several algorithms have been developed to efficiently compute the DFT. These are collectively called fast Fourier transform (or FFT) algorithms. We will study two such algorithms in detail.

5.1 THE DISCRETE FOURIER SERIES

In Chapter 2, we defined the periodic sequence by $\tilde{x}(n)$, satisfying the condition

$$\tilde{x}(n) = \tilde{x}(n + kN), \quad \forall n, k \tag{5.1}$$

where N is the fundamental period of the sequence. From Fourier analysis, we know that the periodic functions can be synthesized as a linear combination of complex exponentials whose frequencies are multiples (or harmonics) of the fundamental frequency (which in our case is $2\pi/N$). From the frequency-domain periodicity of the discrete-time Fourier transform, we conclude that there are a finite number of harmonics; the frequencies are $\left\{\frac{2\pi}{N}k, \quad k = 0, 1, \ldots, N-1\right\}$. Therefore, a periodic sequence $\tilde{x}(n)$ can be expressed as

$$\tilde{x}(n) = \frac{1}{N} \sum_{k=0}^{N-1} \tilde{X}(k) e^{j\frac{2\pi}{N}kn}, \quad n = 0, \pm 1, \ldots \tag{5.2}$$

where $\{\tilde{X}(k), \quad k = 0, \pm 1, \ldots, \}$ are called the discrete Fourier series coefficients, which are given by

$$\tilde{X}(k) = \sum_{n=0}^{N-1} \tilde{x}(n) e^{-j\frac{2\pi}{N}nk}, \quad k = 0, \pm 1, \ldots \tag{5.3}$$

Note that $\tilde{X}(k)$ is itself a (complex-valued) periodic sequence with fundamental period equal to N, that is,

$$\tilde{X}(k + N) = \tilde{X}(k) \tag{5.4}$$

The pair of equations (5.3) and (5.2), taken together, is called the *discrete Fourier series* representation of periodic sequences. Using $W_N \overset{\triangle}{=} e^{-j\frac{2\pi}{N}}$ to denote the complex exponential term, we express (5.3) and (5.2) as

$$\tilde{X}(k) \triangleq \text{DFS}[\tilde{x}(n)] = \sum_{n=0}^{N-1} \tilde{x}(n) W_N^{nk} \qquad \text{Analysis or a} \\ \text{DFS equation}$$

$$\tilde{x}(n) \triangleq \text{IDFS}[\tilde{X}(k)] = \frac{1}{N} \sum_{k=0}^{N-1} \tilde{X}(k) W_N^{-nk} \qquad \text{Synthesis or an inverse} \\ \text{DFS equation}$$

$$(5.5)$$

☐   **EXAMPLE 5.1**   Find the DFS representation of the periodic sequence

$$\tilde{x}(n) = \{\ldots, 0, 1, 2, 3, 0, 1, 2, 3, 0, 1, 2, 3, \ldots\}$$
$$\uparrow$$

Solution   The fundamental period of this sequence is $N = 4$. Hence $W_4 = e^{-j\frac{2\pi}{4}} = -j$. Now

$$\tilde{X}(k) = \sum_{n=0}^{3} \tilde{x}(n) W_4^{nk}, \quad k = 0, \pm 1, \pm 2, \ldots$$

Hence

$$\tilde{X}(0) = \sum_{0}^{3} \tilde{x}(n) W_4^{0 \cdot n} = \sum_{0}^{3} \tilde{x}(n) = \tilde{x}(0) + \tilde{x}(1) + \tilde{x}(2) + \tilde{x}(3) = 6$$

Similarly,

$$\tilde{X}(1) = \sum_{0}^{3} \tilde{x}(n) W_4^{n} = \sum_{0}^{3} \tilde{x}(n)(-j)^{n} = (-2 + 2j)$$

$$\tilde{X}(2) = \sum_{0}^{3} \tilde{x}(n) W_4^{2n} = \sum_{0}^{3} \tilde{x}(n)(-j)^{2n} = -2$$

$$\tilde{X}(3) = \sum_{0}^{3} \tilde{x}(n) W_4^{3n} = \sum_{0}^{3} \tilde{x}(n)(-j)^{3n} = (-2 - 2j)$$

☐

5.1.1 MATLAB IMPLEMENTATION

A careful look at (5.5) reveals that the DFS is a numerically computable representation. It can be implemented in many ways. To compute each sample $\tilde{X}(k)$, we can implement the summation as a `for...end` loop. To compute all DFS coefficients would require another `for...end` loop. This will result in a two nested `for...end` loop implementation. This is clearly inefficient in MATLAB. An efficient implementation in MATLAB would be to use a matrix-vector multiplication for each of the relations in (5.5). We have used this approach earlier in implementing a numerical approximation to the discrete-time Fourier transform. Let $\tilde{\mathbf{x}}$ and $\tilde{\mathbf{X}}$ denote column vectors corresponding to the primary periods of sequences $\tilde{x}(n)$ and $\tilde{X}(k)$, respectively. Then (5.5) is given by

$$\tilde{\mathbf{X}} = \mathbf{W}_N \tilde{\mathbf{x}}$$

$$\tilde{\mathbf{x}} = \frac{1}{N} \mathbf{W}_N^* \tilde{\mathbf{X}} \tag{5.6}$$

where the matrix $\mathbf{W}_N$ is given by

$$\mathbf{W}_N \triangleq \left[W_N^{kn} {}_{0 \le k,n \le N-1} \right] = \begin{matrix} \\ k \\ \downarrow \end{matrix} \overset{n \longrightarrow}{\begin{bmatrix} 1 & 1 & \cdots & 1 \\ 1 & W_N^1 & \cdots & W_N^{(N-1)} \\ \vdots & \vdots & \ddots & \vdots \\ 1 & W_N^{(N-1)} & \cdots & W_N^{(N-1)^2} \end{bmatrix}} \tag{5.7}$$

The matrix $\mathbf{W}_N$ is a square matrix and is called a *DFS matrix*. The following MATLAB function `dfs` implements this procedure.

```matlab
function [Xk] = dfs(xn,N)
% Computes discrete Fourier series coefficients
% ----------------------------------------------
% [Xk] = dfs(xn,N)
% Xk = DFS coeff. array over 0 <= k <= N-1
% xn = One period of periodic signal over 0 <= n <= N-1
%  N = Fundamental period of xn
%
n = [0:1:N-1];              % Row vector for n
k = [0:1:N-1];              % Row vector for k
WN = exp(-j*2*pi/N);        % Wn factor
nk = n'*k;                  % Creates an N by N matrix of nk values
WNnk = WN .^ nk;            % DFS matrix
Xk = xn * WNnk;             % Row vector for DFS coefficients
```

The DFS in Example 5.1 can be computed using MATLAB as

```matlab
>> xn = [0,1,2,3]; N = 4;  Xk = dfs(xn,N)
Xk =
    6.0000            -2.0000 + 2.0000i  -2.0000 - 0.0000i  -2.0000 - 2.0000i
```

The following `idfs` function implements the synthesis equation.

```
function [xn] = idfs(Xk,N)
% Computes inverse discrete Fourier series
% ------------------------------------------
% [xn] = idfs(Xk,N)
% xn = one period of periodic signal over 0 <= n <= N-1
% Xk = DFS coeff. array over 0 <= k <= N-1
%  N = fundamental period of Xk
%
n = [0:1:N-1];              % Row vector for n
k = [0:1:N-1];              % Row vector for k
WN = exp(-j*2*pi/N);        % Wn factor
nk = n'*k;                  % Creates an N by N matrix of nk values
WNnk = WN .^ (-nk);         % IDFS matrix
xn = (Xk * WNnk)/N;         % Row vector for IDFS values
```

Caution: These functions are efficient approaches of implementing (5.5) in MATLAB. They are not computationally efficient, especially for large N. We will deal with this problem later in this chapter.

☐ **EXAMPLE 5.2** A periodic "square wave" sequence is given by

$$
\tilde{x}(n) = \begin{cases} 1, & mN \le n \le mN + L - 1 \\ 0, & mN + L \le n \le (m+1)N - 1 \end{cases} ; \quad m = 0, \pm1, \pm2, \ldots
$$

where N is the fundamental period and L/N is the duty cycle.

a. Determine an expression for $|\tilde{X}(k)|$ in terms of L and N.
b. Plot the magnitude $|\tilde{X}(k)|$ for $L = 5$, $N = 20$; $L = 5$, $N = 40$; $L = 5$, $N = 60$; and $L = 7$, $N = 60$.
c. Comment on the results.

Solution A plot of this sequence for $L = 5$ and $N = 20$ is shown in Figure 5.1.

a. By applying the analysis equation (5.3),

$$
\tilde{X}(k) = \sum_{n=0}^{N-1} \tilde{x}(n) e^{-j\frac{2\pi}{N}nk} = \sum_{n=0}^{L-1} e^{-j\frac{2\pi}{N}nk} = \sum_{n=0}^{L-1} \left(e^{-j\frac{2\pi}{N}k} \right)^n
$$

$$
= \begin{cases} L, & k = 0, \pm N, \pm 2N, \ldots \\[2mm] \dfrac{1 - e^{-j2\pi Lk/N}}{1 - e^{-j2\pi k/N}}, & \text{otherwise} \end{cases}
$$

The last step follows from the sum of the geometric terms formula (2.7) in Chapter 2. The last expression can be simplified to

$$
\frac{1 - e^{-j2\pi Lk/N}}{1 - e^{-j2\pi k/N}} = \frac{e^{-j\pi Lk/N}}{e^{-j\pi k/N}} \frac{e^{j\pi Lk/N} - e^{-j\pi Lk/N}}{e^{j\pi k/N} - e^{-j\pi k/N}}
$$

$$
= e^{-j\pi(L-1)k/N} \frac{\sin(\pi k L/N)}{\sin(\pi k/N)}
$$

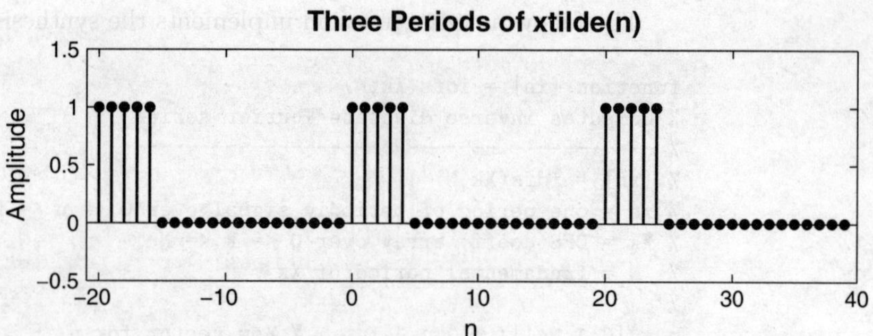

FIGURE 5.1 *Periodic square wave sequence*

or the magnitude of $\tilde{X}(k)$ is given by

$$\left|\tilde{X}(k)\right| = \begin{cases} L, & k = 0, \pm N, \pm 2N, \ldots \\ \left|\dfrac{\sin(\pi k L/N)}{\sin(\pi k/N)}\right|, & \text{otherwise} \end{cases}$$

b. The MATLAB script for $L = 5$ and $N = 20$:

```
>> L = 5; N = 20; k = [-N/2:N/2];         % Sq wave parameters
>> xn = [ones(1,L), zeros(1,N-L)];        % Sq wave x(n)
>> Xk = dfs(xn,N);                        % DFS
>> magXk = abs([Xk(N/2+1:N) Xk(1:N/2+1)]); % DFS magnitude
>> subplot(2,2,1); stem(k,magXk); axis([-N/2,N/2,-0.5,5.5])
>> xlabel('k'); ylabel('Amplitude')
>> title('DFS of SQ. Wave: L=5, N=20')
```

The plots for this and all other cases are shown in Figure 5.2. Note that since $\tilde{X}(k)$ is periodic, the plots are shown from $-N/2$ to $N/2$.

c. Several interesting observations can be made from plots in Figure 5.2. The envelopes of the DFS coefficients of square waves look like "sinc" functions. The amplitude at $k = 0$ is equal to L, while the zeros of the functions are at multiples of N/L, which is the reciprocal of the duty cycle. We will study these functions later in this chapter.   □

5.1.2 RELATION TO THE z-TRANSFORM

Let $x(n)$ be a finite-duration sequence of duration N such that

$$x(n) = \begin{cases} \text{Nonzero}, & 0 \le n \le N - 1 \\ 0, & \text{elsewhere} \end{cases} \tag{5.8}$$

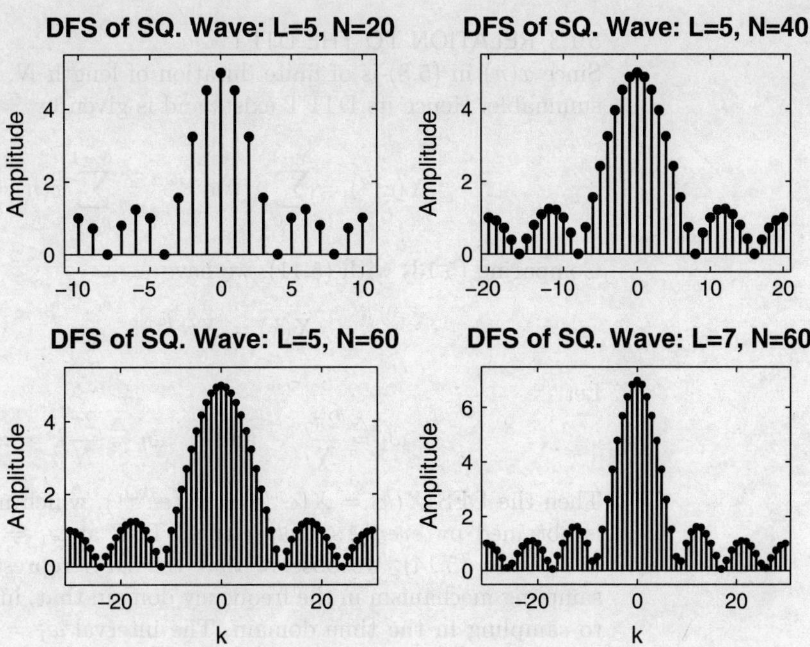

FIGURE 5.2   *The DFS plots of a periodic square wave for various L and N*

Then we can compute its z-transform:

$$X(z) = \sum_{n=0}^{N-1} x(n) z^{-n} \tag{5.9}$$

Now we construct a periodic sequence $\tilde{x}(n)$ by periodically repeating $x(n)$ with period N, that is,

$$x(n) = \begin{cases} \tilde{x}(n), & 0 \le n \le N-1 \\ 0, & \text{elsewhere} \end{cases} \tag{5.10}$$

The DFS of $\tilde{x}(n)$ is given by

$$\tilde{X}(k) = \sum_{n=0}^{N-1} \tilde{x}(n) e^{-j\frac{2\pi}{N}nk} = \sum_{n=0}^{N-1} x(n) \left[e^{j\frac{2\pi}{N}k} \right]^{-n} \tag{5.11}$$

Comparing it with (5.9), we have

$$\tilde{X}(k) = X(z)\big|_{z=e^{j\frac{2\pi}{N}k}} \tag{5.12}$$

which means that the DFS $\tilde{X}(k)$ represents N evenly spaced samples of the z-transform $X(z)$ around the unit circle.

5.1.3 RELATION TO THE DTFT

Since $x(n)$ in (5.8) is of finite duration of length N, it is also absolutely summable. Hence its DTFT exists and is given by

$$X(e^{j\omega}) = \sum_{n=0}^{N-1} x(n)e^{-j\omega n} = \sum_{n=0}^{N-1} \tilde{x}(n)e^{-j\omega n} \qquad \textbf{(5.13)}$$

Comparing (5.13) with (5.11), we have

$$\tilde{X}(k) = X(e^{j\omega})\big|_{\omega = \frac{2\pi}{N}k} \qquad \textbf{(5.14)}$$

Let

$$\omega_1 \triangleq \frac{2\pi}{N} \qquad \text{and} \qquad \omega_k \triangleq \frac{2\pi}{N}k = k\omega_1$$

Then the DFS $X(k) = X(e^{j\omega_k}) = X(e^{jk\omega_1})$, which means that the DFS is obtained by *evenly sampling* the DTFT at $\omega_1 = \frac{2\pi}{N}$ intervals. From (5.12) and (5.14), we observe that the DFS representation gives us a sampling mechanism in the frequency domain that, in principle, is similar to sampling in the time domain. The interval $\omega_1 = \frac{2\pi}{N}$ is the *sampling interval* in the frequency domain. It is also called the *frequency resolution* because it tells us how close the frequency samples (or measurements) are.

□ **EXAMPLE 5.3**   Let $x(n) = \{0, 1, 2, 3\}$.
$\qquad\qquad\qquad\qquad\quad\uparrow$

a. Compute its discrete-time Fourier transform $X(e^{j\omega})$.
b. Sample $X(e^{j\omega})$ at $k\omega_1 = \frac{2\pi}{4}k$, $\;k = 0, 1, 2, 3$ and show that it is equal to $\tilde{X}(k)$ in Example 5.1.

Solution   The sequence $x(n)$ is not periodic but is of finite duration.

a. The discrete-time Fourier transform is given by

$$X(e^{j\omega}) = \sum_{n=-\infty}^{\infty} x(n)e^{-j\omega n} = e^{-j\omega} + 2e^{-j2\omega} + 3e^{-j3\omega}$$

b. Sampling at $k\omega_1 = \frac{2\pi}{4}k$, $\;k = 0, 1, 2, 3$, we obtain

$$X(e^{j0}) = 1 + 2 + 3 = 6 = \tilde{X}(0)$$
$$X(e^{j2\pi/4}) = e^{-j2\pi/4} + 2e^{-j4\pi/4} + 3e^{-j6\pi/4} = -2 + 2j = \tilde{X}(1)$$
$$X(e^{j4\pi/4}) = e^{-j4\pi/4} + 2e^{-j8\pi/4} + 3e^{-j12\pi/4} = 2 = \tilde{X}(2)$$
$$X(e^{j6\pi/4}) = e^{-j6\pi/4} + 2e^{-j12\pi/4} + 3e^{-j18\pi/4} = -2 - 2j = \tilde{X}(3)$$

as expected.   □

5.2 SAMPLING AND RECONSTRUCTION IN THE z-DOMAIN

Let $x(n)$ be an arbitrary absolutely summable sequence, which may be of infinite duration. Its z-transform is given by

$$X(z) = \sum_{m=-\infty}^{\infty} x(m) z^{-m}$$

and we assume that the ROC of $X(z)$ includes the unit circle. We sample $X(z)$ on the unit circle at equispaced points separated in angle by $\omega_1 = 2\pi/N$ and call it a DFS sequence,

$$\tilde{X}(k) \triangleq X(z)\big|_{z=e^{j\frac{2\pi}{N}k}}, \qquad k = 0, \pm 1, \pm 2, \dots$$

$$= \sum_{m=-\infty}^{\infty} x(m) e^{-j\frac{2\pi}{N}km} = \sum_{m=-\infty}^{\infty} x(m) W_N^{km} \qquad \textbf{(5.15)}$$

which is periodic with period N. Finally, we compute the IDFS of $\tilde{X}(k)$,

$$\tilde{x}(n) = \mathrm{IDFS}\big[\tilde{X}(k)\big]$$

which is also periodic with period N. Clearly, there must be a relationship between the arbitrary $x(n)$ and the periodic $\tilde{x}(n)$. This is an important issue. In order to compute the inverse DTFT or the inverse z-transform numerically, we must deal with a finite number of samples of $X(z)$ around the unit circle. Therefore, we must know the effect of such sampling on the time-domain sequence. This relationship is easy to obtain.

$$\tilde{x}(n) = \frac{1}{N} \sum_{k=0}^{N-1} \tilde{X}(k) W_N^{-kn} \qquad \text{[from (5.2)]}$$

$$= \frac{1}{N} \sum_{k=0}^{N-1} \left\{ \sum_{m=-\infty}^{\infty} x(m) W_N^{km} \right\} W_N^{-kn} \qquad \text{[from (5.15)]}$$

or

$$\tilde{x}(n) = \sum_{m=-\infty}^{\infty} x(m) \underbrace{\frac{1}{N} \sum_{0}^{N-1} W_N^{-k(n-m)}}_{= \begin{cases} 1, & n-m = rN \\ 0, & \text{elsewhere} \end{cases}} = \sum_{m=-\infty}^{\infty} x(m) \sum_{r=-\infty}^{\infty} \delta(n-m-rN)$$

$$= \sum_{r=-\infty}^{\infty} \sum_{m=-\infty}^{\infty} x(m) \delta(n-m-rN)$$

or

$$\tilde{x}(n) = \sum_{r=-\infty}^{\infty} x(n - rN) = \cdots + x(n + N) + x(n) + x(n - N) + \cdots \quad \textbf{(5.16)}$$

which means that when we sample $X(z)$ on the unit circle, we obtain a periodic sequence in the time domain. This sequence is a linear combination of the original $x(n)$ and its infinite replicas, each shifted by multiples of $\pm N$. This is illustrated in Example 5.5. From (5.16), we observe that if $x(n) = 0$ for $n < 0$ and $n \geq N$, then there will be no overlap or aliasing in the time domain. Hence we should be able to recognize and recover $x(n)$ from $\tilde{x}(n)$, that is,

$$x(n) = \tilde{x}(n) \text{ for } 0 \leq n \leq (N - 1)$$

or

$$x(n) = \tilde{x}(n)\mathcal{R}_N(n) = \begin{cases} \tilde{x}(n), & 0 \leq n \leq N - 1 \\ 0, & \text{elsewhere} \end{cases}$$

where $\mathcal{R}_N(n)$ is called a *rectangular window* of length N. Therefore, we have the following theorem.

■   **THEOREM 1**   *Frequency Sampling*

If $x(n)$ is time-limited (i.e., of finite duration) to $[0, N - 1]$, then N samples of $X(z)$ on the unit circle determine $X(z)$ for all z.

□   **EXAMPLE 5.4**   Let $x_1(n) = \{6, 5, 4, 3, 2, 1\}$. Its DTFT $X_1(e^{j\omega})$ is sampled at
$\qquad\qquad\qquad\qquad\quad\uparrow$

$$\omega_k = \frac{2\pi k}{4}, \quad k = 0, \pm 1, \pm 2, \pm 3, \ldots$$

to obtain a DFS sequence $\tilde{X}_2(k)$. Determine the sequence $\tilde{x}_2(n)$, which is the inverse DFS of $\tilde{X}_2(k)$.

Solution   Without computing the DTFT, the DFS, or the inverse DFS, we can evaluate $\tilde{x}_2(n)$ by using the aliasing formula (5.16).

$$\tilde{x}_2(n) = \sum_{r=-\infty}^{\infty} x_1(n - 4r)$$

Thus $x(4)$ is aliased into $x(0)$, and $x(5)$ is aliased into $x(1)$. Hence

$$\tilde{x}_2(n) = \{\ldots, 8, 6, 4, 3, 8, 6, 4, 3, 8, 6, 4, 3, \ldots\}$$
$$\uparrow$$
$\qquad\qquad\qquad\qquad\qquad\qquad\qquad\qquad\qquad\qquad\qquad\qquad\qquad$ □

☐ **EXAMPLE 5.5**   Let $x(n) = (0.7)^n\, u(n)$. Sample its z-transform on the unit circle with $N = 5$, 10, 20, 50 and study its effect in the time domain.

Solution   From Table 4.1, the z-transform of $x(n)$ is

$$X(z) = \frac{1}{1 - 0.7z^{-1}} = \frac{z}{z - 0.7}, \quad |z| > 0.7$$

We can now use MATLAB to implement the sampling operation

$$\tilde{X}(k) = X(z)\big|_{z=e^{j2\pi k/N}}, \quad k = 0, \pm 1, \pm 2, \dots$$

and the inverse DFS computation to determine the corresponding time-domain sequence. The MATLAB script for $N = 5$ is as follows.

```
>> N = 5; k = 0:1:N-1;                              % Sample index
>> wk = 2*pi*k/N; zk = exp(j*wk);                   % Samples of z
>> Xk = (zk)./(zk-0.7);                             % DFS as samples of X(z)
>> xn = real(idfs(Xk,N));                           % IDFS
>> xtilde = xn'* ones(1,8); xtilde = (xtilde(:))';  % Periodic sequence
>> subplot(2,2,1); stem(0:39,xtilde);axis([0,40,-0.1,1.5])
>> ylabel('Amplitude'); title('N=5')
```

The plots in Figure 5.3 clearly demonstrate the aliasing in the time domain, especially for $N = 5$ and $N = 10$. For large values of N, the tail end of $x(n)$

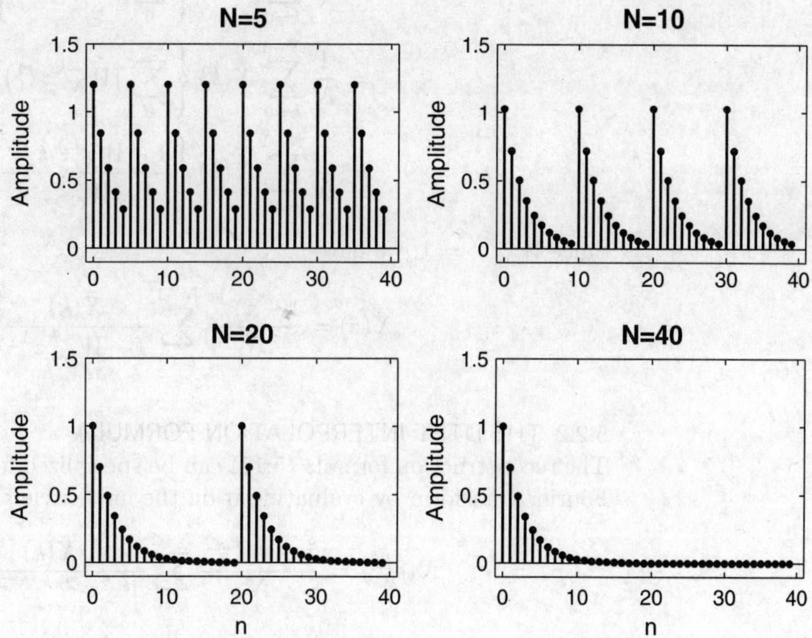

FIGURE 5.3   *Plots in Example 5.5*

is sufficiently small to result in any appreciable amount of aliasing in practice. Such information is useful in effectively truncating an infinite-duration sequence prior to taking its transform.　　　　$\square$

5.2.1 THE z-TRANSFORM RECONSTRUCTION FORMULA

Let $x(n)$ be time-limited to $[0, N-1]$. Then from Theorem 1 we should be able to recover the z-transform $X(z)$ using its samples $\tilde{X}(k)$. This is given by

$$X(z) = \mathcal{Z}\left[x(n)\right] = \mathcal{Z}\left[\tilde{x}(n)\mathcal{R}_N(n)\right]$$

$$= \mathcal{Z}[\,\mathrm{IDFS}\{\underbrace{\tilde{X}(k)}_{\text{Samples of } X(z)}\}\mathcal{R}_N(n)]$$

This approach results in the z-domain reconstruction formula:

$$X(z) = \sum_{0}^{N-1} x(n)z^{-n} = \sum_{0}^{N-1} \tilde{x}(n)z^{-n}$$

$$= \sum_{0}^{N-1}\left\{\frac{1}{N}\sum_{0}^{N-1}\tilde{X}(k)W_N^{-kn}\right\}z^{-n}$$

$$= \frac{1}{N}\sum_{k=0}^{N-1}\tilde{X}(k)\left\{\sum_{0}^{N-1}W_N^{-kn}z^{-n}\right\}$$

$$= \frac{1}{N}\sum_{k=0}^{N-1}\tilde{X}(k)\left\{\sum_{0}^{N-1}\left(W_N^{-k}z^{-1}\right)^n\right\}$$

$$= \frac{1}{N}\sum_{k=0}^{N-1}\tilde{X}(k)\left\{\frac{1-W_N^{-kN}z^{-N}}{1-W_N^{-k}z^{-1}}\right\}$$

Since $W_N^{-kN} = 1$, we have

$$X(z) = \frac{1-z^{-N}}{N}\sum_{k=0}^{N-1}\frac{\tilde{X}(k)}{1-W_N^{-k}z^{-1}} \tag{5.17}$$

5.2.2 THE DTFT INTERPOLATION FORMULA

The reconstruction formula (5.17) can be specialized for the discrete-time Fourier transform by evaluating it on the unit circle $z = e^{j\omega}$. Then

$$X(e^{j\omega}) = \frac{1-e^{-j\omega N}}{N}\sum_{k=0}^{N-1}\frac{\tilde{X}(k)}{1-e^{j2\pi k/N}e^{-j\omega}}$$

$$= \sum_{k=0}^{N-1}\tilde{X}(k)\frac{1-e^{-j\omega N}}{N\left\{1-e^{j2\pi k/N}e^{-j\omega}\right\}}$$

Consider

$$\frac{1 - e^{-j\omega N}}{N\left\{1 - e^{j2\pi k/N}e^{-j\omega}\right\}} = \frac{1 - e^{-j(\omega - \frac{2\pi k}{N})N}}{N\left\{1 - e^{-j(\omega - \frac{2\pi k}{N})}\right\}}$$

$$= \frac{e^{-j\frac{N}{2}(\omega - \frac{2\pi k}{N})}}{e^{-\frac{1}{2}j(\omega - \frac{2\pi k}{N})}}\left\{\frac{\sin\left[(\omega - \frac{2\pi k}{N})\frac{N}{2}\right]}{N\sin\left[(\omega - \frac{2\pi k}{N})\frac{1}{2}\right]}\right\}$$

Let

$$\Phi(\omega) \triangleq \frac{\sin(\frac{\omega N}{2})}{N\sin(\frac{\omega}{2})}e^{-j\omega(\frac{N-1}{2})} : \text{an interpolating function} \qquad (5.18)$$

Then

$$X(e^{j\omega}) = \sum_{k=0}^{N-1} \tilde{X}(k)\Phi\left(\omega - \frac{2\pi k}{N}\right) \qquad (5.19)$$

This is the DTFT interpolation formula to reconstruct $X(e^{j\omega})$ from its samples $\tilde{X}(k)$. Since $\Phi(0) = 1$, we have that $X(e^{j2\pi k/N}) = \tilde{X}(k)$, which means that the interpolation is exact at sampling points. Recall the time-domain interpolation formula (3.33) for analog signals:

$$x_a(t) = \sum_{n=-\infty}^{\infty} x(n)\operatorname{sinc}\left[F_s(t - nT_s)\right] \qquad (5.20)$$

The DTFT interpolating formula (5.19) looks similar.

However, there are some differences. First, the time-domain formula (5.20) reconstructs an arbitrary *nonperiodic* analog signal, while the frequency-domain formula (5.19) gives us a periodic waveform. Second, in (5.19) we use a $\frac{\sin(Nx)}{N\sin x}$ interpolation function instead of our more familiar $\frac{\sin x}{x}$ (sinc) function. The $\Phi(\omega)$ function is a periodic function and hence is known as a *periodic-sinc* function. It is also known as the Dirichlet function. This is the function we observed in Example 5.2.

5.2.3 MATLAB IMPLEMENTATION
The interpolation formula (5.19) suffers the same fate as that of (5.20) while trying to implement it in practice. One has to generate several interpolating functions (5.18) and perform their linear combinations to obtain the discrete-time Fourier transform $X(e^{j\omega})$ from its computed samples $\tilde{X}(k)$. Furthermore, in MATLAB we have to evaluate (5.19) on a finer grid over $0 \leq \omega \leq 2\pi$. This is clearly an inefficient approach. Another approach is to use the cubic spline interpolation function as an efficient approximation to (5.19). This is what we did to implement the time-domain interpolation formula for analog signals in Chapter 3. However, there is an alternate and efficient approach based on the DFT, which we will study in the next section.

5.3 THE DISCRETE FOURIER TRANSFORM

The discrete Fourier series provides a mechanism for numerically computing the discrete-time Fourier transform. It also alerts us to a potential problem of aliasing in the time domain. Mathematics dictates that the sampling of the discrete-time Fourier transform result in a periodic sequence $\tilde{x}(n)$. But most of the signals in practice are not periodic. They are likely to be of finite duration. How can we develop a numerically computable Fourier representation for such signals? Theoretically, we can take care of this problem by defining a periodic signal whose primary shape is that of the finite-duration signal and then using the DFS on this periodic signal. Practically, we define a new transform called the *discrete Fourier transform* (DFT), which is the primary period of the DFS. This DFT is the ultimate numerically computable Fourier transform for arbitrary finite-duration sequences.

First we define a finite-duration sequence $x(n)$ that has N samples over $0 \leq n \leq N-1$ as an N-*point sequence*. Let $\tilde{x}(n)$ be a periodic signal of period N, created using the N-point sequence $x(n)$; that is, from (5.19),

$$\tilde{x}(n) = \sum_{r=-\infty}^{\infty} x(n - rN)$$

This is a somewhat cumbersome representation. Using the modulo-N operation on the argument, we can simplify it to

$$\tilde{x}(n) = x(n \bmod N) \tag{5.21}$$

A simple way to interpret this operation is the following: if the argument n is between 0 and $N-1$, then leave it as it is; otherwise add or subtract multiples of N from n until the result is between 0 and $N-1$. Note carefully that (5.21) is valid only if the length of $x(n)$ is N or less. Furthermore, we use the following convenient notation to denote the modulo-N operation:

$$x((n))_N \triangleq x(n \bmod N) \tag{5.22}$$

Then the compact relationships between $x(n)$ and $\tilde{x}(n)$ are

$$\tilde{x}(n) = x((n))_N \qquad \text{(Periodic extension)}$$

$$x(n) = \tilde{x}(n)\mathcal{R}_N(n) \quad \text{(Window operation)} \tag{5.23}$$

The `rem(n,N)` function in MATLAB determines the remainder after dividing n by N. This function can be used to implement our modulo-N

operation when $n \geq 0$. When $n < 0$, we need to modify the result to obtain correct values. This is shown below in the `m=mod(n,N)` function.

```
function m = mod(n,N)
% Computes m = (n mod N) index
% ----------------------------
% m = mod(n,N)
m = rem(n,N);   m = m+N;   m = rem(m,N);
```

In this function, `n` can be any integer array, and the array `m` contains the corresponding modulo-N values.

From the frequency sampling theorem, we conclude that N equispaced samples of the discrete-time Fourier transform $X(e^{j\omega})$ of the N-point sequence $x(n)$ can uniquely reconstruct $X(e^{j\omega})$. These N samples around the unit circle are called the discrete Fourier transform coefficients. Let $\tilde{X}(k) = \mathrm{DFS}\, \tilde{x}(n)$, which is a periodic sequence (and hence of infinite duration). Its primary interval then is the discrete Fourier transform, which is of finite duration. These notions are made clear in the following definitions. The discrete Fourier transform of an N-point sequence is given by

$$X(k) \stackrel{\triangle}{=} \mathrm{DFT}\,[x(n)] = \begin{cases} \tilde{X}(k), & 0 \leq k \leq N-1 \\ 0, & \text{elsewhere} \end{cases} = \tilde{X}(k)\mathcal{R}_N(k)$$

or

$$X(k) = \sum_{n=0}^{N-1} x(n)W_N^{nk}, \quad 0 \leq k \leq N-1 \qquad (5.24)$$

Note that the DFT $X(k)$ is also an N-point sequence; that is, it is not defined outside of $0 \leq k \leq N-1$. From (5.23), $\tilde{X}(k) = X((k))_N$; that is, outside the $0 \leq k \leq N-1$ interval only the DFS $\tilde{X}(k)$ is defined, which of course is the periodic extension of $X(k)$. Finally, $X(k) = \tilde{X}(k)\mathcal{R}_N(k)$ means that the DFT $X(k)$ is the primary interval of $\tilde{X}(k)$.

The inverse discrete Fourier transform of an N-point DFT $X(k)$ is given by

$$x(n) \stackrel{\triangle}{=} \mathrm{IDFT}\,[X(k)] = \tilde{x}(n)\mathcal{R}_N(n)$$

or

$$x(n) = \frac{1}{N} \sum_{k=0}^{N-1} X(k)W_N^{-kn}, \quad 0 \leq n \leq N-1 \qquad (5.25)$$

Once again, $x(n)$ is not defined outside $0 \leq n \leq N-1$. The extension of $x(n)$ outside this range is $\tilde{x}(n)$.

5.3.1 MATLAB IMPLEMENTATION

It is clear from the discussions at the top of this section that the DFS is practically equivalent to the DFT when $0 \leq n \leq N - 1$. Therefore, the implementation of the DFT can be done in a similar fashion. If $x(n)$ and $X(k)$ are arranged as column vectors $\mathbf{x}$ and $\mathbf{X}$, respectively, then from (5.24) and (5.25) we have

$$\mathbf{X} = \mathbf{W}_N \mathbf{x}$$
$$\mathbf{x} = \frac{1}{N} \mathbf{W}_N^* \mathbf{X} \tag{5.26}$$

where $\mathbf{W}_N$ is the matrix defined in (5.7) and will now be called a *DFT matrix*. Hence the earlier `dfs` and `idfs` MATLAB functions can be renamed as the `dft` and `idft` functions to implement the discrete Fourier transform computations.

```matlab
function [Xk] = dft(xn,N)
% Computes discrete Fourier transform
% ----------------------------------
% [Xk] = dft(xn,N)
% Xk = DFT coeff. array over 0 <= k <= N-1
% xn = N-point finite-duration sequence
%  N = Length of DFT
%
n = [0:1:N-1];                    % Row vector for n
k = [0:1:N-1];                    % Row vector for k
WN = exp(-j*2*pi/N);              % Wn factor
nk = n'*k;                        % Creates an N by N matrix of nk values
WNnk = WN .^ nk;                  % DFT matrix
Xk = xn * WNnk;                   % Row vector for DFT coefficients

function [xn] = idft(Xk,N)
% Computes inverse discrete transform
% ----------------------------------
% [xn] = idft(Xk,N)
% xn = N-point sequence over 0 <= n <= N-1
% Xk = DFT coeff. array over 0 <= k <= N-1
%  N = length of DFT
%
n = [0:1:N-1];                    % Row vector for n
k = [0:1:N-1];                    % Row vector for k
WN = exp(-j*2*pi/N);              % Wn factor
nk = n'*k;                        % Creates an N by N matrix of nk values
WNnk = WN .^ (-nk);               % IDFT matrix
xn = (Xk * WNnk)/N;               % Row vector for IDFT values
```

□   **EXAMPLE 5.6**   Let $x(n)$ be a four-point sequence:

$$x(n) = \begin{cases} 1, & 0 \leq n \leq 3 \\ 0, & \text{otherwise} \end{cases}$$

   a. Compute the discrete-time Fourier transform $X(e^{j\omega})$ and plot its magnitude and phase.
   b. Compute the four-point DFT of $x(n)$.

Solution   **a.** The discrete-time Fourier transform is given by

$$X(e^{j\omega}) = \sum_{0}^{3} x(n)e^{-j\omega n} = 1 + e^{-j\omega} + e^{-j2\omega} + e^{-j3\omega}$$

$$= \frac{1 - e^{-j4\omega}}{1 - e^{-j\omega}} = \frac{\sin(2\omega)}{\sin(\omega/2)} e^{-j3\omega/2}$$

Hence

$$\left| X(e^{j\omega}) \right| = \left| \frac{\sin(2\omega)}{\sin(\omega/2)} \right|$$

and

$$\angle X(e^{j\omega}) = \begin{cases} -\dfrac{3\omega}{2}, & \text{when } \dfrac{\sin(2\omega)}{\sin(\omega/2)} > 0 \\ -\dfrac{3\omega}{2} \pm \pi, & \text{when } \dfrac{\sin(2\omega)}{\sin(\omega/2)} < 0 \end{cases}$$

The plots are shown in Figure 5.4.
   b. Let us denote the four-point DFT by $X_4(k)$. Then

$$X_4(k) = \sum_{n=0}^{3} x(n) W_4^{nk}; \quad k = 0, 1, 2, 3; \quad W_4 = e^{-j2\pi/4} = -j$$

These calculations are similar to those in Example 5.1. We can also use MATLAB to compute this DFT.

```
>> x = [1,1,1,1]; N = 4;  X = dft(x,N);
>> magX = abs(X), phaX = angle(X)*180/pi
magX =
     4.0000     0.0000     0.0000     0.0000
phaX =
          0 -134.9810  -90.0000  -44.9979
```

Hence

$$X_4(k) = \{4, 0, 0, 0\}$$
$$\uparrow$$

Note that when the magnitude sample is zero, the corresponding angle is not zero. This is due to a particular algorithm used by MATLAB to compute the

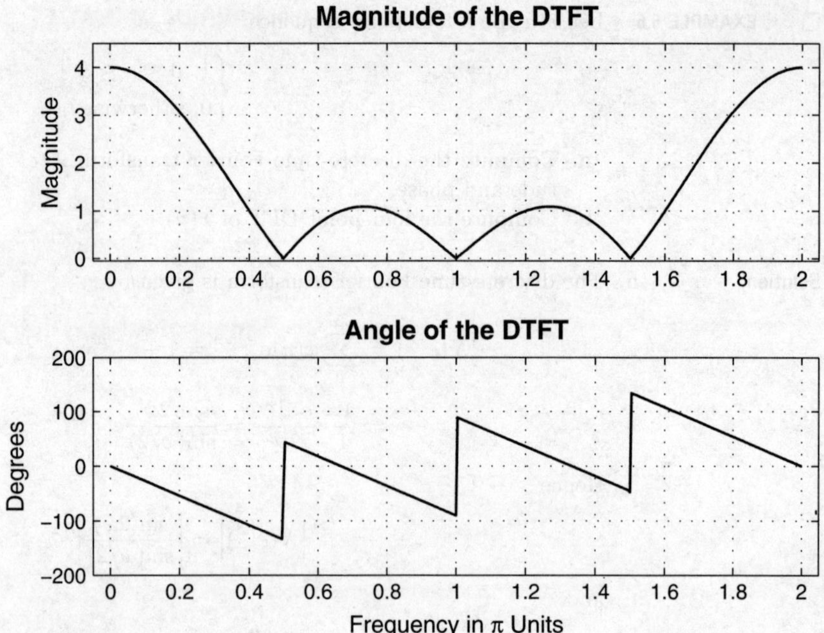

FIGURE 5.4   *The DTFT plots in Example 5.6*

angle part. Generally, these angles should be ignored. The plot of DFT values is shown in Figure 5.5. The plot of $X(e^{j\omega})$ is also shown as a dashed line for comparison. From the plot in Figure 5.5, we observe that X_4 correctly gives four samples of $X(e^{j\omega})$, but it has only one nonzero sample. Is this surprising? By looking at the four-point $x(n)$, which contains all 1's, one must conclude that its periodic extension is

$$\tilde{x}(n) = 1, \ \forall n$$

which is a constant (or a DC) signal. This is what is predicted by the DFT $X_4(k)$, which has a nonzero sample at $k = 0$ (or $\omega = 0$) and has no values at other frequencies.   □

☐   **EXAMPLE 5.7**   How can we obtain other samples of the DTFT $X(e^{j\omega})$?

Solution   It is clear that we should sample at dense (or finer) frequencies; that is, we should increase N. Suppose we take twice the number of points, or $N = 8$ instead of $N = 4$. This we can achieve by treating $x(n)$ as an eight-point sequence by *appending* four zeros.

$$x(n) = \{1, 1, 1, 1, 0, 0, 0, 0\}$$
$$\uparrow$$

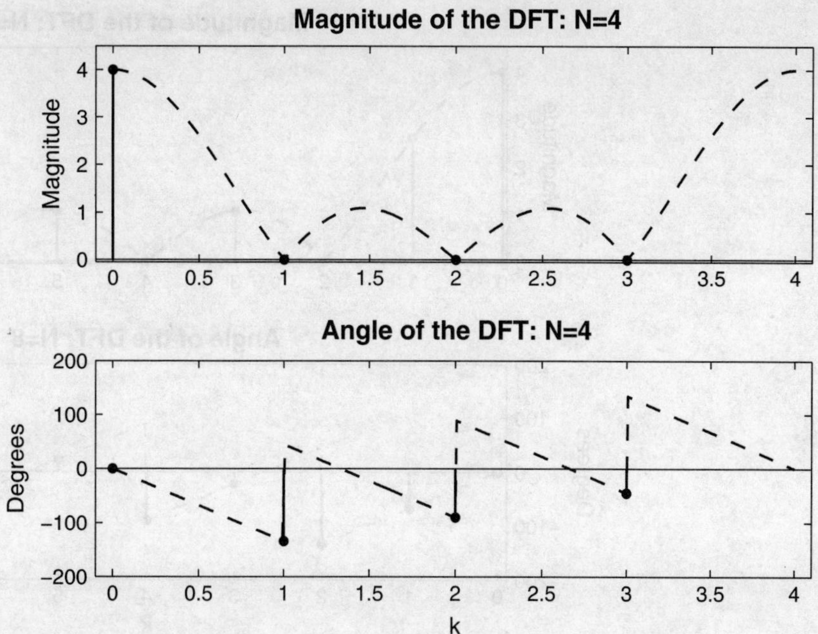

FIGURE 5.5   *The DFT plots of Example 5.6*

This is a very important operation called a *zero-padding operation*. This operation is necessary in practice to obtain a *dense spectrum* of signals, as we shall see. Let $X_8(k)$ be an eight-point DFT, then

$$X_8(k) = \sum_{n=0}^{7} x(n)W_8^{nk}; \quad k = 0, 1, \ldots, 7; \quad W_8 = e^{-j\pi/4}$$

In this case, the frequency resolution is $\omega_1 = 2\pi/8 = \pi/4$.

MATLAB script:

```
>> x = [1,1,1,1, zeros(1,4)]; N = 8;  X = dft(x,N);
>> magX = abs(X), phaX = angle(X)*180/pi
magX =
    4.0000    2.6131    0.0000    1.0824    0.0000    1.0824    0.0000    2.6131
phaX =
         0  -67.5000 -134.9810  -22.5000  -90.0000   22.5000  -44.9979   67.5000
```

Hence
$$X_8(k) = \{4,\ 2.6131e^{-j67.5^\circ},\ 0,\ 1.0824e^{-j22.5^\circ},\ 0,\ 1.0824e^{j22.5^\circ},$$
$$0,\ 2.6131e^{j67.5^\circ}\}$$

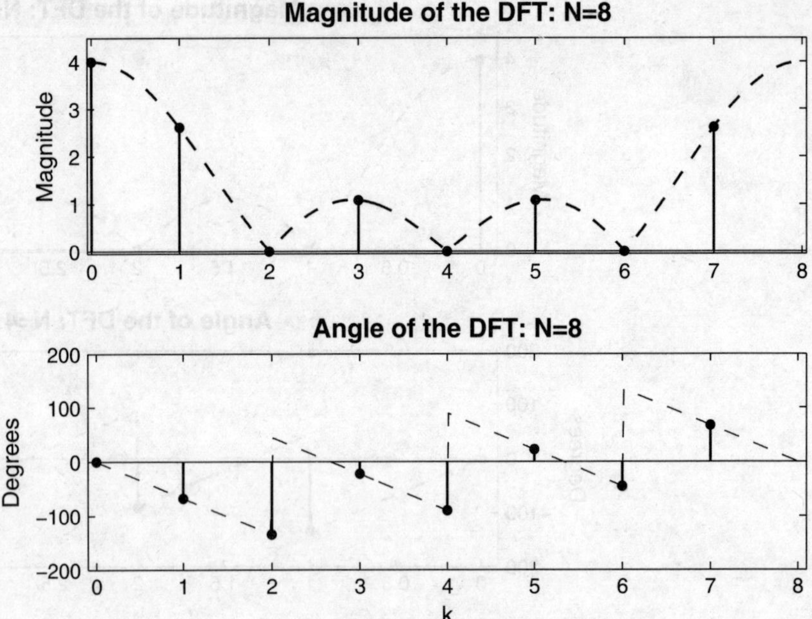

FIGURE 5.6　　*The DFT plots of Example 5.7: $N = 8$*

which is shown in Figure 5.6. Continuing further, if we treat $x(n)$ as a 16-point sequence by padding 12 zeros, such that

$$x(n) = \{\underset{\uparrow}{1}, 1, 1, 1, 0, 0, 0, 0, 0, 0, 0, 0, 0, 0, 0, 0\}$$

then the frequency resolution is $\omega_1 = 2\pi/16 = \pi/8$ and $W_{16} = e^{-j\pi/8}$. Therefore, we get a more dense spectrum with spectral samples separated by $\pi/8$. The sketch of $X_{16}(k)$ is shown in Figure 5.7.

It should be clear then that if we obtain many more spectral samples by choosing a large N value, then the resulting DFT samples will be very close to each other and we will obtain plot values similar to those in Figure 5.4. However, the displayed stem-plots will be dense. In this situation, a better approach to display samples is to either show them using dots or join the sample values using the `plot` command (i.e., using the FOH studied in Chapter 3). Figure 5.8 shows the magnitude and phase of the 128-point DFT $x_{128}(k)$ obtained by padding 120 zeros. The DFT magnitude plot overlaps the DTFT magnitude plot shown as dotted-line, while the phase plot shows discrepancy at discontinuities due to finite N value, which should be expected.　　　　　□

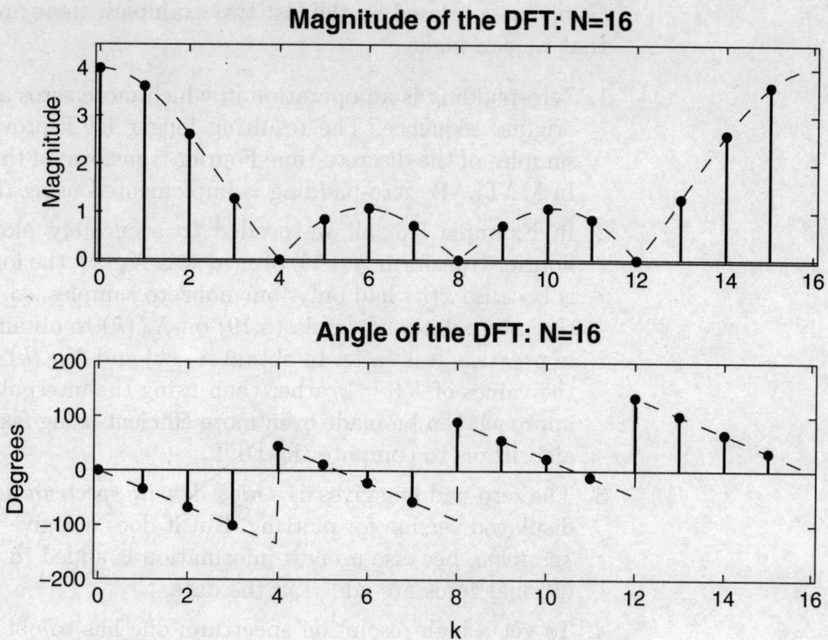

FIGURE 5.7 *The DFT plots of Example 5.7: $N = 16$*

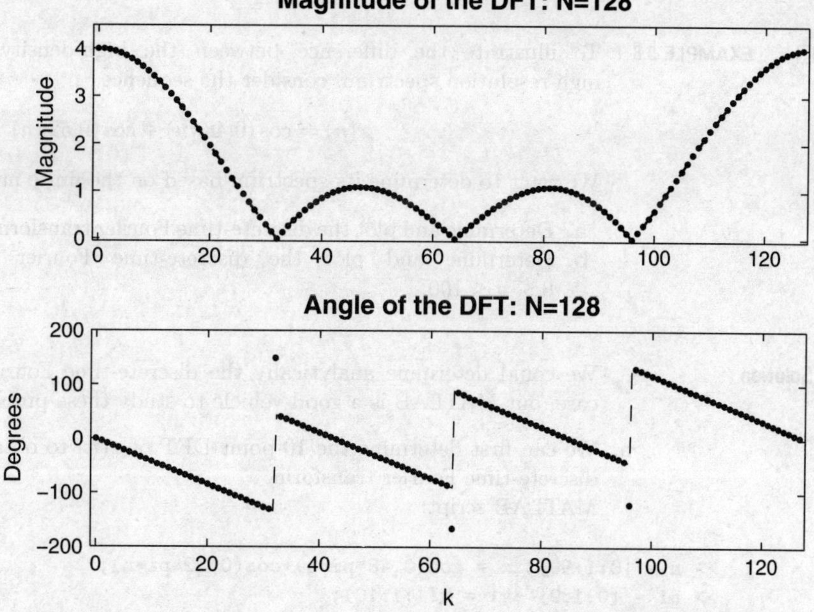

FIGURE 5.8 *The DFT plots of Example 5.7 for $N = 128$ are shown as line plots*

Comments: Based on the last two examples, there are several comments that we can make.

1. Zero-padding is an operation in which more zeros are appended to the original sequence. The resulting longer DFT provides closely spaced samples of the discrete-time Fourier transform of the original sequence. In MATLAB, zero-padding is implemented using the **zeros** function.

2. In Example 5.6, all we needed to accurately plot the discrete-time Fourier transform $X(e^{j\omega})$ of $x(n)$ was $X_4(k)$, the four-point DFT. This is because $x(n)$ had only four nonzero samples, so we could have used the interpolation formula (5.19) on $X_4(k)$ to obtain $X(e^{j\omega})$. However, in practice, it is easier to obtain $X_8(k)$ and $X_{16}(k)$, and so on, to *fill in* the values of $X(e^{j\omega})$ rather than using the interpolation formula. This approach can be made even more efficient using fast Fourier transform algorithms to compute the DFT.

3. The zero-padding gives us a *high-density spectrum* and provides a better displayed version for plotting. But it does not give us a *high-resolution spectrum*, because no new information is added to the signal; only additional zeros are added in the data.

4. To get a high-resolution spectrum, one has to obtain more data from the experiment or observations (see Example 5.8, below). There are also other advanced methods that use additional side information or nonlinear techniques.

□   **EXAMPLE 5.8**   To illustrate the difference between the high-density spectrum and the high-resolution spectrum, consider the sequence

$$x(n) = \cos(0.48\pi n) + \cos(0.52\pi n)$$

We want to determine its spectrum based on the finite number of samples.

    a. Determine and plot the discrete-time Fourier transform of $x(n)$, $0 \le n \le 10$.
    b. Determine and plot the discrete-time Fourier transform of $x(n)$, $0 \le n \le 100$.

Solution   We could determine analytically the discrete-time Fourier transform in each case, but MATLAB is a good vehicle to study these problems.

    a. We can first determine the 10-point DFT of $x(n)$ to obtain an estimate of its discrete-time Fourier transform.
    MATLAB script:

```
>> n = [0:1:99]; x = cos(0.48*pi*n)+cos(0.52*pi*n);
>> n1 = [0:1:9] ;y1 = x(1:1:10);
>> subplot(2,1,1) ;stem(n1,y1); title('signal x(n), 0 <= n <= 9');xlabel('n')
```

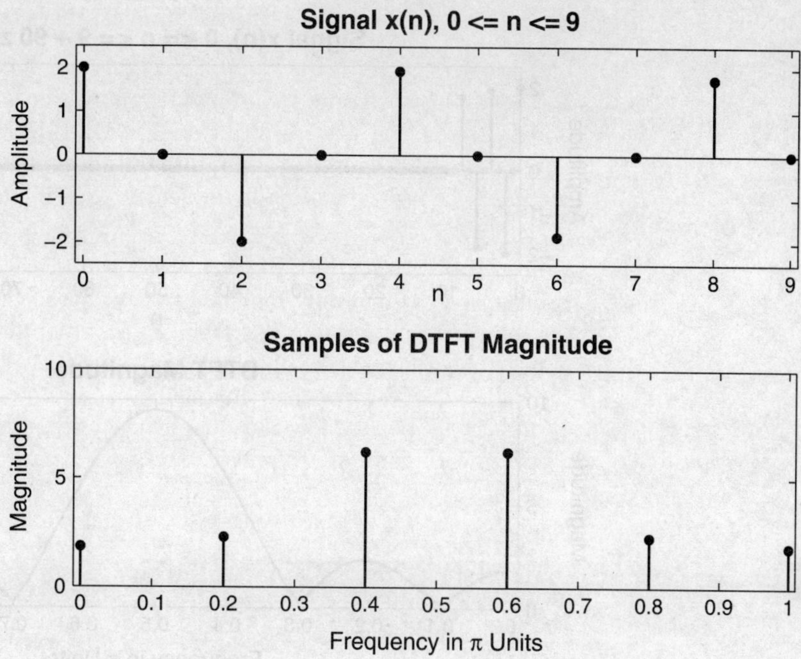

FIGURE 5.9 *Signal and its spectrum in Example 5.8a: $N = 10$*

```
>> Y1 = dft(y1,10); magY1 = abs(Y1(1:1:6));
>> k1 = 0:1:5 ;w1 = 2*pi/10*k1;
>> subplot(2,1,2);stem(w1/pi,magY1);title('Samples of DTFT Magnitude');
>> xlabel('Frequency in \pi Units')
```

The plots in Figure 5.9 show there aren't enough samples to draw any conclusions. Therefore, we will pad 90 zeros to obtain a dense spectrum. As explained in Example 5.7, this spectrum is plotted using the **plot** command.

MATLAB script:

```
>> n2 = [0:1:99]; y2 = [x(1:1:10) zeros(1,90)];
>> subplot(2,1,1) ;stem(n2,y2) ;title('signal x(n), 0 <= n <= 9 + 90 zeros');
>> xlabel('n')
>> Y2 =dft(y2,100); magY2 = abs(Y2(1:1:51));
>> k2 = 0:1:50; w2 = 2*pi/100*k2;
>> subplot(2,1,2); plot(w2/pi,magY2); title('DTFT Magnitude');
>> xlabel('Frequency in \pi Units')
```

Now the plot shows that the sequence has a dominant frequency at $\omega = 0.5\pi$ (Figure 5.10). This fact is not supported by the original sequence, which has two

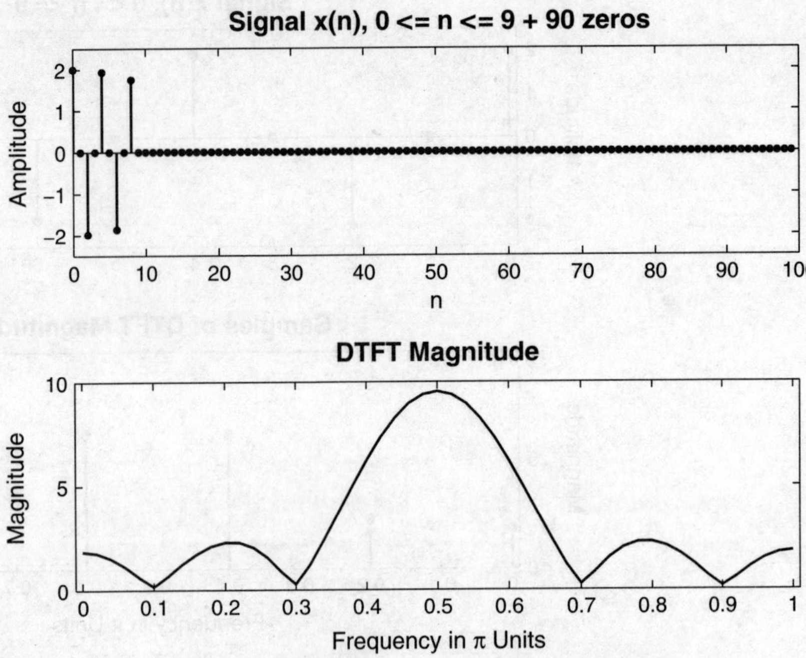

FIGURE 5.10 *Signal and its spectrum in Example 5.8a: $N = 100$*

frequencies. The zero-padding provided a smoother version of the spectrum in Figure 5.9.

b. To get better spectral information, we will take the first 100 samples of $x(n)$ and determine its discrete-time Fourier transform.

MATLAB script:

```
>> subplot(2,1,1); stem(n,x);
>> title('signal x(n), 0 <= n <= 99'); xlabel('n')
>> X = dft(x,100); magX = abs(X(1:1:51));
>> k = 0:1:50; w = 2*pi/100*k;
>> subplot(2,1,2); plot(w/pi,magX); title('DTFT Magnitude');
>> xlabel('Frequency in \pi Units')
```

Now the discrete-time Fourier transform plot clearly shows two frequencies, which are very close to each other (Figure 5.11). This is the high-resolution spectrum of $x(n)$ Note that padding more zeros to the 100-point sequence will result in a smoother rendition of the spectrum in Figure 5.11 but will not reveal any new information. Readers are encouraged to verify this.   □

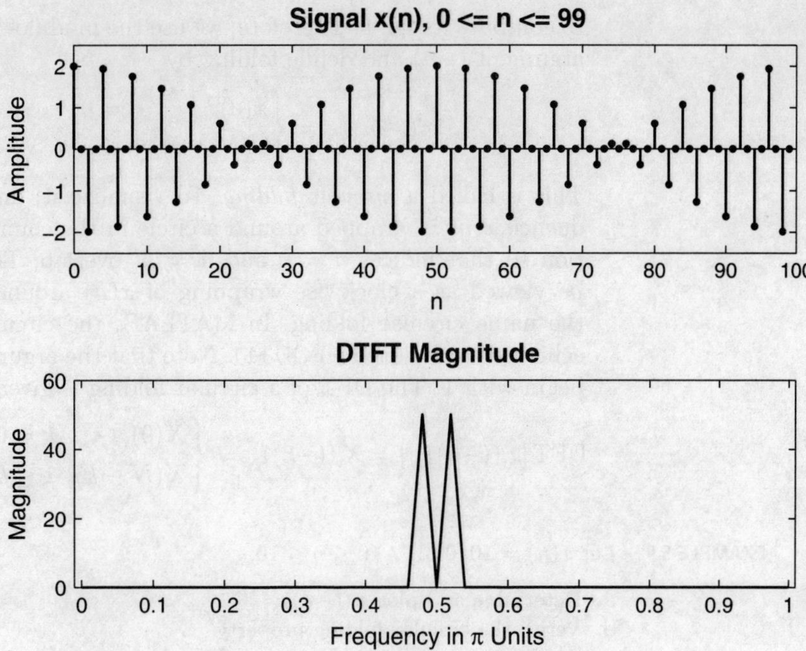

FIGURE 5.11   *Signal and its spectrum in Example 5.8b:* $N = 100$

5.4 PROPERTIES OF THE DISCRETE FOURIER TRANSFORM

The DFT properties are derived from those of the DFS because mathematically DFS is the valid representation. We discuss several useful properties, which are given without proof. These properties also apply to the DFS with necessary changes. Let $X(k)$ be an N-point DFT of the sequence $x(n)$. Unless otherwise stated, the N-point DFTs will be used in these properties.

1. **Linearity:** The DFT is a linear transform

$$\text{DFT}\left[ax_1(n) + bx_2(n)\right] = a\,\text{DFT}\left[x_1(n)\right] + b\,\text{DFT}\left[x_2(n)\right] \qquad \textbf{(5.27)}$$

Note: If $x_1(n)$ and $x_2(n)$ have different durations—that is, they are N_1-point and N_2-point sequences, respectively—then choose $N_3 = \max(N_1, N_2)$ and proceed by taking N_3-point DFTs.

2. **Circular folding:** If an N-point sequence is folded, then the result $x(-n)$ would not be an N-point sequence, and it would not be possible

to compute its DFT. Therefore, we use the modulo-N operation on the argument $(-n)$ and define folding by

$$x\left(\left(-n\right)\right)_N = \begin{cases} x(0), & n = 0 \\ x(N - n), & 1 \le n \le N - 1 \end{cases} \tag{5.28}$$

This is called a *circular folding*. To visualize it, imagine that the sequence $x(n)$ is wrapped around a circle in the counterclockwise direction so that indices $n = 0$ and $n = N$ overlap. Then $x((-n))_N$ can be viewed as a clockwise wrapping of $x(n)$ around the circle; hence the name circular folding. In MATLAB, the circular folding can be achieved by x=x(mod(-n,N)+1). Note that the arguments in MATLAB begin with 1. The DFT of a circular folding is given by

$$\text{DFT}\left[x\left(\left(-n\right)\right)_N\right] = X\left(\left(-k\right)\right)_N = \begin{cases} X(0), & k = 0 \\ X(N - k), & 1 \le k \le N - 1 \end{cases} \tag{5.29}$$

☐   **EXAMPLE 5.9**   Let $x(n) = 10\left(0.8\right)^n$, $0 \le n \le 10$.

     a. Determine and plot $x\left(\left(-n\right)\right)_{11}$.
     b. Verify the circular folding property.

Solution   **a.** MATLAB script:

```
>> n = 0:10; x = 10*(0.8) .^ n;  y = x(mod(-n,11)+1);
>> subplot(2,1,1); stem(n,x); title('Original Sequence')
>> xlabel('n'); ylabel('Amplitude');
>> subplot(2,1,2); stem(n,y);
>> title('Circularly Folded Sequence x((-n))_{11}');
>> xlabel('n'); ylabel('Amplitude');
```

The plots in Figure 5.12 show the effect of circular folding.

b. MATLAB script:

```
>> X = dft(x,11); Y = dft(y,11);
>> subplot(2,2,1); stem(n,real(X));
>> title('Real(DFT[x(n)])'); xlabel('k');
>> subplot(2,2,2); stem(n,imag(X));
>> title('Imag(DFT[x(n)])'); xlabel('k');
>> subplot(2,2,3); stem(n,real(Y));
>> title('Real(DFT[x((-n))_{11}])'); xlabel('k');
>> subplot(2,2,4); stem(n,imag(Y));
>> title('Imag(DFT[x((-n))_{11}])'); xlabel('k');
```

The plots in Figure 5.13 verify the property.   ☐

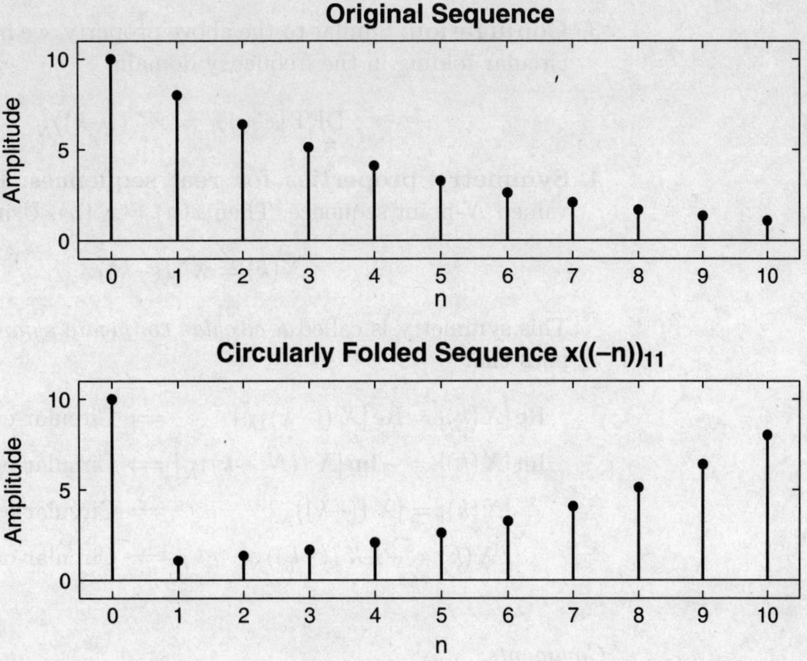

FIGURE 5.12 *Circular folding in Example 5.9a*

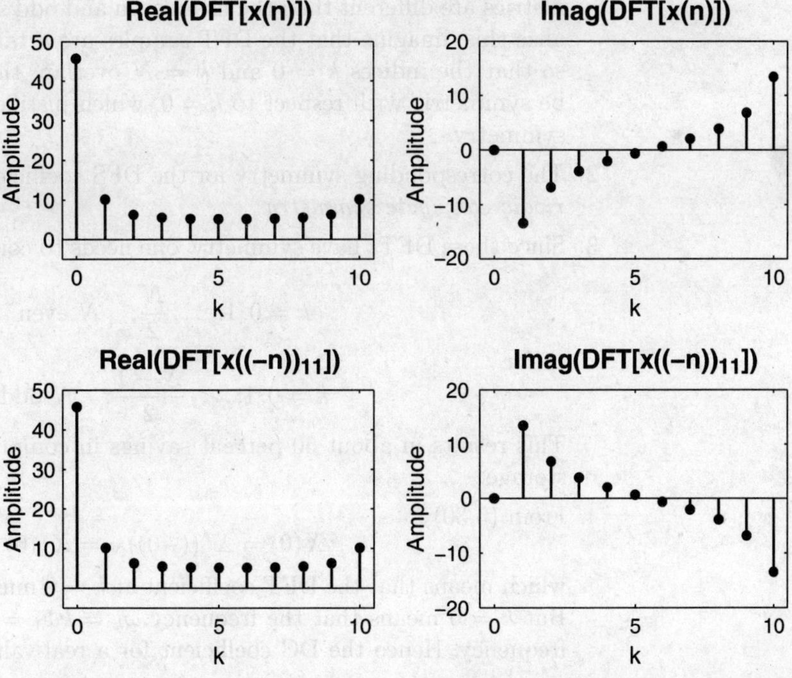

FIGURE 5.13 *Circular folding property in Example 5.9b*

3. **Conjugation:** Similar to the above property, we have to introduce the circular folding in the frequency domain:

$$\mathrm{DFT}\left[x^*(n)\right] = X^*\left((-k)\right)_N \tag{5.30}$$

4. **Symmetry properties for real sequences:** Let $x(n)$ be a real-valued N-point sequence. Then $x(n) = x^*(n)$. Using (5.30),

$$X(k) = X^*\left((-k)\right)_N \tag{5.31}$$

This symmetry is called a *circular conjugate symmetry*. It further implies that

$$
\begin{aligned}
\mathrm{Re}\left[X(k)\right] &= \mathrm{Re}\left[X\left((-k)\right)_N\right] && \Longrightarrow \text{Circular-even sequence} \\
\mathrm{Im}\left[X(k)\right] &= -\,\mathrm{Im}\left[X\left((N-k)\right)_N\right] && \Longrightarrow \text{Circular-odd sequence} \\
\left|X(k)\right| &= \left|X\left((-k)\right)_N\right| && \Longrightarrow \text{Circular-even sequence} \\
\angle X(k) &= -\angle X\left((-k)\right)_N && \Longrightarrow \text{Circular-odd sequence}
\end{aligned}
\tag{5.32}
$$

Comments:

1. Observe the magnitudes and angles of the various DFTs in Examples 5.6 and 5.7. They do satisfy the above circular symmetries. These symmetries are different than the usual even and odd symmetries. To visualize this, imagine that the DFT samples are arranged around a circle so that the indices $k = 0$ and $k = N$ overlap; then the samples will be symmetric with respect to $k = 0$, which justifies the name circular symmetry.

2. The corresponding symmetry for the DFS coefficients is called the *periodic conjugate symmetry*.

3. Since these DFTs have symmetry, one needs to compute $X(k)$ only for

$$k = 0, 1, \ldots, \frac{N}{2}; \quad N \text{ even}$$

or for

$$k = 0, 1, \ldots, \frac{N-1}{2}; \quad N \text{ odd}$$

This results in about 50 percent savings in computation as well as in storage.

4. From (5.30)

$$X(0) = X^*\left((-0)\right)_N = X^*(0)$$

which means that the DFT coefficient at $k = 0$ must be a real number. But $k = 0$ means that the frequency $\omega_k = k\omega_1 = 0$, which is the DC frequency. Hence the DC coefficient for a real-valued $x(n)$ must be a real number. In addition, if N is even, then $N/2$ is also an integer. Then from (5.32),

$$X\left(N/2\right) = X^*\left((-N/2)\right)_N = X^*\left(N/2\right)$$

which means that even the $k = N/2$ component is also real-valued. This component is called the *Nyquist component* since $k = N/2$ means that the frequency $\omega_{N/2} = (N/2)(2\pi/N) = \pi$, which is the digital Nyquist frequency.

The real-valued signals can also be decomposed into their even and odd components, $x_e(n)$ and $x_o(n)$, respectively, as discussed in Chapter 2. However, these components are not N-point sequences, and therefore we cannot take their N-point DFTs. Hence we define a new set of components using the circular folding discussed above. These are called *circular-even* and *circular-odd* components defined by

$$x_{\text{ec}}\left(n\right) \overset{\triangle}{=} \tfrac{1}{2}\left[x(n) + x\left((-n)\right)_N\right] = \begin{cases} x(0), & n = 0 \\ \tfrac{1}{2}\left[x\left(n\right) + x\left(N - n\right)\right], & 1 \le n \le N - 1 \end{cases}$$

$$x_{\text{oc}}\left(n\right) \overset{\triangle}{=} \tfrac{1}{2}\left[x(n) - x\left((-n)\right)_N\right] = \begin{cases} 0, & n = 0 \\ \tfrac{1}{2}\left[x\left(n\right) - x\left(N - n\right)\right], & 1 \le n \le N - 1 \end{cases}$$

$$(5.33)$$

Then

$$\text{DFT}\left[x_{\text{ec}}\left(n\right)\right] = \text{Re}\left[X(k)\right] = \text{Re}\left[X\left((-k)\right)_N\right]$$
$$\text{DFT}\left[x_{\text{oc}}\left(n\right)\right] = \text{Im}\left[X(k)\right] = \text{Im}\left[X\left((-k)\right)_N\right]$$

$$(5.34)$$

Implication: If $x(n)$ is real and circular-even, then its DFT is also real and circular-even. Hence only the first $0 \le n \le N/2$ coefficients are necessary for complete representation.

Using (5.33), it is easy to develop a function to decompose an N-point sequence into its circular-even and circular-odd components. The following `circevod` function uses the `mod` function given earlier to implement the modulo-N operation.

```
function [xec, xoc] = circevod(x)
% Signal decomposition into circular-even and circular-odd parts
% ---------------------------------------------------------------
% [xec, xoc] = circevod(x)
%
if any(imag(x) ~= 0)
    error('x is not a real sequence')
```

```
end
N = length(x); n = 0:(N-1);
xec = 0.5*(x + x(mod(-n,N)+1));   xoc = 0.5*(x - x(mod(-n,N)+1));
```

☐ **EXAMPLE 5.10**   Let $x(n) = 10\,(0.8)^n$, $0 \le n \le 10$ as in Example 5.9.

a. Decompose and plot the $x_{ec}(n)$ and $x_{oc}(n)$ components of $x(n)$.
b. Verify the property in (5.34).

Solution   **a.** MATLAB script:

```
>> n = 0:10; x = 10*(0.8) .^ n;
>> [xec,xoc] = circevod(x);
>> subplot(2,1,1); stem(n,xec); title('Circular-Even Component')
>> xlabel('n'); ylabel('Amplitude'); axis([-0.5,10.5,-1,11])
>> subplot(2,1,2); stem(n,xoc); title('Circular-Odd Component')
>> xlabel('n'); ylabel('Amplitude'); axis([-0.5,10.5,-4,4])
```

The plots in Figure 5.14 show the circularly symmetric components of $x(n)$.

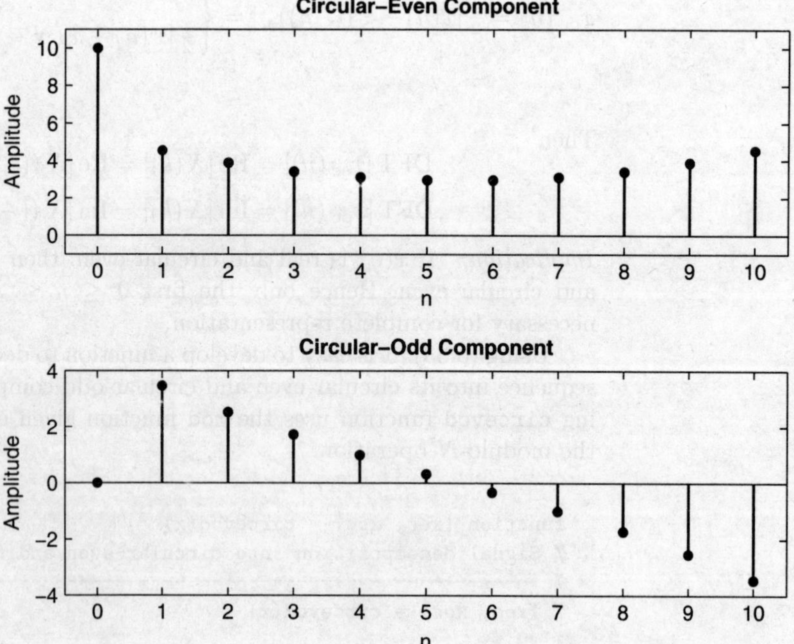

FIGURE 5.14   *Circular-even and circular-odd components of the sequence in Example 5.10a*

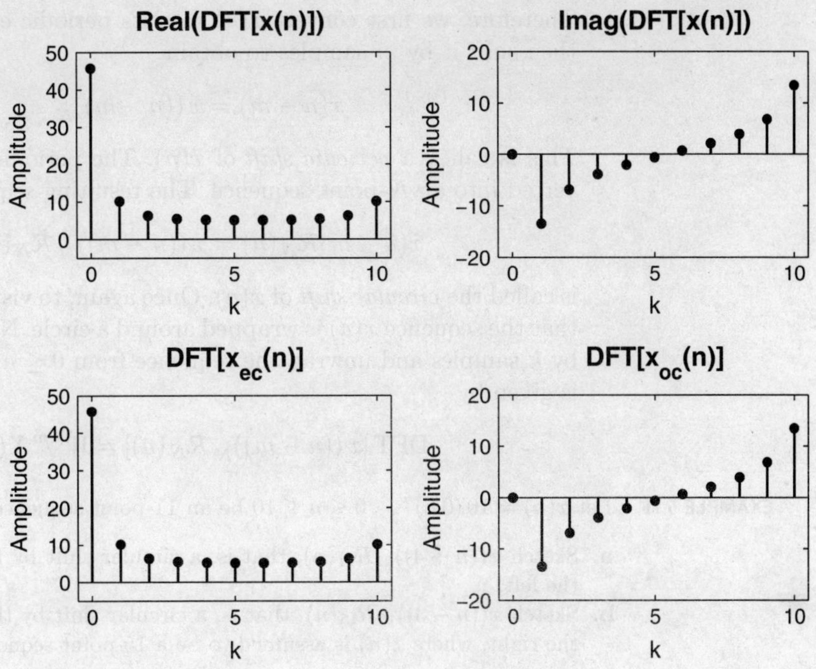

FIGURE 5.15 *Plots of DFT symmetry properties in Example 5.10b*

b. MATLAB script:

```
>> X = dft(x,11); Xec = dft(xec,11); Xoc = dft(xoc,11);
>> subplot(2,2,1); stem(n,real(X)); axis([-0.5,10.5,-5,50])
>> title('Real(DFT[x(n)])'); xlabel('k');
>> subplot(2,2,2); stem(n,imag(X)); axis([-0.5,10.5,-20,20])
>> title('Imag(DFT[x(n)])'); xlabel('k');
>> subplot(2,2,3); stem(n,real(Xec)); axis([-0.5,10.5,-5,50])
>> title('DFT[xec(n)]'); xlabel('k');
>> subplot(2,2,4); stem(n,imag(Xoc)); axis([-0.5,10.5,-20,20])
>> title('DFT[xoc(n)]'); xlabel('k');
```

From the plots in Figure 5.15, we observe that the DFT of $x_{ec}(n)$ is the same as the real part of $X(k)$ and that the DFT of $x_{oc}(n)$ is the same as the imaginary part of $X(k)$. $\square$

A similar property for complex-valued sequences is explored in Problem P5.18.

5. **Circular shift of a sequence:** If an N-point sequence is shifted in either direction, then the result is no longer between $0 \le n \le N - 1$.

Therefore, we first convert $x(n)$ into its periodic extension $\tilde{x}(n)$, and then shift it by m samples to obtain

$$\tilde{x}(n-m) = x\left((n-m)\right)_N \tag{5.35}$$

This is called a *periodic shift* of $\tilde{x}(n)$. The periodic shift is then converted into an N-point sequence. The resulting sequence

$$\tilde{x}(n-m)\mathcal{R}_N(n) = x\left((n-m)\right)_N \mathcal{R}_N(n) \tag{5.36}$$

is called the *circular shift* of $x(n)$. Once again, to visualize this, imagine that the sequence $x(n)$ is wrapped around a circle. Now rotate the circle by k samples and unwrap the sequence from $0 \leq n \leq N-1$. Its DFT is given by

$$\mathrm{DFT}\left[x\left((n-m)\right)_N \mathcal{R}_N(n)\right] = W_N^{km} X(k) \tag{5.37}$$

□   **EXAMPLE 5.11**   Let $x(n) = 10\,(0.8)^n$, $\quad 0 \leq n \leq 10$ be an 11-point sequence.

    a. Sketch $x((n+4))_{11}R_{11}(n)$, that is, a circular shift by four samples toward the left.

    b. Sketch $x((n-3))_{15}R_{15}(n)$, that is, a circular shift by three samples toward the right, where $x(n)$ is assumed to be a 15-point sequence.

Solution   We will use a step-by-step graphical approach to illustrate the circular shifting operation. This approach shows the periodic extension $\tilde{x}(n) = x((n))_N$ of $x(n)$, followed by a linear shift in $\tilde{x}(n)$ to obtain $\tilde{x}(n-m) = x((n-m))_N$, and finally truncating $\tilde{x}(n-m)$ to obtain the circular shift.

    a. Figure 5.16 shows four sequences. The top-left shows $x(n)$, the bottom-left shows $\tilde{x}(n)$, the top-right shows $\tilde{x}(n+4)$, and, finally, the bottom-right shows $x((n+4))_{11}R_{11}(n)$. Note carefully that as samples move out of the $[0, N-1]$ window in one direction, they reappear from the opposite direction. This is the meaning of the circular shift, and it is different from the linear shift.

    b. In this case, the sequence $x(n)$ is treated as a 15-point sequence by padding four zeros. Now the circular shift will be different than when $N = 11$. This is shown in Figure 5.17. In fact, the circular shift $x\left((n-3)\right)_{15}$ looks like a linear shift $x(n-3)$.   □

To implement a circular shift, we do not have to go through the periodic shift as shown in Example 5.11. It can be implemented directly in two ways. In the first approach, the modulo-N operation can be used on the argument $(n-m)$ in the time domain. This is shown below in the `cirshftt` function.

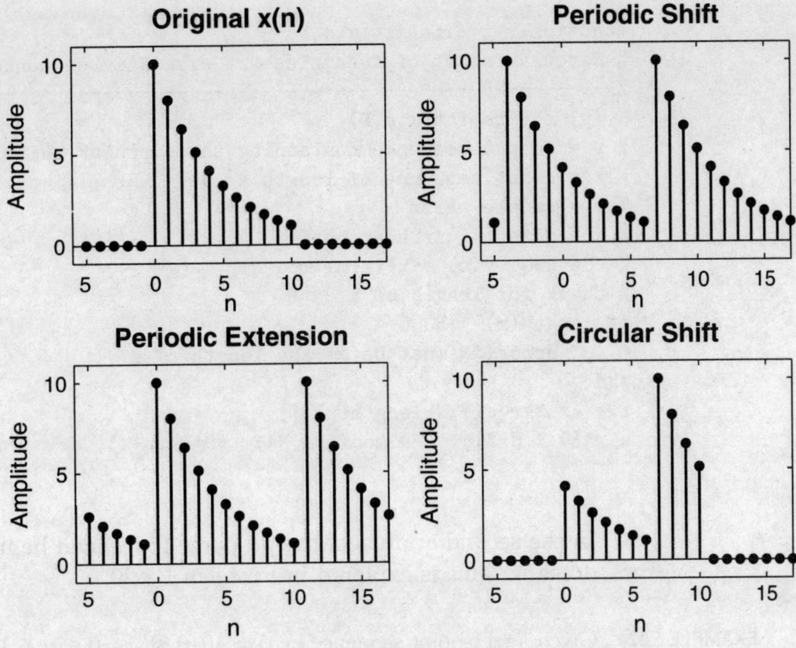

FIGURE 5.16   *Graphical interpretation of circular shift, $N = 11$*

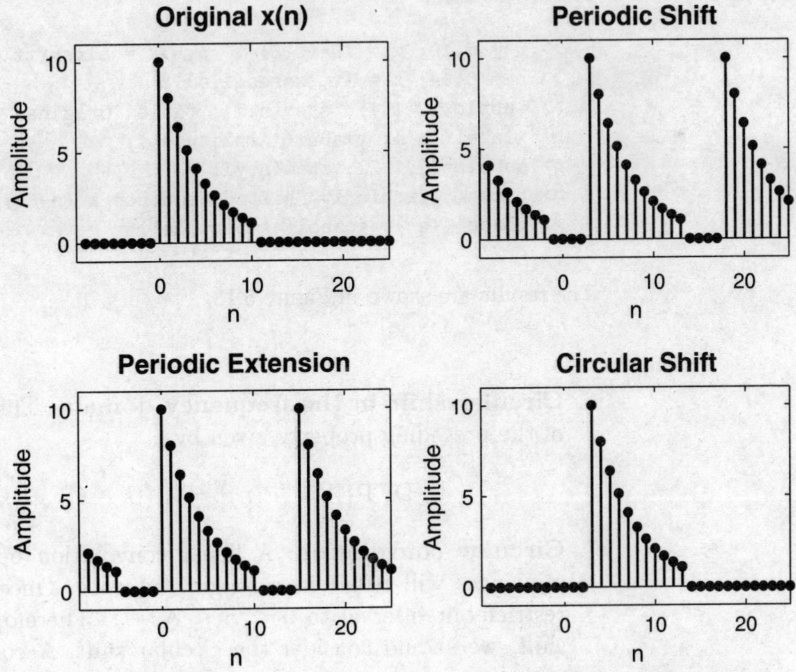

FIGURE 5.17   *Graphical interpretation of circular shift, $N = 15$*

```
function y = cirshftt(x,m,N)
% Circular shift of m samples wrt size N in sequence x: (time domain)
% --------------------------------------------------------------------
% [y] = cirshftt(x,m,N)
% y = output sequence containing the circular shift
% x = input sequence of length <= N
% m = sample shift
% N = size of circular buffer
%  Method: y(n) = x((n-m) mod N)
% Check for length of x
if length(x) > N
      error('N must be >= the length of x')
end
x = [x zeros(1,N-length(x))];
n = [0:1:N-1];  n = mod(n-m,N);  y = x(n+1);
```

In the second approach, the property (5.37) can be used in the frequency
domain. This is explored in Problem P5.20.

☐   **EXAMPLE 5.12**   Given an 11-point sequence $x(n) = 10\,(0.8)^n$, $0 \leq n \leq 10$, determine and plot
$x\,((n-6))_{15}$.

Solution   MATLAB script:

```
>> n = 0:10; x = 10*(0.8) .^ n;  y = cirshftt(x,6,15);
>> n = 0:14; x = [x, zeros(1,4)];
>> subplot(2,1,1); stem(n,x); title('Original Sequence x(n)')
>> xlabel('n'); ylabel('Amplitude');
>> subplot(2,1,2); stem(n,y);
>> title('Circularly Shifted Sequence x((n-6))_{15}')
>> xlabel('n'); ylabel('Amplitude');
```

The results are shown in Figure 5.18.   ☐

6. **Circular shift in the frequency domain:** This property is a dual
of the preceding property given by

$$\text{DFT}\left[W_N^{-\ell n}x(n)\right] = X\,((k - \ell))_N\, R_N(k) \tag{5.38}$$

7. **Circular convolution:** A linear convolution between two N-point
sequences will result in a longer sequence. Once again, we have to
restrict our interval to $0 \leq n \leq N - 1$. Therefore, instead of linear
shift, we should consider the circular shift. A convolution operation

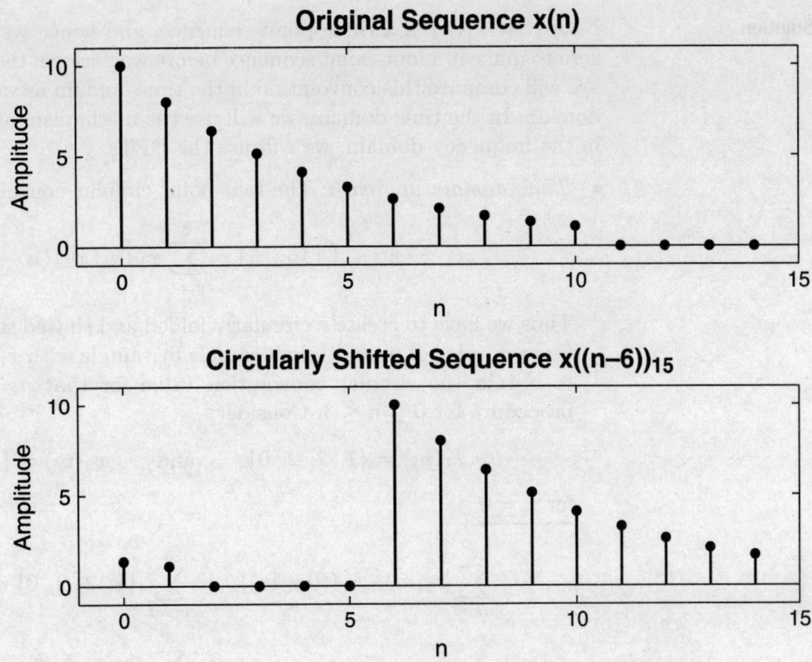

FIGURE 5.18 *Circularly shifted sequence in Example 5.12*

that contains a circular shift is called the *circular convolution* and is given by

$$x_1(n) \ \text{\textcircled{N}} \ x_2(n) = \sum_{m=0}^{N-1} x_1(m) x_2\left((n-m)\right)_N, \quad 0 \le n \le N-1 \quad \textbf{(5.39)}$$

Note that the circular convolution is also an N-point sequence. It has a structure similar to that of a linear convolution. The differences are in the summation limits and in the N-point circular shift. Hence it depends on N and is also called an N-point circular convolution. Therefore, the use of the notation $\text{\textcircled{N}}$ is appropriate. The DFT property for the circular convolution is

$$\text{DFT}\left[x_1(n) \ \text{\textcircled{N}} \ x_2(n)\right] = X_1(k) \cdot X_2(k) \quad \textbf{(5.40)}$$

An alternate interpretation of this property is that when we multiply two N-point DFTs in the frequency domain, we get the circular convolution (and not the usual linear convolution) in the time domain.

☐ **EXAMPLE 5.13** Let $x_1(n) = \{1, 2, 2\}$ and $x_2(n) = \{1, 2, 3, 4\}$. Compute the four-point circular convolution $x_1(n) \ \text{\textcircled{4}} \ x_2(n)$.

Solution

Note that $x_1(n)$ is a three-point sequence, and hence we will have to pad one zero to make it a four-point sequence before we perform the circular convolution. We will compute this convolution in the time domain as well as in the frequency domain. In the time domain, we will use the mechanism of circular convolution; in the frequency domain, we will use the DFTs.

- *Time-domain approach:* The four-point circular convolution is given by

$$x_1(n) \,(\!4\!)\, x_2(n) = \sum_{m=0}^{3} x_1(m)\, x_2\left((n-m)\right)_4$$

Thus we have to create a circularly folded and shifted sequence $x_2((n-m))_N$ for each value of n, multiply it sample by sample with $x_1(m)$, add the samples to obtain the circular convolution value for that n, and then repeat the procedure for $0 \le n \le 3$. Consider

$$x_1(m) = \{1,\, 2,\, 2,\, 0\} \qquad \text{and} \qquad x_2(m) = \{1,\, 2,\, 3,\, 4\}$$

for $n = 0$

$$\sum_{m=0}^{3} x_1(m) \cdot x_2\left((0-m)\right)_5 = \sum_{m=0}^{3} \left[\{1,\, 2,\, 2,\, 0\} \cdot \{1,\, 4,\, 3,\, 2\}\right]$$

$$= \sum_{m=0}^{3} \{1,\, 8,\, 6,\, 0\} = 15$$

for $n = 1$

$$\sum_{m=0}^{3} x_1(m) \cdot x_2\left((1-m)\right)_5 = \sum_{m=0}^{3} \left[\{1,\, 2,\, 2,\, 0\} \cdot \{2,\, 1,\, 4,\, 3\}\right]$$

$$= \sum_{m=0}^{3} \{2,\, 2,\, 8,\, 0\} = 12$$

for $n = 2$

$$\sum_{m=0}^{3} x_1(m) \cdot x_2\left((2-m)\right)_5 = \sum_{m=0}^{3} \left[\{1,\, 2,\, 2,\, 0\} \cdot \{3,\, 2,\, 1,\, 4\}\right]$$

$$= \sum_{m=0}^{3} \{3,\, 4,\, 2,\, 0\} = 9$$

for $n = 3$

$$\sum_{m=0}^{3} x_1(m) \cdot x_2\left((3-m)\right)_5 = \sum_{m=0}^{3} \left[\{1,\, 2,\, 2,\, 0\} \cdot \{4,\, 3,\, 2,\, 1\}\right]$$

$$= \sum_{m=0}^{3} \{4,\, 6,\, 4,\, 0\} = 14$$

Hence

$$x_1(n) \; \textcircled{4} \; x_2(n) = \{15, \, 12, \, 9, \, 14\}$$

- *Frequency-domain approach:* In this approach, we first compute four-point DFTs of $x_1(n)$ and $x_2(n)$, multiply them sample by sample, and then take the inverse DFT of the result to obtain the circular convolution.

<u>DFT of $x_1(n)$</u>

$$x_1(n) = \{1, 2, 2, 0\} \Longrightarrow X_1(k) = \{5, \, -1-j2, \, 1, \, -1+j2\}$$

<u>DFT of $x_2(n)$</u>

$$x_2(n) = \{1, 2, 3, 4\} \Longrightarrow X_2(k) = \{10, \, -2+j2, \, -2, \, -2-j2\}$$

Now

$$X_1(k) \cdot X_2(k) = \{50, \, 6+j2, \, -2, \, 6-j2\}$$

Finally, after IDFT,

$$x_1(n) \; \textcircled{4} \; x_2(n) = \{15, \, 12, \, 9, \, 14\}$$

which is the same as before. $\qquad\square$

Similar to the circular shift implementation, we can implement the circular convolution in a number of different ways. The simplest approach would be to implement (5.39) literally by using the `cirshftt` function and requiring two nested `for...end` loops. Obviously, this is not efficient. Another approach is to generate a sequence $x((n-m))_N$ for each n in $[0, N-1]$ as rows of a matrix and then implement (5.39) as a matrix-vector multiplication similar to our `dft` function. This would require one `for...end` loop. The following `circonvt` function incorporates these steps.

```
function y = circonvt(x1,x2,N)
% N-point circular convolution between x1 and x2: (time-domain)
% --------------------------------------------------------------
% [y] = circonvt(x1,x2,N)
%  y = output sequence containing the circular convolution
% x1 = input sequence of length N1 <= N
% x2 = input sequence of length N2 <= N
%  N = size of circular buffer
%  Method: y(n) = sum (x1(m)*x2((n-m) mod N))
% Check for length of x1
if length(x1) > N
        error('N must be >= the length of x1')
end
```

```
% Check for length of x2
if length(x2) > N
        error('N must be >= the length of x2')
end
x1=[x1 zeros(1,N-length(x1))];
x2=[x2 zeros(1,N-length(x2))];
m = [0:1:N-1];  x2 = x2(mod(-m,N)+1);  H = zeros(N,N);
for n = 1:1:N
H(n,:) = cirshftt(x2,n-1,N);
end
y = x1*conj(H');
```

Problems P5.24 and P5.25 explore an approach to eliminate the `for...` `end` loop in the `circonvt` function. The third approach would be to implement the frequency-domain operation (5.40) using the `dft` function. This is explored in Problem P5.26.

□ **EXAMPLE 5.14**   Let us use MATLAB to perform the circular convolution in Example 5.13.

Solution   The sequences are $x_1(n) = \{1, 2, 2\}$ and $x_2(n) = \{1, 2, 3, 4\}$.

MATLAB script:

```
>> x1 = [1,2,2]; x2 = [1,2,3,4];  y = circonvt(x1, x2, 4)
y =
      15    12    9    14
```

Hence

$$x_1(n) \;\textcircled{4}\; x_2(n) = \{15, \ 12, \ 9, \ 14\}$$

as before.   □

□ **EXAMPLE 5.15**   In this example, we will study the effect of N on the circular convolution. Obviously, $N \geq 4$; otherwise, there will be a time-domain aliasing for $x_2(n)$. We will use the same two sequences from Example 5.13.

a. Compute $x_1(n) \;\textcircled{5}\; x_2(n)$.
b. Compute $x_1(n) \;\textcircled{6}\; x_2(n)$.
c. Comment on the results.

Solution   The sequences are $x_1(n) = \{1, 2, 2\}$ and $x_2(n) = \{1, 2, 3, 4\}$. Even though the sequences are the same as in Example 5.14, we should expect different results for different values of N. This is not the case with the linear convolution, which is unique, given two sequences.

a. MATLAB script for five-point circular convolution:

```
>> x1 = [1,2,2]; x2 = [1,2,3,4];  y = circonvt(x1, x2, 5)
y =
       9      4      9     14     14
```

Hence

$$x_1(n) \; ⑤ \; x_2(n) = \{9, \ 4, \ 9, \ 14, \ 14\}$$

b. MATLAB script for six-point circular convolution:

```
>> x1 = [1,2,2]; x2 = [1,2,3,4];  y = circonvt(x1, x2, 6)
y =
       1      4      9     14     14      8
```

Hence

$$x_1(n) \; ⑥ \; x_2(n) = \{1, \ 4, \ 9, \ 14, \ 14, \ 8\}$$

c. A careful observation of four-, five-, and six-point circular convolutions from this and the previous example indicates some unique features. Clearly, an N-point circular convolution is an N-point sequence. However, some samples in these convolutions have the same values, while other values can be obtained as a sum of samples in other convolutions. For example, the first sample in the five-point convolution is a sum of the first and the last samples of the six-point convolution. The linear convolution between $x_1(n)$ and $x_2(n)$ is given by

$$x_1(n) * x_2(n) = \{1, \ 4, \ 9, \ 14, \ 14, \ 8\}$$

which is equivalent to the six-point circular convolution. These and other issues are explored in the next section. $\qquad\square$

8. **Multiplication:** This is the dual of the circular convolution property. It is given by

$$\mathrm{DFT}\,[x_1(n) \cdot x_2(n)] = \frac{1}{N} X_1(k) \; Ⓝ \; X_2(k) \tag{5.41}$$

in which the circular convolution is performed in the frequency domain. The MATLAB functions developed for circular convolution can also be used here since $X_1(k)$ and $X_2(k)$ are also N-point sequences.

9. **Parseval's relation:** This relation computes the energy in the frequency domain.

$$\mathrm{E}_x = \sum_{n=0}^{N-1} |x(n)|^2 = \frac{1}{N} \sum_{k=0}^{N-1} |X(k)|^2 \tag{5.42}$$

The quantity $\frac{|X(k)|^2}{N}$ is called the *energy spectrum* of finite-duration sequences. Similarly, for periodic sequences, the quantity $|\frac{\tilde{X}(k)}{N}|^2$ is called the *power spectrum*.

5.5 LINEAR CONVOLUTION USING THE DFT

■

One of the most important operations in linear systems is the linear convolution. In fact, FIR filters are generally implemented in practice using this linear convolution. On the other hand, the DFT is a practical approach for implementing linear system operations in the frequency domain. As we shall see later, it is also an efficient operation in terms of computations. However, there is one problem. The DFT operations result in a circular convolution (something that we do not desire), not in a linear convolution that we want. Now we shall see how to use the DFT to perform a linear convolution (or equivalently, how to make a circular convolution identical to the linear convolution). We alluded to this problem in Example 5.15.

Let $x_1(n)$ be an N_1-point sequence, and let $x_2(n)$ be an N_2-point sequence. Define the linear convolution of $x_1(n)$ and $x_2(n)$ by $x_3(n)$, that is,

$$x_3(n) = x_1(n) * x_2(n)$$

$$= \sum_{k=-\infty}^{\infty} x_1(k)x_2(n-k) = \sum_{0}^{N_1-1} x_1(k)x_2(n-k) \qquad \textbf{(5.43)}$$

Then $x_3(n)$ is an $(N_1 + N_2 - 1)$-point sequence. If we choose $N = \max(N_1, N_2)$ and compute an N-point circular convolution $x_1(n)$ Ⓝ $x_2(n)$, then we get an N-point sequence, which obviously is different from $x_3(n)$. This observation also gives us a clue. Why not choose $N = N_1+N_2-1$ and perform an (N_1+N_2-1)-point circular convolution? Then at least both of these convolutions will have an equal number of samples.

Therefore, let $N = N_1 + N_2 - 1$, and let us treat $x_1(n)$ and $x_2(n)$ as N-point sequences. Define the N-point circular convolution by $x_4(n)$.

$$x_4(n) = x_1(n) \,Ⓝ\, x_2(n) \qquad \textbf{(5.44)}$$

$$= \left[\sum_{m=0}^{N-1} x_1(m)x_2((n-m))_N \right] \mathcal{R}_N(n)$$

$$= \left[\sum_{m=0}^{N-1} x_1(m) \sum_{r=-\infty}^{\infty} x_2(n-m-rN) \right] \mathcal{R}_N(n)$$

$$= \left[\sum_{r=-\infty}^{\infty} \underbrace{\sum_{m=0}^{N_1-1} x_1(m)x_2(n-m-rN)}_{x_3(n-rN)} \right] \mathcal{R}_N(n)$$

$$= \left[\sum_{r=-\infty}^{\infty} x_3(n-rN) \right] \mathcal{R}_N(n) \qquad\qquad \text{using (5.43)}$$

This analysis shows that, in general, the circular convolution is an aliased version of the linear convolution. We observed this fact in Example 5.15. Now since $x_3(n)$ is an $N = (N_1 + N_2 - 1)$-point sequence, we have

$$x_4(n) = x_3(n); \quad 0 \le n \le (N-1)$$

which means that there is no aliasing in the time domain.

Conclusion: If we make both $x_1(n)$ and $x_2(n)$ $N = (N_1 + N_2 - 1)$-point sequences by padding an appropriate number of zeros, then the circular convolution is identical to the linear convolution.

☐ **EXAMPLE 5.16**   Let $x_1(n)$ and $x_2(n)$ be the following two four-point sequences:

$$x_1(n) = \{1,\ 2,\ 2,\ 1\}, \quad x_2(n) = \{1,\ -1,\ -1,\ 1\}$$

a. Determine their linear convolution $x_3(n)$.
b. Compute the circular convolution $x_4(n)$ so that it is equal to $x_3(n)$.

Solution   We will use MATLAB to do this problem.

a. MATLAB script:

```
>> x1 = [1,2,2,1]; x2 = [1,-1,-1,1];   x3 = conv(x1,x2)
x3 =     1      1     -1     -2     -1     1     1
```

Hence the linear convolution $x_3(n)$ is a seven-point sequence given by

$$x_3(n) = \{1, 1, -1, -2, -1, 1, 1\}$$

b. We will have to use $N \ge 7$. Choosing $N = 7$, we have

```
>> x4 = circonvt(x1,x2,7)
x4 =     1      1     -1     -2     -1     1     1
```

Hence

$$x_4 = \{1, 1, -1, -2, -1, 1, 1\} = x_3(n)$$

☐

☐ **EXAMPLE 5.17**   Consider the sequences $x_1(n)$ and $x_2(n)$ from the previous example. Evaluate circular convolutions for $N = 6, 5$, and 4. Verify the error relations in each case.

☐

5.5.1 ERROR ANALYSIS

To use the DFT for linear convolution, we must choose N properly. However, in practice it may not be possible to do so, especially when N is very large and there is a limit on memory. Then an error will be introduced when N is chosen less than the required value to perform the circular convolution. We want to compute this error, which is useful in practice. Obviously, $N \geq \max(N_1, N_2)$. Therefore, let

$$\max(N_1, N_2) \leq N < (N_1 + N_2 - 1)$$

Then, from our previous analysis (5.44),

$$x_4(n) = \left[\sum_{r=-\infty}^{\infty} x_3(n - rN) \right] \mathcal{R}_N(n)$$

Let an error $e(n)$ be given by

$$e(n) \triangleq x_4(n) - x_3(n)$$

$$= \left[\sum_{r \neq 0} x_3(n - rN) \right] \mathcal{R}_N(n)$$

Since $N \geq \max(N_1, N_2)$, only two terms corresponding to $r = \pm 1$ remain in the above summation. Hence

$$e(n) = [x_3(n - N) + x_3(n + N)] \mathcal{R}_N(n)$$

Generally, $x_1(n)$ and $x_2(n)$ are causal sequences. Then $x_3(n)$ is also causal, which means that

$$x_3(n - N) = 0; \quad 0 \leq n \leq N - 1$$

Therefore,

$$e(n) = x_3(n + N), \quad 0 \leq n \leq N - 1 \tag{5.45}$$

This is a simple yet important relation. It implies that when $\max(N_1, N_2) \leq N < (N_1 + N_2 - 1)$ the error value at n is the same as the linear convolution value computed N samples away. Now the linear convolution will be zero after $(N_1 + N_2 - 1)$ samples. This means that the first few samples of the circular convolution are in error, while the remaining ones are the correct linear convolution values.

☐ **EXAMPLE 5.17**   Consider the sequences $x_1(n)$ and $x_2(n)$ from the previous example. Evaluate circular convolutions for $N = 6$, 5, and 4. Verify the error relations in each case.

Solution

Clearly, the linear convolution $x_3(n)$ is still the same.

$$x_3(n) = \{1, 1, -1, -2, -1, 1, 1\}$$

When $N = 6$, we obtain a six-point sequence:

$$x_4(n) = x_1(n) \;\textcircled{6}\; x_2(n) = \{2, 1, -1, -2, -1, 1\}$$

Therefore,

$$\begin{aligned}
e(n) &= \{2, 1, -1, -2, -1, 1\} - \{1, 1, -1, -2, -1, 1\}, \quad 0 \le n \le 5 \\
&= \{1, 0, 0, 0, 0, 0\} \\
&= x_3(n + 6)
\end{aligned}$$

as expected. When $N = 5$, we obtain a five-point sequence,

$$x_4(n) = x_1(n) \;\textcircled{5}\; x_2(n) = \{2, 2, -1, -2, -1\}$$

and

$$\begin{aligned}
e(n) &= \{2, 2, -1, -2, -1\} - \{1, 1, -1, -2, -1\}, \quad 0 \le n \le 4 \\
&= \{1, 1, 0, 0, 0\} \\
&= x_3(n + 5)
\end{aligned}$$

Finally, when $N = 4$, we obtain a four-point sequence,

$$x_4(n) = x_1(n) \;\textcircled{4}\; x_2(n) = \{0, 2, 0, -2\}$$

and

$$\begin{aligned}
e(n) &= \{0, 2, 0, -2\} - \{1, 1, -1, -2\}, \quad 0 \le n \le 3 \\
&= \{-1, 1, 1, 0\} \\
&= x_3(n + 4)
\end{aligned}$$

The last case of $N = 4$ also provides the following useful observation.

Observation: When $N = \max(N_1, N_2)$ is chosen for circular convolution, then the first $(M - 1)$ samples are in error (i.e., different from the linear convolution), where $M = \min(N_1, N_2)$. This result is useful in implementing long convolutions in the form of block processing. $\qquad\square$

5.5.2 BLOCK CONVOLUTIONS

When we want to filter an input sequence that is being received continuously, such as a speech signal from a microphone, then for practical purposes we can think of this sequence as an infinite-length sequence. If we want to implement this filtering operation as an FIR filter in which the linear convolution is computed using the DFT, then we experience some practical problems. We will have to compute a large DFT, which is generally impractical. Furthermore, output samples are not available until all input samples are processed. This introduces an unacceptably large amount of delay. Therefore, we have to segment the infinite-length input sequence into smaller sections (or blocks), process each section using the DFT, and finally assemble the output sequence from the outputs of each section. This procedure is called a *block convolution* (or block processing) operation.

Let us assume that the sequence $x(n)$ is sectioned into N-point sequences and that the impulse response of the filter is an M-point sequence, where $M < N$. Then from the observation in Example 5.17, we note that the N-point circular convolution between the input block and the impulse response will yield a block output sequence in which the first $(M-1)$ samples are not the correct output values. If we simply partition $x(n)$ into nonoverlapping sections, then the resulting output sequence will have intervals of incorrect samples. To correct this problem, we can partition $x(n)$ into sections, each overlapping with the previous one by exactly $(M-1)$ samples, save the last $(N-M+1)$ output samples, and finally concatenate these outputs into a sequence. To correct for the first $(M-1)$ samples in the first output block, we set the first $(M-1)$ samples in the first input block to zero. This procedure is called an *overlap-save* method of block convolutions. Clearly, when $N \gg M$, this method is more efficient. We illustrate it using a simple example.

☐   **EXAMPLE 5.18**   Let $x(n) = (n+1)$, $0 \le n \le 9$ and $h(n) = \{1, \overset{\uparrow}{0}, -1\}$. Implement the overlap-save method using $N = 6$ to compute $y(n) = x(n) * h(n)$.

Solution   Since $M = 3$, we will have to overlap each section with the previous one by two samples. Now $x(n)$ is a 10-point sequence, and we will need $(M-1) = 2$ zeros in the beginning. Since $N = 6$, we will need three sections. Let the sections be

$$x_1(n) = \{0, 0, 1, 2, 3, 4\}$$

$$x_2(n) = \{3, 4, 5, 6, 7, 8\}$$

$$x_3(n) = \{7, 8, 9, 10, 0, 0\}$$

Note that we have to pad $x_3(n)$ by two zeros since $x(n)$ runs out of values at $n = 9$. Now we will compute the six-point circular convolution of each section with $h(n)$.

$$y_1 = x_1(n) \,⑥\, h(n) = \{-3, -4, 1, 2, 2, 2\}$$

$$y_2 = x_2(n) \,⑥\, h(n) = \{-4, -4, 2, 2, 2, 2\}$$

$$y_3 = x_3(n) \,⑥\, h(n) = \{7, 8, 2, 2, -9, -10\}$$

Noting that the first two samples in each section are to be discarded, we assemble the output $y(n)$ as

$$y(n) = \{1, 2, 2, 2, 2, 2, 2, 2, 2, 2, -9, -10\}$$
$$\uparrow$$

The linear convolution is given by

$$x(n) * h(n) = \{1, 2, 2, 2, 2, 2, 2, 2, 2, 2, -9, -10\}$$
$$\uparrow$$

which agrees with the overlap-save method. □

5.5.3 MATLAB IMPLEMENTATION

Using this example as a guide, we can develop a MATLAB function to implement the overlap-save method for a very long input sequence $x(n)$. The key step in this function is to obtain a proper indexing for the segmentation. Given $x(n)$ for $n \geq 0$, we have to set the first $(M-1)$ samples to zero to begin the block processing. Let this augmented sequence be

$$\hat{x}(n) \overset{\triangle}{=} \{\underbrace{0, 0, \ldots, 0}_{(M-1) \text{ zeros}}, x(n)\}, \quad n \geq 0$$

and let $L = N - M + 1$; then the kth block $x_k(n)$, $0 \leq n \leq N - 1$, is given by

$$x_k(n) = \hat{x}(m); \quad kL \leq m \leq kL + N - 1, k \geq 0, 0 \leq n \leq N - 1$$

The total number of blocks is given by

$$K = \left\lfloor \frac{N_x + M - 2}{L} \right\rfloor + 1$$

where N_x is the length of $x(n)$ and $\lfloor \cdot \rfloor$ is the truncation operation. Now each block can be circularly convolved with $h(n)$ using the `circonvt` function developed earlier to obtain

$$y_k(n) = x_k(n) \textcircled{N} h(n)$$

Finally, discarding the first $(M-1)$ samples from each $y_k(n)$ and concatenating the remaining samples, we obtain the linear convolution $y(n)$. This procedure is incorporated in the following `ovrlpsav` function.

```
function [y] = ovrlpsav(x,h,N)
% Overlap-Save method of block convolution
% ------------------------------------------
% [y] = ovrlpsav(x,h,N)
% y = output sequence
% x = input sequence
% h = impulse response
% N = block length
%
Lenx = length(x); M = length(h);  M1 = M-1; L = N-M1;
  h = [h zeros(1,N-M)];
  %
  x = [zeros(1,M1), x, zeros(1,N-1)]; % Preappend (M-1) zeros
  K = floor((Lenx+M1-1)/(L));          % # of blocks
  Y = zeros(K+1,N);
  % Convolution with succesive blocks
  for k=0:K
   xk = x(k*L+1:k*L+N);
   Y(k+1,:) = circonvt(xk,h,N);
  end
  Y = Y(:,M:N)';                       % Discard the first (M-1) samples
  y = (Y(:))';                         % Assemble output
```

Note: The `ovrlpsav` function as developed here is not the most efficient approach. We will come back to this issue when we discuss the fast Fourier transform.

□ **EXAMPLE 5.19**   To verify the operation of the `ovrlpsav` function, let us consider the sequences given in Example 5.18.

Solution   MATLAB script:

```
>> n = 0:9; x = n+1; h = [1,0,-1]; N = 6;  y = ovrlpsav(x,h,N)
y =
     1    2    2    2    2    2    2    2    2    2   -9  -10
```

This is the correct linear convolution as expected.   □

There is an alternate method called an *overlap-add* method of block convolutions. In this method, the input sequence $x(n)$ is partitioned into nonoverlapping blocks and convolved with the impulse response. The resulting output blocks are overlapped with the subsequent sections and added to form the overall output. This is explored in Problem P5.32.

5.6 THE FAST FOURIER TRANSFORM

The DFT (5.24) introduced earlier is the only transform that is discrete in both the time and the frequency domains and is defined for finite-duration sequences. Although it is a computable transform, the straightforward implementation of (5.24) is very inefficient, especially when the sequence length N is large. In 1965, Cooley and Tukey [8] showed a procedure to substantially reduce the amount of computations involved in the DFT. This led to the explosion of applications of the DFT, including in the digital signal processing area. Furthermore, it also led to the development of other efficient algorithms. All these efficient algorithms are collectively known as fast Fourier transform (FFT) algorithms.

Consider an N-point sequence $x(n)$. Its N-point DFT is given by (5.24) and reproduced here,

$$X(k) = \sum_{n=0}^{N-1} x(n)W_N^{nk}, \quad 0 \le k \le N-1 \tag{5.46}$$

where $W_N = e^{-j2\pi/N}$. To obtain one sample of $X(k)$, we need N complex multiplications and $(N-1)$ complex additions. Hence to obtain a complete set of DFT coefficients, we need N^2 complex multiplications and $N(N-1)$ $\simeq N^2$ complex additions. Also, one has to store N^2 complex coefficients $\left\{W_N^{nk}\right\}$ (or generate internally at an extra cost). Clearly, the number of DFT computations for an N-point sequence depends quadratically on N, which will be denoted by the notation

$$C_N = \mathrm{o}\left(N^2\right)$$

For large N, $\mathrm{o}\left(N^2\right)$ is unacceptable in practice. Generally, the processing time for one addition is much less than that for one multiplication. Hence from now on we will concentrate on the number of complex multiplications, which itself requires four real multiplications and two real additions.

5.6.1 GOAL OF AN EFFICIENT COMPUTATION

In an efficiently designed algorithm, the number of computations should be constant per data sample, and therefore the total number of computations should be linear with respect to N.

The quadratic dependence on N can be reduced by realizing that most of the computations (which are done again and again) can be eliminated using the periodicity property

$$W_N^{kn} = W_N^{k(n+N)} = W_N^{(k+N)n}$$

and the symmetry property

$$W_N^{kn+N/2} = -W_N^{kn}$$

of the factor $\{W_N^{nk}\}$.

One algorithm that considers only the periodicity of W_N^{nk} is the Goertzel algorithm. This algorithm still requires $C_N = o(N^2)$ multiplications, but it has certain advantages. This algorithm is described in Chapter 12. We first begin with an example to illustrate the advantages of the symmetry and periodicity properties in reducing the number of computations. We then describe and analyze two specific FFT algorithms that require $C_N = o(N \log N)$ operations. They are the *decimation-in-time* (DIT-FFT) and *decimation-in-frequency* (DIF-FFT) algorithms.

☐ **EXAMPLE 5.20**   Let us discuss the computations of a four-point DFT and develop an efficient algorithm for its computation.

$$X(k) = \sum_{n=0}^{3} x(n)W_4^{nk}, \quad 0 \le k \le 3; \quad W_4 = e^{-j2\pi/4} = -j$$

Solution   These computations can be done in the matrix form

$$\begin{bmatrix} X(0) \\ X(1) \\ X(2) \\ X(3) \end{bmatrix} = \begin{bmatrix} W_4^0 & W_4^0 & W_4^0 & W_4^0 \\ W_4^0 & W_4^1 & W_4^2 & W_4^3 \\ W_4^0 & W_4^2 & W_4^4 & W_4^6 \\ W_4^0 & W_4^3 & W_4^6 & W_4^9 \end{bmatrix} \begin{bmatrix} x(0) \\ x(1) \\ x(2) \\ x(3) \end{bmatrix}$$

which requires 16 complex multiplications.

Efficient Approach   Using periodicity,

$$W_4^0 = W_4^4 = 1 \quad ; \quad W_4^1 = W_4^9 = -j$$
$$W_4^2 = W_4^6 = -1 \quad ; \quad W_4^3 = j$$

and substituting in the above matrix form, we get

$$\begin{bmatrix} X(0) \\ X(1) \\ X(2) \\ X(3) \end{bmatrix} = \begin{bmatrix} 1 & 1 & 1 & 1 \\ 1 & -j & -1 & j \\ 1 & -1 & 1 & -1 \\ 1 & j & -1 & -j \end{bmatrix} \begin{bmatrix} x(0) \\ x(1) \\ x(2) \\ x(3) \end{bmatrix}$$

Using symmetry, we obtain

$$X(0) = x(0) + x(1) + x(2) + x(3) = \underbrace{[x(0) + x(2)]}_{g_1} + \underbrace{[x(1) + x(3)]}_{g_2}$$

$$X(1) = x(0) - jx(1) - x(2) + jx(3) = \underbrace{[x(0) - x(2)]}_{h_1} - j\underbrace{[x(1) - x(3)]}_{h_2}$$

$$X(2) = x(0) - x(1) + x(2) - x(3) = \underbrace{[x(0) + x(2)]}_{g_1} - \underbrace{[x(1) + x(3)]}_{g_2}$$

$$X(3) = x(0) + jx(1) - x(2) - jx(3) = \underbrace{[x(0) - x(2)]}_{h_1} + j\underbrace{[x(1) - x(3)]}_{h_2}$$

Hence an efficient algorithm is

$$
\begin{array}{ll|l}
& \text{Step 1} & \text{Step 2} \\
& g_1 = x(0) + x(2) & X(0) = g_1 + g_2 \\
& g_2 = x(1) + x(3) & X(1) = h_1 - jh_2 \\
& h_1 = x(0) - x(2) & X(2) = g_1 - g_2 \\
& h_2 = x(1) - x(3) & X(3) = h_1 + jh_2
\end{array}
\tag{5.47}
$$

which requires only two complex multiplications, which is a considerably smaller number, even for this simple example. A signal flowgraph structure for this algorithm is given in Figure 5.19.

An Interpretation   This efficient algorithm (5.47) can be interpreted differently. First, a four-point sequence $x(n)$ is divided into two two-point sequences, which are arranged into column vectors as shown here:

$$\left[\begin{bmatrix} x(0) \\ x(2) \end{bmatrix}, \begin{bmatrix} x(1) \\ x(3) \end{bmatrix}\right] = \begin{bmatrix} x(0) & x(1) \\ x(2) & x(3) \end{bmatrix}$$

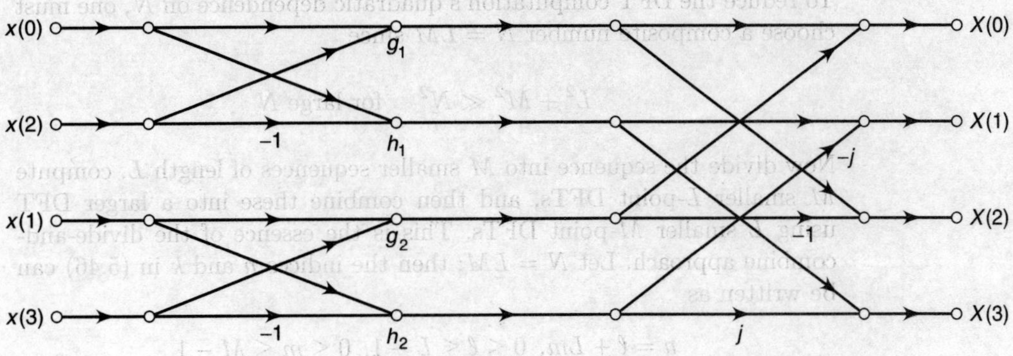

FIGURE 5.19   *Signal flowgraph in Example 5.20*

Second, a smaller two-point DFT of each column is taken.

$$\mathbf{W}_2 \begin{bmatrix} x(0) & x(1) \\ x(2) & x(3) \end{bmatrix} = \begin{bmatrix} 1 & 1 \\ 1 & -1 \end{bmatrix} \begin{bmatrix} x(0) & x(1) \\ x(2) & x(3) \end{bmatrix}$$

$$= \begin{bmatrix} x(0) + x(2) & x(1) + x(3) \\ x(0) - x(2) & x(1) - x(3) \end{bmatrix} = \begin{bmatrix} g_1 & g_2 \\ h_1 & h_2 \end{bmatrix}$$

Then each element of the resultant matrix is multiplied by $\{W_4^{pq}\}$, where p is the row index and q is the column index; that is, the following *dot-product* is performed:

$$\begin{bmatrix} 1 & 1 \\ 1 & -j \end{bmatrix} \cdot * \begin{bmatrix} g_1 & g_2 \\ h_1 & h_2 \end{bmatrix} = \begin{bmatrix} g_1 & g_2 \\ h_1 & -jh_2 \end{bmatrix}$$

Finally, two more smaller two-point DFTs are taken of *row vectors*.

$$\begin{bmatrix} g_1 & g_2 \\ h_1 & -jh_2 \end{bmatrix} \mathbf{W}_2 = \begin{bmatrix} g_1 & g_2 \\ h_1 & -jh_2 \end{bmatrix} \begin{bmatrix} 1 & 1 \\ 1 & -1 \end{bmatrix} = \begin{bmatrix} g_1 + g_2 & g_1 - g_2 \\ h_1 - jh_2 & h_1 + jh_2 \end{bmatrix}$$

$$= \begin{bmatrix} X(0) & X(2) \\ X(1) & X(3) \end{bmatrix}$$

Although this interpretation seems to have more multiplications than the efficient algorithm, it does suggest a systematic approach of computing a larger DFT based on smaller DFTs.   □

5.6.2 DIVIDE-AND-COMBINE APPROACH

To reduce the DFT computation's quadratic dependence on N, one must choose a composite number $N = LM$ since

$$L^2 + M^2 \ll N^2 \quad \text{for large } N$$

Now divide the sequence into M smaller sequences of length L, compute M smaller L-point DFTs, and then combine these into a larger DFT using L smaller M-point DFTs. This is the essence of the divide-and-combine approach. Let $N = LM$; then the indices n and k in (5.46) can be written as

$$n = \ell + Lm, \ 0 \leq \ell \leq L - 1, \ 0 \leq m \leq M - 1$$

$$k = q + Mp, \ 0 \leq p \leq L - 1, \ 0 \leq q \leq M - 1$$

(5.48)

and write sequences $x(n)$ and $X(k)$ as arrays $x(\ell, m)$ and $X(p, q)$, respectively. Then (5.46) can be written as

$$X(p,q) = \sum_{\ell=0}^{L-1} \sum_{m=0}^{M-1} x(\ell, m) W_N^{(\ell+Lm)(q+Mp)}$$

$$= \sum_{\ell=0}^{L-1} \left\{ W_N^{\ell q} \left[\sum_{m=0}^{M-1} x(\ell, m) W_N^{Lmq} \right] \right\} W_N^{M\ell p}$$

$$= \sum_{\ell=0}^{L-1} \left\{ W_N^{\ell q} \underbrace{\left[\sum_{m=0}^{M-1} x(\ell, m) W_M^{mq} \right]}_{M\text{-point DFT}} W_L^{\ell p} \right\} \tag{5.49}$$

$$\underbrace{\phantom{= \sum_{\ell=0}^{L-1} \left\{ W_N^{\ell q} \left[\sum_{m=0}^{M-1} x(\ell, m) W_M^{mq} \right] W_L^{\ell p} \right\}}}_{L\text{-point DFT}}$$

Hence (5.49) can be implemented as a three-step procedure:

1. First, we compute the M-point DFT array

$$F(\ell, q) \triangle \sum_{m=0}^{M-1} x(\ell, m) W_M^{mq}; \quad 0 \leq q \leq M-1 \tag{5.50}$$

for each of the rows $\ell = 0, \ldots, L-1$.

2. Second, we modify $F(\ell, q)$ to obtain another array.

$$G(\ell, q) = W_N^{\ell q} F(\ell, q), \quad \begin{array}{l} 0 \leq \ell \leq L-1 \\ 0 \leq q \leq M-1 \end{array} \tag{5.51}$$

The factor $W_N^{\ell q}$ is called a *twiddle* factor.

3. Finally, we compute the L-point DFTs

$$X(p,q) = \sum_{\ell=0}^{L-1} G(\ell, q) W_L^{\ell p} \quad 0 \leq p \leq L-1 \tag{5.52}$$

for each of the columns $q = 0, \ldots, M-1$.

The total number of complex multiplications for this approach can now be given by

$$C_N = LM^2 + N + ML^2 < \mathrm{o}\left(N^2\right) \tag{5.53}$$

We illustrate this approach in the following example.

□ **EXAMPLE 5.21**   Develop the divide-and-combine FFT algorithm for $N = 15$.

Solution   Let $L = 3$ and $M = 5$. Then from (5.48), we have

$$n = \ell + 3M, \quad 0 \leq \ell \leq 2, \quad 0 \leq m \leq 4 \\ k = q + 5p, \quad 0 \leq p \leq 2, \quad 0 \leq q \leq 4 \tag{5.54}$$

Hence (5.49) becomes

$$X(p,q) = \sum_{\ell=0}^{2} \left\{ W_{15}^{\ell q} \left[\sum_{m=0}^{4} x(\ell,m) W_5^{mq} \right] \right\} W_3^{\ell p} \tag{5.55}$$

To implement (5.55), we arrange the given sequence $x(n)$ in the form of an array $\{x(\ell,m)\}$ using a column-wise ordering as

$$\begin{array}{ccccc} x(0) & x(3) & x(6) & x(9) & x(12) \\ x(1) & x(4) & x(7) & x(10) & x(13) \\ x(2) & x(5) & x(8) & x(11) & x(14) \end{array} \tag{5.56}$$

The first step is to compute five-point DFTs $F(\ell, q)$ for each of the three rows and arrange them back in the same array formation

$$\begin{array}{ccccc} F(0,0) & F(0,1) & F(0,2) & F(0,3) & F(0,4) \\ F(1,0) & F(1,1) & F(1,2) & F(1,3) & F(1,4) \\ F(2,0) & F(2,1) & F(2,2) & F(2,3) & F(2,4) \end{array} \tag{5.57}$$

which requires a total of $3 \times 5^2 = 75$ complex operations. The second step is to modify $F(\ell, q)$ to obtain the array $G(\ell, q)$ using the twiddle factors $W_{15}^{\ell q}$

$$\begin{array}{ccccc} G(0,0) & G(0,1) & G(0,2) & G(0,3) & G(0,4) \\ G(1,0) & G(1,1) & G(1,2) & G(1,3) & G(1,4) \\ G(2,0) & G(2,1) & G(2,2) & G(2,3) & G(2,4) \end{array} \tag{5.58}$$

which requires 15 complex operations. The last step is to perform three-point DFTs $X(p,q)$ for each of the five columns to obtain

$$\begin{array}{ccccc} X(0,0) & X(0,1) & X(0,2) & X(0,3) & X(0,4) \\ X(1,0) & X(1,1) & X(1,2) & X(1,3) & X(1,4) \\ X(2,0) & X(2,1) & X(2,2) & X(2,3) & X(2,4) \end{array} \tag{5.59}$$

using a total of $5 \times 3^2 = 45$ complex operations. According to (5.54), the array in (5.59) is a rearrangement of $X(k)$ as

$$\begin{array}{ccccc} X(0) & X(1) & X(2) & X(3) & X(4) \\ X(5) & X(6) & X(7) & X(8) & X(9) \\ X(10) & X(11) & X(12) & X(13) & X(14) \end{array} \tag{5.60}$$

Finally, after "unwinding" this array in the row-wise fashion, we obtain the required 15-point DFT $X(k)$. The total number of complex operations required for this divide-and-combine approach is 135, whereas the direct approach for the 15-point DFT requires 225 complex operations. Thus the divide-and-combine approach is clearly efficient. $\square$

The divide-and-combine procedure can be further repeated if M or L are composite numbers. Clearly, the most efficient algorithm is obtained when N is a highly composite number, that is, $N = R^\nu$. Such algorithms are called *radix-R* FFT algorithms. When $N = R_1^{\nu_1} R_2^{\nu_2} \ldots$, then such decompositions are called *mixed-radix* FFT algorithms. The one most popular and easily programmable algorithm is the radix-2 FFT algorithm.

5.6.3 RADIX-2 FFT ALGORITHM

Let $N = 2^\nu$; then we choose $L = 2$ and $M = N/2$ and divide $x(n)$ into two $N/2$-point sequences according to (5.48) as

$$\begin{aligned} g_1(n) &= x(2n) \\ g_2(n) &= x(2n+1) \end{aligned}; \quad 0 \le n \le \frac{N}{2} - 1$$

The sequence $g_1(n)$ contains even-ordered samples of $x(n)$, while $g_2(n)$ contains odd-ordered samples of $x(n)$. Let $G_1(k)$ and $G_2(k)$ be $N/2$-point DFTs of $g_1(n)$ and $g_2(n)$, respectively. Then (5.49) reduces to

$$X(k) = G_1(k) + W_N^k G_2(k), \quad 0 \le k \le N - 1 \qquad \textbf{(5.61)}$$

This is called a *merging formula*, which combines two $N/2$-point DFTs into one N-point DFT. The total number of complex multiplications and additions reduces to

$$C_N = \frac{N^2}{2} + N = \mathrm{o}\left(N^2/2\right)$$

This procedure can be repeated again and again. At each stage, the sequences are decimated and the smaller DFTs combined. This decimation ends after ν stages when we have N one-point sequences, which are also one-point DFTs. The resulting procedure is called the *decimation-in-time* FFT (DIT-FFT) algorithm, for which the total number of complex multiplications is

$$C_N = N\nu = N \log_2 N$$

Clearly, if N is large, then C_N is approximately linear in N, which was the goal of our efficient algorithm. Using additional symmetries, C_N can be reduced to $\frac{N}{2} \log_2 N$. The signal flowgraph for this algorithm is shown in Figure 5.20 for $N = 8$.

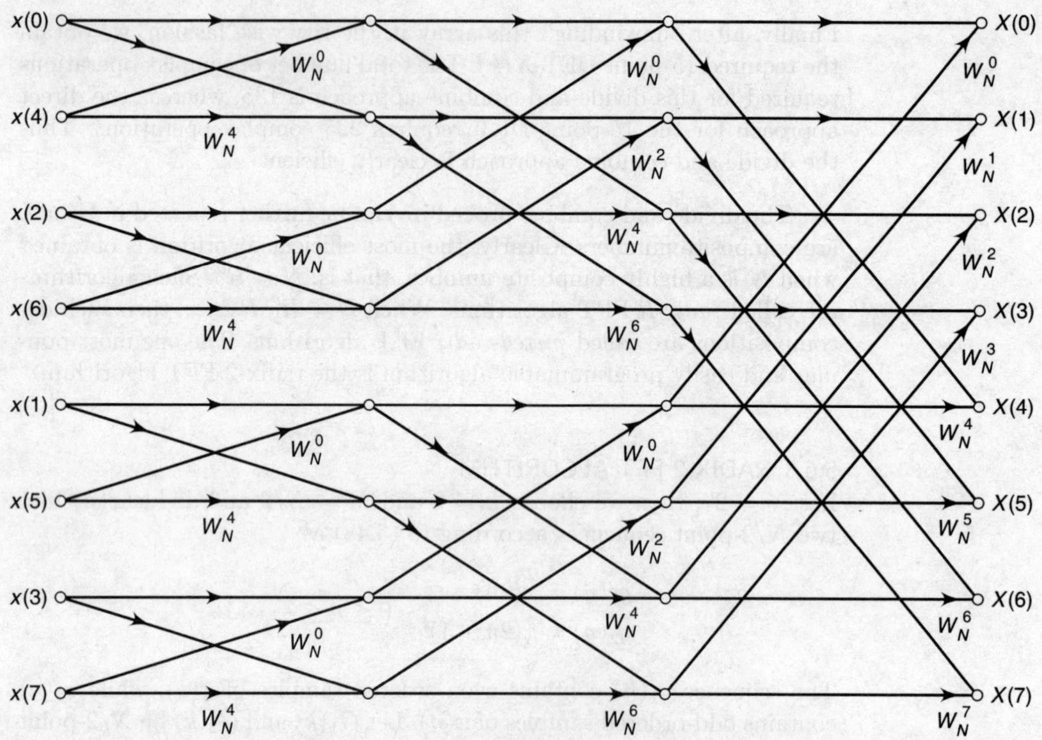

FIGURE 5.20   *Decimation-in-time FFT structure for $N = 8$*

In an alternate approach, we choose $M = 2$, $L = N/2$ and follow the steps in (5.49). Note that the initial DFTs are two-point DFTs, which contain no complex multiplications. From (5.50),

$$F(0, m) = x(0, m) + x(1, m)W_2^0$$
$$= x(n) + x(n + N/2), \quad 0 \le n \le N/2$$
$$F(1, m) = x(0, m) + x(1, m)W_2^1$$
$$= x(n) - x(n + N/2), \quad 0 \le n \le N/2$$

and from (5.51),

$$G(0, m) = F(0, m)W_N^0$$
$$= x(n) + x(n + N/2), \quad 0 \le n \le N/2$$
$$G(1, m) = F(1, m)W_N^m$$
$$= [x(n) - x(n + N/2)]\,W_N^n, \quad 0 \le n \le N/2$$

(5.62)

Let $G(0, m) = d_1(n)$ and $G(1, m) = d_2(n)$ for $0 \leq n \leq N/2 - 1$ (since they can be considered as time-domain sequences); then from (5.52) we have

$$X(0, q) = X(2q) \quad = D_1(q)$$
$$X(1, q) = X(2q + 1) = D_2(q)$$

(5.63)

This implies that the DFT values $X(k)$ are computed in a decimated fashion. Therefore, this approach is called a *decimation-in-frequency* FFT (DIF-FFT) algorithm. Its signal flowgraph is a transposed structure of the DIT-FFT structure, and its computational complexity is also equal to $\frac{N}{2} \log_2 N$.

5.6.4 MATLAB IMPLEMENTATION

MATLAB provides a function called `fft` to compute the DFT of a vector x. It is invoked by `X = fft(x,N)`, which computes the N-point DFT. If the length of x is less than N, then x is padded with zeros. If the argument N is omitted, then the length of the DFT is the length of x. If x is a matrix, then `fft(x,N)` computes the N-point DFT of each column of x.

This `fft` function is written in machine language and not using MATLAB commands (i.e., it is not available as a .m file). Therefore, it executes very fast. It is written as a mixed-radix algorithm. If N is a power of two, then a high-speed radix-2 FFT algorithm is employed. If N is not a power of two, then N is decomposed into prime factors and a slower mixed-radix FFT algorithm is used. Finally, if N is a prime number, then the `fft` function is reduced to the raw DFT algorithm.

The inverse DFT is computed using the `ifft` function, which has the same characteristics as `fft`.

☐ **EXAMPLE 5.22**

In this example, we will study the execution time of the `fft` function for $1 \leq N \leq 2048$. This will reveal the divide-and-combine strategy for various values of N. One note of caution. The results obtained in this example are valid only for MATLAB Versions 5 and earlier. Beginning in Version 6, MATLAB is using a new numerical computing core called LAPACK. It is optimized for memory references and cache usage and not for individual floating-point operations. Therefore, results for Version 6 and later are difficult to interpret. Also, the execution times given here are for a specific computer and may vary on different computers.

Solution

To determine the execution time, MATLAB provides two functions. The `clock` function provides the instantaneous clock reading, while the `etime(t1,t2)` function computes the elapsed time between two time marks `t1` and `t2`. To determine the execution time, we will generate random vectors from length 1 through 2048, compute their FFTs, and save the computation time in an array. Finally, we will plot this execution time versus N.

MATLAB script:

```
>> Nmax = 2048;  fft_time=zeros(1,Nmax);
>> for n=1:1:Nmax
>>    x=rand(1,n);
>>    t=clock;fft(x);fft_time(n)=etime(clock,t);
>> end
>> n=[1:1:Nmax];   plot(n,fft_time,'.')
>> xlabel('N');ylabel('Time in Sec');  title('FFT Execution Times')
```

The plot of the execution times is shown in Figure 5.21. This plot is very informative. The points in the plot do not show one clear function but appear to group themselves into various trends. The uppermost group depicts a $o(N^2)$ dependence on N, which means that these values must be prime numbers between 1 and 2048 for which the FFT algorithm defaults to the DFT algorithm. Similarly, there are groups corresponding to the $o\left(N^2/2\right)$, $o\left(N^2/3\right)$, $o\left(N^2/4\right)$, and so on, dependencies for which the number N has fewer decompositions. The last group shows the (almost linear) $o\left(N\log N\right)$ dependence, which is for

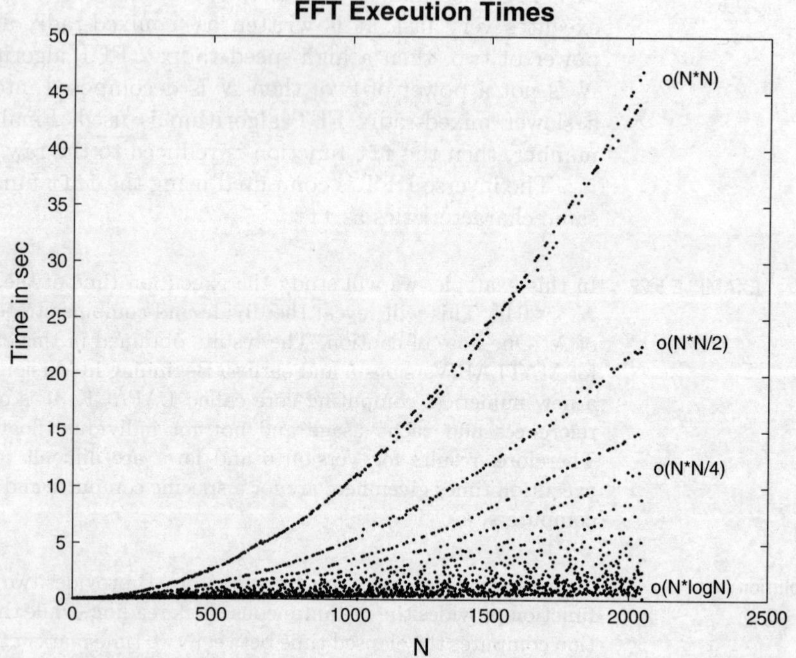

FIGURE 5.21   *FFT execution times for $1 <= N <= 2048$*

$N = 2^\nu, 0 \leq \nu \leq 11$. For these values of N, the radix-2 FFT algorithm is used. For all other values, a mixed-radix FFT algorithm is employed. This shows that the divide-and-combine strategy is very effective when N is highly composite. For example, the execution time is 0.16 sec for $N = 2048$, 2.48 sec for $N = 2047$, and 46.96 sec for $N = 2039$. $\qquad\qquad\qquad\qquad\qquad\qquad\square$

The MATLAB functions developed previously in this chapter should now be modified by substituting the `fft` function in place of the `dft` function. From the preceding example, care must be taken to use a highly composite N. A good practice is to choose $N = 2^\nu$ unless a specific situation demands otherwise.

5.6.5 FAST CONVOLUTIONS

The `conv` function in MATLAB is implemented using the `filter` function (which is written in C) and is very efficient for smaller values of N (<50). For larger values of N, it is possible to speed up the convolution using the FFT algorithm. This approach uses the circular convolution to implement the linear convolution, and the FFT to implement the circular convolution. The resulting algorithm is called a *fast convolution* algorithm. In addition, if we choose $N = 2^\nu$ and implement the radix-2 FFT, then the algorithm is called a *high-speed convolution*. Let $x_1(n)$ be an N_1-point sequence, and let $x_2(n)$ be an N_2-point sequence; then for high-speed convolution N is chosen to be

$$N = 2^{\lceil \log_2(N_1+N_2-1) \rceil} \qquad\qquad (5.64)$$

where $\lceil x \rceil$ is the smallest integer greater than x (also called a *ceiling* function). The linear convolution $x_1(n) * x_2(n)$ can now be implemented by two N-point FFTs, one N-point IFFT, and one N-point dot-product.

$$x_1(n) * x_2(n) = \text{IFFT}\left[\text{FFT}\left[x_1(n)\right] \cdot \text{FFT}\left[x_2(n)\right]\right] \qquad (5.65)$$

For large values of N, (5.65) is faster than the time-domain convolution, as we see in the following example.

$\square$ **EXAMPLE 5.23**   To demonstrate the effectiveness of the high-speed convolution, let us compare the execution times of two approaches. Let $x_1(n)$ be an L-point uniformly distributed random number between $[0, 1]$, and let $x_2(n)$ be an L-point Gaussian random sequence with mean 0 and variance 1. We will determine the average execution times for $1 \leq L \leq 150$, in which the average is computed over the 100 realizations of random sequences. (Please see the cautionary note given in Example 5.22.)

Solution MATLAB script:

```
conv_time = zeros(1,150); fft_time = zeros(1,150);
%
for L = 1:150
    tc = 0; tf=0;
   N = 2*L-1; nu = ceil(log10(N)/log10(2)); N = 2^nu;
    for I=1:100
       h = randn(1,L);  x = rand(1,L);
      t0 = clock; y1 = conv(h,x); t1=etime(clock,t0);  tc = tc+t1;
      t0 = clock; y2 = ifft(fft(h,N).*fft(x,N)); t2=etime(clock,t0);
      tf = tf+t2;
    end
%
    conv_time(L)=tc/100;  fft_time(L)=tf/100;
end
%
n = 1:150; subplot(1,1,1);
plot(n(25:150),conv_time(25:150),n(25:150),fft_time(25:150))
```

Figure 5.22 shows the linear convolution and the high-speed convolution times
for $25 \leq L \leq 150$. It should be noted that these times are affected by the

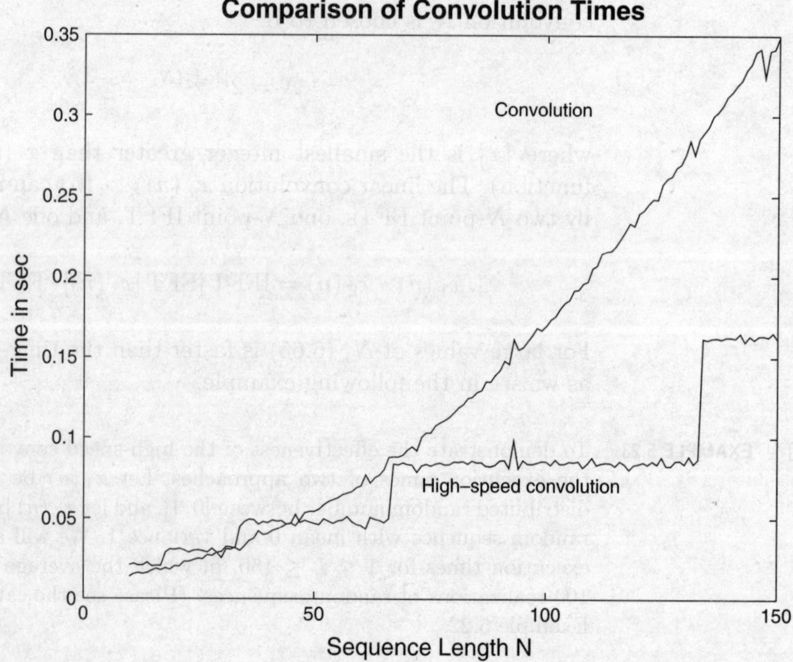

FIGURE 5.22 *Comparison of linear and high-speed convolution times*

computing platform used to execute the MATLAB script. The plot in Figure 5.22 was obtained on a 33 MHz 486 computer. It shows that for low values of L the linear convolution is faster. The crossover point appears to be $L = 50$, beyond which the linear convolution time increases exponentially, while the high-speed convolution time increases fairly linearly. Note that since $N = 2^\nu$, the high-speed convolution time is constant over a range on L. $\square$

5.6.6 HIGH-SPEED BLOCK CONVOLUTIONS

Earlier we discussed a block convolution algorithm called the overlap-and-save method (and its companion the overlap-and-add method), which is used to convolve a very large sequence with a relatively smaller sequence. The MATLAB function `ovrlpsav` developed in that section uses the DFT to implement the linear convolution. We can now replace the DFT by the radix-2 FFT algorithm to obtain a *high-speed* overlap-and-save algorithm. To further reduce the computations, the FFT of the shorter (fixed) sequence can be computed only once. The following `hsolpsav` function shows this algorithm.

```matlab
function [y] = hsolpsav(x,h,N)
% High-speed Overlap-Save method of block convolutions using FFT
% ----------------------------------------------------------------
% [y] = hsolpsav(x,h,N)
% y = output sequence
% x = input sequence
% h = impulse response
% N = block length (must be a power of two)
%
N = 2^(ceil(log10(N)/log10(2)));
Lenx = length(x); M = length(h);
M1 = M-1; L = N-M1;  h = fft(h,N);
%
x = [zeros(1,M1), x, zeros(1,N-1)];
K = floor((Lenx+M1-1)/(L)); % # of blocks
Y = zeros(K+1,N);
for k=0:K
xk = fft(x(k*L+1:k*L+N));
Y(k+1,:) = real(ifft(xk.*h));
end
Y = Y(:,M:N)'; y = (Y(:))';
```

A similar modification can be done to the overlap-and-add algorithm. MATLAB also provides the function `fftfilt` to implement the overlap-and-add algorithm.

5.7 PROBLEMS

P5.1   Compute the DFS coefficients of the following periodic sequences using the DFS definition, and then verify your answers using MATLAB.

1. $\tilde{x}_1(n) = \{4, 1, -1, 1\}$, $N = 4$
2. $\tilde{x}_2(n) = \{2, 0, 0, 0, -1, 0, 0, 0\}$, $N = 8$
3. $\tilde{x}_3(n) = \{1, 0, -1, -1, 0\}$, $N = 5$
4. $\tilde{x}_4(n) = \{0, 0, 2j, 0, 2j, 0\}$, $N = 6$
5. $\tilde{x}_5(n) = \{3, 2, 1\}$, $N = 3$

P5.2   Determine the periodic sequences given the following periodic DFS coefficients. First use the IDFS definition, and then verify your answers using MATLAB.

1. $\tilde{X}_1(k) = \{4, 3j, -3j\}$, $N = 3$
2. $\tilde{X}_2(k) = \{j, 2j, 3j, 4j\}$, $N = 4$
3. $\tilde{X}_3(k) = \{1, 2 + 3j, 4, 2 - 3j\}$, $N = 4$
4. $\tilde{X}_4(k) = \{0, 0, 2, 0, 0\}$, $N = 5$
5. $\tilde{X}_5(k) = \{3, 0, 0, 0, -3, 0, 0, 0\}$, $N = 8$

P5.3   Let $\tilde{x}_1(n)$ be periodic with fundamental period $N = 40$, where one period is given by

$$\tilde{x}_1(n) = \begin{cases} 5\sin(0.1\pi n), & 0 \le n \le 19 \\ 0, & 20 \le n \le 39 \end{cases}$$

and let $\tilde{x}_2(n)$ be periodic with fundamental period $N = 80$, where one period is given by

$$\tilde{x}_2(n) = \begin{cases} 5\sin(0.1\pi n), & 0 \le n \le 19 \\ 0, & 20 \le n \le 79 \end{cases}$$

These two periodic sequences differ in their periodicity but otherwise have the same nonzero samples.

1. Compute the DFS $\tilde{X}_1(k)$ of $\tilde{x}_1(n)$, and plot samples (using the **stem** function) of its magnitude and angle versus k.
2. Compute the DFS $\tilde{X}_2(k)$ of $\tilde{x}_2(n)$, and plot samples of its magnitude and angle versus k.
3. What is the difference between the two preceding DFS plots?

P5.4   Consider the periodic sequence $\tilde{x}_1(n)$ given in Problem P5.3. Let $\tilde{x}_2(n)$ be periodic with fundamental period $N = 40$, where one period is given by

$$\tilde{x}_2(n) = \begin{cases} \tilde{x}_1(n), & 0 \le n \le 19 \\ -\tilde{x}_1(n - 20), & 20 \le n \le 39 \end{cases}$$

1. Determine analytically the DFS $\tilde{X}_2(k)$ in terms of $\tilde{X}_1(k)$.
2. Compute the DFS $\tilde{X}_2(k)$ of $\tilde{x}_2(n)$, and plot samples of its magnitude and angle versus k.
3. Verify your answer in part 1 using the plots of $\tilde{X}_1(k)$ and $\tilde{X}_2(k)$?

P5.5   Consider the periodic sequence $\tilde{x}_1(n)$ given in Problem P5.3. Let $\tilde{x}_3(n)$ be periodic with period 80, obtained by concatenating two periods of $\tilde{x}_1(n)$, that is,

$$\tilde{x}_3(n) = [\tilde{x}_1(n), \tilde{x}_1(n)]_{\text{PERIODIC}}$$

Clearly, $\tilde{x}_3(n)$ is different from $\tilde{x}_2(n)$ of Problem P5.3 even though both of them are periodic with period 80.

1. Compute the DFS $\tilde{X}_3(k)$ of $\tilde{x}_3(n)$, and plot samples of its magnitude and angle versus k.
2. What effect does the periodicity doubling have on the DFS?
3. Generalize this result to M-fold periodicity. In particular, show that if

$$\tilde{x}_M(n) = \left[\underbrace{\tilde{x}_1(n), \tilde{x}_1(n), \ldots, \tilde{x}_1(n)}_{M \text{ times}}\right]_{\text{PERIODIC}}$$

then

$$\tilde{X}_M(Mk) = M\tilde{X}_1(k), \quad k = 0, 1, \ldots, N-1$$
$$\tilde{X}_M(k) = 0, \qquad\qquad k \neq 0, M, \ldots, MN$$

P5.6 Let $X(e^{j\omega})$ be the DTFT of a finite-length sequence

$$x(n) = \begin{cases} n+1, & 0 \leq n \leq 49 \\ 100 - n, & 50 \leq n \leq 99 \\ 0, & \text{otherwise} \end{cases}$$

1. Let

$$y_1(n) = \overset{\text{10-point}}{\text{IDFS}} \left[X(e^{j0}), X(e^{j2\pi/10}), X(e^{j4\pi/10}), \ldots, X(e^{j18\pi/10})\right]$$

Determine $y_1(n)$ using the frequency sampling theorem. Verify your answer using MATLAB.

2. Let

$$y_2(n) = \overset{\text{200-point}}{\text{IDFS}} \left[X(e^{j0}), X(e^{j2\pi/200}), X(e^{j4\pi/200}), \ldots, X(e^{j398\pi/200})\right]$$

Determine $y_2(n)$ using the frequency sampling theorem. Verify your answer using MATLAB.

3. Comment on your results in parts (a) and (b).

P5.7 Let $\tilde{x}(n)$ be a periodic sequence with period N, and let

$$\tilde{y}(n) \overset{\triangle}{=} \tilde{x}(-n) = \tilde{x}(N-n)$$

that is, $\tilde{y}(n)$ is a periodically folded version of $\tilde{x}(n)$. Let $\tilde{X}(k)$ and $\tilde{Y}(k)$ be the DFS sequences.

1. Show that

$$\tilde{Y}(k) = \tilde{X}(-k) = \tilde{X}(N-k)$$

that is, $\tilde{Y}(k)$ is also a periodically folded version of $\tilde{X}(k)$.

2. Let $\tilde{x}(n) = \{2, 4, 6, 1, 3, 5\}_{\text{PERIODIC}}$ with $N = 6$.

(a) *Sketch* $\tilde{y}(n)$ for $0 \leq n \leq 5$.

(b) Compute $\tilde{X}(k)$ for $0 \leq k \leq 5$.

(c) Compute $\tilde{Y}(k)$ for $0 \leq k \leq 5$.

(d) Verify the relation in part 1.

P5.8 Consider the following finite-length sequence:

$$x(n) = \begin{cases} \text{sinc}^2\{(n-50)/2\}, & 0 \leq n \leq 100 \\ 0, & \text{else} \end{cases}$$

1. Determine the DFT $X(k)$ of $x(n)$. Plot (using the **stem** function) its magnitude and phase.
2. Plot the magnitude and phase of the DTFT $X(e^{j\omega})$ of $x(n)$ using MATLAB.
3. Verify that the above DFT is the sampled version of $X(e^{j\omega})$. It might be helpful to combine the above two plots in one graph using the **hold** function.
4. Is it possible to reconstruct the DTFT $X(e^{j\omega})$ from the DFT $X(k)$? If possible, give the necessary interpolation formula for reconstruction. If not possible, state why this reconstruction cannot be done.

P5.9 Let a finite-length sequence be given by

$$x(n) = \begin{cases} 2e^{-0.9|n|}, & -5 \leq n \leq 5 \\ 0, & \text{otherwise} \end{cases}$$

Plot the DTFT $X(e^{j\omega})$ of the above sequence using DFT as a computation tool. Choose the length N of the DFT so that this plot appears to be a smooth graph.

P5.10 Plot the DTFT magnitude and angle of each of the following sequences using the DFT as a computation tool. Make an educated guess about the length N so that your plots are meaningful.

1. $x(n) = (0.6)^{|n|}\left[u(n+10) - u(n-11)\right]$
2. $x(n) = n(0.9)^n\left[u(n) - u(n-21)\right]$
3. $x(n) = [\cos(0.5\pi n) + j\sin(0.5\pi n)][u(n) - u(n-51)]$
4. $x(n) = \{1, 2, 3, 4, 3, 2, 1\}$
   $\phantom{x(n) = \{1,}\uparrow$
5. $x(n) = \{-1, -2, -3, 0, 3, 2, 1\}$
   $\phantom{x(n) = \{-1, -2,}\uparrow$

P5.11 Let $H(e^{j\omega})$ be the frequency response of a real, causal discrete-time LSI system.

1. If

$$\text{Re}\left\{H\left(e^{j\omega}\right)\right\} = \sum_{k=0}^{5} (0.9)^k \cos(k\omega)$$

determine the impulse response $h(n)$ analytically. Verify your answer using DFT as a computation tool. Choose the length N appropriately.

2. If

$$\text{Im}\left\{H\left(e^{j\omega}\right)\right\} = \sum_{\ell=0}^{5} 2\ell \sin(\ell\omega), \quad \text{and} \quad \int_{-\pi}^{\pi} H(e^{j\omega})d\omega = 0$$

determine the impulse response $h(n)$ analytically. Verify your answer using DFT as a computation tool. Again choose the length N appropriately.

P5.12 Let $X(k)$ denote the N-point DFT of an N-point sequence $x(n)$. The DFT $X(k)$ itself is an N-point sequence.

1. If the DFT of $X(k)$ is computed to obtain another N-point sequence $x_1(n)$, show that

$$x_1(n) = Nx((-n))_N, \quad 0 \le n \le N - 1$$

2. Using this property, design a MATLAB function to implement an N-point circular folding operation $x_2(n) = x_1((-n))_N$. The format should be

```
x2 = circfold(x1,N)
% Circular folding using DFT
% x2 = circfold(x1,N)
% x2 = circularly folded output sequence
% x1 = input sequence of length <= N
%  N = circular buffer length
```

3. Determine the circular folding of the following sequence:

$$x_1(n) = \{1, 3, 5, 7, 9, -7, -5, -3, -1\}$$

P5.13 Let $X(k)$ be an N-point DFT of an N-point sequence $x(n)$. Let N be an even integer.

1. If $x(n) = x(n + N/2)$ for all n, then show that $X(k) = 0$ for k odd (i.e., nonzero for k even). Verify this result for $x(n) = \{1, 2, -3, 4, 5, 1, 2, -3, 4, 5\}$.
2. If $x(n) = -x(n + N/2)$ for all n, then show that $X(k) = 0$ for k even (i.e., nonzero for k odd). Verify this result for $x(n) = \{1, 2, -3, 4, 5, -1, -2, 3, -4, -5\}$.

P5.14 Let $X(k)$ be an N-point DFT of an N-point sequence $x(n)$. Let $N = 4\nu$ where ν is an integer.

1. If $x(n) = x(n + \nu)$ for all n, then show that $X(k)$ is nonzero for $k = 4\ell$ for $0 \le \ell \le \nu - 1$. Verify this result for $x(n) = \{1, 2, 3, 1, 2, 3, 1, 2, 3, 1, 2, 3\}$.
2. If $x(n) = -x(n + \nu)$ for all n, then show that $X(k)$ is nonzero for $k = 4\ell + 2$ for $0 \le \ell \le \nu - 1$. Verify this result for $x(n) = \{1, 2, 3, -1, -2, -3, 1, 2, 3, -1, -2, -3\}$.

P5.15 Let $X(k)$ be an N-point DFT of an N-point sequence $x(n)$. Let $N = 2\mu\nu$ where μ and ν are integers.

1. If $x(n) = x(n + \nu)$ for all n, then show that $X(k)$ is nonzero for $k = 2(\mu\ell)$ for $0 \le \ell \le \nu - 1$. Verify this result for $x(n) = \{1, -2, 3, 1, -2, 3, 1, -2, 3, 1, -2, 3, 1, -2, 3, 1, -2, 3\}$.
2. If $x(n) = -x(n + \nu)$ for all n, then show that $X(k)$ is nonzero for $k = 2(\mu\ell + 1)$ for $0 \le \ell \le \nu - 1$. Verify this result for $x(n) = \{1, -2, 3, -1, 2, -3, 1, -2, 3, -1, 2, -3, 1, -2, 3, -1, 2, -3\}$.

P5.16 Let $X(k)$ and $Y(k)$ be 10-point DFTs of two 10-point sequences $x(n)$ and $y(n)$, respectively. If

$$X(k) = \exp(j0.2\pi k), \quad 0 \le k \le 9$$

determine $Y(k)$ in each of the following cases without computing the DFT.

1. $y(n) = x((n-5))_{10}$
2. $y(n) = x((n+4))_{10}$
3. $y(n) = x((3-n))_{10}$
4. $y(n) = x(n)e^{j3\pi n/5}$
5. $y(n) = x(n) \;⑩\; x((-n))_{10}$

Verify your answers using MATLAB.

P5.17 The first six values of the 10-point DFT of a real-valued sequence $x(n)$ are given by

$$\{10, -2+j3, 3+j4, 2-j3, 4+j5, 12\}$$

Determine the DFT of each of the following sequences using DFT properties.

1. $x_1(n) = x((2-n))_{10}$
2. $x_2(n) = x((n+5))_{10}$
3. $x_3(n) = x(n)x((-n))_{10}$
4. $x_4(n) = x(n) \;⑩\; x((-n))_{10}$
5. $x_5(n) = x(n)e^{-j4\pi n/5}$

P5.18 Complex-valued N-point sequence $x(n)$ can be decomposed into N-point circular-conjugate-symmetric and circular-conjugate-antisymmetric sequences using the following relations:

$$x_{\text{ccs}}(n) \triangleq \frac{1}{2}\left[x(n) + x^*((-n))_N\right]$$

$$x_{\text{cca}}(n) \triangleq \frac{1}{2}\left[x(n) - x^*((-n))_N\right]$$

If $X_{\text{R}}(k)$ and $X_{\text{I}}(k)$ are the real and imaginary parts of the N-point DFT of $x(n)$, then

$$\text{DFT}\left[x_{\text{ccs}}(n)\right] = X_{\text{R}}(k) \quad \text{and} \quad \text{DFT}\left[x_{\text{cca}}(n)\right] = jX_{\text{I}}(k)$$

1. Prove these relations property analytically.
2. Modify the `circevod` function developed in the chapter so that it can be used for complex-valued sequences.
3. Let $X(k) = [3\cos(0.2\pi k) + j4\sin(0.1\pi k)][u(k) - u(k-20)]$ be a 20-point DFT. Verify this symmetry property using your `circevod` function.

P5.19 If $X(k)$ is the N-point DFT of an N-point complex-valued sequence

$$x(n) = x_{\text{R}}(n) + jx_{\text{I}}(n)$$

where $x_{\text{R}}(n)$ and $x_{\text{I}}(n)$ are the real and imaginary parts of $x(n)$, then

$$\text{DFT}\left[x_{\text{R}}(n)\right] = X_{\text{ccs}}(k) \quad \text{and} \quad \text{DFT}\left[jx_{\text{I}}(n)\right] = X_{\text{cca}}(k)$$

where $X_{\text{ccs}}(k)$ and $X_{\text{cca}}(k)$ are the circular-even and circular-odd components of $X(k)$ as defined in Problem P5.18.

1. Prove this property analytically.
2. This property can be used to compute the DFTs of two real-valued N-point sequences using one N-point DFT operation. Specifically, let $x_1(n)$ and $x_2(n)$ be two N-point sequences. Then we can form a complex-valued sequence

$$x(n) = x_1(n) + jx_2(n)$$

and use this property. Develop a MATLAB function to implement this approach with the following format.

```
function [X1,X2] = real2dft(x1,x2,N)
% DFTs of two real sequences
% [X1,X2] = real2dft(x1,x2,N)
%   X1 = n-point DFT of x1
%   X2 = n-point DFT of x2
%   x1 = sequence of length <= N
%   x2 = sequence of length <= N
%    N = length of DFT
```

3. Compute and plot the DFTs of the following two sequences using this function:

$$x_1(n) = \cos(0.1\pi n), \; x_2(n) = \sin(0.2\pi n); \quad 0 \le n \le 39$$

P5.20 Using the frequency domain approach, devise a MATLAB function to determine a circular shift $x((n-m))_N$, given an N_1-point sequence $x(n)$ where $N_1 \le N$. Your function should have the following format.

```
function y = cirshftf(x,m,N)
%   Circular shift of m samples wrt size N in sequence x: (freq domain)
%   --------------------------------------------------------------------
%   y = cirshftf(x,m,N)
%        y : output sequence containing the circular shift
%        x : input sequence of length <= N
%        m : sample shift
%        N : size of circular buffer
%   Method: y(n) = idft(dft(x(n))*WN^(mk))
%
%   If m is a scalar then y is a sequence (row vector)
%   If m is a vector then y is a matrix, each row is a circular shift
%        in x corresponding to entries in vector m
%   M and x should not be matrices
```

Verify your function on the following sequence:

$$x(n) = \{5, 4, 3, 2, 1, 0, 0, 1, 2, 3, 4\}, \quad 0 \le n \le 10$$
$$\uparrow$$

with (a) $m = -5$, $N = 12$ and (b) $m = 8$, $N = 15$.

P5.21 Using the analysis and synthesis equations of the DFT, show that the energy of a sequence satisfies

$$\mathcal{E}_X \triangleq \sum_{n=0}^{N-1} |x(n)|^2 = \frac{1}{N} \sum_{k=0}^{N-1} |X(k)|^2$$

This is commonly referred to as a *Parseval's relation for the DFT*. Verify this relation using MATLAB on the sequence in Problem P5.20.

P5.22 A 512-point DFT $X(k)$ of a real-valued sequence $x(n)$ has the DFT values

$$X(0) = 20 + j\alpha; \qquad X(5) = 20 + j30; \qquad X(k_1) = -10 + j15; \quad X(152) = 17 + j23;$$

$$X(k_2) = 20 - j30; \quad X(k_3) = 17 - j23; \qquad X(480) = -10 - j15; \quad X(256) = 30 + j\beta$$

and all other values are known to be zero.

1. Determine the real-valued coefficients α and β.
2. Determine the values of the integers k_1, k_2, and k_3.
3. Determine the energy of the signal $x(n)$.
4. Express the sequence $x(n)$ in a closed form.

P5.23 Let $x(n)$ be a finite length sequence given by

$$x(n) = \left\{ \ldots, 0, 0, 0, 1, 2, -3, 4, -5, 0, \ldots \right\}$$

Determine and sketch the sequence $x((-8 - n))_7 \mathcal{R}_7(n)$ where

$$\mathcal{R}_7(n) = \begin{cases} 1, & 0 \le n \le 6 \\ 0, & \text{elsewhere} \end{cases}$$

P5.24 The `circonvt` function developed in this chapter implements the circular convolution as a matrix-vector multiplication. The matrix corresponding to the circular shifts $\{x((n - m))_N; 0 \le n \le N - 1\}$ has an interesting structure. This matrix is called a *circulant* matrix, which is a special case of Toeplitz matrix introduced in Chapter 2.

1. Consider the sequences given in Example 5.13. Express $x_1(n)$ as a column vector $\mathbf{x}_1$ and $x_2((n - m))_N$ as a circulant matrix $\mathbf{X}_2$ with rows corresponding to $n = 0, 1, 2, 3$. Characterize this matrix $\mathbf{X}_2$. Can it completely be described by its first row (or column)?
2. Determine the circular convolution as $\mathbf{X}_2\mathbf{x}_1$ and verify your calculations.

P5.25 Develop a MATLAB function to construct a circulant matrix $\mathbf{C}$ given an N-point sequence $x(n)$. Use the `toeplitz` function to implement matrix $\mathbf{C}$. Your subroutine function should have the following format.

```
function [C] = circulnt(x,N)
% Circulant Matrix from an N-point sequence
% [C] = circulnt(x,N)
% C = circulant matrix of size NxN
% x = sequence of length <= N
% N = size of circulant matrix
```

Using this function, modify the circular convolution function `circonvt` discussed in the chapter so that the `for...end` loop is eliminated. Verify your functions on the sequences in Problem P5.24.

P5.26 Using the frequency domain approach, devise a MATLAB function to implement the circular convolution operation between two sequences. The format of the sequence should be

```
function x3 = circonvf(x1,x2,N)
% Circular convolution in the frequency domain
%   x3 = circonvf(x1,x2,N)
%   x3 = convolution result of length N
%   x1 = sequence of length <= N
%   x2 = sequence of length <= N
%    N = length of circular buffer
```

Using your function, compute the circular convolution $\{4, 3, 2, 1\}$ $\textcircled{4}$ $\{1, 2, 3, 4\}$.

P5.27 The following four sequences are given:

$$x_1(n) = \{1, 3, 2, -1\}; \quad x_2(n) = \{2, 1, 0, -1\}; \quad x_3(n) = x_1(n) * x_2(n); \quad x_4(n) = x_1(n) \textcircled{5} x_2(n)$$

1. Determine and sketch $x_3(n)$.
2. Using $x_3(n)$ alone, determine and sketch $x_4(n)$. Do not directly compute $x_4(n)$.

P5.28 Compute the N-point circular convolution for the following sequences. Plot their samples.

1. $x_1(n) = \sin(\pi n/3)\mathcal{R}_6(n), \quad x_2(n) = \cos(\pi n/4)\mathcal{R}_8(n); \quad N = 10$
2. $x_1(n) = \cos(2\pi n/N)\mathcal{R}_N(n), \quad x_2(n) = \sin(2\pi n/N)\mathcal{R}_N(n); \quad N = 32$
3. $x_1(n) = (0.8)^n\,\mathcal{R}_N(n), \quad x_2(n) = (-0.8)^n\,\mathcal{R}_N(n); \quad N = 20$
4. $x_1(n) = n\mathcal{R}_N(n), \quad x_2(n) = (N - n)\,\mathcal{R}_N(n); \quad N = 10$
5. $x_1(n) = (0.8)^n R_{20}, \quad x_2(n) = u(n) - u(n - 40); \quad N = 50$

P5.29 Let $x_1(n)$ and $x_2(n)$ be two N-point sequences.

1. If $y(n) = x_1(n) \, \textcircled{N} \, x_2(n)$ show that

$$\sum_{n=0}^{N-1} y(n) = \left(\sum_{n=0}^{N-1} x_1(n)\right) \left(\sum_{n=0}^{N-1} x_2(n)\right)$$

2. Verify this result for the following sequences:

$$x_1(n) = \{9, 4, -1, 4, -4, -1, 8, 3\}; \quad x_2(n) = \{-5, 6, 2, -7, -5, 2, 2, -2\}$$

P5.30 Let $X(k)$ be the eight-point DFT of a three-point sequence $x(n) = \{5, -4, 3\}$. Let $Y(k)$ be the eight-point DFT of a sequence $y(n)$. Determine $y(n)$ when $Y(k) = W_8^{5k}X(-k)_8$.

P5.31 For the following sequences, compute (i) the N-point circular convolution $x_3(n) = x_1(n) \, \textcircled{N} \, x_2(n)$, (ii) the linear convolution $x_4(n) = x_1(n) * x_2(n)$, and (iii) the error sequence $e(n) = x_3(n) - x_4(n)$.

1. $x_1(n) = \{1, 1, 1, 1\}, \quad x_2(n) = \cos(\pi n/4)\mathcal{R}_6(n); \quad N = 8$
2. $x_1(n) = \cos(2\pi n/N)\mathcal{R}_{16}(n), \quad x_2(n) = \sin(2\pi n/N)\mathcal{R}_{16}(n); \quad N = 32$
3. $x_1(n) = (0.8)^n\,\mathcal{R}_{10}(n), \quad x_2(n) = (-0.8)^n\,\mathcal{R}_{10}(n); \quad N = 15$
4. $x_1(n) = n\mathcal{R}_{10}(n), \quad x_2(n) = (N - n)\,\mathcal{R}_{10}(n); \quad N = 10$
5. $x_1(n) = \{1, -1, 1, -1\}, \quad x_2(n) = \{1, 0, -1, 0\}; \quad N = 5$

In each case, verify that $e(n) = x_4(n + N)$.

P5.32 The overlap-add method of block convolution is an alternative to the overlap-save method. Let $x(n)$ be a long sequence of length ML where $M, L \gg 1$. Divide $x(n)$ into M segments $\{x_m(n),\ m = 1, \ldots, M\}$ each of length L

$$x_m(n) = \begin{cases} x(n), & mL \le n \le (m+1)L - 1 \\ 0, & \text{elsewhere} \end{cases} \quad \text{so that} \quad x(n) = \sum_{m=0}^{M-1} x_m(n)$$

Let $h(n)$ be an L-point impulse response. Then

$$y(n) = x(n) * h(n) = \sum_{m=0}^{M-1} x_m(n) * h(n) = \sum_{m=0}^{M-1} y_m(n); \quad y_m(n) \stackrel{\triangle}{=} x_m(n) * h(n)$$

Clearly, $y_m(n)$ is a $(2L - 1)$-point sequence. In this method, we have to save the intermediate convolution results and then properly overlap these before adding to form the final result $y(n)$. To use DFT for this operation, we have to choose $N \ge (2L - 1)$.

1. Develop a MATLAB function to implement the overlap-add method using the circular convolution operation. The format should be

```
function [y] = ovrlpadd(x,h,N)
% Overlap-Add method of block convolution
% [y] = ovrlpadd(x,h,N)
%
% y = output sequence
% x = input sequence
% h = impulse response
% N = block length >= 2*length(h)-1
```

2. Incorporate the radix-2 FFT implementation in this function to obtain a high-speed overlap-add block convolution routine. Remember to choose $N = 2^\nu$.
3. Verify your functions on the following two sequences:

$$x(n) = \cos(\pi n/500)\,\mathcal{R}_{4000}(n), \quad h(n) = \{1, -1, 1, -1\}$$

P5.33 Given the following sequences $x_1(n)$ and $x_2(n)$:

$$x_1(n) = \{2, 1, 1, 2\}, \quad x_2(n) = \{1, -1, -1, 1\}$$

1. Compute the circular convolution $x_1(n)\ \textcircled{N}\ x_2(n)$ for $N = 4$, 7, and 8.
2. Compute the linear convolution $x_1(n) * x_2(n)$.
3. Using results of calculations, determine the minimum value of N necessary so that linear and circular convolutions are the same on the N-point interval.
4. Without performing the actual convolutions, explain how you could have obtained the result of P5.33.3.

P5.34 Let

$$x(n) = \begin{cases} A\cos(2\pi\ell n/N), & 0 \le n \le N - 1 \\ 0, & \text{elsewhere} \end{cases} = A\cos(2\pi\ell n/N)\,\mathcal{R}_N(n)$$

where ℓ is an integer. Notice that $x(n)$ contains *exactly* ℓ periods (or cycles) of the cosine waveform in N samples. This is a windowed cosine sequence containing *no leakage*.

1. Show that the DFT $X(k)$ is a real sequence given by

$$X(k) = \frac{AN}{2}\delta(k - \ell) + \frac{AN}{2}\delta(k - N + \ell); \quad 0 \le k \le (N-1), \quad 0 < \ell < N$$

2. Show that if $\ell = 0$, then the DFT $X(k)$ is given by

$$X(k) = AN\delta(k); \quad 0 \le k \le (N-1)$$

3. Explain clearly how these results should be modified if $\ell < 0$ or $\ell > N$.
4. Verify the results of parts 1, 2, and 3 using the following sequences. Plot the real parts of the DFT sequences using the `stem` function.

   (a) $x_1(n) = 3\cos(0.04\pi n)\,\mathcal{R}_{200}(n)$
   (b) $x_2(n) = 5\mathcal{R}_{50}(n)$
   (c) $x_3(n) = [1 + 2\cos(0.5\pi n) + \cos(\pi n)]\,\mathcal{R}_{100}(n)$
   (d) $x_4(n) = \cos(25\pi n/16)\,\mathcal{R}_{64}(n)$
   (e) $x_5(n) = [4\cos(0.1\pi n) - 3\cos(1.9\pi n)]\,\mathcal{R}_{40}(n)$

P5.35 Let $x(n) = A\cos(\omega_0 n)\,\mathcal{R}_N(n)$, where ω_0 is a real number.

1. Using the properties of the DFT, show that the real and the imaginary parts of $X(k)$ are given by

$$X(k) = X_R(k) + jX_I(k)$$

$$X_R(k) = (A/2)\cos\left[\tfrac{\pi(N-1)}{N}(k - f_0 N)\right]\frac{\sin[\pi(k - f_0 N)]}{\sin[\pi(k - f_0 N)/N]}$$

$$+ (A/2)\cos\left[\tfrac{\pi(N-1)}{N}(k + f_0 N)\right]\frac{\sin[\pi(k - N + f_0 N)]}{\sin[\pi(k - N + f_0 N)/N]}$$

$$X_I(k) = -(A/2)\sin\left[\tfrac{\pi(N-1)}{N}(k - f_0 N)\right]\frac{\sin[\pi(k - f_0 N)]}{\sin[\pi(k - f_0 N)/N]}$$

$$- (A/2)\sin\left[\tfrac{\pi(N-1)}{N}(k + f_0 N)\right]\frac{\sin[\pi(k - N + f_0 N)]}{\sin[\pi(k - N + f_0 N)/N]}$$

2. This result implies that the original frequency ω_0 of the cosine waveform has *leaked* into other frequencies that form the harmonics of the time-limited sequence, and hence it is called the leakage property of cosines. It is a natural result due to the fact that bandlimited periodic cosines are sampled over noninteger periods. Explain this result using the periodic extension $\tilde{x}(n)$ of $x(n)$ and the result in Problem P5.34.1.
3. Verify the leakage property using $x(n) = \cos(5\pi n/99)\,\mathcal{R}_{200}(n)$. Plot the real and the imaginary parts of $X(k)$ using the `stem` function.

P5.36 Let

$$x(n) = \begin{cases} A\sin(2\pi\ell n/N), & 0 \le n \le N-1 \\ 0, & \text{elsewhere} \end{cases} = A\sin(2\pi\ell n/N)\,\mathcal{R}_N(n)$$

where ℓ is an integer. Notice that $x(n)$ contains *exactly* ℓ periods (or cycles) of the sine waveform in N samples. This is a windowed sine sequence containing *no leakage*.

1. Show that the DFT $X(k)$ is a purely imaginary sequence given by

$$X(k) = \frac{AN}{2j}\delta\,(k - \ell) - \frac{AN}{2j}\delta(k - N + \ell); \quad 0 \le k \le (N-1), \quad 0 < \ell < N$$

2. Show that if $\ell = 0$, then the DFT $X(k)$ is given by

$$X(k) = 0; \quad 0 \le k \le (N-1)$$

3. Explain clearly how these results should be modified if $\ell < 0$ or $\ell > N$.
4. Verify the results of parts 1, 2, and 3 using the following sequences. Plot the imaginary parts of the DFT sequences using the **stem** function.

   (a) $x_1(n) = 3\sin\,(0.04\pi n)\,\mathcal{R}_{200}(n)$
   (b) $x_2(n) = 5\sin 10\pi n\mathcal{R}_{50}(n)$
   (c) $x_3(n) = [2\sin\,(0.5\pi n) + \sin\,(\pi n)]\,\mathcal{R}_{100}(n)$
   (d) $x_4(n) = \sin\,(25\pi n/16)\,\mathcal{R}_{64}(n)$
   (e) $x_5(n) = [4\sin\,(0.1\pi n) - 3\sin\,(1.9\pi n)]\,\mathcal{R}_{20}(n)$

P5.37 Let $x(n) = A\sin\,(\omega_0 n)\,\mathcal{R}_N(n)$, where ω_0 is a real number.

1. Using the properties of the DFT, show that the real and the imaginary parts of $X(k)$ are given by

$$X(k) = X_R(k) + jX_I(k)$$

$$X_R(k) = -\,(A/2)\sin\left[\tfrac{\pi(N-1)}{N}\,(k - f_0 N)\right]\frac{\sin\,[\pi\,(k - f_0 N)]}{\sin\,[\pi(k - f_0 N)/N]}$$

$$+\,(A/2)\sin\left[\tfrac{\pi(N-1)}{N}\,(k + f_0 N)\right]\frac{\sin\,[\pi\,(k - N + f_0 N)]}{\sin\,[\pi(k - N + f_0 N)/N]}$$

$$X_I(k) = -\,(A/2)\cos\left[\tfrac{\pi(N-1)}{N}\,(k - f_0 N)\right]\frac{\sin\,[\pi\,(k - f_0 N)]}{\sin\,[\pi(k - f_0 N)/N]}$$

$$+\,(A/2)\cos\left[\tfrac{\pi(N-1)}{N}\,(k + f_0 N)\right]\frac{\sin\,[\pi\,(k - N + f_0 N)]}{\sin\,[\pi(k - N + f_0 N)/N]}$$

2. This result is the leakage property of sines. Explain it using the periodic extension $\tilde{x}(n)$ of $x(n)$ and the result in Problem P5.36.1.
3. Verify the leakage property using $x(n) = \sin\,(5\pi n/99)\,\mathcal{R}_{100}(n)$. Plot the real and the imaginary parts of $X(k)$ using the **stem** function.

P5.38 An analog signal $x_a(t) = 2\sin\,(4\pi t) + 5\cos\,(8\pi t)$ is sampled at $t = 0.01n$ for $n = 0, 1, \ldots, N - 1$ to obtain an N-point sequence $x(n)$. An N-point DFT is used to obtain an estimate of the magnitude spectrum of $x_a(t)$.

1. From the following values of N, choose the one that will provide the accurate estimate of the spectrum of $x_a(t)$. Plot the real and imaginary parts of the DFT spectrum $X(k)$.
   (a) $N = 40$,   (b) $N = 50$,   (c) $N = 60$.

2. From the following values of N, choose the one that will provide the least amount of leakage in the spectrum of $x_a(t)$. Plot the real and imaginary parts of the DFT spectrum $X(k)$.
   (a) $N = 90$,   (b) $N = 95$,   (c) $N = 99$.

P5.39 Using (5.49), determine and draw the signal flow graph for the $N = 8$ point, radix-2 decimation-in-frequency FFT algorithm. Using this flow graph, determine the DFT of the sequence

$$x(n) = \cos(\pi n/2), \quad 0 \le n \le 7$$

P5.40 Using (5.49), determine and draw the signal flow graph for the $N = 16$ point, radix-4 decimation-in-time FFT algorithm. Using this flow graph, determine the DFT of the sequence

$$x(n) = \cos(\pi n/2), \quad 0 \le n \le 15$$

P5.41 Let $x(n)$ be a uniformly distributed random number between $[-1, 1]$ for $0 \le n \le 10^6$. Let

$$h(n) = \sin(0.4\pi n), \quad 0 \le n \le 100$$

1. Using the **conv** function, determine the output sequence $y(n) = x(n) * h(n)$.
2. Consider the overlap-and-save method of block convolution along with the FFT algorithm to implement high-speed block convolution. Using this approach, determine $y(n)$ with FFT sizes of 1024, 2048, and 4096.
3. Compare these approaches in terms of the convolution results and their execution times.

CHAPTER 6

Implementation of Discrete-Time Filters

In earlier chapters, we studied the theory of discrete systems in both the time and frequency domains. We will now use this theory for the processing of digital signals. To process signals, we have to design and implement systems called *filters* (or spectrum analyzers in some contexts). The filter design issue is influenced by such factors as the type of the filter (i.e., IIR or FIR) and the form of its implementation (structures). Hence, before we discuss the design issue, we first concern ourselves with how these filters can be implemented in practice. This is an important concern because different filter structures dictate different design strategies.

IIR filters, as designed and used in DSP, can be modeled by rational system functions or, equivalently, by difference equations. Such filters are termed *autoregressive moving average* (*ARMA*) or, more generally, as *recursive* filters. Although ARMA filters include moving average filters that are FIR filters, we will treat FIR filters separately from IIR filters for both design and implementation purposes.

In addition to describing various filter structures, we also begin to consider problems associated with quantization effects when finite-precision arithmetic is used in the implementation. Digital hardware contains processing elements that use finite-precision arithmetic. When filters are implemented either in hardware or in software, filter coefficients as well as filter operations are subjected to the effects of these finite-precision operations. In this chapter, we treat the effects on filter frequency response characteristics due to coefficient quantization. In Chapter 10, we will consider the round-off noise effects in the digital filter implementations.

We begin with a description of basic building blocks that are used to describe filter structures. In the subsequent sections, we briefly describe IIR, FIR, and lattice filter structures, respectively, and provide MATLAB functions to implement these structures. This is followed by a brief treatment of the representation of numbers and the resulting error characteristics, which is then used to analyze coefficient quantization effects.

6.1 BASIC ELEMENTS

Since our filters are LTI systems, we need the following three elements to describe digital filter structures. These elements are shown in Figure 6.1.

1. **Adder:** This element has two inputs and one output and is shown in Figure 6.1a. Note that the addition of three or more signals is implemented by successive two-input adders.

2. **Multiplier (gain):** This is a single-input, single-output element and is shown in Figure 6.1b. Note that the multiplication by 1 is understood and hence not explicitly shown.

3. **Delay element (shifter or memory):** This element delays the signal passing through it by one sample, as shown in Figure 6.1c. It is implemented by using a shift register.

Using these basic elements, we can now describe various structures of both IIR and FIR filters. MATLAB is a convenient tool in the development of these structures that require operations on polynomials.

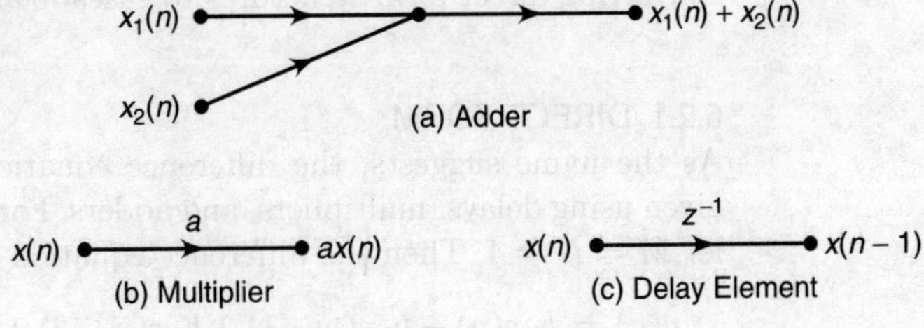

FIGURE 6.1 *Three basic elements*

6.2 IIR FILTER STRUCTURES

The system function of an IIR filter is given by

$$H(z) = \frac{B(z)}{A(z)} = \frac{\sum_{n=0}^{M} b_n z^{-n}}{\sum_{n=0}^{N} a_n z^{-n}} = \frac{b_0 + b_1 z^{-1} + \cdots + b_M z^{-M}}{1 + a_1 z^{-1} + \cdots + a_N z^{-N}}; \; a_0 = 1$$

(6.1)

where b_n and a_n are the coefficients of the filter. We have assumed without loss of generality that $a_0 = 1$. The order of such an IIR filter is called N if $a_N \neq 0$. The difference equation representation of an IIR filter is expressed as

$$y(n) = \sum_{m=0}^{M} b_m x(n - m) - \sum_{m=1}^{N} a_m y(n - m)$$

(6.2)

Three different structures can be used to implement an IIR filter:

1. **Direct form:** In this form, the difference equation (6.2) is implemented directly as given. There are two parts to this filter, namely the moving average part and the recursive part (or equivalently, the numerator and denominator parts). Therefore, this implementation leads to two versions: direct form I and direct form II structures.
2. **Cascade form:** In this form, the system function $H(z)$ in equation (6.1) is factored into smaller second-order sections, called *biquads*. The system function is then represented as a *product* of these biquads. Each biquad is implemented in a direct form, and the entire system function is implemented as a *cascade* of biquad sections.
3. **Parallel form:** This is similar to the cascade form, but after factorization, a partial fraction expansion is used to represent $H(z)$ as a *sum* of smaller second-order sections. Each section is again implemented in a direct form, and the entire system function is implemented as a *parallel* network of sections.

We will briefly discuss these forms in this section. IIR filters are generally described using the rational form version (or the direct form structure) of the system function. Hence we will provide MATLAB functions for converting direct form structures to cascade and parallel form structures.

6.2.1 DIRECT FORM

As the name suggests, the difference equation (6.2) is implemented as given using delays, multipliers, and adders. For the purpose of illustration, let $M = N = 4$. Then the difference equation is

$$y(n) = b_0 x(n) + b_1 x(n - 1) + b_2 x(n - 2) + b_3 x(n - 3) + b_4 x(n - 4)$$
$$- a_1 y(n - 1) - a_2 y(n - 2) - a_3 y(n - 3) - a_4 y(n - 4)$$

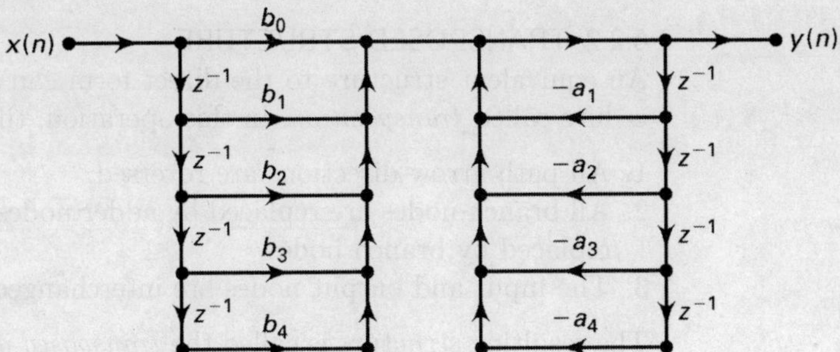

FIGURE 6.2 *Direct form I structure*

which can be implemented as shown in Figure 6.2. This block diagram is
called *direct form I* structure.

The direct form I structure implements each part of the rational function $H(z)$ separately with a cascade connection between them. The numerator part is a tapped delay line followed by the denominator part,
which is a feedback tapped delay line. Thus there are two separate delay lines in this structure, and hence it requires eight delay elements. We
can reduce this delay element count or eliminate one delay line by inter-
changing the order in which the two parts are connected in the cascade.
Now the two delay lines are close to each other, connected by a unity
gain branch. Therefore, one delay line can be removed, and this reduction
leads to a canonical structure called *direct form II* structure, shown in
Figure 6.3. It should be noted that both direct forms are equivalent from
the input-output point of view. Internally, however, they have different
signals.

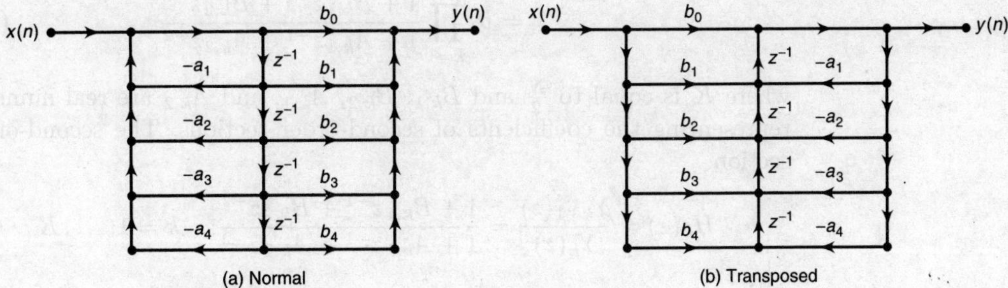

FIGURE 6.3 *Direct form II structure*

6.2.2 TRANSPOSED STRUCTURE

An equivalent structure to the direct form can be obtained using a procedure called *transposition*. In this operation, three steps are performed:

1. All path arrow directions are reversed.
2. All branch nodes are replaced by adder nodes, and all adder nodes are replaced by branch nodes.
3. The input and output nodes are interchanged.

The resulting structure is called the *transposed direct form* structure. The transposed direct form II structure is shown in Figure 6.3b. Problem P6.3 explains this equivalent structure.

6.2.3 MATLAB IMPLEMENTATION

In MATLAB, the direct form structure is described by two row vectors: **b** containing the $\{b_n\}$ coefficients and **a** containing the $\{a_n\}$ coefficients. The `filter` function, which is discussed in Chapter 2, implements the transposed direct form II structure.

6.2.4 CASCADE FORM

In this form, the system function $H(z)$ is written as a product of second-order sections with real coefficients. This is done by factoring the numerator and denominator polynomials into their respective roots and then combining either a complex conjugate root pair or any two real roots into second-order polynomials. In the remainder of this chapter, we assume that N is an even integer. Then

$$
\begin{aligned}
H(z) &= \frac{b_0 + b_1 z^{-1} + \cdots + b_N z^{-N}}{1 + a_1 z^{-1} + \cdots + a_N z^{-N}} \\[2mm]
&= b_0 \frac{1 + \frac{b_1}{b_0} z^{-1} + \cdots + \frac{b_N}{b_0} z^{-N}}{1 + a_1 z^{-1} + \cdots + a_N z^{-N}} \\[2mm]
&= b_0 \prod_{k=1}^{K} \frac{1 + B_{k,1} z^{-1} + B_{k,2} z^{-2}}{1 + A_{k,1} z^{-1} + A_{k,2} z^{-2}}
\end{aligned}
\tag{6.3}
$$

where K is equal to $\frac{N}{2}$ and $B_{k,1}$, $B_{k,2}$, $A_{k,1}$, and $A_{k,2}$ are real numbers representing the coefficients of second-order sections. The second-order section

$$
H_k(z) = \frac{Y_{k+1}(z)}{Y_k(z)} = \frac{1 + B_{k,1} z^{-1} + B_{k,2} z^{-2}}{1 + A_{k,1} z^{-1} + A_{k,2} z^{-2}}; \quad k = 1, \ldots, K
$$

with

$$
Y_1(z) = b_0 X(z); \quad Y_{K+1}(z) = Y(z)
$$

is called the kth biquad section. The input to the kth biquad section is the output from the $(k-1)$th biquad section, and the output from the

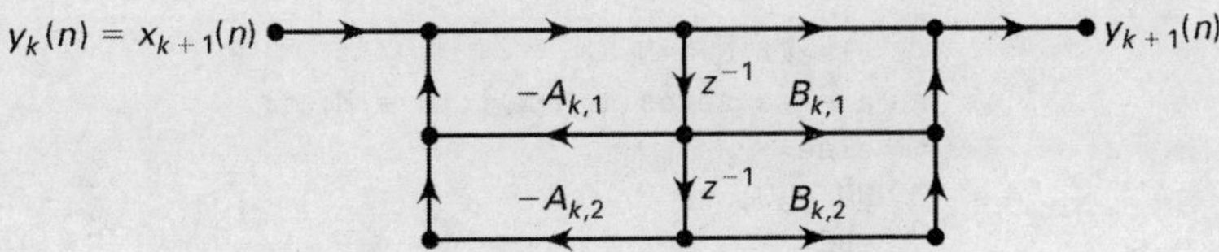

FIGURE 6.4 *Biquad section structure*

kth biquad is the input to the $(k+1)$th biquad. Now each biquad section $H_k(z)$ can be implemented in direct form II, as shown in Figure 6.4. The entire filter is then implemented as a cascade of biquads.

As an example, consider $N = 4$. Figure 6.5 shows a cascade form structure for this fourth-order IIR filter.

6.2.5 MATLAB IMPLEMENTATION

Given the coefficients $\{b_n\}$ and $\{a_n\}$ of the direct form filter, we have to obtain the coefficients b_0, $\{B_{k,i}\}$, and $\{A_{k,i}\}$. This is done by the following function `dir2cas`.

```matlab
function [b0,B,A] = dir2cas(b,a)
% DIRECT form to CASCADE form conversion (cplxpair version)
% -------------------------------------------------------------
% [b0,B,A] = dir2cas(b,a)
% b0 = gain coefficient
%  B = K by 3 matrix of real coefficients containing bk's
%  A = K by 3 matrix of real coefficients containing ak's
%  b = numerator polynomial coefficients of DIRECT form
%  a = denominator polynomial coefficients of DIRECT form

% Compute gain coefficient b0
b0 = b(1); b = b/b0;  a0 = a(1); a = a/a0;  b0 = b0/a0;
%
M = length(b); N = length(a);
if N > M
b = [b zeros(1,N-M)];
```

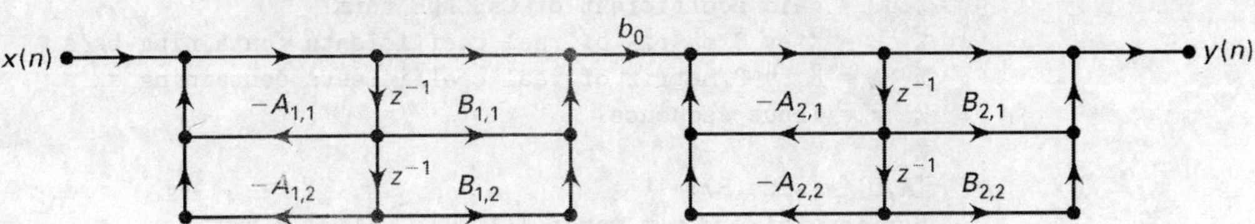

FIGURE 6.5 *Cascade form structure for $N = 4$*

```
elseif M > N
a = [a zeros(1,M-N)]; N = M;
else
NM = 0;
end
%
K = floor(N/2); B = zeros(K,3); A = zeros(K,3);
if K*2 == N
b = [b 0];  a = [a 0];
end
%
broots = cplxpair(roots(b));  aroots = cplxpair(roots(a));
for i=1:2:2*K
Brow = broots(i:1:i+1,:);    Brow = real(poly(Brow));
B(fix((i+1)/2),:) = Brow;
Arow = aroots(i:1:i+1,:);    Arow = real(poly(Arow));
A(fix((i+1)/2),:) = Arow;
end
```

This function converts the b and a vectors into $K \times 3$ size B and A matrices. It begins by computing b_0, which is equal to b_0/a_0 (assuming $a_0 \neq 1$). It then makes the vectors b and a of equal length by zero-padding the shorter vector. This ensures that each biquad has a nonzero numerator and denominator. Next, it computes the roots of the $B(z)$ and $A(z)$ polynomials. Using the `cplxpair` function, these roots are ordered in complex conjugate pairs. Now every pair is converted back into a second-order numerator or denominator polynomial using the `poly` function. The SP toolbox function, `tf2sos` (transfer function to second-order section), also performs a similar operation.

The cascade form is implemented using the following `casfiltr` function.

```
function y = casfiltr(b0,B,A,x)
% CASCADE form realization of IIR and FIR filters
% ------------------------------------------------
% y = casfiltr(b0,B,A,x);
%  y = output sequence
% b0 = gain coefficient of CASCADE form
%  B = K by 3 matrix of real coefficients containing bk's
%  A = K by 3 matrix of real coefficients containing ak's
%  x = input sequence
%
[K,L] = size(B);
N = length(x);  w = zeros(K+1,N);  w(1,:) = x;
```

```
for i = 1:1:K
      w(i+1,:) = filter(B(i,:),A(i,:),w(i,:));
end
y = b0*w(K+1,:);
```

This function employs the `filter` function in a loop using the coefficients of each biquad stored in `B` and `A` matrices. The input is scaled by `b0`, and the output of each filter operation is used as an input to the next filter operation. The output of the final filter operation is the overall output.

The following MATLAB function, `cas2dir`, converts a cascade form to a direct form. This is a simple operation that involves multiplication of several second-order polynomials. For this purpose, the MATLAB function `conv` is used in a loop over K factors. The SP toolbox function `sos2tf` also performs a similar operation.

```
function [b,a] = cas2dir(b0,B,A)
% CASCADE-to-DIRECT form conversion
% ----------------------------------
% [b,a] = cas2dir(b0,B,A)
%  b = numerator polynomial coefficients of DIRECT form
%  a = denominator polynomial coefficients of DIRECT form
% b0 = gain coefficient
%  B = K by 3 matrix of real coefficients containing bk's
%  A = K by 3 matrix of real coefficients containing ak's
%
[K,L] = size(B);
b = [1];   a = [1];
for i=1:1:K
b=conv(b,B(i,:));   a=conv(a,A(i,:));
end
b = b*b0;
```

□   **EXAMPLE 6.1**   A filter is described by the following difference equation:

$$16y(n) + 12y(n-1) + 2y(n-2) - 4y(n-3) - y(n-4)$$
$$= x(n) - 3x(n-1) + 11x(n-2) - 27x(n-3) + 18x(n-4)$$

Determine its cascaded form structure.

Solution   MATLAB script:

```
>> b=[1 -3 11 -27 18];  a=[16 12 2 -4 -1];
>> [b0,B,A]=dir2cas(b,a)
 b0 = 0.0625
  B =
        1.0000   -0.0000    9.0000
        1.0000   -3.0000    2.0000
  A =
        1.0000  1.0000    0.5000
        1.0000   -0.2500   -0.1250
```

The resulting structure is shown in Figure 6.6. To check that our cascade structure is correct, let us compute the first eight samples of the impulse response
using both forms.

```
>> delta = impseq(0,0,7)
delta =
     1    0    0    0    0    0    0    0
>> format long
>> hcas=casfiltr(b0,B,A,delta)
hcas =
  Columns 1 through 4
    0.06250000000000   -0.23437500000000    0.85546875000000   -2.28417968750000
  Columns 5 through 8
    2.67651367187500   -1.52264404296875    0.28984069824219    0.49931716918945
>> hdir=filter(b,a,delta)
hdir =
  Columns 1 through 4
    0.06250000000000   -0.23437500000000    0.85546875000000   -2.28417968750000
  Columns 5 through 8
    2.67651367187500   -1.52264404296875    0.28984069824219    0.49931716918945
```

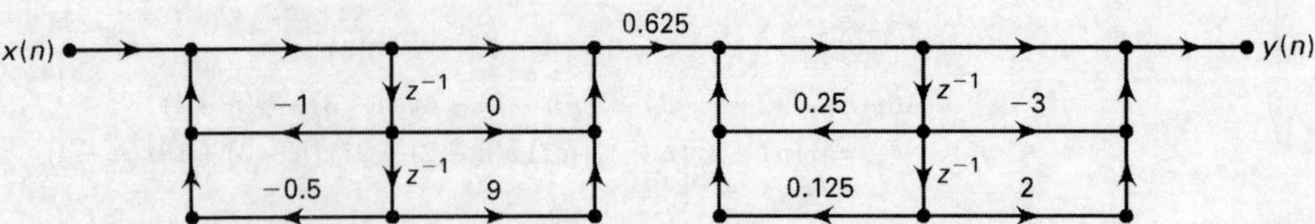

FIGURE 6.6 *Cascade structure in Example 6.1*

6.2.6 PARALLEL FORM

In this form, the system function $H(z)$ is written as a sum of second-order sections using partial fraction expansion.

$$H(z) = \frac{B(z)}{A(z)} = \frac{b_0 + b_1 z^{-1} + \cdots + b_M z^{-M}}{1 + a_1 z^{-1} + \cdots + a_N z^{-N}}$$

$$= \frac{\hat{b}_0 + \hat{b}_1 z^{-1} + \cdots + \hat{b}_{N-1} z^{1-N}}{1 + a_1 z^{-1} + \cdots + a_N z^{-N}} + \underbrace{\sum_0^{M-N} C_k z^{-k}}_{\text{Only if } M \geq N}$$

$$= \sum_{k=1}^{K} \frac{B_{k,0} + B_{k,1} z^{-1}}{1 + A_{k,1} z^{-1} + A_{k,2} z^{-2}} + \underbrace{\sum_0^{M-N} C_k z^{-k}}_{\text{Only if } M \geq N} \qquad \textbf{(6.4)}$$

where K is equal to $\frac{N}{2}$ and $B_{k,0}$, $B_{k,1}$, $A_{k,1}$, and $A_{k,2}$ are real numbers representing the coefficients of second-order sections. The second-order section

$$H_k(z) = \frac{Y_k(z)}{X(z)} = \frac{B_{k,0} + B_{k,1} z^{-1}}{1 + A_{k,1} z^{-1} + A_{k,2} z^{-2}}; \quad k = 1, \ldots, K$$

with

$$Y_k(z) = H_k(z) X(z), \quad Y(z) = \sum Y_k(z), \quad M < N$$

is the kth proper rational biquad section. The filter input is available to all biquad sections as well as to the polynomial section if $M \geq N$ (which is an FIR part). The output from these sections is summed to form the filter output. Now each biquad section $H_k(z)$ can be implemented in direct form II. Due to the summation of subsections, a parallel structure can be built to realize $H(z)$. As an example, consider $M = N = 4$. Figure 6.7 shows a parallel form structure for this fourth-order IIR filter.

6.2.7 MATLAB IMPLEMENTATION

The following function `dir2par` converts the direct form coefficients $\{b_n\}$ and $\{a_n\}$ into parallel form coefficients $\{B_{k,i}\}$ and $\{A_{k,i}\}$.

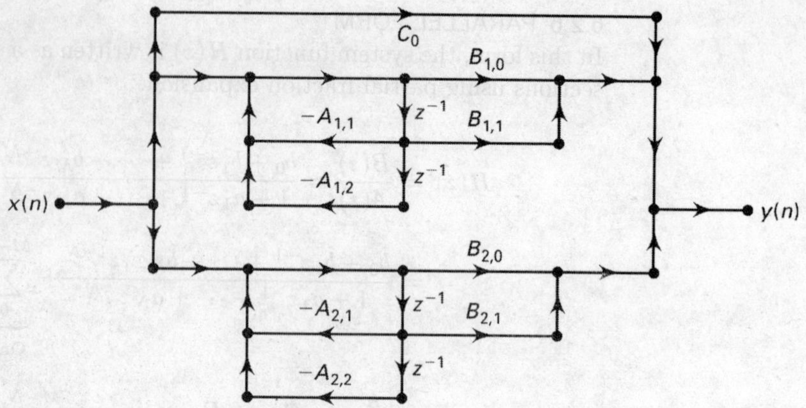

FIGURE 6.7 *Parallel form structure for* $N = 4$

```
function [C,B,A] = dir2par(b,a)
% DIRECT form to PARALLEL form conversion
% -------------------------------------------
% [C,B,A] = dir2par(b,a)
%  C = polynomial part when length(b) >= length(a)
%  B = K by 2 matrix of real coefficients containing bk's
%  A = K by 3 matrix of real coefficients containing ak's
%  b = numerator polynomial coefficients of DIRECT form
%  a = denominator polynomial coefficients of DIRECT form
%
M = length(b); N = length(a);

[r1,p1,C] = residuez(b,a);
p = cplxpair(p1,10000000*eps);   I = cplxcomp(p1,p);   r = r1(I);

K = floor(N/2); B = zeros(K,2); A = zeros(K,3);
if K*2 == N; %N even, order of A(z) odd, one factor is first order
 for i=1:2:N-2
 Brow = r(i:1:i+1,:);   Arow = p(i:1:i+1,:);
 [Brow,Arow] = residuez(Brow,Arow,[]);
 B(fix((i+1)/2),:) = real(Brow);   A(fix((i+1)/2),:) = real(Arow);
 end
 [Brow,Arow] = residuez(r(N-1),p(N-1),[]);
 B(K,:) = [real(Brow) 0]; A(K,:) = [real(Arow) 0];
else
for i=1:2:N-1
```

```
Brow = r(i:1:i+1,:);   Arow = p(i:1:i+1,:);
[Brow,Arow] = residuez(Brow,Arow,[]);
B(fix((i+1)/2),:) = real(Brow);   A(fix((i+1)/2),:) = real(Arow);
end
end
```

The `dir2cas` function first computes the z-domain partial fraction expansion using the `residuez` function. We need to arrange pole-and-residue pairs into complex conjugate pole-and-residue pairs followed by real pole-and-residue pairs. To do this, the `cplxpair` function from MATLAB can be used; it sorts a complex array into complex conjugate pairs. However, two consecutive calls to this function, one each for pole and residue arrays, will not guarantee that poles and residues will correspond to each other. Therefore, a new `cplxcomp` function is developed, which compares two shuffled complex arrays and returns the index of one array, which can be used to rearrange another array.

```
function I = cplxcomp(p1,p2)
%  I = cplxcomp(p1,p2)
% Compares two complex pairs which contain the same scalar elements
%  but (possibly) at differrent indices.  This routine should be
%  used after CPLXPAIR routine for rearranging pole vector and its
%  corresponding residue vector.
%      p2 = cplxpair(p1)
%
I=[];
for j=1:1:length(p2)
    for i=1:1:length(p1)
        if (abs(p1(i)-p2(j)) < 0.0001)
           I=[I,i];
        end
    end
end
I=I';
```

After collecting these pole-and-residue pairs, the `dir2cas` function computes the numerator and denominator of the biquads by employing the `residuez` function in the reverse fashion.

These parallel form coefficients are then used in the function `parfiltr`, which implements the parallel form. The `parfiltr` function uses the `filter` function in a loop using the coefficients of each biquad stored in the B and A matrices. The input is first filtered through the FIR part C and stored in the first row of a w matrix. Then the outputs of all biquad filters are computed for the same input and stored as subsequent rows in the w matrix. Finally, all the columns of the w matrix are summed to yield the output.

```
function y = parfiltr(C,B,A,x)
% PARALLEL form realization of IIR filters
% -----------------------------------------
%   [y] = parfiltr(C,B,A,x);
%   y = output sequence
%   C = polynomial (FIR) part when M >= N
%   B = K by 2 matrix of real coefficients containing bk's
%   A = K by 3 matrix of real coefficients containing ak's
%   x = input sequence
%
[K,L] = size(B);  N = length(x);  w = zeros(K+1,N);
w(1,:) = filter(C,1,x);
for i = 1:1:K
        w(i+1,:) = filter(B(i,:),A(i,:),x);
end
y = sum(w);
```

To obtain a direct form from a parallel form, the function `par2dir` can be used. It computes poles and residues of each proper biquad and combines these into system poles and residues. Another call of the `residuez` function in reverse order computes the numerator and denominator polynomials.

```
function [b,a] = par2dir(C,B,A)
% PARALLEL-to-DIRECT form conversion
% ----------------------------------
% [b,a] = par2dir(C,B,A)
%   b = numerator polynomial coefficients of DIRECT form
%   a = denominator polynomial coefficients of DIRECT form
%   C = polynomial part of PARALLEL form
%   B = K by 2 matrix of real coefficients containing bk's
%   A = K by 3 matrix of real coefficients containing ak's
%
[K,L] = size(A); R = []; P = [];

for i=1:1:K
[r,p,k]=residuez(B(i,:),A(i,:));  R = [R;r]; P = [P;p];
end
[b,a] = residuez(R,P,C);  b = b(:)'; a = a(:)';
```

☐ **EXAMPLE 6.2** Consider the filter given in Example 6.1.

$$16y(n) + 12y(n-1) + 2y(n-2) - 4y(n-3) - y(n-4)$$
$$= x(n) - 3x(n-1) + 11x(n-2) - 27x(n-3) + 18x(n-4)$$

Now determine its parallel form.

Solution MATLAB script:

```
>> b=[1 -3 11 -27 18];   a=[16 12 2 -4 -1];
>> [C,B,A]=dir2par(b,a)
C =
   -18
B =
  -10.0500    -3.9500
   28.1125   -13.3625
A =
    1.0000     1.0000     0.5000
    1.0000    -0.2500    -0.1250
```

The resulting structure is shown in Figure 6.8. To check our parallel structure,
let us compute the first eight samples of the impulse response using both forms.

```
>> format long; delta = impseq(0,0,7);   hpar=parfiltr(C,B,A,delta)
hpar =
  Columns 1 through 4
    0.06250000000000   -0.23437500000000    0.85546875000000   -2.28417968750000
```

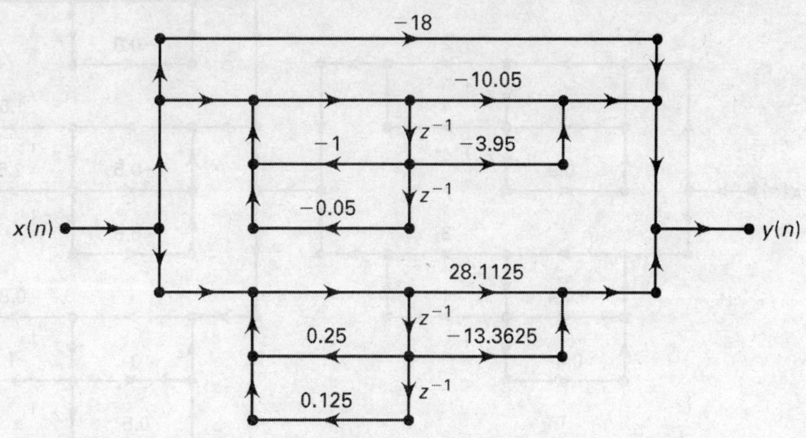

FIGURE 6.8 *Parallel form structure in Example 6.2*

```
    Columns 5 through 8
       2.67651367187500   -1.52264404296875      0.28984069824219      0.49931716918945
>> hdir = filter(b,a,delta)
hdir =
    Columns 1 through 4
       0.06250000000000   -0.23437500000000      0.85546875000000   -2.28417968750000
    Columns 5 through 8
       2.67651367187500   -1.52264404296875      0.28984069824219      0.49931716918945
```

$\square$

☐ **EXAMPLE 6.3**   What would be the overall direct, cascade, or parallel form if a structure contains a combination of these forms? Consider the block diagram shown in Figure 6.9.

Solution   This structure contains a cascade of two parallel sections. The first parallel section contains two biquads, while the second one contains three biquads. We will have to convert each parallel section into a direct form using the `par2dir` function, giving us a cascade of two direct forms. The overall direct form can be computed by convolving the corresponding numerator and denominator polynomials. The overall cascade and parallel forms can now be derived from the direct form.

MATLAB script:

```
>> C0=0; B1=[2 4;3 1]; A1=[1 1 0.9; 1 0.4 -0.4];
>> B2=[0.5 0.7;1.5 2.5;0.8 1]; A2=[1 -1 0.8;1 0.5 0.5;1 0 -0.5];
>> [b1,a1]=par2dir(C0,B1,A1)
b1 =
    5.0000    8.8000    4.5000   -0.7000
```

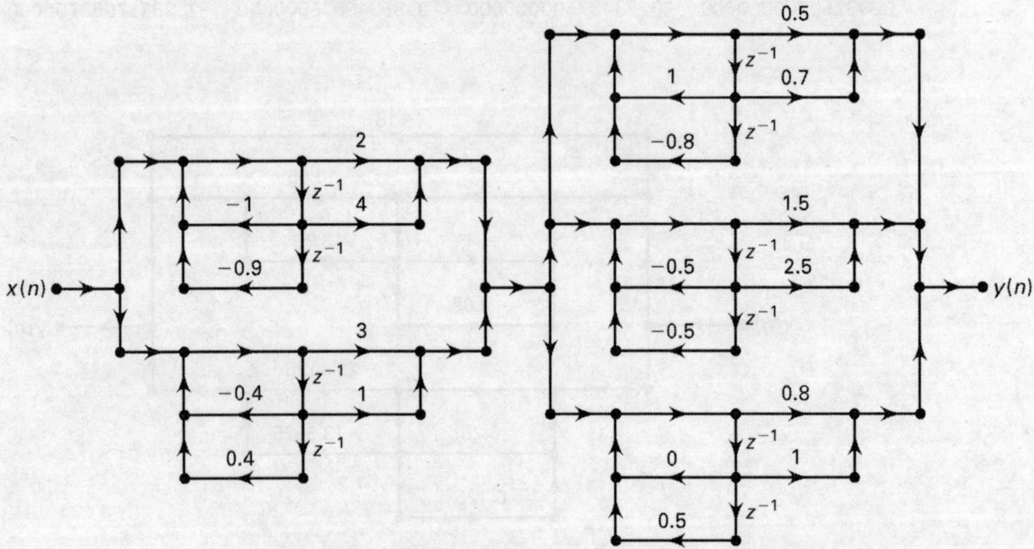

FIGURE 6.9   *Block diagram in Example 6.3*

```
a1 =
    1.0000    1.4000    0.9000   -0.0400   -0.3600
>> [b2,a2]=par2dir(C0,B2,A2)
b2 =
    2.8000    2.5500   -1.5600    2.0950    0.5700   -0.7750
a2 =
    1.0000   -0.5000    0.3000    0.1500    0.0000    0.0500   -0.2000
>> b=conv(b1,b2) % Overall direct form numerator
b =
  Columns 1 through 7
   14.0000   37.3900   27.2400    6.2620   12.4810   11.6605   -5.7215
  Columns 8 through 9
   -3.8865    0.5425
>> a=conv(a1,a2) % Overall direct form denominator
a =
  Columns 1 through 7
    1.0000    0.9000    0.5000    0.0800    0.1400    0.3530   -0.2440
  Columns 8 through 11
   -0.2890   -0.1820   -0.0100    0.0720
>> [b0,Bc,Ac]=dir2cas(b,a) % Overall cascade form
b0 =
   14.0000
Bc =
    1.0000    1.8836    1.1328
    1.0000   -0.6915    0.6719
    1.0000    2.0776    0.8666
    1.0000         0         0
    1.0000   -0.5990    0.0588
Ac =
    1.0000    1.0000    0.9000
    1.0000    0.5000    0.5000
    1.0000   -1.0000    0.8000
    1.0000    1.5704    0.6105
    1.0000   -1.1704    0.3276
>> [C0,Bp,Ap]=dir2par(b,a) % Overall parallel form
C0 = []
Bp =
  -20.4201   -1.6000
   24.1602    5.1448
    2.4570    3.3774
   -0.8101   -0.2382
    8.6129   -4.0439
Ap =
    1.0000    1.0000    0.9000
    1.0000    0.5000    0.5000
    1.0000   -1.0000    0.8000
    1.0000    1.5704    0.6105
    1.0000   -1.1704    0.3276
```

This example shows that by using the MATLAB functions developed in this section, we can probe and construct a wide variety of structures. $\square$

6.3 FIR FILTER STRUCTURES

A finite-duration impulse response filter has a system function of the form

$$H(z) = b_0 + b_1 z^{-1} + \cdots + b_{M-1} z^{1-M} = \sum_{n=0}^{M-1} b_n z^{-n} \qquad \textbf{(6.5)}$$

Hence the impulse response $h(n)$ is

$$h(n) = \begin{cases} b_n, & 0 \le n \le M-1 \\ 0, & \text{else} \end{cases} \qquad \textbf{(6.6)}$$

and the difference equation representation is

$$y(n) = b_0 x(n) + b_1 x(n-1) + \cdots + b_{M-1} x(n-M+1) \qquad \textbf{(6.7)}$$

which is a linear convolution of finite support.

The order of the filter is $M-1$, and the *length* of the filter (which is equal to the number of coefficients) is M. The FIR filter structures are always stable, and they are relatively simple compared to IIR structures. Furthermore, FIR filters can be designed to have a linear-phase response, which is desirable in some applications.

We will consider the following four structures.

1. **Direct form:** In this form, the difference equation (6.7) is implemented directly as given.
2. **Cascade form:** In this form, the system function $H(z)$ in (6.5) is factored into second-order factors, which are then implemented in a cascade connection.
3. **Linear-phase form:** When an FIR filter has a linear-phase response, its impulse response exhibits certain symmetry conditions. In this form, we exploit these symmetry relations to reduce multiplications by about half.
4. **Frequency-sampling form**: This structure is based on the DFT of the impulse response $h(n)$ and leads to a parallel structure. It is also suitable for a design technique based on the sampling of frequency response $H(e^{j\omega})$.

We will briefly describe these four forms along with some examples. The MATLAB function `dir2cas` developed in the previous section is also applicable for the cascade form.

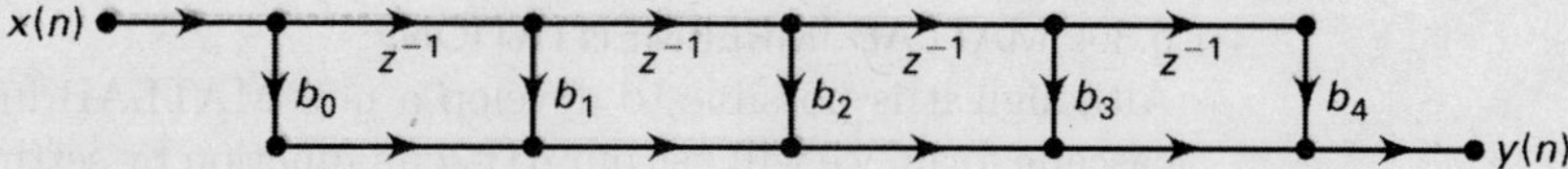

FIGURE 6.10 *Direct form FIR structure*

6.3.1 DIRECT FORM

The difference equation (6.7) is implemented as a tapped delay line since there are no feedback paths. Let $M = 5$ (i.e., a fourth-order FIR filter); then

$$y(n) = b_0 x(n) + b_1 x(n-1) + b_2 x(n-2) + b_3 x(n-3) + b_4 x(n-4)$$

The direct form structure is given in Figure 6.10. Note that since the denominator is equal to unity, there is only one direct form structure.

6.3.2 MATLAB IMPLEMENTATION

In MATLAB, the direct form FIR structure is described by the row vector **b** containing the $\{b_n\}$ coefficients. The structure is implemented by the `filter` function, in which the vector **a** is set to the scalar value 1, as discussed in Chapter 2.

6.3.3 CASCADE FORM

This form is similar to that of the IIR form. The system function $H(z)$ is converted into products of second-order sections with real coefficients. These sections are implemented in direct form and the entire filter as a cascade of second-order sections. From (6.5),

$$H(z) = b_0 + b_1 z^{-1} + \cdots + b_{M-1} z^{-M+1} \tag{6.8}$$

$$= b_0 \left(1 + \frac{b_1}{b_0} z^{-1} + \cdots + \frac{b_{M-1}}{b_0} z^{-M+1} \right)$$

$$= b_0 \prod_{k=1}^{K} \left(1 + B_{k,1} z^{-1} + B_{k,2} z^{-2} \right)$$

where K is equal to $\lfloor \frac{M}{2} \rfloor$ and $B_{k,1}$ and $B_{k,2}$ are real numbers representing the coefficients of second-order sections. For $M = 7$, the cascade form is shown in Figure 6.11.

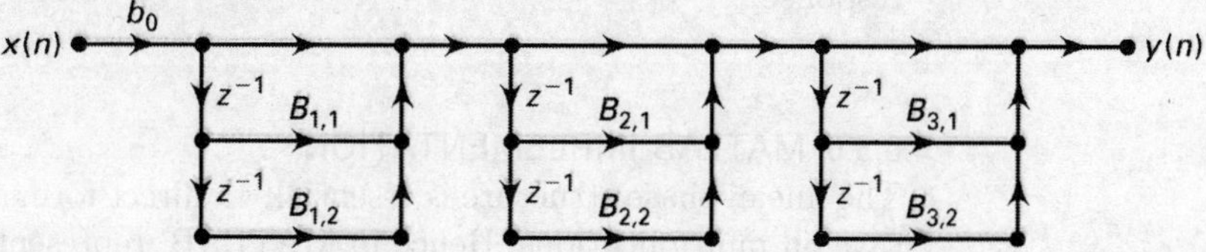

FIGURE 6.11 *Cascade form FIR structure*

6.3.4 MATLAB IMPLEMENTATION

Although it is possible to develop a new MATLAB function for the FIR cascade form, we will use our `dir2cas` function by setting the denominator vector `a` equal to 1. Similarly, `cas2dir` can be used to obtain the direct form from the cascade form.

6.3.5 LINEAR-PHASE FORM

For frequency-selective filters (e.g., lowpass filters), it is generally desirable to have a phase response that is a linear function of frequency; that is, we want

$$\angle H(e^{j\omega}) = \beta - \alpha\omega, \quad -\pi < \omega \le \pi \tag{6.9}$$

where $\beta = 0$ or $\pm\pi/2$ and α is a constant. For a causal FIR filter with impulse response over $[0,\ M-1]$ interval, the linear-phase condition (6.9) imposes the following symmetry conditions on the impulse response $h(n)$ (see Problem P6.15):

$$h(n) = h(M-1-n); \quad \beta = 0, \alpha = \frac{M-1}{2}, 0 \le n \le M-1 \tag{6.10}$$

$$h(n) = -h(M-1-n); \quad \beta = \pm\pi/2, \alpha = \frac{M-1}{2}, 0 \le n \le M-1 \tag{6.11}$$

An impulse response that satisfies (6.10) is called a *symmetric impulse response* and that in (6.11) is called an *antisymmetric impulse response*. These symmetry conditions can now be exploited in a structure called the linear-phase form.

Consider the difference equation given in (6.7) with a symmetric impulse response in (6.10). We have

$$\begin{aligned}
y(n) &= b_0 x(n) + b_1 x(n-1) + \cdots + b_1 x(n-M+2) + b_0 x(n-M+1) \\
&= b_0[x(n) + x(n-M+1)] + b_1[x(n-1) + x(n-M+2)] + \cdots
\end{aligned}$$

The block diagram implementation of this difference equation is shown in Figure 6.12 for both odd and even M.

Clearly, this structure requires 50% fewer multiplications than the direct form. A similar structure can be derived for an antisymmetric impulse response.

6.3.6 MATLAB IMPLEMENTATION

The linear-phase structure is essentially a direct form drawn differently to save on multiplications. Hence in MATLAB, representation of the linear-phase structure is equivalent to the direct form.

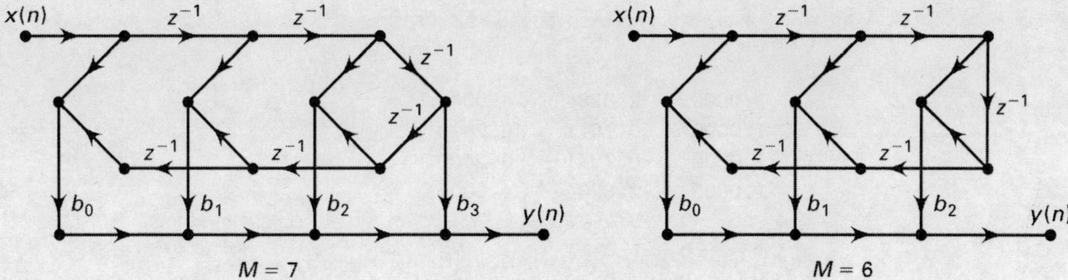

FIGURE 6.12 *Linear-phase form FIR structures (symmetric impulse response)*

☐   **EXAMPLE 6.4**   An FIR filter is given by the system function

$$H(z) = 1 + 16\frac{1}{16}z^{-4} + z^{-8}$$

Determine and draw the direct, linear-phase, and cascade form structures.

a. Direct form: The difference equation is given by

$$y(n) = x(n) + 16.0625x(n-4) + x(n-8)$$

and the direct form structure is shown in Figure 6.13(a).

b. Linear-phase form: The difference equation can be written in the form

$$y(n) = [x(n) + x(n-8)] + 16.0625x(n-4)$$

and the resulting structure is shown in Figure 6.13b.

c. Cascade form: We use the following MATLAB script.

```
>> b=[1,0,0,0,16+1/16,0,0,0,1];   [b0,B,A] = dir2cas(b,1)
```

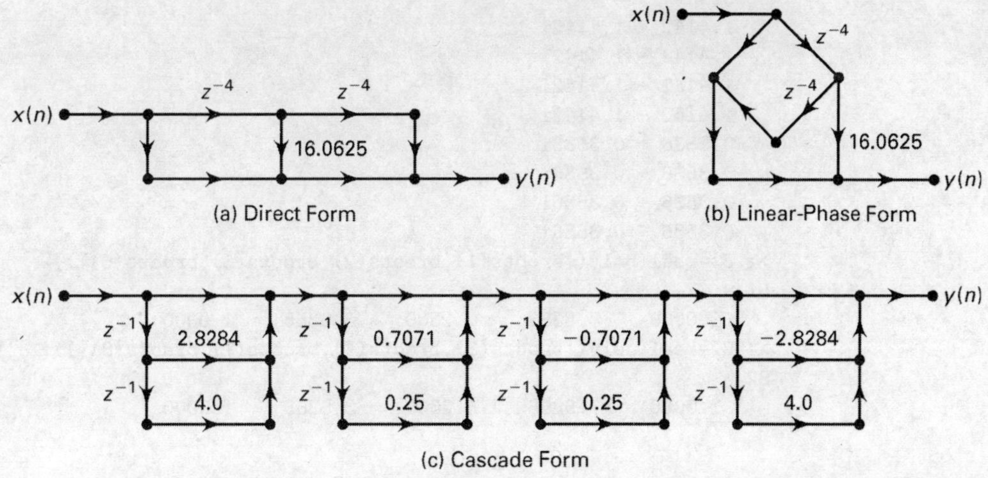

FIGURE 6.13 *FIR filter structures in Example 6.4*

```
b0 = 1
B =
    1.0000    2.8284    4.0000
    1.0000    0.7071    0.2500
    1.0000   -0.7071    0.2500
    1.0000   -2.8284    4.0000
A =
    1    0    0
    1    0    0
    1    0    0
    1    0    0
```

The cascade form structure is shown in Figure 6.13c. □

□   **EXAMPLE 6.5**   For the filter in Example 6.4, what would be the structure if we desire a cascade form containing linear-phase components with real coefficients?

Solution   We are interested in cascade sections that have symmetry and real coefficients. From the properties of linear-phase FIR filters (see Chapter 7), if such a filter has an arbitrary zero at $z = r\angle\theta$, then there must be three other zeros at $(1/r)\angle\theta$, $r\angle -\theta$, and $(1/r)\angle -\theta$ to have real filter coefficients. We can now make use of this property. First we will determine the zero locations of the given eighth-order polynomial. Then we will group four zeros that satisfy this property to obtain one (fourth-order) linear-phase section. There are two such sections, which we will connect in cascade.

MATLAB script:

```
>> b=[1,0,0,0,16+1/16,0,0,0,1];  broots=roots(b)
broots =
  -1.4142 + 1.4142i
  -1.4142 - 1.4142i
   1.4142 + 1.4142i
   1.4142 - 1.4142i
  -0.3536 + 0.3536i
  -0.3536 - 0.3536i
   0.3536 + 0.3536i
   0.3536 - 0.3536i
>> B1=real(poly([broots(1),broots(2),broots(5),broots(6)]))
B1 =
    1.0000    3.5355    6.2500    3.5355    1.0000
>> B2=real(poly([broots(3),broots(4),broots(7),broots(8)]))
B2 =
    1.0000   -3.5355    6.2500   -3.5355    1.0000
```

The structure is shown in Figure 6.14. □

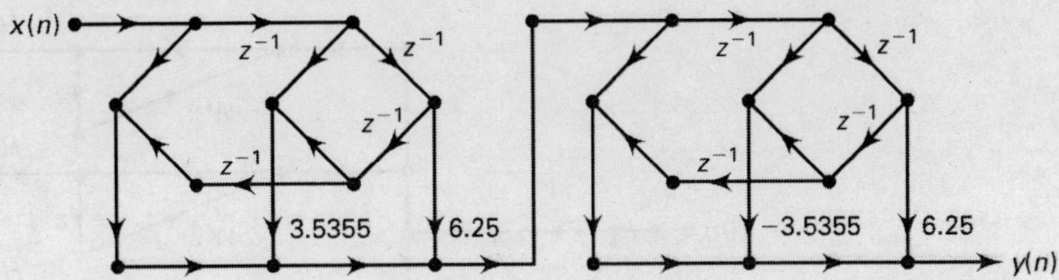

FIGURE 6.14 *Cascade of FIR linear-phase elements*

6.3.7 FREQUENCY-SAMPLING FORM

In this form, we use the fact that the system function $H(z)$ of an FIR filter can be reconstructed from its samples on the unit circle. From our discussions on the DFT in Chapter 5, we recall that these samples are in fact the M-point DFT values $\{H(k),\ 0 \leq k \leq M-1\}$ of the M-point impulse response $h(n)$. Therefore, we have

$$H(z) = \mathcal{Z}[h(n)] = \mathcal{Z}[\text{IDFT}\{H(k)\}]$$

Using this procedure, we obtain [see (5.17) in Chapter 5]

$$H(z) = \left(\frac{1 - z^{-M}}{M}\right) \sum_{k=0}^{M-1} \frac{H(k)}{1 - W_M^{-k} z^{-1}} \tag{6.12}$$

This shows that the DFT $H(k)$, rather than the impulse response $h(n)$ (or the difference equation), is used in this structure. Also note that the FIR filter described by (6.12) has a recursive form similar to an IIR filter because (6.12) contains both poles and zeros. The resulting filter is an FIR filter since the poles at W_M^{-k} are canceled by the roots of

$$1 - z^{-M} = 0$$

The system function in (6.12) leads to a parallel structure, as shown in Figure 6.15 for $M = 4$.

One problem with the structure in Figure 6.15 is that it requires a complex arithmetic implementation. Since an FIR filter is almost always a real-valued filter, it is possible to obtain an alternate realization in which only real arithmetic is used. This realization is derived using the symmetry properties of the DFT and the W_M^{-k} factor. Then (6.12) can be expressed as (see Problem P6.18)

$$H(z) = \frac{1 - z^{-M}}{M} \left\{ \sum_{k=1}^{L} 2|H(k)| H_k(z) + \frac{H(0)}{1 - z^{-1}} + \frac{H(M/2)}{1 + z^{-1}} \right\} \tag{6.13}$$

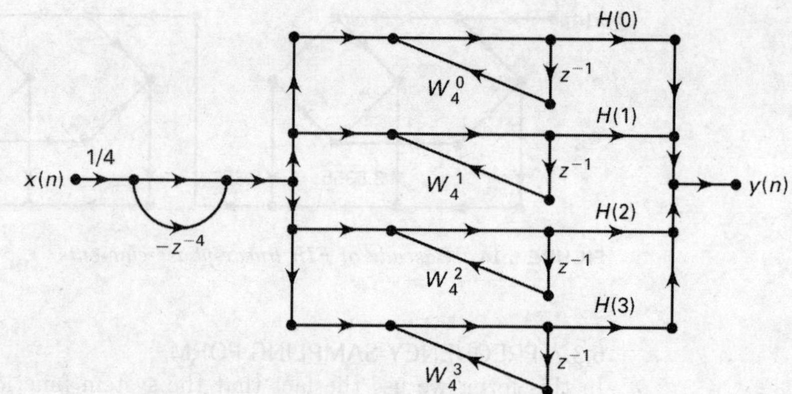

FIGURE 6.15   *Frequency-sampling structure for $M = 4$*

where $L = \frac{M-1}{2}$ for M odd, $L = \frac{M}{2} - 1$ for M even, and $\{H_k(z),\ k = 1,$ $\dots, L\}$ are second-order sections given by

$$H_k(z) = \frac{\cos\left[\angle H(k)\right] - z^{-1}\cos\left[\angle H(k) - \frac{2\pi k}{M}\right]}{1 - 2z^{-1}\cos\left(\frac{2\pi k}{M}\right) + z^{-2}} \tag{6.14}$$

Note that the DFT samples $H(0)$ and $H(M/2)$ are real-valued and that the third term on the right-hand side of (6.13) is absent if M is odd. Using (6.13) and (6.14), we show a frequency-sampling structure in Figure 6.16 for $M = 4$ containing real coefficients.

6.3.8 MATLAB IMPLEMENTATION

Given the impulse response $h(n)$ or the DFT $H(k)$, we have to determine the coefficients in (6.13) and (6.14). The following MATLAB function, `dir2fs`, converts a direct form $h(n)$ to the frequency-sampling form by directly implementing (6.13) and (6.14).

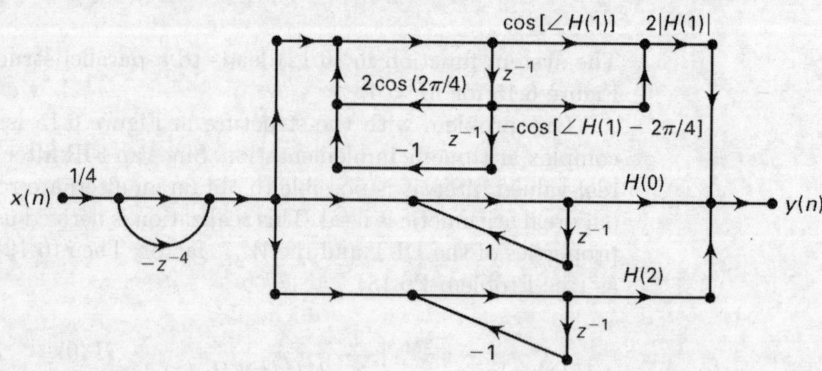

FIGURE 6.16   *Frequency-sampling structure for $M = 4$ with real coefficients*

```
function [C,B,A] = dir2fs(h)
% Direct form to frequency-sampling form conversion
% -------------------------------------------------
% [C,B,A] = dir2fs(h)
% C = row vector containing gains for parallel sections
% B = matrix containing numerator coefficients arranged in rows
% A = matrix containing denominator coefficients arranged in rows
% h = impulse response vector of an FIR filter
%
M = length(h);  H = fft(h,M);
magH = abs(H); phaH = angle(H)';
% Check even or odd M
if (M == 2*floor(M/2))
      L = M/2-1;   % M is even
     A1 = [1,-1,0;1,1,0];  C1 = [real(H(1)),real(H(L+2))];
else
      L = (M-1)/2; % M is odd
     A1 = [1,-1,0];  C1 = [real(H(1))];
end
k = [1:L]';
% Initialize B and A arrays
B = zeros(L,2); A = ones(L,3);
% Compute denominator coefficients
A(1:L,2) = -2*cos(2*pi*k/M); A = [A;A1];
% Compute numerator coefficients
B(1:L,1) = cos(phaH(2:L+1));
B(1:L,2) = -cos(phaH(2:L+1)-(2*pi*k/M));
% Compute gain coefficients
C = [2*magH(2:L+1),C1]';
```

In this function, the impulse response values are supplied through the
h array. After conversion, the C array contains the gain values for each
parallel section. The gain values for the second-order parallel sections
are given first, followed by $H(0)$ and $H(M/2)$ (if M is even). The B
matrix contains the numerator coefficients, which are arranged in length-
2 row vectors for each second-order section. The A matrix contains the
denominator coefficients, which are arranged in length-3 row vectors for
the second-order sections corresponding to those in B, followed by the
coefficients for the first-order sections.

A practical problem with the structure in Figure 6.16 is that it has
poles on the unit circle, which makes this filter critically unstable. If the
filter is not excited by one of the pole frequencies, then the output is
bounded. We can avoid this problem by sampling $H(z)$ on a circle $|z| = r$,

where the radius r is very close to 1 but is less than 1 (e.g., $r = 0.99$), which results in

$$H(z) = \frac{1 - r^M z^{-M}}{M} \sum_{k=0}^{M-1} \frac{H(k)}{1 - rW_M^{-k} z^{-k}}; \quad H(k) = H\left(re^{j2\pi k/M}\right)$$

$$(6.15)$$

Now approximating $H\left(re^{j2\pi k/M}\right) \approx H\left(e^{j2\pi k/M}\right)$ for $r \approx 1$, we can obtain a stable structure similar to the one in Figure 6.16 containing real values. This is explored in Problem P6.19.

□ **EXAMPLE 6.6** Let $h(n) = \frac{1}{9}\{1, 2, 3, 2, 1\}$. Determine and draw the frequency-sampling form.

Solution MATLAB script:

```
>> h = [1,2,3,2,1]/9;  [C,B,A] = dir2fs(h)
C =
    0.5818
    0.0849
    1.0000
B =
   -0.8090    0.8090
    0.3090   -0.3090
A =
    1.0000   -0.6180    1.0000
    1.0000    1.6180    1.0000
    1.0000   -1.0000         0
```

Since $M = 5$ is odd, there is only one first-order section. Hence

$$H(z) = \frac{1 - z^{-5}}{5}\left[0.5818\frac{-0.809 + 0.809z^{-1}}{1 - 0.618z^{-1} + z^{-2}}\right.$$

$$\left. + 0.0849\frac{0.309 - 0.309z^{-1}}{1 + 1.618z^{-1} + z^{-2}} + \frac{1}{1 - z^{-1}}\right]$$

The frequency-sampling form is shown in Figure 6.17.   □

□ **EXAMPLE 6.7** The frequency samples of a 32-point linear-phase FIR filter are given by

$$|H(k)| = \begin{cases} 1, & k = 0, 1, 2 \\ 0.5, & k = 3 \\ 0, & k = 4, 5, \ldots, 15 \end{cases}$$

Determine its frequency-sampling form, and compare its computational complexity with the linear-phase form.

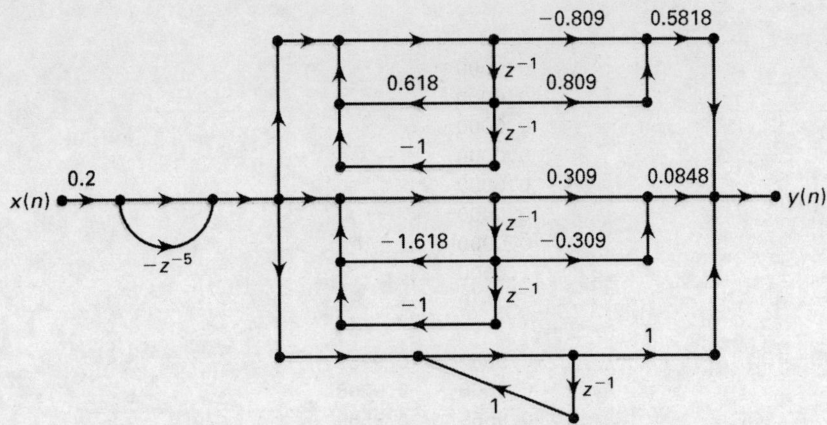

FIGURE 6.17 *Frequency-sampling structure in Example 6.6*

Solution

In this example, since the samples of the DFT $H(k)$ are given, we could use (6.13) and (6.14) directly to determine the structure. However, we will use the `dir2fs` function for which we will have to determine the impulse response $h(n)$. Using the symmetry property and the linear-phase constraint, we assemble the DFT $H(k)$ as

$$H(k) = |H(k)|\, e^{j\angle H(k)}, \quad k = 0, 1, \ldots, 31$$

$$|H(k)| = |H(32-k)|, \quad k = 1, 2, \ldots, 31; \; H(0) = 1$$

$$\angle H(k) = -\frac{31}{2}\frac{2\pi}{32}k = -\angle H(32-k), \quad k = 0, 1, \ldots, 31$$

Now the IDFT of $H(k)$ will result in the desired impulse response.

MATLAB script:

```
>> M = 32; alpha = (M-1)/2;
>> magHk = [1,1,1,0.5,zeros(1,25),0.5,1,1];
>> k1 = 0:15; k2 = 16:M-1;
>> angHk = [-alpha*(2*pi)/M*k1, alpha*(2*pi)/M*(M-k2)];
>> H = magHk.*exp(j*angHk);  h = real(ifft(H,M));  [C,B,A] = dir2fs(h)
```

```
C =
    2.0000
    2.0000
    1.0000
    0.0000
    0.0000
    0.0000
    0.0000
         0
```

```
        0.0000
        0.0000
        0.0000
        0.0000
        0.0000
        0.0000
        0.0000
        1.0000
             0
B =
   -0.9952      0.9952
    0.9808     -0.9808
   -0.9569      0.9569
   -0.8944      0.3162
    0.9794     -0.7121
    0.8265      0.2038
   -0.6754      0.8551
    1.0000      0.0000
    0.6866     -0.5792
    0.5191      0.9883
   -0.4430      0.4993
   -0.8944     -0.3162
   -0.2766      0.3039
    0.9343      0.9996
   -0.9077     -0.8084
A =
    1.0000     -1.9616      1.0000
    1.0000     -1.8478      1.0000
    1.0000     -1.6629      1.0000
    1.0000     -1.4142      1.0000
    1.0000     -1.1111      1.0000
    1.0000     -0.7654      1.0000
    1.0000     -0.3902      1.0000
    1.0000      0.0000      1.0000
    1.0000      0.3902      1.0000
    1.0000      0.7654      1.0000
    1.0000      1.1111      1.0000
    1.0000      1.4142      1.0000
    1.0000      1.6629      1.0000
    1.0000      1.8478      1.0000
    1.0000      1.9616      1.0000
    1.0000     -1.0000           0
    1.0000      1.0000           0
```

Note that only four gain coefficients are nonzero. Hence the frequency-sampling form is

$$H\left(z\right) = \frac{1 - z^{-32}}{32}\left[2\frac{-0.9952 + 0.9952z^{-1}}{1 - 1.9616z^{-1} + z^{-2}} + 2\frac{0.9808 - 0.9808z^{-1}}{1 - 1.8478z^{-1} + z^{-2}} + \frac{-0.9569 + 0.9569z^{-1}}{1 - 1.6629z^{-1} + z^{-2}} + \frac{1}{1 - z^{-1}}\right]$$

To determine the computational complexity, note that since $H\left(0\right) = 1$, the first-order section requires no multiplication, whereas the three second-order sections require three multiplications each for a total of nine multiplications per output sample. The total number of additions is 13. To implement the linear-phase structure would require 16 multiplications and 31 additions per output sample. Therefore, the frequency-sampling structure of this FIR filter is more efficient than the linear-phase structure. $\qquad\square$

6.4 OVERVIEW OF FINITE-PRECISION NUMERICAL EFFECTS

Until now, we have considered digital filter designs and implementations in which both the filter coefficients and the filter operations such as additions and multiplications were expressed using infinite-precision numbers. When discrete-time systems are implemented in hardware or in software, all parameters and arithmetic operations are implemented using finite-precision numbers, and hence their effect is unavoidable.

Consider a typical digital filter implemented as a direct form II structure, which is shown in Figure 6.18a. When finite-precision representation is used in its implementation, there are three possible considerations that affect the overall quality of its output. We have to

1. quantize the filter coefficients $\{a_k,\ b_k\}$ to obtain their finite word-length representations $\{\hat{a}_k,\ \hat{b}_k\}$,
2. quantize the input sequence $x(n)$ to obtain $\hat{x}(n)$, and
3. consider all internal arithmetic that must be converted to their next best representations.

Thus the output, $y(n)$, is also a quantized value $\hat{y}(n)$. This gives us a new filter realization, $\hat{H}(z)$, which is shown in Figure 6.18b. We hope that this new filter $\hat{H}(z)$ and its output $\hat{y}(n)$ are as close as possible to the original filter $H(z)$ and the original output $y(n)$.

Since the quantization operation is a nonlinear operation, the overall analysis that takes into account all three effects described above is very difficult and tedious. Therefore, we will study each of these effects separately as though it were the only one acting at the time. This makes the analysis easier and the results more interpretable.

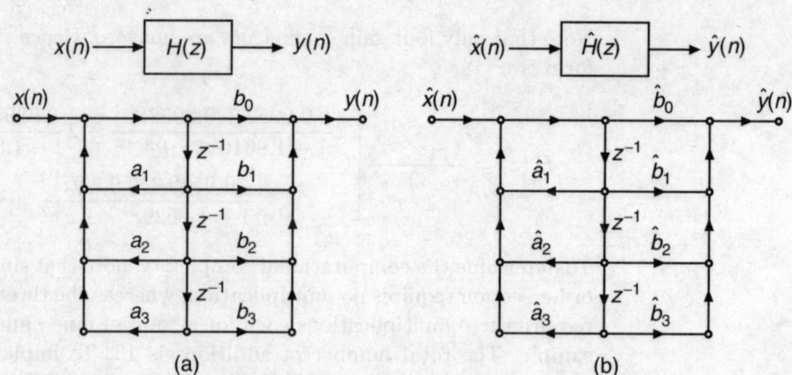

FIGURE 6.18 *Direct form II digital filter implementation: (a) infinite precision, (b) finite precision*

We begin by discussing the number representation in a computer—more accurately, a central processing unit (CPU). This leads to the process of number quantization and the resulting error characterization. We then analyze the effects of filter coefficient quantization on digital filter frequency responses. The effects of multiplication and addition quantization (collectively known as arithmetic round-off errors) on filter output are discussed in Chapter 10.

6.5 REPRESENTATION OF NUMBERS

In computers, numbers (real-valued or complex-valued, integers or fractions) are represented using binary digits (*bits*), which take the value of either a 0 or a 1. The finite word-length arithmetic needed for processing these numbers is implemented using two different approaches, depending on the ease of implementation and the accuracy as well as dynamic range needed in processing. The *fixed-point* arithmetic is easy to implement but has only a fixed dynamic range and accuracy (i.e., very large numbers or very small numbers). The *floating-point* arithmetic, on the other hand, has a wide dynamic range and a variable accuracy (relative to the magnitude of a number) but is more complicated to implement and analyze.

Since a computer can operate only on a binary variable (e.g., a 1 or a 0), positive numbers can straightforwardly be represented using binary numbers. The problem arises as to how to represent the negative numbers. There are three different formats used in each of these arithmetics: *sign-magnitude* format, *one's-complement* format, and *two's-complement* format. In discussing and analyzing these representations, we will mostly consider a binary number system containing bits. However, this discussion and analysis is also valid for any radix numbering system—for example, the hexadecimal, octal, or decimal system.

In the following discussion, we will first begin with fixed-point signed integer arithmetic. A B-bit binary representation of an integer x is given by[1]

$$x \equiv b_{B-1}\, b_{B-2}\, \cdots\, b_0 = b_{B-1} \times 2^{B-1} + b_{B-2} \times 2^{B-2} + \cdots + b_0 \times 2^0 \quad \textbf{(6.16)}$$

where each bit b_i represents either a 0 or a 1. This representation will help us to understand the advantages and disadvantages of each signed format and to develop simple MATLAB functions. We will then extend these concepts to fractional real numbers for both fixed-point and floating-point arithmetic.

6.5.1 FIXED-POINT SIGNED INTEGER ARITHMETIC

In this arithmetic, positive numbers are coded using their binary representation. For example, using 3 bits, we can represent numbers from 0 to 7 as

```
     0    1    2    3    4    5    6    7
    -+----+----+----+----+----+----+----+-
    000  001  010  011  100  101  110  111
```

Thus, with 8 bits the numbers represented can be 0 to 255, with 10 bits we can represent the numbers from 0 to 1023, and with 16 bits the range covered is 0 to 65535. For negative numbers, the following three formats are used: sign-magnitude, one's-complement, and two's-complement.

Sign-magnitude format   In this format, positive numbers are represented using bits as before. However, the leftmost bit (also known as the most-significant bit, or MSB) is used as the sign bit (0 is +, and 1 is −), and the remaining bits hold the absolute magnitude of the number as shown here:

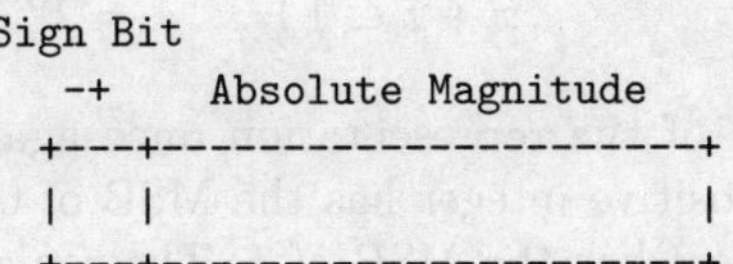

This system has thus two different codes for 0, one for the positive 0, the other one for the negative 0. For example, using 3 bits, we can represent numbers from −3 to 3 as

```
     -3   -2   -1   -0    0    1    2    3
    -+----+----+----+----+----+----+----+-
    111  110  101  100  000  001  010  011
```

Thus, 8 bits cover the interval $[-127, +127]$, while 16 bits cover $[-32,767, +32,767]$. If we use B bits in the sign-magnitude format, then we can represent integers from $-(2^{B-1} - 1)$ to $+(2^{B-1} - 1)$ only.

---

[1] Here the letter b is used to represent a binary bit. It is also used for filter coefficients $\{b_k\}$. Its use in the text should be clear from the context.

This format has two drawbacks. First, there are two representations for 0. Second, the arithmetic using the sign-magnitude format requires one rule to compute addition, another rule to compute subtraction, and a way to compare two magnitudes to determine their relative value before subtraction.

MATLAB Implementation   MATLAB is a 64-bit floating-point computation engine that provides results in decimal numbers. Therefore, fixed-point binary operations must be simulated in MATLAB. It provides the function `dec2bin` to convert a positive decimal integer into a B-bit representation, which is a symbol (or a code) and not a number. Hence it cannot be used in computation. Similarly, the function `bin2dec` converts a B-bit binary character code into a decimal integer. For example, `dec2bin(3,3)` gives 011 and `bin2dec('111')` results in 7. To obtain a sign-magnitude format, a sign bit must be prefixed. Similarly, to convert a sign-magnitude format, the leading bit must be used to impart a positive or negative value. These functions are explored in Problem P9.1.

One's-complement format   In this format, the negation (or complementation) of an integer x is obtained by complementing every bit (i.e., a 0 is replaced by 1 and a 1 by 0) in the binary representation of x. Suppose the B-bit binary representation of x is $b_{B-1} b_{B-2} \cdots b_0$; then the B-bit *one's-complement*, $\bar{x}$, of x is given by

$$\bar{x} \triangleq \bar{b}_{B-1} \bar{b}_{B-2} \cdots \bar{b}_0$$

where each bit $\bar{b}_i$ is a complement of bit b_i. Clearly then

$$x + \bar{x} \equiv 1\,1 \ldots 1 = 2^B - 1 \qquad (6.17)$$

The MSB of the representation once again represents the sign bit, because the positive integer has the MSB of 0 so that its negation (or a negative integer) has the MSB of 1. The remaining bits represent either the number x (if positive) or its one's-complement (if negative). Thus, using (6.17) the one's-complement format representation[2] is given by

$$x_{(1)} \triangleq \begin{cases} x, & x \geq 0 \\ |\bar{x}|, & x < 0 \end{cases} = \begin{cases} x, & x \geq 0 \\ 2^B - 1 - |x|, & x < 0 \end{cases} = \begin{cases} x, & x \geq 0 \\ 2^B - 1 + x, & x < 0 \end{cases} \qquad (6.18)$$

Clearly, if B bits are available, then we can represent only integers from $(-2^{B-1}+1)$ to $(+2^{B-1}-1)$, which is similar to the sign-magnitude format.

---

[2]The one's-complement format refers to the representation of positive and negative numbers, whereas the one's-complement of a number refers to the negation of that number.

For example, using 3 bits, we can represent numbers from -3 to 3 as

```
-3    -2    -1    -0     0     1     2     3
-+----+----+----+----+----+----+----+----+-
100   101   110   111   000   001   010   011
```

which is a different bit arrangement for negative numbers compared to the sign-magnitude format.

The advantage of this format is that subtraction can be achieved by adding the complement, which is very easy to obtain by simply complementing a number's bits. However, there are many drawbacks. There are still two different codes for 0, the addition is a bit tricky to implement, and overflow management requires addition of the overflow bit to the least significant bit (or 2^0).

MATLAB Implementation The one's-complement of a positive integer x using B bits can be obtained by using the built-in function `bitcmp(x,B)`, which complements the number's bits. The result is a decimal number between 0 and $2^B - 1$. As before, the `dec2bin` can be used to obtain the binary code. Using (6.18), we can develop the MATLAB function `OnesComplement`, which obtains the one's-complement format representation. It uses the sign of a number to determine when to use one's-complement and can use scalar as well as vector values. The result is a decimal equivalent of the representation.

```matlab
function y = OnesComplement(x,B)
% y = OnesComplement(x,B)
% ----------------
% Decimal equivalent of
%  sign-magnitude format integer to b-bit ones'-complement format conversion
%
%    x: integer between -2^(b-1) <  x <  2^(b-1) (sign-magnitude)
%    y: integer between        0 <= y <= 2^b-1   (1's-complement)

if any((x <= -2^(B-1) | (x >= 2^(B-1))))
    error('Numbers must satisfy -2^(B-1) < x <  2^(B-1)')
end
s = sign(x); % sign of x (-1 if x<0, 0 if x=0, 1 if x>0)
sb = (s < 0); % sign-bit  (0 if x>=0, 1 if x<0));
y = (1-sb).*x + sb.*bitcmp(abs(x),B);
```

☐ **EXAMPLE 6.8**   Using the function `OnesComplement`, obtain one's-complement format representation of integers from -7 to 7 using 4 bits.

Solution   MATLAB script:

```
>> x = -7:7
x =
    -7  -6  -5  -4  -3  -2  -1   0   1   2   3   4   5   6   7
>> y = OnesComplement(x,4)
y =
     8   9  10  11  12  13  14   0   1   2   3   4   5   6   7
```

Note that the number 15 is missing since we do not have -0 in our original array.   □

Two's-complement format   The disadvantage of having two codes for the number 0 is eliminated in this format. Positive numbers are coded as usual. The B-bit two's-complement, $\tilde{x}$, of a positive integer x is given by

$$\tilde{x} = \bar{x} + 1 = 2^B - x \quad \text{or} \quad x + \tilde{x} = 2^B \tag{6.19}$$

where the second equality is obtained from (6.18). Once again, the MSB of the representation provides the sign bit. Thus using (6.19), the two's-complement format representation[3] is given by

$$x_{(2)} = \begin{cases} x, & x \geq 0 \\ |\tilde{x}|, & x < 0 \end{cases} = \begin{cases} x, & x \geq 0 \\ 2^B - |x|, & x < 0 \end{cases} = \begin{cases} x, & x \geq 0 \\ 2^B + x, & x < 0 \end{cases} \tag{6.20}$$

Thus in B-bit two's-complement format negative numbers are obtained by adding 2^B to them. Clearly, if B bits are available, then we can represent 2^B integers from (-2^{B-1}) to $(+2^{B-1} - 1)$. For example, using 3 bits, we can represent numbers from -4 to 3 as

```
-4   -3   -2   -1    0    1    2    3
-+----+----+----+----+----+----+----+-
100  101  110  111  000  001  010  011
```

This format, by shifting to the right (e.g., by incrementing) the code of the negative numbers, straightforwardly removes the problem of having two codes for 0 and gives access to an additional negative number at the left of the line. Thus 4 bits go from -8 to $+7$, 8 bits cover the interval $[-127, +127]$, and 16 bits cover $[-32768, +32767]$.

---

[3]Again, the two's-complement format refers to the representation of positive and negative numbers, whereas the two's-complement of a number refers to the negation of that number.

MATLAB Implementation Using (6.20), we can develop the MATLAB function `TwosComplement`, which obtains the two's-complement format representation. We can use the `bitcmp` function and then add 1 to the result to obtain the two's-complement. However, we will use the last equality in (6.20) to obtain the two's-complement since this approach will also be useful for fractional numbers. The function can use scalar as well as vector values. The result is a decimal equivalent of the two's-complement representation. As before, the `dec2bin` can be used to obtain the binary code.

```
function y = TwosComplement(x,b)
% y = TwosComplement(x,b)
% ----------------
% Decimal equivalent of
%  sign-magnitude format integer to b-bit ones'-complement format conversion
%
%    x: integer between -2^(b-1) <= x <  2^(b-1) (sign-magnitude)
%    y: integer between          0 <= y <= 2^b-1   (two's-complement)
if any((x < -2^(b-1) | (x >= 2^(b-1))))
    error('Numbers must satisfy -2^(b-1) <= x <  2^(b-1)')
end
s = sign(x); % Sign of x (-1 if x<0, 0 if x=0, 1 if x>0)
sb = (s < 0); % Sign-bit  (0 if x>=0, 1 if x<0));
y = (1-sb).*x + sb.*(2^b+x); % or y = (1-sb).*x + sb.*(bitcmp(abs(x),b)+1);
```

☐   **EXAMPLE 6.9**   Using the function `TwosComplement`, obtain the two's-complement format representation of integers from -8 to 7 using 4 bits.

Solution   MATLAB script:

```
>> x = -8:7
x =
    -8   -7   -6   -5   -4   -3   -2   -1    0    1    2    3    4    5    6    7
>> y = TwosComplement(x,4)
y =
     8    9   10   11   12   13   14   15    0    1    2    3    4    5    6    7
>> y = dec2bin(y,4); disp(sprintf('%s',[y';char(ones(1,16)*32)]))
1000 1001 1010 1011 1100 1101 1110 1111 0000 0001 0010 0011 0100 0101 0110 0111
```

☐

The two's-complement format has many interesting characteristics and advantages. These will be given after we discuss the next format— namely, the ten's-complement.

Ten's-complement format This is a representation for decimal integers. We will describe it so that we can explore characteristics of two's-complement through decimal integers, which is much easier to understand. Following (6.19), the N-digit ten's-complement of a positive integer x is given by

$$\tilde{x} = 10^N - x \quad or \quad x + \tilde{x} = 10^N \tag{6.21}$$

Using (6.21), the N-digit ten's-complement format representation is given by

$$x_{(10^N)} \triangleq \begin{cases} x, & x \geq 0 \\ |\tilde{x}|, & x < 0 \end{cases} = \begin{cases} x, & x \geq 0 \\ 10^N - |x|, & x < 0 \end{cases} = \begin{cases} x, & x \geq 0 \\ 10^N + x, & x < 0 \end{cases} \tag{6.22}$$

Thus in N-digit ten's-complement format (which is sometimes referred to as 10^N-complement format), negative numbers are obtained by adding 10^N to them. Clearly, when N digits are available, we can represent 10^N integers from $(-\frac{10^N}{2})$ to $(+\frac{10^N}{2} - 1)$. For example, using one digit, we can represent numbers from -5 to 4 as

```
     -5   -4   -3   -2   -1    0    1    2    3    4
     -+----+----+----+----+----+----+----+----+----+
      5    6    7    8    9    0    1    2    3    4
```

<table>
<tr><td>☐ EXAMPLE 6.10</td><td>Using the two-digit ten's-complement, i.e., hundred's-complement format, perform the following operations:
1. $16 - 32$,   2. $32 - 16$,   3. $-30 - 40$,   4. $40 + 20 - 30$,   5. $-40 - 20 + 30$.</td></tr>
<tr><td>Solution</td><td>

1. $16 - 32$
First, we note that $16 - 32 = -16$. If we use the usual subtraction rule to proceed from right to left generating carries in the process, we cannot complete the operation. To use the hundred's-complement format, we first note that in the hundred's-complement format we have

$$16_{(100)} = 16, \quad -16_{(100)} = 100 - 16 = 84, \quad and \quad -32_{(100)} = 100 - 32 = 68$$

Hence $16 - 32 \equiv 16 + 68 = 84 \equiv -16$ in the sign-magnitude format, as expected.

2. $32 - 16$
In this case, the hundred's-complement format gives

$$32 + 84 = 116 \equiv 16$$

in the sign-magnitude format by ignoring the generated carry digit. This is because the sign bits were different; therefore, the operation cannot generate an overflow. Hence we check for overflow only if the sign bits are same.

3. $-30 - 40$
In this case, the hundred's-complement format gives

$$(100 - 30) + (100 - 40) = 70 + 60 = 130$$

</td></tr>
</table>

Since the sign bits were the same, an overflow is generated and the result is invalid.

4. $40 + 20 - 30$

This is an example of more than one addition or subtraction. Since the final result is well within the range, the overflow can be ignored—that is,

$$40 + 20 + (100 - 30) = 40 + 20 + 70 = 130 \equiv 30$$

which is a correct result.

5. $-40 - 20 + 30$

In this case, we have

$$(100 - 40) + (100 - 20) + 30 = 60 + 80 + 30 = 170 \equiv -30$$

in the sign-magnitude format, which is, again, a correct result. $\qquad\square$

MATLAB Implementation Using (6.22), one can develop the MATLAB function, `TensComplement`, which obtains ten's-complement format representation. It is similar to the `TwosComplement` function and is explored in Problem P6.23.

Advantages of two's-complement format Using the results of the Example 6.10, we now state the benefits of the two's-complement format. These also hold (with obvious modifications) for the ten's-complement format.

1. It provides for all 2^{B+1} distinct representations for a B-bit fractional representation. There is only one representation for zero.
2. This complement is compatible with our notion of negation: the complement of a complement is the number itself.
3. It unifies the subtraction and addition operations (subtractions are essentially additions).
4. In a sum of more than two numbers, the internal overflows do not affect the final result so long as the result is within the range (i.e., adding two positive numbers gives a positive result, and adding two negative numbers gives a negative result).

Hence in most A/D converters and processors, negative numbers are represented using two's-complement format. Almost all current processors implement signed arithmetic using this format and provide special functions (e.g., an overflow flag) to support it.

Excess-2^{B-1} format This format is used in describing the exponent of floating-point arithmetic; hence it is briefly discussed here. In excess-2^{B-1} signed format (also known as a *biased* format), all positive and negative integers between -2^{B-1} and $2^{B-1}-1$ are given by

$$x_{(e)} \triangleq 2^{B-1} + x \qquad (6.23)$$

For example, using 3 bits, we can represent the numbers from -4 to 3 as

```
  -4    -3    -2    -1     0     1     2     3
 -+----+----+----+----+----+----+----+----+-
  000   001   010   011   100   101   110   111
```

Notice that this format is very similar to the two's-complement format, but the sign bit is complemented. The arithmetic for this format is similar to that of the two's-complement format. It is used in the exponent of floating-point number representation.

6.5.2 GENERAL FIXED-POINT ARITHMETIC

Using the discussion of integer arithmetic from the last section as a guide, we can extend the fixed-point representation to arbitrary real (integer and fractional) numbers. We assume that a given infinite-precision real number x is approximated by a binary number $\hat{x}$ with the following bit arrangement:

$$\hat{x} = \pm \underbrace{\mathtt{XX\cdots X}}_{\substack{\text{``}L\text{''} \\ \text{Integer bits}}} \blacktriangle \underbrace{\mathtt{XX\cdots X}}_{\substack{\text{``}B\text{''} \\ \text{Fraction bits}}} \qquad (6.24)$$

where the sign bit $\pm$ is 0 for positive numbers and 1 for negative numbers, $\mathtt{x}$ represents either a 0 or a 1, and $\blacktriangle$ represents the *binary point*. This representation is in fact the sign-magnitude format for real numbers, as we will see. The total *word length* of the number $\hat{x}$ is then equal to $L + B + 1$ bits.

☐ **EXAMPLE 6.11**   Let $L = 4$ and $B = 5$, which means $\hat{x}$ is a 10-bit number. Represent $11010\blacktriangle01110$ in decimal.

Solution

$$\hat{x} = -\left(1 \times 2^3 + 0 \times 2^2 + 1 \times 2^1 + 0 \times 2^0 + 0 \times 2^{-1} + 1 \times 2^{-2} + 1 \times 2^{-3} + 1 \times 2^{-4} + 0 \times 2^{-5}\right)$$
$$= -10.4375$$

in decimal.   ☐

In many A/D converters and processors, the real numbers are scaled so that the fixed-point representation is in the $(-1, 1)$ range. This has the advantage that the multiplication of two fractions is always a fraction and, as such, there is no overflow. Hence we will consider the following representation:

$$\hat{x} = A(\pm \blacktriangle \underbrace{\text{xxxxxx} \cdots \text{x}}_{B \text{ fraction bits}}) \tag{6.25}$$

where A is a positive *scaling factor*.

☐   **EXAMPLE 6.12**   Represent the number $\hat{x} = -10.4375$ in Example 6.11 using a fraction-only arrangement.

Solution   Choose $A = 2^4 = 16$ and $B = 9$. Then

$$\hat{x} = -10.4375 = 16\,(1 \blacktriangle 101001110)$$

Hence by properly choosing A and B, one can obtain any fraction-only representation.

Note: The scalar A need not be a power of two. In fact, by choosing any real number A we can obtain an arbitrary range. The power-of-two choice for A, however, makes hardware implementation a little easier.   ☐

As discussed in the previous section, there are three main formats for fixed-point arithmetic, depending on how negative numbers are obtained. For all these formats, positive numbers have exactly the same representation. In the following, we assume the fraction-only arrangement.

Sign-magnitude format   As the name suggests, the magnitude is given by the B-bit fraction, and the sign is given by the MSB. Thus

$$\hat{x} = \begin{cases} 0 \blacktriangle \text{x}_1 \text{x}_2 \cdots \text{x}_B & \text{if } x \geq 0 \\ 1 \blacktriangle \text{x}_1 \text{x}_2 \cdots \text{x}_B & \text{if } x < 0 \end{cases} \tag{6.26}$$

For example, when $B = 2$, $\hat{x} = +1/4$ is represented by $\hat{x} = 0 \blacktriangle 01$, and $\hat{x} = -1/4$ is represented by $\hat{x} = 1 \blacktriangle 01$.

One's-complement format   In this format, the positive numbers have the same representation as the sign-magnitude format. When the number is negative, then its magnitude is given by its bit-complement arrangement. Thus

$$\hat{x} = \begin{cases} 0 \blacktriangle \text{x}_1 \text{x}_2 \cdots \text{x}_B & \text{if } x \geq 0 \\ 1 \blacktriangle \bar{\text{x}}_1 \bar{\text{x}}_2 \cdots \bar{\text{x}}_B & \text{if } x < 0 \end{cases} \tag{6.27}$$

For example, when $B = 2$, $\hat{x} = +1/4$ is represented by $\hat{x} = 0 \blacktriangle 01$, and $\hat{x} = -1/4$ is represented by $\hat{x} = 1 \blacktriangle 10$.

Two's-complement format   Once again, the positive numbers have the same representation. Negative numbers are obtained by first complementing the magnitude and then modulo-2 adding 1 to the last bit or the *least-significant bit* (LSB). Stated differently, two's-complement is formed by subtracting the magnitude of the number from 2. Thus

$$
\hat{x} = \begin{cases} 0_{\blacktriangle}\mathsf{x}_1\mathsf{x}_2\cdots\mathsf{x}_B & \text{if } x \geq 0 \\ 2 - |x| = 1_{\blacktriangle}\bar{\mathsf{x}}_1\bar{\mathsf{x}}_2\cdots\bar{\mathsf{x}}_B \oplus 0_{\blacktriangle}00\cdots1 = 1_{\blacktriangle}\mathsf{y}_1\mathsf{y}_2\cdots\mathsf{y}_B & \text{if } x < 0 \end{cases}
$$

$$(6.28)$$

where $\oplus$ represents modulo-2 addition and bit y is, in general, different from bit $\bar{\mathsf{x}}$. For example, when $B = 2$, $\hat{x} = +1/4$ is represented by $\hat{x} = 0_{\blacktriangle}01$, and $\hat{x} = -1/4$ is represented by $\hat{x} = 1_{\blacktriangle}10 \oplus 0_{\blacktriangle}01 = 1_{\blacktriangle}11$.

☐   **EXAMPLE 6.13**   Let $B = 3$; then $\hat{x}$ is a 4-bit number (sign plus 3 bits). Provide all possible values that $\hat{x}$ can take in each of the three formats.

Solution   There are $2^4 = 16$ possible values that $\hat{x}$ can take for each of the three formats, as shown in the following table.

Binary	Sign-Magnitude	one's	two's
$0_{\blacktriangle}111$	7/8	7/8	7/8
$0_{\blacktriangle}110$	6/8	6/8	6/8
$0_{\blacktriangle}101$	5/8	5/8	5/8
$0_{\blacktriangle}100$	4/8	4/8	4/8
$0_{\blacktriangle}011$	3/8	3/8	3/8
$0_{\blacktriangle}010$	2/8	2/8	2/8
$0_{\blacktriangle}001$	1/8	1/8	1/8
$0_{\blacktriangle}000$	0	0	0
$1_{\blacktriangle}000$	-0	$-7/8$	-1
$1_{\blacktriangle}001$	$-1/8$	$-6/8$	$-7/8$
$1_{\blacktriangle}010$	$-2/8$	$-5/8$	$-6/8$
$1_{\blacktriangle}011$	$-3/8$	$-4/8$	$-5/8$
$1_{\blacktriangle}100$	$-4/8$	$-3/8$	$-4/8$
$1_{\blacktriangle}101$	$-5/8$	$-2/8$	$-3/8$
$1_{\blacktriangle}110$	$-6/8$	$-1/8$	$-2/8$
$1_{\blacktriangle}111$	$-7/8$	-0	$-1/8$

☐

In Example 6.13, observe that the bit arrangement is exactly the same as in the integer case for 4 bits. The only difference is in the position of the binary point. Thus the MATLAB programs developed in the previous section can easily be used with proper modifications. The MATLAB function `sm2oc` converts a decimal sign-magnitude fraction into its one's-complement format, while the function `oc2sm` performs the inverse operation. These functions are explored in Problem P6.24. Similarly, MATLAB functions `sm2tc` and `tc2sm` convert a decimal sign-magnitude fraction into its two's-complement format and vice versa, respectively; they are explored in Problem P6.25.

6.5.3 FLOATING-POINT ARITHMETIC

In many applications, the range of numbers needed is very large. For example, in physics one might need, at the same time, the mass of the sun (e.g., 2.10^{30}kg) and the mass of the electron (e.g., 9.10^{-31}kg). These two numbers cover a range of over 10^{60}. For fixed-point arithmetic, we would need 62-digit numbers (or 62-digit precision). However, even the mass of the sun is not accurately known with a precision of 5 digits, and there is almost no measurement in physics that could be made with a precision of 62 digits. One could then imagine making all calculations with a precision of 62 digits and throwing away 50 or 60 of them before printing out the final results. This would be wasteful of both CPU time and memory space. So what is needed is a system for representing numbers in which the range of expressible numbers is independent of the number of significant digits.

Decimal numbers   The floating-point representation for a decimal number x is based on expressing the number in the scientific notation:

$$x = \pm M \times 10^{\pm E}$$

where M is called the *mantissa* and E is the *exponent*. However, there are different possible representations of the same number, depending on the actual position of the decimal point—for example,

$$1234 = 0.1234 \times 10^4 = 1.234 \times 10^3 = 12.34 \times 10^2 = \cdots$$

To fix this problem, a floating-point number is always stored using a unique representation, which has only one nonzero digit to the left of the decimal point. This representation of a floating-point number is called a *normalized form*. The normalized form of the preceding number is 1.234×10^3, because it is the only representation resulting in a unique nonzero digit to the left of the decimal point. The digit arrangement for the normalized form is given by

$$\hat{x} = \underset{}{\pm}\ \ \text{x}_{\blacktriangle}\ \underbrace{\text{xx}\cdots\text{x}}_{N\text{-bit } M}\ \underset{}{\pm}\ \underbrace{\text{xx}\cdots\text{x}}_{L\text{-bit } E} \qquad (6.29)$$

sign of M   sign of E

For the negative numbers, we have the same formats as the fixed-point representations, including the ten's-complement format.

The number of digits used in the exponent determine the range of representable numbers, whereas the number of digits used in the mantissa determine the precision of the numbers. For example, if the mantissa is expressed using two digits plus the sign, and the exponent is expressed using two digits plus the sign, then the real number line will be covered as

```
                99             -99                        -99            99
      -9.99x10       -1.0x10            0         1.0x10         9.99x10
  ---------+----------------+-----------+-----------+----------------+-------->
           | accessible |           0           | accessible |
  negative | negative   | negative | positive | positive   | positive
  overflow | numbers    | underflow| underflow| numbers    | overflow
```

The range of accessible floating-point numbers with a given representation can be large, but it is still finite. In the preceding example (e.g., with two digits for the mantissa and two digits for the exponent), there are only $9 \times 10 \times 10 \times 199 = 179{,}100$ positive numbers, and as many negative numbers, plus the number zero, for a total of $358{,}201$ numbers that can be represented.

Binary numbers   Although the fraction-only fixed-point arithmetic does not have any overflow problems when two numbers are multiplied, it does suffer from overflow problems when two numbers are added. Also, the fixed-point numbers have limited dynamic range. Both of these aspects are unacceptable for an intensive computational job. These limitations can be removed by making the binary point ▲ floating rather than fixed.

The floating-point bit arrangement for binary-number representation is similar to that for the decimal numbers. In practice, however, two exceptions are made. The exponent is expressed using L-bit excess-2^{L-1} format, and the B-bit normalized mantissa is a fractional number with a 1 following the binary point. Note that the sign bit is the MSB of the bit pattern. Thus the B-bit mantissa and L-bit exponent (for a total of $B + L + 1$ word length) bit pattern is given by (note the reversal of the mantissa and exponent places)

$$\hat{x} = \underset{}{\pm} \; \underbrace{\texttt{xx}\cdots\texttt{x}}_{L\text{-bit }E} \; \blacktriangle \; \underbrace{\texttt{1x}\cdots\texttt{x}}_{B\text{-bit }M} \tag{6.30}$$

where the $\pm$ is the Sign of M.

where exponent E is adjusted so that we have a normalized mantissa—that is, $1/2 \leq M < 1$. Hence the first bit after the binary point is always 1. The decimal equivalent of $\hat{x}$ is given by

$$\hat{x} = \pm M \times 2^{E} \tag{6.31}$$

For the negative numbers, we can have the same formats as the fixed-point representations for the mantissa including two's-complement format.

However, the most widely used format for the mantissa is the sign-magnitude one.

☐ **EXAMPLE 6.14**   Consider a 32-bit floating-point word with the following arrangement:

$$\hat{x} = \pm \underbrace{\text{xx}\cdots\text{x}}_{\text{8-bit } E} \; \blacktriangle \; \underbrace{\text{1x}\cdots\text{x}}_{\text{23-bit } M}$$

Determine the decimal equivalent of

$$01000001111000000000000000000000$$

Solution   Since the exponent is 8-bit, it is expressed in excess-2^7 or in excess-128 format. Then the bit pattern can be partitioned into

$$\hat{x} = \overset{\overset{\text{Sign}}{\downarrow}}{0} \; \underbrace{10000011}_{E=131} \; \blacktriangle \; \underbrace{11000000000000000000000}_{M=2^{-1}+2^{-2}}$$

The sign bit is 0, which means that the number is positive. The exponent code is 131, which means that its decimal value is $131 - 128 = 3$. Thus the bit pattern represents the decimal number $\hat{x} = + \left(2^{-1} + 2^{-2}\right)\left(2^3\right) = 2^2 + 2^1 = 6$.   ☐

☐ **EXAMPLE 6.15**   Let $\hat{x} = -0.1875$. Represent $\hat{x}$ using the format given in (6.30), in which $B = 11$, $L = 4$ (for a total of 16 bits), and sign-magnitude format is used for the mantissa.

Solution   We can write

$$\hat{x} = -0.1875 = -0.75 \times 2^{-2}$$

Hence the exponent is -2, the mantissa is 0.75, and the sign is negative. The 4-bit exponent, in excess-8 format, is expressed as $8 - 2 = 6$ or with bit pattern 0110. The mantissa is expressed as 11000000000. Since $\hat{x}$ is negative, the bit pattern is

$$\hat{x} \equiv 1011011000000000$$

☐

The advantages of the floating-point representation are that it has a large dynamic range and that its resolution, defined as the interval between two consecutive representable levels, is proportional to the magnitude. The disadvantages include no representation for the number 0 and the fact that the arithmetic operations are more complicated than their fixed-point representations.

IEEE 754 standard   In the early days of the digital computer revolution, each processor design had its own internal representation for floating-point numbers. Since floating-point arithmetic is more complicated to implement, some of these designs did incorrect arithmetic. Therefore, in 1985 IEEE issued a standard (IEEE standard 754-1985, or IEEE-754 for short) to allow floating-point data exchange among different computers and to provide hardware designers with a model known to be correct. Currently, almost all manufacturers design main processors or a dedicated coprocessor for floating-point operations using the IEEE-754 standard representation.

The IEEE-754 standard defines three formats for binary numbers: a 32-bit single-precision format, a 64-bit double-precision format, and an 80-bit temporary format (which is used internally by the processors or arithmetic coprocessors to minimize rounding errors).

We will briefly describe the 32-bit single-precision standard. This standard has many similarities with the floating-point representation discussed above, but there are also differences. Remember, this is another model advocated by IEEE. The form of this model is

$$\hat{x} = \overset{\text{sign of M}}{\underset{\downarrow}{\pm}}\ \underbrace{\mathrm{XX\cdots X}}_{\text{8-bit E}}\ \blacktriangle\ \underbrace{\mathrm{XX\cdots X}}_{\text{23-bit M}} \tag{6.32}$$

The mantissa's value is called the *significand* in this standard. Features of this model are as follows:

- If the sign bit is 0, the number is positive; if the sign bit is 1, the number is negative.
- The exponent is coded in 8-bit excess-127 (and not 128) format. Hence the uncoded exponents are between -127 and 128.
- The mantissa is in 23-bit binary. A normalized mantissa always starts with a bit 1, followed by the binary point, followed by the rest of the 23-bit mantissa. However, the leading bit 1, which is always present in a normalized mantissa, is hidden (not stored) and needs to be restored for computation. Again, note that this is different from the usual definition of the normalized mantissa. If all the 23 bits representing the mantissa are set to 0, the significand is 1 (remember the implicit leading 1). If all 23 bits are set to 1, the significand is almost 2 (in fact $2 - 2^{-23}$). All IEEE 754 normalized numbers have a significand that is in the interval $1 \le M < 2$.
- The smallest normalized number is 2^{-126}, and the largest normalized number is almost 2^{128}. The resulting positive decimal range is roughly 10^{-38} to 10^{38} with a similar negative range.
- If $E = 0$ and $M = 0$, then the representation is interpreted as a *denormalized* number (i.e., the hidden bit is 0) and is assigned a value

of ± 0, depending on the sign bit (called the *soft zero*). Thus 0 has two representations.

- If $E = 255$ and $M \neq 0$, then the representation is interpreted as a *not-a-number* (abbreviated as NaN). MATLAB assigns a variable `NaN` when this happens—for example, $0/0$.
- If $E = 255$ and $M = 0$, then the representation is interpreted as $\pm\infty$. MATLAB assigns a variable `inf` when this happens—for example, $1/0$.

☐   **EXAMPLE 6.16**   Consider the bit pattern given in Example 6.14. Assuming IEEE-754 format, determine its decimal equivalent.

Solution   The sign bit is 0 and the exponent code is 131, which means that the exponent is $131 - 127 = 4$. The significand is $1 + 2^{-1} + 2^{-2} = 1.75$. Hence the bit pattern represents

$$\hat{x} = +(1 + 2^{-1} + 2^{-2})(2^4) = 2^4 + 2^3 + 2^2 = 28$$

which is different from the number in Example 6.14.   ☐

MATLAB employs the 64-bit double-precision IEEE-754 format for all its number representations and the 80-bit temporary format for its internal computations. Hence all calculations that we perform in MATLAB are in fact floating-point computations. Simulating a different floating-point format in MATLAB would be much more complicated and would not add any more insight to our understanding than the native format. Hence we will not consider a MATLAB simulation of floating-point arithmetic as we did for fixed-point.

6.6 THE PROCESS OF QUANTIZATION AND ERROR CHARACTERIZATIONS

From the discussion of number representations in the previous section, it should be clear that a general infinite-precision real number must be assigned to one of the finite representable numbers, given a specific structure for the finite-length register (i.e., the arithmetic as well as the format). Usually, in practice, there are two different operations by which this assignment is made to the nearest number or level: the *truncation* operation and the *rounding* operation. These operations affect the accuracy as well as general characteristics of digital filters and DSP operations.

We assume, without loss of generality, that there are $B + 1$ bits in the fixed-point (fractional) arithmetic or in the mantissa of floating-point arithmetic including the sign bit. Then the resolution (Δ) is given by

$$\Delta = 2^{-B} \begin{cases} \text{absolute in the case of fixed-point arithmetic} \\ \text{relative in the case of floating-point arithmetic} \end{cases} \tag{6.33}$$

6.6.1 FIXED-POINT ARITHMETIC

The quantizer block diagram in this case is given by

$$x \quad \longrightarrow \boxed{\begin{array}{c} \text{Quantizer} \;\; \mathcal{Q}[\cdot] \\ B, \, \Delta \end{array}} \longrightarrow \quad \mathcal{Q}[x]$$

Infinite-precision   Finite-precision

where B, the number of fractional bits, and Δ, the resolution, are the parameters of the quantizer. We will denote the finite word-length number, after quantization, by $\mathcal{Q}[x]$ for an input number x. Let the quantization error be given by

$$e \stackrel{\triangle}{=} \mathcal{Q}[x] - x \tag{6.34}$$

We will analyze this error for both the truncation and the rounding operations.

Truncation operation In this operation, the number x is truncated beyond B significant bits (i.e., the rest of the bits are eliminated) to obtain $\mathcal{Q}_{\mathrm{T}}[x]$. In MATLAB, to obtain a B-bit truncation, we have to first scale the number x upward by 2^B, then use the `fix` function on the scaled number, and finally scale the result down by 2^{-B}. Thus the MATLAB statement `xhat = fix(x*2^B)/2^B;` implements the desired operation. We will now consider each of the three formats.

Sign-magnitude format If the number x is positive, then after truncation $\mathcal{Q}_{\mathrm{T}}[x] \leq x$ since some value in x is lost. Hence quantizer error for truncation denoted by e_{T} is less than or equal to 0 or $e_{\mathrm{T}} \leq 0$. However, since there are B bits in the quantizer, the maximum error in terms of magnitude is

$$|e_{\mathrm{T}}| = 0.\underbrace{00\cdots0}_{B \text{ bits}} 111\cdots = 2^{-B} \text{ (decimal)} \tag{6.35}$$

or

$$-2^{-B} \leq e_{\mathrm{T}} \leq 0, \quad \text{for } x \geq 0 \tag{6.36}$$

Similarly, if the $x < 0$ then after truncation $\mathcal{Q}_{\mathrm{T}}[x] \geq x$ since $\mathcal{Q}_{\mathrm{T}}[x]$ is less negative, or $e_{\mathrm{T}} \geq 0$. The largest magnitude of this error is again 2^{-B}, or

$$0 \leq e_{\mathrm{T}} \leq 2^{-B}, \quad \text{for } x < 0 \tag{6.37}$$

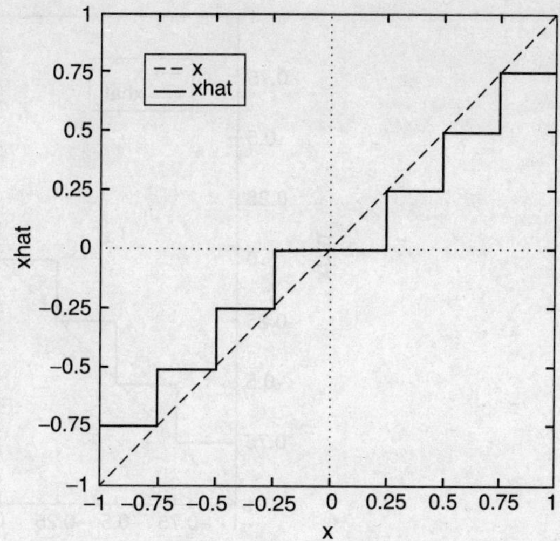

FIGURE 6.19 *Truncation error characteristics in the sign-magnitude format*

☐ **EXAMPLE 6.17** Let $-1 < x < 1$, and let $B = 2$. Using MATLAB, verify the truncation error characteristics.

Solution The resolution is $\Delta = 2^{-2} = 0.25$. Using the following MATLAB script, we can verify the truncation error e_T relations given in (6.36) and (6.37).

```
x = [-1+2^(-10):2^(-10):1-2^(-10)];    % Sign-Mag numbers between -1 and 1
B = 2;                                 % Number of bits for truncation
xhat = fix(x*2^B)/2^B                  % Truncation
plot(x,x,'g',x,xhat,'r','linewidth',1); % Plot
```

The resulting plots of x and $\hat{x}$ are shown in Figure 6.19. Note that the plot of $\hat{x}$ has a staircase shape and that it satisfies (6.36) and (6.37). ☐

One's-complement format For $x \geq 0$, we have the same characteristics for e_T as in sign-magnitude format—that is,

$$-2^{-B} \leq e_T \leq 0, \quad \text{for } x \geq 0 \tag{6.38}$$

For $x < 0$, the representation is obtained by complementing all bits, including the sign bit. To compute the maximum error, let

$$x = 1_\blacktriangle b_1 b_2 \cdots b_B 000 \cdots = -\left\{ _\blacktriangle (1 - b_1)(1 - b_2) \cdots (1 - b_B) 111 \cdots \right\}$$

After truncation, we obtain

$$\mathcal{Q}_T[x] = 1_\blacktriangle b_1 b_2 \cdots b_B = -\left\{ _\blacktriangle (1 - b_1)(1 - b_2) \cdots (1 - b_B) \right\}$$

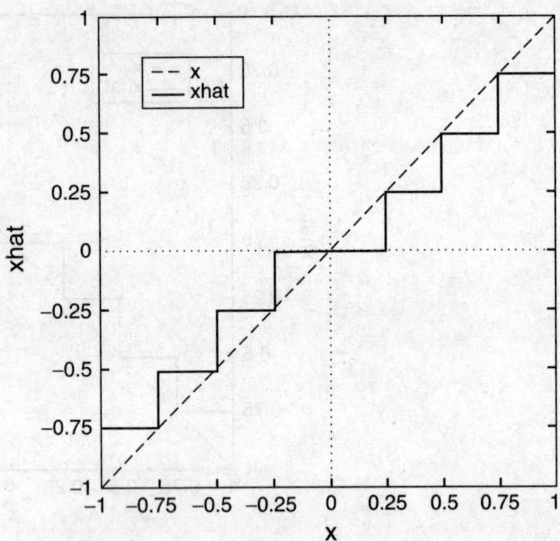

FIGURE 6.20 *Truncation error characteristics in the one's-complement format*

Clearly, x is more negative than $\mathcal{Q}_T[x]$ or $x \leq \mathcal{Q}_T[x]$ or $e_T \geq 0$. In fact, the maximum truncation error is

$$e_{T\max} = 0{\blacktriangle}00\cdots 0111\cdots = 2^{-B} \ \text{(decimal)}$$

Hence

$$0 \leq e_T \leq 2^{-B}, \quad \text{for } x < 0 \tag{6.39}$$

☐ **EXAMPLE 6.18** Again let $-1 < x < 1$ and $B = 2$ with the resolution $\Delta = 2^{-2} = 0.25$. Using MATLAB, verify the truncation error e_T relations given in (6.38) and (6.39).

Solution The MATLAB script uses functions **sm2oc** and **oc2sm**, which are explored in Problem P6.24.

```
x = [-1+2^(-10):2^(-10):1-2^(-10)];    % Sign-Magnitude numbers between -1 and 1
B = 2;                                  % Select bits for truncation
y = sm2oc(x,B);                         % Sign-mag to one's complement
yhat = fix(y*2^B)/2^B;                  % Truncation
xhat = oc2sm(yhat,B);                   % One's-complement to sign-mag
plot(x,x,'g',x,xhat,'r','linewidth',1); % Plot
```

The resulting plots of x and $\hat{x}$ are shown in Figure 6.20. Note that the plot of $\hat{x}$ is identical to the plot in Figure 6.19 and that it satisfies (6.38) and (6.39).   ☐

Two's-complement format   Once again, for $x \geq 0$, we have

$$-2^{-B} \leq e_T \leq 0, \quad \text{for } x \geq 0 \qquad (6.40)$$

For $x < 0$, the representation is given by $2 - |x|$ where $|x|$ is the magnitude. Hence the magnitude of x is given by

$$|x| = 2 - x \qquad (6.41)$$

with $x = 1{\blacktriangle}b_1b_2 \cdots b_Bb_{B+1}\cdots$. After truncation to B bits, we obtain $\mathcal{Q}_T[x] = 1{\blacktriangle}b_1b_2 \cdots b_B$, the magnitude of which is

$$|\mathcal{Q}_T[x]| = 2 - \mathcal{Q}_T[x] \qquad (6.42)$$

From (6.41) and (6.42),

$$|\mathcal{Q}_T[x]| - |x| = x - \mathcal{Q}_T[x] = 1{\blacktriangle}b_1b_2 \cdots b_Bb_{B+1} \cdots - 1{\blacktriangle}b_1b_2 \cdots b_B$$
$$= 0{\blacktriangle}00 \cdots 0b_{B+1} \cdots \qquad (6.43)$$

The largest change in magnitude from (6.43) is

$$0{\blacktriangle}00 \cdots 0111 \cdots = 2^{-B} \text{ (decimal)} \qquad (6.44)$$

Since the change in the magnitude is positive, then after truncation $\mathcal{Q}_T[x]$ becomes more negative, which means that $\mathcal{Q}_T[x] \leq x$. Hence

$$-2^{-B} \leq e_T \leq 0, \quad \text{for } x < 0 \qquad (6.45)$$

☐ **EXAMPLE 6.19**   Again consider $-1 < x < 1$ and $B = 2$ with the resolution $\Delta = 2^{-2} = 0.25$. Using MATLAB, verify the truncation error e_T relations given in (6.40) and (6.45).

Solution   The MATLAB script uses functions `sm2tc` and `tc2sm`, which are explored in Problem P6.25.

```
x = [-1+2^(-10):2^(-10):1-2^(-10)]; % Sign-magnitude numbers between -1 and 1
B = 2;                              % Select bits for truncation
y = sm2tc(x);                       % Sign-mag to two's complement
yhat = fix(y*2^B)/2^B;              % Truncation
xq = tc2sm(yq );                    % Two's-complement to sign-mag
plot(x,x,'g',x,xhat,'r','linewidth',1); % Plot
```

The resulting plots of x and $\hat{x}$ are shown in Figure 6.21. Note that the plot of $\hat{x}$ is also a staircase graph but is below the x graph and that it satisfies (6.40) and (6.45). ☐

Collecting results (6.36)–(6.40) and (6.45) along with those in Figures 6.19–6.21, we conclude that the truncation characteristics for fixed-point arithmetic are the same for the sign-magnitude and the one's-complement formats but are different for the two's-complement format.

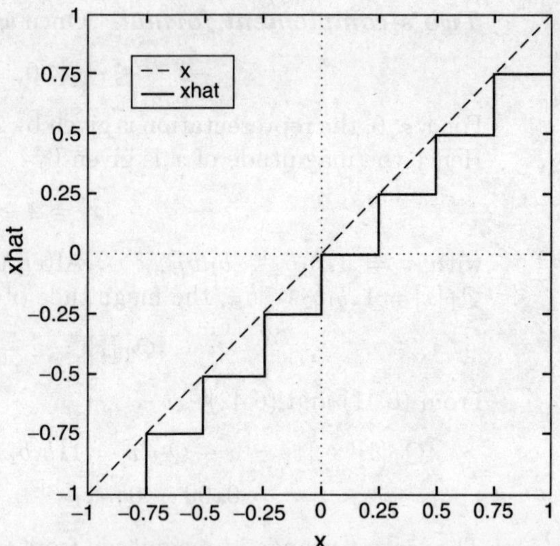

FIGURE 6.21   *Truncation error characteristics in the two's-complement format*

Rounding operation   In this operation, the real number x is rounded to the *nearest* representable level, which we will refer to as $\mathcal{Q}_\mathrm{R}[x]$. In MATLAB, to obtain a B-bit rounding approximation, we have to first scale the number x up by 2^B, then use the `round` function on the scaled number, and finally scale the result down by 2^{-B}. Thus the MATLAB statement `xhat = round(x*2^B)/2^B;` implements the desired operation.

Since the quantization step or resolution is $\Delta = 2^{-B}$, the magnitude of the maximum error is

$$|e_\mathrm{R}|_{\max} = \frac{\Delta}{2} = \frac{1}{2}2^{-B} \tag{6.46}$$

Hence for all three formats, the quantizer error due to rounding, denoted by e_R, satisfies

$$-\frac{1}{2}2^{-B} \le e_\mathrm{R} \le \frac{1}{2}2^{-B} \tag{6.47}$$

☐ **EXAMPLE 6.20**   Demonstrate the rounding operations and the corresponding error characteristics on the signal of Examples 6.17–6.19 using the three formats.

Solution   Since the rounding operation assigns values that can be larger than the unquantized values, which can create problems for the two's- and one's-complement formats, we will restrict the signal over the interval $[-1, 1 - 2^{-B-1}]$. The following MATLAB script shows the two's-complement format rounding, but other scripts are similar (readers are encouraged to verify).

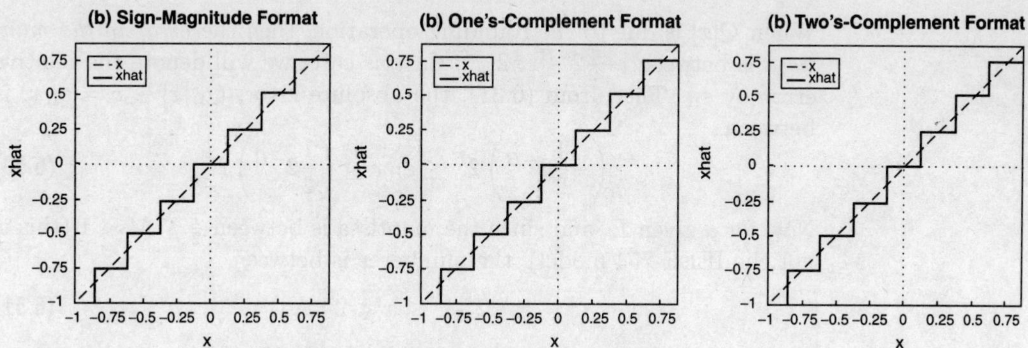

FIGURE 6.22   *Rounding error characteristics in the fixed-point representation*

```
B = 2;                              % Select bits for rounding
x = [-1:2^(-10):1-2^(-B-1)];        % Sign-magnitude numbers between -1 and 1
y = sm2tc(x);                       % Sign-mag to two's complement
yq = round(y*2^B)/2^B;              % Rounding
xq = tc2sm(yq);                     % Two's-complement to sign-mag
```

The resulting plots for the sign-magnitude, one's-, and two's-complement formats are shown in Figure 6.22. These plots do satisfy (6.47). □

Comparing the error characteristics of the truncation and rounding operations given in Figures 6.19 through 6.22, it is clear that the rounding operation is a superior one for the quantization error. This is because the error is symmetric with respect to zero (or equal positive and negative distribution) and because the error is the same across all three formats. Hence we will mostly consider the rounding operation for the floating-point arithmetic as well as for further analysis.

6.6.2 FLOATING-POINT ARITHMETIC

In this arithmetic, the quantizer affects only the mantissa M. However, the number x is represented by $M \times 2^E$ where E is the exponent. Hence the quantizer errors are multiplicative and depend on the magnitude of x. Therefore, the more appropriate measure of error is the relative error rather than the absolute error, $(\mathcal{Q}[x] - x)$. Let us define the relative error, ε, as

$$\varepsilon \triangleq \frac{\mathcal{Q}[x] - x}{x} \tag{6.48}$$

Then the quantized value $\mathcal{Q}[x]$ can be written as

$$\mathcal{Q}[x] = x + \varepsilon x = x\left(1 + \varepsilon\right) \tag{6.49}$$

When $\mathcal{Q}[x]$ is due to the rounding operation, then the *error in the mantissa* is between $[-\frac{1}{2}2^{-B}, \frac{1}{2}2^{-B}]$. In this case, we will denote the relative error by ε_R. Then from (6.31), the absolute error, $\mathcal{Q}_R[x] - x = \varepsilon_R x$, is between

$$\left(-\frac{1}{2}2^{-B}\right)2^E \leq \varepsilon_R x \leq \left(\frac{1}{2}2^{-B}\right)2^E \tag{6.50}$$

Now for a given E, and since the mantissa is between $\frac{1}{2} \leq M < 1$ (this is not the IEEE-754 model), the number x is between

$$2^{E-1} \leq x < 2^E \tag{6.51}$$

Hence from (6.50) and using the smallest value in (6.51), we obtain

$$-2^{-B} \leq \varepsilon_R \leq 2^{-B} \tag{6.52}$$

This relative error relation, (6.52), will be used in subsequent analysis.

6.7 QUANTIZATION OF FILTER COEFFICIENTS

We now study the finite word-length effects on the filter responses, pole-zero locations, and stability when the filter coefficients are quantized. We will separately discuss the issues relating to IIR and FIR filters since we can obtain simpler results for FIR filters. We begin with the case of IIR filters.

6.7.1 IIR FILTERS

Consider a general IIR filter described by

$$H(z) = \frac{\sum_{k=0}^{M} b_k z^{-k}}{1 + \sum_{k=1}^{N} a_k z^{-k}} \tag{6.53}$$

where a_ks and b_ks are the filter coefficients. Now assume that these coefficients are represented by their finite-precision numbers $\hat{a}_k$s and $\hat{b}_k$s. Then we get a new filter system function

$$H(z) \rightarrow \hat{H}(z) \triangleq \frac{\sum_{k=0}^{M} \hat{b}_k z^{-k}}{1 + \sum_{k=1}^{N} \hat{a}_k z^{-k}} \tag{6.54}$$

Since this is a new filter, we want to know how "different" this filter is from the original one $H(z)$. Various aspects can be compared; for example, we may want to compare their magnitude responses, or phase responses, or change in their pole-zero locations, and so on. A general analytical expression to compute this change in all these aspects is difficult to derive. This is where MATLAB can be used to investigate this change and its overall effect on the usability of the filter.

6.7.2 EFFECT ON POLE-ZERO LOCATIONS

One aspect can be reasonably analyzed, which is the movement of filter poles when a_k is changed to $\hat{a}_k$. This can be used to check the stability of IIR filters. A similar movement of zeros to changes in numerator coefficients can also be analyzed.

To evaluate this movement, consider the denominator polynomial of $H(z)$ in (6.53),

$$D(z) \overset{\triangle}{=} 1 + \sum_{k=1}^{N} a_k z^{-k} = \prod_{\ell=1}^{N} \left(1 - p_\ell z^{-1}\right) \tag{6.55}$$

where $\{p_\ell\}$s are the poles of $H(z)$. We will regard $D(z)$ as a function $D(p_1, \ldots, p_N)$ of poles $\{p_1, \ldots, p_N\}$ where each pole p_ℓ is a function of the filter coefficients $\{a_1, \ldots, a_N\}$—that is, $p_\ell = f_\ell(a_1, \ldots, a_N)$, $\ell = 1, \ldots N$. Then the change in the denominator $D(z)$ due to a change in the kth coefficient a_k is given by

$$\left(\frac{\partial D(z)}{\partial a_k}\right) = \left(\frac{\partial D(z)}{\partial p_1}\right)\left(\frac{\partial p_1}{\partial a_k}\right) + \left(\frac{\partial D(z)}{\partial p_2}\right)\left(\frac{\partial p_2}{\partial a_k}\right) + \cdots + \left(\frac{\partial D(z)}{\partial p_N}\right)\left(\frac{\partial p_N}{\partial a_k}\right) \tag{6.56}$$

where, from (6.55),

$$\left(\frac{\partial D(z)}{\partial p_i}\right) = \frac{\partial}{\partial p_i}\left[\prod_{\ell=1}^{N}\left(1 - p_\ell z^{-1}\right)\right] = -z^{-1}\prod_{\ell \neq i}\left(1 - p_\ell z^{-1}\right) \tag{6.57}$$

From (6.57), note that $\left(\frac{\partial D(z)}{\partial p_i}\right)\Big|_{z=p_\ell} = 0$ for $\ell \neq i$. Hence from (6.56) we obtain

$$\left(\frac{\partial D(z)}{\partial a_k}\right)\Big|_{z=p_\ell} = \left(\frac{\partial D(z)}{\partial p_\ell}\right)\Big|_{z=p_\ell}\left(\frac{\partial p_\ell}{\partial a_k}\right) \quad \text{or} \quad \left(\frac{\partial p_\ell}{\partial a_k}\right) = \frac{\left(\frac{\partial D(z)}{\partial a_k}\right)\Big|_{z=p_\ell}}{\left(\frac{\partial D(z)}{\partial p_\ell}\right)\Big|_{z=p_\ell}} \tag{6.58}$$

Now

$$\left(\frac{\partial D(z)}{\partial a_k}\right)\Big|_{z=p_\ell} = \frac{\partial}{\partial a_k}\left(1 + \sum_{i=1}^{N} a_i z^{-i}\right)\Big|_{z=p_\ell} = z^{-k}\Big|_{z=p_\ell} = p_\ell^{-k} \tag{6.59}$$

From (6.57), (6.58), and (6.59), we obtain

$$\left(\frac{\partial p_\ell}{\partial a_k}\right) = \frac{p_\ell^{-k}}{-z^{-1}\prod_{i \neq \ell}\left(1 - p_i z^{-1}\right)\Big|_{z=p_\ell}} = -\frac{p_\ell^{N-k}}{\prod_{i \neq \ell}\left(p_\ell - p_i\right)} \tag{6.60}$$

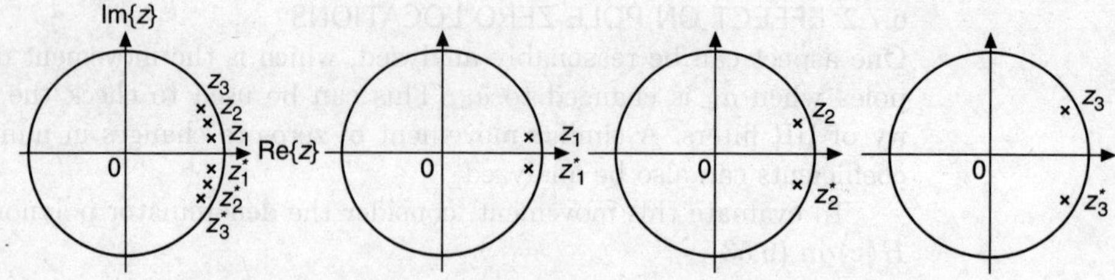

FIGURE 6.23 *z-plane plots of tightly clustered poles of a digital filter*

Finally, the total perturbation error $\triangle p_\ell$ can be expressed as

$$\triangle p_\ell = \sum_{k=1}^{N} \frac{\partial p_\ell}{\partial a_k} \triangle a_k \qquad (6.61)$$

This formula measures the movement of the ℓth pole, p_ℓ, to changes in each of the coefficient $\{a_k\}$; hence it is known as a *sensitivity* formula. It shows that if the coefficients $\{a_k\}$ are such that if the poles p_ℓ and p_i are very close for some ℓ, i, then $(p_\ell - p_i)$ is very small and as a result the filter is very sensitive to the changes in filter coefficients. A similar result can be obtained for the sensitivity of zeros to changes in the parameters $\{b_k\}$.

To investigate this further in the light of various filter realizations, consider the z-plane plot shown in Figure 6.23(a), where poles are tightly clustered. This situation arises in wideband frequency selective filters such as lowpass or highpass filters. Now if we were to realize this filter using the direct form (either I or II), then the filter has all these tightly clustered poles, which makes the direct form realization very sensitive to coefficient changes due to finite word length. Thus the direct form realizations will suffer severely from coefficient quantization effects.

On the other hand, if we were to use either the cascade or the parallel forms, then we would realize the filter using second-order sections containing widely separated poles, as shown in Figure 6.23(b). Thus each second-order section will have low sensitivity in that its pole locations will be perturbed only slightly. Consequently, we expect that the overall system function $H(z)$ will be perturbed only slightly. Thus the cascade or the parallel forms, when realized properly, will have low sensitivity to the changes or errors in filter coefficients.

☐ **EXAMPLE 6.21** Consider a digital resonator that is a second-order IIR filter given by

$$H(z) = \frac{1}{1 - (2r\cos\theta)\,z^{-1} + r^2 z^{-2}} \qquad (6.62)$$

Analyze its sensitivity to pole locations when a 3-bit sign-magnitude format is used for the coefficient representation.

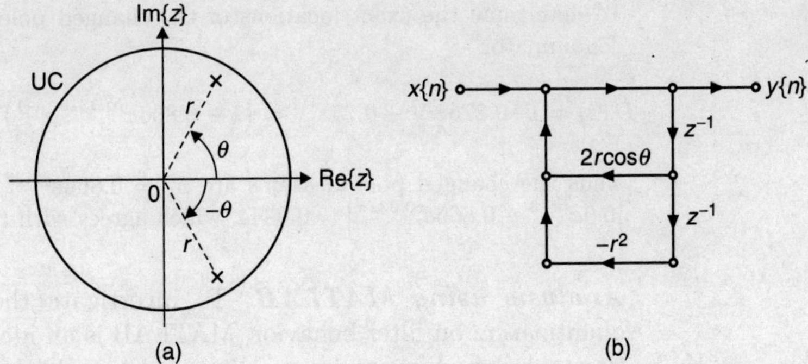

FIGURE 6.24 *Digital filter in Example 6.21: (a) pole-zero plot, (b) filter realization*

Solution

The filter has two complex-conjugate poles at

$$p_1 = re^{j\theta} \quad \text{and} \quad p_2 = re^{-j\theta} = p_1^*$$

For a proper operation as a resonator, the poles must be close to the unit circle—that is, $r \simeq 1$ (but $r < 1$). Then the resonant frequency $\omega_r \simeq \theta$. The zero-pole diagram is shown in Figure 6.24 along with the filter realization. Let $r = 0.9$ and $\theta = \pi/3$. Then from (6.62),

$$a_1 = -2r\cos\theta = -0.9 \quad \text{and} \quad a_2 = r^2 = 0.81$$

We now represent a_1 and a_2, each using 3-bit sign-magnitude format representation—that is,

$$a_k = \pm \blacktriangle b_1\, b_2\, b_3 = \pm \left(b_1 2^{-1} + b_2 2^{-2} + b_3 2^{-3} \right), \quad k = 1, 2$$

where b_j represents the jth bit and $\blacktriangle$ represents the binary point. Then for the closest representation, we must have

$$\hat{a}_1 = 1\blacktriangle 1\,1\,1 = -0.875 \qquad \text{and} \qquad \hat{a}_2 = 0\blacktriangle 1\,1\,0 = +0.75$$

Hence $|\triangle a_1| = 0.025$ and $|\triangle a_2| = 0.06$. Consider the sensitivity formula (6.61), in which

$$\frac{\partial p_1}{\partial a_1} = -\frac{p_1^{2-1}}{(p_1 - p_1^*)} = \frac{-p_1}{2\operatorname{Im}\{p_1\}} = \frac{-re^{j\theta}}{2r(\sin\theta)} = \frac{e^{j\pi/3}}{\sqrt{3}}, \text{ and}$$

$$\frac{\partial p_1}{\partial a_2} = -\frac{p_1^{2-2}}{(p_1 - p_1^*)} = \frac{-1}{2\operatorname{Im}\{p_1\}} = \frac{1}{0.9\sqrt{3}}$$

Using (6.61), we obtain

$$|\triangle p_1| \leq \left|\frac{\partial p_1}{\partial a_1}\right| |\triangle a_1| + \left|\frac{\partial p_1}{\partial a_2}\right| |\triangle a_2|$$

$$= \frac{1}{\sqrt{3}}(0.025) + \frac{1}{0.9\sqrt{3}}(0.06) = 0.0529 \tag{6.63}$$

To determine the exact locations of the changed poles, consider the changed denominator

$$\hat{D}(z) = 1 - 0.875z^{-1} + 0.75z^{-2} = \left(1 - 0.866e^{j0.331\pi}z^{-1}\right)\left(1 - 0.866e^{-j0.331\pi}z^{-1}\right)$$

Thus the changed pole locations are $\hat{p}_1 = 0.866e^{j0.331\pi} = \hat{p}_2^*$. Then $|\triangle p_1| = \left|0.9e^{i\pi/3} - 0.866e^{i0.331\pi}\right| = 0.0344$, which agrees with (6.63). $\quad\square$

Analysis using MATLAB To investigate the effect of coefficient quantization on filter behavior, MATLAB is an ideal vehicle. Using functions developed in previous sections, we can obtain quantized coefficients and then study such aspects as pole-zero movements, frequency response, or impulse response. We will have to represent all filter coefficients using the same number of integer and fraction bits. Hence, instead of quantizing each coefficient separately, we will develop the function `QCoeff` for coefficient quantization. This function implements quantization using rounding operation on sign-magnitude format. Although similar functions can be written for truncation as well as for other formats, we will analyze the effects using the `Qcoeff` function as explained previously.

```
function [y,L,B] = QCoeff(x,N)
%   [y,L,B] = QCoeff(x,N)
%       Coefficient quantization using N=1+L+B bit representation
%       with rounding operation
%       y: quantized array (same dim as x)
%       L: number of integer bits
%       B: number of fractional bits
%       x: a scalar, vector, or matrix
%       N: total number of bits

xm = abs(x);
 L = max(max(0,fix(log2(xm(:)+eps)+1))); % Integer bits
if (L > N)
    errmsg = [' *** N must be at least ',num2str(L),' ***']; error(errmsg);
end
B = N-L;                                 % Fractional bits
y = xm./(2^L); y = round(y.*(2^N));      % Rounding to N bits
y = sign(x).*y*(2^(-B));                 % L+B+1 bit representation
```

The `Qcoeff` function represents each coefficient in the `x` array using N+1-bit (including the sign bit) representation. First, it determines the number of bits L needed for integer representation for the magnitude-wise largest coefficient, and then it assigns N-L bits to the fraction part. The resulting number is returned in B. Thus all coefficients have the same bit pattern L+B+1. Clearly, $N \geq L$.

☐ **EXAMPLE 6.22** Consider the digital resonator in Example 6.21. Determine the change in the pole locations using MATLAB.

Solution The filter coefficients, $a_1 = -0.9$ and $a_2 = 0.81$, can be quantized using

```
>> x = [-0.9,0.81]; [y,L,B] = Qcoeff(x,3)
y = -0.8750    0.7500
L = 0
B = 3
```

as expected. Now using the following MATLAB script, we can determine the change in the location of the poles.

```
% Unquantized parameters
r = 0.9; theta = pi/3; a1 = -2*r*cos(theta); a2 = r*r;
p1 = r*exp(j*theta); p2 = p1';
% Quantized parameters: N = 3;
[ahat,L,B] = Qcoeff([a1,a2],3); rhat = sqrt(ahat(2));
thetahat = acos(-ahat(1)/(2*rhat)); p1hat = rhat*exp(j*thetahat); p2 = p1';
% Changes in pole locations
Dp1 = abs(p1-p1hat)
Dp1 = 0.0344
```

This is the same as before. ☐

☐ **EXAMPLE 6.23** Consider the following IIR filter with 10 poles closely packed at a radius of $r = 0.9$ around angles $\pm45°$ with a separation of $5°$. Due to large number of poles, the denominator coefficients have values that require 6 bits for the integer part. Using 9 bits for the fractional part for a total of 16-bit representation, we compute and plot the new locations of poles:

```
r = 0.9; theta = (pi/180)*[-55:5:-35,35:5:55]';
p = r*exp(j*theta); a = poly(p); b = 1;

% Direct form: quantized coefficients
N = 15; [ahat,L,B] = Qcoeff(a,N);
TITLE = sprintf('%i-bit (1+%i+%i) Precision',N+1,L,B);

% Comparison of pole-zero plots
subplot(1,2,1); [HZ,HP,H1] = zplane(1,a);
set(HZ,'color','g','linewidth',1); set(HP,'color','g','linewidth',1);
set(H1,'color','w'); axis([-1.1,1.1,-1.1,1.1]);
title('Infinite Precision','fontsize',10,'fontweight','bold');
```

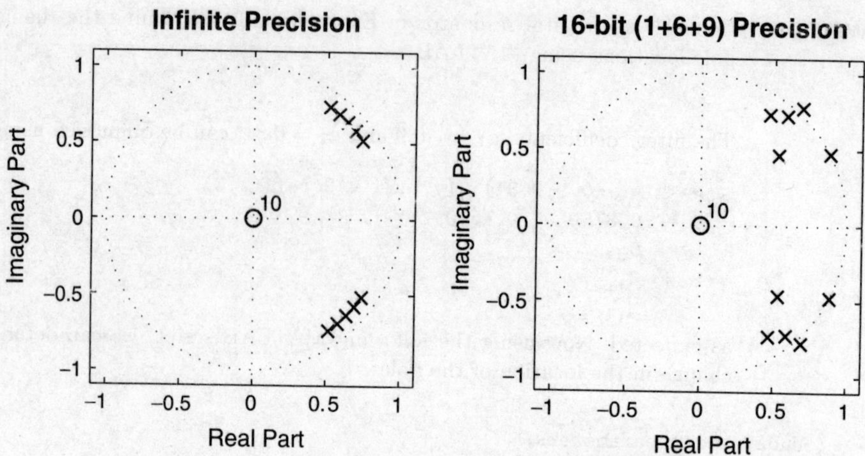

FIGURE 6.25 *Pole-zero plots for direct form structure in Example 6.23*

```
subplot(1,2,2); [HZhat,HPhat,Hlhat] = zplane(1,ahat);
set(HZhat,'color','r','linewidth',1); set(HPhat,'color','r','linewidth',1);
set(Hlhat,'color','w'); title(TITLE,'fontsize',10,'fontweight','bold');
axis([-1.1,1.1,-1.1,1.1]);
```

Figure 6.25 shows the pole-zero plots for filters with both infinite and 16-bit precision coefficients. Clearly, with 16-bit word length, the resulting filter is completely different from the original one and is unstable. To investigate the effect of finite word length on the cascade form structure, we first converted the direct form coefficients into the cascade form coefficients using the **dir2cas** function, quantized the resulting set of coefficients, and then converted back to the direct form for pole-zero plotting. We show results for two different word lengths. In the first case, we used the same 16-bit word length. Since the cascade coefficients have smaller integer parts that require only one integer bit, the number of fractional bits is 14. In the second case, we used 9 fractional bits (same as those in the direct form) for a total word length of 11 bits.

```
% Cascade form: quantized coefficients: same N
[b0,B0,A0] = dir2cas(b,a);   [BAhat1,L1,B1] = Qcoeff([B0,A0],N);
TITLE1 = sprintf('%i-bit (1+%i+%i) Precision',N+1,L1,B1);
Bhat1 = BAhat1(:,1:3); Ahat1 = BAhat1(:,4:6);
[bhat1,ahat1] = cas2dir(b0,Bhat1,Ahat1);

subplot(1,2,1);   [HZhat1,HPhat1,Hlhat1] = zplane(bhat1,ahat1);
set(HZhat1,'color','g','linewidth',1); set(HPhat1,'color','g','linewidth',1);
set(Hlhat1,'color','w'); axis([-1.1,1.1,-1.1,1.1]);
title(TITLE1,'fontsize',10,'fontweight','bold');
```

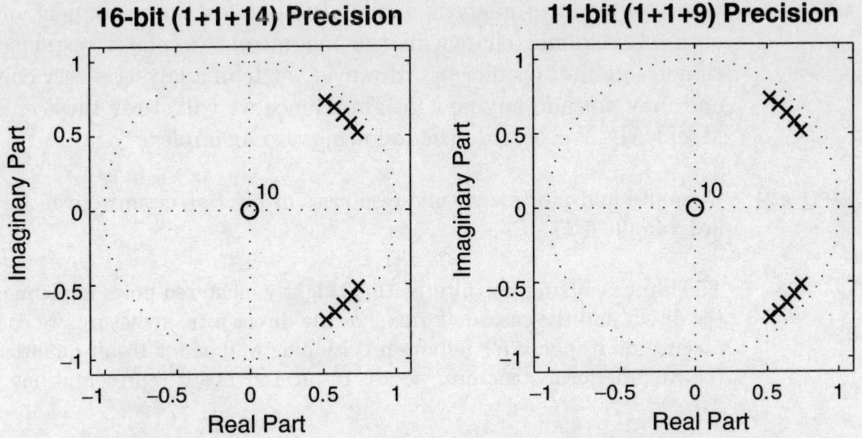

FIGURE 6.26 *Pole-zero plots for cascade form structure in Example 6.23*

```
% Cascade form: quantized coefficients: same B (N=L1+B)
N1 = L1+B; [BAhat2,L2,B2] = Qcoeff([B0,A0],N1);
TITLE2 = sprintf('%i-bit (1+%i+%i) Precision',N1+1,L2,B2);
Bhat2 = BAhat2(:,1:3); Ahat2 = BAhat2(:,4:6);
[bhat2,ahat2] = cas2dir(b0,Bhat2,Ahat2);

subplot(1,2,2);  [HZhat2,HPhat2,Hlhat2] = zplane(bhat2,ahat2);
set(HZhat2,'color','r','linewidth',1); set(HPhat2,'color','r','linewidth',1);
set(Hlhat2,'color','w');title(TITLE2,'fontsize',10,'fontweight','bold');
axis([-1.1,1.1,-1.1,1.1]);
```

The results are shown in Figure 6.26. We observe that not only for 16-bit representation but also for 11-bit representation, the resulting filter is essentially the same as the original one and is stable. Clearly, the cascade form structure has better finite-word-length properties than the direct form structure. $\quad\square$

6.7.3 EFFECTS ON FREQUENCY RESPONSE

The frequency response of the IIR filter in (6.38) is given by

$$H(e^{\jmath\omega}) = \frac{\sum_{k=0}^{M} b_k\, e^{-\jmath\omega k}}{1 + \sum_{k=1}^{N} a_k\, e^{-\jmath\omega k}} \tag{6.64}$$

When the coefficients $\{a_k\}$ and $\{b_k\}$ are quantized to $\{\hat{a}_k\}$ and $\{\hat{b}_k\}$, respectively, the new frequency response is given by

$$\hat{H}(e^{\jmath\omega}) = \frac{\sum_{k=0}^{M} \hat{b}_k\, e^{-\jmath\omega k}}{1 + \sum_{k=1}^{N} \hat{a}_k\, e^{-\jmath\omega k}} \tag{6.65}$$

One can perform analysis similar to that for the movement of poles to obtain maximum change in the magnitude or phase responses due to changes in filter coefficients. However, such an analysis is very complicated and may not add any new insight. Hence we will study these effects using MATLAB. We provide the following two examples.

☐   **EXAMPLE 6.24**   Compute and plot magnitude responses of filter structures given for the filter in Example 6.23.

Solution   The filter is a bandpass filter with 10 tightly clustered poles implemented using the direct and the cascade forms. For the direct form structure, we compute the magnitude response for infinite precision as well as for 16-bit quantization. For the cascade form structure, we use 16-bit and 11-bit representations.

```
r = 0.9; theta = (pi/180)*[-55:5:-35,35:5:55]';
p = r*exp(j*theta); a = poly(p); b = 1;
w = [0:500]*pi/500; H = freqz(b*1e-4,a,w);
magH = abs(H); magHdb = 20*log10(magH);

% Direct form: quantized coefficients
N = 15; [ahat,L,B] = Qcoeff(a,N);
TITLE = sprintf('%i-bit (1+%i+%i) Precision (DF)',N+1,L,B);
Hhat = freqz(b*1e-4,ahat,w); magHhat = abs(Hhat);

% Cascade form: quantized coefficients: Same N
[b0,B0,A0] = dir2cas(b,a);
[BAhat1,L1,B1] = Qcoeff([B0,A0],N);
TITLE1 = sprintf('%i-bit (1+%i+%i) Precision (CF)',N+1,L1,B1);
Bhat1 = BAhat1(:,1:3); Ahat1 = BAhat1(:,4:6);
[bhat1,ahat1] = cas2dir(b0,Bhat1,Ahat1);
Hhat1 = freqz(b*1e-4,ahat1,w); magHhat1 = abs(Hhat1);

% Cascade form: quantized coefficients: Same B (N=L1+B)
N1 = L1+B; [BAhat2,L2,B2] = Qcoeff([B0,A0],N1);
TITLE2 = sprintf('%i-bit (1+%i+%i) Precision (CF)',N1+1,L2,B2);
Bhat2 = BAhat2(:,1:3); Ahat2 = BAhat2(:,4:6);
[bhat2,ahat2] = cas2dir(b0,Bhat2,Ahat2);
Hhat2 = freqz(b*1e-4,ahat2,w); magHhat2 = abs(Hhat2);

% Comparison of Magnitude Plots
Hf_1 = figure('paperunits','inches','paperposition',[0,0,6,4]);
subplot(2,2,1); plot(w/pi,magH,'g','linewidth',2); axis([0,1,0,0.7]);
%xlabel('Digital Frequency in \pi units','fontsize',10);
ylabel('Magnitude Response','fontsize',10);
title('Infinite Precision (DF)','fontsize',10,'fontweight','bold');
subplot(2,2,2); plot(w/pi,magHhat,'r','linewidth',2); axis([0,1,0,0.7]);
```

```
%xlabel('Digital Frequency in \pi units','fontsize',10);
ylabel('Magnitude Response','fontsize',10);
title(TITLE,'fontsize',10,'fontweight','bold');
subplot(2,2,3); plot(w/pi,magHhat1,'r','linewidth',2); axis([0,1,0,0.7]);
xlabel('Digital Frequency in \pi units','fontsize',10);
ylabel('Magnitude Response','fontsize',10);
title(TITLE1,'fontsize',10,'fontweight','bold');
subplot(2,2,4); plot(w/pi,magHhat2,'r','linewidth',2); axis([0,1,0,0.7]);
xlabel('Digital Frequency in \pi units','fontsize',10);
ylabel('Magnitude Response','fontsize',10);
title(TITLE2,'fontsize',10,'fontweight','bold');
```

The plots are shown in Figure 6.27. The top row shows plots for the direct form, and the bottom row shows those for the cascade form. As expected, the magnitude plot of the direct form is severely distorted for 16-bit representation, while those for the cascade form are preserved even for 11-bit word length. $\square$

□ **EXAMPLE 6.25** An eighth-order bandpass filter was obtained using the elliptic filter design approach. This and other design methods will be discussed in Chapter 8. The MATLAB functions needed for this design are shown in the script below. This design produces direct form filter coefficients b_k and a_k, using 64-bit floating-point arithmetic, which gives the precision of 15 decimals and hence can be considered as *unquantized* coefficients. Table 6.1 shows these filter coefficients.

Represent the unquantized filter coefficients using 16-bit and 8-bit word lengths. Plot the filter log-magnitude responses and pole-zero locations for both the infinite and finite word-length coefficients.

TABLE 6.1 *Unquantized IIR filter coefficients used in Example 6.25*

k	b_k	a_k
0	0.021985541264351	1.000000000000000
1	0.000000000000000	−0.000000000000004
2	−0.032498273955222	2.344233276056572
3	0.000000000000000	−0.000000000000003
4	0.046424673058794	2.689868616770005
5	0.000000000000000	0.000000000000001
6	−0.032498273955221	1.584557559015230
7	0.000000000000000	0.000000000000001
8	0.021985541264351	0.413275250482975

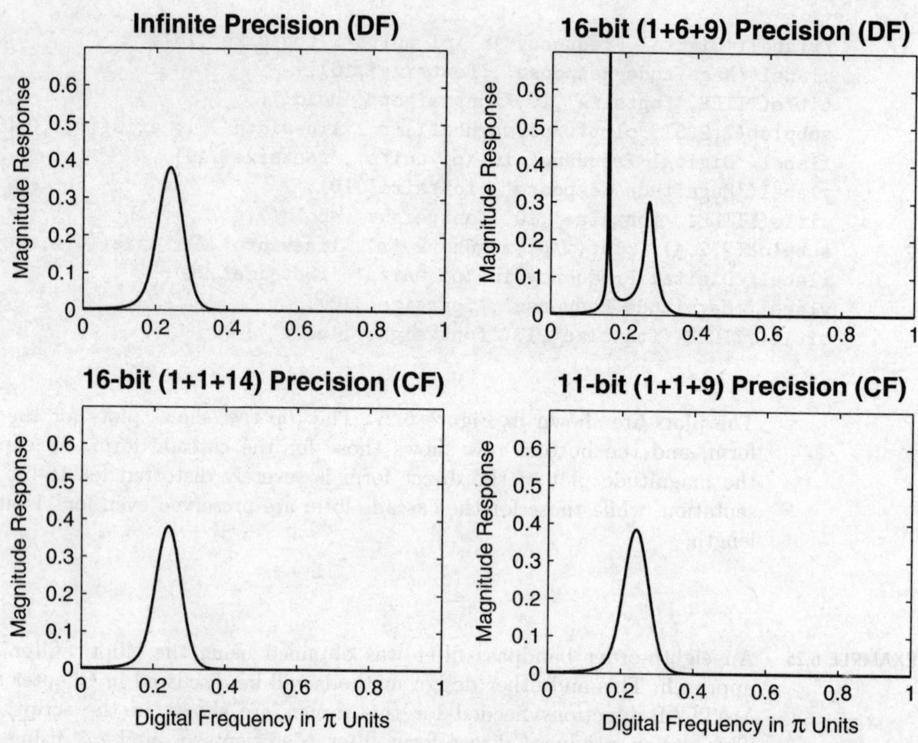

FIGURE 6.27 *Magnitude plots for direct and cascade form structures in Example 6.24*

Solution

Unlike the previous example, some of the filter coefficient values (specifically those of the autoregressive part) are greater than 1 and hence require bits for the integer part. This assignment is done for all coefficients since, in practice, the same bit-pattern is used for the filter representation. These and other steps are given in the following MATLAB script.

```matlab
% The following 3 lines produce filter coefficients shown in Table 6.1.
wp = [0.35,0.65]; ws = [0.25,0.75]; Rp = 1; As = 50;
[N, wn] = ellipord(wp, ws, Rp, As);
[b,a] = ellip(N,Rp,As,wn);
w = [0:500]*pi/500; H = freqz(b,a,w); magH = abs(H);
magHdb = 20*log10(magH);

% 16-bit word-length quantization
N1 = 15; [bahat,L1,B1] = QCoeff([b;a],N1);
TITLE1 = sprintf('%i-bits (1+%i+%i)',N1+1,L1,B1);
bhat1 = bahat(1,:); ahat1 = bahat(2,:);
Hhat1 = freqz(bhat1,ahat1,w); magHhat1 = abs(Hhat1);
magHhat1db = 20*log10(magHhat1); zhat1 = roots(bhat1);
```

```matlab
% 8-bit word-length quantization
N2 = 7; [bahat,L2,B2] = QCoeff([b;a],N2);
TITLE2 = sprintf('%i-bits (1+%i+%i)',N2+1,L2,B2);
bhat2 = bahat(1,:); ahat2 = bahat(2,:);
Hhat2 = freqz(bhat2,ahat2,w); magHhat2 = abs(Hhat2);
magHhat2db = 20*log10(magHhat2); zhat2 = roots(bhat2);

% Plots
Hf_1 = figure('paperunits','inches','paperposition',[0,0,6,5]);

% Comparison of log-magnitude responses: 16 bits
subplot(2,2,1); plot(w/pi,magHdb,'g','linewidth',1.5); axis([0,1,-80,5]);
hold on; plot(w/pi,magHhat1db,'r','linewidth',1); hold off;
xlabel('Digital Frequency in \pi units','fontsize',10);
ylabel('Decibels','fontsize',10);
title(['Log-Mag plot: ',TITLE1],'fontsize',10,'fontweight','bold');

% Comparison of pole-zero plots: 16 bits
subplot(2,2,3); [HZ,HP,Hl] = zplane([b],[a]); axis([-2,2,-2,2]); hold on;
set(HZ,'color','g','linewidth',1,'markersize',4);
set(HP,'color','g','linewidth',1,'markersize',4);
plot(real(zhat1),imag(zhat1),'r+','linewidth',1);
title(['PZ Plot: ',TITLE1],'fontsize',10,'fontweight','bold');
hold off;

% Comparison of log-magnitude responses: 8 bits
subplot(2,2,2); plot(w/pi,magHdb,'g','linewidth',1.5); axis([0,1,-80,5]);
hold on; plot(w/pi,magHhat2db,'r','linewidth',1); hold off;
xlabel('Digital Frequency in \pi units','fontsize',10);
ylabel('Decibels','fontsize',10);
title(['Log-Mag plot: ',TITLE2],'fontsize',10,'fontweight','bold');

% Comparison of pole-zero plots: 8 bits
subplot(2,2,4); [HZ,HP,Hl] = zplane([b],[a]); axis([-2,2,-2,2]); hold on;
set(HZ,'color','g','linewidth',1,'markersize',4);
set(HP,'color','g','linewidth',1,'markersize',4);
plot(real(zhat2),imag(zhat2),'r+','linewidth',1);
title(['PZ Plot: ',TITLE2],'fontsize',10,'fontweight','bold');
hold off;
```

The log-magnitude responses and zero-pole locations of the resulting filters are
plotted in Figure 6.28 along with those of the original filter. When 16 bits
are used, the resulting filter is virtually indistinguishable from the original one.
However, when 8 bits are used, the filter behavior is severely distorted. The filter
is still stable, but it does not satisfy the design specifications.   □

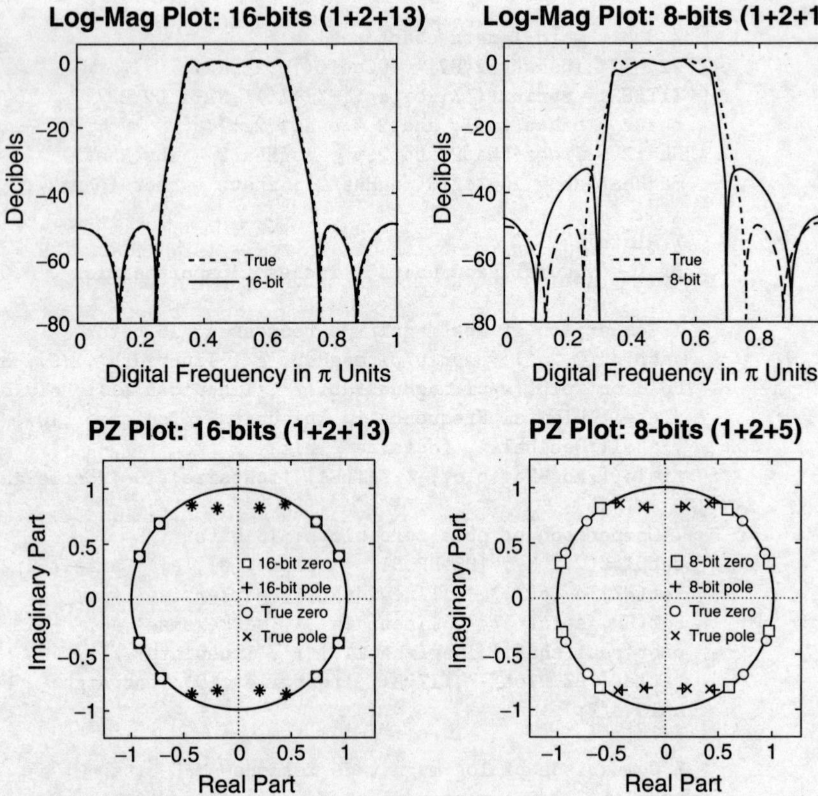

FIGURE 6.28   *Plots for the IIR filter in Example 6.25*

6.7.4 FIR FILTERS

A similar analysis can be done for FIR filters. Let the impulse response
of an FIR filter be $h(n)$ with system response

$$H(z) = \sum_{n=0}^{M-1} h(n)z^{-n} \tag{6.66}$$

Then

$$\Delta H(z) = \sum_{n=0}^{M-1} \Delta h(n)z^{-n} \tag{6.67}$$

where $\Delta H(z)$ is the change due to change in the impulse response $h(n)$.
Hence

$$\Delta H\left(e^{j\omega}\right) = \sum_{n=0}^{M-1} \Delta h(n)\, e^{-j\omega n} \quad \text{or} \quad |\Delta H(e^{j\omega})| \le \sum_{n=0}^{M-1} |\Delta h(n)| \tag{6.68}$$

Now, if each coefficient is quantized to B fraction bits (i.e., total register length is $B + 1$), then

$$|\Delta h(n)| \le \frac{1}{2}2^{-B}$$

Therefore,

$$|\Delta H(e^{j\omega})| \le \frac{1}{2}2^{-B}M = \frac{M}{2}2^{-B} \tag{6.69}$$

Thus the change in frequency response depends not only on the number of bits used but also on the length M of the filter. For large M and small b, this difference can be significant and can destroy the desirable behavior of the filter, as we see in the following example.

☐ **EXAMPLE 6.26** An order-30 lowpass FIR filter is designed using the `firpm` function. This and other FIR filter design functions will be discussed in Chapter 7. The resulting filter coefficients are symmetric and are shown in Table 6.2. We will consider these coefficients as essentially unquantized. The coefficients are quantized to 16 bits (15 fractional plus 1 sign bit) and to 8 bits (7 fractional and 1 sign bit). The resulting filter frequency responses and pole-zero plots are determined and compared. These and other relevant steps are shown in the following MATLAB script.

TABLE 6.2 *Unquantized FIR filter coefficients used in Example 6.26*

k	b_k	k
0	0.000199512328641	30
1	−0.002708453461401	29
2	−0.002400461099957	28
3	0.003546543555809	27
4	0.008266607456720	26
5	0.000012109690648	25
6	−0.015608300819736	24
7	−0.012905580320708	23
8	0.017047710292001	22
9	0.036435951059014	21
10	0.000019292305776	20
11	−0.065652005307521	19
12	−0.057621325403582	18
13	0.090301607282890	17
14	0.300096964940136	16
15	0.400022084144842	15

```
% Filter coefficients given in Table 6.2 are computed using the firpm function
    b = firpm(30,[0,0.3,0.5,1],[1,1,0,0]);
    w = [0:500]*pi/500; H = freqz(b,1,w); magH = abs(H);
```

```matlab
magHdb = 20*log10(magH);
N1 = 15; [bhat1,L1,B1] = Qcoeff(b,N1);
TITLE1 = sprintf('%i-bits (1+%i+%i)',N1+1,L1,B1);
Hhat1 = freqz(bhat1,1,w); magHhat1 = abs(Hhat1);
magHhat1db = 20*log10(magHhat1);
zhat1 = roots(bhat1);

N2 = 7; [bhat2,L2,B2] = Qcoeff(b,N2);
TITLE2 = sprintf('%i-bits (1+%i+%i)',N2+1,L2,B2);
Hhat2 = freqz(bhat2,1,w); magHhat2 = abs(Hhat2);
magHhat2db = 20*log10(magHhat2);
zhat2 = roots(bhat2);

% Plots
Hf_1 = figure('paperunits','inches','paperposition',[0,0,6,5]);

% Comparison of log-magnitude responses: 16 bits
subplot(2,2,1); plot(w/pi,magHdb,'g','linewidth',1.5); axis([0,1,-80,5]);
hold on; plot(w/pi,magHhat1db,'r','linewidth',1); hold off;
xlabel('Digital Frequency in \pi units','fontsize',10);
ylabel('Decibels','fontsize',10);
title(['Log-Mag plot: ',TITLE1],'fontsize',10,'fontweight','bold');

% Comparison of pole-zero plots: 16 bits
subplot(2,2,3); [HZ,HP,Hl] = zplane([b],[1]); axis([-2,2,-2,2]); hold on;
set(HZ,'color','g','linewidth',1,'markersize',4);
set(HP,'color','g','linewidth',1,'markersize',4);
plot(real(zhat1),imag(zhat1),'r+','linewidth',1);
title(['PZ Plot: ',TITLE1],'fontsize',10,'fontweight','bold');
hold off;

% Comparison of log-magnitude responses: 8 bits
subplot(2,2,2); plot(w/pi,magHdb,'g','linewidth',1.5); axis([0,1,-80,5]);
hold on; plot(w/pi,magHhat2db,'r','linewidth',1); hold off;
xlabel('Digital Frequency in \pi units','fontsize',10);
ylabel('Decibels','fontsize',10);
title(['Log-Mag plot: ',TITLE2],'fontsize',10,'fontweight','bold');

% Comparison of pole-zero plots: 8 bits
subplot(2,2,4); [HZ,HP,Hl] = zplane([b],[1]); axis([-2,2,-2,2]); hold on;
set(HZ,'color','g','linewidth',1,'markersize',4);
set(HP,'color','g','linewidth',1,'markersize',4);
plot(real(zhat2),imag(zhat2),'r+','linewidth',1);
title(['PZ Plot: ',TITLE2],'fontsize',10,'fontweight','bold');
hold off;
```

The log-magnitude responses and zero-pole locations of the resulting filters are computed and plotted in Figure 6.29 along with those of the original filter.

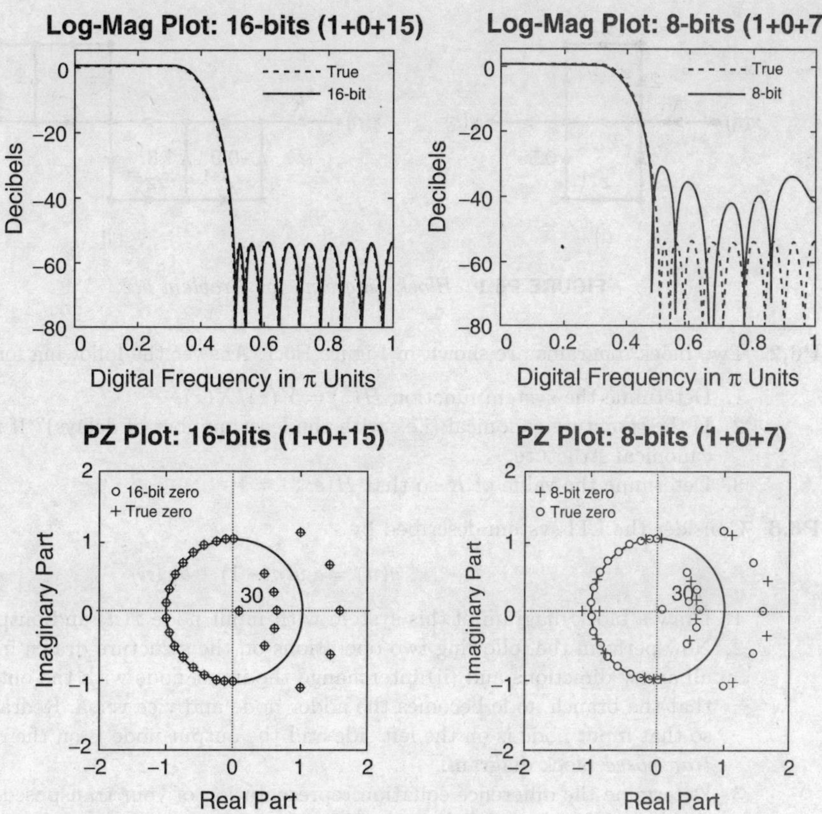

FIGURE 6.29 *Plots for the FIR filter in Example 6.26*

When 16 bits are used, the resulting filter is virtually indistinguishable from the original one. However, when 8 bits are used, the filter behavior is severely distorted and the filter does not satisfy the design specifications. ☐

6.8 PROBLEMS

P6.1 Draw direct form I block diagram structures for each of the following LTI systems with input node $x(n)$ and output node $y(n)$.

1. $y(n) = x(n) + 2x(n-1) + 3x(n-2)$

2. $H(z) = \dfrac{1}{1 - 1.7z^{-1} + 1.53z^{-2} - 0.648z^{-3}}$

3. $y(n) = 1.7y(n-1) - 1.36y(n-2) + 0.576y(n-3) + x(n)$

4. $y(n) = 1.6y(n-1) + 0.64y(n-2) + x(n) + 2x(n-1) + x(n-2)$

5. $H(z) = \dfrac{1 - 3z^{-1} + 3z^{-2} + z^{-3}}{1 + 0.2z^{-1} - 0.14z^{-2} + 0.44z^{-3}}$

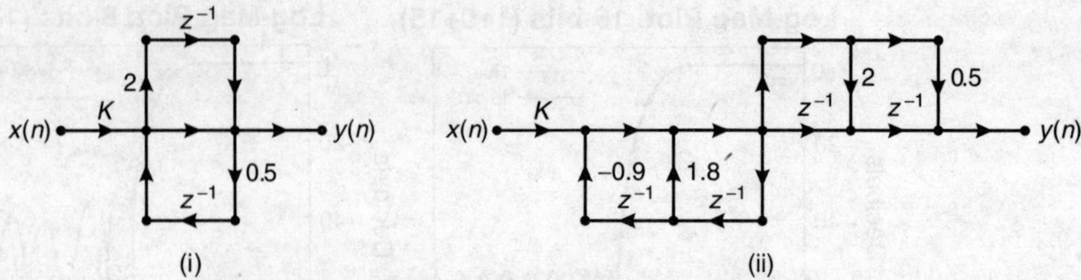

FIGURE P6.1   *Block diagrams for Problem 6.2*

P6.2   Two block diagrams are shown in Figure P6.1. Answer the following for each structure.

1. Determine the system function $H(z) = Y(z)/X(z)$.
2. Is the structure canonical (i.e., with the least number of delays)? If not, draw a canonical structure.
3. Determine the value of K so that $H(e^{j0}) = 1$.

P6.3   Consider the LTI system described by

$$y(n) = a\,y(n-1) + b\,x(n) \tag{6.70}$$

1. Draw a block diagram of this system with input node $x(n)$ and output node $y(n)$.
2. Now perform the following two operations on the structure drawn in part 1: (i) reverse all arrow directions and (ii) interchange the input node with the output node. Notice that the branch node becomes the adder node and vice versa. Redraw the block diagram so that input node is on the left side and the output node is on the right side. This is the *transposed* block diagram.
3. Determine the difference equation representation of your transposed structure in part 2, and verify that it is the same equation as (6.70).

P6.4   Consider the LTI system given by

$$H(z) = \frac{1 - 2.818z^{-1} + 3.97z^{-2} - 2.8180z^{-3} + z^{-4}}{1 - 2.536z^{-1} + 3.215z^{-2} - 2.054z^{-3} + 0.6560z^{-4}} \tag{6.71}$$

1. Draw the normal direct form I structure block diagram.
2. Draw the transposed direct form I structure block diagram.
3. Draw the normal direct form II structure block diagram. Observe that it looks very similar to that in part 2.
4. Draw the transposed direct form II structure block diagram. Observe that it looks very similar to that in part 1.

P6.5   Consider the LTI system given in Problem P6.4.

1. Draw a cascade structure containing second-order normal direct form II sections.
2. Draw a cascade structure containing second-order transposed direct form II sections.
3. Draw a parallel structure containing second-order normal direct form II sections.
4. Draw a parallel structure containing second-order transposed direct form II sections.

P6.6   A causal linear time-invariant system is described by

$$y(n) = \sum_{k=0}^{4} \cos(0.1\pi k)x(n-k) - \sum_{k=1}^{5} (0.8)^k \sin(0.1\pi k)y(n-k)$$

Determine and draw the block diagrams of the following structures. Compute the response of the system to

$$x(n) = [1 + 2(-1)^n], \quad 0 \le n \le 50$$

in each case, using the following structures.

1. Normal direct form I
2. Transposed direct form II
3. Cascade form containing second-order normal direct form II sections
4. Parallel form containing second-order transposed direct form II sections

P6.7 An IIR filter is described by system function

$$H(z) = 2\left(\frac{1 + 0z^{-1} + z^{-2}}{1 - 0.8z^{-1} + 0.64z^{-2}}\right) + \left(\frac{2 - z^{-1}}{1 - 0.75z^{-1}}\right) + \left(\frac{1 + 2z^{-1} + z^{-2}}{1 + 0.81z^{-2}}\right)$$

Determine and draw the following structures.

1. Transposed direct form I
2. Normal direct form II
3. Cascade form containing transposed second-order direct form II sections
4. Parallel form containing normal second-order direct form II sections

P6.8 An IIR filter is described by the system function

$$H(z) = \left(\frac{-14.75 - 12.9z^{-1}}{1 - \frac{7}{8}z^{-1} + \frac{3}{32}z^{-2}}\right) + \left(\frac{24.5 + 26.82z^{-1}}{1 - z^{-1} + \frac{1}{2}z^{-2}}\right)\left(\frac{1 + 2z^{-1} + z^{-2}}{1 + 0.81z^{-2}}\right)$$

Determine and draw the following structures.

1. Normal direct form I
2. Normal direct form II
3. Cascade form containing transposed second-order direct form II sections
4. Parallel form containing transposed second-order direct form II sections

P6.9 A linear time-invariant system with system function

$$H(z) = \frac{0.05 - 0.01z^{-1} - 0.13z^{-2} + 0.13z^{-4} + 0.01z^{-5} - 0.05z^{-6}}{1 - 0.77z^{-1} + 1.59z^{-2} - 0.88z^{-3} + 1.2z^{-4} - 0.35z^{-5} + 0.31z^{-6}}$$

is to be implemented using a flow graph of the form shown in Figure P6.2.

1. Fill in all the coefficients in the diagram.
2. Is your solution unique? Explain.

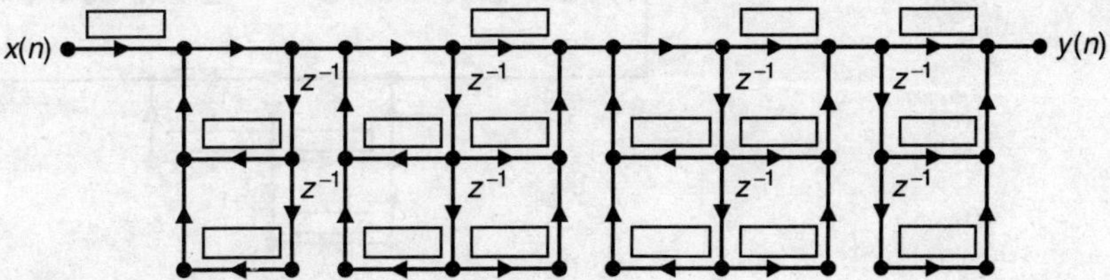

FIGURE P6.2 *Structure for Problem 6.9*

P6.10 A linear time-invariant system with system function

$$H(z) = \frac{0.051 + 0.088z^{-1} + 0.06z^{-2} - 0.029z^{-3} - 0.069z^{-4} - 0.046z^{-5}}{1 - 1.34z^{-1} + 1.478z^{-2} - 0.789z^{-3} + 0.232z^{-4}}$$

is to be implemented using a flow graph of the form shown in Figure P6.3. Fill in all the
coefficients in the diagram.

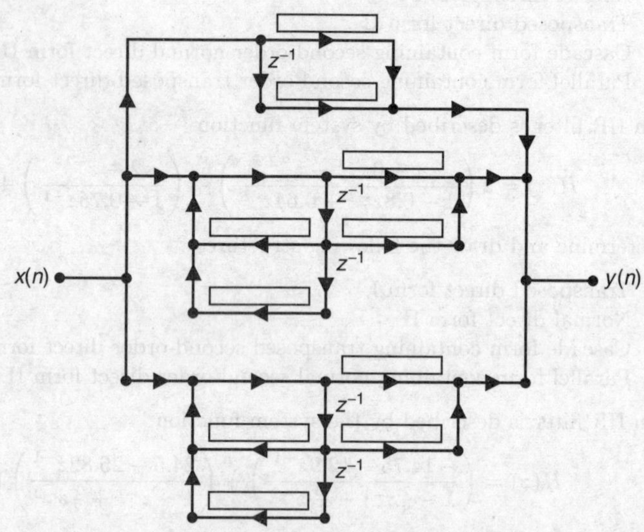

FIGURE P6.3   *Structure for Problem 6.10*

P6.11 Consider the linear time-invariant system given in Problem P6.9.

$$H(z) = \frac{0.05 - 0.01z^{-1} - 0.13z^{-2} + 0.13z^{-4} + 0.01z^{-5} - 0.05z^{-6}}{1 - 0.77z^{-1} + 1.59z^{-2} - 0.88z^{-3} + 1.2z^{-4} - 0.35z^{-5} + 0.31z^{-6}}$$

It is to be implemented using a flow graph of the form shown in Figure P6.4.

1. Fill in all the coefficients in the diagram.
2. Is your solution unique? Explain.

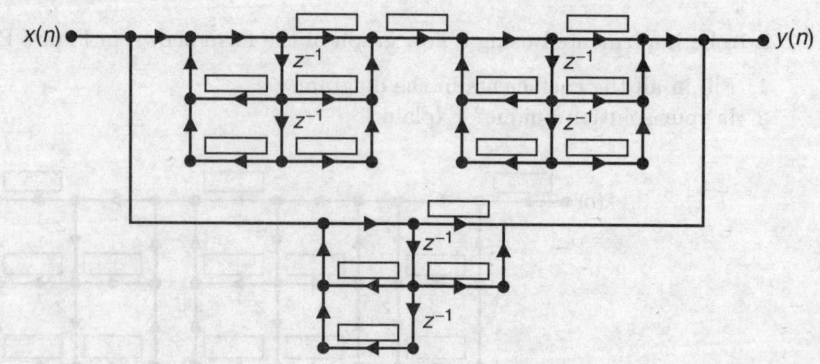

FIGURE P6.4   *Structure for Problem 6.11*

P6.12 The filter structure shown in Figure P6.5 contains a parallel connection of cascade sections. Determine and draw the overall

1. direct form (normal) structure,
2. direct form (transposed) structure,
3. cascade form structure containing second-order sections,
4. parallel form structure containing second-order sections.

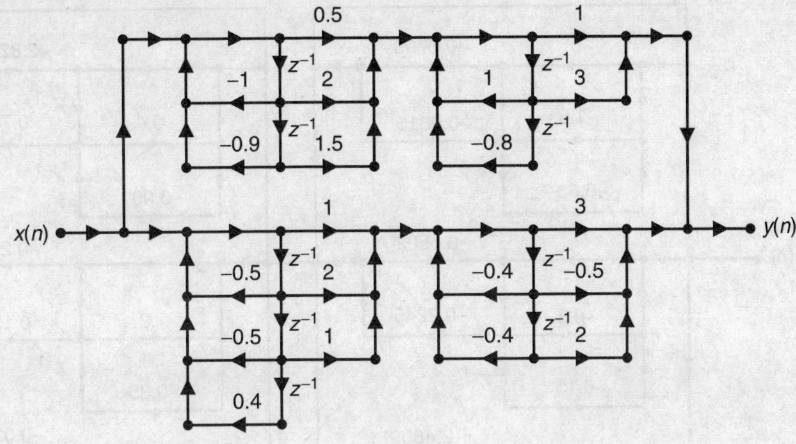

FIGURE P6.5 *Structure for Problem 6.12*

P6.13 In the filter structure shown in Figure P6.6, systems $H_1(z)$ and $H_2(z)$ are subcomponents of a larger system $H(z)$. The system function $H_1(z)$ is given in the parallel form

$$H_1(z) = 2 + \frac{0.2 - 0.3z^{-1}}{1 + 0.9z^{-1} + 0.9z^{-2}} + \frac{0.4 + 0.5z^{-1}}{1 - 0.8z^{-1} + 0.8z^{-2}}$$

and the system function $H_2(z)$ is given in the cascade form

$$H_2(z) = \left(\frac{2 + z^{-1} - z^{-2}}{1 + 1.7z^{-1} + 0.72z^{-2}} \right) \left(\frac{3 + 4z^{-1} + 5z^{-2}}{1 - 1.5z^{-1} + 0.56z^{-2}} \right)$$

1. Express $H(z)$ as a rational function.
2. Draw the block diagram of $H(z)$ as a cascade form structure.
3. Draw the block diagram of $H(z)$ as a parallel form structure.

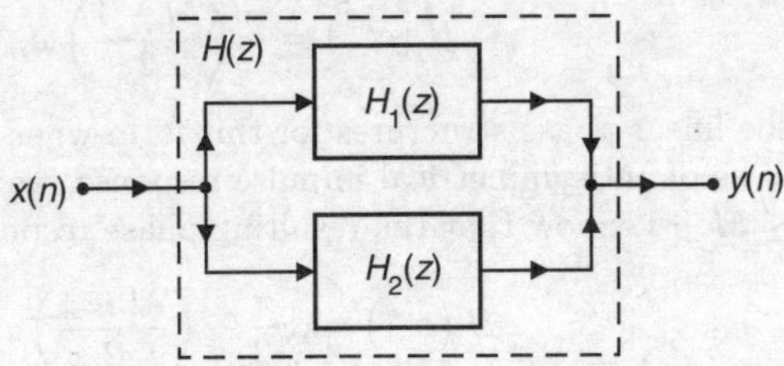

FIGURE P6.6 *Structure for Problem 6.13*

P6.14 The digital filter structure shown in Figure P6.7 is a cascade of two parallel sections and corresponds to a tenth-order IIR digital filter system function

$$H(z) = \frac{1 - 2.2z^{-2} + 1.6368z^{-4} - 0.48928z^{-6} + 5395456 \times 10^{-8}z^{-8} - 147456 \times 10^{-8}z^{-10}}{1 - 1.65z^{-2} + 0.8778z^{-4} - 0.17281z^{-6} + 1057221 \times 10^{-8}z^{-8} - 893025 \times 10^{-10}z^{-10}}$$

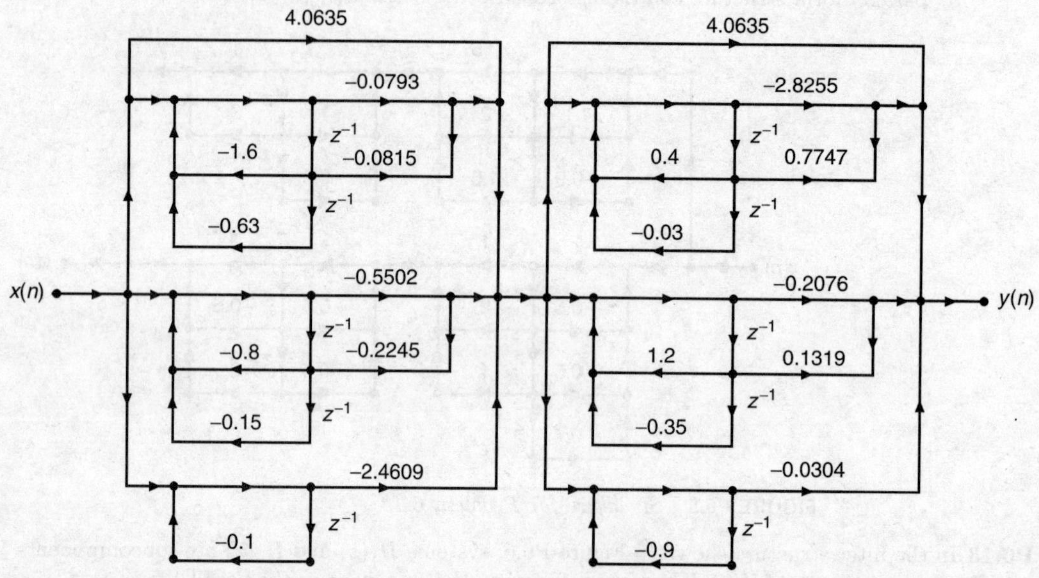

FIGURE P6.7   *Structure for Problem 6.14*

1. Due to an error in labeling, two of the multiplier coefficients (rounded to four decimals) in this structure have incorrect values. Locate these two multipliers and determine their correct values.
2. Determine and draw an overall cascade structure containing second-order sections and which contains the least number of multipliers.

P6.15 As described in this chapter, a linear-phase FIR filter is obtained by requiring certain symmetry conditions on its impulse responses.

1. In the case of symmetrical impulse response, we have $h(n) = h(M - 1 - n)$, $0 \le n \le M - 1$. Show that the resulting phase response is linear in ω and is given by

$$\angle H\left(e^{j\omega}\right) = -\left(\frac{M-1}{2}\right)\omega, \quad -\pi < \omega \le \pi$$

2. Draw the linear-phase structures for this form when $M = 5$ and $M = 6$.
3. In the case of antisymmetrical impulse response, we have $h(n) = -h(M - 1 - n)$, $0 \le n \le M - 1$. Show that the resulting phase response is given by

$$\angle H\left(e^{j\omega}\right) = \pm\frac{\pi}{2} - \left(\frac{M-1}{2}\right)\omega, \quad -\pi < \omega \le \pi$$

4. Draw the linear-phase structures for this form when $M = 5$ and $M = 6$.

P6.16 An FIR filter is described by the difference equation

$$y(n) = \sum_{k=0}^{6} e^{-0.9|k-3|} x(n-k)$$

Determine and draw the block diagrams of the following structures.

1. Direct form
2. Linear-phase form
3. Cascade form
4. Frequency-sampling form

P6.17 A linear time-invariant system is given by the system function

$$H(z) = 2 + 3z^{-1} + 5z^{-2} - 3z^{-3} + 4z^{-5} + 8z^{-7} - 7z^{-8} + 4z^{-9}$$

Determine and draw the block diagrams of the following structures.

1. Direct form
2. Cascade form
3. Frequency-sampling form

P6.18 Using the conjugate symmetry property of the DFT

$$H(k) = \begin{cases} H(0), & k = 0 \\ H^*(M-k), & k = 1, \ldots, M-1 \end{cases}$$

and the conjugate symmetry property of the W_M^{-k} factor, show that (6.12) can be put in the form (6.13) and (6.14) for real FIR filters.

P6.19 To avoid poles on the unit circle in the frequency-sampling structure, one samples $H(z)$ at $z_k = re^{j2\pi k/M}$, $k = 0, \ldots, M-1$ where $r \approx 1$(but < 1), as discussed in Section 6.3.

1. Using

$$H\left(re^{j2\pi k/M}\right) \approx H(k)$$

show that the frequency-sampling structure is given by

$$H(z) = \frac{1 - (rz)^{-M}}{M} \left\{ \sum_{k=1}^{L} 2\,|H(k)|\,H_k(z) + \frac{H(0)}{1 - rz^{-1}} + \frac{H(M/2)}{1 + rz^{-1}} \right\}$$

where

$$H_k(z) = \frac{\cos\left[\angle H(k)\right] - rz^{-1}\cos\left[\angle H(k) - \frac{2\pi k}{M}\right]}{1 - 2rz^{-1}\cos\left(\frac{2\pi k}{M}\right) + r^2 z^{-2}}, \quad k = 1, \ldots, L$$

and M is even.

2. Modify the MATLAB function `dir2fs` (which was developed in Section 6.3) to implement this frequency-sampling form. The format of this function should be

```
[C,B,A,rM] = dir2fs(h,r)
% Direct form to frequency-sampling form conversion
% ----------------------------------------------------
% [C,B,A,rM] = dir2fs(h,r)
%  C = Row vector containing gains for parallel sections
%  B = Matrix containing numerator coefficients arranged in rows
%  A = Matrix containing denominator coefficients arranged in rows
% rM = r^M factor needed in the feedforward loop
%  h = impulse response vector of an FIR filter
%  r = radius of the circle over which samples are taken (r<1)
%
```

3. Determine the frequency sampling structure for the impulse response given in Example 6.6 using this function.

P6.20 Consider the following system function of an FIR filter:

$$H(z) = 1 - 4z^{-1} + 6.4z^{-2} - 5.12z^{-3} + 2.048z^{-4} - 0.32768z^{-5}$$

1. Provide block diagram structures in the following forms.

   (a) Normal and transposed direct forms
   (b) Cascade of five first-order sections
   (c) Cascade of one first-order section and two second-order sections
   (d) Cascade of one second-order section and one third-order section
   (e) Frequency-sampling structure with real coefficients

2. The computational complexity of a digital filter structure can be given by the total number of multiplications and the total number of 2-input additions that are required per output point. Assume that $x(n)$ is real and that multiplication by 1 is not counted as a multiplication. Compare the computational complexity of each of these structures.

P6.21 A causal digital filter is described by the following zeros:

$$z_1 = 0.5\,e^{j60°}, \quad z_2 = 0.5\,e^{-j60°}, \quad z_3 = 2\,e^{j60°}, \quad z_4 = 2\,e^{-j60°},$$

$$z_5 = 0.25\,e^{j30°}, \quad z_6 = 0.25\,e^{-j30°}, \quad z_7 = 4\,e^{j30°}, \quad z_8 = 4\,e^{-j30°}$$

and poles: $\{p_i\}_{i=1}^8 = 0$.

1. Determine the phase response of this filter, and show that it is a linear-phase FIR filter.
2. Determine the impulse response of the filter.
3. Draw a block diagram of the filter structure in the direct form.
4. Draw a block diagram of the filter structure in the linear-phase form.

P6.22 MATLAB provides the built-in functions `dec2bin` and `bin2dec` to convert nonnegative decimal integers into binary codes and vice versa, respectively.

1. Develop a function B = `sm2bin(D)` to convert a sign-magnitude format decimal integer D into its binary representation B. Verify your function on the following numbers:

   (a) $D = 1001$ (b) $D = -63$ (c) $D = -449$ (d) $D = 978$ (e) $D = -205$

2. Develop a function `D = bin2sm(B)` to convert a binary representation B into its sign-magnitude format decimal integer D. Verify your function on the following representations:

    (a) $B = 1010$ (b) $B = 011011011$ (c) $B = 11001$
    (d) $B = 1010101$ (e) $B = 011011$

P6.23 Using the function `TwosComplement` as a model, develop a function `y = TensComplement(x,N)` that converts a sign-magnitude format integer x into the N-digit ten's-complement integer y.

1. Verify your function using the following integers:

    (a) $x = 1234, N = 6$ (b) $x = -603, N = 4$ (c) $x = -843, N = 5$
    (d) $x = -1978, N = 6$ (e) $x = 50, N = 3$

2. Using the ten's-complement format, perform the following arithmetic operations. In each case, choose an appropriate value on N for the meaningful result.

    (a) $123 + 456 - 789$ (b) $648 + 836 - 452$ (c) $2001 + 3756$
    (d) $-968 + 4539$ (e) $888 - 666 + 777$

Verify your results using decimal operations.

P6.24 The function `OnesComplement` developed in this chapter converts signed integers into one's-complement-format decimal representations. In this problem, we will develop functions that will operate on fractional numbers.

1. Develop a MATLAB function `y = sm2oc(x, B)` that converts the sign-magnitude format fraction x into the B-bit one's-complement-format decimal equivalent number y. Verify your function on the following numbers. In each case, the numbers to be considered are both positive and negative. Also, in each case select the appropriate number of bits B.

    (a) $x = \pm 0.5625$ (b) $x = \pm 0.40625$ (c) $x = \pm 0.953125$
    (d) $x = \pm 0.1328125$ (e) $x = \pm 0.7314453125$

2. Develop a MATLAB function `x = oc2sm(y, B)` that converts the B-bit one's-complement-format decimal equivalent number y into the sign-magnitude-format fraction x. Verify your function on the following fractional binary representations:

    (a) $y = 1{\blacktriangle}10110$ (b) $y = 0.{\blacktriangle}011001$ (c) $y = 1{\blacktriangle}00110011$
    (d) $y = 1{\blacktriangle}11101110$ (e) $y = 0{\blacktriangle}00010001$

P6.25 The function `TwosComplement` developed in this chapter converts signed integers into two's-complement-format decimal representations. In this problem, we will develop functions that will operate on fractional numbers.

1. Develop a MATLAB function `y = sm2tc(x, B)` that converts the sign-magnitude-format fraction x into the B-bit two's-complement-format decimal equivalent number y. Verify your function on the following numbers. In each case, the numbers to be considered are both positive and negative. Also, in each case select the appropriate number of bits B.

    (a) $x = \pm 0.5625$ (b) $x = \pm 0.40625$ (c) $x = \pm 0.953125$
    (d) $x = \pm 0.1328125$ (f) $x = \pm 0.7314453125$

Compare your representations with those in Problem P6.24, part 1.

2. Develop a MATLAB function x = `tc2sm(y, B)` that converts the B-bit two's-complement-format decimal equivalent number y into the sign-magnitude-format fraction x. Verify your function on the following fractional binary representations:

(a) $y = 1{\blacktriangle}10110$ (b) $y = 0{\blacktriangle}011001$ (c) $y = 1{\blacktriangle}00110011$
(d) $y = 1{\blacktriangle}11101110$ (e) $y = 0{\blacktriangle}00010001$

Compare your representations with those in Problem P6.24, part 2.

P6.26 Determine the 10-bit sign-magnitude, one's-complement, and two's-complement representation of the following decimal numbers:

(a) 0.12345   (b) −0.56789   (c) 0.38452386   (d) −0.762349   (e) −0.90625

P6.27 Consider a 32-bit floating-point number representation with a 6-bit exponent and a 25-bit mantissa.

1. Determine the value of the smallest number that can be represented.
2. Determine the value of the largest number that can be represented.
3. Determine the dynamic range of this floating-point representation and compare it with the dynamic range of a 32-bit fixed-point signed integer representation.

P6.28 Show that the magnitudes of floating-point numbers in a 32-bit IEEE standard range from 1.18×10^{-38} to 3.4×10^{38}.

P6.29 Compute and plot the truncation error characteristics when $B = 4$ for the sign-magnitude, one's-complement, and two's-complement formats.

P6.30 Consider the third-order elliptic lowpass filter.

$$H(z) = \frac{0.1214 \left(1 - 1.4211z^{-1} + z^{-2}\right) \left(1 + z^{-1}\right)}{\left(1 - 1.4928z^{-1} + 0.8612z^{-2}\right) \left(1 - 0.6183z^{-1}\right)}$$

1. If the filter is realized using a direct form structure, determine its pole sensitivity.
2. If the filter is realized using a cascade form structure, determine its pole sensitivity.

P6.31 Consider the filter described by the difference equation

$$y(n) = \frac{1}{\sqrt{2}}y(n-1) - x(n) + \sqrt{2}x(n-1) \tag{6.72}$$

1. Show that this filter is an allpass filter, that is, $|H(e^{j\omega})|$ is a constant over the entire frequency range $-\pi \leq \omega \leq \pi$. Verify your answer by plotting the magnitude response $|H(e^{j\omega})|$ over the normalized frequency range $0 \leq \omega/\pi \leq 1$. Use `subplot(3,1,1)`.
2. Round the coefficients of the difference equation in (6.72) to three decimals. Is the filter still allpass? Verify your answer by plotting the resulting magnitude response, $|\hat{H}_1(e^{j\omega})|$, over the normalized frequency range $0 \leq \omega/\pi \leq 1$. Use `subplot(3,1,2)`.
3. Round the coefficients of the difference equation in (6.72) to two decimals. Is the filter still allpass? Verify your answer by plotting the resulting magnitude response, $|\hat{H}_2(e^{j\omega})|$, over the normalized frequency range $0 \leq \omega/\pi \leq 1$. Use `subplot(3,1,3)`.
4. Explain why the magnitude $|\hat{H}_1(e^{j\omega})|$ is "different" from the magnitude $|\hat{H}_2(e^{j\omega})|$.

P6.32 An IIR lowpass filter designed to meet the specifications of 0.5 dB ripple in the passband, 60 dB ripple in the stopband, a passband edge frequency $\omega_\mathrm{p} = 0.25\pi$, and a stopband edge frequency $\omega_\mathrm{s} = 0.3\pi$ is obtained using the following MATLAB script.

```
wp = 0.25*pi; ws = 0.3*pi; Rp = 0.5; As = 60;
[N, Wn] = ellipord(wp/pi, ws/pi, Rp, As);
[b,a] = ellip(N,Rp,As,Wn);
```

The filter coefficients b_k and a_k are in the arrays b and a, respectively, and can be considered to have infinite precision.

1. Using infinite precision, plot the log-magnitude and phase responses of the designed filter. Use two rows and one column of subplots.
2. Quantize the direct form coefficients to four decimals (by rounding). Now plot the log-magnitude and phase responses of the resulting filter. Use two rows and one column of subplots.
3. Quantize the direct form coefficients to three decimals (by rounding). Now plot the log-magnitude and phase responses of the resulting filter. Use two rows and one column of subplots.
4. Comment on the plots in parts 1, 2, and 3.

P6.33 Consider the digital lowpass filter used in Problem P6.32.

1. Using infinite precision and cascade form realization, plot the log-magnitude and phase responses of the designed filter. Use two rows and one column of subplots.
2. Quantize the cascade form coefficients to four decimals (by rounding). Now plot the log-magnitude and phase responses of the resulting filter. Use two rows and one column of subplots.
3. Quantize the cascade form coefficients to three decimals (by rounding). Now plot the log-magnitude and phase responses of the resulting filter. Use two rows and one column of subplots.
4. Comment on the plots in the above three parts and compare them with the similar plots in Problem P6.32.

P6.34 A length-32 linear-phase FIR bandpass filter that satisfies the requirements of 60 dB stopband attenuation, lower stopband edge frequency $\omega_{s_1} = 0.2\pi$, and upper stopband edge frequency $\omega_{s_2} = 0.8\pi$ is obtained using the following MATLAB script.

```
ws1 = 0.2*pi; ws2 = 0.8*pi; As = 60;
M = 32; Df = 0.2115;
fp1 = ws1/pi+Df; fp2 = ws2/pi-Df;
h = firpm(M-1,[0,ws1/pi,fp1,fp2,ws2/pi,1],[0,0,1,1,0,0]);
```

The filter impulse response $h(n)$ is in the array h and can be considered to have infinite precision.

1. Using infinite precision, plot the log-magnitude and amplitude responses of the designed filter. Use two rows and one column of subplots.
2. Quantize the direct form coefficients to four decimals (by rounding). Now plot the log-magnitude and amplitude responses of the resulting filter. Use two rows and one column of subplots.

3. Quantize the direct form coefficients to three decimals (by rounding). Now plot the log-magnitude and amplitude responses of the resulting filter. Use two rows and one column of subplots.

4. Comment on the plots in parts 1, 2, and 3.

5. Based on the results of this problem, determine how many significant *bits* (and not decimals) are needed in practice to represent FIR direct form realizations.

P6.35 The digital filter structure shown in Figure P6.8 is a cascade of two parallel sections and corresponds to a tenth-order IIR digital filter system function

$$H(z) = \frac{1 - 2.2z^{-2} + 1.6368z^{-4} - 0.48928z^{-6} + 5395456 \times 10^{-8}z^{-8} - 147456 \times 10^{-8}z^{-10}}{1 - 1.65z^{-2} + 0.8778z^{-4} - 0.17281z^{-6} + 1057221 \times 10^{-8}z^{-8} - 893025 \times 10^{-10}z^{-10}}$$

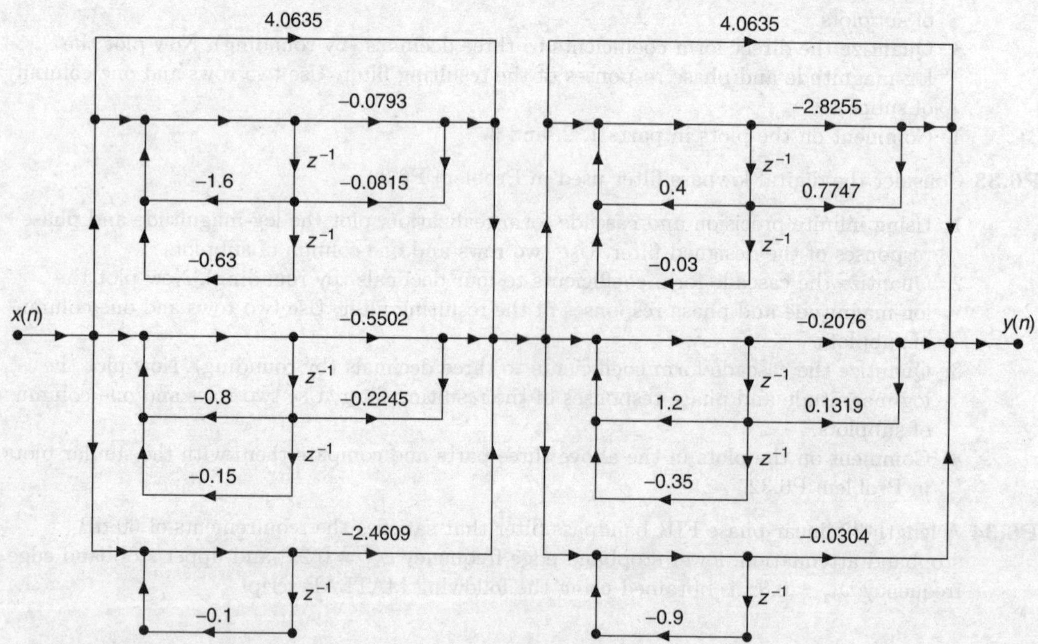

FIGURE P6.8 *Structure for Problem P6.35*

1. Due to an error in labeling, two of the multiplier coefficients (rounded to four decimals) in this structure have incorrect values. Locate these two multipliers and determine their correct values.

2. By inspecting the pole locations of the system function $H(z)$, you should realize that this structure is sensitive to the coefficient quantization. Suggest, with justification, an alternative structure that in *your opinion* is least sensitive to coefficient quantization.

P6.36 An IIR bandstop digital filter that satisfies the requirements:

$$0.95 \leq |H(e^{j\omega})| \leq 1.05, \qquad 0 \leq |\omega| \leq 0.25\pi$$
$$0 \leq |H(e^{j\omega})| \leq 0.01, \ 0.35\pi \leq |\omega| \leq 0.65\pi$$
$$0.95 \leq |H(e^{j\omega})| \leq 1.05, \ 0.75\pi \leq |\omega| \leq \pi$$

can be obtained using the following MATLAB script:

```
wp = [0.25,0.75]; ws = [0.35,0.65]; delta1 = 0.05; delta2 = 0.01;
[Rp,As] = delta2db(delta1,delta2);
[N, wn] = cheb2ord(wp, ws, Rp, As);
[b,a] = cheby2(N,As,wn,'stop');
```

The filter coefficients b_k and a_k are in the arrays b and a, respectively, and can be considered to have infinite precision.

1. Using infinite precision, provide the log-magnitude response plot and the pole-zero plot of the designed filter.
2. Assuming direct-form structure and a 12-bit representation for filter coefficients, provide the log-magnitude response plot and the pole-zero plot of the designed filter. Use the **Qcoeff** function.
3. Assuming cascade-form structure and a 12-bit representation for filter coefficients, provide the log-magnitude response plot and the pole-zero plot of the designed filter. Use the **Qcoeff** function.

P6.37 An IIR lowpass digital filter that satisfies the specifications:

$$\text{passband edge:} \quad 0.4\pi, \quad R_p = 0.5 \text{ dB}$$
$$\text{stopband edge:} \quad 0.6\pi, \quad A_s = 50 \text{ dB}$$

can be obtained using the following MATLAB script:

```
wp = 0.4; ws = 0.6; Rp = 0.5; As = 50;
[N, wn] = buttord(wp, ws, Rp, As);
[b,a] = butter(N,wn);
```

The filter coefficients b_k and a_k are in the arrays b and a, respectively, and can be considered to have infinite precision.

1. Using infinite precision, provide the magnitude response plot and the pole-zero plot of the designed filter.
2. Assuming direct-form structure and a 10-bit representation for filter coefficients, provide the magnitude response plot and the pole-zero plot of the designed filter. Use the **Qcoeff** function.
3. Assuming cascade-form structure and a 10-bit representation for filter coefficients, provide the magnitude response plot and the pole-zero plot of the designed filter. Use the **Qcoeff** function.

P6.38 An IIR highpass digital filter that satisfies the specifications:

$$\text{stopband edge:} \quad 0.4\pi, \quad A_s = 60 \text{ dB}$$
$$\text{passband edge:} \quad 0.6\pi, \quad R_p = 0.5 \text{ dB}$$

can be obtained using the following MATLAB script:

```
wp = 0.6; ws = 0.4; Rp = 0.5; As = 60;
[N,wn] = ellipord(wp, ws, Rp, As);
[b,a] = ellip(N,Rp,As,wn,'high');
```

The filter coefficients b_k and a_k are in the arrays b and a, respectively, and can be considered to have infinite precision.

1. Using infinite precision, provide the magnitude response plot and the pole-zero plot of the designed filter.
2. Assuming direct-form structure and a 10-bit representation for filter coefficients, provide the magnitude response plot and the pole-zero plot of the designed filter. Use the `Qcoeff` function.
3. Assuming parallel-form structure and a 10-bit representation for filter coefficients, provide the magnitude response plot and the pole-zero plot of the designed filter. Use the `Qcoeff` function.

P6.39 A bandstop linear-phase FIR filter that satisfies the specifications:

$$\begin{array}{ll} \text{lower stopband edge:} & 0.4\pi \\ \text{upper stopband edge:} & 0.6\pi \end{array} \quad A_s = 50 \text{ dB}$$

$$\begin{array}{ll} \text{lower passband edge:} & 0.3\pi \\ \text{upper passband edge:} & 0.7\pi \end{array} \quad R_p = 0.2 \text{ dB}$$

can be obtained using the following MATLAB script:

```
wp1 = 0.3; ws1 = 0.4; ws2 = 0.6; wp2 = 0.7; Rp = 0.2; As = 50;
[delta1,delta2] = db2delta(Rp,As);
b = firpm(44,[0,wp1,ws1,ws2,wp2,1],[1,1,0,0,1,1],...
    [delta2/delta1,1,delta2/delta1]);
```

The filter impulse response $h(n)$ is in the array b and can be considered to have infinite precision.

P6.40 A bandpass linear-phase FIR filter that satisfies the specifications:

$$\begin{array}{rcccl} 0 & \leq & |H(e^{j\omega})| & \leq & 0.01, \quad\quad 0 \leq \omega \leq 0.25\pi \\ 0.95 & \leq & |H(e^{j\omega})| & \leq & 1.05, \; 0.35\pi \leq \omega \leq 0.65\pi \\ 0 & \leq & |H(e^{j\omega})| & \leq & 0.01, \; 0.75\pi \leq \omega \leq \pi \end{array}$$

can be obtained using the following MATLAB script:

```
ws1 = 0.25; wp1 = 0.35; wp2 = 0.65; ws2 = 0.75;
delta1 = 0.05; delta2 = 0.01;
b = firpm(40,[0,ws1,wp1,wp2,ws2,1],[0,0,1,1,0,0],...
    [1,delta2/delta1,1]);
```

The filter impulse response $h(n)$ is in the array b and can be considered to have infinite precision.

CHAPTER 7

FIR Filter Design

We now turn our attention to the inverse problem of designing systems from the given specifications. It is an important as well as difficult problem. In digital signal processing, there are two important types of systems. The first type of systems perform signal filtering in the time domain and hence are called *digital filters*. The second type of systems provide signal representation in the frequency domain and are called *spectrum analyzers*. In Chapter 5, we described signal representations using the DFT. In this and the next chapter, we will study several basic design algorithms for both FIR and IIR filters. These designs are mostly of the *frequency selective* type; that is, we will design primarily multiband lowpass, highpass, bandpass, and bandstop filters. In FIR filter design, we will also consider systems like differentiators or Hilbert transformers, which, although not frequency-selective filters, nevertheless follow the design techniques being considered. More sophisticated filter designs are based on arbitrary frequency-domain specifications and require tools that are beyond the scope of this book.

We first begin with some preliminary issues related to design philosophy and design specifications. These issues are applicable to both FIR and IIR filter designs. We will then study FIR filter design algorithms in the rest of this chapter. In Chapter 8, we will provide a similar treatment for IIR filters.

7.1 PRELIMINARIES

The design of a digital filter is carried out in three steps:

- **Specifications:** Before we can design a filter, we must have some specifications. These specifications are determined by the applications.

- **Approximations:** Once the specifications are defined, we use various concepts and mathematics that we studied so far to come up with a filter description that approximates the given set of specifications. This step is the topic of filter design.

- **Implementation:** The product of the above step is a filter description in the form of a difference equation, a system function $H(z)$, or an impulse response $h(n)$. From this description, we implement the filter in hardware or through software on a computer as we discussed in Chapter 6.

In this and the next chapter, we will discuss in detail only the second step, which is the conversion of specifications into a filter description.

In many applications like speech or audio signal processing, digital filters are used to implement frequency-selective operations. Therefore, specifications are required in the frequency domain in terms of the desired magnitude and phase response of the filter. Generally, a linear phase response in the passband is desirable. In the case of FIR filters, it is possible to have exact linear phase, as we have seen in Chapter 6. In the case of IIR filters, a linear phase in the passband is not achievable. Hence we will consider *magnitude-only* specifications.

The magnitude specifications are given in one of two ways. The first approach is called *absolute specifications*, which provide a set of requirements on the magnitude response function $|H(e^{j\omega})|$. These specifications are generally used for FIR filters. IIR filters are specified in a somewhat different way, which we will discuss in Chapter 8. The second approach is called *relative specifications*, which provide requirements in *decibels* (dB), given by

$$\text{dB scale} = -20 \log_{10} \frac{|H(e^{j\omega})|}{|H(e^{j\omega})|_{\max}} \geq 0$$

This approach is the most popular one in practice and is used for both FIR and IIR filters. To illustrate these specifications, we will consider a lowpass filter design as an example.

7.1.1 ABSOLUTE SPECIFICATIONS

A typical absolute specification of a lowpass filter is shown in Figure 7.1a, in which

- band $[0, \omega_p]$ is called the *passband* and δ_1 is the tolerance (or ripple) that we are willing to accept in the ideal passband response,

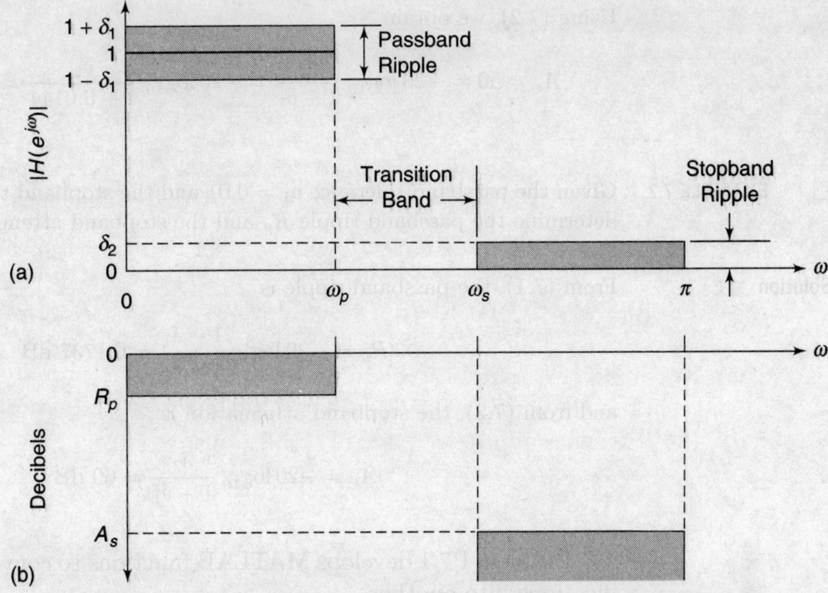

FIGURE 7.1 *FIR filter specifications: (a) absolute (b) relative*

- band $[\omega_s, \pi]$ is called the *stopband* and δ_2 is the corresponding tolerance (or ripple), and
- band $[\omega_p, \omega_s]$ is called the *transition band* that imposes no restrictions on the magnitude response.

7.1.2 RELATIVE (DB) SPECIFICATIONS

A typical relative specification of a lowpass filter is shown in Figure 7.1b, in which

- R_p is the passband ripple in dB, and
- A_s is the stopband attenuation in dB.

The parameters given in these two specifications are obviously related. Since $|H(e^{j\omega})|_{\max}$ in absolute specifications is equal to $(1 + \delta_1)$, we have

$$R_p = -20 \log_{10} \frac{1 - \delta_1}{1 + \delta_1} > 0 \; (\approx 0) \tag{7.1}$$

and

$$A_s = -20 \log_{10} \frac{\delta_2}{1 + \delta_1} > 0 \; (\gg 1) \tag{7.2}$$

□   **EXAMPLE 7.1**   In a certain filter's specifications, the passband ripple is 0.25 dB and the stopband attenuation is 50 dB. Determine δ_1 and δ_2.

Solution   Using (7.1), we obtain

$$R_p = 0.25 = -20 \log_{10} \frac{1 - \delta_1}{1 + \delta_1} \Rightarrow \delta_1 = 0.0144$$

Using (7.2), we obtain

$$A_s = 50 = -20 \log_{10} \frac{\delta_2}{1+\delta_1} = -20 \log_{10} \frac{\delta_2}{1+0.0144} \Rightarrow \delta_2 = 0.0032 \qquad \square$$

□ EXAMPLE 7.2   Given the passband tolerance $\delta_1 = 0.01$ and the stopband tolerance $\delta_2 = 0.001$, determine the passband ripple R_p and the stopband attenuation A_s.

Solution   From (7.1), the passband ripple is

$$R_p = -20 \log_{10} \frac{1-\delta_1}{1+\delta_1} = 0.1737 \text{ dB}$$

and from (7.2), the stopband attenuation is

$$A_s = -20 \log_{10} \frac{\delta_2}{1+\delta_1} = 60 \text{ dB} \qquad \square$$

Problem P7.1 develops MATLAB functions to convert one set of specifications into another.

These specifications were given for a lowpass filter. Similar specifications can also be given for other types of frequency-selective filters, such as highpass or bandpass. However, the most important design parameters are *frequency-band tolerances* (or ripples) and *band-edge frequencies.* Whether the given band is a passband or a stopband is a relatively minor issue. Therefore, in describing design techniques, we will concentrate on a lowpass filter. In the next chapter, we will discuss how to transform a lowpass filter into other types of frequency-selective filters. Hence it makes more sense to develop techniques for a lowpass filter so that we can compare these techniques. However, we will also provide examples of other types of filters. In light of this discussion, our design goal is the following.

Problem statement   Design a lowpass filter (i.e., obtain its system function $H(z)$ or its difference equation) that has a passband $[0, \omega_p]$ with tolerance δ_1 (or R_p in dB) and a stopband $[\omega_s, \pi]$ with tolerance δ_2 (or A_s in dB).

In this chapter, we turn our attention to the design and approximation of FIR digital filters. These filters have several design and implementational advantages:

- The phase response can be exactly linear.
- They are relatively easy to design since there are no stability problems.
- They are efficient to implement.
- The DFT can be used in their implementation.

As we discussed in Chapter 6, we are generally interested in linear-phase frequency-selective FIR filters. Linear-phase response filters have several advantages:

- The design problem contains only real arithmetic and not complex arithmetic
- Linear-phase filters provide no delay distortion and only a fixed amount of delay
- For the filter of length M (or order $M - 1$), the number of operations are of the order of $M/2$, as we discussed in the linear-phase filter implementation

We first begin with a discussion of the properties of the linear-phase FIR filters, which are required in design algorithms. Then we will discuss three design techniques—namely, the window design, the frequency-sampling design, and the optimal equiripple design techniques for linear-phase FIR filters.

7.2 PROPERTIES OF LINEAR-PHASE FIR FILTERS

In this section, we discuss shapes of impulse and frequency responses and locations of system function zeros of linear-phase FIR filters. Let $h(n)$, $0 \leq n \leq M - 1$, be the impulse response of length (or duration) M. Then the system function is

$$H(z) = \sum_{n=0}^{M-1} h(n)z^{-n} = z^{-(M-1)} \sum_{n=0}^{M-1} h(n)z^{M-1-n}$$

which has $(M - 1)$ poles at the origin $z = 0$ (trivial poles) and $(M - 1)$ zeros located anywhere in the z-plane. The frequency response function is

$$H(e^{j\omega}) = \sum_{n=0}^{M-1} h(n)e^{-j\omega n}, \quad -\pi < \omega \leq \pi$$

Now we will discuss specific requirements on the forms of $h(n)$ and $H(e^{j\omega})$ as well as requirements on the specific locations of $(M - 1)$ zeros that the linear-phase constraint imposes.

7.2.1 IMPULSE RESPONSE $h(n)$
We impose a linear-phase constraint

$$\angle H(e^{j\omega}) = -\alpha\omega, \quad -\pi < \omega \leq \pi$$

Symmetric Impulse Response: M Odd

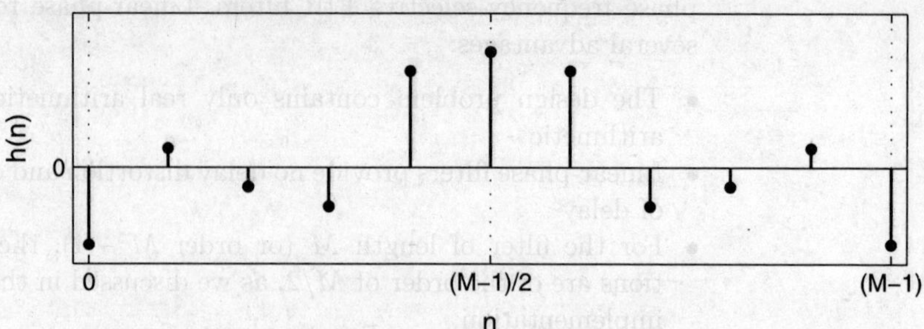

where α is a *constant phase delay*. Then we know from Chapter 6 that $h(n)$ must be symmetric, that is,

$$h(n) = h(M - 1 - n), \quad 0 \le n \le (M - 1) \text{ with } \alpha = \frac{M - 1}{2} \tag{7.3}$$

Hence $h(n)$ is symmetric about α, which is the index of symmetry. There are two possible types of symmetry:

- *M odd.* In this case, $\alpha = (M - 1)/2$ is an integer. The impulse response is as shown above.
- *M even.* In this case, $\alpha = (M - 1)/2$ is not an integer. The impulse response is as shown here.

Symmetric Impulse Response: M Even

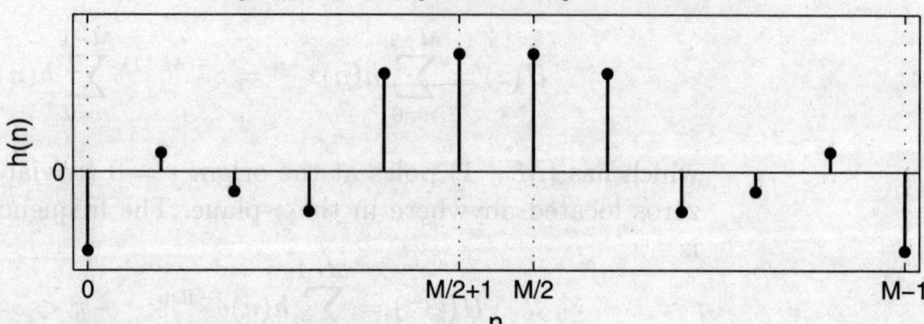

We also have a second type of "linear-phase" FIR filter if we require that the phase response $\angle H(e^{j\omega})$ satisfy the condition

$$\angle H(e^{j\omega}) = \beta - \alpha\omega$$

which is a straight line, but not through the origin. In this case, α is not a constant phase delay, but

$$\frac{d\angle H(e^{j\omega})}{d\omega} = -\alpha$$

is constant, which is the group delay. Therefore, α is called a *constant group delay*. In this case, as a group, frequencies are delayed at a constant rate. But some frequencies may get delayed more and others delayed less. For this type of linear phase, one can show that

$$h\,(n) = -h(M-1-n), \quad 0 \le n \le (M-1); \;\; \alpha = \frac{M-1}{2}, \; \beta = \pm\frac{\pi}{2} \qquad \textbf{(7.4)}$$

This means that the impulse response $h(n)$ is *antisymmetric*. The index of symmetry is still $\alpha = (M-1)/2$. Once again, we have two possible types, one for M odd and one for M even.

- *M odd.* In this case, $\alpha = (M-1)/2$ is an integer and the impulse response is as shown.

Antisymmetric Impulse Response: M Odd

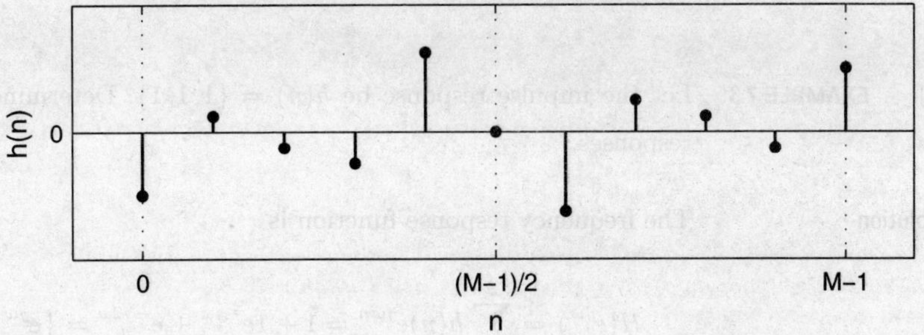

Note that the sample $h(\alpha)$ at $\alpha = (M-1)/2$ must necessarily be equal to zero, that is, $h((M-1)/2) = 0$.

- *M even.* In this case, $\alpha = (M-1)/2$ is not an integer and the impulse response is as shown.

Antisymmetric Impulse Response: M Even

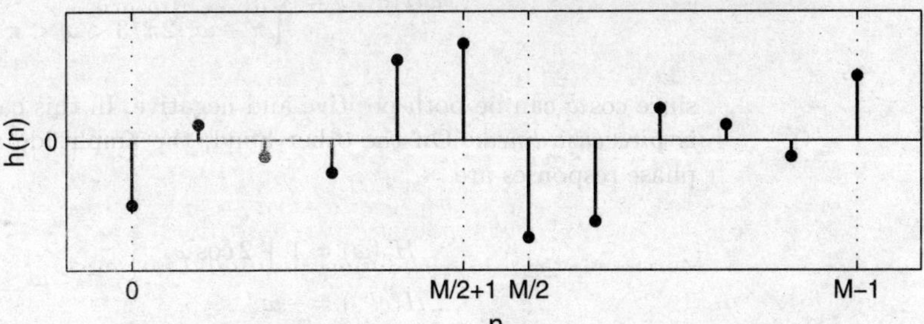

7.2.2 FREQUENCY RESPONSE $H(e^{j\omega})$

When the cases of symmetry and antisymmetry are combined with odd and even M, we obtain four types of linear-phase FIR filters. Frequency response functions for each of these types have some peculiar expressions and shapes. To study these responses, we write $H(e^{j\omega})$ as

$$H(e^{j\omega}) = H_r(\omega)e^{j(\beta - \alpha\omega)}; \quad \beta = \pm\frac{\pi}{2}, \ \alpha = \frac{M-1}{2} \qquad \textbf{(7.5)}$$

where $H_r(\omega)$ is an *amplitude response* function and not a magnitude response function. The amplitude response is a real function, but unlike the magnitude response, which is always positive, the amplitude response may be both positive and negative. The phase response associated with the magnitude response is a *discontinuous* function, while that associated with the amplitude response is a *continuous linear* function. To illustrate the difference between these two types of responses, consider the following example.

□   **EXAMPLE 7.3**   Let the impulse response be $h(n) = \{1, 1, 1\}$. Determine and draw frequency responses.

Solution   The frequency response function is

$$H(e^{j\omega}) = \sum_{0}^{2} h(n)e^{j\omega n} = 1 + 1e^{-j\omega} + e^{-j2\omega} = \left\{e^{j\omega} + 1 + e^{-j\omega}\right\}e^{-j\omega}$$

$$= \{1 + 2\cos\omega\}\, e^{-j\omega}$$

From this, the magnitude and the phase responses are

$$|H(e^{j\omega})| = |1 + 2\cos\omega|, \quad 0 < \omega \le \pi$$

$$\angle H(e^{j\omega}) = \begin{cases} -\omega, & 0 < \omega < 2\pi/3 \\ \pi - \omega, & 2\pi/3 < \omega < \pi \end{cases}$$

since $\cos\omega$ can be both positive and negative. In this case, the phase response is *piecewise linear*. On the other hand, the amplitude and the corresponding phase responses are

$$H_r(\omega) = 1 + 2\cos\omega,$$
$$\angle H(e^{j\omega}) = -\omega, \qquad -\pi < \omega \le \pi$$

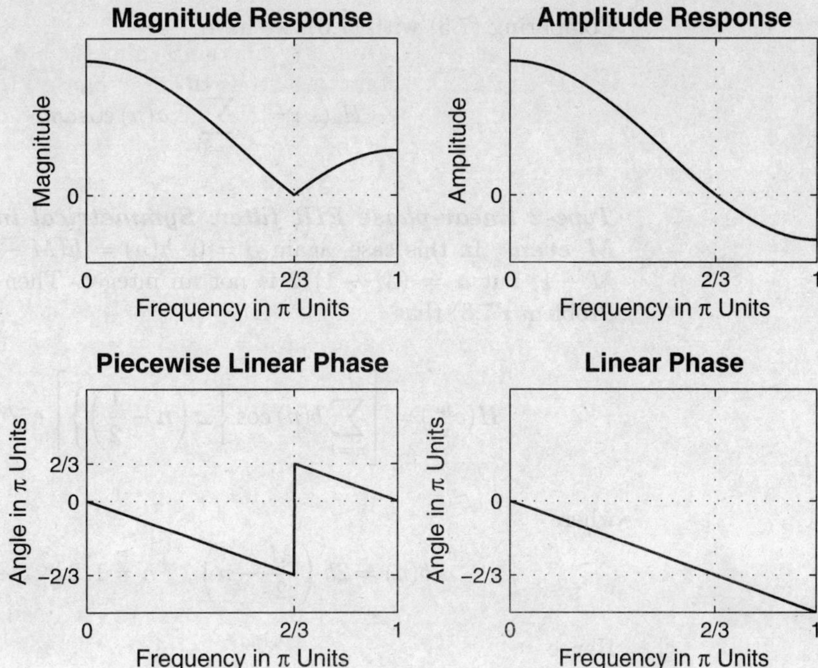

FIGURE 7.2 *Frequency responses in Example 7.3*

In this case, the phase response is *truly linear*. These responses are shown in Figure 7.2. From this example, the difference between the magnitude and the amplitude (or between the piecewise linear and the linear-phase) responses should be clear. ◻

Type-1 linear-phase FIR filter: Symmetrical impulse response, M odd   In this case, $\beta = 0$, $\alpha = (M-1)/2$ is an integer and $h(n) = h(M-1-n)$, $0 \leq n \leq M-1$. Then we can show (see Problem P7.2) that

$$H(e^{j\omega}) = \left[\sum_{n=0}^{(M-1)/2} a(n) \cos \omega n \right] e^{-j\omega(M-1)/2} \qquad (7.6)$$

where sequence $a(n)$ is obtained from $h(n)$ as

$$a(0) = h\left(\frac{M-1}{2}\right) \qquad \text{(the middle sample)}$$

$$a(n) = 2h\left(\frac{M-1}{2} - n\right), \quad 1 \leq n \leq \frac{M-3}{2} \qquad (7.7)$$

Comparing (7.5) with (7.6), we have

$$H_r(\omega) = \sum_{n=0}^{(M-1)/2} a(n) \cos \omega n \tag{7.8}$$

Type-2 linear-phase FIR filter: Symmetrical impulse response, M even In this case, again $\beta = 0$, $h(n) = h(M - 1 - n)$, $0 \leq n \leq M - 1$, but $\alpha = (M - 1)/2$ is not an integer. Then we can show (see Problem P7.3) that

$$H(e^{j\omega}) = \left[\sum_{n=1}^{M/2} b(n) \cos \left\{ \omega \left(n - \frac{1}{2} \right) \right\} \right] e^{-j\omega(M-1)/2} \tag{7.9}$$

where

$$b(n) = 2h \left(\frac{M}{2} - n \right), \quad n = 1, 2, \ldots, \frac{M}{2} \tag{7.10}$$

Hence

$$H_r(\omega) = \sum_{n=1}^{M/2} b(n) \cos \left\{ \omega \left(n - \frac{1}{2} \right) \right\} \tag{7.11}$$

Note: At $\omega = \pi$, we get

$$H_r(\pi) = \sum_{n=1}^{M/2} b(n) \cos \left\{ \pi \left(n - \frac{1}{2} \right) \right\} = 0$$

regardless of $b(n)$ or $h(n)$. Hence we cannot use this type (i.e., symmetric $h(n)$, M even) for highpass or bandstop filters.

Type-3 linear-phase FIR filter: Antisymmetric impulse response, M odd In this case, $\beta = \pi/2$, $\alpha = (M - 1)/2$ is an integer, $h(n) = -h(M - 1 - n)$, $0 \leq n \leq M - 1$, and $h((M - 1)/2) = 0$. Then we can show (see Problem P7.4) that

$$H(e^{j\omega}) = \left[\sum_{n=1}^{(M-1)/2} c(n) \sin \omega n \right] e^{j\left[\frac{\pi}{2} - \left(\frac{M-1}{2} \right)\omega \right]} \tag{7.12}$$

where

$$c(n) = 2h\left(\frac{M-1}{2} - n\right), \quad n = 1, 2, \ldots, \frac{M-1}{2} \tag{7.13}$$

and

$$H_r(\omega) = \sum_{n=1}^{(M-1)/2} c(n) \sin \omega n \tag{7.14}$$

Note: At $\omega = 0$ and $\omega = \pi$, we have $H_r(\omega) = 0$, regardless of $c(n)$ or $h(n)$. Furthermore, $e^{j\pi/2} = j$, which means that $jH_r(\omega)$ is purely imaginary. Hence this type of filter is not suitable for designing a lowpass filter or a highpass filter. However, this behavior is suitable for approximating ideal digital Hilbert transformers and differentiators. An ideal Hilbert transformer [79] is an allpass filter that imparts a 90° phase shift on the input signal. It is frequently used in communication systems for modulation purposes. Differentiators are used in many analog and digital systems to take the derivative of a signal.

Type-4 linear-phase FIR filter: Antisymmetric impulse response, M even   This case is similar to Type-2. We have (see Problem P7.5)

$$H(e^{j\omega}) = \left[\sum_{n=1}^{M/2} d(n) \sin\left\{\omega\left(n - \frac{1}{2}\right)\right\}\right] e^{j[\frac{\pi}{2} - \omega(M-1)/2]} \tag{7.15}$$

where

$$d(n) = 2h\left(\frac{M}{2} - n\right), \quad n = 1, 2, \ldots, \frac{M}{2} \tag{7.16}$$

and

$$H_r(\omega) = \sum_{n=1}^{M/2} d(n) \sin\left\{\omega\left(n - \frac{1}{2}\right)\right\} \tag{7.17}$$

Note: At $\omega = 0$, $H_r(0) = 0$ and $e^{j\pi/2} = j$. Hence this type is also suitable for designing digital Hilbert transformers and differentiators.

7.2.3 MATLAB IMPLEMENTATION

The MATLAB function `freqz` computes the frequency response from which we can determine the magnitude response but not the amplitude response. The SP toolbox now provides the function `zerophase` that can compute the amplitude response. However, it is easy to write simple functions to compute amplitude responses for each of the four types. We provide four functions to do this.

1. Hr_type1:

```
function [Hr,w,a,L] = Hr_Type1(h);
% Computes amplitude response Hr(w) of a Type-1 LP FIR filter
% -------------------------------------------------------------
% [Hr,w,a,L] = Hr_Type1(h)
% Hr = amplitude response
%  w = 500 frequencies between [0 pi] over which Hr is computed
%  a = type-1 LP filter coefficients
%  L = order of Hr
%  h = type-1 LP filter impulse response
%
 M = length(h);   L = (M-1)/2;
 a = [h(L+1) 2*h(L:-1:1)]; % 1x(L+1) row vector
 n = [0:1:L];              % (L+1)x1 column vector
 w = [0:1:500]'*pi/500;  Hr = cos(w*n)*a';
```

2. Hr_type2:

```
function [Hr,w,b,L] = Hr_Type2(h);
% Computes amplitude response of a Type-2 LP FIR filter
% ------------------------------------------------------------
% [Hr,w,b,L] = Hr_Type2(h)
% Hr = amplitude response
%  w = frequencies between [0 pi] over which Hr is computed
%  b = type-2 LP filter coefficients
%  L = order of Hr
%  h = type-2 LP impulse response
%
 M = length(h);   L = M/2;
 b = 2*[h(L:-1:1)];   n = [1:1:L]; n = n-0.5;
 w = [0:1:500]'*pi/500;  Hr = cos(w*n)*b';
```

3. Hr_type3:

```
function [Hr,w,c,L] = Hr_Type3(h);
% Computes amplitude response Hr(w) of a Type-3 LP FIR filter
% -------------------------------------------------------------
% [Hr,w,c,L] = Hr_Type3(h)
% Hr = amplitude response
%  w = frequencies between [0 pi] over which Hr is computed
%  c = type-3 LP filter coefficients
%  L = order of Hr
%  h = type-3 LP impulse response
%
 M = length(h);   L = (M-1)/2;
 c = [2*h(L+1:-1:1)];   n = [0:1:L];
 w = [0:1:500]'*pi/500;  Hr = sin(w*n)*c';
```

4. `Hr_type4`:

```
function [Hr,w,d,L] = Hr_Type4(h);
% Computes amplitude response of a Type-4 LP FIR filter
% -------------------------------------------------------
% [Hr,w,d,L] = Hr_Type4(h)
% Hr = amplitude response
%  w = frequencies between [0 pi] over which Hr is computed
%  d = type-4 LP filter coefficients
%  L = order of d
%  h = type-4 LP impulse response
%
 M = length(h);   L = M/2;
 d = 2*[h(L:-1:1)];   n = [1:1:L]; n = n-0.5;
 w = [0:1:500]'*pi/500;   Hr = sin(w*n)*d';
```

These four functions can be combined into one function, called
ampl_res, that can be written to determine the type of the linear-phase
filter and to implement the appropriate amplitude response expression.
This is explored in Problem P7.6. The use of these functions is described
in Examples 7.4 through 7.7.

The `zerophase` function from the SP toolbox is similar in use to the
`freqz` function. The invocation [Hr,w, phi] = zerophase(b,a) returns
the amplitude response in `Hr`, evaluated at 512 values around the top half
of the unit circle in the array `w` and the continuous phase response in
`phi`. Thus this function can be used for both FIR and IIR filters. Other
invocations are also available.

7.2.4 ZERO LOCATIONS

Recall that for an FIR filter there are $(M - 1)$ (trivial) poles at the origin
and $(M - 1)$ zeros located somewhere in the z-plane. For linear-phase
FIR filters, these zeros possess certain symmetries that are due to the
symmetry constraints on $h(n)$. It can be shown (see reference [79] and
Problem P7.7) that if $H(z)$ has a zero at

$$z = z_1 = re^{j\theta}$$

then for the linear-phase constraint, there must be a zero at

$$z = \frac{1}{z_1} = \frac{1}{r}e^{-j\theta}$$

For a real-valued filter, we also know that if z_1 is complex, then there must
be a conjugate zero at $z_1^* = re^{-j\theta}$, which implies that there must be a

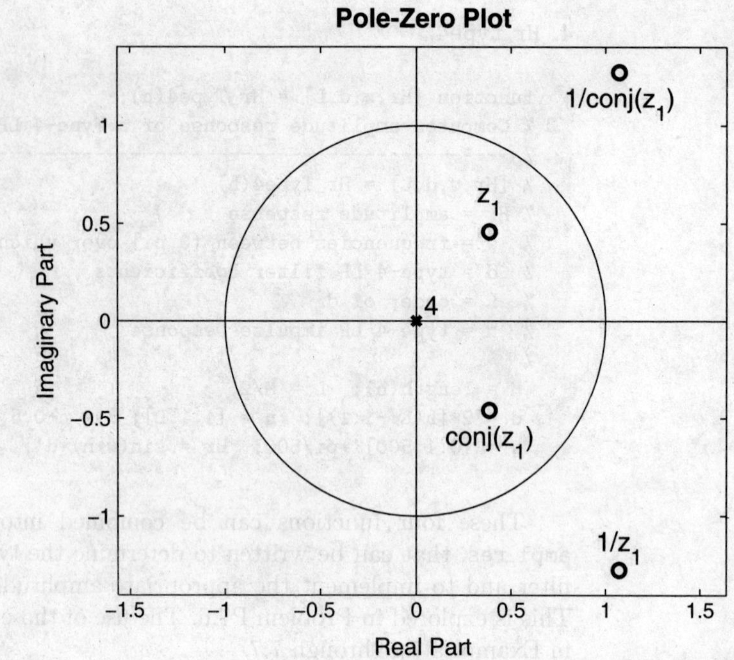

FIGURE 7.3 *A general zero constellation*

zero at $1/z_1^* = (1/r)\, e^{j\theta}$. Thus a general *zero constellation* is a quadruplet

$$re^{j\theta}, \qquad \frac{1}{r}e^{j\theta}, \qquad re^{-j\theta}, \qquad \text{and} \qquad \frac{1}{r}e^{-j\theta}$$

as shown in Figure 7.3. Clearly, if $r = 1$, then $1/r = 1$, and hence the zeros are on the unit circle and occur in pairs

$$e^{j\theta} \qquad \text{and} \qquad e^{-j\theta}$$

If $\theta = 0$ or $\theta = \pi$, then the zeros are on the real line and occur in pairs

$$r \qquad \text{and} \qquad \frac{1}{r}$$

Finally, if $r = 1$ and $\theta = 0$ or $\theta = \pi$, the zeros are either at $z = 1$ or $z = -1$. These symmetries can be used to implement cascade forms with linear-phase sections.

In the following examples, we illustrate the preceding properties of linear-phase FIR filters.

☐ **EXAMPLE 7.4**   Let $h(n) = \{-4, 1, -1, -2, 5, 6, 5, -2, -1, 1, -4\}$. Determine the amplitude response $H_r(\omega)$ and the locations of the zeros of $H(z)$.

Solution   Since $M = 11$, which is odd, and since $h(n)$ is symmetric about $\alpha = (11-1)/2 = 5$, this is a Type-1 linear-phase FIR filter. From (7.7), we have

$$a(0) = h\,(\alpha) = h(5) = 6, \ a(1) = 2h(5-1) = 10, \ a(2) = 2h(5-2) = -4$$

$$a\,(3) = 2h\,(5-3) = -2, \ a\,(4) = 2h\,(5-4) = 2, \ a\,(5) = 2h\,(5-5) = -8$$

From (7.8), we obtain

$$H_r(\omega) = a(0) + a(1)\cos\omega + a(2)\cos 2\omega + a(3)\cos 3\omega + a(4)\cos 4\omega + a(5)\cos 5\omega$$

$$= 6 + 10\cos\omega - 4\cos 2\omega - 2\cos 3\omega + 2\cos 4\omega - 8\cos 5\omega$$

MATLAB script:

```
>> h = [-4,1,-1,-2,5,6,5,-2,-1,1,-4];
>> M = length(h); n = 0:M-1;
>> [Hr,w,a,L] = Hr_Type1(h);
>> a,L
a = 6      10     -4     -2     2     -8
L = 5
>> % plotting commands follow
```

The plots and the zero locations are shown in Figure 7.4. From these plots, we observe that there are no restrictions on $H_r\,(\omega)$ either at $\omega = 0$ or at $\omega = \pi$. There is one zero-quadruplet constellation and three zero pairs. $\square$

$\square$ **EXAMPLE 7.5**   Let $h(n) = \{-4, 1, -1, -2, 5, 6, 6, 5, -2, -1, 1, -4\}$. Determine the amplitude response $H_r\,(\omega)$ and the locations of the zeros of $H\,(z)$.

Solution   This is a Type-2 linear-phase FIR filter since $M = 12$ and since $h\,(n)$ is symmetric with respect to $\alpha = (12 - 1)\,/2 = 5.5$. From (7.10), we have

$$b(1) = 2h\left(\tfrac{12}{2} - 1\right) = 12, \ \ b(2) = 2h\left(\tfrac{12}{2} - 2\right) = 10, \ b(3) = 2h\left(\tfrac{12}{2} - 3\right) = -4$$

$$b(4) = 2h\left(\tfrac{12}{2} - 4\right) = -2, \ b(5) = 2h\left(\tfrac{12}{2} - 5\right) = 2, \ \ b(6) = 2h\left(\tfrac{12}{2} - 6\right) = -8$$

Hence from (7.11) we obtain

$$H_r(\omega) = b(1)\cos\left[\omega\left(1 - \tfrac{1}{2}\right)\right] + b(2)\cos\left[\omega\left(2 - \tfrac{1}{2}\right)\right] + b(3)\cos\left[\omega\left(3 - \tfrac{1}{2}\right)\right]$$

$$+ b(4)\cos\left[\omega\left(4 - \tfrac{1}{2}\right)\right] + b(5)\cos\left[\omega\left(5 - \tfrac{1}{2}\right)\right] + b(6)\cos\left[\omega\left(6 - \tfrac{1}{2}\right)\right]$$

$$= 12\cos\left(\frac{\omega}{2}\right) + 10\cos\left(\frac{3\omega}{2}\right) - 4\cos\left(\frac{5\omega}{2}\right) - 2\cos\left(\frac{7\omega}{2}\right)$$

$$+ 2\cos\left(\frac{9\omega}{2}\right) - 8\cos\left(\frac{11\omega}{2}\right)$$

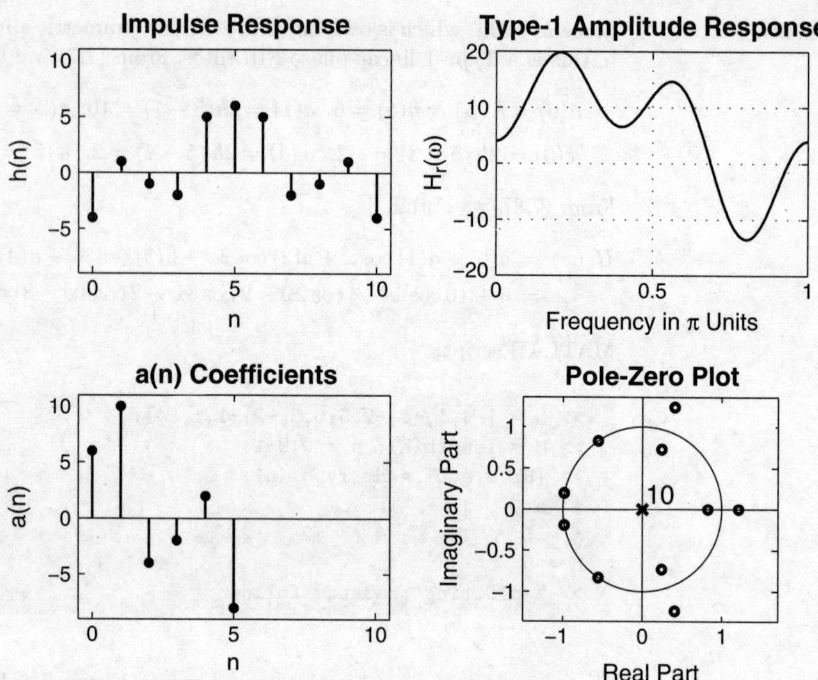

FIGURE 7.4 *Plots in Example 7.4*

MATLAB script:

```
>> h = [-4,1,-1,-2,5,6,6,5,-2,-1,1,-4];
>> M = length(h); n = 0:M-1;  [Hr,w,b,L] = Hr_Type2(h);
>> b,L
b = 12      10      -4      -2      2      -8
L = 6
>> % plotting commands follow
```

The plots and the zero locations are shown in Figure 7.5. From these plots, we observe that $H_r(\omega)$ is zero at $\omega = \pi$. There is one zero-quadruplet constellation, three zero pairs, and one zero at $\omega = \pi$, as expected. □

□ **EXAMPLE 7.6** Let $h(n) = \{-4, 1, -1, -2, 5, 0, -5, 2, 1, -1, 4\}$. Determine the amplitude response $H_r(\omega)$ and the locations of the zeros of $H(z)$.

Solution Since $M = 11$, which is odd, and since $h(n)$ is antisymmetric about $\alpha = (11-1)/2 = 5$, this is a Type-3 linear-phase FIR filter. From (7.13), we have

$$c(0) = h(\alpha) = h(5) = 0, \ c(1) = 2h(5-1) = 10, \ c(2) = 2h(2-2) = -4$$

$$c(3) = 2h(5-3) = -2, \ c(4) = 2h(5-4) = 2, \ c(5) = 2h(5-5) = -8$$

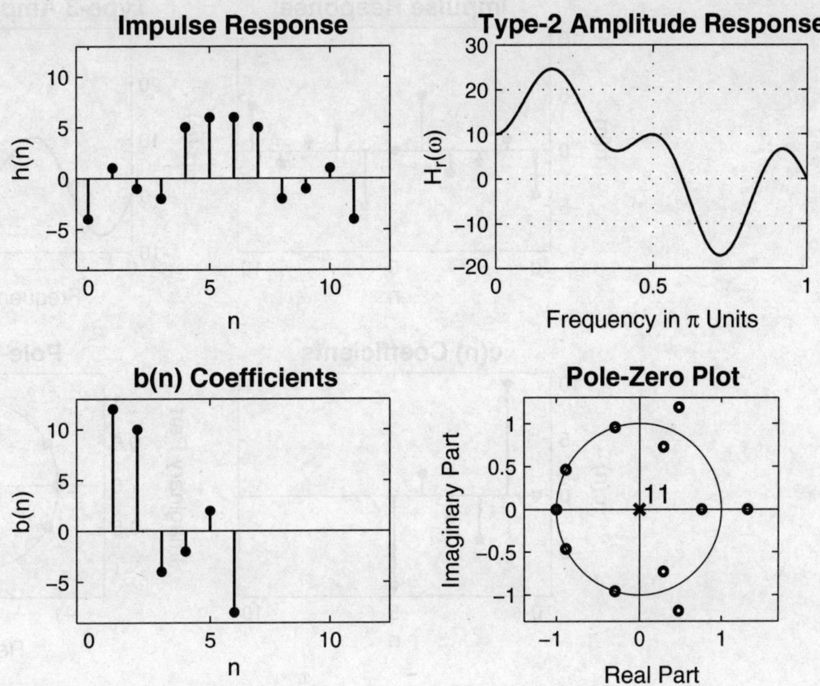

FIGURE 7.5 *Plots in Example 7.5*

From (7.14), we obtain

$$H_r(\omega) = c(0) + c(1)\sin\omega + c(2)\sin 2\omega + c(3)\sin 3\omega + c(4)\sin 4\omega + c(5)\sin 5\omega$$
$$= 0 + 10\sin\omega - 4\sin 2\omega - 2\sin 3\omega + 2\sin 4\omega - 8\sin 5\omega$$

MATLAB script:

```
>> h = [-4,1,-1,-2,5,0,-5,2,1,-1,4];
>> M = length(h); n = 0:M-1; [Hr,w,c,L] = Hr_Type3(h);
>> c,L
a = 0     10     -4     -2     2     -8
L = 5
>> % plotting commands follow
```

The plots and the zero locations are shown in Figure 7.6. From these plots, we observe that $H_r(\omega) = 0$ at $\omega = 0$ and at $\omega = \pi$. There is one zero-quadruplet constellation, two zero pairs, and zeros at $\omega = 0$ and $\omega = \pi$, as expected. □

□   **EXAMPLE 7.7**   Let $h(n) = \{-4, 1, -1, -2, 5, 6, -6, -5, 2, 1, -1, 4\}$. Determine the amplitude

response $H_r(\omega)$ and the locations of the zeros of $H(z)$.

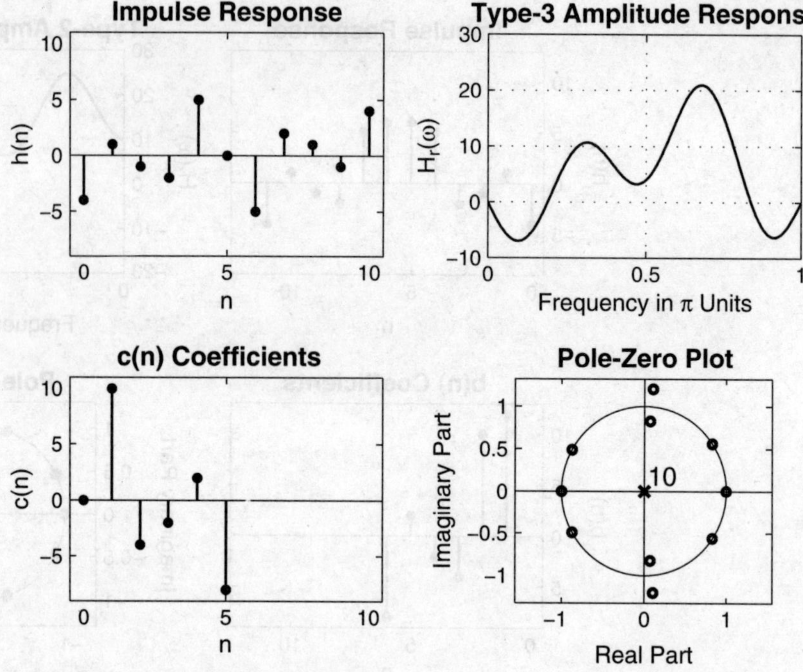

FIGURE 7.6 *Plots in Example 7.6*

Solution

This is a Type-4 linear-phase FIR filter since $M = 12$ and since $h(n)$ is anti-symmetric with respect to $\alpha = (12 - 1)/2 = 5.5$. From (7.16), we have

$$d(1) = 2h\left(\tfrac{12}{2} - 1\right) = 12, \ \ d(2) = 2h\left(\tfrac{12}{2} - 2\right) = 10, \ \ d(3) = 2h\left(\tfrac{12}{2} - 3\right) = -4$$

$$d(4) = 2h\left(\tfrac{12}{2} - 4\right) = -2, \ \ d(5) = 2h\left(\tfrac{12}{2} - 5\right) = 2, \ \ d(6) = 2h\left(\tfrac{12}{2} - 6\right) = -8$$

Hence from (7.17), we obtain

$$H_r(\omega) = d(1)\sin\left[\omega\left(1 - \tfrac{1}{2}\right)\right] + d(2)\sin\left[\omega\left(2 - \tfrac{1}{2}\right)\right] + d(3)\sin\left[\omega\left(3 - \tfrac{1}{2}\right)\right]$$

$$+ d(4)\sin\left[\omega\left(4 - \tfrac{1}{2}\right)\right] + d(5)\sin\left[\omega\left(5 - \tfrac{1}{2}\right)\right] + d(6)\sin\left[\omega\left(6 - \tfrac{1}{2}\right)\right]$$

$$= 12\sin\left(\tfrac{\omega}{2}\right) + 10\sin\left(\tfrac{3\omega}{2}\right) - 4\sin\left(\tfrac{5\omega}{2}\right) - 2\sin\left(\tfrac{7\omega}{2}\right)$$

$$+ 2\sin\left(\tfrac{9\omega}{2}\right) - 8\sin\left(\tfrac{11\omega}{2}\right)$$

MATLAB script:

```
>> h = [-4,1,-1,-2,5,6,-6,-5,2,1,-1,4];
>> M = length(h); n = 0:M-1;  [Hr,w,d,L] = Hr_Type4(h);
>> d,L
d = 12    10    -4    -2    2    -8
L = 6
>> % plotting commands follow
```

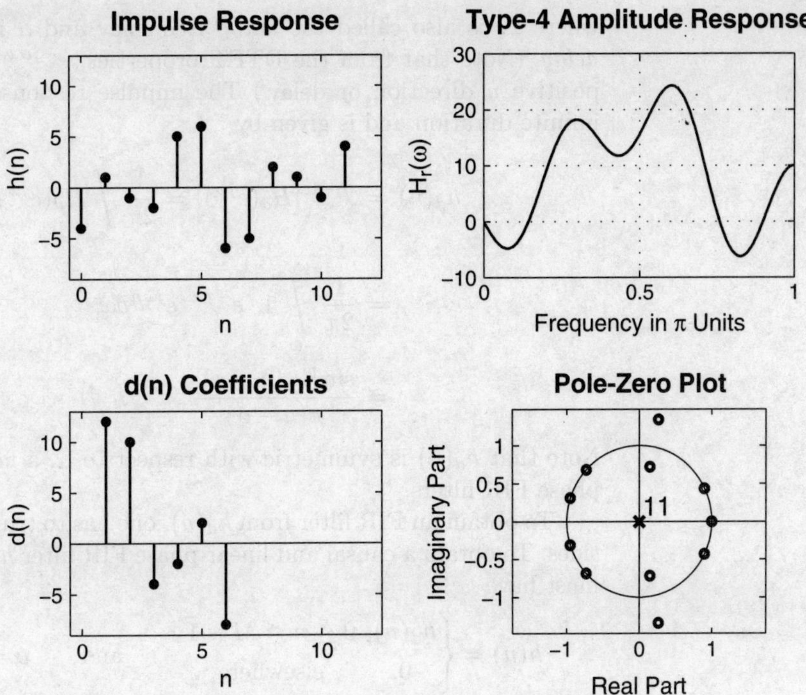

FIGURE 7.7 *Plots in Example 7.7*

The plots and the zero locations are shown in Figure 7.7. From these plots, we observe that $H_r(\omega)$ is zero at $\omega = 0$. There is one zero-quadruplet constellation, three zero pairs, and one zero at $\omega = 0$, as expected. $\qquad\square$

7.3 WINDOW DESIGN TECHNIQUE

The basic idea behind the window design is to choose a proper ideal frequency-selective filter (which always has a noncausal, infinite-duration impulse response) and then to truncate (or window) its impulse response to obtain a linear-phase and causal FIR filter. Therefore, the emphasis in this method is on selecting an appropriate *windowing* function and an appropriate *ideal* filter. We will denote an ideal frequency-selective filter by $H_d(e^{j\omega})$, which has a unity magnitude gain and linear-phase characteristics over its passband, and zero response over its stopband. An ideal LPF of bandwidth $\omega_c < \pi$ is given by

$$H_d(e^{j\omega}) = \begin{cases} 1 \cdot e^{-j\alpha\omega}, & |\omega| \leq \omega_c \\ 0, & \omega_c < |\omega| \leq \pi \end{cases} \qquad (7.18)$$

where ω_c is also called the *cutoff* frequency and α is called the sample *delay*. (Note that from the DTFT properties, $e^{-j\alpha\omega}$ implies shift in the positive n direction or delay.) The impulse response of this filter is of infinite duration and is given by

$$h_d(n) = \mathcal{F}^{-1}\left[H_d(e^{j\omega})\right] = \frac{1}{2\pi}\int_{-\pi}^{\pi} H_d(e^{j\omega})e^{j\omega n}d\omega \qquad (7.19)$$

$$= \frac{1}{2\pi}\int_{-\omega_c}^{\omega_c} 1 \cdot e^{-j\alpha\omega}e^{j\omega n}d\omega$$

$$= \frac{\sin\left[\omega_c(n-\alpha)\right]}{\pi(n-\alpha)}$$

Note that $h_d(n)$ is symmetric with respect to α, a fact useful for linear-phase FIR filters.

To obtain an FIR filter from $h_d(n)$, one has to truncate $h_d(n)$ on both sides. To obtain a causal and linear-phase FIR filter $h(n)$ of length M, we must have

$$h(n) = \begin{cases} h_d(n), & 0 \le n \le M - 1 \\ 0, & \text{elsewhere} \end{cases} \qquad \text{and} \qquad \alpha = \frac{M-1}{2} \qquad (7.20)$$

This operation is called "windowing." In general, $h(n)$ can be thought of as being formed by the product of $h_d(n)$ and a window function $w(n)$ as follows:

$$h(n) = h_d(n)w(n) \qquad (7.21)$$

where
$$w(n) = \begin{cases} \text{some symmetric function with respect to} \\ \alpha \text{ over } 0 \le n \le M - 1 \\ 0, \text{ otherwise} \end{cases}$$

Depending on how we define $w(n)$, we obtain different window designs. For example, in (7.20)

$$w(n) = \begin{cases} 1, & 0 \le n \le M - 1 \\ 0, & \text{otherwise} \end{cases} = \mathcal{R}_M(n)$$

which is the *rectangular window* defined earlier.

In the frequency domain, the causal FIR filter response $H(e^{j\omega})$ is given by the periodic convolution of $H_d(e^{j\omega})$ and the window response $W(e^{j\omega})$; that is,

$$H(e^{j\omega}) = H_d(e^{j\omega}) \circledast W(e^{j\omega}) = \frac{1}{2\pi}\int_{-\pi}^{\pi} W\left(e^{j\lambda}\right) H_d\left(e^{j(\omega-\lambda)}\right) d\lambda$$

$$(7.22)$$

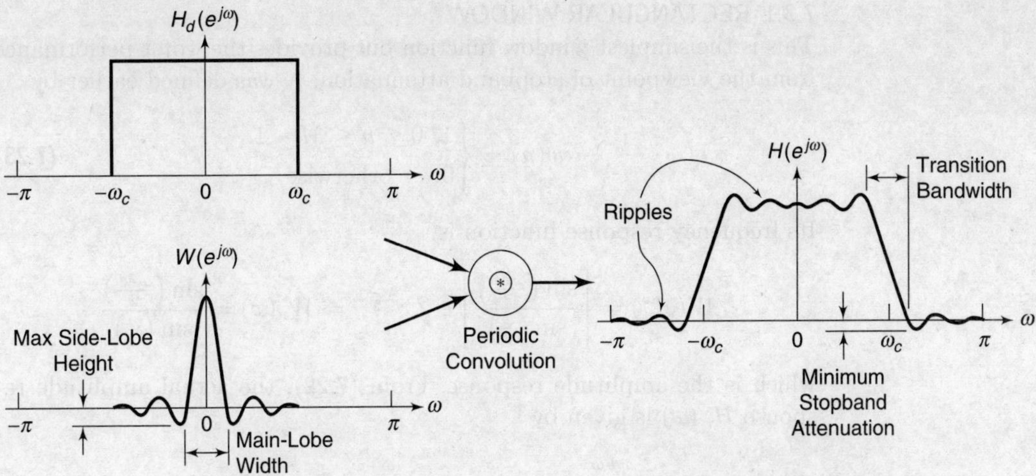

FIGURE 7.8   *Windowing operation in the frequency domain*

This is shown pictorially in Figure 7.8 for a typical window response, from which we have the following observations.

1. Since the window $w(n)$ has a finite length equal to M, its response has a *peaky main-lobe* whose width is proportional to $1/M$ and has side-lobes of smaller heights.
2. The periodic convolution (7.22) produces a smeared version of the ideal response $H_d(e^{j\omega})$.
3. The main lobe produces a transition band in $H(e^{j\omega})$ whose width is responsible for the transition width. This width is then proportional to $1/M$. The wider the main lobe, the wider will be the transition width.
4. The side lobes produce ripples that have similar shapes in both the passband and stopband.

Basic window design idea   For the given filter specifications, choose the filter length M and a window function $w(n)$ for the narrowest main-lobe width and the smallest side-lobe attenuation possible.

From observation 4, we note that the passband tolerance δ_1 and the stopband tolerance δ_2 cannot be specified independently. We generally take care of δ_2 alone, which results in $\delta_2 = \delta_1$. We now briefly describe various well-known window functions. We will use the rectangular window as an example to study their performances in the frequency domain.

7.3.1 RECTANGULAR WINDOW

This is the simplest window function but provides the worst performance
from the viewpoint of stopband attenuation. It was defined earlier by

$$w(n) = \begin{cases} 1, \ 0 \le n \le M - 1 \\ 0, \quad \text{otherwise} \end{cases} \tag{7.23}$$

Its frequency response function is

$$W(e^{j\omega}) = \left[\frac{\sin\left(\frac{\omega M}{2}\right)}{\sin\left(\frac{\omega}{2}\right)} \right] e^{-j\omega \frac{M-1}{2}} \Rightarrow W_r(\omega) = \frac{\sin\left(\frac{\omega M}{2}\right)}{\sin\left(\frac{\omega}{2}\right)}$$

which is the amplitude response. From (7.22), the actual amplitude response $H_r(\omega)$ is given by

$$H_r(\omega) \simeq \frac{1}{2\pi} \int\limits_{-\pi}^{\omega+\omega_c} W_r(\lambda)\, d\lambda = \frac{1}{2\pi} \int\limits_{-\pi}^{\omega+\omega_c} \frac{\sin\left(\frac{\omega M}{2}\right)}{\sin\left(\frac{\omega}{2}\right)} d\lambda, \quad M \gg 1 \tag{7.24}$$

This implies that the running integral of the window amplitude response
(or *integrated* amplitude response) is necessary in the accurate analysis of
the transition bandwidth and the stopband attenuation. Figure 7.9 shows
the rectangular window function $w(n)$, its amplitude response $W(\omega)$, the
amplitude response in dB, and the integrated amplitude response (7.24)
in dB. From the observation of plots in Figure 7.9, we can make several
observations.

1. The amplitude response $W_r(\omega)$ has the first zero at $\omega = \omega_1$, where

$$\frac{\omega_1 M}{2} = \pi \qquad \text{or} \qquad \omega_1 = \frac{2\pi}{M}$$

   Hence the width of the main lobe is $2\omega_1 = 4\pi/M$. Therefore, the
   approximate transition bandwidth is $4\pi/M$.

2. The magnitude of the first side lobe (which is also the peak side-lobe
   magnitude) is approximately at $\omega = 3\pi/M$ and is given by

$$\left| W_r\left(\omega = \frac{3\pi}{M}\right) \right| = \left| \frac{\sin\left(\frac{3\pi}{2}\right)}{\sin\left(\frac{3\pi}{2M}\right)} \right| \simeq \frac{2M}{3\pi} \qquad \text{for } M \gg 1$$

   Comparing this with the main-lobe amplitude, which is equal to M,
   the *peak side-lobe magnitude* is

$$\frac{2}{3\pi} = 21.22\% \equiv 13 \text{ dB}$$

   below the main-lobe magnitude of 0 dB.

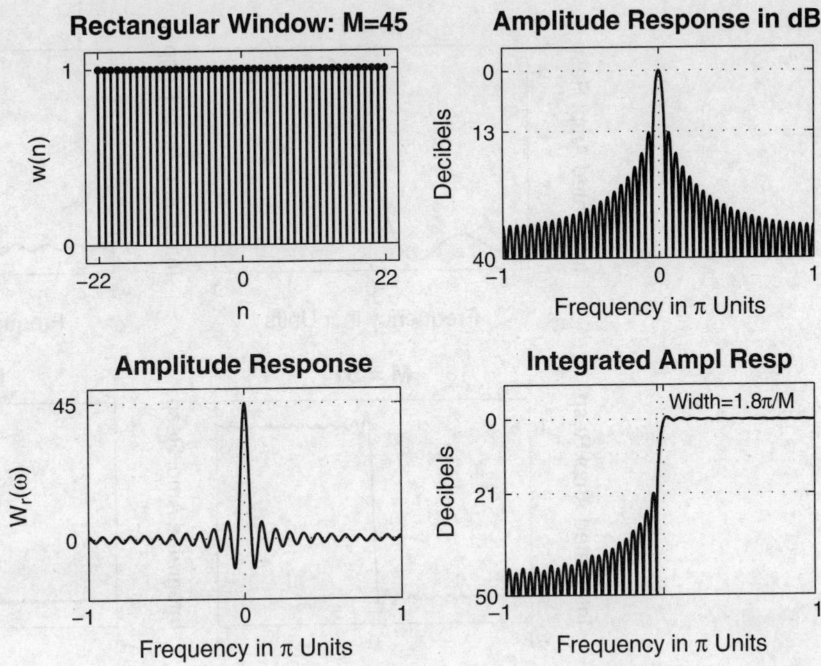

FIGURE 7.9 *Rectangular window:* $M = 45$

3. The integrated amplitude response has the first side-lobe magnitude at 21 dB. This results in the *minimum stopband attenuation* of 21 dB irrespective of the window length M.

4. Using the minimum stopband attenuation, the transition bandwidth can be accurately computed. It is shown in the accumulated amplitude response plot in Figure 7.9. This computed *exact transition bandwidth* is

$$\omega_s - \omega_p = \frac{1.8\pi}{M}$$

which is less than half the approximate bandwidth of $4\pi/M$.

Clearly, this is a simple window operation in the time domain and an easy function to analyze in the frequency domain. However, there are two main problems. First, the minimum stopband attenuation of 21 dB is insufficient in practical applications. Second, the rectangular windowing being a direct truncation of the infinite length $h_d(n)$, it suffers from the *Gibbs phenomenon*. If we increase M, the width of each side lobe will decrease, but the area under each lobe will remain constant. Therefore, the *relative amplitudes* of side lobes will remain constant, and the minimum stopband attenuation will remain at 21 dB. This implies that all ripples will bunch up near the band edges. This is shown in Figure 7.10.

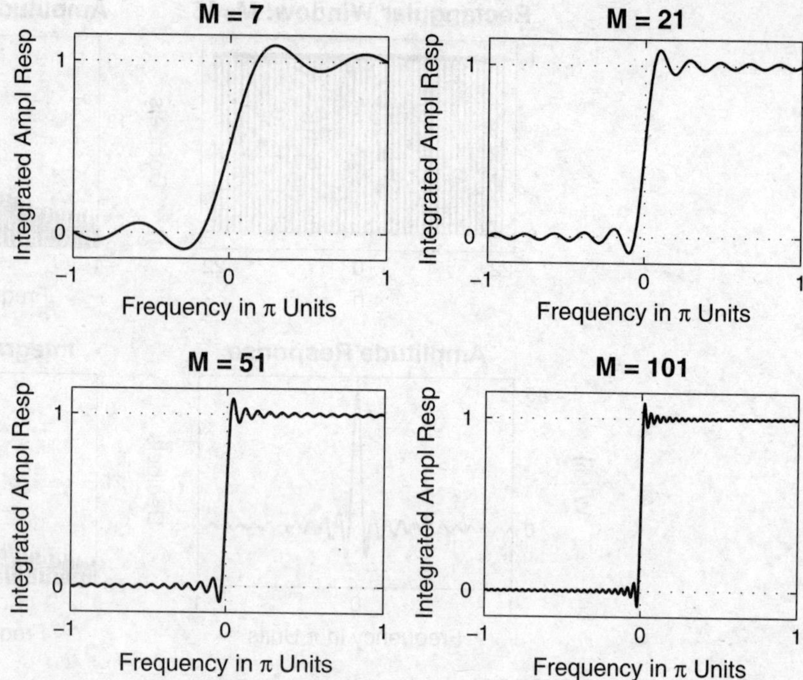

FIGURE 7.10 *Gibbs phenomenon*

Since the rectangular window is impractical in many applications, we consider other fixed window functions that provide a fixed amount of attenuation. These window functions bear the names of the people who first proposed them. Although these window functions can also be analyzed similar to the rectangular window, we present their results using MATLAB simulations.

7.3.2 BARTLETT WINDOW

Since the Gibbs phenomenon results from the fact that the rectangular window has a sudden transition from 0 to 1 (or 1 to 0), Bartlett suggested a more gradual transition in the form of a triangular window, which is given by

$$
w(n) = \begin{cases} \dfrac{2n}{M-1}, & 0 \le n \le \dfrac{M-1}{2} \\[2ex] 2 - \dfrac{2n}{M-1}, & \dfrac{M-1}{2} \le n \le M-1 \\[2ex] 0, & \text{otherwise} \end{cases} \tag{7.25}
$$

This window and its frequency-domain responses are shown in Figure 7.11.

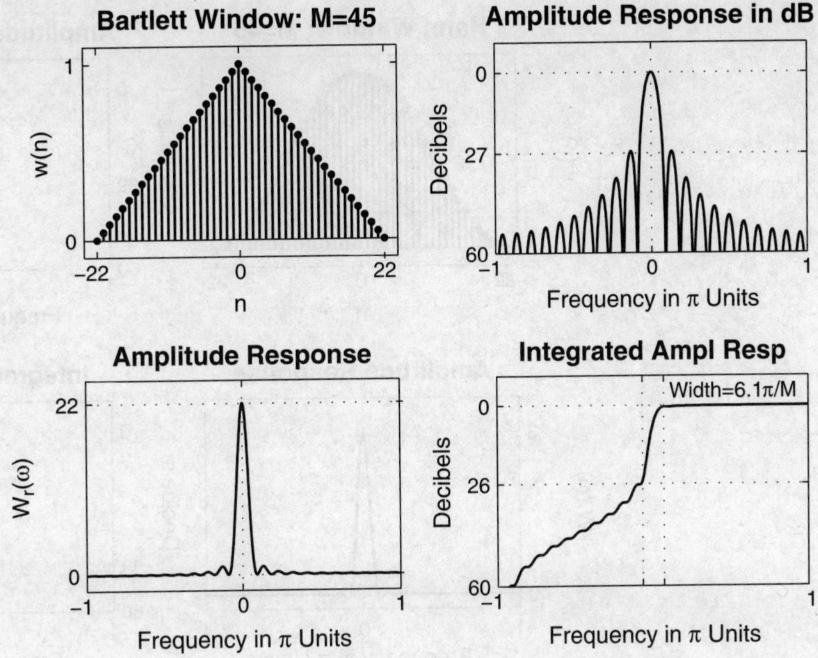

FIGURE 7.11 *Bartlett window: $M = 45$*

7.3.3 HANN WINDOW

This is a raised cosine window function given by

$$w(n) = \begin{cases} 0.5 \left[1 - \cos\left(\frac{2\pi n}{M-1}\right) \right], & 0 \leq n \leq M-1 \\ 0, & \text{otherwise} \end{cases} \tag{7.26}$$

This window and its frequency-domain responses are shown in Figure 7.12.

7.3.4 HAMMING WINDOW

This window is similar to the Hann window except that it has a small amount of discontinuity and is given by

$$w(n) = \begin{cases} 0.54 - 0.46\cos\left(\frac{2\pi n}{M-1}\right), & 0 \leq n \leq M-1 \\ 0, & \text{otherwise} \end{cases} \tag{7.27}$$

This window and its frequency-domain responses are shown in Figure 7.13.

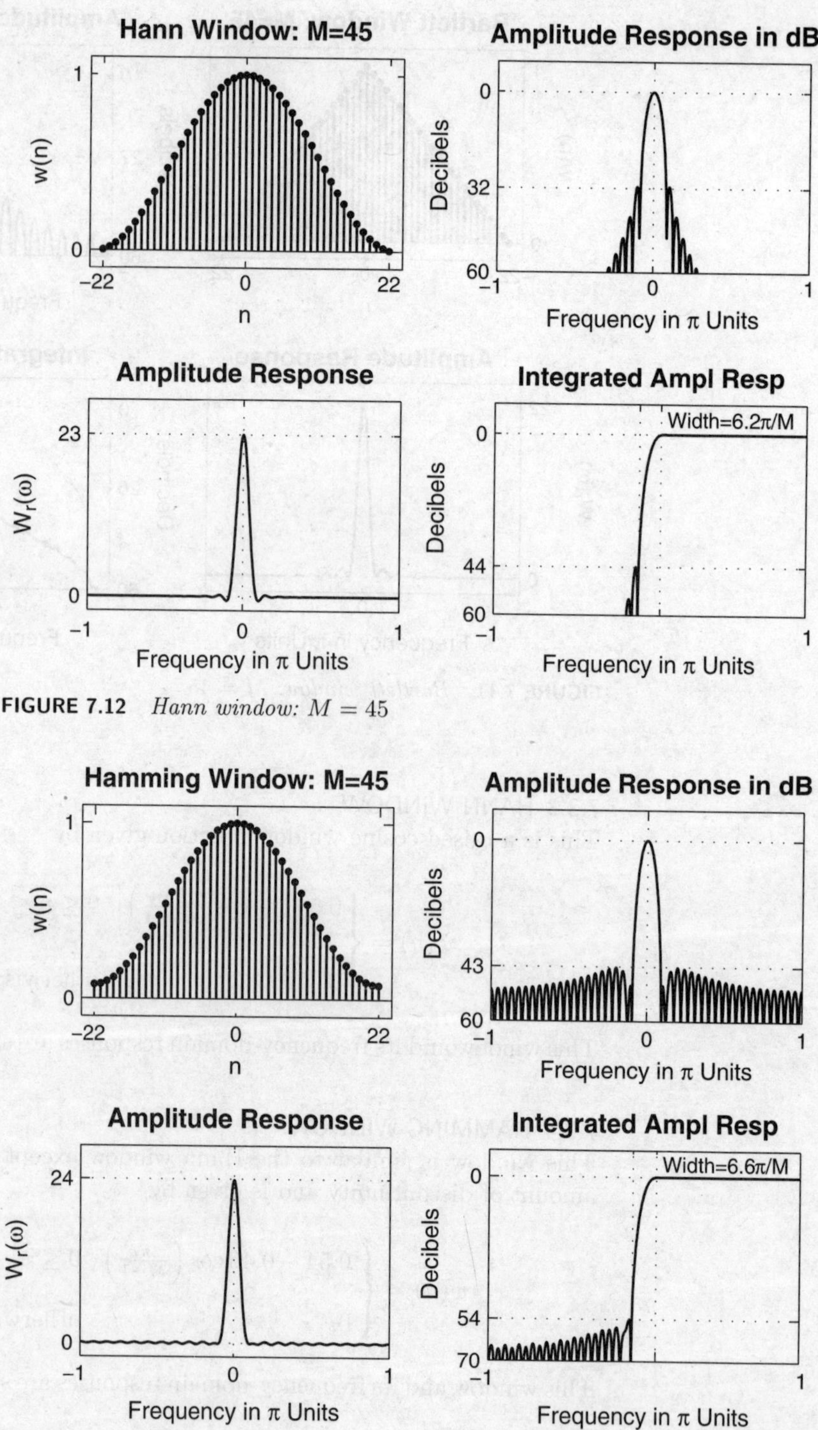

FIGURE 7.12   *Hann window:* $M = 45$

FIGURE 7.13   *Hamming window:* $M = 45$

7.3.5 BLACKMAN WINDOW

This window is also similar to the previous two but contains a second harmonic term and is given by

$$
w(n) = \begin{cases} 0.42 - 0.5\cos\left(\frac{2\pi n}{M-1}\right) + 0.08\cos\left(\frac{4\pi n}{M-1}\right), & 0 \le n \le M-1 \\ 0, & \text{otherwise} \end{cases}
$$

$$(7.28)$$

This window and its frequency-domain responses are shown in Figure 7.14.

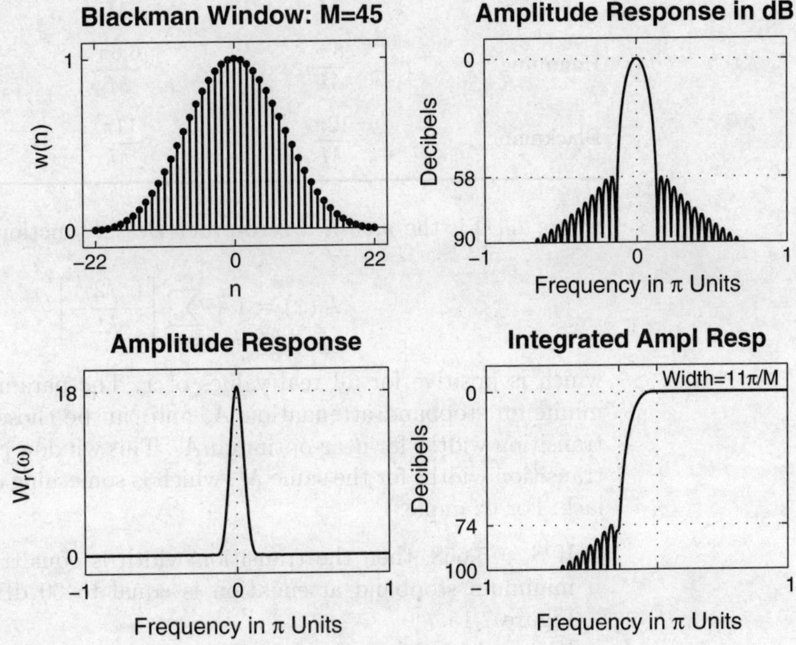

FIGURE 7.14 *Blackman window: $M = 45$*

In Table 7.1, we provide a summary of fixed window function characteristics in terms of their transition widths (as a function of M) and their minimum stopband attenuations in dB. Both the approximate as well as the exact transition bandwidths are given. Note that the transition widths and the stopband attenuations increase as we go down the table. The Hamming window appears to be the best choice for many applications.

7.3.6 KAISER WINDOW

This is an adjustable window function that is widely used in practice. The window function is due to J.F. Kaiser and is given by

$$
w(n) = \frac{I_0\left[\beta\sqrt{1 - (1 - \frac{2n}{M-1})^2}\right]}{I_0\left[\beta\right]}, \quad 0 \le n \le M-1 \tag{7.29}
$$

TABLE 7.1 *Summary of commonly used window function characteristics*

Window Name	Transition Width $\Delta\omega$ Approximate	Exact Values	Min. Stopband Attenuation
Rectangular	$\dfrac{4\pi}{M}$	$\dfrac{1.8\pi}{M}$	21 dB
Bartlett	$\dfrac{8\pi}{M}$	$\dfrac{6.1\pi}{M}$	25 dB
Hann	$\dfrac{8\pi}{M}$	$\dfrac{6.2\pi}{M}$	44 dB
Hamming	$\dfrac{8\pi}{M}$	$\dfrac{6.6\pi}{M}$	53 dB
Blackman	$\dfrac{12\pi}{M}$	$\dfrac{11\pi}{M}$	74 dB

where $I_0[\,\cdot\,]$ is the *modified* zero-*order Bessel* function given by

$$I_0(x) = 1 + \sum_{k=0}^{\infty} \left[\frac{(x/2)^k}{k!} \right]^2$$

which is positive for all real values of x. The parameter β controls the minimum stopband attenuation A_s and can be chosen to yield different transition widths for near-optimum A_s. This window can provide different transition widths for the same M, which is something other fixed windows lack. For example:

- If $\beta = 5.658$, then the transition width is equal to $7.8\pi/M$, and the minimum stopband attenuation is equal to 60 dB. This is shown in Figure 7.15.
- If $\beta = 4.538$, then the transition width is equal to $5.8\pi/M$, and the minimum stopband attenuation is equal to 50 dB.

Hence the performance of this window is comparable to that of the Hamming window. In addition, the Kaiser window provides flexible transition bandwidths. Due to the complexity involved in the Bessel functions, the design equations for this window are not easy to derive. Fortunately, Kaiser has developed *empirical* design equations, which we provide here without proof. Given ω_p, ω_s, R_p, and A_s, the parameters M and β are given by

$$\text{Transition width} = \Delta\omega = \omega_s - \omega_p \tag{7.30a}$$

$$\text{Filter length } M \simeq \frac{A_s - 7.95}{2.285\Delta\omega} + 1 \tag{7.30b}$$

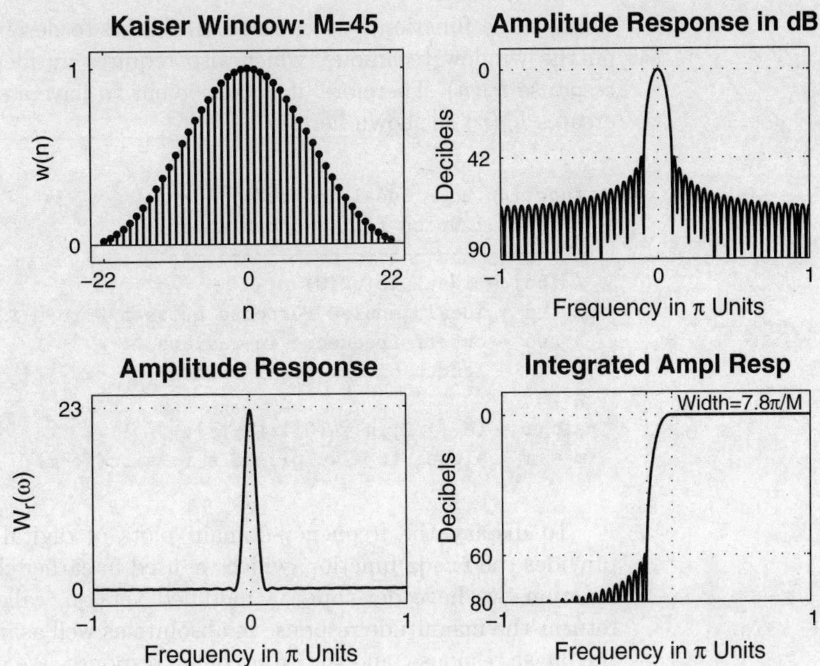

FIGURE 7.15 *Kaiser window: $M = 45$, $\beta = 5.658$*

$$\text{Parameter } \beta = \begin{cases} 0.1102(A_s - 8.7), & A_s \geq 50 \\ \\ 0.5842\,(A_s - 21)^{0.4} \\ \quad + 0.07886(A_s - 21), & 21 < A_s < 50 \end{cases} \qquad (7.30c)$$

7.3.7 MATLAB IMPLEMENTATION

MATLAB provides several functions to implement window functions discussed in this section. A brief description of these functions follow.

- `w=boxcar(M)` returns the M-point rectangular window function in array `w`.
- `w=bartlett(M)` returns the M-point Bartlett window function in array `w`.
- `w=hann(M)` returns the M-point Hann window function in array `w`.
- `w=hamming(M)` returns the M-point Hamming window function in array `w`.
- `w=blackman(M)` returns the M-point Blackman window function in array `w`.
- `w=kaiser(M,beta)` returns the `beta`-valued M-point rectangular window function in array `w`.

Using these functions, we can use MATLAB to design FIR filters based on the window technique, which also requires an ideal lowpass impulse response $h_d(n)$. Therefore, it is convenient to have a simple routine that creates $h_d(n)$ as shown here.

```
function hd = ideal_lp(wc,M);
% Ideal lowpass filter computation
% ---------------------------------
% [hd] = ideal_lp(wc,M)
%  hd = ideal impulse response between 0 to M-1
%  wc = cutoff frequency in radians
%   M = length of the ideal filter
%
alpha = (M-1)/2; n = [0:1:(M-1)];
m = n - alpha; fc = wc/pi; hd = fc*sinc(fc*m);
```

To display the frequency-domain plots of digital filters, MATLAB provides the `freqz` function, which we used in earlier chapters. Using this function, we have developed a modified version, called `freqz_m`, which returns the magnitude response in absolute as well as in relative dB scale, the phase response, and the group delay response. We will need the group delay response in the next chapter.

```
function [db,mag,pha,grd,w] = freqz_m(b,a);
% Modified version of freqz subroutine
% -------------------------------------
% [db,mag,pha,grd,w] = freqz_m(b,a);
%  db = relative magnitude in dB computed over 0 to pi radians
% mag = absolute magnitude computed over 0 to pi radians
% pha = phase response in radians over 0 to pi radians
% grd = group delay over 0 to pi radians
%   w = 501 frequency samples between 0 to pi radians
%   b = numerator polynomial of H(z)   (for FIR: b=h)
%   a = denominator polynomial of H(z) (for FIR: a=[1])
%
[H,w] = freqz(b,a,1000,'whole');
    H = (H(1:1:501))'; w = (w(1:1:501))';
  mag = abs(H);   db = 20*log10((mag+eps)/max(mag));
  pha = angle(H);   grd = grpdelay(b,a,w);
```

7.3.8 DESIGN EXAMPLES

We now provide several examples of FIR filter design using window techniques and MATLAB functions.

☐ **EXAMPLE 7.8** Design a digital FIR lowpass filter with the following specifications:

$$\omega_p = 0.2\pi, \quad R_p = 0.25 \text{ dB}$$

$$\omega_s = 0.3\pi, \quad A_s = 50 \text{ dB}$$

Choose an appropriate window function from Table 7.1. Determine the impulse response and provide a plot of the frequency response of the designed filter.

Solution Both the Hamming and Blackman windows can provide attenuation of more than 50 dB. Let us choose the Hamming window, which provides the smaller transition band and hence has the smaller order. Although we do not use the passband ripple value of $R_p = 0.25$ dB in the design, we will have to check the actual ripple from the design and verify that it is indeed within the given tolerance. The design steps are given in the following MATLAB script.

```
>> wp = 0.2*pi; ws = 0.3*pi;  tr_width = ws - wp;
>> M = ceil(6.6*pi/tr_width) + 1
M = 67
>> n=[0:1:M-1];
>> wc = (ws+wp)/2, % Ideal LPF cutoff frequency
>> hd = ideal_lp(wc,M);  w_ham = (hamming(M))';  h = hd .* w_ham;
>> [db,mag,pha,grd,w] = freqz_m(h,[1]);  delta_w = 2*pi/1000;
>> Rp = -(min(db(1:1:wp/delta_w+1)));    % Actual passband ripple
Rp = 0.0394
>> As = -round(max(db(ws/delta_w+1:1:501))) % Min stopband attenuation
As = 52
% plotting commands follow
```

Note that the filter length is $M = 67$, the actual stopband attenuation is 52 dB, and the actual passband ripple is 0.0394 dB. Clearly, the passband ripple is satisfied by this design. This practice of verifying the passband ripple is strongly recommended. The time- and the frequency-domain plots are shown in Figure 7.16. ☐

☐ **EXAMPLE 7.9** For the design specifications given in Example 7.8, choose the Kaiser window to design the necessary lowpass filter.

Solution The design steps are given in the following MATLAB script.

```
>> wp = 0.2*pi; ws = 0.3*pi; As = 50;  tr_width = ws - wp;
>> M = ceil((As-7.95)/(2.285*tr_width)+1) + 1
M = 61
>> n=[0:1:M-1];  beta = 0.1102*(As-8.7)
beta = 4.5513
>> wc = (ws+wp)/2;  hd = ideal_lp(wc,M);
>> w_kai = (kaiser(M,beta))';  h = hd .* w_kai;
>> [db,mag,pha,grd,w] = freqz_m(h,[1]);  delta_w = 2*pi/1000;
>> As = -round(max(db(ws/delta_w+1:1:501))) % Min stopband attenuation
As = 52
% plotting commands follow
```

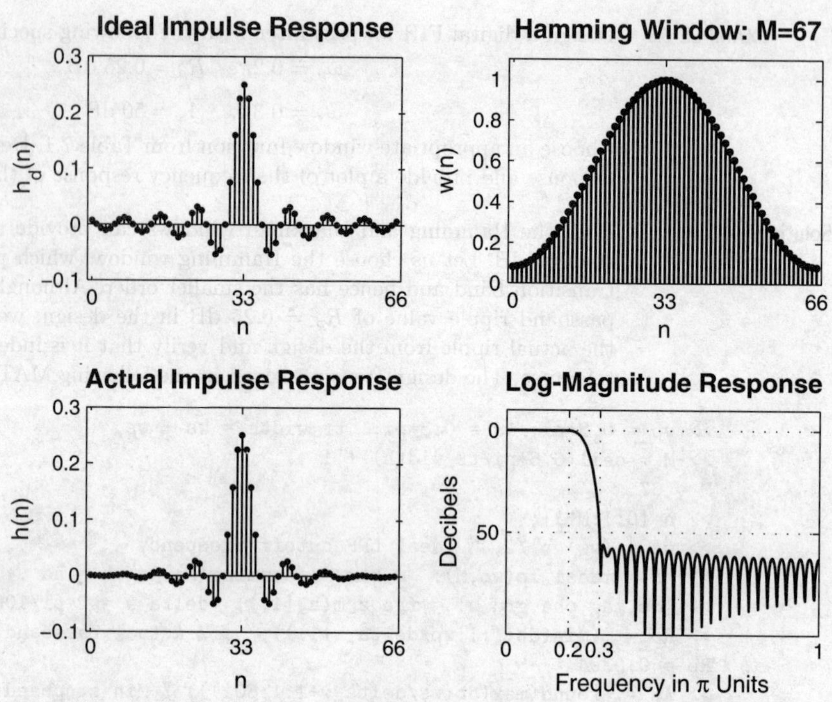

FIGURE 7.16   *Lowpass filter plots for Example 7.8*

Note that the Kaiser window parameters are $M = 61$ and $\beta = 4.5513$ and that the actual stopband attenuation is 52 dB. The time- and the frequency-domain plots are shown in Figure 7.17.   □

□   **EXAMPLE 7.10**   Let us design the following digital bandpass filter.

$$\text{lower stopband edge: } \omega_{1s} = 0.2\pi, \quad A_s = 60 \text{ dB}$$
$$\text{lower passband edge: } \omega_{1p} = 0.35\pi, \quad R_p = 1 \text{ dB}$$
$$\text{upper passband edge: } \omega_{2p} = 0.65\pi \quad R_p = 1 \text{ dB}$$
$$\text{upper stopband edge: } \omega_{2s} = 0.8\pi \quad A_s = 60 \text{ dB}$$

These quantities are shown in Figure 7.18.

Solution   There are two transition bands, namely, $\Delta\omega_1 \triangleq \omega_{1p} - \omega_{1s}$ and $\Delta\omega_2 \triangleq \omega_{2s} - \omega_{2p}$. These two bandwidths must be the same in the window design; that is, there is no independent control over $\Delta\omega_1$ and $\Delta\omega_2$. Hence $\Delta\omega_1 = \Delta\omega_2 = \Delta\omega$. For this design, we can use either the Kaiser window or the Blackman window. Let us

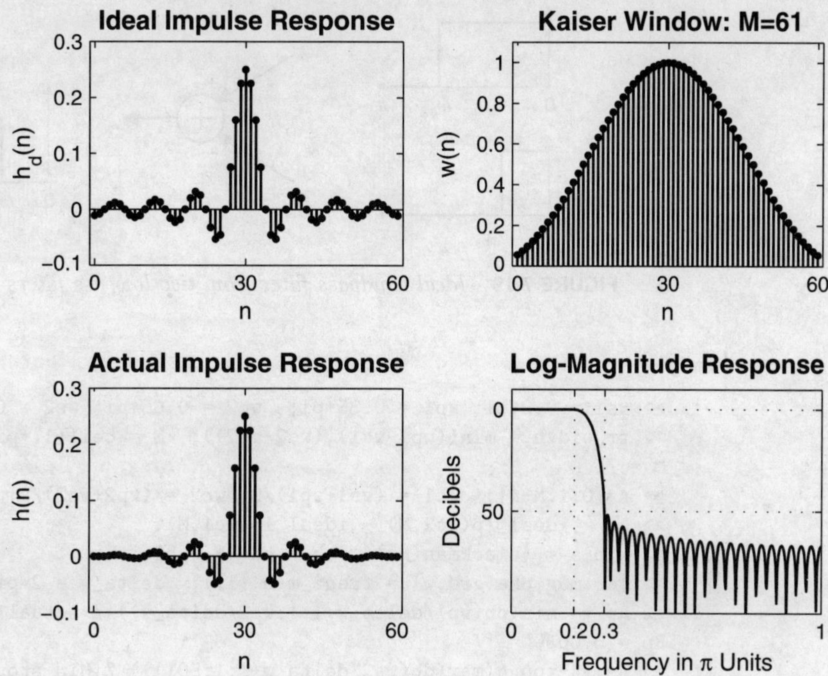

FIGURE 7.17 *Lowpass filter plots for Example 7.9*

use the Blackman Window. We will also need the ideal bandpass filter impulse response $h_d(n)$. Note that this impulse response can be obtained from two ideal lowpass magnitude responses, provided they have the same phase response. This is shown in Figure 7.19. Therefore, the MATLAB routine `ideal_lp(wc,M)` is sufficient to determine the impulse response of an ideal bandpass filter. The design steps are given in the following MATLAB script.

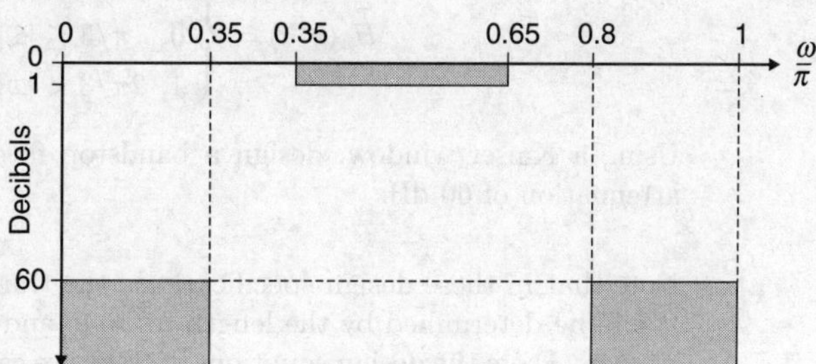

FIGURE 7.18 *Bandpass filter specifications in Example 7.10*

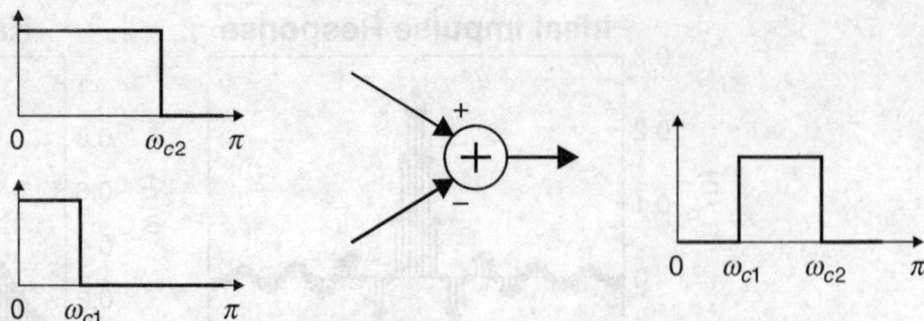

FIGURE 7.19 *Ideal bandpass filter from two lowpass filters*

```
>> ws1 = 0.2*pi; wp1 = 0.35*pi;  wp2 = 0.65*pi; ws2 = 0.8*pi;  As = 60;
>> tr_width = min((wp1-ws1),(ws2-wp2));  M = ceil(11*pi/tr_width) + 1
M = 75
>> n=[0:1:M-1];  wc1 = (ws1+wp1)/2; wc2 = (wp2+ws2)/2;
>> hd = ideal_lp(wc2,M) - ideal_lp(wc1,M);
>> w_bla = (blackman(M))';  h = hd .* w_bla;
>> [db,mag,pha,grd,w] = freqz_m(h,[1]);  delta_w = 2*pi/1000;
>> Rp = -min(db(wp1/delta_w+1:1:wp2/delta_w)) % Actual passband ripple
Rp = 0.0030
>> As = -round(max(db(ws2/delta_w+1:1:501))) % Min stopband attenuation
As = 75
% plotting commands follow
```

Note that the Blackman window length is $M = 75$ and that the actual stopband attenuation is 75 dB. The time- and the frequency-domain plots are shown in Figure 7.20. □

□ **EXAMPLE 7.11** The frequency response of an ideal bandstop filter is given by

$$H_e(e^{j\omega}) = \begin{cases} 1, & 0 \leq |\omega| < \pi/3 \\ 0, & \pi/3 \leq |\omega| \leq 2\pi/3 \\ 1, & 2\pi/3 < |\omega| \leq \pi \end{cases}$$

Using a Kaiser window, design a bandstop filter of length 45 with stopband attenuation of 60 dB.

Solution Note that in these design specifications, the transition bandwidth is not given. It will be determined by the length $M = 45$ and the parameter β of the Kaiser window. From the design equations (7.30b), we can determine β from A_s; that is,

$$\beta = 0.1102 \times (A_s - 8.7)$$

The ideal bandstop impulse response can also be determined from the ideal lowpass impulse response using a method similar to Figure 7.19. We can now

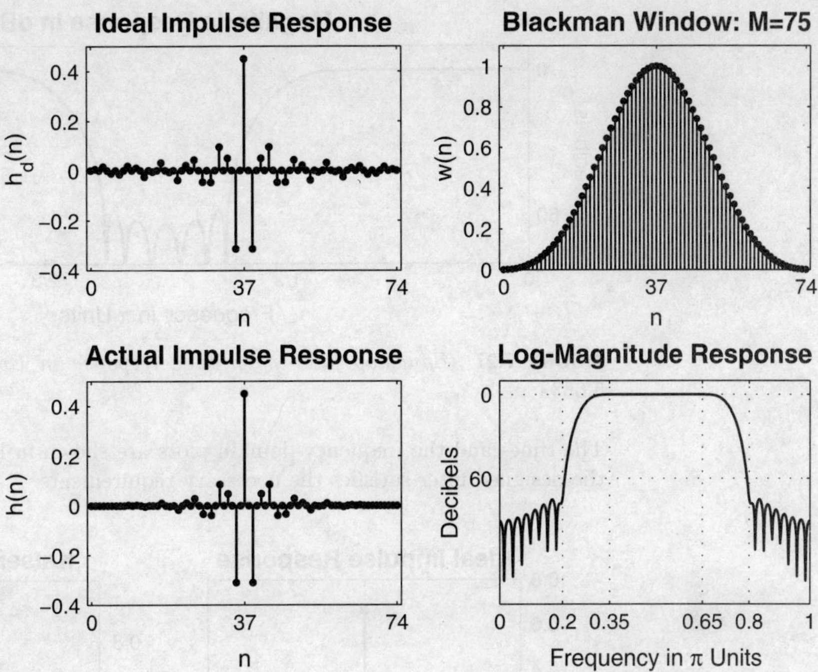

FIGURE 7.20 *Bandpass filter plots in Example 7.10*

implement the Kaiser window design and check for the minimum stopband attenuation. This is shown in the following MATLAB script.

```
>> M = 45; As = 60; n=[0:1:M-1];
>> beta = 0.1102*(As-8.7)
beta = 5.6533
>> w_kai = (kaiser(M,beta))';  wc1 = pi/3; wc2 = 2*pi/3;
>> hd = ideal_lp(wc1,M) + ideal_lp(pi,M) - ideal_lp(wc2,M);
>> h = hd .* w_kai;  [db,mag,pha,grd,w] = freqz_m(h,[1]);
```

The β parameter is equal to 5.6533, and, from the magnitude plot in Figure 7.21, we observe that the minimum stopband attenuation is smaller than 60 dB. Clearly, we have to increase β to increase the attenuation to 60 dB. The required value was found to be $\beta = 5.9533$.

```
>> M = 45; As = 60; n=[0:1:M-1];
>> beta = 0.1102*(As-8.7)+0.3
beta = 5.9533
>> w_kai = (kaiser(M,beta))';  wc1 = pi/3; wc2 = 2*pi/3;
>> hd = ideal_lp(wc1,M) + ideal_lp(pi,M) - ideal_lp(wc2,M);
>> h = hd .* w_kai;  [db,mag,pha,grd,w] = freqz_m(h,[1]);
>> plotting commands follow
```

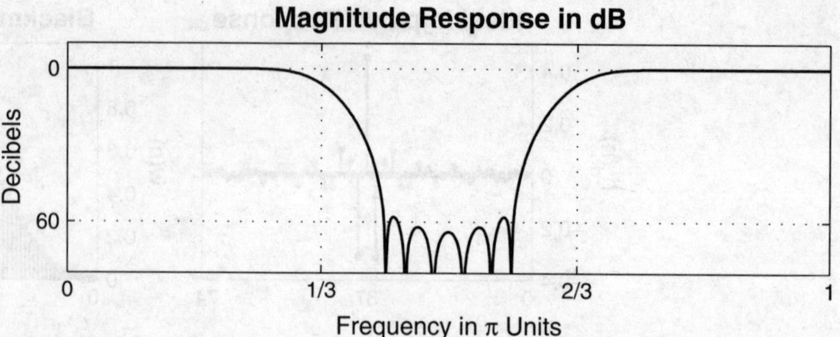

FIGURE 7.21 *Bandstop filter magnitude response in Example 7.11 for* $\beta =$ 5.6533

The time- and the frequency-domain plots are shown in Figure 7.22, in which the designed filter satisfies the necessary requirements. □

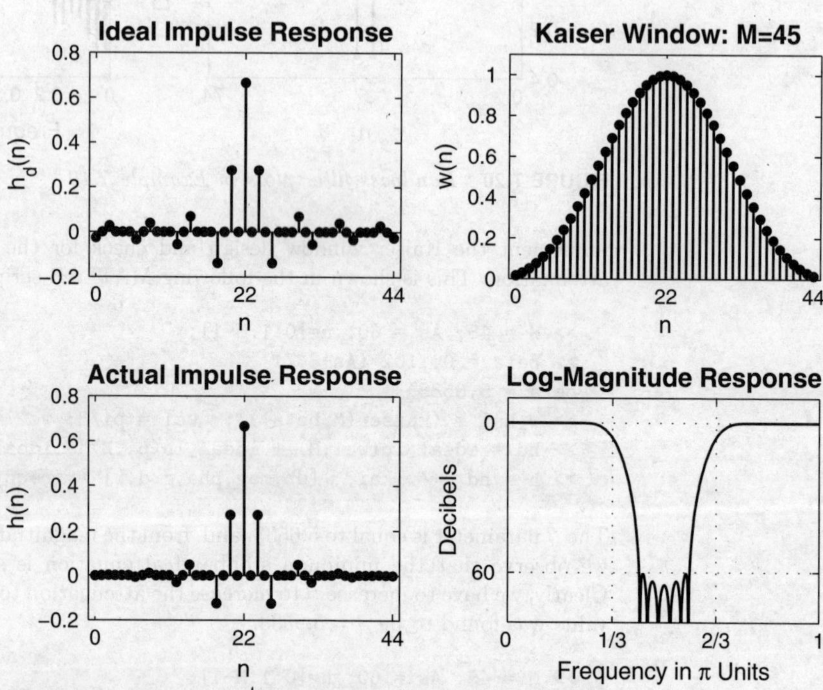

FIGURE 7.22 *Bandstop filter plots in Example 7.11:* $\beta = 5.9533$

□ **EXAMPLE 7.12** The frequency response of an ideal digital differentiator is given by

$$H_d(e^{j\omega}) = \begin{cases} j\omega, & 0 < \omega \le \pi \\ -j\omega, & -\pi < \omega < 0 \end{cases} \tag{7.31}$$

Using a Hamming window of length 21, design a digital FIR differentiator. Plot the time- and the frequency-domain responses.

Solution The ideal impulse response of a digital differentiator with linear phase is given by

$$h_d(n) = \mathcal{F}\left[H_d(e^{j\omega})e^{-j\alpha\omega}\right] = \frac{1}{2\pi}\int_{-\pi}^{\pi} H_d(e^{j\omega})e^{-j\alpha\omega}e^{j\omega n}d\omega$$

$$= \frac{1}{2\pi}\int_{-\pi}^{0}(-j\omega)\,e^{-j\alpha\omega}e^{j\omega n}d\omega + \frac{1}{2\pi}\int_{0}^{\pi}(j\omega)\,e^{-j\alpha\omega}e^{j\omega n}d\omega$$

$$= \begin{cases} \dfrac{\cos\pi(n-\alpha)}{(n-\alpha)}, & n \neq \alpha \\[2mm] 0, & n = \alpha \end{cases}$$

This impulse response can be implemented in MATLAB, along with the Hamming window to design the required differentiator. Note that if M is an even number, then $\alpha = (M-1)/2$ is not an integer and $h_d(n)$ will be zero for all n. Hence M must be an odd number, and this will be a Type-3 linear-phase FIR filter. However, the filter will not be a full-band differentiator, since $H_r(\pi) = 0$ for Type-3 filters.

```
>> M = 21; alpha = (M-1)/2;  n = 0:M-1;
>> hd = (cos(pi*(n-alpha)))./(n-alpha); hd(alpha+1)=0;
>> w_ham = (hamming(M))';  h = hd .* w_ham;  [Hr,w,P,L] = Hr_Type3(h);
% plotting commands follow
```

The plots are shown in Figure 7.23. $\qquad\square$

$\square$ **EXAMPLE 7.13** Design a length-25 digital Hilbert transformer using a Hann window.

Solution The ideal frequency response of a linear-phase Hilbert transformer is given by

$$H_d(e^{j\omega}) = \begin{cases} -je^{-j\alpha\omega}, & 0 < \omega < \pi \\ +je^{-j\alpha\omega}, & -\pi < \omega < 0 \end{cases} \tag{7.32}$$

After inverse transformation, the ideal impulse response is given by

$$h_d(n) = \begin{cases} \dfrac{2}{\pi}\dfrac{\sin^2\pi(n-\alpha)/2}{n-\alpha}, & n \neq \alpha \\[2mm] 0, & n = \alpha \end{cases}$$

which can be easily implemented in MATLAB. Note that since $M = 25$, the designed filter is of Type-3.

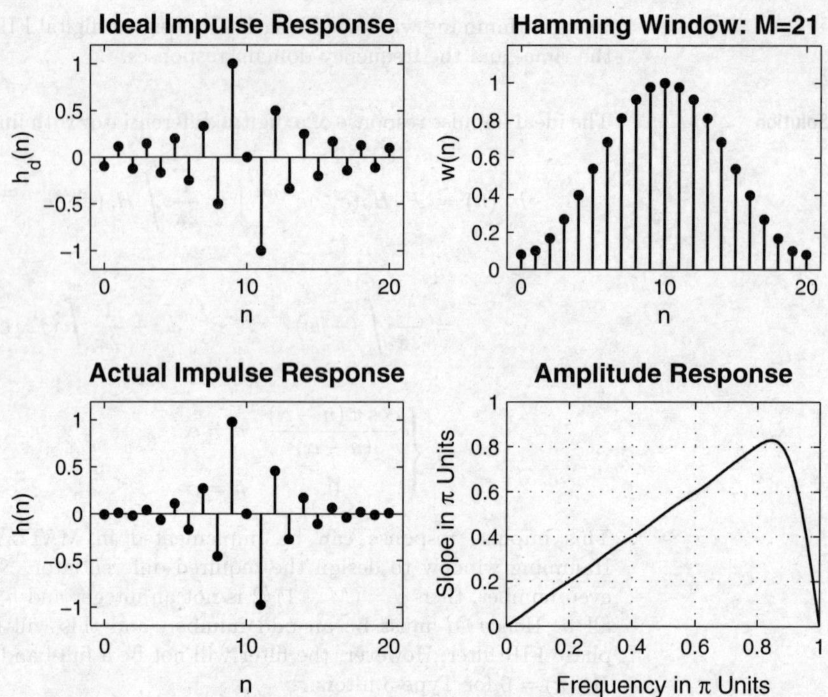

FIGURE 7.23 *FIR differentiator design in Example 7.12*

MATLAB script:

```
>> M = 25; alpha = (M-1)/2;   n = 0:M-1;
>> hd = (2/pi)*((sin((pi/2)*(n-alpha)).^2)./(n-alpha)); hd(alpha+1)=0;
>> w_han = (hann(M))';   h = hd .* w_han;   [Hr,w,P,L] = Hr_Type3(h);
>> plotting commands follow
```

The plots are shown in Figure 7.24. Observe that the amplitude response is
plotted over $-\pi \leq \omega \leq \pi$.   □

The SP toolbox provides a function called `fir1`, which designs conventional lowpass, highpass, and other multiband FIR filters using the
window technique. This function's syntax has several forms, including:

- `h = fir1(N,wc)` designs an Nth-order $(N = M - 1)$ lowpass FIR
  filter and returns the impulse response in vector `h`. By default this
  is a Hamming-window based, linear-phase design with a normalized
  cutoff frequency in `wc` that is a number between 0 and 1, where 1
  corresponds to π rad/sample. If `wc` is a two-element vector, that is,

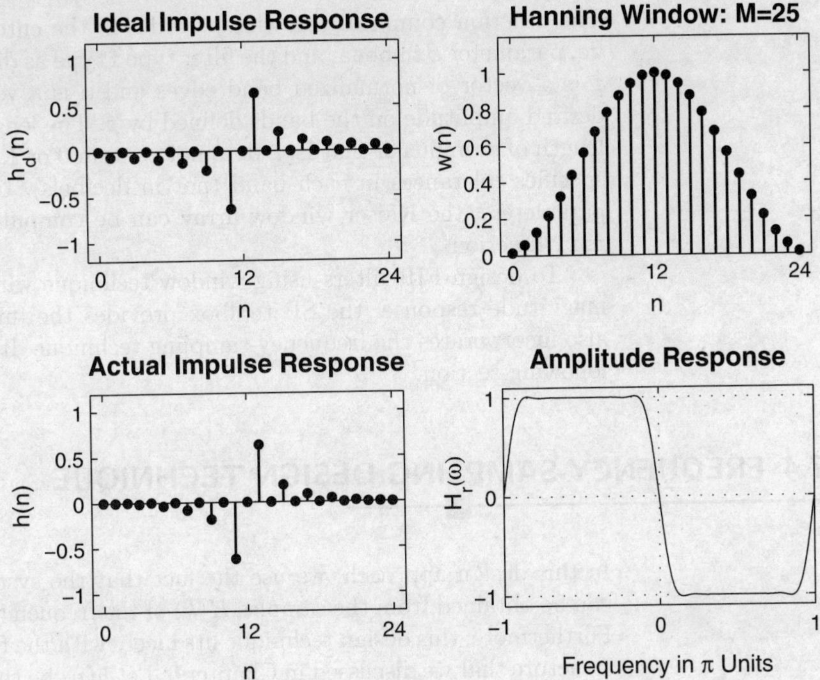

FIGURE 7.24 *FIR Hilbert transformer design in Example 7.13*

`wc = [wc1 wc2]`, then `fir1` returns a bandpass filter with passband cutoffs `wc1` and `wc2`. If `wc` is a multi-element (more than two) vector, then `fir1` returns a multiband filter with cutoffs given in `wc`.

- `h = fir1(N,wc,'ftype')` specifies a filter type, where `'ftype'` is:

  a. `'high'` for a highpass filter with cutoff frequency Wn.
  b. `'stop'` for a bandstop filter, if `Wc = [wc1 wc2]`. The stopband frequency range is specified by this interval.
  c. `'DC-1'` to make the first band of a multiband filter a passband.
  d. `'DC-0'` to make the first band of a multiband filter a stopband.

- `h = fir1(N,wc,'ftype',window)` or `h = fir1(N,wc,window)` uses the vector `window` of length N+1 obtained from one of the specified MATLAB window functions. The default window function used is the Hamming window.

To design FIR filters using the Kaiser window, the SP toolbox provides the function `kaiserord`, which estimates window parameters that can be used in the `fir1` function. The basic syntax is

```
[N,wc,beta,ftype] = kaiserord(f,m,ripple);
```

The function computes the window order N, the cutoff frequency vector wc, parameter β in beta, and the filter type ftype as discussed. The vector f is a vector of normalized band edges and m is a vector specifying the desired amplitude on the bands defined by f. The length of f is twice the length of m, minus 2; that is, f does not contain 0 or 1. The vector ripple specifies tolerances in each band (not in decibels). Using the estimated parameters, the Kaiser window array can be computed and used in the fir1 function.

To design FIR filters using window technique with arbitrary-shaped magnitude response, the SP toolbox provides the function fir2, which also incorporates the frequency-sampling technique. It is explained in the following section.

7.4 FREQUENCY-SAMPLING DESIGN TECHNIQUE

In this design approach, we use the fact that the system function $H(z)$ can be obtained from the samples $H(k)$ of the frequency response $H(e^{j\omega})$. Furthermore, this design technique fits nicely with the frequency-sampling structure that we discussed in Chapter 6. Let $h(n)$ be the impulse response of an M-point FIR filter, let $H(k)$ be its M-point DFT, and let $H(z)$ be its system function. Then from (6.12), we have

$$H(z) = \sum_{n=0}^{M-1} h(n) z^{-n} = \frac{1 - z^{-M}}{M} \sum_{k=0}^{M-1} \frac{H(k)}{1 - z^{-1}e^{j2\pi k/M}} \tag{7.33}$$

and

$$H(e^{j\omega}) = \frac{1 - e^{-j\omega M}}{M} \sum_{k=0}^{M-1} \frac{H(k)}{1 - e^{-j\omega}e^{j2\pi k/M}} \tag{7.34}$$

with

$$H(k) = H\left(e^{j2\pi k/M}\right) = \begin{cases} H(0), & k = 0 \\ H^*(M-k), & k = 1, \ldots, M-1 \end{cases}$$

For a linear-phase FIR filter, we have

$$h(n) = \pm h(M-1-n), \quad n = 0, 1, \ldots, M-1$$

where the positive sign is for the Type-1 and Type-2 linear-phase filters, while the negative sign is for the Type-3 and Type-4 linear-phase filters. Then $H(k)$ is given by

$$H(k) = H_r\left(\frac{2\pi k}{M}\right) e^{j\angle H(k)} \tag{7.35}$$

where

$$H_r\left(\frac{2\pi k}{M}\right) = \begin{cases} H_r\left(0\right), & k = 0 \\ H_r\left(\frac{2\pi(M-k)}{M}\right), & k = 1,\ldots,M-1 \end{cases} \tag{7.36}$$

and

$$\angle H\left(k\right) = \begin{cases} -\left(\dfrac{M-1}{2}\right)\left(\dfrac{2\pi k}{M}\right), & k = 0,\ldots,\left\lfloor\dfrac{M-1}{2}\right\rfloor \\ +\left(\dfrac{M-1}{2}\right)\dfrac{2\pi}{M}\left(M-k\right), & k = \left\lfloor\dfrac{M-1}{2}\right\rfloor+1,\ldots,M-1 \end{cases} \quad \text{(Type-1 \& -2)} \tag{7.37}$$

or

$$\angle H\left(k\right) = \begin{cases} \left(\pm\dfrac{\pi}{2}\right)-\left(\dfrac{M-1}{2}\right)\left(\dfrac{2\pi k}{M}\right), & k = 0,\ldots,\left\lfloor\dfrac{M-1}{2}\right\rfloor \\ -\left(\pm\dfrac{\pi}{2}\right)+\left(\dfrac{M-1}{2}\right)\dfrac{2\pi}{M}\left(M-k\right), & \text{(Type-3 \& -4)} \\ \\ k = \left\lfloor\dfrac{M-1}{2}\right\rfloor+1,\ldots,M-1 \end{cases} \tag{7.38}$$

Finally, we have

$$h(n) = \text{IDFT}\left[H(k)\right] \tag{7.39}$$

Note that several textbooks (e.g., [71, 79, 83]) provide explicit formulas to compute $h(n)$, given $H(k)$. We will use MATLAB's `ifft` function to compute $h(n)$ from (7.39).

Basic idea   Given an ideal filter $H_d(e^{j\omega})$, choose the filter length M and then sample $H_d(e^{j\omega})$ at M equispaced frequencies between 0 and 2π. The actual response $H(e^{j\omega})$ is the interpolation of the samples $H(k)$ given by (7.34). This is shown in Figure 7.25. The impulse response is given by (7.39). Similar steps apply to other frequency-selective filters. Furthermore, this idea can also be extended for approximating arbitrary frequency-domain specifications.

From Figure 7.25, we observe the following:

1. The approximation error—that is, the difference between the ideal and the actual response—is zero at the sampled frequencies.
2. The approximation error at all other frequencies depends on the shape of the ideal response; that is, the sharper the ideal response, the larger the approximation error.
3. The error is larger near the band edges and smaller within the band.

There are two design approaches. In the first approach, we use the basic idea literally and provide no constraints on the approximation error;

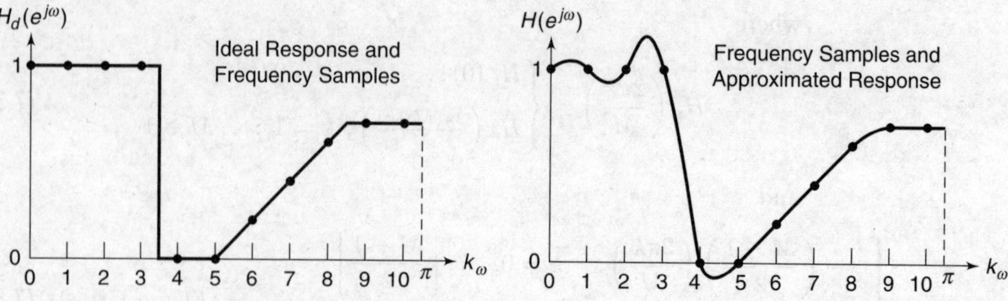

FIGURE 7.25 *Pictorial description of frequency-sampling technique*

that is, we accept whatever error we get from the design. This approach is called a *naive design* method. In the second approach, we try to minimize error in the stopband by varying values of the transition band samples. It results in a much better design called an *optimum design* method.

7.4.1 NAIVE DESIGN METHOD

In this method, we set $H(k) = H_d(e^{j2\pi k/M})$, $k = 0, \ldots, M-1$, and use (7.35) through (7.39) to obtain the impulse response $h(n)$.

□ **EXAMPLE 7.14**   Consider the lowpass filter specifications from Example 7.8:

$$\omega_p = 0.2\pi, \ R_p = 0.25 \text{ dB}$$

$$\omega_s = 0.3\pi, \ A_s = 50 \text{ dB}$$

Design an FIR filter using the frequency-sampling approach.

Solution   Let us choose $M = 20$ so that we have a frequency sample at ω_p, that is, at $k = 2$,

$$\omega_p = 0.2\pi = \frac{2\pi}{20}2$$

and the next sample at ω_s, that is, at $k = 3$,

$$\omega_s = 0.3\pi = \frac{2\pi}{20}3$$

Thus we have three samples in the passband $[0 \leq \omega \leq \omega_p]$ and seven samples in the stopband $[\omega_s \leq \omega \leq \pi]$. From (7.36), we have

$$H_r(k) = [1, 1, 1, \underbrace{0, \ldots, 0}_{15 \text{ zeros}}, 1, 1]$$

Since $M = 20$, $\alpha = \frac{20-1}{2} = 9.5$ and since this is a Type-2 linear-phase filter, from (7.37) we have

$$\angle H(k) = \begin{cases} -9.5\dfrac{2\pi}{20}k = -0.95\pi k, & 0 \le k \le 9 \\ +0.95\pi(20-k), & 10 \le k \le 19 \end{cases}$$

Now, from (7.35), we assemble $H(k)$ and from (7.39) determine the impulse response $h(n)$. The MATLAB script follows.

```
>> M = 20; alpha = (M-1)/2; l = 0:M-1; wl = (2*pi/M)*l;
>> Hrs = [1,1,1,zeros(1,15),1,1]; %Ideal amp res sampled
>> Hdr = [1,1,0,0]; wdl = [0,0.25,0.25,1]; %Ideal amp res for plotting
>> k1 = 0:floor((M-1)/2); k2 = floor((M-1)/2)+1:M-1;
>> angH = [-alpha*(2*pi)/M*k1, alpha*(2*pi)/M*(M-k2)];
>> H = Hrs.*exp(j*angH);  h = real(ifft(H,M));
>> [db,mag,pha,grd,w] = freqz_m(h,1);  [Hr,ww,a,L] = Hr_Type2(h);
>> plotting commands follow
```

The time- and the frequency-domain plots are shown in Figure 7.26. Observe that the minimum stopband attenuation is about 16 dB, which is clearly unacceptable. If we increase M, then there will be samples in the transition band, for which we do not precisely know the frequency response. Therefore, the naive design method is seldom used in practice. $\square$

7.4.2 OPTIMUM DESIGN METHOD

To obtain more attenuation, we will have to increase M and make the transition band samples free samples—that is, we vary their values to obtain the largest attenuation for the given M and the transition width. This problem is known as an optimization problem, and it is solved using linear programming techniques. We demonstrate the effect of transition band sample variation on the design using the following example.

$\square$ **EXAMPLE 7.15**   Using the optimum design method, design a better lowpass filter of Example 7.14.

Solution   Let us choose $M = 40$ so that we have one sample in the transition band $0.2\pi < \omega < 0.3\pi$. Since $\omega_1 \triangleq 2\pi/40$, the transition band samples are at $k = 5$ and at $k = 40 - 5 = 35$. Let us denote the value of these samples by T_1, $0 < T_1 < 1$; then the sampled amplitude response is

$$H_r(k) = [1,1,1,1,1,T_1,\underbrace{0,\ldots,0}_{29 \text{ zeros}},T_1,1,1,1,1]$$

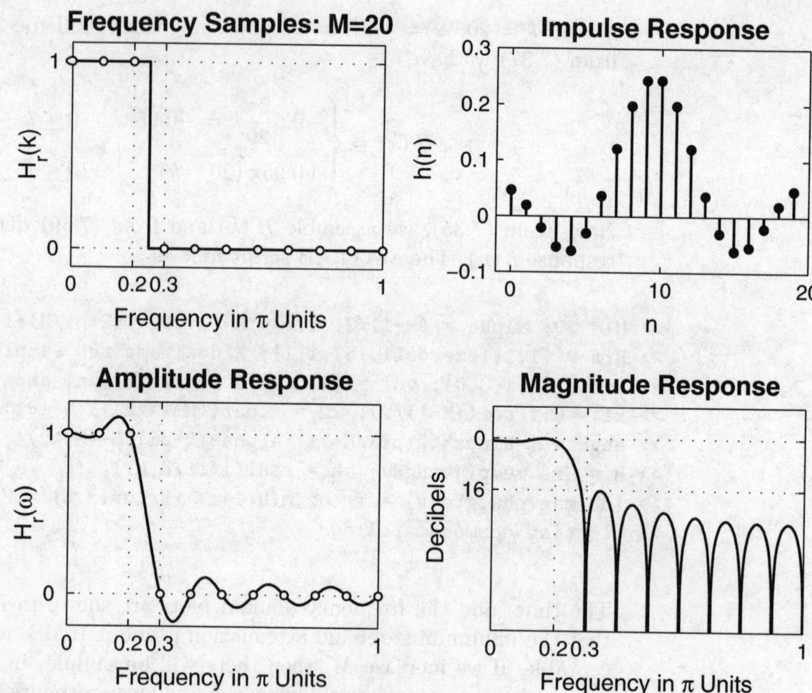

FIGURE 7.26 *Naive frequency sampling design method in Example 7.14*

Since $\alpha = \frac{40-1}{2} = 19.5$, the samples of the phase response are

$$\angle H(k) = \begin{cases} -19.5\dfrac{2\pi}{40}k = -0.975\pi k, & 0 \le k \le 19 \\[2mm] +0.975\pi(40-k), & 20 \le k \le 39 \end{cases}$$

Now we can vary T_1 to get the best minimum stopband attenuation. This will result in the widening of the transition width. We first see what happens when $T_1 = 0.5$ using the following MATLAB script.

```
% T1 = 0.5
>> M = 40; alpha = (M-1)/2;
>> Hrs = [ones(1,5),0.5,zeros(1,29),0.5,ones(1,4)];
>> k1 = 0:floor((M-1)/2); k2 = floor((M-1)/2)+1:M-1;
>> angH = [-alpha*(2*pi)/M*k1, alpha*(2*pi)/M*(M-k2)];
>> H = Hrs.*exp(j*angH);
>> h = real(ifft(H,M));
```

From the plots of this design in Figure 7.27, we observe that the minimum stopband attenuation is now 30 dB, which is better than the naive design attenuation but is still not at the acceptable level of 50 dB. The best value for T_1

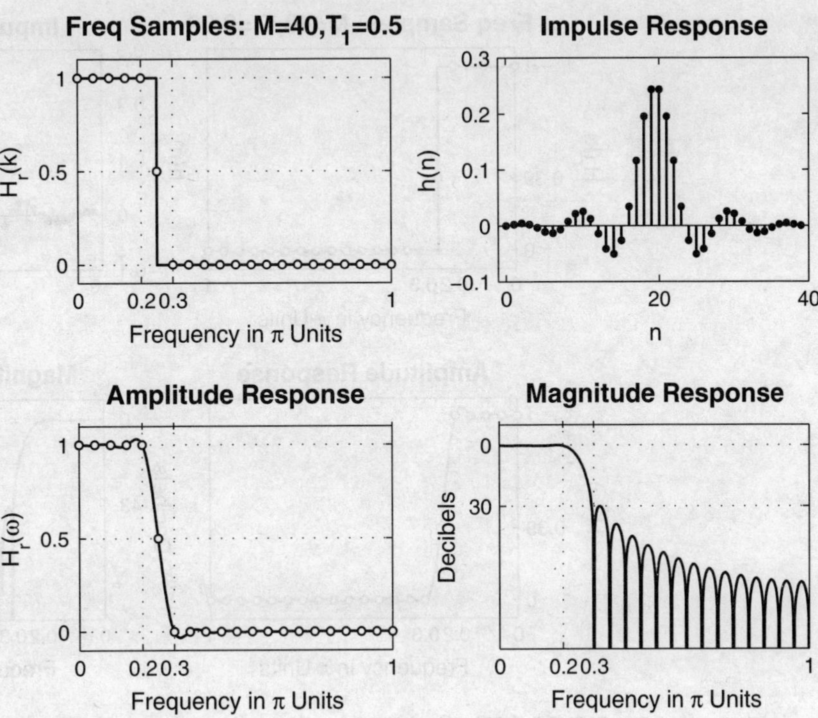

FIGURE 7.27 *Optimum frequency design method: $T_1 = 0.5$ in Example 7.15*

was obtained by varying it manually (although more efficient linear programming techniques are available, these were not used in this case), and the near optimum solution was found at $T_1 = 0.39$. The resulting filter is obtained using the following MATLAB script.

```
% T1 = 0.39
>> M = 40; alpha = (M-1)/2;
>> Hrs = [ones(1,5),0.39,zeros(1,29),0.39,ones(1,4)];
>> k1 = 0:floor((M-1)/2); k2 = floor((M-1)/2)+1:M-1;
>> angH = [-alpha*(2*pi)/M*k1, alpha*(2*pi)/M*(M-k2)];
>> H = Hrs.*exp(j*angH);  h = real(ifft(H,M));
```

From the plots in Figure 7.28, we observe that the optimum stopband attenuation is 43 dB. It is obvious that to further increase the attenuation, we will have to vary more than one sample in the transition band. □

Clearly, this method is superior in that by varying one sample we can get a much better design. In practice, the transition bandwidth is

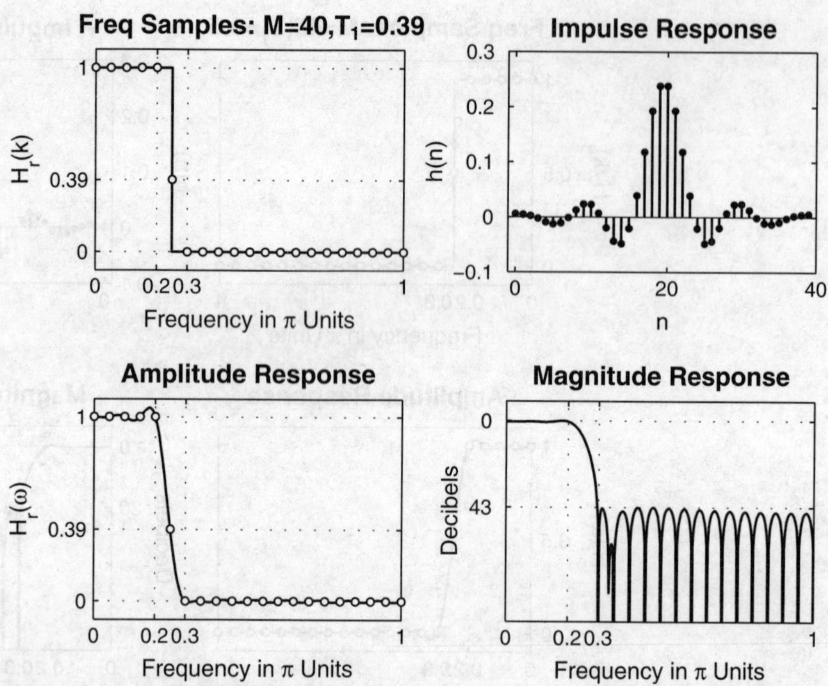

FIGURE 7.28 *Optimum frequency design method:* $T_1 = 0.39$ *in Example 7.15*

generally small, containing either one or two samples. Hence we need to optimize at most two samples to obtain the largest minimum stopband attenuation. This is also equivalent to minimizing the maximum side-lobe magnitudes in the absolute sense. Hence this optimization problem is also called a *minimax* problem. This problem is solved by Rabiner et al. [83], and the solution is available in the form of tables of transition values. A selected number of tables are also available in [79, Appendix B]. This problem can also be solved in MATLAB, but it would require the use of the Optimization toolbox. We will consider a more general version of this problem in the next section. We now illustrate the use of these tables in the following examples.

□ **EXAMPLE 7.16** Let us revisit our lowpass filter design in Example 7.14. We will solve it using two samples in the transition band so that we can get a better stopband attenuation.

Solution Let us choose $M = 60$ so that there are two samples in the transition band. Let the values of these transition band samples be T_1 and T_2. Then $H_r(\omega)$ is given by

$$H(\omega) = [\underbrace{1, \ldots, 1}_{7 \text{ ones}}, T_1, T_2, \underbrace{0, \ldots, 0}_{43 \text{ zeros}}, T_2, T_1, \underbrace{1, \ldots, 1}_{6 \text{ ones}}]$$

From tables in [79, Appendix B], $T_1 = 0.5925$ and $T_2 = 0.1099$. Using these values, we use MATLAB to compute $h(n)$.

```
>> M = 60; alpha = (M-1)/2; l = 0:M-1; wl = (2*pi/M)*l;
>> Hrs = [ones(1,7),0.5925,0.1099,zeros(1,43),0.1099,0.5925,ones(1,6)];
>> Hdr = [1,1,0,0]; wdl = [0,0.2,0.3,1];
>> k1 = 0:floor((M-1)/2); k2 = floor((M-1)/2)+1:M-1;
>> angH = [-alpha*(2*pi)/M*k1, alpha*(2*pi)/M*(M-k2)];
>> H = Hrs.*exp(j*angH);  h = real(ifft(H,M));
>> [db,mag,pha,grd,w] = freqz_m(h,1);   [Hr,ww,a,L] = Hr_Type2(h);
```

The time- and the frequency-domain plots are shown in Figure 7.29. The minimum stopband attenuation is now at 63 dB, which is acceptable. $\qquad\square$

$\square$ **EXAMPLE 7.17**   Design the bandpass filter of Example 7.10 using the frequency sampling technique. The design specifications are as follows.

$$\text{lower stopband edge: } \omega_{1s} = 0.2\pi, \quad A_s = 60 \text{ dB}$$

$$\text{lower passband edge: } \omega_{1p} = 0.35\pi, \quad R_p = 1 \text{ dB}$$

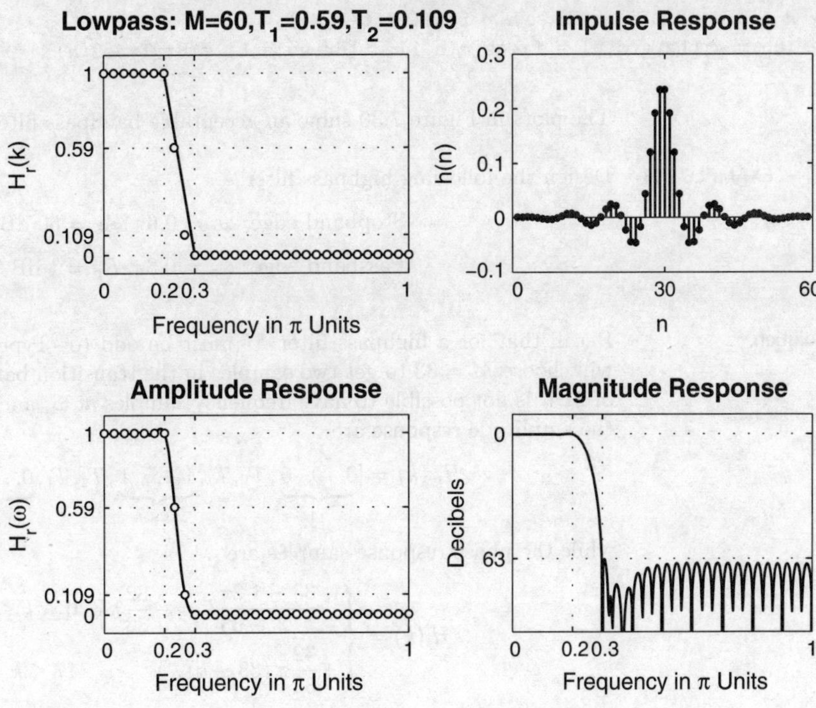

FIGURE 7.29   *Lowpass filter design plots in Example 7.16*

$$\text{upper passband edge: } \omega_{2p} = 0.65\pi \quad R_p = 1 \text{ dB}$$

$$\text{upper stopband edge: } \omega_{2s} = 0.8\pi \quad A_s = 60 \text{ dB}$$

Solution Let us choose $M = 40$ so that we have two samples in the transition band. Let the frequency samples in the lower transition band be T_1 and T_2. Then the samples of the amplitude response are

$$H_r\left(\omega\right) = [\underbrace{0,\ldots,0}_{5},T_1,T_2,\underbrace{1,\ldots,1}_{7},T_2,T_1,\underbrace{0,\ldots,0}_{9},T_1,T_2,\underbrace{1,\ldots,1}_{7},T_2,T_1,\underbrace{0,\ldots,0}_{4}]$$

The optimum values of T_1 and T_2 for $M = 40$ and seven samples in the passband [79, Appendix B] are

$$T_1 = 0.109021, \quad T_2 = 0.59417456$$

MATLAB script:

```
>> M = 40; alpha = (M-1)/2; l = 0:M-1; wl = (2*pi/M)*l;
>> T1 = 0.109021; T2 = 0.59417456;
>> Hrs=[zeros(1,5),T1,T2,ones(1,7),T2,T1,zeros(1,9),T1,T2,ones(1,7),T2,T1,zeros(1,4)];
>> Hdr = [0,0,1,1,0,0]; wdl = [0,0.2,0.35,0.65,0.8,1];
>> k1 = 0:floor((M-1)/2); k2 = floor((M-1)/2)+1:M-1;
>> angH = [-alpha*(2*pi)/M*k1, alpha*(2*pi)/M*(M-k2)];
>> H = Hrs.*exp(j*angH);  h = real(ifft(H,M));
>> [db,mag,pha,grd,w] = freqz_m(h,1);   [Hr,ww,a,L] = Hr_Type2(h);
```

The plots in Figure 7.30 show an acceptable bandpass filter design. □

□ **EXAMPLE 7.18** Design the following highpass filter.

$$\text{Stopband edge: } \omega_s = 0.6\pi \quad A_s = 50 \text{ dB}$$

$$\text{Passband edge: } \omega_p = 0.8\pi \quad R_p = 1 \text{ dB}$$

Solution Recall that for a highpass filter M must be odd (or Type-1 filter). Hence we will choose $M = 33$ to get two samples in the transition band. With this choice of M it is not possible to have frequency samples at ω_s and ω_p. The samples of the amplitude response are

$$H_r\left(k\right) = [\underbrace{0,\ldots,0}_{11},T_1,T_2,\underbrace{1,\ldots,1}_{8},T_2,T_1,\underbrace{0,\ldots,0}_{10}]$$

while the phase response samples are

$$\angle H\left(k\right) = \begin{cases} -\dfrac{33-1}{2}\dfrac{2\pi}{33}k = -\dfrac{32}{33}\pi k, & 0 \le k \le 16 \\ +\dfrac{32}{33}\pi\left(33-k\right), & 17 \le k \le 32 \end{cases}$$

The optimum values of transition samples are $T_1 = 0.1095$ and $T_2 = 0.598$. Using these values, the MATLAB design is given in the following script.

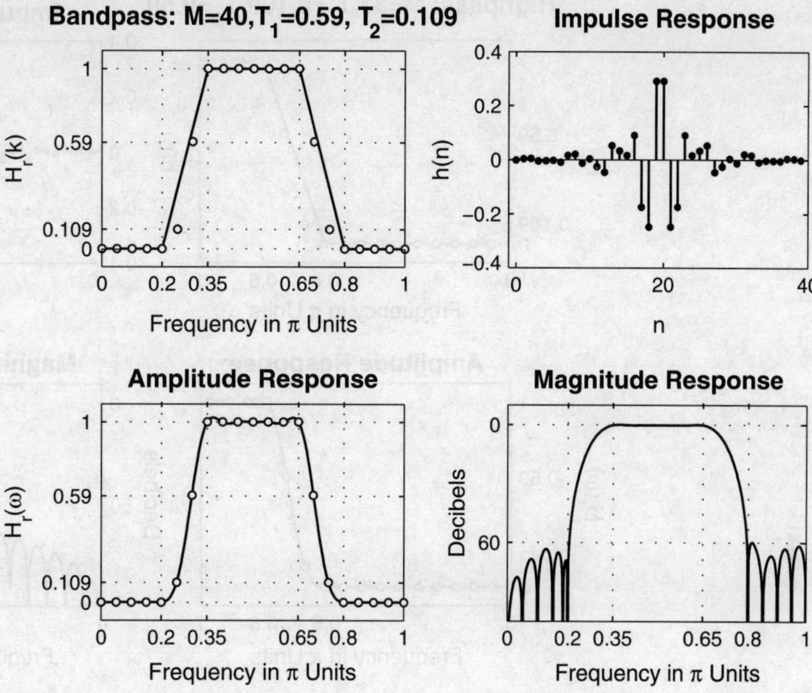

FIGURE 7.30   *Bandpass filter design plots in Example 7.17*

```
>> M = 33; alpha = (M-1)/2; l = 0:M-1; wl = (2*pi/M)*l;
>> T1 = 0.1095; T2 = 0.598;
>> Hrs = [zeros(1,11),T1,T2,ones(1,8),T2,T1,zeros(1,10)];
>> Hdr = [0,0,1,1]; wdl = [0,0.6,0.8,1];
>> k1 = 0:floor((M-1)/2); k2 = floor((M-1)/2)+1:M-1;
>> angH = [-alpha*(2*pi)/M*k1, alpha*(2*pi)/M*(M-k2)];
>> H = Hrs.*exp(j*angH);  h = real(ifft(H,M));
>> [db,mag,pha,grd,w] = freqz_m(h,1);  [Hr,ww,a,L] = Hr_Type1(h);
```

The time- and the frequency-domain plots of the design are shown in
Figure 7.31.   □

☐   **EXAMPLE 7.19**   Design a 33-point digital differentiator based on the ideal differentiator of (7.31)
given in Example 7.12.

Solution   From (7.31), the samples of the (imaginary-valued) amplitude response are
given by

$$
jH_r(k) = \begin{cases} +j\dfrac{2\pi}{M}k, & k = 0,\ldots,\left\lfloor\dfrac{M-1}{2}\right\rfloor \\[2ex] -j\dfrac{2\pi}{M}(M-k), & k = \left\lfloor\dfrac{M-1}{2}\right\rfloor+1,\ldots,M-1 \end{cases}
$$

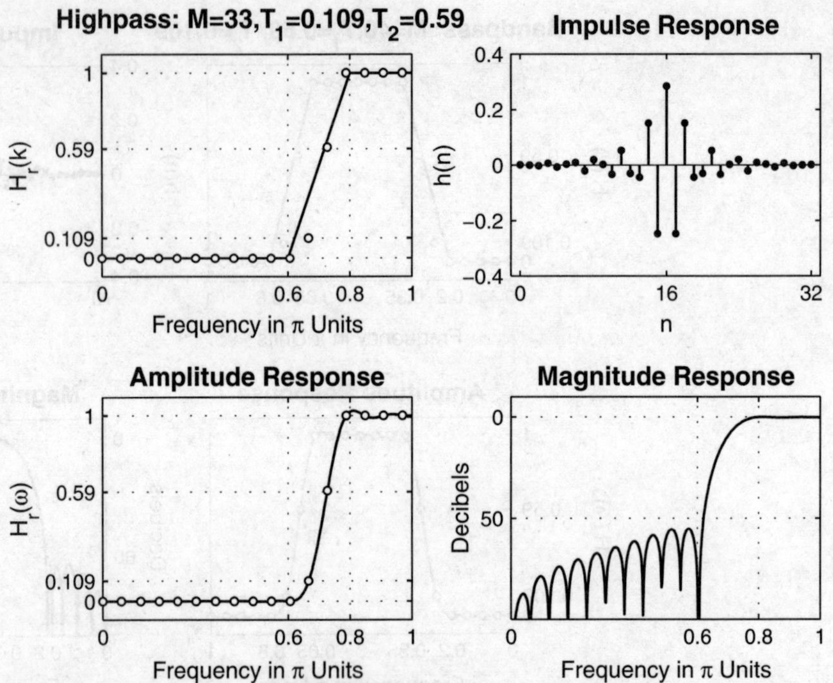

FIGURE 7.31   *Highpass filter design plots in Example 7.18*

and for linear phase the phase samples are

$$\angle H\left(k\right) = \begin{cases} -\dfrac{M-1}{2}\dfrac{2\pi}{M}k = -\dfrac{M-1}{M}\pi k, & k = 0,\ldots,\left\lfloor\dfrac{M-1}{2}\right\rfloor \\[2ex] +\dfrac{M-1}{M}\pi\left(M-k\right), & k = \left\lfloor\dfrac{M-1}{2}\right\rfloor + 1,\ldots,M-1 \end{cases}$$

Therefore,

$$H\left(k\right) = jH_r\left(k\right)e^{j\angle H(k)}, \quad 0 \le k \le M-1 \quad \text{and} \quad h\left(n\right) = \text{IDFT}\left[H\left(k\right)\right]$$

MATLAB script:

```
>> M = 33; alpha = (M-1)/2; Dw = 2*pi/M;  l = 0:M-1; wl = Dw*l;
>> k1 = 0:floor((M-1)/2); k2 = floor((M-1)/2)+1:M-1;
>> Hrs = [j*Dw*k1,-j*Dw*(M-k2)];
>> angH = [-alpha*Dw*k1, alpha*Dw*(M-k2)];
>> H = Hrs.*exp(j*angH);  h = real(ifft(H,M));  [Hr,ww,a,P]=Hr_Type3(h);
```

The time- and the frequency-domain plots are shown in Figure 7.32. We observe
that the differentiator is not a full-band differentiator.   □

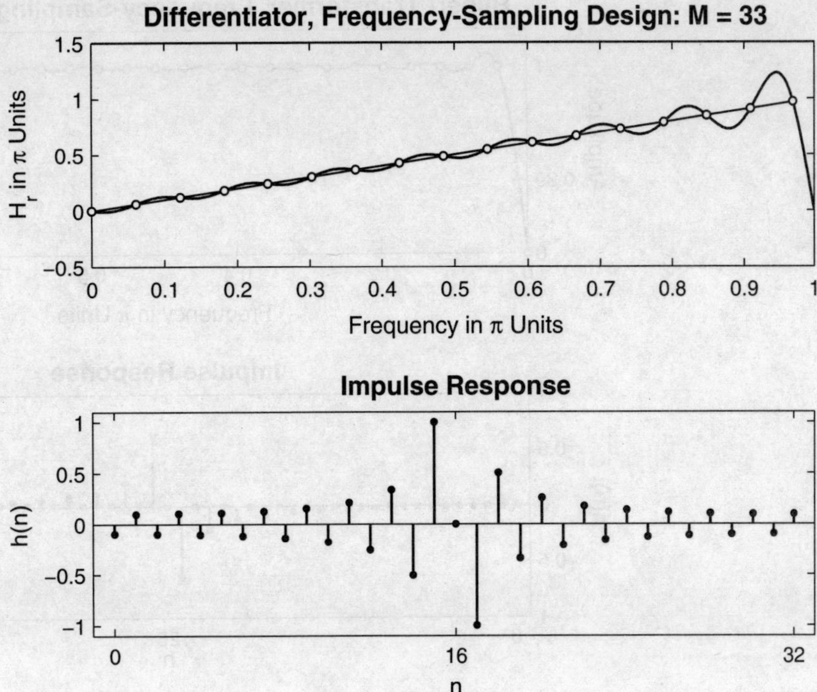

FIGURE 7.32 *Differentiator design plots in Example 7.19*

☐ **EXAMPLE 7.20**   Design a 51-point digital Hilbert transformer based on the ideal Hilbert transformer of (7.32).

Solution   From (7.32), the samples of the (imaginary-valued) amplitude response are given by

$$
jH_r\left(k\right) =
\begin{cases}
-j, \; k = 1, \ldots, \left\lfloor \dfrac{M-1}{2} \right\rfloor \\[2ex]
0, \quad k = 0 \\[2ex]
+j, \; k = \left\lfloor \dfrac{M-1}{2} \right\rfloor + 1, \ldots, M-1
\end{cases}
$$

Since this is a Type-3 linear-phase filter, the amplitude response will be zero at $\omega = \pi$. Hence to reduce the ripples, we should choose the two samples (in transition bands) near $\omega = \pi$, optimally between 0 and j. Using our previous experience, we could select this value as $0.39j$. The samples of the phase response are selected similar to those in Example 7.19.

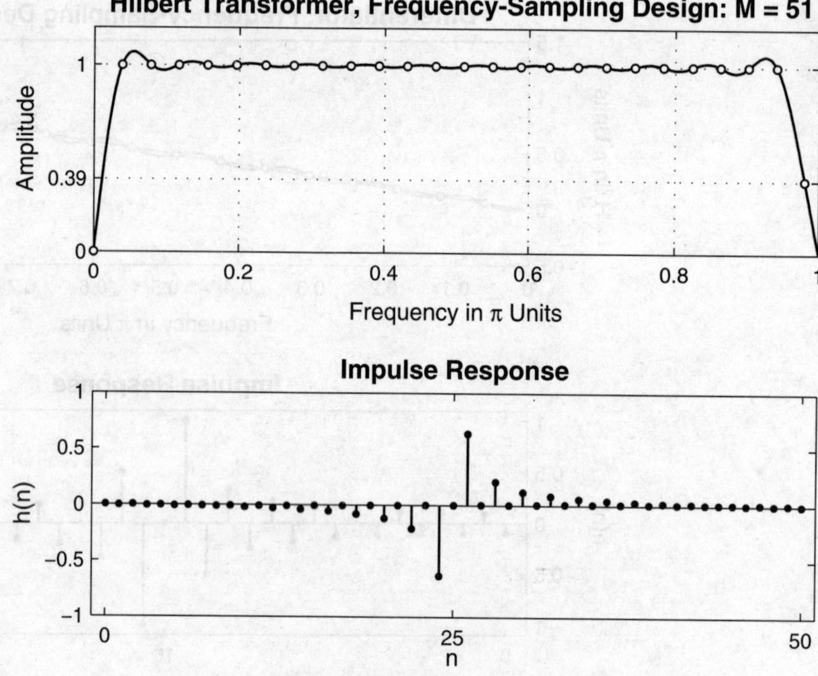

FIGURE 7.33 *Digital Hilbert transformer design plots in Example 7.20*

MATLAB script:

```
>> M = 51; alpha = (M-1)/2; Dw = 2*pi/M;  l = 0:M-1; wl = Dw*l;
>> k1 = 0:floor((M-1)/2); k2 = floor((M-1)/2)+1:M-1;
>> Hrs = [0,-j*ones(1,(M-3)/2),-0.39j,0.39j,j*ones(1,(M-3)/2)];
>> angH = [-alpha*Dw*k1, alpha*Dw*(M-k2)];
>> H = Hrs.*exp(j*angH);  h = real(ifft(H,M));  [Hr,ww,a,P]=Hr_Type3(h);
```

The plots in Figure 7.33 show the effect of the transition band samples.   □

The SP toolbox provides a function called `fir2`, which combines
the frequency-sampling technique with the window technique to design
arbitrary-shaped magnitude response FIR filters. After computing the filter impulse response using the naive design method, `fir2` then applies a
selected window to minimize ripples near the band-edge frequencies. This
function's syntax also has several forms, including:

- `h = fir2(N,f,m)` designs an Nth-order ($N = M-1$) lowpass FIR filter
  and returns the impulse response in vector `h`. The desired magnitude

response of the filter is supplied in vectors `f` and `m`, which must be of the same length. The vector `f` contains normalized frequencies in the range from 0 to 1, where 1 corresponds to π rad/sample. The first value of `f` must be 0 and the last value 1. The vector `m`, contains the samples of the desired magnitude response at the values specified in `f`. The desired frequency response is then interpolated onto a dense, evenly spaced grid of length 512. Thus this syntax corresponds to the naive design method.

- `h = fir2(N,f,m,window)` uses the vector `window` of length N+1 obtained from one of the specified MATLAB window functions. The default window function used is the Hamming window.

- `h = fir2(N,f,m,npt)` or `h = fir2(N,f,m,npt,window)` specifies the number of points `npt` for the grid onto which `fir2` interpolates the frequency response. The default `npt` value is 512.

Note that the `fir2` does not implement the classic optimum frequency-sampling method. By incorporating window design, `fir2` has found an alternative (and somewhat clever) approach to do away with the optimum transition band values and the associated tables. By densely sampling values in the entire band, interpolation errors are reduced (but not minimized), and stopband attenuation is increased to an acceptable level. However, the basic design is contaminated by the window operation; hence, the frequency response does not go through the original sampled values. It is more suitable for designing FIR filters with arbitrary-shaped frequency responses.

The type of frequency-sampling filter that we considered is called a Type-A filter, in which the sampled frequencies are

$$\omega_k = \frac{2\pi}{M}k, \quad 0 \le k \le M-1$$

There is a second set of uniformly spaced samples given by

$$\omega_k = \frac{2\pi\left(k + \frac{1}{2}\right)}{M}, \quad 0 \le k \le M-1$$

This is called a Type-B filter, for which a frequency-sampling structure is also available. The expressions for the magnitude response $H(e^{j\omega})$ and the impulse response $h(n)$ are somewhat more complicated and are available in Proakis and Manolakis [79]. Their design can also be done in MATLAB using the approach discussed in this section.

7.5 OPTIMAL EQUIRIPPLE DESIGN TECHNIQUE

The last two techniques—namely, the window design and the frequency-sampling design—were easy to understand and implement. However, they have some disadvantages. First, we cannot specify the band frequencies ω_p and ω_s precisely in the design; that is, we have to accept whatever values we obtain after the design. Second, we cannot specify both δ_1 and δ_2 ripple factors simultaneously. Either we have $\delta_1 = \delta_2$ in the window design method, or we can optimize only δ_2 in the frequency-sampling method. Finally, the approximation error—that is, the difference between the ideal response and the actual response—is not uniformly distributed over the band intervals. It is higher near the band edges and smaller in the regions away from band edges. By distributing the error uniformly, we can obtain a lower-order filter satisfying the same specifications. Fortunately, a technique exists that can eliminate these three problems. This technique is somewhat difficult to understand and requires a computer for its implementation.

For linear-phase FIR filters, it is possible to derive a set of conditions for which it can be proved that the design solution is optimal in the sense of *minimizing the maximum approximation error* (sometimes called the *minimax* or the *Chebyshev* error). Filters that have this property are called *equiripple* filters because the approximation error is uniformly distributed in both the passband and the stopband. This results in lower-order filters.

In the following, we first formulate a minimax optimal FIR design problem and discuss the total number of maxima and minima (collectively called *extrema*) that one can obtain in the amplitude response of a linear-phase FIR filter. Using this, we then discuss a general equiripple FIR filter design algorithm, which uses polynomial interpolation for its solution. This algorithm is known as the Parks–McClellan algorithm, and it incorporates the Remez exchange algorithm for polynomial solution. This algorithm is available as a subroutine on many computing platforms. In this section, we will use MATLAB to design equiripple FIR filters.

7.5.1 DEVELOPMENT OF THE MINIMAX PROBLEM

Earlier in this chapter, we showed that the frequency response of the four cases of linear-phase FIR filters can be written in the form

$$H(e^{j\omega}) = e^{j\beta} e^{-j\frac{M-1}{2}\omega} H_r(w)$$

where the values for β and the expressions for $H_r(\omega)$ are given in Table 7.2.

TABLE 7.2 *Amplitude response and β-values for linear-phase FIR filters*

Linear-phase FIR Filter Type	β	$H_r(e^{j\omega})$
Type-1: M odd, symmetric $h(n)$	0	$\displaystyle\sum_{0}^{(M-1)/2} a(n)\cos\omega n$
Type-2: M even, symmetric $h(n)$	0	$\displaystyle\sum_{1}^{M/2} b(n)\cos\left[\omega(n-1/2)\right]$
Type-3: M odd, antisymmetric $h(n)$	$\dfrac{\pi}{2}$	$\displaystyle\sum_{1}^{(M-1)/2} c(n)\sin\omega n$
Type-4: M even, antisymmetric $h(n)$	$\dfrac{\pi}{2}$	$\displaystyle\sum_{1}^{M/2} d(n)\sin\left[\omega(n-1/2)\right]$

Using simple trigonometric identities, each expression for $H_r(\omega)$ can be written as a product of a fixed function of ω (call this $Q(\omega)$) and a function that is a sum of cosines (call this $P(\omega)$). For details, see Proakis and Manolakis [79] and Problems P7.2–P7.5. Thus

$$H_r(\omega) = Q(\omega)P(\omega) \tag{7.40}$$

where $P(\omega)$ is of the form

$$P(\omega) = \sum_{n=0}^{L} \alpha(n)\cos\omega n \tag{7.41}$$

and $Q(\omega)$, L, $P(\omega)$ for the four cases are given in Table 7.3.

TABLE 7.3 *$Q(\omega)$, L, and $P(\omega)$ for linear-phase FIR filters*

LP FIR Filter Type	$Q(\omega)$	L	$P(\omega)$
Type-1	1	$\dfrac{M-1}{2}$	$\displaystyle\sum_{0}^{L} a(n)\cos\omega n$
Type-2	$\cos\dfrac{\omega}{2}$	$\dfrac{M}{2}-1$	$\displaystyle\sum_{0}^{L} \tilde{b}(n)\cos\omega n$
Type-3	$\sin\omega$	$\dfrac{M-3}{2}$	$\displaystyle\sum_{0}^{L} \tilde{c}(n)\cos\omega n$
Type-4	$\sin\dfrac{\omega}{2}$	$\dfrac{M}{2}-1$	$\displaystyle\sum_{0}^{L} \tilde{d}(n)\cos\omega n$

The purpose of the previous analysis was to have a *common form* for $H_r(\omega)$ across all four cases. It makes the problem formulation much easier. To formulate our problem as a Chebyshev approximation problem, we have to define the desired amplitude response $H_{dr}(\omega)$ and a weighting function $W(\omega)$, both defined over passbands and stopbands. The weighting function is necessary so that we can have an independent control over δ_1 and δ_2. The weighted error is defined as

$$E(\omega) \triangleq W(\omega)\left[H_{dr}(\omega) - H_r(\omega)\right], \quad \omega \in \mathcal{S} \triangleq [0, \omega_p] \cup [\omega_s, \pi] \tag{7.42}$$

These concepts are made clear in the following set of figures. It shows a typical equiripple filter response along with its ideal response.

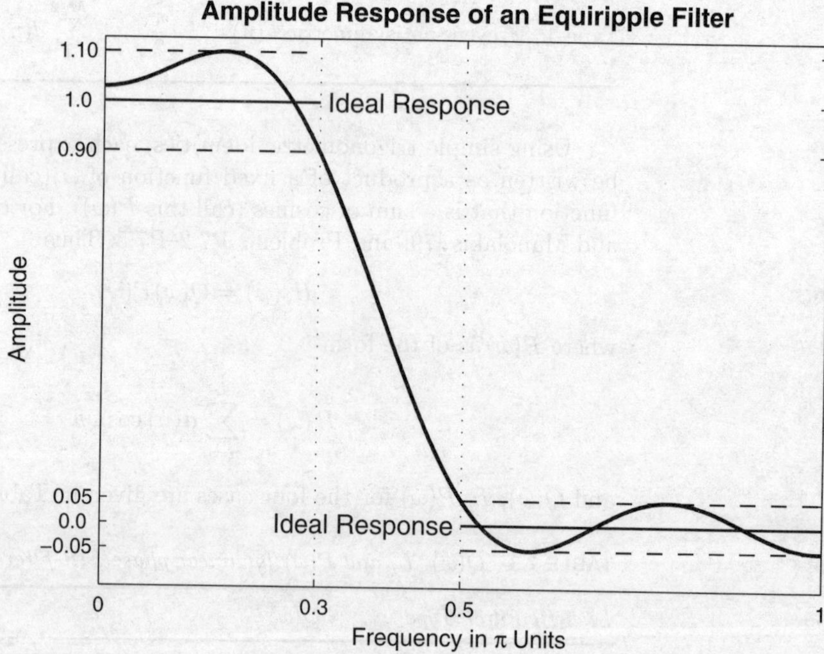

The error $[H_{dr}(\omega) - H_r(\omega)]$ response is shown here.

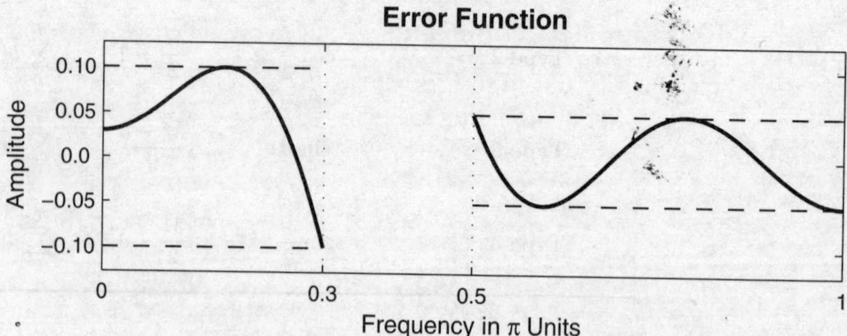

Now if we choose

$$W\left(\omega\right) = \begin{cases} \dfrac{\delta_2}{\delta_1}, & \text{in the passband} \\[2mm] 1, & \text{in the stopband} \end{cases} \tag{7.43}$$

then the weighted error $E(\omega)$ response is

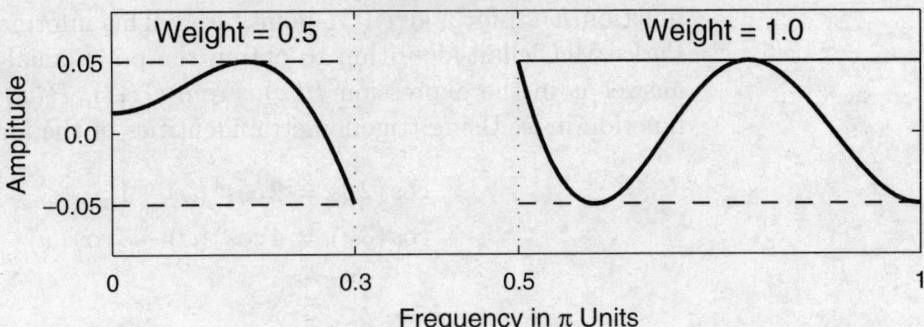

Thus the maximum error in both the passband and stopband is δ_2. Therefore, if we succeed in minimizing the maximum weighted error to δ_2, we automatically also satisfy the specification in the passband to δ_1. Substituting $H_r(\omega)$ from (7.40) into (7.42), we obtain

$$\begin{aligned} E\left(\omega\right) &= W\left(\omega\right)\left[H_{dr}\left(\omega\right) - Q\left(\omega\right)P\left(\omega\right)\right] \\ &= W\left(\omega\right)Q\left(\omega\right)\left[\frac{H_{dr}\left(\omega\right)}{Q\left(\omega\right)} - P\left(\omega\right)\right], \quad \omega \in \mathcal{S} \end{aligned}$$

If we define

$$\hat{W}(\omega) \triangleq W(\omega)Q(w) \quad \text{and} \quad \hat{H}_{dr}\left(\omega\right) \triangleq \frac{H_{dr}\left(\omega\right)}{Q\left(\omega\right)}$$

then we obtain

$$E(\omega) = \hat{W}(\omega)\left[\hat{H}_{dr}(\omega) - P(\omega)\right], \quad \omega \in \mathcal{S} \tag{7.44}$$

Thus we have a common form of $E(\omega)$ for all four cases.

Problem statement The Chebyshev approximation problem can now be defined as follows:

Determine the set of coefficients $a(n)$ or $\tilde{b}(n)$ or $\tilde{c}(n)$ or $\tilde{d}(n)$ [or equivalently $a(n)$ or $b(n)$ or $c(n)$ or $d(n)$] to minimize the maximum absolute value of $E\left(\omega\right)$ over the passband and stopband, that is,

$$\min_{\substack{\text{over coeff.}}} \left[\max_{\omega \in S}\left|E\left(\omega\right)\right|\right] \tag{7.45}$$

Now we have succeeded in specifying the exact ω_p, ω_s, δ_1, and δ_2. In addition, the error can now be distributed uniformly in both the passband and stopband.

7.5.2 CONSTRAINT ON THE NUMBER OF EXTREMA

Before we give the solution to this above problem, we will first discuss the following issue: How many local maxima and minima exist in the error function $E(\omega)$ for a given M-point filter? This information is used by the Parks–McClellan algorithm to obtain the polynomial interpolation. The answer is in the expression $P(\omega)$. From (7.41), $P(\omega)$ is a trigonometric function in ω. Using trigonometric identities of the form

$$\cos(2\omega) = 2\cos^2(\omega) - 1$$
$$\cos(3\omega) = 4\cos^3(\omega) - 3\cos(\omega)$$
$$\vdots \quad = \quad \vdots$$

$P(\omega)$, given in (7.41) can be converted to a trigonometric polynomial in $\cos(\omega)$, as follows

$$P(\omega) = \sum_{n=0}^{L} \beta(n) \cos^n \omega \tag{7.46}$$

□ **EXAMPLE 7.21** Let $h(n) = \frac{1}{15}[1, 2, 3, 4, 3, 2, 1]$. Then $M = 7$ and $h(n)$ is symmetric, which means that we have a Type-1 linear-phase filter. Hence $L = (M - 1)/2 = 3$. Now from (7.7),

$$\alpha(n) = a(n) = 2h(3 - n), \quad 1 \le n \le 2; \qquad \text{and} \qquad \alpha(0) = a(0) = h(3)$$

or $\alpha(n) = \frac{1}{15}[4, 6, 4, 2]$. Hence

$$P(\omega) = \sum_{0}^{3} \alpha(n) \cos \omega n = \frac{1}{15}(4 + 6\cos\omega + 4\cos 2\omega + 2\cos 3\omega)$$

$$= \frac{1}{15}\left\{4 + 6\cos\omega + 4(2\cos^2\omega - 1) + 2(4\cos^3\omega - 3\cos\omega)\right\}$$

$$= 0 + 0 + \frac{8}{15}\cos^2\omega + \frac{8}{15}\cos^3\omega = \sum_{0}^{3} \beta(n)\cos^n\omega$$

or $\beta(n) = \left[0, 0, \dfrac{8}{15}, \dfrac{8}{15}\right]$. □

From (7.46), we note that $P(\omega)$ is an Lth-order polynomial in $\cos(\omega)$. Since $\cos(\omega)$ is a *monotone* function in the *open* interval $0 < \omega < \pi$, then it follows that the Lth-order polynomial $P(\omega)$ in $\cos(\omega)$ should behave like an ordinary Lth-order polynomial $P(x)$ in x. Therefore, $P(\omega)$ has *at most* (i.e., no more than) $(L-1)$ local extrema in the open interval $0 < \omega < \pi$. For example,

$$\cos^2(\omega) = \frac{1 + \cos 2\omega}{2}$$

has only one minimum at $\omega = \pi/2$. However, it has three extrema in the closed interval $0 \le \omega \le \pi$ (i.e., a maximum at $\omega = 0$, a minimum at $\omega = \pi/2$, and a maximum at $\omega = \pi$). Thus if we include the end points $\omega = 0$ and $\omega = \pi$, then $P(\omega)$ has at most $(L+1)$ local extrema in the closed interval $0 \le \omega \le \pi$. Finally, we would like the filter specifications to be met exactly at band edges ω_p and ω_s. Then the specifications can be met at no more than $(L+3)$ extremal frequencies in the $0 \le \omega \le \pi$ interval.

Conclusion   The error function $E(\omega)$ has at most $(L+3)$ extrema in $\mathcal{S}$.

☐   **EXAMPLE 7.22**   Let us plot the amplitude response of the filter given in Example 7.21 and count the total number of extrema in the corresponding error function.

Solution   The impulse response is

$$h(n) = \frac{1}{15}[1, 2, 3, 4, 3, 2, 1], \quad M = 7 \quad \text{or} \quad L = 3$$

and $\alpha(n) = \frac{1}{15}[4, 6, 4, 2]$ and $\beta(n) = \left[0, 0, \frac{8}{15}, \frac{8}{15}\right]$ from Example 7.21. Hence

$$P(\omega) = \frac{8}{15}\cos^2 \omega + \frac{8}{15}\cos^3 \omega$$

which is shown in Figure 7.34. Clearly, $P(\omega)$ has $(L-1) = 2$ extrema in the open interval $0 < \omega < \pi$. Also shown in Figure 7.34 is the error function, which has $(L+3) = 6$ extrema.   ☐

Let us now turn our attention to the problem statement and equation (7.45). It is a well-known problem in *approximation theory*, and the solution is given by the following important theorem.

■   **THEOREM 1**   ***Alternation Theorem***
Let $\mathcal{S}$ be any closed subset of the closed interval $[0, \pi]$. In order that $P(\omega)$ be the unique minimax approximation to $H_{dr}(\omega)$ on $\mathcal{S}$, it is necessary and sufficient that the error function $E(\omega)$ exhibit at least $(L+2)$ "alternations" or extremal frequencies in $\mathcal{S}$; that is, there must exist $(L+2)$ frequencies ω_i in $\mathcal{S}$ such that

$$E(\omega_i) = -E(\omega_{i-1}) = \pm \max_{S} |E(\omega)| \tag{7.47}$$

$$\triangleq \pm\delta, \; \forall \, \omega_0 < \omega_1 < \cdots < \omega_{L+1} \in \mathcal{S}$$

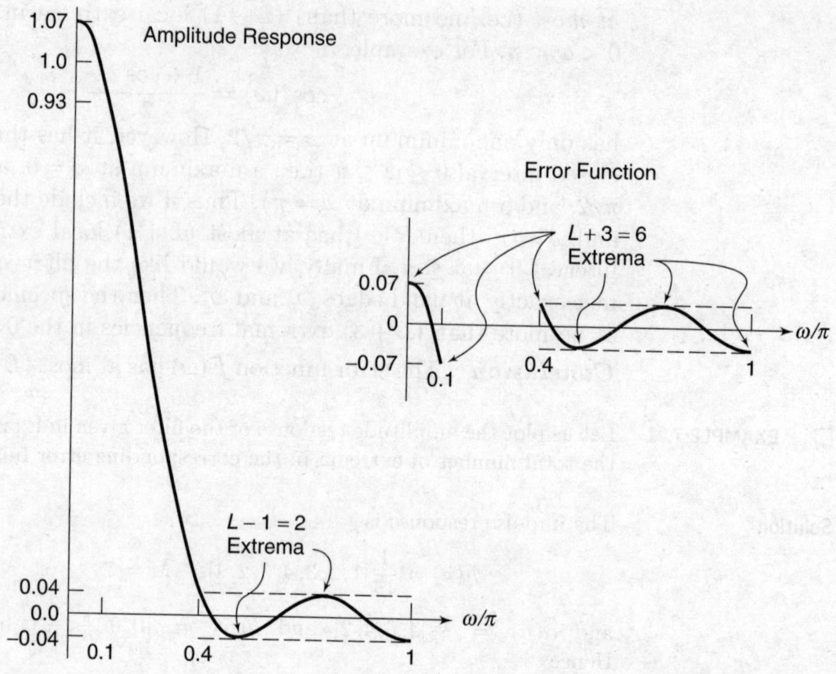

FIGURE 7.34 *Amplitude response and the error function in Example 7.22*

Combining this theorem with our earlier conclusion, we infer that the optimal equiripple filter has either $(L + 2)$ or $(L + 3)$ alternations in its error function over $\mathcal{S}$. Most of the equiripple filters have $(L + 2)$ alternations. However, for some combinations of ω_p and ω_s, we can get filters with $(L+3)$ alternations. These filters have one extra ripple in their response and hence are called *extraripple* filters.

7.5.3 PARKS–McCLELLAN ALGORITHM

The alternation theorem ensures that the solution to our minimax approximation problem exists and is unique, but it does not tell us how to obtain this solution. We know neither the order M (or equivalently, L), nor the extremal frequencies ω_i, nor the parameters $\{\alpha(n)\}$, nor the maximum error δ. Parks and McClellan [74] provided an iterative solution using the Remez exchange algorithm. It assumes that the filter length M (or L) and the ratio δ_2/δ_1 are known. If we choose the weighting function as in (7.43), and if we choose the order M correctly, then $\delta = \delta_2$ when the solution is obtained. Clearly, δ and M are related; the larger the M, the smaller the δ. In the filter specifications, δ_1, δ_2, ω_p, and ω_s are given.

Therefore, M has to be assumed. Fortunately, a simple formula, due to Kaiser, exists for approximating M. It is given by

$$\hat{M} = \frac{-20\log_{10}\sqrt{\delta_1\delta_2} - 13}{2.285\Delta\omega} + 1; \quad \Delta\omega = \omega_s - \omega_p \qquad (7.48)$$

The Parks–McClellan algorithm begins by guessing $(L+2)$ extremal frequencies $\{\omega_i\}$ and estimating the maximum error δ at these frequencies. It then fits an Lth-order polynomial (7.46) through points given in (7.47). Local maximum errors are determined over a finer grid, and the extremal frequencies $\{\omega_i\}$ are adjusted at these new extremal values. A new Lth-order polynomial is fit through these new frequencies, and the procedure is repeated. This iteration continues until the optimum set $\{\omega_i\}$ and the global maximum error δ are found. The iterative procedure is guaranteed to converge, yielding the polynomial $P(\omega)$. From (7.46), coefficients $\beta(n)$ are determined. Finally, the coefficients $a(n)$ as well as the impulse response $h(n)$ are computed. This algorithm is available in MATLAB as the `firpm` function, which is described shortly.

Since we approximated M, the maximum error δ may not be equal to δ_2. If this is the case, then we have to increase M (if $\delta > \delta_2$) or decrease M (if $\delta < \delta_2$) and use the `firpm` algorithm again to determine a new δ. We repeat this procedure until $\delta \leq \delta_2$. The optimal equiripple FIR filter, which satisfies all the three requirements discussed earlier, is now determined.

7.5.4 MATLAB IMPLEMENTATION

The Parks–McClellan algorithm is available in MATLAB as a function called `firpm`, the most general syntax of which is

```
[h] = firpm(N,f,m,weights,ftype)
```

There are several versions of this syntax:

- `[h] = firpm(N,f,m)` designs an Nth-order (note that the length of the filter is $M = N + 1$) FIR digital filter whose frequency response is specified by the arrays `f` and `m`. The filter coefficients (or the impulse response) are returned in array `h` of length M. The array `f` contains band-edge frequencies in units of π, that is, $0.0 \leq f \leq 1.0$. These frequencies must be in increasing order, starting with 0.0 and ending with 1.0. The array `m` contains the desired magnitude response at frequencies specified in `f`. The lengths of `f` and `m` arrays must be the same and must be an even number. The weighting function used in each band is equal to unity, which means that the tolerances (δ_i's) in every band are the same.

- `[h] = firpm(N,f,m,weights)` is similar to the preceding case except that the array `weights` specifies the weighting function in each band.
- `[h] = firpm(N,f,m,ftype)` is similar to the first case except that when `ftype` is the string 'differentiator' or 'hilbert', it designs digital differentiators or digital Hilbert transformers, respectively. For the digital Hilbert transformer, the lowest frequency in the `f` array should not be 0, and the highest frequency should not be 1. For the digital differentiator, the `m` vector does not specify the desired slope in each band but the desired magnitude.
- `[h] = firpm(N,f,m,weights,ftype)` is similar to the above case except that the array `weights` specifies the weighting function in each band.

To estimate the filter order N, the SP toolbox provides the function `firpmord`, which also estimates other parameters that can be used in the `firpm` function. The basic syntax is

```
[N,f0,m0,weights] = firpmord(f,m,delta);
```

The function computes the window order `N`, the normalized frequency band edges in `f0`, amplitude response in `a0`, and the band weights in `weights`. The vector `f` is a vector of normalized band edges and `m` is a vector specifying the desired amplitude on the bands defined by `f`. The length of `f` is 2 less than twice the length of `m`; that is, `f` does not contain 0 or 1. The vector `delta` specifies tolerances in each band (not in decibels). The estimated parameters can now be used in the `firpm` function.

As explained during the description of the Parks–McClellan algorithm, we have to first guess the order of the filter using (7.48) to use the function `firpm`. After we obtain the filter coefficients in array `h`, we have to check the minimum stopband attenuation and compare it with the given A_s and then increase (or decrease) the filter order. We have to repeat this procedure until we obtain the desired A_s. We illustrate this procedure in the following several MATLAB examples. These examples also use the ripple conversion function `db2delta`, which is developed in Problem P7.1.

☐ **EXAMPLE 7.23**   Let us design the lowpass filter described in Example 7.8 using the Parks–McClellan algorithm. The design parameters are

$$\omega_p = 0.2\pi, \quad R_p = 0.25 \text{ dB}$$

$$\omega_s = 0.3\pi, \quad A_s = 50 \text{ dB}$$

We provide a MATLAB script to design this filter.

```
>> wp = 0.2*pi; ws = 0.3*pi; Rp = 0.25; As = 50;
>> [delta1,delta2] = db2delta(Rp,As);
>> [N,f,m,weights] = firpmord([wp,ws]/pi,[1,0],[delta1,delta2]);
>> h = firpm(N,f,m,weights);
>> [db,mag,pha,grd,w] = freqz_m(h,[1]);
>> delta_w = 2*pi/1000; wsi=ws/delta_w+1; wpi = wp/delta_w;
>> Asd = -max(db(wsi:1:501))
Asd = 47.8404
>> N = N+1
N = 43
>> h = firpm(N,f,m,weights); [db,mag,pha,grd,w] = freqz_m(h,[1]);
>> Asd = -max(db(wsi:1:501))
Asd = 48.2131
>> N = N+1
N =  44
>> h = firpm(N,f,m,weights); [db,mag,pha,grd,w] = freqz_m(h,[1]);
>> Asd = -max(db(wsi:1:501))
Asd = 48.8689
>> N = N+1
N = 45
>> h = firpm(N,f,m,weights); [db,mag,pha,grd,w] = freqz_m(h,[1]);
>> Asd = -max(db(wsi:1:501))
Asd = 49.8241
>> N = N+1
N = 46
>> h = firpm(N,f,m,weights); [db,mag,pha,grd,w] = freqz_m(h,[1]);
>> Asd = -max(db(wsi:1:501))
Asd = 51.0857
>> M = N+1
M = 47
```

Note that we stopped this iterative procedure when the computed stopband attenuation exceeded the given stopband attenuation A_s and the optimal value of M was found to be 47. This value is considerably lower than the window design techniques ($M = 61$ for a Kaiser window) or the frequency-sampling technique ($M = 60$). In Figure 7.35, we show the time- and the frequency-domain plots of the designed filter along with the error function in both the passband and the stopband to illustrate the equiripple behavior.

EXAMPLE 7.24   Let us design the bandpass filter described in Example 7.10 using the Parks–McClellan algorithm. The design parameters are

$$\begin{matrix} \omega_{1s} = 0.2\pi \\ \omega_{1p} = 0.35\pi \end{matrix} \;;\quad R_p = 1 \text{ dB}$$

$$\begin{matrix} \omega_{2p} = 0.65\pi \\ \omega_{2s} = 0.8\pi \end{matrix} \;;\quad A_s = 60 \text{ db}$$

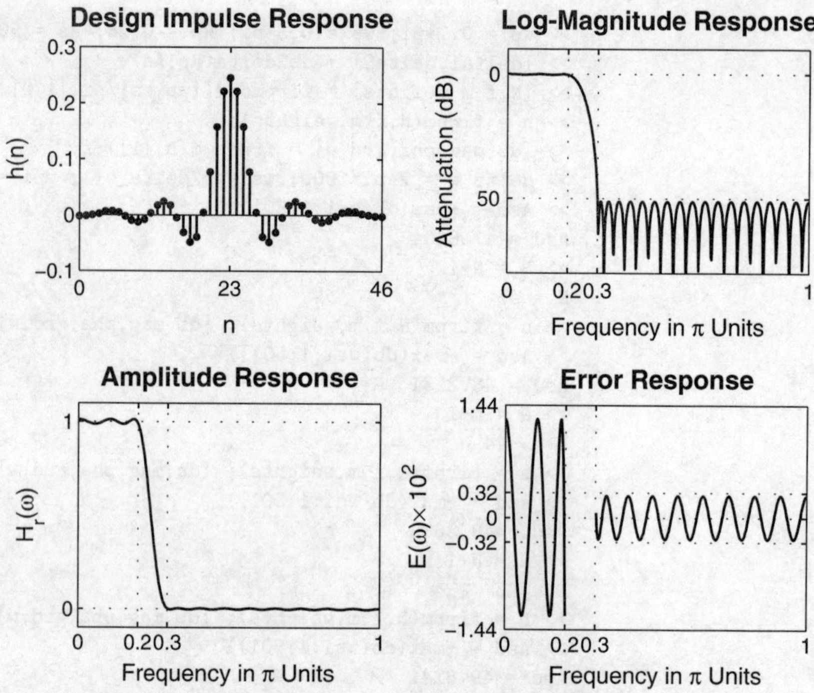

FIGURE 7.35 *Plots for equiripple lowpass FIR filter in Example 7.23*

Solution   The following MATLAB script shows how to design this filter.

```
>> ws1 = 0.2*pi; wp1 = 0.35*pi; wp2 = 0.65*pi; ws2 = 0.8*pi;
>> Rp = 1.0; As = 60;
>> [delta1,delta2] = db2delta(Rp,As);
>> f = [ws1,wp1,wp2,ws2]/pi; m = [0,1,0]; delta = [delta2,delta1,delta2];
>> [N,f,m,weights] = firpmord(f,m,delta); N
N = 26
>> h = firpm(N,f,m,weights);
>> [db,mag,pha,grd,w] = freqz_m(h,[1]);
>> delta_w=2*pi/1000;
>> ws1i=floor(ws1/delta_w)+1; wp1i = floor(wp1/delta_w)+1;
>> ws2i=floor(ws2/delta_w)+1; wp2i = floor(wp2/delta_w)+1;
>> Asd = -max(db(1:1:ws1i))
Asd = 54.7756
>> N = N+1;
>> h = firpm(N,f,m,weights);
>> [db,mag,pha,grd,w] = freqz_m(h,[1]);
>> Asd = -max(db(1:1:ws1i))
```

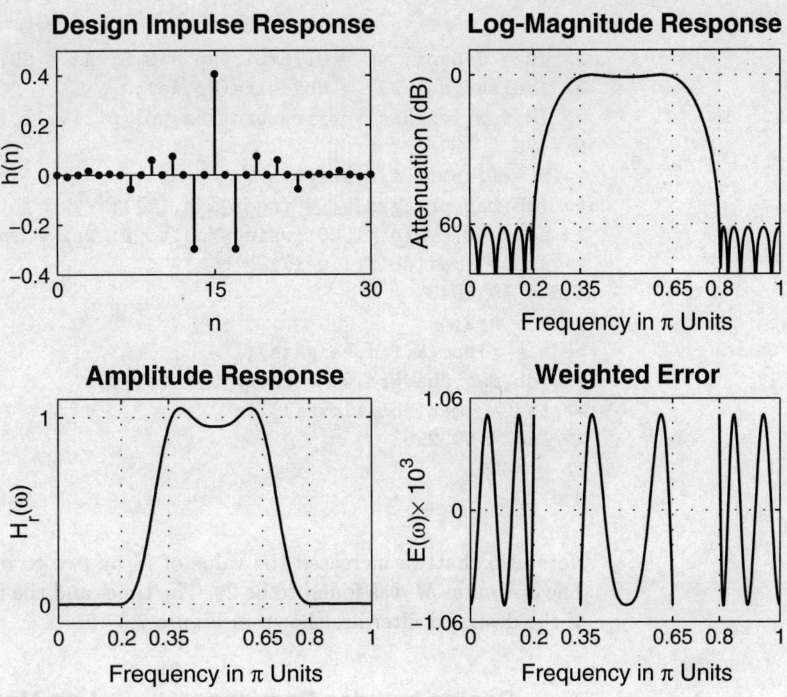

FIGURE 7.36 *Plots for equiripple bandpass FIR filter in Example 7.24*

```
Asd = 56.5910
>> N = N+1;
>> h = firpm(N,f,m,weights);
>> [db,mag,pha,grd,w] = freqz_m(h,[1]);
Asd = -max(db(1:1:ws1i))
>> Asd = 61.2843
>> M = N+1
M = 29
```

The optimal value of M was found to be 29. The time- and the frequency-domain plots of the designed filter are shown in Figure 7.36. □

□ **EXAMPLE 7.25**   Design a highpass filter that has the following specifications:

$$\omega_s = 0.6\pi, \quad A_s = 50 \text{ dB}$$

$$\omega_p = 0.75\pi, \quad R_p = 0.5 \text{ dB}$$

Solution   Since this is a highpass filter, we must ensure that the length M is an odd number. This is shown in the following MATLAB script.

```
>> ws = 0.6*pi; wp = 0.75*pi; Rp = 0.5; As = 50;
>> [delta1,delta2] = db2delta(Rp,As);
>> [N,f,m,weights] = firpmord([ws,wp]/pi,[0,1],[delta2,delta1]); N
N = 26
>> h = firpm(N,f,m,weights);
>> [db,mag,pha,grd,w] = freqz_m(h,[1]);
>> delta_w = 2*pi/1000; wsi=ws/delta_w; wpi = wp/delta_w;
>> Asd = -max(db(1:1:wsi))
Asd = 49.5918
>> N = N+2;
>> h = firpm(N,f,m,weights);
>> [db,mag,pha,grd,w] = freqz_m(h,[1]);
>> Asd = -max(db(1:1:wsi))
>> Asd = 50.2253
>> M = N+1
M = 29
```

Note also that we increased the value of N by two to maintain its even value.
The optimum M was found to be 29. The time- and the frequency-domain plots
of the designed filter are shown in Figure 7.37.   □

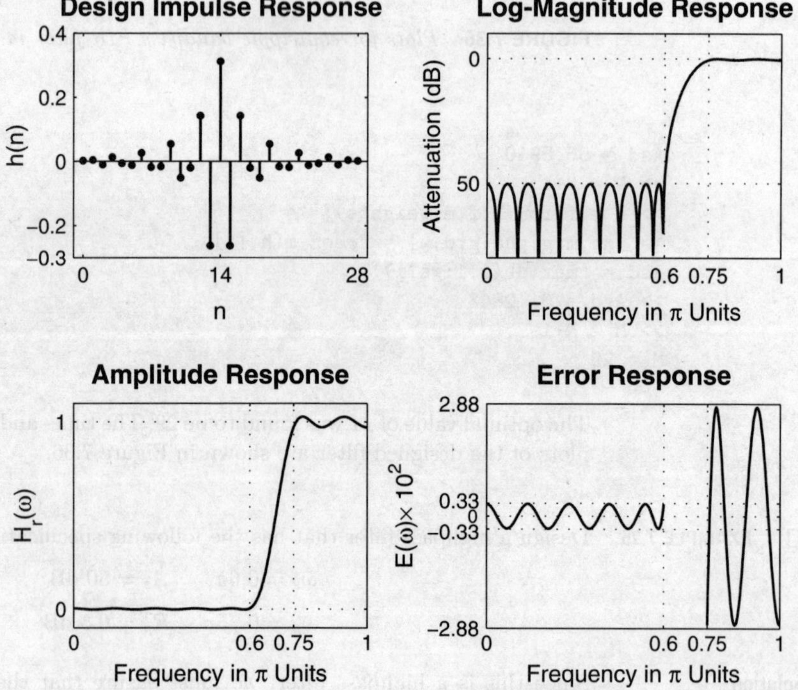

FIGURE 7.37 *Plots for equiripple highpass FIR filter in Example 7.25*

☐ **EXAMPLE 7.26**   In this example, we will design a "staircase" filter, which has 3 bands with different ideal responses and different tolerances in each band. The design specifications are as follows.

$$\text{Band-1:} \quad 0 \leq \omega \leq 0.3\pi, \text{ Ideal gain} = 1, \quad \text{Tolerance } \delta_1 = 0.01$$

$$\text{Band-2:} \quad 0.4\pi \leq \omega \leq 0.7\pi, \text{ Ideal gain} = 0.5, \text{ Tolerance } \delta_2 = 0.005$$

$$\text{Band-3:} \quad 0.8\pi \leq \omega \leq \pi, \quad \text{ Ideal gain} = 0, \quad \text{Tolerance } \delta_3 = 0.001$$

Solution   The following MATLAB script describes the design procedure.

```
>> w1 = 0; w2 = 0.3*pi; delta1 = 0.01;
>> w3 = 0.4*pi; w4 = 0.7*pi; delta2 = 0.005;
>> w5 = 0.8*pi; w6 = pi; delta3 = 0.001;
>> weights = [delta3/delta1 delta3/delta2 1];
>> Dw = min((w3-w2), (w5-w3));
>> M = ceil((-20*log10((delta1*delta2*delta3)^(1/3))-13)/(2.285*Dw)+1)
>> M = 51
>> f = [0 w2/pi w3/pi w4/pi w5/pi 1];
>> m = [1 1 0.5 0.5 0 0];
>> h = firpm(M-1,f,m,weights);
>> [db,mag,pha,grd,w] = freqz_m(h,[1]);
>> delta_w = 2*pi/1000;
>> w1i=floor(w1/delta_w)+1; w2i = floor(w2/delta_w)+1;
>> w3i=floor(w3/delta_w)+1; w4i = floor(w4/delta_w)+1;
>> w5i=floor(w5/delta_w)+1; w6i = floor(w6/delta_w)+1;
>> Asd = -max(db(w5i:w6i))
Asd = 62.0745
>> M = M-1; h = firpm(M-1,f,m,weights);
>> [db,mag,pha,grd,w] = freqz_m(h,[1]);
>> Asd = -max(db(w5i:w6i))
Asd = 60.0299
>> M = M-1; h = firpm(M-1,f,m,weights);
>> [db,mag,pha,grd,w] = freqz_m(h,[1]);
>> Asd = -max(db(w5i:w6i))
Asd = 60.6068
>> M
M = 49
```

The time- and the frequency-domain plots of the designed filter are shown in Figure 7.38.   ☐

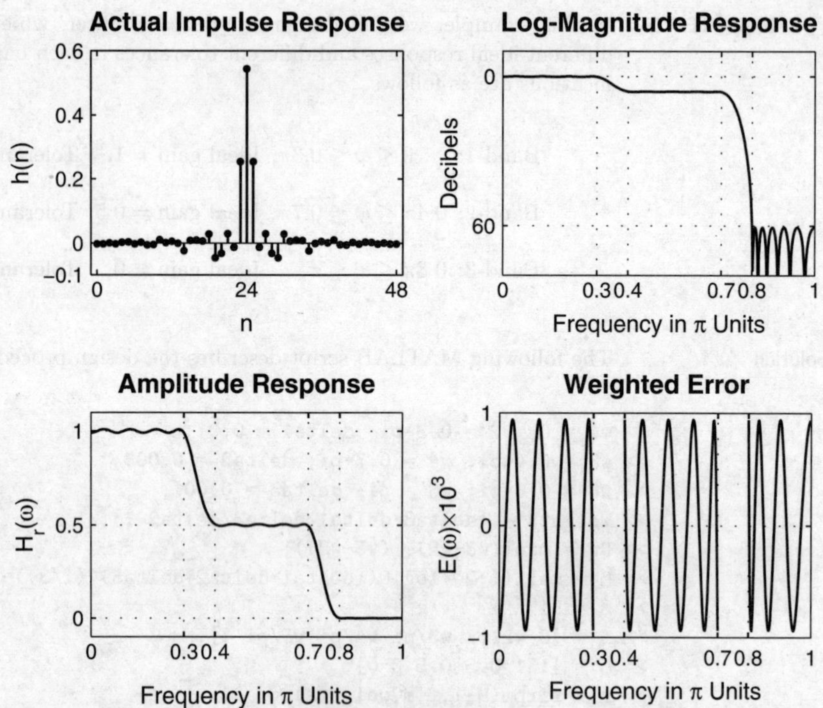

FIGURE 7.38 *Plots for equiripple staircase FIR filter in Example 7.26*

□ **EXAMPLE 7.27**   In this example, we will design a digital differentiator with different slopes in each band. The specifications are as follows.

$$\text{Band-1:} \qquad 0 \leq \omega \leq 0.2\pi, \ \text{Slope} = 1 \ \text{sam/cycle}$$

$$\text{Band-2:} \ 0.4\pi \leq \omega \leq 0.6\pi, \ \text{Slope} = 2 \ \text{sam/cycle}$$

$$\text{Band-3:} \ 0.8\pi \leq \omega \leq \pi, \qquad \text{Slope} = 3 \ \text{sam/cycle}$$

Solution   We need desired magnitude response values in each band. These can be obtained by multiplying band-edge frequencies in cycles/sam by the slope values in sam/cycle.

$$\text{Band-1:} \quad 0 \leq f \leq 0.1, \ \text{Slope} = 1 \ \text{sam/cycle} \Rightarrow 0.0 \leq |H| \leq 0.1$$

$$\text{Band-2:} \ 0.2 \leq f \leq 0.3, \ \text{Slope} = 2 \ \text{sam/cycle} \Rightarrow 0.4 \leq |H| \leq 0.6$$

$$\text{Band-3:} \ 0.4 \leq f \leq 0.5, \ \text{Slope} = 3 \ \text{sam/cycle} \Rightarrow 1.2 \leq |H| \leq 1.5$$

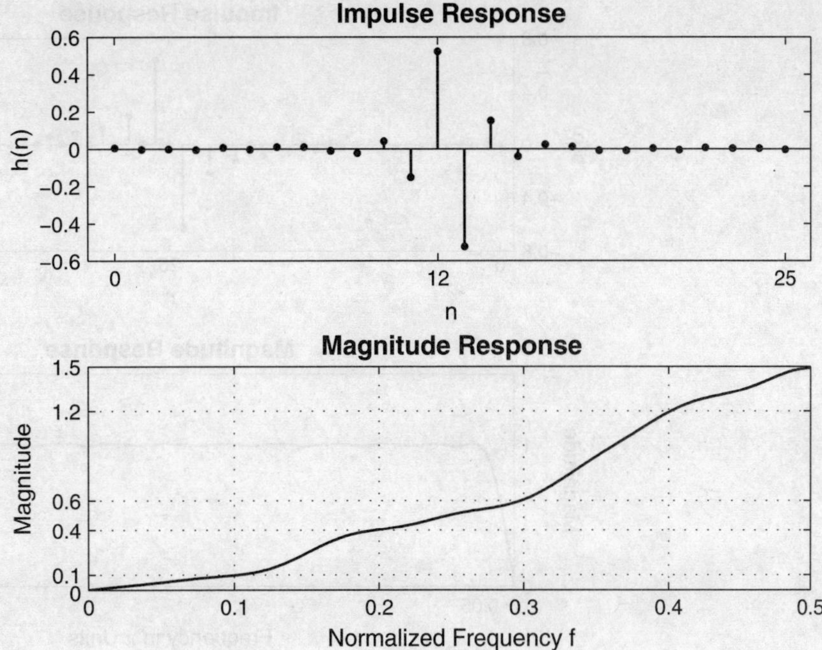

FIGURE 7.39 *Plots of the differentiator in Example 7.27*

Let the weights be equal in all bands. MATLAB script:

```
>> f = [0 0.2 0.4 0.6 0.8 1];            % In w/pi units
>> m = [0,0.1,0.4,0.6,1.2,1.5];          % Magnitude values
>> h = firpm(25,f,m,'differentiator');
>> [db,mag,pha,grd,w] = freqz_m(h,[1]);
% Plot commands follow
```

The frequency-domain response is shown in Figure 7.39.   □

☐ **EXAMPLE 7.28**   Finally, we design a Hilbert transformer over the band $0.05\pi \leq \omega \leq 0.95\pi$.

Solution   Since this is a wideband Hilbert transformer, we will choose an odd length for our filter (i.e., a Type-3 filter). Let us choose $M = 51$. MATLAB script:

```
>> f = [0.05,0.95]; m = [1 1];  h = firpm(50,f,m,'hilbert');
>> [db,mag,pha,grd,w] = freqz_m(h,[1]);
% Plot commands follow
```

The plots of this Hilbert transformer are shown in Figure 7.40.   □

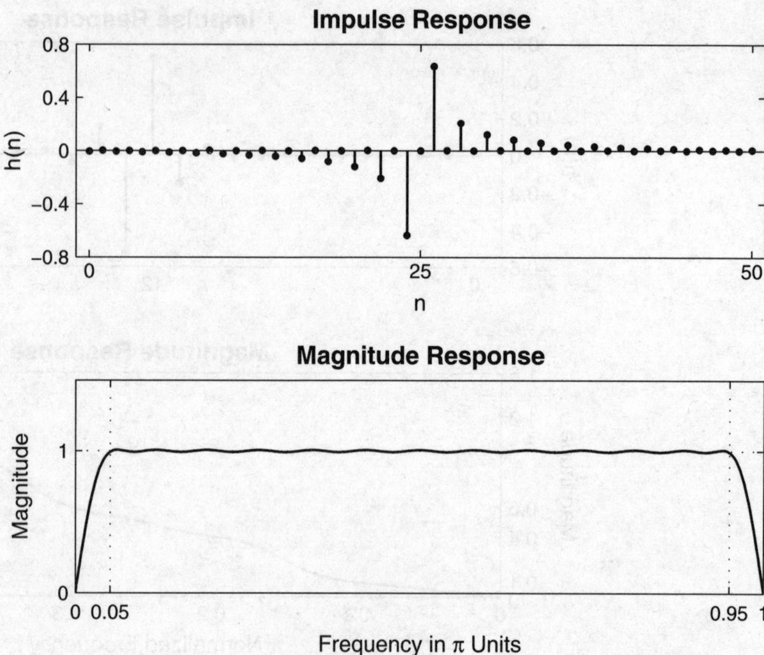

FIGURE 7.40 *Plots of the Hilbert transformer in Example 7.28*

7.6 PROBLEMS

P7.1 The absolute and relative (dB) specifications for a lowpass filter are related by (7.1) and (7.2). In this problem, we will develop a simple MATLAB function to convert one set of specifications into another.

1. Write a MATLAB function to convert absolute specifications δ_1 and δ_2 into the relative specifications R_p and A_s in dB. The format of the function should be

```
function [Rp,As] = delta2db(delta1,delta2)
% Converts absolute specs delta1 and delta2 into dB specs Rp and As
% [Rp,As] = delta2db(delta1,delta2)
```

Verify your function using the specifications given in Example 7.2.

2. Write a MATLAB function to convert relative (dB) specifications R_p and A_s into the absolute specifications δ_1 and δ_2. The format of the function should be

```
function [delta1,delta2] = db2delta(Rp,As)
% Converts dB specs Rp and As into absolute specs delta1 and delta2
% [delta1,delta2] = db2delta(Rp,As)
```

Verify your function using the specifications given in Example 7.1.

P7.2 The Type-1 linear-phase FIR filter is characterized by

$$h(n) = h(M - 1 - n), \quad 0 \le n \le M - 1, \quad M \text{ odd}$$

Show that its amplitude response $H_r(\omega)$ is given by

$$H_r(\omega) = \sum_{n=0}^{L} a(n) \cos(\omega n), \quad L = \frac{M - 1}{2}$$

where coefficients $\{a(n)\}$ are obtained as defined in (7.7).

P7.3 The Type-2 linear-phase FIR filter is characterized by

$$h(n) = h(M - 1 - n), \quad 0 \le n \le M - 1, \quad M \text{ even}$$

1. Show that its amplitude response $H_r(\omega)$ is given by

$$H_r(\omega) = \sum_{n=1}^{M/2} b(n) \cos\left\{\omega\left(n - \tfrac{1}{2}\right)\right\}$$

where coefficients $\{b(n)\}$ are obtained as defined in (7.10).

2. Show that $H_r(\omega)$ can be further expressed as

$$H_r(\omega) = \cos\left(\frac{\omega}{2}\right) \sum_{n=0}^{L} \tilde{b}(n) \cos(\omega n), \quad L = \frac{M}{2} - 1$$

where coefficients $\tilde{b}(n)$ are given by

$$b(1) = \tilde{b}(0) + \tfrac{1}{2}\tilde{b}(1),$$

$$b(n) = \frac{1}{2}\left[\tilde{b}(n - 1) + \tilde{b}(n)\right], \quad 2 \le n \le \frac{M}{2} - 1,$$

$$b\left(\tfrac{M}{2}\right) = \frac{1}{2}\tilde{b}\left(\tfrac{M}{2} - 1\right).$$

P7.4 The Type-3 linear-phase FIR filter is characterized by

$$h(n) = -h(M - 1 - n), \quad 0 \le n \le M - 1, \quad M \text{ odd}$$

1. Show that its amplitude response $H_r(\omega)$ is given by

$$H_r(\omega) = \sum_{n=1}^{(M-1)/2} c(n) \sin(\omega n)$$

where coefficients $\{c(n)\}$ are obtained as defined in (7.13).

2. Show that $H_r(\omega)$ can be further expressed as

$$H_r(\omega) = \sin(\omega) \sum_{n=0}^{L} \tilde{c}(n) \cos(\omega n), \quad L = \frac{M - 3}{2}$$

where coefficients $\tilde{c}(n)$ are given by

$$c(1) = \tilde{c}(0) - \tfrac{1}{2}\tilde{c}(1),$$

$$c(n) = \frac{1}{2}\left[\tilde{c}(n-1) - \tilde{c}(n)\right], \quad 2 \le n \le \frac{M-3}{2},$$

$$c\left(\frac{M-1}{2}\right) = \frac{1}{2}\tilde{c}\left(\frac{M-3}{2}\right).$$

P7.5 The Type-4 linear-phase FIR filter is characterized by

$$h(n) = -h(M-1-n), \quad 0 \le n \le M-1, \quad M \text{ even}$$

1. Show that its amplitude response $H_r(\omega)$ is given by

$$H_r(\omega) = \sum_{n=1}^{M/2} d(n)\sin\left\{\omega\left(n - \tfrac{1}{2}\right)\right\}$$

where coefficients $\{d(n)\}$ are obtained as defined in (7.16).
2. Show that the above $H_r(\omega)$ can be further expressed as

$$H_r(\omega) = \sin\left(\frac{\omega}{2}\right)\sum_{n=0}^{L}\tilde{d}(n)\cos(\omega n), \quad L = \frac{M}{2} - 1$$

where coefficients $\tilde{d}(n)$ are given by

$$d(1) = \tilde{d}(0) - \tfrac{1}{2}\tilde{d}(1),$$

$$d(n) = \frac{1}{2}\left[\tilde{d}(n-1) - \tilde{d}(n)\right], \quad 2 \le n \le \frac{M}{2} - 1,$$

$$d\left(\frac{M}{2}\right) = \frac{1}{2}\tilde{d}\left(\frac{M}{2} - 1\right).$$

P7.6 Write a MATLAB function to compute the amplitude response $H_r(\omega)$ given a linear phase impulse response $h(n)$. The format of this function should be

```
function [Hr,w,P,L] = Ampl_Res(h);
% Computes amplitude response Hr(w) and its polynomial P of order L,
%    given a linear-phase FIR filter impulse response h.
% The type of filter is determined automatically by the subroutine.
%
% [Hr,w,P,L] = Ampl_Res(h)
% Hr = amplitude response
% w = frequencies between [0 pi] over which Hr is computed
% P = polynomial coefficients
% L = Order of P
% h = Linear-phase filter impulse response
```

The function should first determine the type of the linear-phase FIR filter and then use the appropriate `Hr_Type#` function discussed in this chapter. It should also check if the given $h(n)$ is of a linear-phase type. Verify your function on sequences given here.

$$h_\mathrm{I}(n) = (0.9)^{|n-5|} \cos[\pi(n-5)/12]\,[u(n) - u(n-11)]$$
$$h_\mathrm{II}(n) = (0.9)^{|n-4.5|} \cos[\pi(n-4.5)/11]\,[u(n) - u(n-10)]$$
$$h_\mathrm{III}(n) = (0.9)^{|n-5|} \sin[\pi(n-5)/12]\,[u(n) - u(n-11)]$$
$$h_\mathrm{IV}(n) = (0.9)^{|n-4.5|} \sin[\pi(n-4.5)/11]\,[u(n) - u(n-10)]$$
$$h(n) = (0.9)^{n} \cos[\pi(n-5)/12]\,[u(n) - u(n-11)]$$

P7.7 Prove the following properties of linear-phase FIR filters.

1. If $H(z)$ has four zeros at $z_1 = re^{j\theta}$, $z_2 = \frac{1}{r}e^{-j\theta}$, $z_3 = re^{-j\theta}$, and $z_4 = \frac{1}{r}e^{-j\theta}$, then $H(z)$ represents a linear-phase FIR filter.
2. If $H(z)$ has two zeros at $z_1 = e^{j\theta}$ and $z_2 = e^{-j\theta}$, then $H(z)$ represents a linear-phase FIR filter.
3. If $H(z)$ has two zeros at $z_1 = r$ and $z_2 = \frac{1}{r}$, then $H(z)$ represents a linear-phase FIR filter.
4. If $H(z)$ has a zero at $z_1 = 1$ or a zero at $z_1 = -1$, then $H(z)$ represents a linear-phase FIR filter.
5. For each of the sequences given in Problem P7.6, plot the locations of zeros. Determine which sequences imply linear-phase FIR filters.

P7.8 A notch filter is an LTI system, which is used to eliminate an arbitrary frequency $\omega = \omega_0$. The ideal linear-phase notch filter frequency response is given by

$$H_d\left(e^{j\omega}\right) = \begin{cases} 0, & |\omega| = \omega_0; \\ 1 \cdot e^{-j\alpha\omega}, & \text{otherwise.} \end{cases} \quad (\alpha \text{ is a delay in samples})$$

1. Determine the ideal impulse response, $h_d(n)$, of the ideal notch filter.
2. Using $h_d(n)$, design a linear-phase FIR notch filter using a length 51 rectangular window to eliminate the frequency $\omega_0 = \pi/2$ rad/sample. Plot the amplitude response of the resulting filter.
3. Repeat part 2 using a length 51 Hamming window. Compare your results.

P7.9 Design a linear-phase bandpass filter using the Hann window design technique. The specifications are

$$\begin{array}{ll} \text{lower stopband edge:} & 0.2\pi \\ \text{upper stopband edge:} & 0.75\pi \end{array} \quad A_s = 40 \text{ dB}$$
$$\begin{array}{ll} \text{lower passband edge:} & 0.35\pi \\ \text{upper passband edge:} & 0.55\pi \end{array} \quad R_p = 0.25 \text{ dB}$$

Plot the impulse response and the magnitude response (in dB) of the designed filter. Do not use the `fir1` function.

P7.10 Design a bandstop filter using the Hamming window design technique. The specifications are

$$\begin{array}{ll} \text{lower stopband edge:} & 0.4\pi \\ \text{upper stopband edge:} & 0.6\pi \end{array} \quad A_s = 50 \text{ dB}$$
$$\begin{array}{ll} \text{lower passband edge:} & 0.3\pi \\ \text{upper passband edge:} & 0.7\pi \end{array} \quad R_p = 0.2 \text{ dB}$$

Plot the impulse response and the magnitude response (in dB) of the designed filter. Do not use the `fir1` function.

P7.11 Design a bandpass filter using the Hamming window design technique. The specifications are

$$\begin{aligned}
&\text{lower stopband edge: } 0.3\pi \\
&\text{upper stopband edge: } 0.6\pi
\end{aligned} \quad A_s = 50 \text{ dB}$$

$$\begin{aligned}
&\text{lower passband edge: } 0.4\pi \\
&\text{upper passband edge: } 0.5\pi
\end{aligned} \quad R_p = 0.5 \text{ dB}$$

Plot the impulse response and the magnitude response (in dB) of the designed filter. Do not use the `fir1` function.

P7.12 Design a highpass filter using one of the fixed window functions. The specifications are

$$\begin{aligned}
&\text{stopband edge: } 0.4\pi, \ A_s = 50 \text{ dB} \\
&\text{passband edge: } 0.6\pi, \ R_p = 0.004 \text{ dB}
\end{aligned}$$

Plot the zoomed magnitude response (in dB) of the designed filter in the passband to verify the passband ripple R_p. Do not use the `fir1` function.

P7.13 Using the Kaiser window method, design a linear-phase FIR digital filter that meets the following specifications:

$$\begin{aligned}
0.975 &\le |H(e^{j\omega})| \le 1.025, & 0 \le \omega \le 0.25\pi \\
0 &\le |H(e^{j\omega})| \le 0.005, & 0.35\pi \le \omega \le 0.65\pi \\
0.975 &\le |H(e^{j\omega})| \le 1.025, & 0.75\pi \le \omega \le \pi
\end{aligned}$$

Determine the minimum-length impulse response $h(n)$ of such a filter. Provide a plot containing subplots of the amplitude response and the magnitude response in dB. Do not use the `fir1` function.

P7.14 We wish to use the Kaiser window method to design a linear-phase FIR digital filter that meets the following specifications:

$$\begin{aligned}
0 &\le |H(e^{j\omega})| \le 0.01, & 0 \le \omega \le 0.25\pi \\
0.95 &\le |H(e^{j\omega})| \le 1.05, & 0.35\pi \le \omega \le 0.65\pi \\
0 &\le |H(e^{j\omega})| \le 0.01, & 0.75\pi \le \omega \le \pi
\end{aligned}$$

Determine the minimum-length impulse response $h(n)$ of such a filter. Provide a plot containing subplots of the amplitude response and the magnitude response in dB. Do not use the `fir1` function.

P7.15 Design the staircase filter of Example 7.26 using the Kaiser window approach. The specifications are as follows.

$$\begin{aligned}
&\text{Band-1:} & 0 \le \omega \le 0.3\pi, & \ \text{Ideal gain } = 1, & \delta_1 = 0.01 \\
&\text{Band-2:} & 0.4\pi \le \omega \le 0.7\pi, & \ \text{Ideal gain } = 0.5, & \delta_2 = 0.005 \\
&\text{Band-3:} & 0.8\pi \le \omega \le \pi, & \ \text{Ideal gain } = 0, & \delta_3 = 0.001
\end{aligned}$$

Compare the filter length of this design with that of Example 7.26. Provide a plot of the magnitude response in dB. Do not use the `fir1` function.

P7.16 Design a bandpass filter using a fixed window design technique that has the minimum length and that satisfies the following specifications:

$$\left.\begin{array}{l} \text{lower stopband edge} = 0.3\pi \\ \text{upper stopband edge} = 0.6\pi \end{array}\right\} A_s = 40 \text{ dB}$$

$$\left.\begin{array}{l} \text{lower passband edge} = 0.4\pi \\ \text{upper passband edge} = 0.5\pi \end{array}\right\} R_p = 0.5 \text{ dB}$$

Provide a plot of the log-magnitude response in dB and `stem` plot of the impulse response.

P7.17 Repeat Problem P7.9 using the `fir1` function.

P7.18 Repeat Problem P7.10 using the `fir1` function.

P7.19 Repeat Problem P7.11 using the `fir1` function.

P7.20 Repeat Problem P7.12 using the `fir1` function.

P7.21 Repeat Problem P7.13 using the `fir1` function.

P7.22 Repeat Problem P7.14 using the `fir1` function.

P7.23 Consider an ideal lowpass filter with the cutoff frequency $\omega_c = 0.3\pi$. We want to approximate this filter using a frequency-sampling design in which we choose 40 samples.

1. Choose the sample at ω_c equal to 0.5, and use the naive design method to compute $h(n)$. Determine the minimum stopband attenuation.
2. Now vary the sample at ω_c, and determine the optimum value to obtain the largest minimum stopband attenuation.
3. Plot the magnitude responses in dB of the preceding two designs in one plot; comment on the results.

P7.24 Design the bandstop filter of Problem P7.10 using the frequency-sampling method. Choose the order of the filter appropriately so that there are two samples in the transition band. Use optimum values for these samples. Compare your results with those obtained using the `fir2` function.

P7.25 Design the bandpass filter of Problem P7.11 using the frequency-sampling method. Choose the order of the filter appropriately so that there are two samples in the transition band. Use optimum values for these samples. Compare your results with those obtained using the `fir2` function.

P7.26 Design the highpass filter of Problem P7.12 using the frequency-sampling method. Choose the order of the filter appropriately so that there are two samples in the transition band. Use optimum values. Compare your results with those obtained using the `fir2` function.

P7.27 Consider the filter specifications given in Figure P7.1. Use the `fir2` function and a Hamming window to design a linear-phase FIR filter via the frequency-sampling method. Experiment with the filter length to achieve the required design. Plot the amplitude response of the resulting filter.

P7.28 Design a bandpass filter using the frequency-sampling method. Choose the order of the filter appropriately so that there is one sample in the transition band. Use optimum value for this sample. The specifications are as follows:

$$\left.\begin{array}{l} \text{lower stopband edge} = 0.3\pi \\ \text{upper stopband edge} = 0.7\pi \end{array}\right\} A_s = 40 \text{ dB}$$

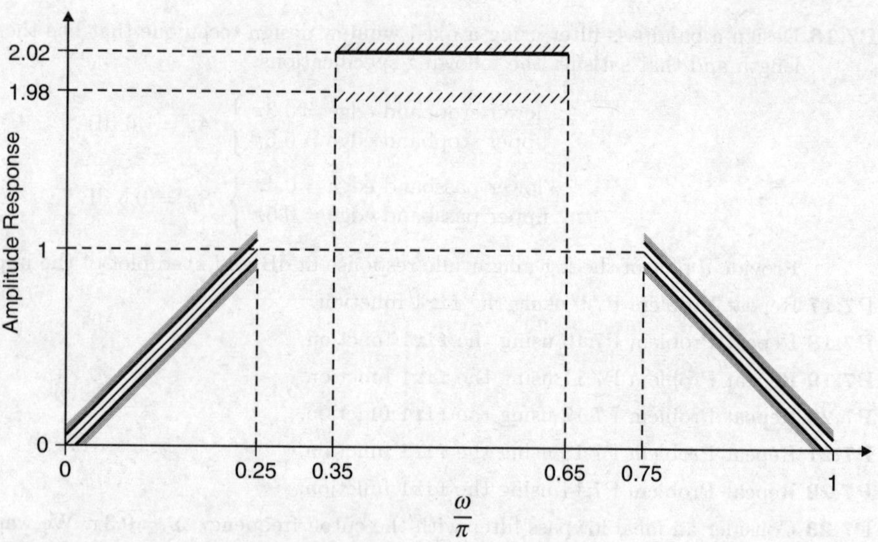

FIGURE P7.1 *Filter specifications for Problem P7.27*

$$\left.\begin{array}{l} \text{lower passband edge} = 0.4\pi \\ \text{upper passband edge} = 0.6\pi \end{array}\right\}\ R_p = 0.5 \text{ dB}.$$

Provide a plot of the log-magnitude response in dB and `stem` plot of the impulse response.

P7.29 The frequency response of an ideal bandpass filter is given by

$$H_d(e^{j\omega}) = \begin{cases} 0, & 0 \leq |\omega| \leq \pi/3 \\ 1, & \pi/3 \leq |\omega| \leq 2\pi/3 \\ 0, & 2\pi/3 \leq |\omega| \leq \pi \end{cases}$$

1. Determine the coefficients of a 25-tap filter based on the Parks–McClellan algorithm with stopband attenuation of 50 dB. The designed filter should have the smallest possible transition width.
2. Plot the amplitude response of the filter using the function developed in Problem P7.6.

P7.30 Consider the bandstop filter given in Problem P7.10.

1. Design a linear-phase bandstop FIR filter using the Parks–McClellan algorithm. Note that the length of the filter must be odd. Provide a plot of the impulse response and the magnitude response in dB of the designed filter.
2. Plot the amplitude response of the designed filter and count the total number of extrema in stopband and passbands. Verify this number with the theoretical estimate of the total number of extrema.
3. Compare the order of this filter with those of the filters in Problems P7.10 and P7.24.
4. Verify the operation of the designed filter on the following signal:

$$x(n) = 5 - 5\cos\left(\frac{\pi n}{2}\right); \quad 0 \leq n \leq 300$$

P7.31 Using the Parks–McClellan algorithm, design a 25-tap FIR differentiator with slope equal to 1 sample/cycle.

1. Choose the frequency band of interest between 0.1π and 0.9π. Plot the impulse response and the amplitude response.
2. Generate 100 samples of the sinusoid

$$x(n) = 3\sin(0.25\pi n), \quad n = 0, ..., 100$$

and process through the preceding FIR differentiator. Compare the result with the theoretical "derivative" of $x(n)$. *Note:* Don't forget to take the 12-sample delay of the FIR filter into account.

P7.32 Design a lowest-order equiripple linear-phase FIR filter to satisfy the specifications given in Figure P7.2. Provide a plot of the amplitude response and a plot of the impulse response.

P7.33 A digital signal $x(n)$ contains a sinusoid of frequency $\pi/2$ and a Gaussian noise $w(n)$ of zero mean and unit variance; that is,

$$x(n) = 2\cos\frac{\pi n}{2} + w(n)$$

We want to filter out the noise component using a 50th-order causal and linear-phase FIR filter.

1. Using the Parks–McClellan algorithm, design a narrow bandpass filter with passband width of no more than 0.02π and stopband attenuation of at least 30 dB. Note that no other parameters are given and that you have to choose the remaining parameters for the `firpm` function to satisfy the requirements. Provide a plot of the log-magnitude response in dB of the designed filter.
2. Generate 200 samples of the sequence $x(n)$ and processed through the preceding filter to obtain the output $y(n)$. Provide subplots of $x(n)$ and $y(n)$ for $100 \le n \le 200$ on one plot and comment on your results.

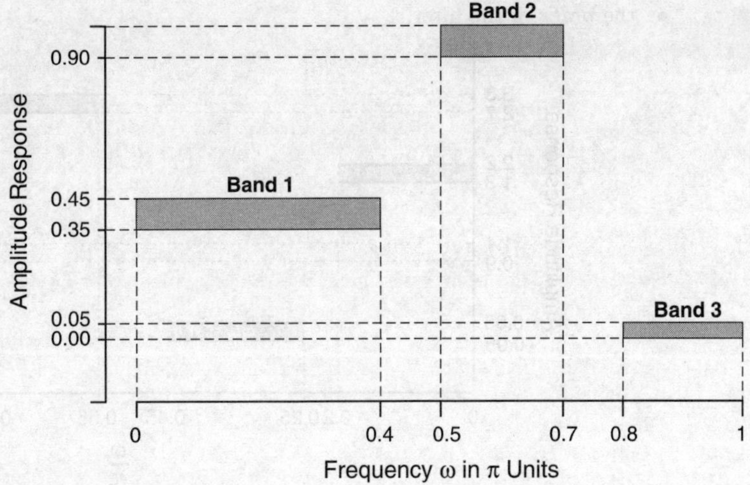

FIGURE P7.2 *Filter specifications for Problem P7.32*

P7.34 Design a minimum-order linear-phase FIR filter, using the Parks–McClellan algorithm, to satisfy the requirements given in Figure P7.1.

1. Provide a plot of the amplitude response with grid lines and axis labeling as shown in Figure P7.1.
2. Generate the following signals:

$$x_1(n) = \cos(0.25\pi n), \quad x_2(n) = \cos(0.5\pi n), \quad x_3(n) = \cos(0.75\pi n); \quad 0 \le n \le 100$$

Process these signals through this filter to obtain the corresponding output signals $y_1(n)$, $y_2(n)$, and $y_3(n)$. Provide stem plots of all input and output signals in one figure.

P7.35 Design a minimum-order linear-phase FIR filter, using the Parks–McClellan algorithm, to satisfy the requirements given in Figure P7.3. Provide a plot of the amplitude response with grid lines and axis labeling as shown in Figure P7.3.

P7.36 The specifications on the amplitude response (not to scale) of an FIR filter are given in Figure P7.4.

1. Using a window design approach and a *fixed* window function, design a minimum-length linear-phase FIR filter to satisfy the given requirements. Provide a plot of the amplitude response with grid lines as shown in Figure P7.4.
2. Using a window design approach and the Kaiser window function, design a minimum-length linear-phase FIR filter to satisfy the given requirements. Provide a plot of the amplitude response with grid lines as shown in Figure P7.4.
3. Using a frequency-sampling design approach and with no more than two samples in the transition bands, design a minimum-length linear-phase FIR filter to satisfy the given requirements. Provide a plot of the amplitude response with grid lines as shown in Figure P7.4.
4. Using the Parks–McClellan design approach, design a minimum-length linear-phase FIR filter to satisfy the given requirements. Provide a plot of the amplitude response with grid lines as shown in Figure P7.4.
5. Compare the preceding four design methods in terms of

   - the *order* of the filter,

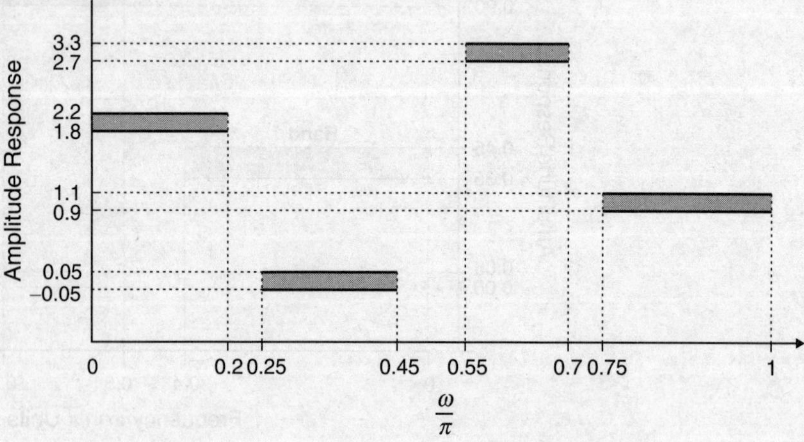

FIGURE P7.3   *Filter specifications for Problem P7.35*

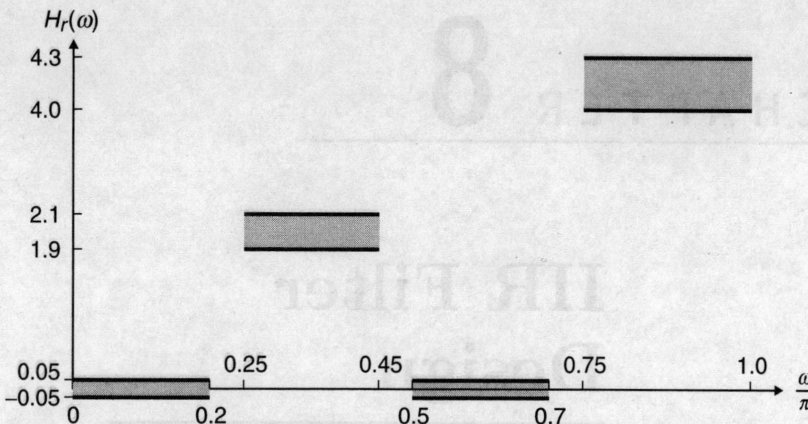

FIGURE P7.4   *Filter specifications for Problem P7.36*

- the *exact* band-edge frequencies,
- the *exact* tolerances in each band.

P7.37 Design a minimum-order linear-phase FIR filter, using the Parks–McClellan algorithm, to satisfy the requirements given in Figure P7.5. Provide a plot of the amplitude response with grid lines as shown in Figure P7.5.

P7.38 Design a minimum-length linear-phase bandpass filter of Problem P7.9 using the Parks–McClellan algorithm.

1. Plot the impulse response and the magnitude response in dB of the designed filter in one figure plot.
2. Plot the amplitude response of the designed filter and count the total number of extrema in passband and stopbands. Verify this number with the theoretical estimate of the total number of extrema.
3. Compare the order of this filter with that of the filter in Problem P7.9.

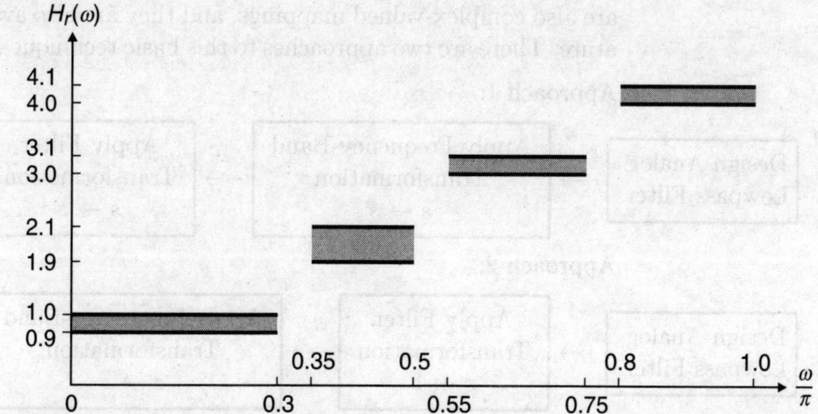

FIGURE P7.5   *Filter specifications for Problem P7.37*

CHAPTER 8

IIR Filter Design

IIR filters have infinite-duration impulse responses, and hence they can be matched to analog filters, all of which generally have infinitely long impulse responses. Therefore, the basic technique of IIR filter design transforms well-known analog filters into digital filters using *complex-valued* mappings. The advantage of this technique lies in the fact that both analog filter design (AFD) tables and the mappings are available extensively in the literature. This basic technique is called the A/D (analog-to-digital) filter transformation. However, the AFD tables are available only for lowpass filters. We also want to design other frequency-selective filters (highpass, bandpass, bandstop, etc.). To do this, we need to apply frequency-band transformations to lowpass filters. These transformations are also complex-valued mappings, and they are also available in the literature. There are two approaches to this basic technique of IIR filter design:

Approach 1:

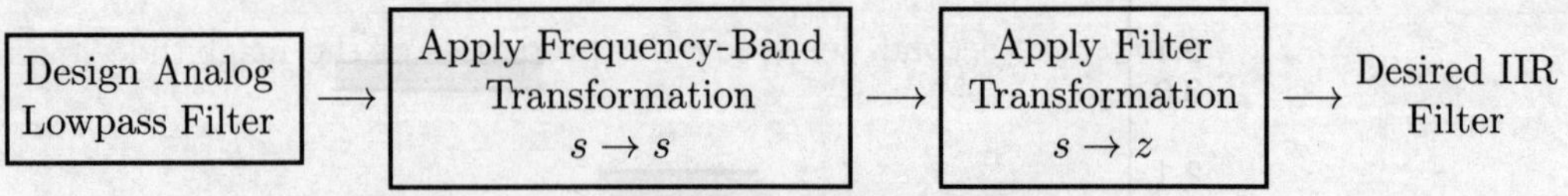

$$
\boxed{\text{Design Analog Lowpass Filter}} \longrightarrow \boxed{\begin{array}{c}\text{Apply Frequency-Band}\\ \text{Transformation}\\ s \to s\end{array}} \longrightarrow \boxed{\begin{array}{c}\text{Apply Filter}\\ \text{Transformation}\\ s \to z\end{array}} \longrightarrow \text{Desired IIR Filter}
$$

Approach 2:

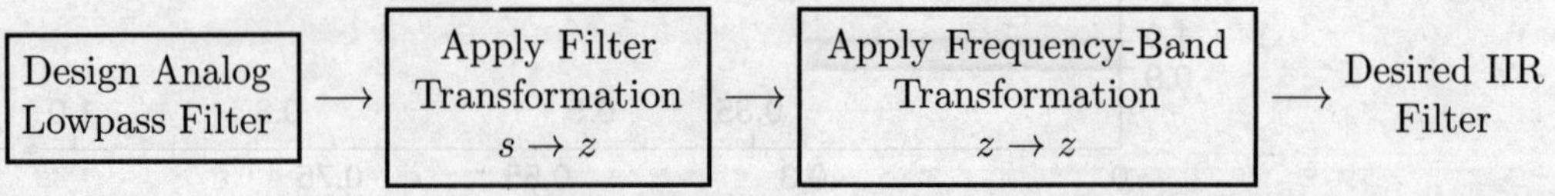

$$
\boxed{\text{Design Analog Lowpass Filter}} \longrightarrow \boxed{\begin{array}{c}\text{Apply Filter}\\ \text{Transformation}\\ s \to z\end{array}} \longrightarrow \boxed{\begin{array}{c}\text{Apply Frequency-Band}\\ \text{Transformation}\\ z \to z\end{array}} \longrightarrow \text{Desired IIR Filter}
$$

The first approach is used in MATLAB to design IIR filters. A straightforward use of these MATLAB functions does not provide any insight into the design methodology. Therefore, we will study the second approach because it involves the frequency-band transformation in the digital domain. Hence in this IIR filter design technique, we will follow the following steps:

- Design analog lowpass filters.
- Study and apply filter transformations to obtain digital lowpass filters.
- Study and apply frequency-band transformations to obtain other digital filters from digital lowpass filters.

The main problem with these approaches is that we have no control over the phase characteristics of the IIR filter. Hence IIR filter designs will be treated as *magnitude-only* designs. More sophisticated techniques, which can simultaneously approximate both the magnitude and the phase responses, require advanced optimization tools and hence will not be covered in this book.

We begin with a discussion on the analog filter specifications and the properties of the magnitude-squared response used in specifying analog filters. Next, before we delve into basic techniques for general IIR filters, we consider the design of special types of digital filters—for example, resonators, notch filters, comb filters, and so on. This is followed by a brief description of the characteristics of three widely used analog filters: *Butterworth*, *Chebyshev*, and *elliptic* filters. Finally, we will study transformations to convert these prototype analog filters into different frequency-selective digital filters and conclude this chapter with several IIR filter designs using MATLAB.

8.1 SOME PRELIMINARIES

We discuss two preliminary issues in this section. First, we consider the magnitude-squared response specifications, which are more typical of analog (and hence of IIR) filters. These specifications are given on the *relative linear scale*. Second, we study the properties of the magnitude-squared response.

8.1.1 RELATIVE LINEAR SCALE

Let $H_a(j\Omega)$ be the frequency response of an analog filter. Then the lowpass filter specifications on the magnitude-squared response are given by

$$\frac{1}{1+\epsilon^2} \leq |H_a(j\Omega)|^2 \leq 1, \quad |\Omega| \leq \Omega_p$$

$$0 \leq |H_a(j\Omega)|^2 \leq \frac{1}{A^2}, \quad \Omega_s \leq |\Omega| \tag{8.1}$$

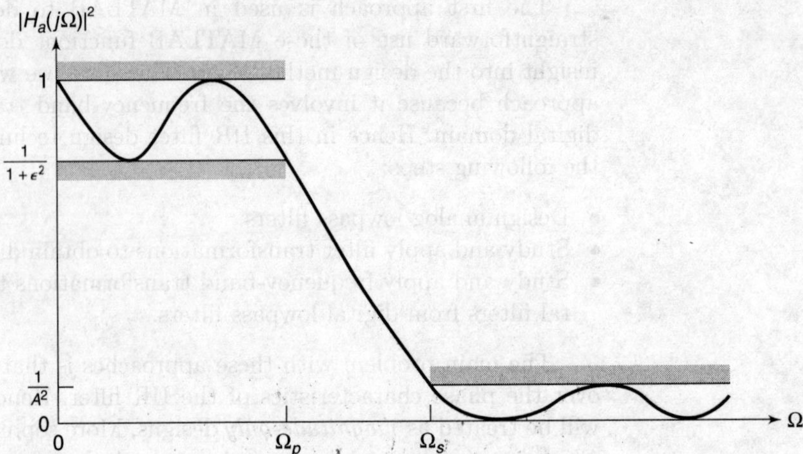

FIGURE 8.1 *Analog lowpass filter specifications*

where ϵ is a passband *ripple parameter*, Ω_p is the passband cutoff frequency in rad/sec, A is a stopband *attenuation parameter*, and Ω_s is the stopband cutoff in rad/sec. These specifications are shown in Figure 8.1, from which we observe that $|H_a(j\Omega)|^2$ must satisfy

$$
\begin{aligned}
|H_a(j\Omega_p)|^2 &= \frac{1}{1+\epsilon^2} \quad \text{at } \Omega = \Omega_p \\[2mm]
|H_a(j\Omega_s)|^2 &= \frac{1}{A^2} \quad \text{at } \Omega = \Omega_s
\end{aligned}
\tag{8.2}
$$

The parameters ϵ and A are related to parameters R_p and A_s, respectively, of the dB scale. These relations are given by

$$
R_p = -10\log_{10}\frac{1}{1+\epsilon^2} \Longrightarrow \epsilon = \sqrt{10^{R_p/10}-1}
\tag{8.3}
$$

and

$$
A_s = -10\log_{10}\frac{1}{A^2} \Longrightarrow A = 10^{A_s/20}
\tag{8.4}
$$

The ripples, δ_1 and δ_2, of the absolute scale are related to ϵ and A by

$$
\frac{1-\delta_1}{1+\delta_1} = \sqrt{\frac{1}{1+\epsilon^2}} \Longrightarrow \epsilon = \frac{2\sqrt{\delta_1}}{1-\delta_1}
$$

and

$$
\frac{\delta_2}{1+\delta_1} = \frac{1}{A} \Longrightarrow A = \frac{1+\delta_1}{\delta_2}
$$

8.1.2 PROPERTIES OF $|H_a(j\Omega)|^2$

Analog filter specifications (8.1), which are given in terms of the magnitude-squared response, contain no phase information. Now to evaluate the s-domain system function $H_a(s)$, consider

$$H_a(j\Omega) = H_a(s)|_{s=j\Omega}$$

Then we have

$$|H_a(j\Omega)|^2 = H_a(j\Omega)H_a^*(j\Omega) = H_a(j\Omega)H_a(-j\Omega) = H_a(s)H_a(-s)|_{s=j\Omega}$$

or

$$H_a(s)H_a(-s) = |H_a(j\Omega)|^2\Big|_{\Omega=s/j} \tag{8.5}$$

Therefore, the poles and zeros of the magnitude-squared function are distributed in a *mirror-image symmetry* with respect to the $j\Omega$ axis. Also for real filters, poles and zeros occur in complex conjugate pairs (or mirror-image symmetry with respect to the real axis). A typical pole-zero pattern of $H_a(s)H_a(-s)$ is shown in Figure 8.2. From this pattern, we can construct $H_a(s)$, which is the system function of our analog filter. We want $H_a(s)$ to represent a *causal* and *stable* filter. Then all poles of $H_a(s)$ must lie within the left half-plane. Thus we assign all left-half poles of $H_a(s)H_a(-s)$ to $H_a(s)$. However, zeros of $H_a(s)$ can lie anywhere in the s-plane. Therefore, they are not uniquely determined unless they all are on the $j\Omega$ axis. We will choose the zeros of $H_a(s)H_a(-s)$ lying left to or on the $j\Omega$ axis as the zeros of $Ha(s)$. The resulting filter is then called a *minimum-phase* filter.

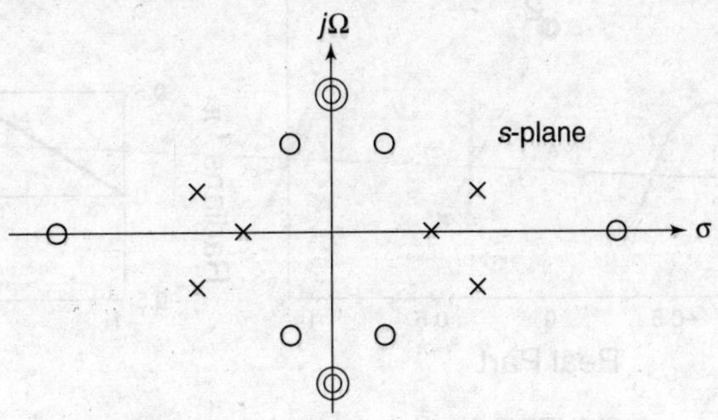

FIGURE 8.2 *Typical pole-zero pattern of $H_a(s)H_a(-s)$*

8.2 SOME SPECIAL FILTER TYPES

In this section, we consider the design of several special types of digital filters and describe their frequency response characteristics. We begin by describing the design and characteristics of a digital resonator.

8.2.1 DIGITAL RESONATORS

A digital resonator is a special two-pole bandpass filter with a pair of complex-conjugate poles located very near the unit circle, as shown in the left plot of Figure 8.3. The magnitude of the frequency response of the filter is shown in the top right plot of Figure 8.3. The name *resonator* refers to the fact that the filter has a large magnitude response in the vicinity of the pole position. The angle of the pole location determines the resonant frequency of the filter. Digital resonators are useful in many applications, including simple bandpass filtering and speech generation.

Let us consider the design of a digital resonator with a resonant peak at or near $\omega = \omega_0$. Hence we select the pole position as

$$p_{1,2} = re^{\pm j\omega_0} \tag{8.6}$$

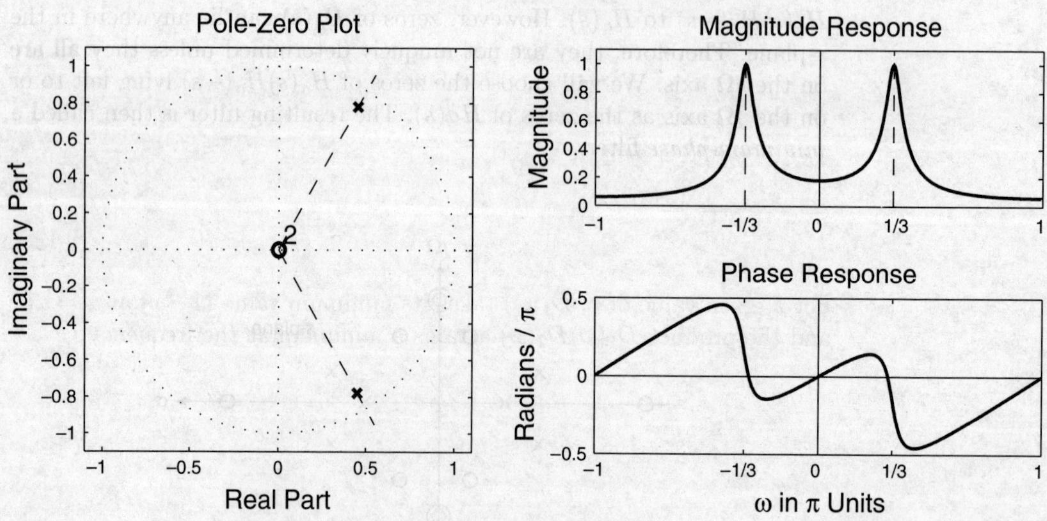

FIGURE 8.3 *Pole positions and frequency response of a digital resonator with* $r = 0.9$ *and* $\omega_0 = \pi/3$

The corresponding system function is

$$H(z) = \frac{b_0}{(1 - re^{j\omega_0}z^{-1})(1 - re^{-j\omega_0}z^{-1})}$$

$$= \frac{b_0}{1 - (2r\cos\omega_0)z^{-1} + r^2 z^{-2}} \tag{8.7}$$

where b_0 is a gain parameter. The frequency response of the resonator is

$$H(e^{j\omega}) = \frac{b_0}{\left[1 - re^{-j(\omega-\omega_0)}\right]\left[1 - re^{-j(\omega+\omega_0)}\right]} \tag{8.8}$$

Since $\left|H(e^{j\omega})\right|$ has its peak at or near $\omega = \omega_0$, we select the gain parameter b_0 so that $\left|H(e^{j\omega_0})\right| = 1$. Hence

$$\left|H(e^{j\omega_0})\right| = \frac{b_0}{|(1-r)(1 - re^{-j2\omega_0})|}$$

$$= \frac{b_0}{(1-r)\sqrt{1 + r^2 - 2r\cos 2\omega_0}} \tag{8.9}$$

Consequently, the desired gain parameter is

$$b_0 = (1-r)\sqrt{1 + r^2 - 2r\cos 2\omega_0} \tag{8.10}$$

The magnitude of the frequency response $H(\omega)$ may be expressed as

$$\left|H(e^{j\omega})\right| = \frac{b_0}{D_1(\omega)D_2(\omega)} \tag{8.11}$$

where $D_1(\omega)$ and $D_2(\omega)$ are given as

$$D_1(\omega) = \sqrt{1 + r^2 - 2r\cos(\omega - \omega_0)} \tag{8.12a}$$

$$D_2(\omega) = \sqrt{1 + r^2 - 2r\cos(\omega + \omega_0)} \tag{8.12b}$$

For a given value of r, $D_1(\omega)$ takes its minimum value $(1-r)$ at $\omega = \omega_0$, and the product $D_1(\omega)D_2(\omega)$ attains a minimum at the frequency

$$\omega_r = \cos^{-1}\left(\frac{1+r^2}{2r}\cos\omega_0\right) \tag{8.13}$$

which defines precisely the resonant frequency of the filter. Note that when r is very close to unity, $\omega_r \approx \omega_0$, which is the angular position of the pole. Furthermore, as r approaches unity, the resonant peak becomes sharper (narrower) because $D_1(\omega)$ changes rapidly in the vicinity of ω_0.

A quantitative measure of the width of the peak is the $3\,\text{dB}$ bandwidth of the filter, denoted as $\Delta(\omega)$. For values of r close to unity,

$$\Delta\omega \approx 2(1 - r) \tag{8.14}$$

Figure 8.3 illustrates the magnitude and phase responses of a digital resonator with $\omega_0 = \pi/3$, $r = 0.90$. Note that the phase response has its greatest rate of change near the resonant frequency $\omega_r \approx \omega_0 = \pi/3$.

This resonator has two zeros at $z = 0$. Instead of placing zeros at the origin, an alternative choice is to locate the zeros at $z = 1$ and $z = -1$. This choice completely eliminates the response of the filter at the frequencies $\omega = 0$ and $\omega = \pi$, which may be desirable in some applications. The corresponding resonator has the system function

$$H(z) = \frac{G(1 - z^{-1})(1 + z^{-1})}{(1 - re^{j\omega_0}z^{-1})(1 - re^{-j\omega_0}z^{-1})}$$

$$= G\frac{1 - z^{-2}}{1 - (2r\cos\omega_0)z^{-1} + r^2z^{-2}} \tag{8.15}$$

and the frequency response characteristic

$$H\!\left(e^{j\omega}\right) = G\frac{1 - e^{-j2\omega}}{\left[1 - re^{j(\omega_0-\omega)}\right]\!\left[1 - re^{-j(\omega_0+\omega)}\right]} \tag{8.16}$$

where G is a gain parameter that is selected so that $\left|H\!\left(e^{j\omega_0}\right)\right| = 1$.

The introduction of zeros at $z = \pm 1$ alters both the magnitude and phase response of the resonator. The magnitude response may be expressed as

$$\left|H\!\left(e^{j\omega}\right)\right| = G\frac{N(\omega)}{D_1(\omega)D_2(\omega)} \tag{8.17}$$

where $N(\omega)$ is defined as

$$N(\omega) = \sqrt{2(1 - \cos 2\omega)} \tag{8.18}$$

Due to the presence of the zeros at $z = \pm 1$, the resonant frequency of the resonator is altered from the expression given by (8.13). The bandwidth of the filter is also altered. Although exact values for these two parameters are rather tedious to derive, we can easily compute the frequency response when the zeros are at $z = \pm 1$ and $z = 0$ and compare the results.

Figure 8.4 illustrates the magnitude and phase responses for the cases $z = \pm 1$ and $z = 0$, for pole location at $\omega = \pi/3$ and $r = 0.90$. We observe that the resonator with $z = \pm 1$ has a slightly smaller bandwidth than the resonator with zeros at $z = 0$. In addition, there appears to be a very small shift in the resonant frequency between the two cases.

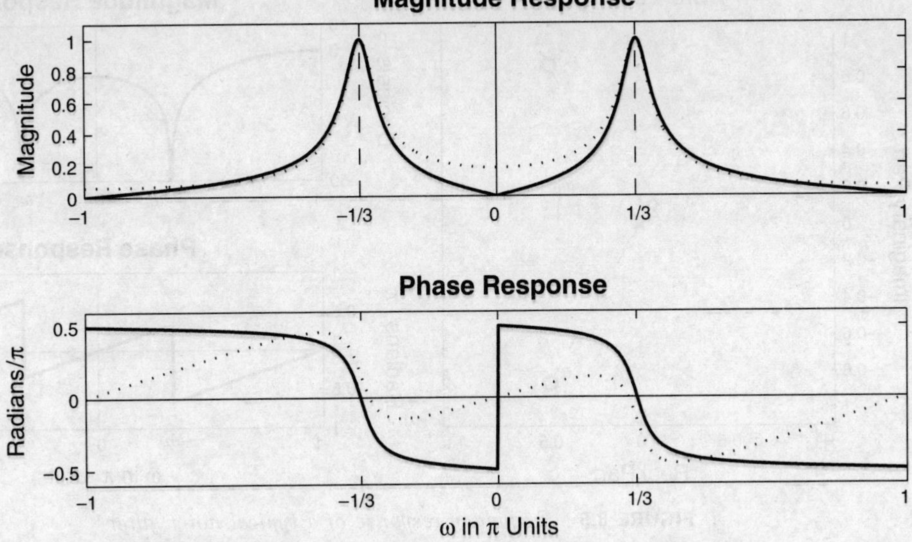

FIGURE 8.4 *Magnitude and phase responses of digital resonator with zeros at $z = \pm 1$ (solid lines) and $z = 0$ (dotted lines) for $r = 0.9$ and $\omega_0 = \pi/3$*

8.2.2 NOTCH FILTERS

A notch filter is a filter that contains one or more deep notches or, ideally, perfect nulls in its frequency response. Figure 8.5 illustrates the frequency response of a notch filter with a null at the frequency $\omega = \omega_0$. Notch filters are useful in many applications where specific frequency components must be eliminated. For example, instrumentation systems require that the power line frequency of 60 Hz and its harmonics be eliminated.

To create a null in the frequency response of a filter at a frequency ω_0, we simply introduce a pair of complex-conjugate zeros on the unit circle at the angle ω_0. Hence the zeros are selected as

$$z_{1,2} = e^{\pm j\omega_0} \tag{8.19}$$

Then the system function for the notch filter is

$$H(z) = b_0(1 - e^{j\omega_0}z^{-1})(1 - e^{-j\omega_0}z^{-1})$$
$$= b_0(1 - (2\cos\omega_0)z^{-1} + z^{-2}) \tag{8.20}$$

where b_0 is a gain factor. Figure 8.6 illustrates the magnitude response of a notch filter having a null at $\omega = \pi/4$.

The major problem with this notch filter is that the notch has a relatively large bandwidth, which means that other frequency components

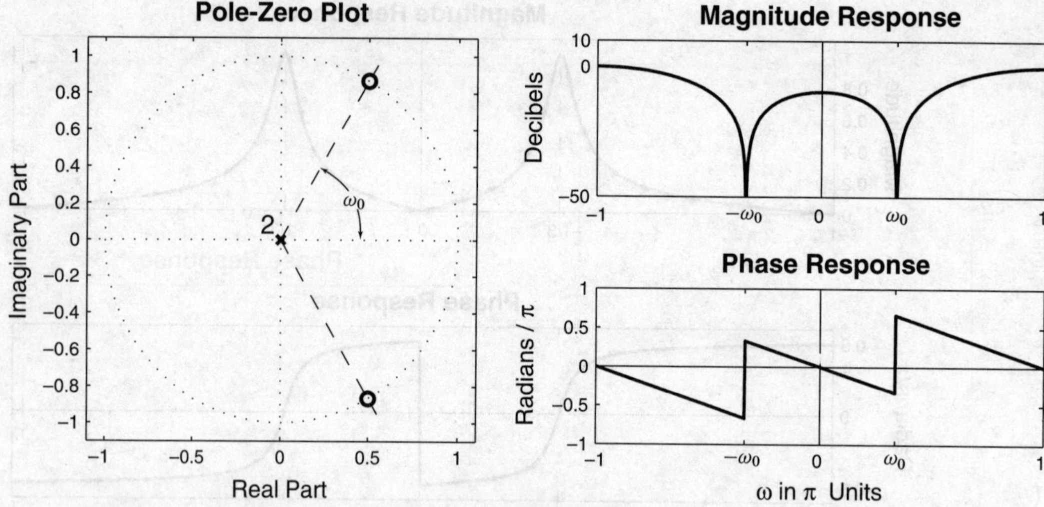

FIGURE 8.5 *Frequency response of a typical notch filter*

around the desired null are severely attenuated. To reduce the bandwidth of the null, we may resort to the more sophisticated, longer FIR filter designed according to the optimum equiripple design method described in Chapter 7. Alternatively, we could attempt to improve the frequency response of the filter by introducing poles in the system function.

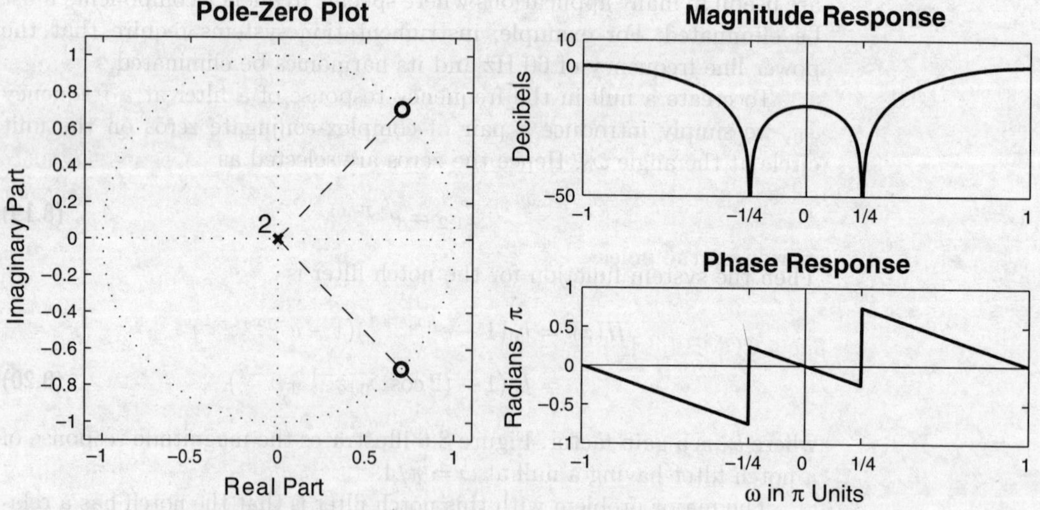

FIGURE 8.6 *Frequency response of a notch filter with $\omega_0 = \pi/4$*

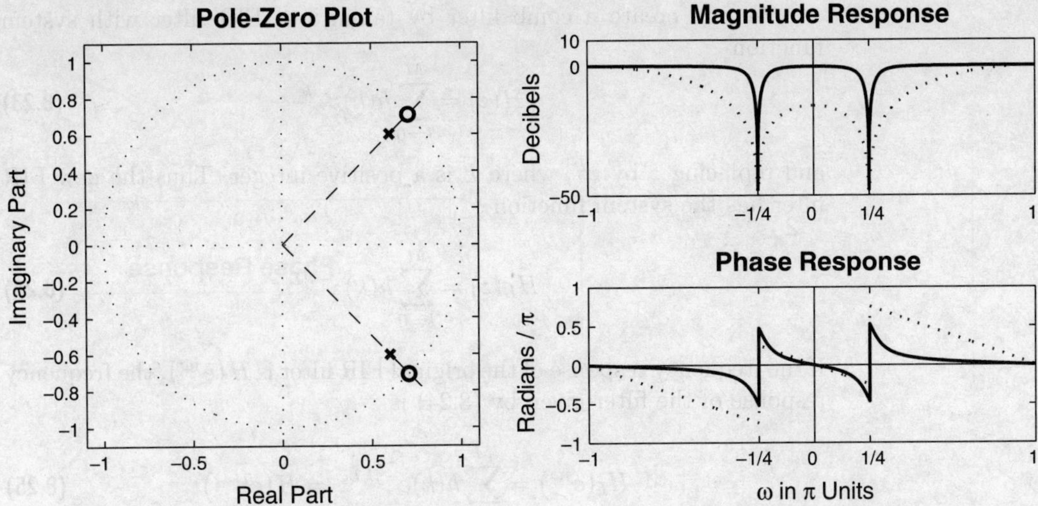

FIGURE 8.7 *Magnitude and phase responses of notch filter with poles (solid lines) and without poles (dotted lines) for $\omega_0 = \pi/4$ and $r = 0.85$*

In particular, suppose that we select the poles at

$$p_{1,2} = re^{\pm j\omega_0} \tag{8.21}$$

Hence the system function becomes

$$H(z) = b_0 \frac{1 - (2\cos\omega_0)z^{-1} + z^2}{1 - (2r\cos\omega_0)z^{-1} + r^2 z^{-2}} \tag{8.22}$$

The magnitude of the frequency response $\left|H\left(e^{j\omega}\right)\right|$ of this filter is illustrated in Figure 8.7 for $\omega_0 = \pi/4$ and $r = 0.85$. Also plotted in this figure is the frequency response without the poles. We observe that the effect of the pole is to introduce a resonance in the vicinity of the null and, thus, to reduce the bandwidth of the notch. In addition to reducing the bandwidth of the notch, the introduction of a pole in the vicinity of the null may result in a small ripple in the passband of the filter due to the resonance created by the pole.

8.2.3 COMB FILTERS

In its simplest form, a comb filter may be viewed as a notch filter in which the nulls occur periodically across the frequency band, hence the analogy to an ordinary comb that has periodically spaced teeth. Comb filters are used in many practical systems, including the rejections of power-line harmonics and the suppression of clutter from fixed objects in moving-target indicator (MTI) radars.

We can create a comb filter by taking our FIR filter with system function

$$H(z) = \sum_{k=0}^{M} h(k) z^{-k} \tag{8.23}$$

and replacing z by z^L, where L is a positive integer. Thus the new FIR filter has the system function

$$H_L(z) = \sum_{k=0}^{M} h(k) z^{-kL} \tag{8.24}$$

If the frequency response of the original FIR filter is $H\!\left(e^{j\omega}\right)$, the frequency response of the filter given by (8.24) is

$$H_L\!\left(e^{j\omega}\right) = \sum_{k=0}^{M} h(k) e^{-jkL\omega} = H\!\left(e^{jL\omega}\right) \tag{8.25}$$

Consequently, the frequency response characteristic $H_L\!\left(e^{j\omega}\right)$ is an L-order repetition of $H\!\left(e^{j\omega}\right)$ in the range $0 \le \omega \le 2\pi$. Figure 8.8 illustrates the relationship between $H_L\!\left(e^{j\omega}\right)$ and $H\!\left(e^{j\omega}\right)$ for $L = 4$. The introduction of a pole at each notch may be used to narrow the bandwidth of each notch, as just described.

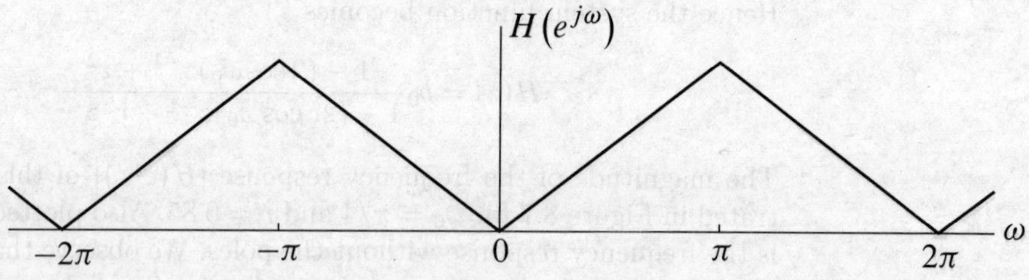

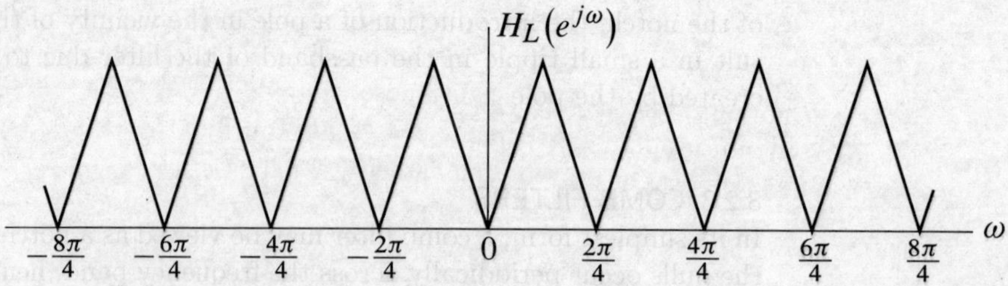

FIGURE 8.8 *Comb filters with frequency response* $H_L\!\left(e^{j\omega}\right)$ *obtained from* $H\!\left(e^{j\omega}\right)$ *for* $L = 4$

8.2.4 ALLPASS FILTERS

An *allpass filter* is characterized by a system function that has a constant magnitude response for all frequencies, that is,

$$\left|H(e^{j\omega})\right| = 1, \qquad 0 \le \omega \le \pi \tag{8.26}$$

A simple example of an allpass system is a system that introduces a pure delay to an input signal, that is,

$$H(z) = z^{-k} \tag{8.27}$$

This system passes all frequency components of an input signal without any frequency-dependent attenuation. It simply delays all frequency components by k samples.

A more general characterization of an allpass filter is one having a system function of the form

$$H(z) = \frac{a_N + a_{N-1}z^{-1} + \cdots + a_1 z^{-N+1} + z^{-N}}{1 + a_1 z^{-1} + \cdots + a_{N-1}z^{-N+1} + a_N z^{-N}} \tag{8.28}$$

which may be expressed in the compact form as

$$H(z) = z^{-N}\,\frac{A(z^{-1})}{A(z)} \tag{8.29}$$

where

$$A(z) = \sum_{k=0}^{N} a_k z^{-k}, \qquad a_0 = 1 \tag{8.30}$$

We observe that

$$\left|H(e^{j\omega})\right|^2 = H(z)H(z^{-1})\big|_{z=e^{j\omega}} = 1 \tag{8.31}$$

for all frequencies. Hence the system is allpass.

From the form of $H(z)$ given by (8.28), we observe that if z_0 is a pole of $H(z)$, then $1/z_0$ is a zero of $H(z)$. That is, the poles and zeros are reciprocals of one another. Figure 8.9 illustrates the typical pole-zero pattern for a single-pole, single-zero filter and a two-pole, two-zero filter. Graphs of the magnitude and phase characteristics of these two filters are shown in Figure 8.10 for $a = 0.6$ and $r = 0.9$, $\omega_0 = \pi/4$, where $A(z)$ for the two filters is, respectively, given as

$$A(z) = 1 + az^{-1} \tag{8.32a}$$

$$A(z) = 1 - (2r\cos\omega_0)z^{-1} + r^2 z^{-2} \tag{8.32b}$$

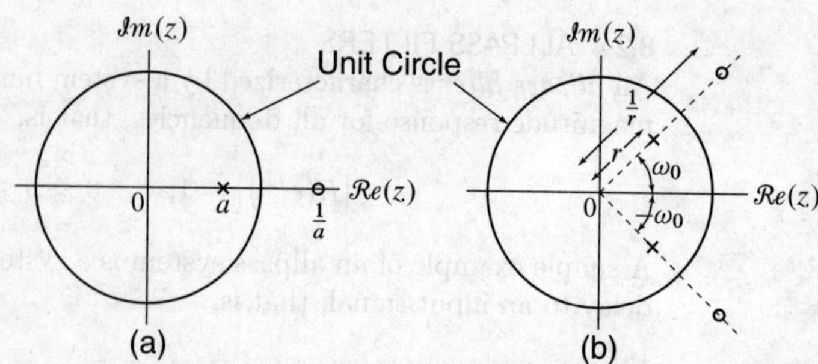

FIGURE 8.9   *Pole-zero locations for (a) one-pole and (b) two-pole allpass filter*

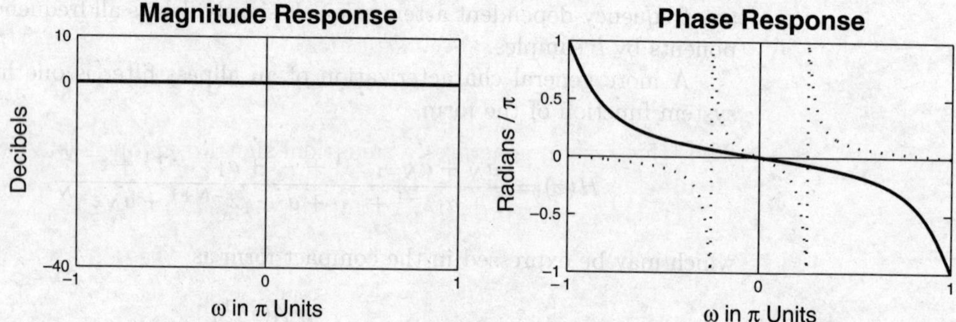

FIGURE 8.10   *Magnitude and phase responses for one-pole (solid line) and two-pole (dotted line) allpass filters*

The general form for the system function of an allpass filter with real coefficients may be expressed in factored form as

$$H(z) = \prod_{k=1}^{N_R} \frac{z^{-1} - \alpha_k}{1 - \alpha_k z^{-1}} \prod_{k=1}^{N_C} \frac{(z^{-1} - \beta_k)(z^{-1} - \beta_k^*)}{(1 - \beta_k z^{-1})(1 - \beta_k^* z^{-1})} \tag{8.33}$$

where N_R is the number of real poles and zeros and N_C is the number of complex-conjugate pairs of poles and zeros. For a causal and stable system, we require that $|\alpha_k| < 1$ and $|\beta_k| < 1$.

Allpass filters are usually employed as phase equalizers. When placed in cascade with a system that has an undesirable phase response, a phase equalizer is designed to compensate for the poor phase characteristics of the system and thus result in an overall linear phase system.

8.2.5 DIGITAL SINUSOIDAL OSCILLATORS

A digital sinusoidal oscillator can be viewed as a limiting form of a two-pole resonator for which the complex-conjugate poles are located on the unit circle. From our previous discussion of resonators, the system function for a resonator with poles at $re^{\pm j\omega_0}$ is

$$H(z) = \frac{b_0}{1 - (2r\cos\omega_0)z^{-1} + r^2 z^{-2}} \tag{8.34}$$

When we set $r = 1$ and select the gain parameter b_0 as

$$b_0 = A\sin\omega_0 \tag{8.35}$$

the system function becomes

$$H(z) = \frac{A\sin\omega_0}{1 - (2\cos\omega_0)z^{-1} + z^{-2}} \tag{8.36}$$

and the corresponding impulse response of the system becomes

$$h(n) = A\sin(n+1)\omega_0 \; u(n) \tag{8.37}$$

Thus this system generates a sinusoidal signal of frequency ω_0 when excited by an impulse $\delta(n) = 1$.

The block diagram representation of the system function given by (8.36) is illustrated in Figure 8.11. The corresponding difference equation for this system is

$$y(n) = (2\cos\omega_0)\, y(n-1) - y(n-2) + b_0\delta(n) \tag{8.38}$$

where $b_0 = A\sin\omega_0$.

Note that the sinusoidal oscillation obtained from the difference equation in (8.38) can also be obtained by setting the input to zero and setting the initial conditions to $y(-1) = 0$, $y(-2) = -A\sin\omega_0$. Thus the zero-input response to the second-order system described by the homogeneous difference equation

$$y(n) = (2\cos\omega_0)\, y(n-1) - y(n-2) \tag{8.39}$$

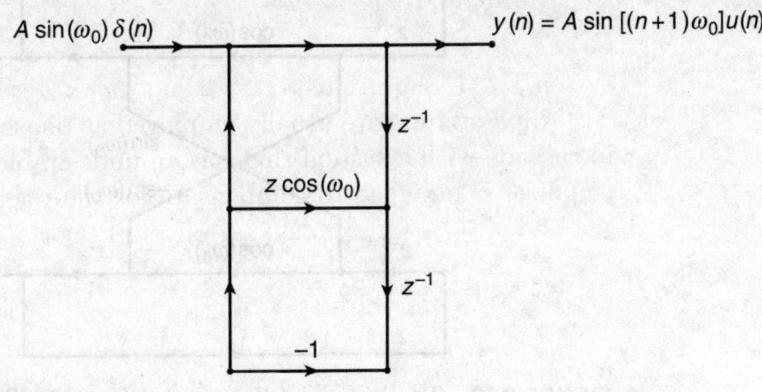

FIGURE 8.11 *Digital sinusoidal oscillator*

with initial conditions $y(-1) = 0$, $y(-2) = -A\sin\omega_0$ is exactly the same as the response of (8.38) to an impulse excitation. In fact, the homogeneous difference equation in (8.39) can be obtained directly from the trigonometric identity

$$\sin\alpha + \sin\beta = 2\sin\left(\frac{\alpha+\beta}{2}\right)\cos\left(\frac{\alpha-\beta}{2}\right) \tag{8.40}$$

where, by definition, $\alpha = (n+1)\omega_0$, $\beta = (n-1)\omega_0$, and $y(n) = \sin(n+1)\omega_0$.

In practical applications involving modulation of two sinusoidal carrier signals in phase quadrature, there is a need to generate the sinusoids $A\sin\omega_0 n$ and $A\cos\omega_0 n$. These quadrature carrier signals can be generated by the so-called coupled-form oscillator, which can be obtained with the aid of the trigonometric formulas

$$\cos(\alpha + \beta) = \cos\alpha\cos\beta - \sin\alpha\sin\beta \tag{8.41}$$

$$\sin(\alpha + \beta) = \sin\alpha\cos\beta + \cos\alpha\sin\beta \tag{8.42}$$

where by definition, $\alpha = n\omega_0$, $\beta = \omega_0$, $y_c(n) = \cos(n+1)\omega_0$, and $y_s(n) = \sin(n+1)\omega_0$. Thus, with substitution of these quantities into the two trigonometric identities, we obtain the two coupled difference equations

$$y_c(n) = (\cos\omega_0)\,y_c(n-1) - (\sin\omega_0)\,y_s(n-1) \tag{8.43}$$

$$y_s(n) = (\sin\omega_0)\,y_c(n-1) + (\cos\omega_0)\,y_s(n-1) \tag{8.44}$$

The structure for the realization of the coupled-form oscillator is illustrated in Figure 8.12. Note that this is a two-output system that does not require any input excitation, but it does require setting the initial conditions. $y_c(-1) = A\cos\omega_0$ and $y_s(-1) = -A\sin\omega_0$ in order to begin its self-sustaining oscillations.

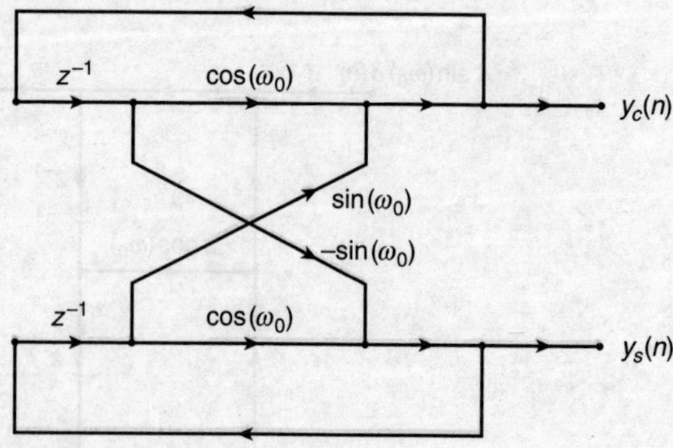

FIGURE 8.12 *Realization of the coupled form oscillator*

8.3 CHARACTERISTICS OF PROTOTYPE ANALOG FILTERS

IIR filter design techniques rely on existing analog filters to obtain digital filters. We designate these analog filters as *prototype* filters. Three prototypes are widely used in practice. In this section, we briefly summarize the characteristics of the lowpass versions of these prototypes: Butterworth lowpass, Chebyshev lowpass (Type I and II), and Elliptic lowpass. Although we will use MATLAB functions to design these filters, it is necessary to learn the characteristics of these filters so that we can use proper parameters in MATLAB functions to obtain correct results.

8.3.1 BUTTERWORTH LOWPASS FILTERS

This filter is characterized by the property that its magnitude response is flat in both passband and stopband. The magnitude-squared response of an Nth-order lowpass filter is given by

$$|H_a(j\Omega)|^2 = \frac{1}{1 + \left(\dfrac{\Omega}{\Omega_c}\right)^{2N}} \tag{8.45}$$

where N is the order of the filter and Ω_c is the cutoff frequency in rad/sec. The plot of the magnitude-squared response is as follows.

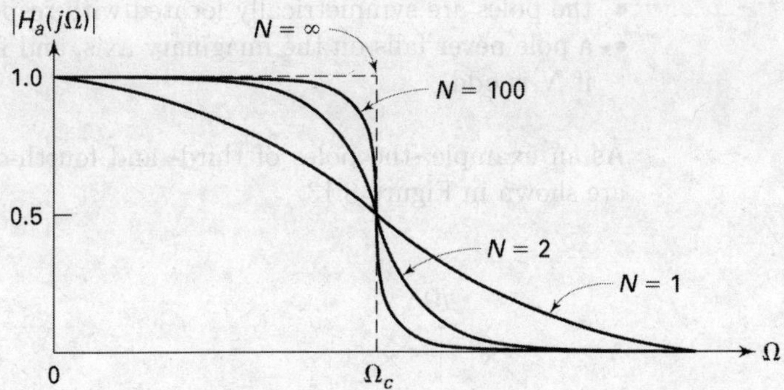

From this plot, we can observe the following properties:

- At $\Omega = 0$, $|H_a(j0)|^2 = 1$ for all N.
- At $\Omega = \Omega_c$, $|H_a(j\Omega_c)|^2 = \frac{1}{2}$ for all N, which implies a 3 dB attenuation at Ω_c.
- $|H_a(j\Omega)|^2$ is a monotonically decreasing function of Ω.

- $|H_a(j\Omega)|^2$ approaches an ideal lowpass filter as $N \to \infty$.
- $|H_a(j\Omega)|^2$ is *maximally flat* at $\Omega = 0$ since derivatives of all orders exist and are equal to zero.

To determine the system function $H_a(s)$, we put (8.45) in the form of (8.5) to obtain

$$H_a(s)H_a(-s) = |H_a(j\Omega)|^2 \Big|_{\Omega=s/j} = \frac{1}{1 + \left(\dfrac{s}{j\Omega_c}\right)^{2N}} = \frac{(j\Omega)^{2N}}{s^{2N} + (j\Omega_c)^{2N}}$$

$$(8.46)$$

The roots of the denominator polynomial (or poles of $H_a(s)H_a(-s)$) from (8.46) are given by

$$p_k = (-1)^{\frac{1}{2N}}(j\Omega) = \Omega_c e^{j\frac{\pi}{2N}(2k+N+1)}, \quad k = 0, 1, \ldots, 2N-1 \qquad (8.47)$$

An interpretation of (8.47) is that

- there are $2N$ poles of $H_a(s)H_a(-s)$, which are equally distributed on a circle of radius Ω_c with angular spacing of π/N radians;
- for N odd the poles are given by $p_k = \Omega_c e^{jk\pi/N}, \quad k = 0, 1, \ldots, 2N-1$;
- for N even the poles are given by $p_k = \Omega_c e^{j\left(\frac{\pi}{2N}+\frac{k\pi}{N}\right)}, \quad k = 0, 1, \ldots, 2N-1$;
- the poles are symmetrically located with respect to the $j\Omega$ axis;
- a pole never falls on the imaginary axis, and falls on the real axis only if N is odd.

As an example, the poles of third- and fourth-order Butterworth filters are shown in Figure 8.13.

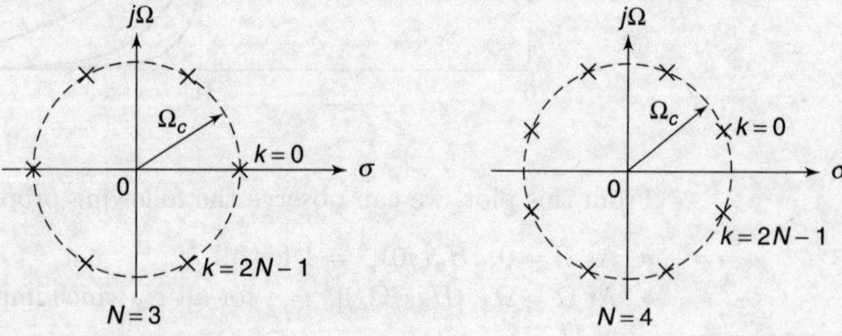

FIGURE 8.13 *Pole plots for Butterworth filters*

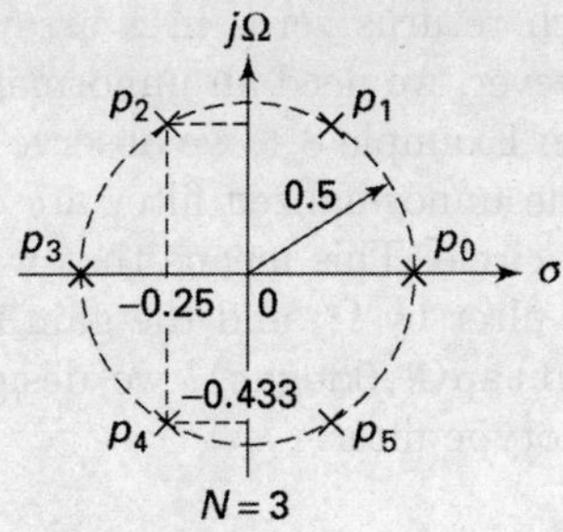

FIGURE 8.14 *Pole plot for Example 8.1*

A stable and causal filter $H_a(s)$ can now be specified by selecting poles in the left half-plane, and $H_a(s)$ can be written in the form

$$H_a(s) = \frac{\Omega_c^N}{\displaystyle\prod_{\text{LHP poles}} (s - p_k)} \tag{8.48}$$

☐ **EXAMPLE 8.1** Given that $|H_a(j\Omega)|^2 = \dfrac{1}{1 + 64\Omega^6}$, determine the analog filter system function $H_a(s)$.

Solution From the given magnitude-squared response,

$$|H_a(j\Omega)|^2 = \frac{1}{1 + 64\Omega^6} = \frac{1}{1 + \left(\dfrac{\Omega}{0.5}\right)^{2(3)}}$$

Comparing this with expression (8.45), we obtain $N = 3$ and $\Omega_c = 0.5$. The poles of $H_a(s)H_a(-s)$ are as shown in Figure 8.14.

Hence

$$H_a(j\Omega) = \frac{\Omega_c^3}{(s - p_2)(s - p_3)(s - p_4)}$$

$$= \frac{1/8}{(s + 0.25 - j0.433)(s + 0.5)(s + 0.25 + j0.433)}$$

$$= \frac{0.125}{(s + 0.5)(s^2 + 0.5s + 0.25)}$$

☐

8.3.2 MATLAB IMPLEMENTATION

MATLAB provides a function called `[z,p,k]=buttap(N)` to design a *normalized* (i.e., $\Omega_c = 1$) Butterworth analog prototype filter of order N, which returns zeros in z array, poles in p array, and the gain value k. However, we need an unnormalized Butterworth filter with arbitrary Ω_c. From Example 8.1, we observe that there are no zeros and that the poles of the unnormalized filter are on a circle with radius Ω_c instead of on a unit circle. This means that we have to scale the array p of the normalized filter by Ω_c and the gain k by Ω_c^N. In the following function, called U_buttap(N,Omegac), we design the unnormalized Butterworth analog prototype filter.

```
function [b,a] = u_buttap(N,Omegac);
% Unnormalized Butterworth analog lowpass filter prototype
% ------------------------------------------------------------
% [b,a] = u_buttap(N,Omegac);
%       b = numerator polynomial coefficients of Ha(s)
%       a = denominator polynomial coefficients of Ha(s)
%       N = Order of the Butterworth Filter
% Omegac = Cutoff frequency in radians/sec
%
[z,p,k] = buttap(N);
        p = p*Omegac;
        k = k*Omegac^N;
        B = real(poly(z));
        b0 = k;  b = k*B;  a = real(poly(p));
```

This function provides a direct form (or numerator-denominator) structure. Often, we also need a cascade form structure. In Chapter 6, we have already studied how to convert a direct form into a cascade form. The following sdir2cas function describes the procedure that is suitable for analog filters.

```
function [C,B,A] = sdir2cas(b,a);
% DIRECT form to CASCADE form conversion in s-plane
% ---------------------------------------------------
% [C,B,A] = sdir2cas(b,a)
%  C = gain coefficient
%  B = K by 3 matrix of real coefficients containing bk's
%  A = K by 3 matrix of real coefficients containing ak's
%  b = numerator polynomial coefficients of DIRECT form
%  a = denominator polynomial coefficients of DIRECT form
%
Na = length(a)-1; Nb = length(b)-1;
```

```matlab
% Compute gain coefficient C
b0 = b(1); b = b/b0;  a0 = a(1); a = a/a0;  C = b0/a0;
%
% Denominator second-order sections:
p= cplxpair(roots(a)); K = floor(Na/2);
if K*2 == Na       % Computation when Na is even
   A = zeros(K,3);
   for n=1:2:Na
       Arow = p(n:1:n+1,:);  Arow = poly(Arow);
       A(fix((n+1)/2),:) = real(Arow);
   end

elseif Na == 1    % Computation when Na = 1
       A = [0 real(poly(p))];

else               % Computation when Na is odd and > 1
   A = zeros(K+1,3);
   for n=1:2:2*K
       Arow = p(n:1:n+1,:);  Arow = poly(Arow);
       A(fix((n+1)/2),:) = real(Arow);
       end
       A(K+1,:) = [0 real(poly(p(Na)))];
end

% Numerator second-order sections:
z = cplxpair(roots(b)); K = floor(Nb/2);
if Nb == 0          % Computation when Nb = 0
   B = [0 0 poly(z)];

elseif K*2 == Nb     % Computation when Nb is even
   B = zeros(K,3);
   for n=1:2:Nb
       Brow = z(n:1:n+1,:);  Brow = poly(Brow);
       B(fix((n+1)/2),:) = real(Brow);
   end

elseif Nb == 1       % Computation when Nb = 1
       B = [0 real(poly(z))];

else                 % Computation when Nb is odd and > 1
   B = zeros(K+1,3);
   for n=1:2:2*K
       Brow = z(n:1:n+1,:);  Brow = poly(Brow);
       B(fix((n+1)/2),:) = real(Brow);
   end
   B(K+1,:) = [0 real(poly(z(Nb)))];
end
```

□   **EXAMPLE 8.2**   Design a third-order Butterworth analog prototype filter with $\Omega_c = 0.5$ given in Example 8.1.

Solution   MATLAB script:

```
>> N = 3; OmegaC = 0.5;  [b,a] = u_buttap(N,OmegaC);
>> [C,B,A] = sdir2cas(b,a)
C = 0.1250
B = 0       0      1
A = 1.0000    0.5000    0.2500
          0    1.0000    0.5000
```

The cascade form coefficients agree with those in Example 8.1.   □

8.3.3 DESIGN EQUATIONS

The analog lowpass filter is specified by the parameters Ω_p, R_p, Ω_s, and A_s. Therefore, the essence of the design in the case of Butterworth filter is to obtain the order N and the cutoff frequency Ω_c, given these specifications. We want

- at $\Omega = \Omega_p$, $-10 \log_{10} |H_a(j\Omega)|^2 = R_p$, or

$$-10 \log_{10} \left(\frac{1}{1 + \left(\dfrac{\Omega_p}{\Omega_c}\right)^{2N}} \right) = R_p$$

and
- at $\Omega = \Omega_s$, $-10 \log_{10} |H_a(j\Omega)|^2 = A_s$, or

$$-10 \log_{10} \left(\frac{1}{1 + \left(\dfrac{\Omega_s}{\Omega_c}\right)^{2N}} \right) = A_s$$

Solving these two equations for N and Ω_c, we have

$$N = \frac{\log_{10} \left[\left(10^{R_p/10} - 1\right) / \left(10^{A_s/10} - 1\right) \right]}{2 \log_{10} \left(\Omega_p/\Omega_s\right)}$$

In general, N will not be an integer. Since we want N to be an integer, we must choose

$$N = \left\lceil \frac{\log_{10} \left[\left(10^{R_p/10} - 1\right) / \left(10^{A_s/10} - 1\right) \right]}{2 \log_{10} \left(\Omega_p/\Omega_s\right)} \right\rceil \tag{8.49}$$

where the operation $\lceil x \rceil$ means "choose the smallest integer larger than x"—for example, $\lceil 4.5 \rceil = 5$. Since the actual N chosen is larger than required, specifications can be either met or exceeded either at Ω_p or at Ω_s. To satisfy the specifications exactly at Ω_p,

$$\Omega_c = \frac{\Omega_p}{\sqrt[2N]{\left(10^{R_p/10} - 1\right)}} \tag{8.50}$$

or, to satisfy the specifications exactly at Ω_s,

$$\Omega_c = \frac{\Omega_s}{\sqrt[2N]{\left(10^{A_s/10} - 1\right)}} \tag{8.51}$$

☐   **EXAMPLE 8.3**   Design a lowpass Butterworth filter to satisfy the following specifications.

$$\text{Passband cutoff: } \Omega_p = 0.2\pi \; ; \; \text{Passband ripple: } R_p = 7\,\text{dB}$$

$$\text{Stopband cutoff: } \Omega_s = 0.3\pi \; ; \; \text{Stopband ripple: } A_s = 16\,\text{dB}$$

Solution   From (8.49),

$$N = \left\lceil \frac{\log_{10}\left[\left(10^{0.7} - 1\right)/\left(10^{1.6} - 1\right)\right]}{2\log_{10}\left(0.2\pi/0.3\pi\right)} \right\rceil = \lceil 2.79 \rceil = 3$$

To satisfy the specifications exactly at Ω_p, from (8.50) we obtain

$$\Omega_c = \frac{0.2\pi}{\sqrt[6]{\left(10^{0.7} - 1\right)}} = 0.4985$$

To satisfy specifications exactly at Ω_s, from (8.51) we obtain

$$\Omega_c = \frac{0.3\pi}{\sqrt[6]{\left(10^{1.6} - 1\right)}} = 0.5122$$

Now we can choose any Ω_c between the above two numbers. Let us choose $\Omega_c = 0.5$. We have to design a Butterworth filter with $N = 3$ and $\Omega_c = 0.5$, which we did in Example 8.1. Hence

$$H_a(j\Omega) = \frac{0.125}{(s + 0.5)\left(s^2 + 0.5s + 0.25\right)}$$

☐

8.3.4 MATLAB IMPLEMENTATION

The preceding design procedure can be implemented in MATLAB as a simple function. Using the U_buttap function, we provide the afd_butt function to design an analog Butterworth lowpass filter, given its specifications. This function uses (8.50).

```
function [b,a] = afd_butt(Wp,Ws,Rp,As);
% Analog lowpass filter design: Butterworth
% ------------------------------------------
% [b,a] = afd_butt(Wp,Ws,Rp,As);
%  b = numerator coefficients of Ha(s)
%  a = denominator coefficients of Ha(s)
% Wp = passband-edge frequency in rad/sec; Wp > 0
% Ws = stopband-edge frequency in rad/sec; Ws > Wp > 0
% Rp = passband ripple in +dB; (Rp > 0)
% As = stopband attenuation in +dB; (As > 0)
%
if Wp <= 0
        error('Passband edge must be larger than 0')
end
if Ws <= Wp
        error('Stopband edge must be larger than Passband edge')
end
if (Rp <= 0) | (As < 0)
        error('PB ripple and/or SB attenuation must be larger than 0')
end


N = ceil((log10((10^(Rp/10)-1)/(10^(As/10)-1)))/(2*log10(Wp/Ws)));
fprintf('\n*** Butterworth Filter Order = %2.0f \n',N)
OmegaC = Wp/((10^(Rp/10)-1)^(1/(2*N)));
[b,a]=u_buttap(N,OmegaC);
```

To display the frequency-domain plots of analog filters, we provide a function called freqs_m, which is a modified version of a function freqs provided by MATLAB. This function computes the magnitude response in absolute as well as in relative dB scale and the phase response. This function is similar to the freqz_m function discussed earlier. One main difference between them is that in the freqs_m function the responses are computed up to a maximum frequency $\Omega_{\max}$.

```
function [db,mag,pha,w] = freqs_m(b,a,wmax);
% Computation of s-domain frequency response: Modified version
% ------------------------------------------------------------
% [db,mag,pha,w] = freqs_m(b,a,wmax);
```

```
%    db = relative magnitude in db over [0 to wmax]
%   mag = absolute magnitude over [0 to wmax]
%   pha = phase response in radians over [0 to wmax]
%     w = array of 500 frequency samples between [0 to wmax]
%     b = numerator polynomial coefficents of Ha(s)
%     a = denominator polynomial coefficents of Ha(s)
% wmax = maximum frequency in rad/sec over which response is desired
%
w = [0:1:500]*wmax/500;   H = freqs(b,a,w);
mag = abs(H);   db = 20*log10((mag+eps)/max(mag));   pha = angle(H);
```

The impulse response $h_a(t)$ of the analog filter is computed using MATLAB's `impulse` function.

☐   **EXAMPLE 8.4**   Design the analog Butterworth lowpass filter specified in Example 8.3 using MATLAB.

Solution   MATLAB script:

```
>> Wp = 0.2*pi; Ws = 0.3*pi; Rp = 7; As = 16;
>> Ripple = 10 ^ (-Rp/20); Attn = 10 ^ (-As/20);
>> % Analog filter design:
>> [b,a] = afd_butt(Wp,Ws,Rp,As);
*** Butterworth Filter Order =  3
>> % Calculation of second-order sections:
>> [C,B,A] = sdir2cas(b,a)
C = 0.1238
B = 0        0        1
A = 1.0000    0.4985    0.2485
         0    1.0000    0.4985
>> % Calculation of frequency response:
>> [db,mag,pha,w] = freqs_m(b,a,0.5*pi);
>> % Calculation of impulse response:
>> [ha,x,t] = impulse(b,a);
```

The system function is given by

$$H_a(s) = \frac{0.1238}{\left(s^2 + 0.4985s + 0.2485\right)\left(s + 0.4985\right)}$$

This $H_a(s)$ is slightly different from the one in Example 8.3 because in that example we used $\Omega_c = 0.5$, while in the `afd_butt` function Ω_c is chosen to satisfy the specifications at Ω_p. The filter plots are shown in Figure 8.15.   ☐

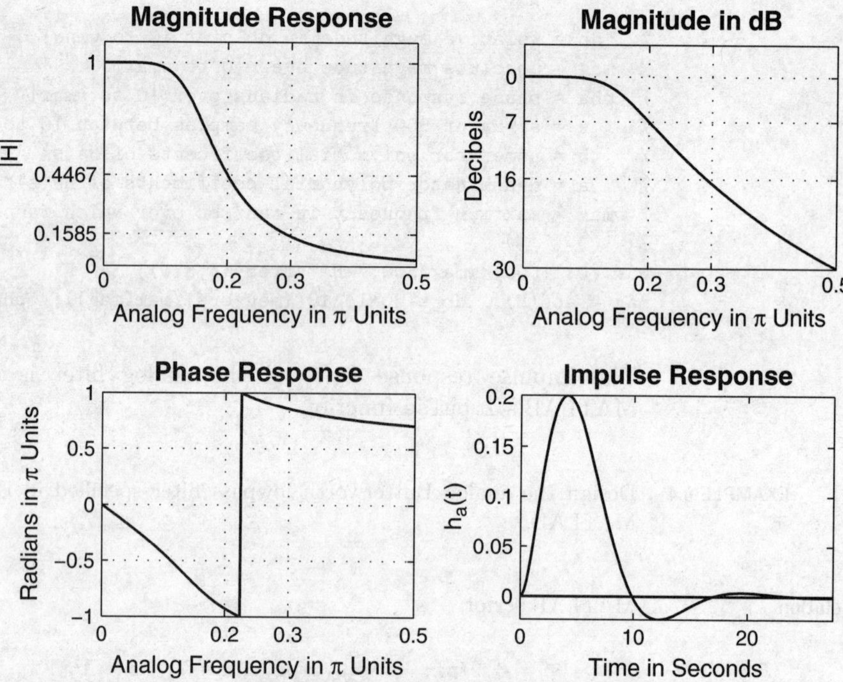

FIGURE 8.15 *Butterworth analog filter in Example 8.4*

8.3.5 CHEBYSHEV LOWPASS FILTERS

There are two types of Chebyshev filters. The Chebyshev-I filters have *equiripple response in the passband*, while the Chebyshev-II filters have *equiripple response in the stopband*. Butterworth filters have monotonic response in both bands. Recall our discussions regarding equiripple FIR filters. We noted that by choosing a filter that has an equiripple rather than a monotonic behavior, we can obtain a lower-order filter. Therefore, Chebyshev filters provide lower order than Butterworth filters for the same specifications.

The magnitude-squared response of a Chebyshev-I filter is

$$|H_a(j\Omega)|^2 = \frac{1}{1 + \epsilon^2 T_N^2 \left(\dfrac{\Omega}{\Omega_c} \right)} \tag{8.52}$$

where N is the order of the filter, ϵ is the passband ripple factor, which is related to R_p, and $T_N(x)$ is the Nth-order Chebyshev polynomial given by

$$T_N(x) = \begin{cases} \cos\left(N\cos^{-1}(x) \right), & 0 \le x \le 1 \\ \cosh\left(\cosh^{-1}(x) \right), & 1 < x < \infty \end{cases} \quad \text{where } x = \frac{\Omega}{\Omega_c}$$

The equiripple response of the Chebyshev filters is due to this polynomial $T_N(x)$. Its key properties are (a) for $0 < x < 1$, $T_N(x)$ oscillates between -1 and 1, and (b) for $1 < x < \infty$, $T_N(x)$ increases monotonically to ∞.

There are two possible shapes of $|H_a(j\Omega)|^2$, one for N odd and one for N even as shown here. Note that $x = \Omega/\Omega_c$ is the normalized frequency.

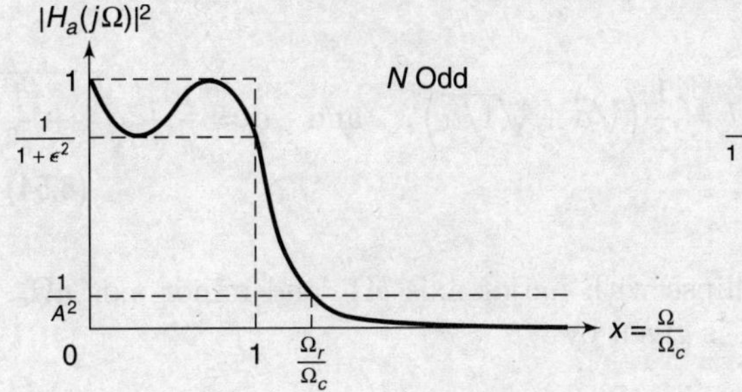

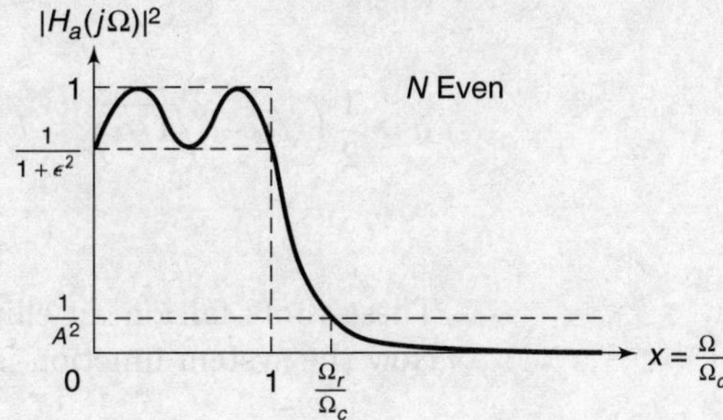

From these two response plots we observe the following properties:

- At $x = 0$ (or $\Omega = 0$), $\quad |H_a(j0)|^2 = 1 \quad$ for N odd,

$$|H_a(j0)|^2 = \frac{1}{1+\epsilon^2} \quad \text{for } N \text{ even.}$$

- At $x = 1$ (or $\Omega = \Omega_c$), $\quad |H_a(j1)|^2 = \frac{1}{1+\epsilon^2} \quad$ for all N.

- For $0 \le x \le 1$ (or $0 \le \Omega \le \Omega_c$), $|H_a(jx)|^2$ oscillates between 1 and $\dfrac{1}{1+\epsilon^2}$.

- For $x > 1$ (or $\Omega > \Omega_c$), $|H_a(jx)|^2$ decreases monotonically to 0.

- At $x = \Omega_r$, $|H_a(jx)|^2 = \dfrac{1}{A^2}$.

To determine a causal and stable $H_a(s)$, we must find the poles of $H_a(s)H_a(-s)$ and select the left half-plane poles for $H_a(s)$. The poles of $H_a(s)H_a(-s)$ are obtained by finding the roots of

$$1 + \epsilon^2 T_N^2\left(\frac{s}{j\Omega_c}\right)$$

The solution of this equation is tedious if not difficult to obtain. It can be shown that if $p_k = \sigma_k + j\Omega_k$, $\quad k = 0, \ldots, N-1$ are the (left half-plane) roots of these polynomial, then

$$\sigma_k = (a\Omega_c)\cos\left[\frac{\pi}{2} + \frac{(2k+1)\pi}{2N}\right]$$

$$\Omega_k = (b\Omega_c)\sin\left[\frac{\pi}{2} + \frac{(2k+1)\pi}{2N}\right] \quad k = 0, \dots, N-1 \qquad (8.53)$$

where

$$a = \frac{1}{2}\left(\sqrt[N]{\alpha} - \sqrt[N]{1/\alpha}\right), \quad b = \frac{1}{2}\left(\sqrt[N]{\alpha} + \sqrt[N]{1/\alpha}\right), \quad \text{and} \quad \alpha = \frac{1}{\epsilon} + \sqrt{1 + \frac{1}{\epsilon^2}}$$

$$(8.54)$$

These roots fall on an ellipse with major axis $b\Omega_c$ and minor axis $a\Omega_c$. Now the system function is given by

$$H_a(s) = \frac{K}{\prod\limits_{k}(s - p_k)} \qquad (8.55)$$

where K is a normalizing factor chosen to make

$$H_a(j0) = \begin{cases} 1, & N \text{ odd}, \\[2ex] \dfrac{1}{\sqrt{1 + \epsilon^2}}, & N \text{ even} \end{cases} \qquad (8.56)$$

8.3.6 MATLAB IMPLEMENTATION

MATLAB provides a function called [z,p,k]=cheb1ap(N,Rp) to design a *normalized* Chebyshev-I analog prototype filter of order N and passband ripple Rp and that returns zeros in z array, poles in p array, and the gain value k. We need an unnormalized Chebyshev-I filter with arbitrary Ω_c. This is achieved by scaling the array p of the normalized filter by Ω_c. Similar to the Butterworth prototype, this filter has no zeros. The new gain k is determined using (8.56), which is achieved by scaling the old k by the ratio of the unnormalized to the normalized denominator polynomials evaluated at $s = 0$. In the following function, called U_chb1ap(N,Rp,Omegac), we design an unnormalized Chebyshev-I analog prototype filter that returns $H_a(s)$ in the direct form.

```
function [b,a] = u_chb1ap(N,Rp,Omegac);
% Unnormalized Chebyshev-1 analog lowpass filter prototype
% -----------------------------------------------------------
% [b,a] = u_chb1ap(N,Rp,Omegac);
%        b = numerator polynomial coefficients
%        a = denominator polynomial coefficients
%        N = order of the elliptic filter
%       Rp = passband ripple in dB; Rp > 0
% Omegac = cutoff frequency in radians/sec
%
[z,p,k] = cheb1ap(N,Rp);  a = real(poly(p));  aNn = a(N+1);
        p = p*Omegac;  a = real(poly(p));  aNu = a(N+1);
        k = k*aNu/aNn;
        b0 = k;  B = real(poly(z));  b = k*B;
```

8.3.7 DESIGN EQUATIONS

Given Ω_p, Ω_s, R_p, and A_S, three parameters are required to determine a Chebyshev-I filter: ϵ, Ω_c, and N. From equations (8.3) and (8.4), we obtain

$$\epsilon = \sqrt{10^{0.1R_p} - 1} \qquad \text{and} \qquad A = 10^{A_s/20}$$

From these properties, we have

$$\Omega_c = \Omega_p \qquad \text{and} \qquad \Omega_r = \frac{\Omega_s}{\Omega_p} \tag{8.57}$$

The order N is given by

$$g = \sqrt{(A^2 - 1)/\epsilon^2} \tag{8.58}$$

$$N = \left\lceil \frac{\log_{10}\left[g + \sqrt{g^2 - 1}\right]}{\log_{10}\left[\Omega_r + \sqrt{\Omega_r^2 - 1}\right]} \right\rceil \tag{8.59}$$

Now using (8.54), (8.53), and (8.55), we can determine $H_a(s)$.

☐ **EXAMPLE 8.5**   Design a lowpass Chebyshev-I filter to satisfy the following specifications.

$$\text{Passband cutoff: } \Omega_p = 0.2\pi \text{ ; Passband ripple: } R_p = 1\,\text{dB}$$

$$\text{Stopband cutoff: } \Omega_s = 0.3\pi \text{ ; Stopband ripple: } A_s = 16\,\text{dB}$$

Solution   First, compute the necessary parameters.

$$\epsilon = \sqrt{10^{0.1(1)} - 1} = 0.5088 \qquad A = 10^{16/20} = 6.3096$$

$$\Omega_c = \Omega_p = 0.2\pi \qquad \Omega_r = \frac{0.3\pi}{0.2\pi} = 1.5$$

$$g = \sqrt{(A^2 - 1)/\epsilon^2} = 12.2429 \qquad N = 4$$

Now we can determine $H_a(s)$.

$$\alpha = \frac{1}{\epsilon} + \sqrt{1 + \frac{1}{\epsilon^2}} = 4.1702$$

$$a = 0.5 \left(\sqrt[N]{\alpha} - \sqrt[N]{1/\alpha} \right) = 0.3646$$

$$b = 0.5 \left(\sqrt[N]{\alpha} + \sqrt[N]{1/\alpha} \right) = 1.0644$$

There are four poles for $H_a(s)$:

$$p_{0,3} = (a\Omega_c)\cos\left[\frac{\pi}{2} + \frac{\pi}{8}\right] \pm (b\Omega_c)\sin\left[\frac{\pi}{2} + \frac{\pi}{8}\right] = -0.0877 \pm j0.6179$$

$$p_{1,2} = (a\Omega_c)\cos\left[\frac{\pi}{2} + \frac{3\pi}{8}\right] \pm (b\Omega_c)\sin\left[\frac{\pi}{2} + \frac{3\pi}{8}\right] = -0.2117 \pm j0.2559$$

Hence

$$H_a(s) = \frac{K}{\displaystyle\prod_{k=0}^{3} (s - p_k)} = \frac{\overbrace{0.89125 \times .1103 \times .3895}^{0.03829}}{(s^2 + 0.1754s + 0.3895)(s^2 + 0.4234s + 0.1103)}$$

Note that the numerator is such that

$$H_a(j0) = \frac{1}{\sqrt{1 + \epsilon^2}} = 0.89125$$

□

8.3.8 MATLAB IMPLEMENTATION

Using the U_chb1ap function, we provide a function called **afd_chb1** to design an analog Chebyshev-II lowpass filter, given its specifications. This is shown below and uses the procedure described in Example 8.5.

```
function [b,a] = afd_chb1(Wp,Ws,Rp,As);
% Analog lowpass filter design: Chebyshev-1
% -----------------------------------------
% [b,a] = afd_chb1(Wp,Ws,Rp,As);
%  b = numerator coefficients of Ha(s)
%  a = denominator coefficients of Ha(s)
% Wp = passband-edge frequency in rad/sec; Wp > 0
% Ws = stopband-edge frequency in rad/sec; Ws > Wp > 0
% Rp = passband ripple in +dB; (Rp > 0)
% As = stopband attenuation in +dB; (As > 0)
```

```
%
if Wp <= 0
        error('Passband edge must be larger than 0')
end
if Ws <= Wp
        error('Stopband edge must be larger than Passband edge')
end
if (Rp <= 0) | (As < 0)
        error('PB ripple and/or SB attenuation must be larger than 0')
end

ep = sqrt(10^(Rp/10)-1);  A = 10^(As/20);
OmegaC = Wp;  OmegaR = Ws/Wp;  g = sqrt(A*A-1)/ep;
N = ceil(log10(g+sqrt(g*g-1))/log10(OmegaR+sqrt(OmegaR*OmegaR-1)));
fprintf('\n*** Chebyshev-1 Filter Order = %2.0f \n',N)
[b,a]=u_chb1ap(N,Rp,OmegaC);
```

☐ **EXAMPLE 8.6**   Design the analog Chebyshev-I lowpass filter given in Example 8.5 using MATLAB.

Solution   MATLAB script:

```
>> Wp = 0.2*pi; Ws = 0.3*pi; Rp = 1; As = 16;
>> Ripple = 10 ^ (-Rp/20); Attn = 10 ^ (-As/20);
>> % Analog filter design:
>> [b,a] = afd_chb1(Wp,Ws,Rp,As);
*** Chebyshev-1 Filter Order =  4
>> % Calculation of second-order sections:
>> [C,B,A] = sdir2cas(b,a)
C = 0.0383
B = 0      0      1
A = 1.0000    0.4233    0.1103
    1.0000    0.1753    0.3895
>> % Calculation of frequency response:
>> [db,mag,pha,w] = freqs_m(b,a,0.5*pi);
>> % Calculation of impulse response:
>> [ha,x,t] = impulse(b,a);
```

The specifications are satisfied by a fourth-order Chebyshev-I filter whose system function is

$$H_a(s) = \frac{0.0383}{(s^2 + 4233s + 0.1103)\,(s^2 + 0.1753s + 0.3895)}$$

The filter plots are shown in Figure 8.16.   ☐

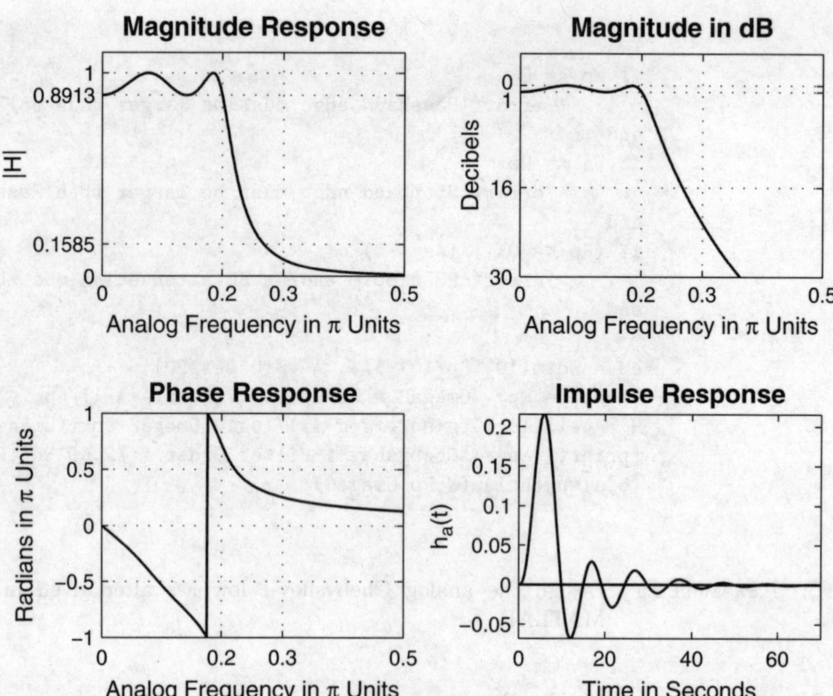

FIGURE 8.16   *Chebyshev-I analog filter in Example 8.6*

A Chebyshev-II filter is related to the Chebyshev-I filter through a simple transformation. It has a monotone passband and an equiripple stopband, which implies that this filter has both poles and zeros in the s-plane. Therefore, the group delay characteristics are better (and the phase response more linear) in the passband than those of the Chebyshev-I prototype. If we replace the term $\epsilon^2 T_N^2(\Omega/\Omega_c)$ in (8.52) by its reciprocal and also the argument $x = \Omega/\Omega_c$ by its reciprocal, we obtain the magnitude-squared response of Chebyshev-II as

$$|H_a(j\Omega)|^2 = \frac{1}{1 + \left[\epsilon^2 T_N^2(\Omega_c/\Omega)\right]^{-1}} \tag{8.60}$$

One approach to designing a Chebyshev-II filter is to design the corresponding Chebyshev-I first and then apply these transformations. We will not discuss the details of this filter but will use a function from MATLAB to design a Chebyshev-II filter.

8.3.9 MATLAB IMPLEMENTATION

MATLAB provides a function called `[z,p,k]=cheb2ap(N,As)` to design a *normalized* Chebyshev-II analog prototype filter of order `N` and passband ripple `As` and that returns zeros in `z` array, poles in `p` array, and the gain value **k**. We need an unnormalized Chebyshev-I filter with arbitrary Ω_c. This is achieved by scaling the array **p** of the normalized filter by Ω_c. Since this filter has zeros, we also have to scale the array **z** by Ω_c. The new gain **k** is determined using (8.56), which is achieved by scaling the old **k** by the ratio of the unnormalized to the normalized rational functions evaluated at $s = 0$. In the following function, called `U_chb2ap(N,As,Omegac)`, we design an unnormalized Chebyshev-II analog prototype filter that returns $H_a(s)$ in the direct form.

```matlab
function [b,a] = u_chb2ap(N,As,Omegac);
% Unnormalized Chebyshev-2 analog lowpass filter prototype
% -----------------------------------------------------------
% [b,a] = u_chb2ap(N,As,Omegac);
%      b = numerator polynomial coefficients
%      a = denominator polynomial coefficients
%      N = order of the Elliptic Filter
%     As = stopband Ripple in dB; As > 0
% Omegac = cutoff frequency in radians/sec
%
[z,p,k] = cheb2ap(N,As);
      a = real(poly(p));   aNn = a(N+1);
      p = p*Omegac;  a = real(poly(p));   aNu = a(N+1);
      b = real(poly(z));   M = length(b);   bNn = b(M);
      z = z*Omegac;  b = real(poly(z));   bNu = b(M);
      k = k*(aNu*bNn)/(aNn*bNu);
     b0 = k;   b = k*b;
```

The design equations for the Chebyshev-II prototype are similar to those of the Chebyshev-I except that $\Omega_c = \Omega_s$ since the ripples are in the stopband. Therefore, we can develop a MATLAB function similar to the `afd_chb1` function for the Chebyshev-II prototype.

```matlab
function [b,a] = afd_chb2(Wp,Ws,Rp,As);
% Analog lowpass filter design: Chebyshev-2
% -----------------------------------------
% [b,a] = afd_chb2(Wp,Ws,Rp,As);
%  b = numerator coefficients of Ha(s)
%  a = denominator coefficients of Ha(s)
% Wp = passband-edge frequency in rad/sec; Wp > 0
% Ws = stopband-edge frequency in rad/sec; Ws > Wp > 0
% Rp = passband ripple in +dB; (Rp > 0)
% As = stopband attenuation in +dB; (As > 0)
%
if Wp <= 0
        error('Passband edge must be larger than 0')
end
```

```
if Ws <= Wp
        error('Stopband edge must be larger than Passband edge')
end
if (Rp <= 0) | (As < 0)
        error('PB ripple and/or SB attenuation must be larger than 0')
end

ep = sqrt(10^(Rp/10)-1);  A = 10^(As/20);
OmegaC = Wp;  OmegaR = Ws/Wp;  g = sqrt(A*A-1)/ep;
N = ceil(log10(g+sqrt(g*g-1))/log10(OmegaR+sqrt(OmegaR*OmegaR-1)));
fprintf('\n*** Chebyshev-2 Filter Order = %2.0f \n',N)
[b,a]=u_chb2ap(N,As,Ws);
```

☐ **EXAMPLE 8.7** Design a Chebyshev-II analog lowpass filter to satisfy the specifications given in Example 8.5:

$$\text{Passband cutoff: } \Omega_p = 0.2\pi \ ; \ \text{Passband ripple: } R_p = 1\,\text{dB}$$

$$\text{Stopband cutoff: } \Omega_s = 0.3\pi \ ; \ \text{Stopband ripple: } A_s = 16\,\text{dB}$$

Solution   MATLAB script:

```
>> Wp = 0.2*pi; Ws = 0.3*pi; Rp = 1; As = 16;
>> Ripple = 10 ^ (-Rp/20); Attn = 10 ^ (-As/20);
>> % Analog filter design:
>> [b,a] = afd_chb2(Wp,Ws,Rp,As);
*** Chebyshev-2 Filter Order =  4
>> % Calculation of second-order sections:
>> [C,B,A] = sdir2cas(b,a)
C = 0.1585
B = 1.0000         0      6.0654
    1.0000         0      1.0407
A = 1.0000    1.9521      1.4747
    1.0000    0.3719      0.6784
>> % Calculation of frequency response:
>> [db,mag,pha,w] = freqs_m(b,a,0.5*pi);
>> % Calculation of impulse response:
>> [ha,x,t] = impulse(b,a);
```

The specifications are satisfied by a fourth-order Chebyshev-II filter whose system function is

$$H_a(s) = \frac{0.1585\left(s^2 + 6.0654\right)\left(s^2 + 1.0407\right)}{\left(s^2 + 1.9521s + 1.4747\right)\left(s^2 + 0.3719s + 0.6784\right)}$$

The filter plots are shown in Figure 8.17.   ☐

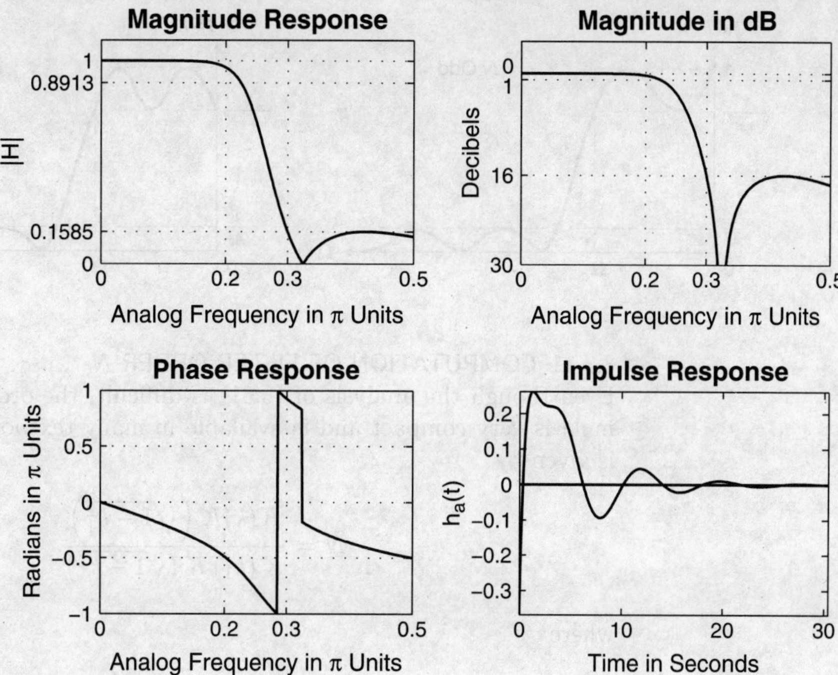

FIGURE 8.17   *Chebyshev-II analog filter in Example 8.7*

8.3.10 ELLIPTIC LOWPASS FILTERS

These filters exhibit equiripple behavior in the passband as well as in the stopband. They are similar in magnitude response characteristics to the FIR equiripple filters. Therefore, elliptic filters are optimum filters in that they achieve the minimum order N for the given specifications (or alternately, achieve the sharpest transition band for the given order N). These filters, for obvious reasons, are very difficult to analyze and, therefore, to design. It is not possible to design them using simple tools, and often programs or tables are needed to design them.

The magnitude-squared response of elliptic filters is given by

$$|H_a(j\Omega)|^2 = \frac{1}{1 + \epsilon^2 U_N^2 \left(\dfrac{\Omega}{\Omega_c}\right)} \tag{8.61}$$

where N is the order, ϵ is the passband ripple (which is related to R_p), and $U_N(\cdot)$ is the Nth-order Jacobian elliptic function. The analysis of this function, even on a superficial level, is beyond the scope of this book. Note the similarity between the preceding response (8.61) and that of the Chebyshev filters given by (8.52). Typical responses for odd and even N are as follows:

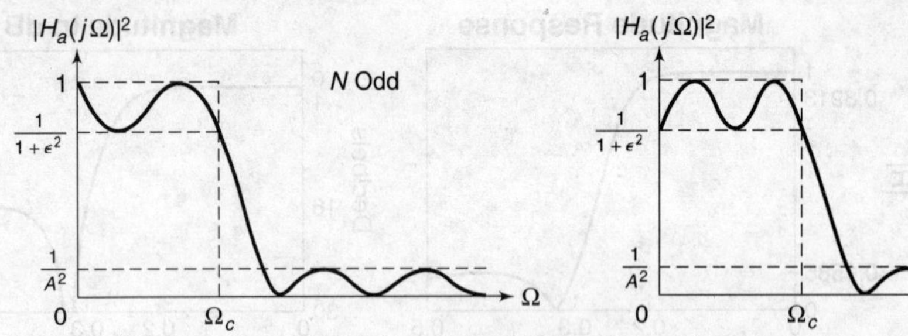

8.3.11 COMPUTATION OF FILTER ORDER N

Even though the analysis of (8.61) is difficult, the order calculation formula is very compact and is available in many textbooks [71, 79, 83]. It is given by

$$N = \frac{K(k)K\left(\sqrt{1-k_1^2}\right)}{K\left(k_1\right)K\left(\sqrt{1-k^2}\right)} \tag{8.62}$$

where

$$k = \frac{\Omega_p}{\Omega_s}, \quad k_1 = \frac{\epsilon}{\sqrt{A^2-1}}$$

and

$$K(x) = \int_0^{\pi/2} \frac{d\theta}{\sqrt{1-x^2\sin^2\theta}}$$

is the complete elliptic integral of the first kind. MATLAB provides the function `ellipke` to numerically compute the above integral, which we will use to compute N and to design elliptic filters.

8.3.12 MATLAB IMPLEMENTATION

MATLAB provides a function called `[z,p,k]=ellipap(N,Rp,As)` to design a *normalized* elliptic analog prototype filter of order `N`, passband ripple `Rp`, and stopband attenuation `As`, and that returns zeros in `z` array, poles in `p` array, and the gain value `k`. We need an unnormalized elliptic filter with arbitrary Ω_c. This is achieved by scaling the arrays `p` and `z` of the normalized filter by Ω_c and the gain `k` by the ratio of the unnormalized to the normalized rational functions evaluated at $s = 0$. In the following function, called `U_elipap(N,Rp,As,Omegac)`, we design an unnormalized elliptic analog prototype filter that returns $H_a(s)$ in the direct form.

```
function [b,a] = u_elipap(N,Rp,As,Omegac);
% Unnormalized elliptic analog lowpass filter prototype
% ------------------------------------------------------
% [b,a] = u_elipap(N,Rp,As,Omegac);
%       b = numerator polynomial coefficients
%       a = denominator polynomial coefficients
%       N = order of the elliptic filter
%      Rp = passband ripple in dB; Rp > 0
%      As = stopband attenuation in dB; As > 0
% Omegac = cutoff frequency in radians/sec
%
[z,p,k] = ellipap(N,Rp,As);
      a = real(poly(p));   aNn = a(N+1);
      p = p*Omegac;  a = real(poly(p));   aNu = a(N+1);
      b = real(poly(z));   M = length(b);   bNn = b(M);
      z = z*Omegac;  b = real(poly(z));   bNu = b(M);
      k = k*(aNu*bNn)/(aNn*bNu);
      b0 = k;   b = k*b;
```

Using the `U_elipap` function, we provide a function called `afd_elip`
to design an analog elliptic lowpass filter, given its specifications. This
follows and uses the filter order computation formula given in (8.62).

```
function [b,a] = afd_elip(Wp,Ws,Rp,As);
% Analog lowpass filter design: Elliptic
% --------------------------------------
% [b,a] = afd_elip(Wp,Ws,Rp,As);
% b = numerator coefficients of Ha(s)
% a = denominator coefficients of Ha(s)
% Wp = passband-edge frequency in rad/sec; Wp > 0
% Ws = stopband-edge frequency in rad/sec; Ws > Wp > 0
% Rp = passband ripple in +dB; (Rp > 0)
% As = stopband attenuation in +dB; (As > 0)
%
if Wp <= 0
      error('Passband edge must be larger than 0')
end
if Ws <= Wp
      error('Stopband edge must be larger than Passband edge')
end
if (Rp <= 0) | (As < 0)
      error('PB ripple and/or SB attenuation must be larger than 0')
end

ep = sqrt(10^(Rp/10)-1);   A = 10^(As/20);
OmegaC = Wp;   k = Wp/Ws;   k1 = ep/sqrt(A*A-1);
```

```
capk = ellipke([k.^2 1-k.^2]); % Version 4.0 code
capk1 = ellipke([(k1 .^2) 1-(k1 .^2)]); % Version 4.0 code
N = ceil(capk(1)*capk1(2)/(capk(2)*capk1(1)));
fprintf('\n*** Elliptic Filter Order = %2.0f \n',N)
[b,a]=u_elipap(N,Rp,As,OmegaC);
```

☐ **EXAMPLE 8.8**   Design an analog elliptic lowpass filter to satisfy the following specifications of
Example 8.5:

$$\Omega_p = 0.2\pi, \; R_p = 1\,\text{dB}$$

$$\Omega_s = 0.3\pi, \; A_s = 16\,\text{dB}$$

Solution   MATLAB script:

```
>> Wp = 0.2*pi; Ws = 0.3*pi; Rp = 1; As = 16;
>> Ripple = 10 ^ (-Rp/20); Attn = 10 ^ (-As/20);
>> % Analog filter design:
>> [b,a] = afd_elip(Wp,Ws,Rp,As);
*** Elliptic Filter Order =  3
>> % Calculation of second-order sections:
>> [C,B,A] = sdir2cas(b,a)
C = 0.2740
B = 1.0000        0     0.6641
A = 1.0000    0.1696    0.4102
         0    1.0000    0.4435
>> % Calculation of frequency response:
>> [db,mag,pha,w] = freqs_m(b,a,0.5*pi);
>> % Calculation of impulse response:
>> [ha,x,t] = impulse(b,a);
```

The specifications are satisfied by a third-order elliptic filter whose system function is

$$H_a(s) = \frac{0.274\left(s^2 + 0.6641\right)}{\left(s^2 + 0.1696s + 0.4102\right)\left(s + 0.4435\right)}$$

The filter plots are shown in Figure 8.18.   ☐

8.3.13 PHASE RESPONSES OF PROTOTYPE FILTERS
Elliptic filters provide optimal performance in the magnitude-squared response but have highly nonlinear phase response in the passband (which is
undesirable in many applications). Even though we decided not to worry

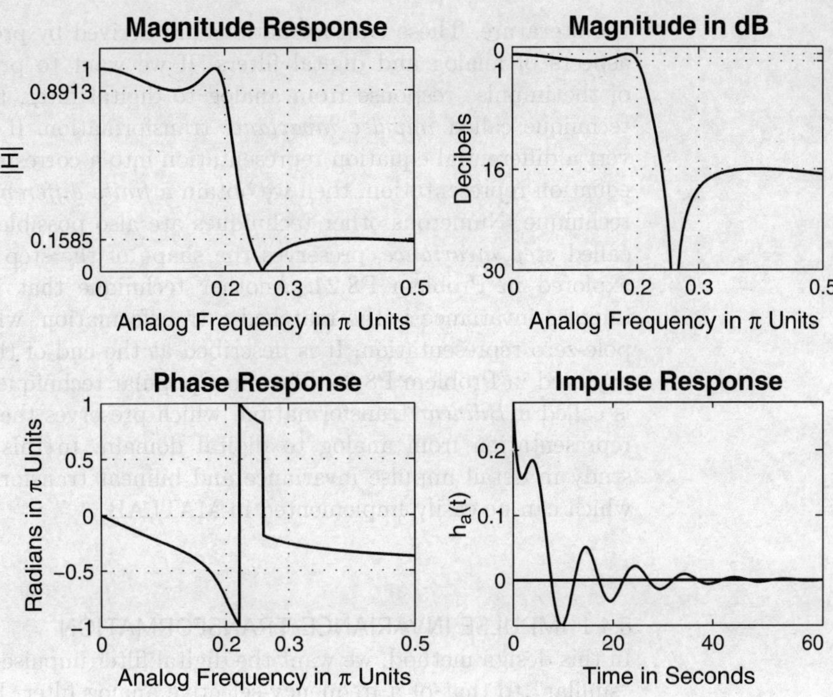

FIGURE 8.18 *Elliptic analog lowpass filter in Example 8.8*

about phase response in our designs, phase is still an important issue in the overall system. At the other end of the performance scale are the Butterworth filters, which have maximally flat magnitude response and require a higher-order N (more poles) to achieve the same stopband specification. However, they exhibit a fairly linear phase response in their passband. The Chebyshev filters have phase characteristics that lie somewhere in between. Therefore, in practical applications, we do consider Butterworth as well as Chebyshev filters, in addition to elliptic filters. The choice depends on both the filter order (which influences processing speed and implementation complexity) and the phase characteristics (which control the distortion).

8.4 ANALOG-TO-DIGITAL FILTER TRANSFORMATIONS

After discussing different approaches to the design of analog filters, we are now ready to transform them into digital filters. These transformations are complex-valued mappings that are extensively studied in the literature. These transformations are derived by preserving different aspects of analog and digital filters. If we want to preserve the shape of the impulse response from analog to digital filter, then we obtain a technique called *impulse invariance* transformation. If we want to convert a differential equation representation into a corresponding difference equation representation, then we obtain a *finite difference approximation* technique. Numerous other techniques are also possible. One technique, called *step invariance*, preserves the shape of the step response; this is explored in Problem P8.24. Another technique that is similar to the impulse invariance is the matched-z transformation, which matches the pole-zero representation. It is described at the end of this section and is explored in Problem P8.26. The most popular technique used in practice is called a *Bilinear* transformation, which preserves the system function representation from analog to digital domain. In this section, we will study in detail impulse invariance and bilinear transformations, both of which can be easily implemented in MATLAB.

8.4.1 IMPULSE INVARIANCE TRANSFORMATION

In this design method, we want the digital filter impulse response to look "similar" to that of a frequency-selective analog filter. Hence we sample $h_a(t)$ at some sampling interval T to obtain $h(n)$; that is,

$$h(n) = h_a(nT)$$

The parameter T is chosen so that the shape of $h_a(t)$ is "captured" by the samples. Since this is a sampling operation, the analog and digital frequencies are related by

$$\omega = \Omega T \text{ or } e^{j\omega} = e^{j\Omega T}$$

Since $z = e^{j\omega}$ on the unit circle and $s = j\Omega$ on the imaginary axis, we have the following transformation from the s-plane to the z-plane:

$$z = e^{sT} \tag{8.63}$$

The system functions $H(z)$ and $H_a(s)$ are related through the frequency-domain aliasing formula (3.27):

$$H(z) = \frac{1}{T} \sum_{k=-\infty}^{\infty} H_a\left(s - j\frac{2\pi}{T}k\right)$$

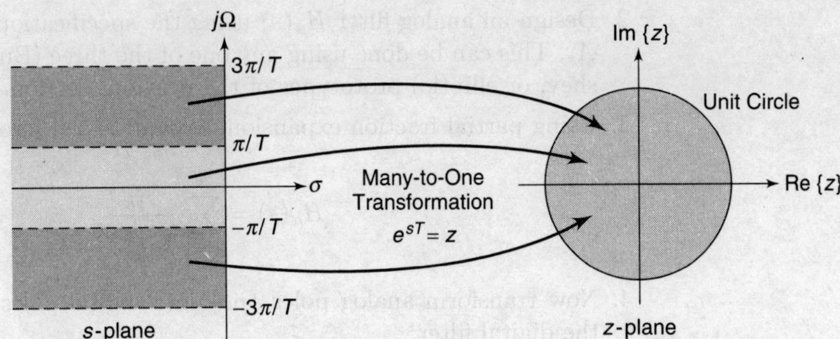

FIGURE 8.19 *Complex-plane mapping in impulse invariance transformation*

The complex plane transformation under the mapping (8.63) is shown in Figure 8.19, from which we have the following observations.

1. Using $\sigma = \text{Re}(s)$, we note that

$$\sigma < 0 \text{ maps into } |z| < 1 \text{ (inside of the UC)}$$

$$\sigma = 0 \text{ maps onto } |z| = 1 \text{ (on the UC)}$$

$$\sigma > 0 \text{ maps into } |z| > 1 \text{ (outside of the UC)}$$

2. All semi-infinite strips (shown above) of width $2\pi/T$ map into $|z| < 1$. Thus this mapping is not unique but a *many-to-one* mapping.

3. Since the entire left half of the s-plane maps into the unit circle, a causal and stable analog filter maps into a causal and stable digital filter.

4. If $H_a(j\Omega) = H_a(j\omega/T) = 0$ for $|\Omega| \geq \pi/T$, then

$$H(e^{j\omega}) = \frac{1}{T}H_a(j\omega/T), \quad |\omega| \leq \pi$$

and there will be no aliasing. However, no analog filter of finite order can be exactly band-limited. Therefore some aliasing error will occur in this design procedure, and hence the sampling interval T plays a minor role in this design method.

8.4.2 DESIGN PROCEDURE

Given the digital lowpass filter specifications ω_p, ω_s, R_p, and A_s, we want to determine $H(z)$ by first designing an equivalent analog filter and then mapping it into the desired digital filter. The steps required for this procedure are as follows.

1. Choose T and determine the analog frequencies

$$\Omega_p = \frac{\omega_p}{T_p} \qquad \text{and} \qquad \Omega_s = \frac{\omega_s}{T}$$

2. Design an analog filter $H_a(s)$ using the specifications Ω_p, Ω_s, R_p, and A_s. This can be done using any one of the three (Butterworth, Chebyshev, or elliptic) prototypes of the previous section.

3. Using partial fraction expansion, expand $H_a(s)$ into

$$H_a(s) = \sum_{k=1}^{N} \frac{R_k}{s - p_k}$$

4. Now transform analog poles $\{p_k\}$ into digital poles $\{e^{p_k T}\}$ to obtain the digital filter:

$$H(z) = \sum_{k=1}^{N} \frac{R_k}{1 - e^{p_k T} z^{-1}} \tag{8.64}$$

☐ **EXAMPLE 8.9**   Transform

$$H_a(s) = \frac{s+1}{s^2 + 5s + 6}$$

into a digital filter $H(z)$ using the impulse invariance technique in which $T = 0.1$.

Solution   We first expand $H_a(s)$ using partial fraction expansion:

$$H_a(s) = \frac{s+1}{s^2 + 5s + 6} = \frac{2}{s+3} - \frac{1}{s+2}$$

The poles are at $p_1 = -3$ and $p_2 = -2$. Then from (8.64) and using $T = 0.1$, we obtain

$$H(z) = \frac{2}{1 - e^{-3T} z^{-1}} - \frac{1}{1 - e^{-2T} z^{-1}} = \frac{1 - 0.8966 z^{-1}}{1 - 1.5595 z^{-1} + 0.6065 z^{-2}}$$

It is easy to develop a MATLAB function to implement the impulse invariance mapping. Given a rational function description of $H_a(s)$, we can use the `residue` function to obtain its pole-zero description. Then each analog pole is mapped into a digital pole using (8.63). Finally, the `residuez` function can be used to convert $H(z)$ into rational function form. This procedure is given in the function `imp_invr`.

```
function [b,a] = imp_invr(c,d,T)
% Impulse invariance transformation from analog to digital filter
% ----------------------------------------------------------------
% [b,a] = imp_invr(c,d,T)
%  b = numerator polynomial in z^(-1) of the digital filter
%  a = denominator polynomial in z^(-1) of the digital filter
%  c = numerator polynomial in s of the analog filter
```

```
%  d = denominator polynomial in s of the analog filter
%  T = sampling (transformation) parameter
%
[R,p,k] = residue(c,d);  p = exp(p*T);
[b,a] = residuez(R,p,k);  b = real(b'); a = real(a');
```

A similar function called `impinvar` is available in the SP toolbox of MATLAB.

   □

□ **EXAMPLE 8.10** We demonstrate the use of the `imp_invr` function on the system function from Example 8.9.

Solution MATLAB script:

```
>> c = [1,1]; d = [1,5,6]; T = 0.1;
>> [b,a] = imp_invr(c,d,T)
b =   1.0000   -0.8966
a =   1.0000   -1.5595      0.6065
```

The digital filter is

$$H(z) = \frac{1 - 0.8966z^{-1}}{1 - 1.5595z^{-1} + 0.6065z^{-2}}$$

as expected. In Figure 8.20, we show the impulse responses and the magnitude responses (plotted up to the sampling frequency $1/T$) of the analog and the resulting digital filter. Clearly, the aliasing in the frequency domain is evident.

   □

In the next several examples, we illustrate the impulse invariance design procedure on all three prototypes.

□ **EXAMPLE 8.11** Design a lowpass digital filter using a Butterworth prototype to satisfy

$$\omega_p = 0.2\pi, \; R_p = 1\,\text{dB}$$

$$\omega_s = 0.3\pi, \; A_s = 15\,\text{dB}$$

Solution The design procedure is described in the following MATLAB script.

```
>> % Digital filter specifications:
>> wp = 0.2*pi;                          % Digital passband freq in Hz
>> ws = 0.3*pi;                          % Digital stopband freq in Hz
>> Rp = 1;                               % Passband ripple in dB
>> As = 15;                              % Stopband attenuation in dB
```

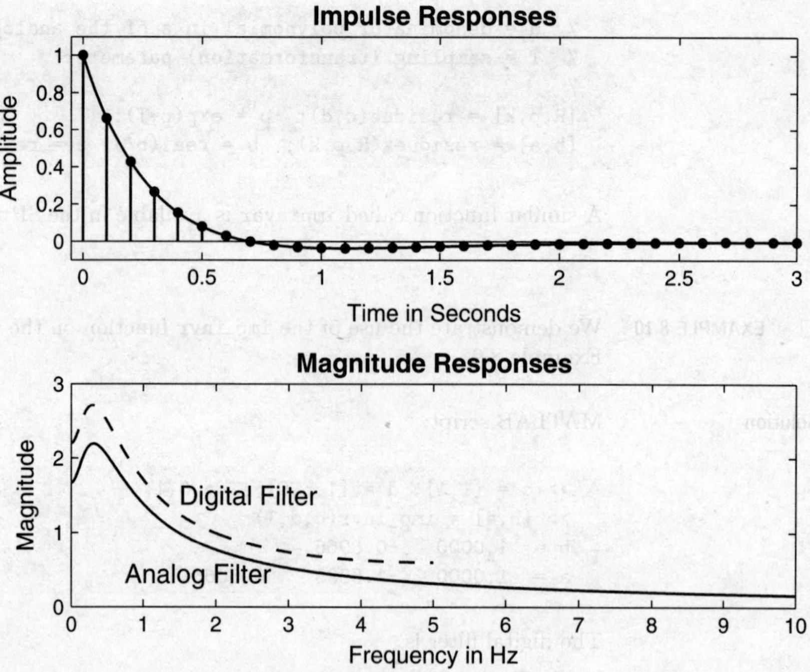

FIGURE 8.20 *Impulse and frequency response plots in Example 8.10*

as expected in Figure 8.20, we show, the impulse responses and the magnitude responses (blown up to the sampling frequency π/T) of the analog and the resulting digital filter. Clearly, the aliasing in the frequency domain is evident.

```
>> % Analog prototype specifications: Inverse mapping for frequencies
>> T = 1;                                % Set T=1
>> OmegaP = wp / T;                       % Prototype passband freq
>> OmegaS = ws / T;                       % Prototype stopband freq

>> % Analog Butterworth prototype filter calculation:
>> [cs,ds] = afd_butt(OmegaP,OmegaS,Rp,As);
*** Butterworth Filter Order =  6

>> % Impulse invariance transformation:
>> [b,a] = imp_invr(cs,ds,T);   [C,B,A] = dir2par(b,a)
C =   []
B = 1.8557    -0.6304
   -2.1428     1.1454
    0.2871    -0.4466
A = 1.0000    -0.9973     0.2570
    1.0000    -1.0691     0.3699
    1.0000    -1.2972     0.6949
```

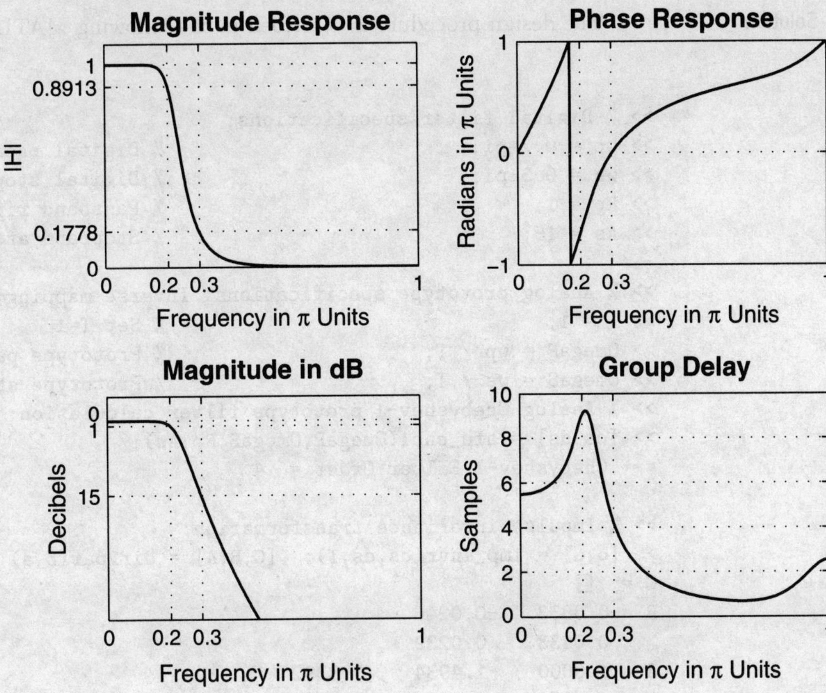

FIGURE 8.21 *Digital Butterworth lowpass filter using impulse invariance design*

The desired filter is a sixth-order Butterworth filter whose system function $H(z)$ is given in the parallel form

$$H(z) = \frac{1.8587 - 0.6304z^{-1}}{1 - 0.9973z^{-1} + 0.257z^{-2}} + \frac{-2.1428 + 1.1454z^{-1}}{1 - 1.0691z^{-1} + 0.3699z^{-2}}$$

$$+ \frac{0.2871 - 0.4463z^{-1}}{1 - 1.2972z^{-1} + 0.6449z^{-2}}$$

The frequency response plots are given in Figure 8.21. $\square$

□ **EXAMPLE 8.12** Design a lowpass digital filter using a Chebyshev-I prototype to satisfy

$$\omega_p = 0.2\pi, \ R_p = 1\,\mathrm{dB}$$
$$\omega_s = 0.3\pi, \ A_s = 15\,\mathrm{dB}$$

Solution   The design procedure is described in the following MATLAB script.

```
>> % Digital filter specifications:
>> wp = 0.2*pi;                        % Digital passband freq in rad
>> ws = 0.3*pi;                        % Digital stopband freq in rad
>> Rp = 1;                             % Passband ripple in dB
>> As = 15;                            % Stopband attenuation in dB

>> % Analog prototype specifications: Inverse mapping for frequencies
>> T = 1;                              % Set T=1
>> OmegaP = wp / T;                    % Prototype passband freq
>> OmegaS = ws / T;                    % Prototype stopband freq
>> % Analog Chebyshev-1 prototype filter calculation:
>> [cs,ds] = afd_chb1(OmegaP,OmegaS,Rp,As);
*** Chebyshev-1 Filter Order =  4

>> % Impulse invariance transformation:
>> [b,a] = imp_invr(cs,ds,T);   [C,B,A] = dir2par(b,a)
C =  []
B =-0.0833    -0.0246
    0.0833     0.0239
A = 1.0000    -1.4934     0.8392
    1.0000    -1.5658     0.6549
```

The desired filter is a fourth-order Chebyshev-I filter whose system function $H(z)$ is

$$H(z) = \frac{-0.0833 - 0.0246z^{-1}}{1 - 1.4934z^{-1} + 0.8392z^{-2}} + \frac{-0.0833 + 0.0239z^{-1}}{1 - 1.5658z^{-1} + 0.6549z^{-2}}$$

The frequency response plots are given in Figure 8.22.   □

□   **EXAMPLE 8.13**   Design a lowpass digital filter using a Chebyshev-II prototype to satisfy

$$\omega_p = 0.2\pi, \ R_p = 1\,\mathrm{dB}$$

$$\omega_s = 0.3\pi, \ A_s = 15\,\mathrm{dB}$$

Solution   Recall that the Chebyshev-II filter is equiripple in the stopband. This means that this analog filter has a response that does not go to zero at high frequencies in the stopband. Therefore, after impulse invariance transformation, the aliasing

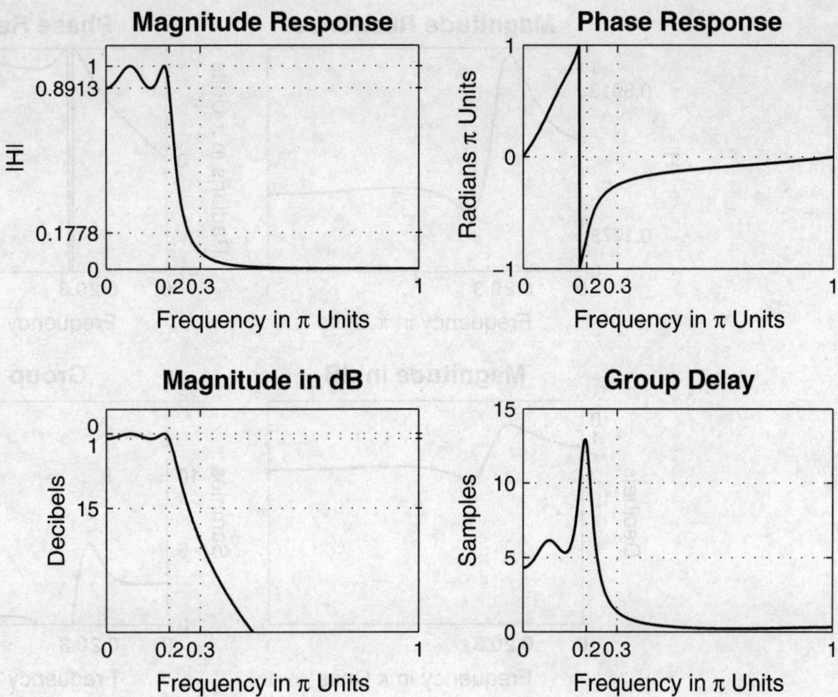

FIGURE 8.22 *Digital Chebyshev-I lowpass filter using impulse invariance design*

effect will be significant; this can degrade the passband response. The MATLAB script follows:

```
>> % Digital filter specifications:
>> wp = 0.2*pi;                    % Digital passband freq in rad
>> ws = 0.3*pi;                    % Digital stopband freq in rad
>> Rp = 1;                         % Passband ripple in dB
>> As = 15;                        % Stopband attenuation in dB

>> % Analog prototype specifications: Inverse mapping for frequencies
>> T = 1;                          % Set T=1
>> OmegaP = wp / T;                % Prototype passband freq
>> OmegaS = ws / T;                % Prototype stopband freq

>> % Analog Chebyshev-1 prototype filter calculation:
>> [cs,ds] = afd_chb2(OmegaP,OmegaS,Rp,As);
*** Chebyshev-2 Filter Order =  4

>> % Impulse invariance transformation:
>> [b,a] = imp_invr(cs,ds,T);   [C,B,A] = dir2par(b,a);
```

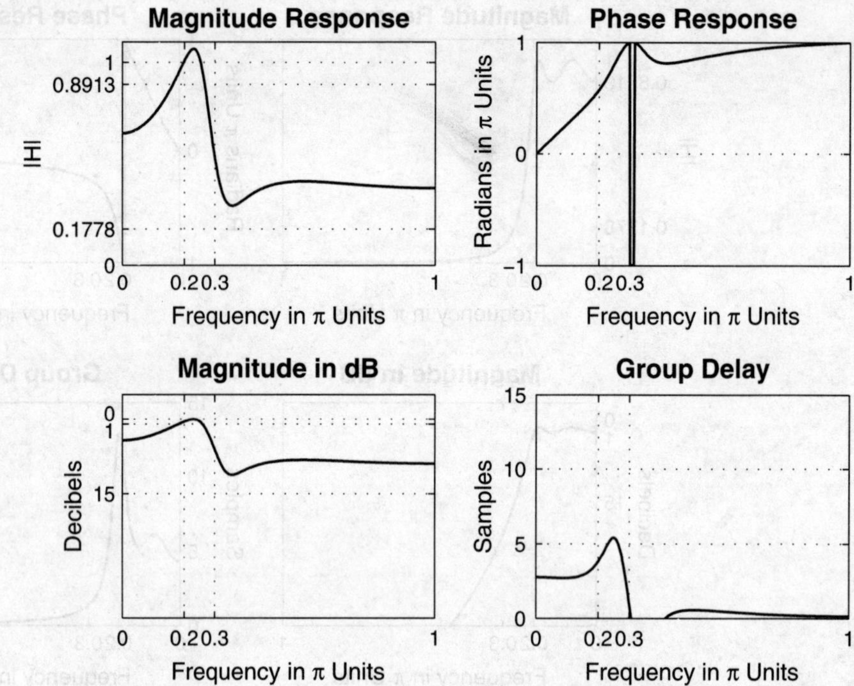

FIGURE 8.23 *Digital Chebyshev-II lowpass filter using impulse invariance design*

From the frequency response plots in Figure 8.23, we clearly observe the passband as well as stopband degradation. Hence the impulse invariance design technique has failed to produce a desired digital filter. □

☐ **EXAMPLE 8.14**   Design a lowpass digital filter using an elliptic prototype to satisfy

$$\omega_p = 0.2\pi,\ R_p = 1\text{ dB}$$

$$\omega_s = 0.3\pi,\ A_s = 15\text{ dB}$$

Solution   The elliptic filter is equiripple in both bands. Hence this situation is similar to that of the Chebyshev-II filter, and we should not expect a good digital filter. MATLAB script:

```
>> % Digital filter specifications:
>> wp = 0.2*pi;                          % Digital passband freq in rad
>> ws = 0.3*pi;                          % Digital stopband freq in rad
>> Rp = 1;                               % Passband ripple in dB
>> As = 15;                              % Stopband attenuation in dB
```

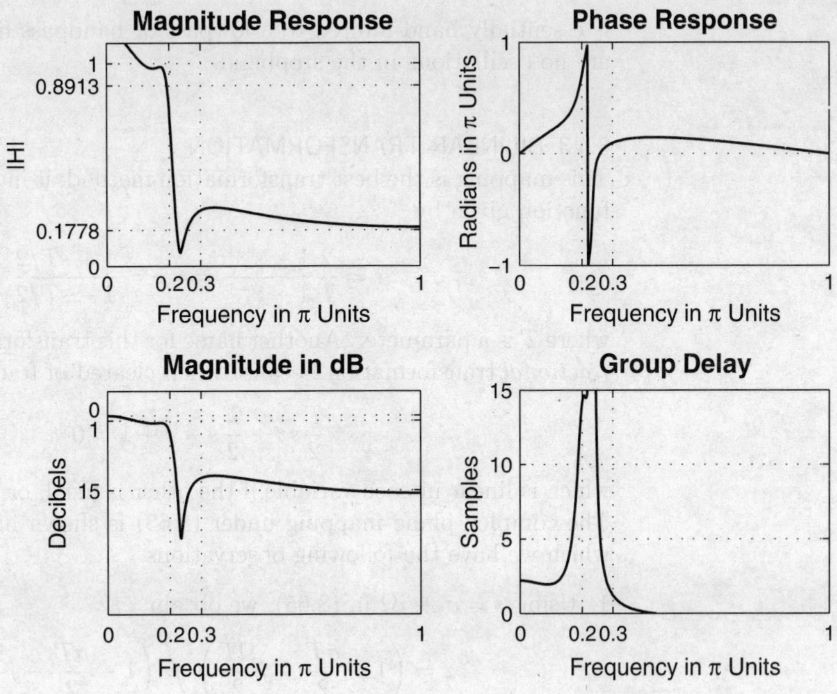

FIGURE 8.24 *Digital elliptic lowpass filter using impulse invariance design*

```
>> % Analog prototype specifications: Inverse mapping for frequencies
>> T = 1;                               % Set T=1
>> OmegaP = wp / T;                     % Prototype passband freq
>> OmegaS = ws / T;                     % Prototype stopband freq

>> % Analog elliptic prototype filter calculation:
>> [cs,ds] = afd_elip(OmegaP,OmegaS,Rp,As);
*** Elliptic Filter Order =  3

>> % Impulse invariance transformation:
>> [b,a] = imp_invr(cs,ds,T);   [C,B,A] = dir2par(b,a);
```

From the frequency response plots in Figure 8.24, we clearly observe that once again the impulse invariance design technique has failed. □

The advantages of the impulse invariance mapping are that it is a stable design and that the frequencies Ω and ω are linearly related. But the disadvantage is that we should expect some aliasing of the analog frequency response, and in some cases this aliasing is intolerable. Consequently, this design method is useful only when the analog filter is essentially band-limited to a lowpass or bandpass filter in which there are no oscillations in the stopband.

8.4.3 BILINEAR TRANSFORMATION

This mapping is the best transformation method; it involves a well-known function given by

$$s = \frac{2}{T}\frac{1 - z^{-1}}{1 + z^{-1}} \implies z = \frac{1 + sT/2}{1 - sT/2} \tag{8.65}$$

where T is a parameter. Another name for this transformation is the *linear fractional* transformation because when cleared of fractions, we obtain

$$\frac{T}{2}sz + \frac{T}{2}s - z + 1 = 0$$

which is linear in each variable if the other is fixed, or *bilinear* in s and z. The complex plane mapping under (8.65) is shown in Figure 8.25, from which we have the following observations.

1. Using $s = \sigma + j\Omega$ in (8.65), we obtain

$$z = \left(1 + \frac{\sigma T}{2} + j\frac{\Omega T}{2}\right) \Big/ \left(1 - \frac{\sigma T}{2} - j\frac{\Omega T}{2}\right) \tag{8.66}$$

Hence

$$\sigma < 0 \implies |z| = \left|\frac{1 + \frac{\sigma T}{2} + j\frac{\Omega T}{2}}{1 - \frac{\sigma T}{2} - j\frac{\Omega T}{2}}\right| < 1$$

$$\sigma = 0 \implies |z| = \left|\frac{1 + j\frac{\Omega T}{2}}{1 - j\frac{\Omega T}{2}}\right| = 1$$

$$\sigma > 0 \implies |z| = \left|\frac{1 + \frac{\sigma T}{2} + j\frac{\Omega T}{2}}{1 - \frac{\sigma T}{2} - j\frac{\Omega T}{2}}\right| > 1$$

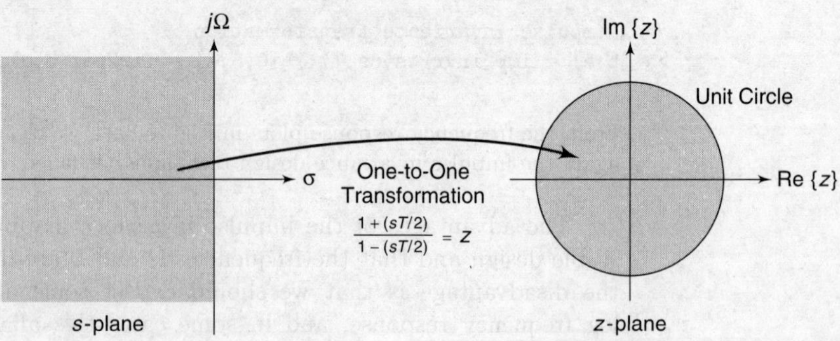

FIGURE 8.25 *Complex-plane mapping in bilinear transformation*

2. The entire left half-plane maps into the inside of the unit circle. Hence this is a stable transformation.

3. The imaginary axis maps onto the unit circle in a one-to-one fashion. Hence there is no aliasing in the frequency domain.

Substituting $\sigma = 0$ in (8.66), we obtain

$$z = \frac{1 + j\frac{\Omega T}{2}}{1 - j\frac{\Omega T}{2}} = e^{j\omega}$$

since the magnitude is 1. Solving for ω as a function of Ω, we obtain

$$\omega = 2\tan^{-1}\left(\frac{\Omega T}{2}\right) \qquad \text{or} \qquad \Omega = \frac{2}{T}\tan\left(\frac{\omega}{2}\right) \qquad \textbf{(8.67)}$$

This shows that Ω is nonlinearly related to (or warped into) ω but that there is no aliasing. Hence, in (8.67), we will say that ω is prewarped into Ω.

☐   **EXAMPLE 8.15**   Transform $H_a(s) = \dfrac{s+1}{s^2 + 5s + 6}$ into a digital filter using the bilinear transformation. Choose $T = 1$.

Solution   Using (8.65), we obtain

$$H(z) = H_a\left(\frac{2}{T}\frac{1 - z^{-1}}{1 + z^{-1}}\bigg|_{T=1}\right) = H_a\left(2\frac{1 - z^{-1}}{1 + z^{-1}}\right)$$

$$= \frac{2\dfrac{1 - z^{-1}}{1 + z^{-1}} + 1}{\left(2\dfrac{1 - z^{-1}}{1 + z^{-1}}\right)^2 + 5\left(2\dfrac{1 - z^{-1}}{1 + z^{-1}}\right) + 6}$$

Simplifying,

$$H(z) = \frac{3 + 2z^{-1} - z^{-2}}{20 + 4z^{-1}} = \frac{0.15 + 0.1z^{-1} - 0.05z^{-2}}{1 + 0.2z^{-1}}$$

☐

MATLAB provides a function called `bilinear` to implement this mapping. Its invocation is similar to the `imp_invr` function, but it also takes several forms for different input-output quantities. The SP toolbox manual should be consulted for more details. Its use is shown in the following example.

☐ **EXAMPLE 8.16**   Transform the system function $H_a(s)$ in Example 8.15 using the `bilinear` function.

Solution   MATLAB script:

```
>> c = [1,1]; d = [1,5,6]; T = 1; Fs = 1/T;
>> [b,a] = bilinear(c,d,Fs)
b = 0.1500    0.1000    -0.0500
a = 1.0000    0.2000    0.0000
```

The filter is

$$H(z) = \frac{0.15 + 0.1z^{-1} - 0.05z^{-2}}{1 + 0.2z^{-1}}$$

as before.   ☐

8.4.4 DESIGN PROCEDURE

Given digital filter specifications ω_p, ω_s, R_p, and A_s, we want to determine $H(z)$. The design steps in this procedure are the following.

1. Choose a value for T. This is arbitrary, and we may set $T = 1$.

2. Prewarp the cutoff frequencies ω_p and ω_s; that is, calculate Ω_p and Ω_s using (8.67):

$$\Omega_p = \frac{2}{T} \tan\left(\frac{\omega_p}{2}\right), \quad \Omega_s = \frac{2}{T} \tan\left(\frac{\omega_s}{2}\right) \tag{8.68}$$

3. Design an analog filter $H_a(s)$ to meet the specifications Ω_p, Ω_s, R_p, and A_s. We have already described how to do this in the previous section.

4. Finally, set

$$H(z) = H_a\left(\frac{2}{T}\frac{1 - z^{-1}}{1 + z^{-1}}\right)$$

and simplify to obtain $H(z)$ as a rational function in z^{-1}.

In the next several examples, we demonstrate this design procedure on our analog prototype filters.

☐ **EXAMPLE 8.17**   Design the digital Butterworth filter of Example 8.11. The specifications are

$$\omega_p = 0.2\pi, \; R_p = 1 \text{ dB}$$

$$\omega_s = 0.3\pi, \; A_s = 15 \text{ dB}$$

Solution   MATLAB script:

```
>> % Digital filter specifications:
>> wp = 0.2*pi;                        % Digital passband freq in rad
>> ws = 0.3*pi;                        % Digital stopband freq in rad
>> Rp = 1;                             % Passband ripple in dB
>> As = 15;                            % Stopband attenuation in dB
>> % Analog prototype specifications: Inverse mapping for frequencies
>> T = 1; Fs = 1/T;                    % Set T=1
>> OmegaP = (2/T)*tan(wp/2);           % Prewarp prototype passband freq
>> OmegaS = (2/T)*tan(ws/2);           % Prewarp prototype stopband freq
>> % Analog Butterworth prototype filter calculation:
>> [cs,ds] = afd_butt(OmegaP,OmegaS,Rp,As);
*** Butterworth Filter Order =  6
>> % Bilinear transformation:
>> [b,a] = bilinear(cs,ds,Fs);  [C,B,A] = dir2cas(b,a)
C = 5.7969e-004
B = 1.0000     2.0183     1.0186
    1.0000     1.9814     0.9817
    1.0000     2.0004     1.0000
A = 1.0000    -0.9459     0.2342
    1.0000    -1.0541     0.3753
    1.0000    -1.3143     0.7149
```

The desired filter is once again a sixth-order filter and has six zeros. Since the sixth-order zero of $H_a(s)$ at $s = -\infty$ is mapped to $z = -1$, these zeros should be at $z = -1$. Due to the finite precision of MATLAB, these zeros are not exactly at $z = -1$. Hence the system function should be

$$H(z) = \frac{0.00057969\left(1 + z^{-1}\right)^6}{\left(1 - 0.9459z^{-1} + 0.2342z^{-2}\right)\left(1 - 1.0541z^{-1} + 0.3753z^{-2}\right)\left(1 - 1.3143z^{-1} + 0.7149z^{-2}\right)}$$

The frequency response plots are given in Figure 8.26. Comparing these plots with those in Figure 8.21, we observe that these two designs are very similar.
$\square$

☐ **EXAMPLE 8.18**   Design the digital Chebyshev-I filter of Example 8.12. The specifications are

$$\omega_p = 0.2\pi, \ R_p = 1 \text{ dB}$$
$$\omega_s = 0.3\pi, \ A_s = 15 \text{ dB}$$

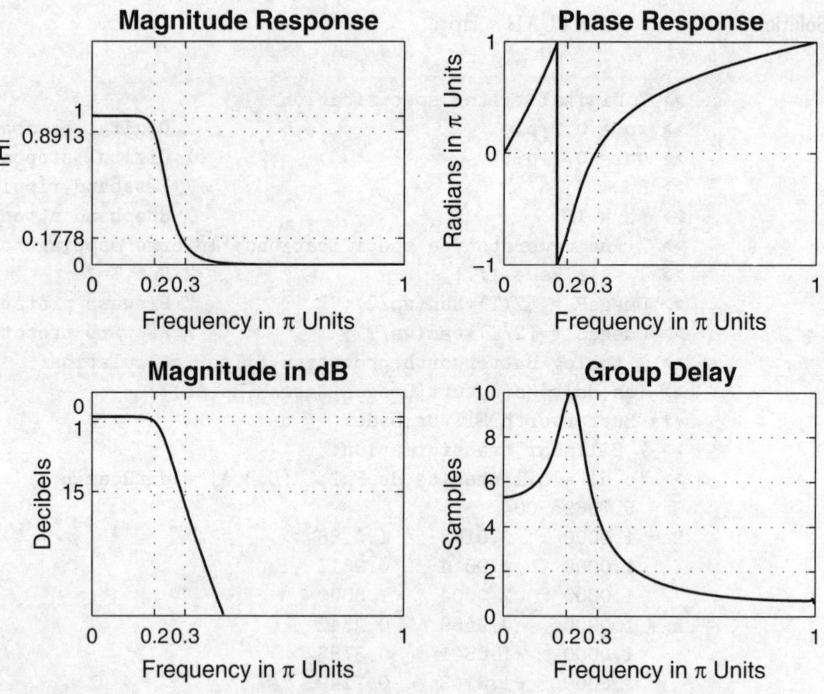

FIGURE 8.26 *Digital Butterworth lowpass filter using bilinear transformation*

Solution   MATLAB script:

```
>> % Digital filter specifications:
>> wp = 0.2*pi;                    % Digital passband freq in rad
>> ws = 0.3*pi;                    % Digital stopband freq in rad
>> Rp = 1;                         % Passband ripple in dB
>> As = 15;                        % Stopband attenuation in dB
>> % Analog prototype specifications: Inverse mapping for frequencies
>> T = 1; Fs = 1/T;               % Set T=1
>> OmegaP = (2/T)*tan(wp/2);       % Prewarp prototype passband freq
>> OmegaS = (2/T)*tan(ws/2);       % Prewarp prototype stopband freq
>> % Analog Chebyshev-1 prototype filter calculation:
>> [cs,ds] = afd_chb1(OmegaP,OmegaS,Rp,As);
*** Chebyshev-1 Filter Order =  4
>> % Bilinear transformation:
>> [b,a] = bilinear(cs,ds,Fs);  [C,B,A] = dir2cas(b,a)
C = 0.0018
B = 1.0000    2.0000    1.0000
    1.0000    2.0000    1.0000
A = 1.0000   -1.4996    0.8482
    1.0000   -1.5548    0.6493
```

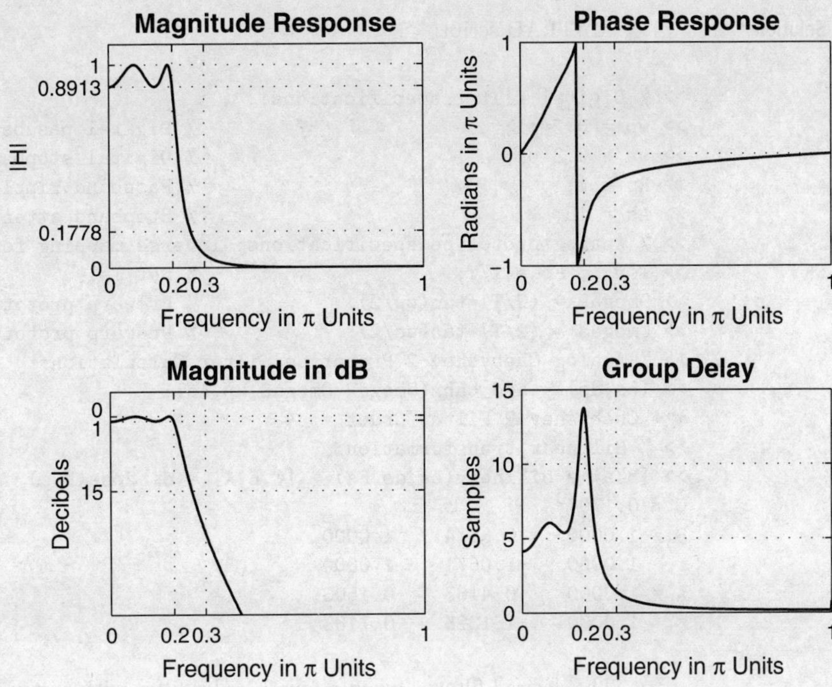

FIGURE 8.27 *Digital Chebyshev-I lowpass filter using bilinear transformation*

The desired filter is a fourth-order filter and has four zeros at $z = -1$. The system function is

$$H(z) = \frac{0.0018 \left(1 + z^{-1}\right)^4}{\left(1 - 1.4996z^{-1} + 0.8482z^{-2}\right)\left(1 - 1.5548z^{-1} + 0.6493z^{-2}\right)}$$

The frequency response plots are given in Figure 8.27, which are similar to those in Figure 8.22. □

□ **EXAMPLE 8.19** Design the digital Chebyshev-II filter of Example 8.13. The specifications are

$$\omega_p = 0.2\pi, \ R_p = 1 \text{ dB}$$

$$\omega_s = 0.3\pi, \ A_s = 15 \text{ dB}$$

Solution   MATLAB script:

```
>> % Digital filter specifications:
>> wp = 0.2*pi;                          % Digital passband freq in rad
>> ws = 0.3*pi;                          % Digital stopband freq in rad
>> Rp = 1;                               % Passband ripple in dB
>> As = 15;                              % Stopband attenuation in dB
>> % Analog prototype specifications: Inverse mapping for frequencies
>> T = 1; Fs = 1/T;                      % Set T=1
>> OmegaP = (2/T)*tan(wp/2);             % Prewarp prototype passband freq
>> OmegaS = (2/T)*tan(ws/2);             % Prewarp prototype stopband freq
>> % Analog Chebyshev-2 Prototype Filter Calculation:
>> [cs,ds] = afd_chb2(OmegaP,OmegaS,Rp,As);
*** Chebyshev-2 Filter Order =  4
>> % Bilinear transformation:
>> [b,a] = bilinear(cs,ds,Fs);   [C,B,A] = dir2cas(b,a)
C = 0.1797
B = 1.0000      0.5574     1.0000
    1.0000     -1.0671     1.0000
A = 1.0000     -0.4183     0.1503
    1.0000     -1.1325     0.7183
```

The desired filter is again a fourth-order filter with system function

$$H(z) = \frac{0.1797\left(1 + 0.5574z^{-1} + z^{-2}\right)\left(1 - 1.0671z^{-1} + z^{-2}\right)}{\left(1 - 0.4183z^{-1} + 0.1503z^{-2}\right)\left(1 - 1.1325z^{-1} + 0.7183z^{-2}\right)}$$

The frequency response plots are given in Figure 8.28. Note that the bilinear transformation has properly designed the Chebyshev-II digital filter.   □

□ **EXAMPLE 8.20**   Design the digital elliptic filter of Example 8.14. The specifications are

$$\omega_p = 0.2\pi,\ R_p = 1 \text{ dB}$$

$$\omega_s = 0.3\pi,\ A_s = 15 \text{ dB}$$

Solution   MATLAB script:

```
>> % Digital filter specifications:
>> wp = 0.2*pi;                          % Digital passband freq in rad
>> ws = 0.3*pi;                          % Digital stopband freq in rad
>> Rp = 1;                               % Passband ripple in dB
>> As = 15;                              % Stopband attenuation in dB
>> % Analog prototype specifications: Inverse mapping for frequencies
>> T = 1; Fs = 1/T;                      % Set T=1
```

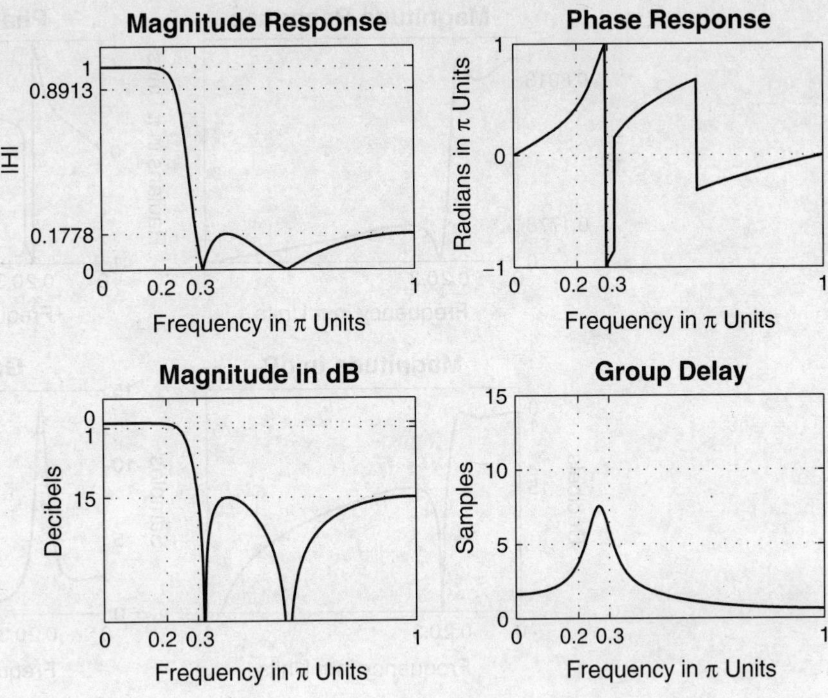

FIGURE 8.28 *Digital Chebyshev-II lowpass filter using bilinear transformation*

```
>> OmegaP = (2/T)*tan(wp/2);            % Prewarp prototype passband freq
>> OmegaS = (2/T)*tan(ws/2);            % Prewarp prototype stopband freq
>> % Analog elliptic prototype filter calculation:
>> [cs,ds] = afd_elip(OmegaP,OmegaS,Rp,As);
*** Elliptic Filter Order = 3
>> % Bilinear transformation:
>> [b,a] = bilinear(cs,ds,Fs);   [C,B,A] = dir2cas(b,a)
C = 0.1214
B = 1.0000    -1.4211     1.0000
    1.0000     1.0000          0
A = 1.0000    -1.4928     0.8612
    1.0000    -0.6183          0
```

The desired filter is a third-order filter with system function

$$H(z) = \frac{0.1214\left(1 - 1.4211z^{-1} + z^{-2}\right)\left(1 + z^{-1}\right)}{\left(1 - 1.4928z^{-1} + 0.8612z^{-2}\right)\left(1 - 0.6183z^{-1}\right)}$$

The frequency response plots are given in Figure 8.29. Note that the bilinear transformation has again properly designed the elliptic digital filter. □

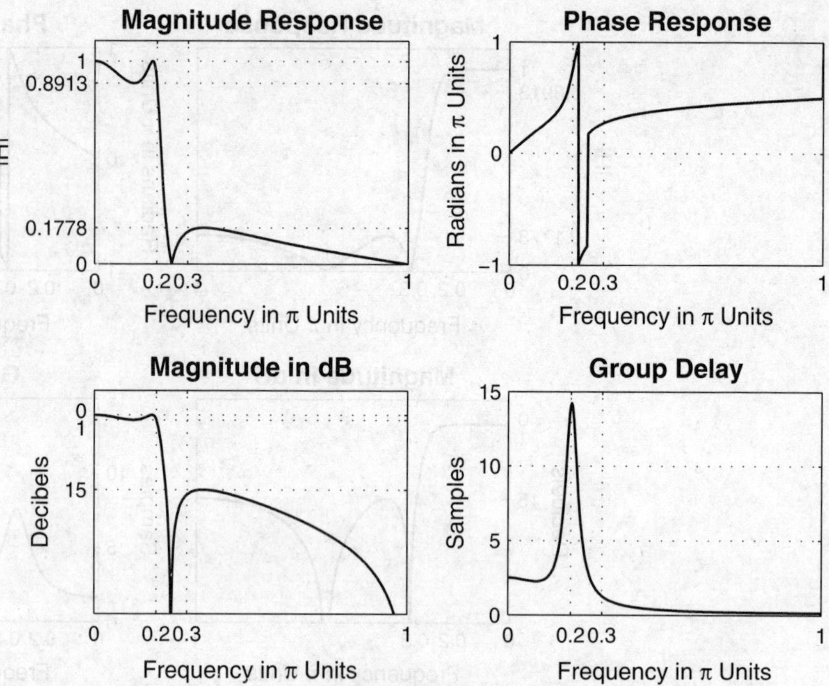

FIGURE 8.29 *Digital elliptic lowpass filter using bilinear transformation*

The advantages of this mapping are that (a) it is a stable design, (b) there is no aliasing, and (c) there is no restriction on the type of filter that can be transformed. Therefore, this method is used exclusively in computer programs including MATLAB, as we shall see next.

8.4.5 MATCHED-z TRANSFORMATION

In this method of filter transformation, zeros and poles of $H_a(s)$ are directly mapped into zeros and poles in the z-plane using an exponential function. Given a root (zero or pole) at the location $s = a$ in the s-plane, we map it in the z-plane at $z = e^{aT}$ where T is a sampling interval. Thus the system function $H_a(s)$ with zeros $\{z_k\}$ and poles $\{p_\ell\}$ is mapped into the digital filter system function $H(z)$ as

$$H_a(s) = \frac{\prod_{k=1}^{M} (s - z_k)}{\prod_{\ell=1}^{N} (s - p_\ell)} \quad \rightarrow \quad H(z) = \frac{\prod_{k=1}^{M} \left(1 - e^{z_k T} z^{-1}\right)}{\prod_{\ell=1}^{N} \left(s - e^{p_\ell T} z^{-1}\right)} \quad \textbf{(8.69)}$$

Clearly, the z-transform system function is "matched" to the s-domain system function.

Note that this technique appears to be similar to the impulse invariance mapping in that the pole locations are identical and aliasing is unavoidable. However, these two techniques differ in zero locations. Also, the matched-z transformation does not preserve either the impulse response or the frequency response characteristics. Hence it is suitable when designing using pole-zero placement, but it is generally unsuitable when the frequency-domain specifications are given.

8.5 LOWPASS FILTER DESIGN USING MATLAB

In this section, we will demonstrate the use of MATLAB's filter design functions to design digital lowpass filters. These functions use the bilinear transformation because of its desirable advantages as discussed in the previous section. These functions are as follows.

1. `[b,a]=butter(N,wn)`
   This function designs an Nth-order lowpass digital Butterworth filter and returns the filter coefficients in length $N+1$ vectors `b` and `a`. The filter order is given by (8.49), and the cutoff frequency `wn` is determined by the prewarping formula (8.68). However, in MATLAB all digital frequencies are given in *units of* π. Hence `wn` is computed by using the following relation:

$$\omega_n = \frac{2}{\pi}\tan^{-1}\left(\frac{\Omega_c T}{2}\right)$$

   The use of this function is given in Example 8.21.

2. `[b,a]=cheby1(N,Rp,wn)`
   This function designs an Nth-order lowpass digital Chebyshev-I filter with `Rp` decibels of ripple in the passband. It returns the filter coefficients in length $N+1$ vectors `b` and `a`. The filter order is given by (8.59), and the cutoff frequency `wn` is the digital passband frequency in units of π; that is,

$$\omega_n = \omega_p/\pi$$

   The use of this function is given in Example 8.22.

3. `[b,a]=cheby2(N,As,wn)`
   This function designs an Nth-order lowpass digital Chebyshev-II filter with the stopband attenuation `As` decibels. It returns the filter coefficients in length $N+1$ vectors `b` and `a`. The filter order is given by (8.59), and the cutoff frequency `wn` is the digital stopband frequency in units of π; that is,

$$\omega_n = \omega_s/\pi$$

   The use of this function is given in Example 8.23.

4. [b,a]=ellip(N,Rp,As,wn)

This function designs an Nth-order lowpass digital elliptic filter with the passband ripple of Rp decibels and a stopband attenuation of As decibels. It returns the filter coefficients in length $N+1$ vectors b and a. The filter order is given by (8.62), and the cutoff frequency wn is the digital passband frequency in units of π; that is,

$$\omega_n = \omega_p/\pi$$

The use of this function is given in Example 8.24.

All these above functions can also be used to design other frequency-selective filters, such as highpass and bandpass. We will discuss their additional capabilities in Section 8.6.

There is also another set of filter functions—namely, the buttord, cheb1ord, cheb2ord, and ellipord functions—that can provide filter order N and filter cutoff frequency ω_n, given the specifications. These functions are available in the Signal Processing toolbox. In the examples to follow, we will determine these parameters using the formulas given earlier. We will discuss the filter-order functions in the next section.

In the following examples, we will redesign the same lowpass filters of previous examples and compare their results. The specifications of the lowpass digital filter are

$$\omega_p = 0.2\pi,\ R_p = 1 \text{ dB}$$

$$\omega_s = 0.3\pi,\ A_s = 15 \text{ dB}$$

☐ **EXAMPLE 8.21**   Digital Butterworth lowpass filter design:

```
>> % Digital filter specifications:
>> wp = 0.2*pi;                        % Digital passband freq in rad
>> ws = 0.3*pi;                        % Digital stopband freq in rad
>> Rp = 1;                             % Passband ripple in dB
>> As = 15;                            % Stopband attenuation in dB

>> % Analog Prototype Specifications:
>> T = 1;                              % Set T=1
>> OmegaP = (2/T)*tan(wp/2);           % Prewarp prototype passband freq
>> OmegaS = (2/T)*tan(ws/2);           % Prewarp prototype stopband freq
>> % Analog Prototype Order Calculation:
>> N =ceil((log10((10^(Rp/10)-1)/(10^(As/10)-1)))/(2*log10(OmegaP/OmegaS)));
>> fprintf('\n*** Butterworth Filter Order = %2.0f \n',N)
** Butterworth Filter Order =   6
>> OmegaC = OmegaP/((10^(Rp/10)-1)^(1/(2*N))); % Analog BF prototype cutoff
>> wn = 2*atan((OmegaC*T)/2);          % Digital BF cutoff freq
```

```
>> % Digital butterworth filter design:
>> wn = wn/pi;                              % Digital BF cutoff in pi units
>> [b,a]=butter(N,wn);   [b0,B,A] = dir2cas(b,a)
C = 5.7969e-004
B = 1.0000     2.0297     1.0300
    1.0000     1.9997     1.0000
    1.0000     1.9706     0.9709
A = 1.0000    -0.9459     0.2342
    1.0000    -1.0541     0.3753
    1.0000    -1.3143     0.7149
```

The system function is

$$H(z) = \frac{0.00057969 \left(1 + z^{-1}\right)^6}{\left(1 - 0.9459z^{-1} + 0.2342z^{-2}\right)\left(1 - 1.0541z^{-1} + 0.3753z^{-2}\right)\left(1 - 1.3143z^{-1} + 0.7149z^{-2}\right)}$$

which is the same as in Example 8.17. The frequency-domain plots were shown in Figure 8.26.   □

□ **EXAMPLE 8.22**   Digital Chebyshev-I lowpass filter design:

```
>> % Digital filter specifications:
>> wp = 0.2*pi;                             % Digital passband freq in rad
>> ws = 0.3*pi;                             % Digital stopband freq in rad
>> Rp = 1;                                  % Passband ripple in dB
>> As = 15;                                 % Stopband attenuation in dB

>> % Analog prototype specifications:
>> T = 1;                                   % Set T=1
>> OmegaP = (2/T)*tan(wp/2);                % Prewarp prototype passband freq
>> OmegaS = (2/T)*tan(ws/2);                % Prewarp prototype stopband freq

>> % Analog prototype order calculation:
>> ep = sqrt(10^(Rp/10)-1);                 % Passband ripple factor
>> A = 10^(As/20);                          % Stopband attenuation factor
>> OmegaC = OmegaP;                         % Analog prototype cutoff freq
>> OmegaR = OmegaS/OmegaP;                  % Analog prototype transition ratio
>> g = sqrt(A*A-1)/ep;                      % Analog prototype intermediate cal.
>> N = ceil(log10(g+sqrt(g*g-1))/log10(OmegaR+sqrt(OmegaR*OmegaR-1)));
>> fprintf('\n*** Chebyshev-1 Filter Order = %2.0f \n',N)
*** Chebyshev-1 Filter Order =  4
>> % Digital Chebyshev-I Filter Design:
>> wn = wp/pi;                              % Digital passband freq in pi units
>> [b,a]=cheby1(N,Rp,wn);   [b0,B,A] = dir2cas(b,a)
```

```
b0 = 0.0018
B = 1.0000      2.0000     1.0000
    1.0000      2.0000     1.0000
A = 1.0000     -1.4996     0.8482
    1.0000     -1.5548     0.6493
```

The system function is

$$H(z) = \frac{0.0018 \left(1 + z^{-1}\right)^4}{\left(1 - 1.4996z^{-1} + 0.8482z^{-2}\right)\left(1 - 1.5548z^{-1} + 0.6493z^{-2}\right)}$$

which is the same as in Example 8.18. The frequency-domain plots were shown
in Figure 8.27.   □

□   **EXAMPLE 8.23**   Digital Chebyshev-II lowpass filter design:

```
>> % Digital filter specifications:
>> wp = 0.2*pi;                      % Digital passband freq in rad
>> ws = 0.3*pi;                      % Digital stopband freq in rad
>> Rp = 1;                           % Passband ripple in dB
>> As = 15;                          % Stopband attenuation in dB

>> % Analog prototype specifications:
>> T = 1;                            % Set T=1
>> OmegaP = (2/T)*tan(wp/2);         % Prewarp prototype passband freq
>> OmegaS = (2/T)*tan(ws/2);         % Prewarp prototype stopband freq

>> % Analog prototype order calculation:
>> ep = sqrt(10^(Rp/10)-1);          % Passband ripple factor
>> A = 10^(As/20);                   % Stopband attenuation factor
>> OmegaC = OmegaP;                  % Analog prototype cutoff freq
>> OmegaR = OmegaS/OmegaP;           % Analog prototype transition ratio
>> g = sqrt(A*A-1)/ep;               % Analog prototype intermediate cal.
>> N = ceil(log10(g+sqrt(g*g-1))/log10(OmegaR+sqrt(OmegaR*OmegaR-1)));
>> fprintf('\n*** Chebyshev-2 Filter Order = %2.0f \n',N)
*** Chebyshev-2 Filter Order =  4

>> % Digital Chebyshev-II filter design:
>> wn = ws/pi;                       % Digital stopband freq in pi units
>> [b,a]=cheby2(N,As,wn);   [b0,B,A] = dir2cas(b,a)
b0 = 0.1797
B = 1.0000      0.5574     1.0000
    1.0000     -1.0671     1.0000
A = 1.0000     -0.4183     0.1503
    1.0000     -1.1325     0.7183
```

The system function is

$$H(z) = \frac{0.1797 \left(1 + 0.5574z^{-1} + z^{-2}\right)\left(1 - 1.0671z^{-1} + z^{-2}\right)}{\left(1 - 0.4183z^{-1} + 0.1503z^{-2}\right)\left(1 - 1.1325z^{-1} + 0.7183z^{-2}\right)}$$

which is the same as in Example 8.19. The frequency-domain plots were shown in Figure 8.28. $\square$

$\square$ **EXAMPLE 8.24**   Digital elliptic lowpass filter design:

```
>> % Digital filter specifications:
>> wp = 0.2*pi;                       % Digital passband freq in rad
>> ws = 0.3*pi;                       % Digital stopband freq in rad
>> Rp = 1;                            % Passband ripple in dB
>> As = 15;                           % Stopband attenuation in dB

>> % Analog prototype specifications:
>> T = 1;                             % Set T=1
>> OmegaP = (2/T)*tan(wp/2);          % Prewarp prototype passband freq
>> OmegaS = (2/T)*tan(ws/2);          % Prewarp prototype stopband freq

>> % Analog elliptic filter order calculations:
>> ep = sqrt(10^(Rp/10)-1);          % Passband ripple factor
>> A = 10^(As/20);                    % Stopband attenuation factor
>> OmegaC = OmegaP;                   % Analog prototype cutoff freq
>> k = OmegaP/OmegaS;                 % Analog prototype transition ratio
>> k1 = ep/sqrt(A*A-1);              % Analog prototype intermediate cal.
>> capk = ellipke([k.^2 1-k.^2]);
>> capk1 = ellipke([(k1 .^2) 1-(k1 .^2)]);
>> N = ceil(capk(1)*capk1(2)/(capk(2)*capk1(1)));
>> fprintf('\n*** Elliptic Filter Order = %2.0f \n',N)
*** Elliptic Filter Order =  3

>> % Digital elliptic filter design:
>> wn = wp/pi;                        % Digital passband freq in pi units
>> [b,a]=ellip(N,Rp,As,wn);   [b0,B,A] = dir2cas(b,a)
b0 = 0.1214
B = 1.0000    -1.4211    1.0000
    1.0000     1.0000         0
A = 1.0000    -1.4928    0.8612
    1.0000    -0.6183         0
```

The system function is

$$H(z) = \frac{0.1214 \left(1 - 1.4211z^{-1} + z^{-2}\right)\left(1 + z^{-1}\right)}{\left(1 - 1.4928z^{-1} + 0.8612z^{-2}\right)\left(1 - 0.6183z^{-1}\right)}$$

which is the same as in Example 8.20. The frequency-domain plots were shown in Figure 8.29. $\square$

TABLE 8.1   *Comparison of four prototype filters*

Prototype	Order N	Actual R_p	Actual A_s
Butterworth	6	1	17.6
Chebyshev-I	4	1	23.6
Chebyshev-II	4	0.15	15
Elliptic	3	1	16

8.5.1 COMPARISON OF FOUR PROTOTYPE FILTERS

In Examples 8.17–8.20, we designed a lowpass digital filter using the bilinear mapping on four different prototype analog filters satisfying the specifications $\omega_p = 0.2\pi$, $R_p = 1\,$dB, $\omega_s = 0.3\pi$, and $A_s = 15\,$dB. Let us now compare their performance in terms of order N, the actual passband ripple R_p measured at ω_p, and the actual stopband attenuation A_s measured at ω_s. This comparison is shown in Table 8.1. The Butterworth, Chebyshev-I, and elliptic filters satisfy R_p specification exactly at ω_p but exceed A_s specification at ω_s while the Chebyshev-II filter performs exactly opposite.

Clearly, the elliptic prototype gives the best design in terms of the smallest order while satisfying magnitude specifications almost exactly. However, if we compare phase responses of all four filters, then the elliptic design has the most nonlinear phase response in the passband, while Butterworth has the least nonlinear phase response.

8.6 FREQUENCY-BAND TRANSFORMATIONS

In the preceding two sections, we designed digital lowpass filters from their corresponding analog filters. Certainly, we would like to design other types of frequency-selective filters, such as highpass, bandpass, and bandstop. This is accomplished by transforming the frequency axis (or band) of a lowpass filter so that it behaves as another frequency-selective filter. These transformations on the complex variable z are very similar to bilinear transformations, and the design equations are algebraic. The procedure to design a general frequency-selective filter is to first design a *digital prototype* (of fixed bandwidth—say, unit bandwidth) lowpass filter and then to apply these algebraic transformations. In this section, we will describe the basic philosophy behind these mappings and illustrate their mechanism through examples. MATLAB provides functions that incorporate frequency-band transformation in the s-plane. We will first demonstrate the use of the z-plane mapping and then illustrate the use of MATLAB functions. Typical specifications for most commonly used types of frequency-selective digital filters are shown in Figure 8.30.

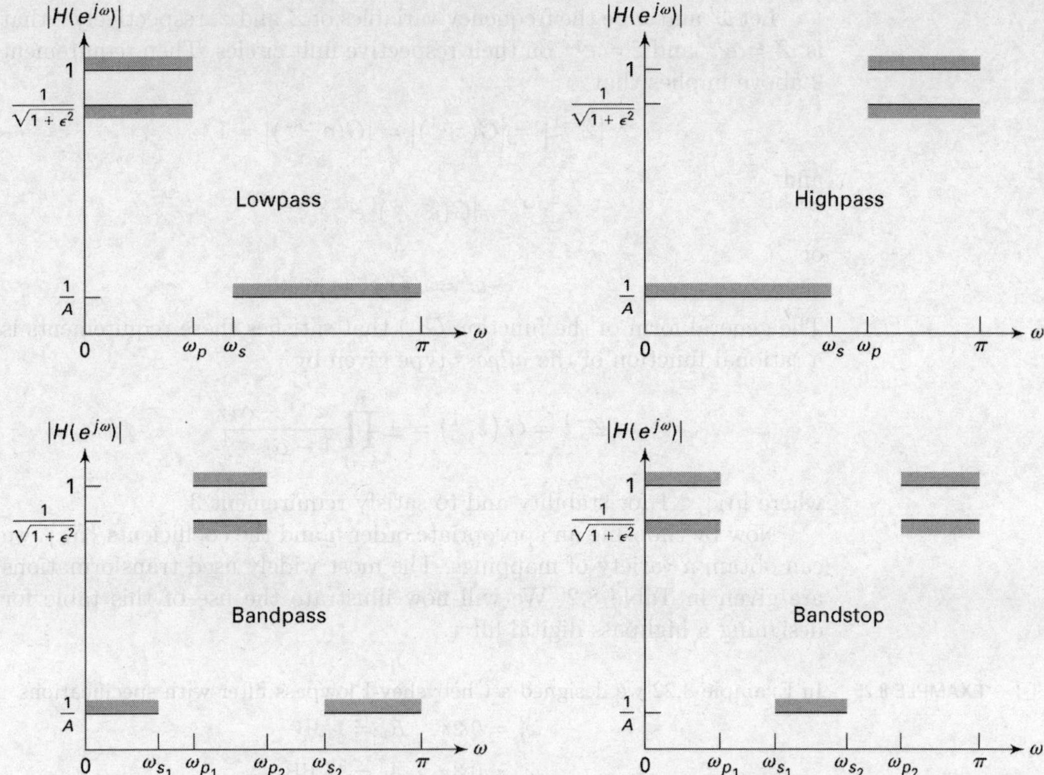

FIGURE 8.30   *Specifications of frequency-selective filters*

Let $H_{LP}(Z)$ be the given prototype lowpass digital filter, and let $H(z)$ be the desired frequency-selective digital filter. Note that we are using two different frequency variables, Z and z, with H_{LP} and H, respectively. Define a mapping of the form

$$Z^{-1} = G(z^{-1})$$

such that

$$H(z) = H_{LP}(Z)\big|_{Z^{-1}=G(z^{-1})}$$

To do this, we simply replace Z^{-1} everywhere in H_{LP} by the function $G(z^{-1})$. Given that $H_{LP}(Z)$ is a stable and causal filter, we also want $H(z)$ to be stable and causal. This imposes the following requirements.

1. $G(\cdot)$ must be a rational function in z^{-1} so that $H(z)$ is implementable.
2. The unit circle of the Z-plane must map onto the unit circle of the z-plane.
3. For stable filters, the inside of the unit circle of the Z-plane must also map onto the inside of the unit circle of the z-plane.

Let ω' and ω be the frequency variables of Z and z, respectively—that is, $Z = e^{j\omega'}$ and $z = e^{j\omega}$ on their respective unit circles. Then requirement 2 above implies that

$$\left|Z^{-1}\right| = \left|G(z^{-1})\right| = \left|G(e^{-j\omega})\right| = 1$$

and

$$e^{-j\omega'} = \left|G(e^{-j\omega})\right| e^{j\angle G(e^{-j\omega})}$$

or

$$-\omega' = \angle G(e^{-j\omega})$$

The general form of the function $G(\cdot)$ that satisfies these requirements is a rational function of the *allpass* type given by

$$Z^{-1} = G\left(z^{-1}\right) = \pm \prod_{k=1}^{n} \frac{z^{-1} - \alpha_k}{1 - \alpha_k z^{-1}}$$

where $|\alpha_k| < 1$ for stability and to satisfy requirement 3.

Now by choosing an appropriate order n and the coefficients $\{\alpha_k\}$, we can obtain a variety of mappings. The most widely used transformations are given in Table 8.2. We will now illustrate the use of this table for designing a highpass digital filter.

□ **EXAMPLE 8.25**   In Example 8.22 we designed a Chebyshev-I lowpass filter with specifications

$$\omega'_p = 0.2\pi, \quad R_p = 1 \text{ dB}$$

$$\omega'_s = 0.3\pi, \quad A_s = 15 \text{ dB}$$

and determined its system function

$$H_{LP}(Z) = \frac{0.001836(1 + Z^{-1})^4}{(1 - 1.4996Z^{-1} + 0.8482Z^{-2})(1 - 1.5548Z^{-1} + 0.6493Z^{-2})}$$

Design a highpass filter with these tolerances but with passband beginning at $\omega_p = 0.6\pi$.

Solution   We want to transform the given lowpass filter into a highpass filter such that the cutoff frequency $\omega'_p = 0.2\pi$ is mapped onto the cutoff frequency $\omega_p = 0.6\pi$. From Table 8.2,

$$\alpha = -\frac{\cos[(0.2\pi + 0.6\pi)/2]}{\cos[(0.2\pi - 0.6\pi)/2]} = -0.38197 \tag{8.70}$$

Hence

$$H_{LP}(z) = H(Z)\big|_{Z = -\frac{z^{-1} - 0.38197}{1 - 0.38197z^{-1}}}$$

$$= \frac{0.02426(1 - z^{-1})^4}{(1 + 0.5661z^{-1} + 0.7657z^{-2})(1 + 1.0416z^{-1} + 0.4019z^{-2})}$$

which is the desired filter. The frequency response plots of the lowpass filter and the new highpass filter are shown in Figure 8.31.   □

TABLE 8.2 *Frequency transformation for digital filters (prototype lowpass filter has cutoff frequency ω_c')*

Type of Transformation	Transformation	Parameters
Lowpass	$z^{-1} \longrightarrow \dfrac{z^{-1} - \alpha}{1 - \alpha z^{-1}}$	$\omega_c = $ cutoff frequency of new filter $\alpha = \dfrac{\sin\left[\left(\omega_c' - \omega_c\right)/2\right]}{\sin\left[\left(\omega_c' + \omega_c\right)/2\right]}$
Highpass	$z^{-1} \longrightarrow -\dfrac{z^{-1} + \alpha}{1 + \alpha z^{-1}}$	$\omega_c = $ cutoff frequency of new filter $\alpha = -\dfrac{\cos\left[\left(\omega_c' + \omega_c\right)/2\right]}{\cos\left[\left(\omega_c' - \omega_c\right)/2\right]}$
Bandpass	$z^{-1} \longrightarrow -\dfrac{z^{-2} - \alpha_1 z^{-1} + \alpha_2}{\alpha_2 z^{-2} - \alpha_1 z^{-1} + 1}$	$\omega_\ell = $ lower cutoff frequency $\omega_u = $ upper cutoff frequency $\alpha_1 = -2\beta K/(K+1)$ $\alpha_2 = (K-1)/(K+1)$ $\beta = \dfrac{\cos\left[\left(\omega_u + \omega_\ell\right)/2\right]}{\cos\left[\left(\omega_u - \omega_\ell\right)/2\right]}$ $K = \cot\dfrac{\omega_u - \omega_\ell}{2}\tan\dfrac{\omega_c'}{2}$
Bandstop	$z^{-1} \longrightarrow \dfrac{z^{-2} - \alpha_1 z^{-1} + \alpha_2}{\alpha_2 z^{-2} - \alpha_1 z^{-1} + 1}$	$\omega_\ell = $ lower cutoff frequency $\omega_u = $ upper cutoff frequency $\alpha_1 = -2\beta/(K+1)$ $\alpha_2 = (K-1)/(K+1)$ $\beta = \dfrac{\cos\left[\left(\omega_u + \omega_\ell\right)/2\right]}{\cos\left[\left(\omega_u - \omega_\ell\right)/2\right]}$ $K = \tan\dfrac{\omega_u - \omega_\ell}{2}\tan\dfrac{\omega_c'}{2}$

From this example, it is obvious that to obtain the rational function of a new digital filter from the prototype lowpass digital filter, we should be able to implement rational function substitutions from Table 8.2. This appears to be a difficult task, but since these are algebraic functions, we can use the `conv` function repetitively for this purpose. The following `zmapping` function illustrates this approach.

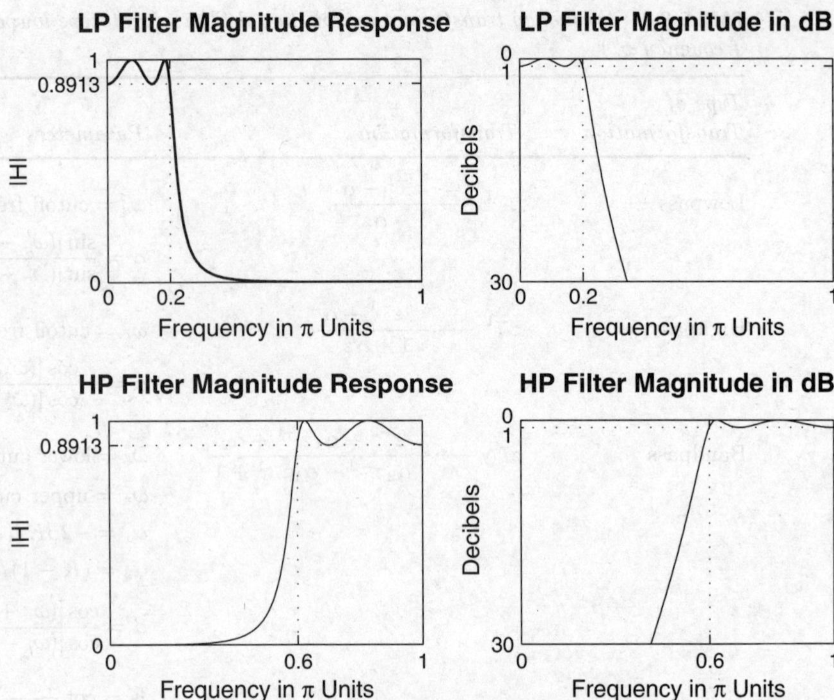

FIGURE 8.31 *Magnitude response plots for Example 8.25*

```
function [bz,az] = zmapping(bZ,aZ,Nz,Dz)
% Frequency-band transformation from Z-domain to z-domain
% ---------------------------------------------------------
% [bz,az] = zmapping(bZ,aZ,Nz,Dz)
% performs:
%           b(z)    b(Z)|
%           ---- = ----|        N(z)
%           a(z)    a(Z)|@Z = ----
%                             D(z)
%

bNzord = (length(bZ)-1)*(length(Nz)-1);
aDzord = (length(aZ)-1)*(length(Dz)-1);
bzord = length(bZ)-1; azord = length(aZ)-1;
bz = zeros(1,bNzord+1);
for k = 0:bzord
    pln = [1];
    for l = 0:k-1
        pln = conv(pln,Nz);
    end
    pld = [1];
```

```
            for l = 0:bzord-k-1
                pld = conv(pld,Dz);
            end
            bz = bz+bZ(k+1)*conv(pln,pld);
        end
    az = zeros(1,aDzord+1);
    for k = 0:azord
        pln = [1];
        for l = 0:k-1
            pln = conv(pln,Nz);
        end
        pld = [1];
        for l = 0:azord-k-1
                pld = conv(pld,Dz);
        end
        az = az+aZ(k+1)*conv(pln,pld);
    end
```

☐ **EXAMPLE 8.26** Use the `zmapping` function to perform the lowpass-to-highpass transformation in Example 8.25.

Solution First we will design the lowpass digital filter in MATLAB using the bilinear transformation procedure and then use the `zmapping` function.

MATLAB script:

```
>> % Digital lowpass filter specifications:
>> wplp = 0.2*pi;                          % Digital passband freq in rad
>> wslp = 0.3*pi;                          % Digital stopband freq in rad
>>   Rp = 1;                               % Passband ripple in dB
>>   As = 15;                              % Stopband attenuation in dB

>> % Analog prototype specifications: Inverse mapping for frequencies
>> T = 1; Fs = 1/T;                        % Set T=1
>> OmegaP = (2/T)*tan(wplp/2);             % Prewarp prototype passband freq
>> OmegaS = (2/T)*tan(wslp/2);             % Prewarp prototype stopband freq

>> % Analog Chebyshev prototype filter calculation:
>> [cs,ds] = afd_chb1(OmegaP,OmegaS,Rp,As);
** Chebyshev-1 Filter Order =  4

>> % Bilinear transformation:
>> [blp,alp] = bilinear(cs,ds,Fs);
```

```
>> % Digital highpass filter cutoff frequency:
>> wphp = 0.6*pi;                                 % Passband-edge frequency

>> % LP-to-HP frequency-band transformation:
>> alpha = -(cos((wplp+wphp)/2))/(cos((wplp-wphp)/2))
alpha = -0.3820

>> Nz = -[alpha,1]; Dz = [1,alpha];
>> [bhp,ahp] = zmapping(blp,alp,Nz,Dz);   [C,B,A] = dir2cas(bhp,ahp)
C = 0.0243
B = 1.0000   -2.0000    1.0000
    1.0000   -2.0000    1.0000
A = 1.0000    1.0416    0.4019
    1.0000    0.5561    0.7647
```

The system function of the highpass filter is

$$H(z) = \frac{0.0243(1 - z^{-1})^4}{(1 + 0.5661z^{-1} + 0.7647z^{-2})(1 + 1.0416z^{-1} + 0.4019z^{-2})}$$

which is essentially identical to that in Example 8.25. □

8.6.1 DESIGN PROCEDURE

In Example 8.26, a lowpass prototype digital filter was available to transform into a highpass filter so that a particular band-edge frequency was properly mapped. In practice, we have to first design a prototype lowpass digital filter whose specifications should be obtained from specifications of other frequency-selective filters as given in Figure 8.30. We will now show that the lowpass prototype filter specifications can be obtained from the transformation formulas given in Table 8.2.

Let us use the highpass filter of Example 8.25 as an example. The passband-edge frequencies were transformed using the parameter $\alpha = -0.38197$ in (8.70). What is the stopband-edge frequency of the highpass filter, say ω_s, corresponding to the stopband edge $\omega_s' = 0.3\pi$ of the prototype lowpass filter? This can be answered by (8.70). Since α is fixed for the transformation, we set the equation

$$\alpha = -\frac{\cos[(0.3\pi + \omega_s)/2]}{\cos[(0.3\pi - \omega_s)/2]} = -0.38197$$

This is a transcendental equation whose solution can be obtained iteratively from an initial guess. It can be done using MATLAB, and the solution is

$$\omega_s = 0.4586\pi$$

Now, in practice, we will know the desired highpass frequencies ω_s and ω_p, and we are required to find the prototype lowpass cutoff frequencies ω'_s and ω'_p. We can choose the passband frequency ω'_p with a reasonable value—say, $\omega'_p = 0.2\pi$—and determine α from ω_p using the formula from Table 8.2. Now ω'_s can be determined (for our highpass filter example) from α and

$$Z = -\frac{z^{-1} + \alpha}{1 + \alpha z^{-1}}$$

where $Z = e^{j\omega'_s}$ and $z = e^{j\omega_s}$, or

$$\omega'_s = \angle\left(-\frac{e^{-j\omega_s} + \alpha}{1 + \alpha e^{-j\omega_s}}\right) \tag{8.71}$$

Continuing our highpass filter example, let $\omega_p = 0.6\pi$ and $\omega_s = 0.4586\pi$ be the band-edge frequencies. Let us choose $\omega'_p = 0.2\pi$. Then $\alpha = -0.38197$ from (8.70), and from (8.71)

$$\omega'_s = \angle\left(-\frac{e^{-j0.4586\pi} - 0.38197}{1 - 0.38197e^{-j \cdot 0.38197}}\right) = 0.3\pi$$

as expected. Now we can design a digital lowpass filter and transform it into a highpass filter using the `zmapping` function to complete our design procedure. For designing a highpass Chebyshev-I digital filter, the above procedure can be incorporated into a MATLAB function called the `cheb1hpf` function, shown here.

```
function [b,a] = cheb1hpf(wp,ws,Rp,As)
% IIR highpass filter design using Chebyshev-1 prototype
% function [b,a] = cheb1hpf(wp,ws,Rp,As)
%    b = numerator polynomial of the highpass filter
%    a = denominator polynomial of the highpass filter
%   wp = passband frequency in radians
%   ws = stopband frequency in radians
%   Rp = passband ripple in dB
%   As = stopband attenuation in dB
%
% Determine the digital lowpass cutoff frequencies:
wplp = 0.2*pi;
alpha = -(cos((wplp+wp)/2))/(cos((wplp-wp)/2));
wslp = angle(-(exp(-j*ws)+alpha)/(1+alpha*exp(-j*ws)));
%
```

```
% Compute analog lowpass prototype specifications:
T = 1; Fs = 1/T;
OmegaP = (2/T)*tan(wplp/2);
OmegaS = (2/T)*tan(wslp/2);

% Design analog Chebyshev prototype lowpass filter:
[cs,ds] = afd_chb1(OmegaP,OmegaS,Rp,As);

% Perform bilinear transformation to obtain digital lowpass
[blp,alp] = bilinear(cs,ds,Fs);

% Transform digital lowpass into highpass filter
Nz = -[alpha,1]; Dz = [1,alpha];
[b,a] = zmapping(blp,alp,Nz,Dz);
```

We will demonstrate this procedure in the following example.

☐   **EXAMPLE 8.27**   Design a highpass digital filter to satisfy

$$\omega_p = 0.6\pi, \qquad R_p = 1 \text{ dB}$$
$$\omega_s = 0.4586\pi, \quad A_s = 15 \text{ dB}$$

Use the Chebyshev-I prototype.

Solution   MATLAB script:

```
>> % Digital highpass filter specifications:
>> wp = 0.6*pi;                        % Digital passband freq in rad
>> ws = 0.4586*pi;                     % Digital stopband freq in rad
>> Rp = 1;                             % Passband ripple in dB
>> As = 15;                            % Stopband attenuation in dB

>> [b,a] = cheb1hpf(wp,ws,Rp,As);   [C,B,A] = dir2cas(b,a)
C = 0.0243
B = 1.0000    -2.0000     1.0000
    1.0000    -2.0000     1.0000
A = 1.0000     1.0416     0.4019
    1.0000     0.5561     0.7647
```

The system function is

$$H(z) = \frac{0.0243(1 - z^{-1})^4}{(1 + 0.5661z^{-1} + 0.7647z^{-2})(1 + 1.0416z^{-1} + 0.4019z^{-2})}$$

which is identical to that in Example 8.26.   ☐

This highpass filter design procedure can be easily extended to other frequency-selective filters using the transformation functions in Table 8.2. These design procedures are explored in Problems P8.34, P8.36, P8.38, and P8.40. We now describe MATLAB's filter design functions for designing arbitrary frequency-selective filters.

8.6.2 MATLAB IMPLEMENTATION

In the preceding section, we discussed four MATLAB functions to design digital lowpass filters. These same functions can also be used to design highpass, bandpass, and bandstop filters. The frequency-band transformations in these functions are done in the s-plane; that is, they use Approach-1 discussed on page 370. For the purpose of illustration, we will use the function `butter`. It can be used with the following variations in its input arguments.

- `[b,a] = BUTTER(N,wn,'high')` designs an Nth-order *highpass* filter with digital 3 dB cutoff frequency `wn` in units of π.
- `[b,a] = BUTTER(N,wn,)` designs an order 2N *bandpass* filter if `wn` is a two-element vector, `wn=[w1 w2]`, with 3 dB passband `w1 < w < w2` in units of π.
- `[b,a] = BUTTER(N,wn,'stop')` is an order 2N *bandstop* filter if `wn=[w1 w2]` with 3 dB stopband `w1 < w < w2` in units of π.

To design any frequency-selective Butterworth filter, we need to know the order `N` and the 3 dB cutoff frequency vector `wn`. In this chapter, we described how to determine these parameters for lowpass filters. However, these calculations are more complicated for bandpass and bandstop filters. In their SP toolbox, MATLAB provides a function called `buttord` to compute these parameters. Given the specifications, ω_p, ω_s, R_p, and A_s, this function determines the necessary parameters. Its syntax is

```
[N,wn] = buttord(wp,ws,Rp,As)
```

The parameters `wp` and `ws` have some restrictions, depending on the type of filter:

- For lowpass filters `wp < ws`.
- For highpass filters `wp > ws`.
- For bandpass filters `wp` and `ws` are two-element vectors, `wp=[wp1, wp2]` and `ws=[ws1,ws2]`, such that `ws1 < wp1 < wp2 < ws2`.
- For bandstop filters `wp1 < ws1 < ws2 < wp2`.

Now using the `buttord` function in conjunction with the `butter` function, we can design any Butterworth IIR filter. Similar discussions apply for `cheby1`, `cheby2`, and `ellip` functions with appropriate modifications. We illustrate the use of these functions through the following examples.

□ **EXAMPLE 8.28** In this example, we will design a Chebyshev-I highpass filter whose specifications were given in Example 8.27.

Solution MATLAB script:

```
>> % Digital filter specifications:        % Type: Chebyshev-I highpass
>> ws = 0.4586*pi;                         % Dig. stopband-edge frequency
>> wp = 0.6*pi;                            % Dig. passband-edge frequency
>> Rp = 1;                                 % Passband ripple in dB
>> As = 15;                                % Stopband attenuation in dB

>> % Calculations of Chebyshev-I filter parameters:
>> [N,wn] = cheb1ord(wp/pi,ws/pi,Rp,As);

>> % Digital Chebyshev-I highpass filter design:
>> [b,a] = cheby1(N,Rp,wn,'high');

>> % Cascade form realization:
>> [b0,B,A] = dir2cas(b,a)
b0 = 0.0243
B = 1.0000    -1.9991     0.9991
    1.0000    -2.0009     1.0009
A = 1.0000     1.0416     0.4019
    1.0000     0.5561     0.7647
```

The cascade form system function

$$H(z) = \frac{0.0243(1 - z^{-1})^4}{(1 + 0.5661z^{-1} + 0.7647z^{-2})(1 + 1.0416z^{-1} + 0.4019z^{-2})}$$

is identical to the filter designed in Example 8.27, which demonstrates that the two approaches described on page 370 are identical. The frequency-domain plots are shown in Figure 8.32.   □

□ **EXAMPLE 8.29** In this example, we will design an elliptic bandpass filter whose specifications are given in the following MATLAB script.

```
>> % Digital filter specifications:        % Type: Elliptic bandpass
>> ws = [0.3*pi 0.75*pi];                  % Dig. stopband-edge frequency
>> wp = [0.4*pi 0.6*pi];                   % Dig. passband-edge frequency
>> Rp = 1;                                 % Passband ripple in dB
>> As = 40;                                % Stopband attenuation in dB
```

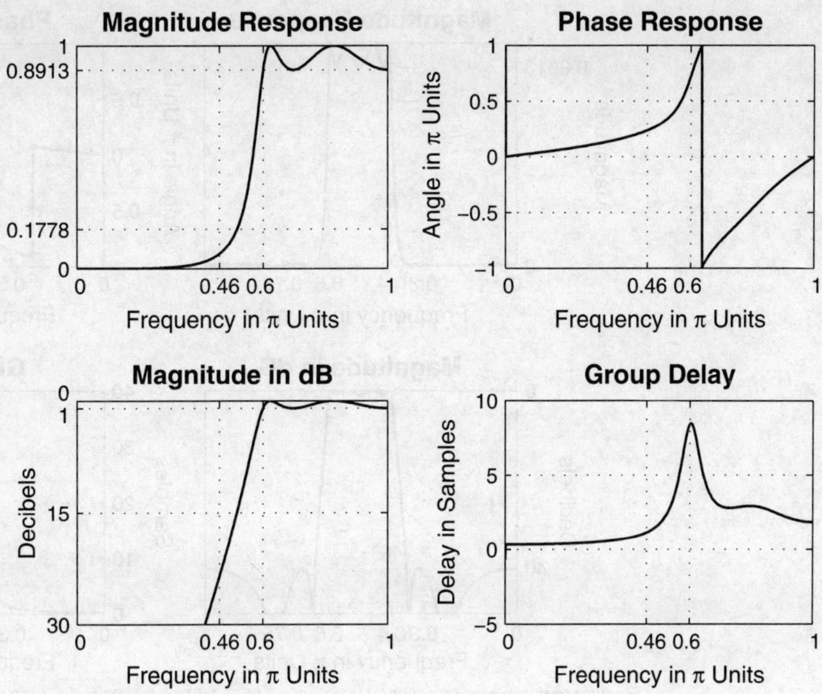

FIGURE 8.32 *Digital Chebyshev-I highpass filter in Example 8.28*

```
>> % Calculations of elliptic filter parameters:
>> [N,wn] = ellipord(wp/pi,ws/pi,Rp,As);

>> % Digital elliptic bandpass filter design:
>> [b,a] = ellip(N,Rp,As,wn);

>> % Cascade form realization:
>> [b0,B,A] = dir2cas(b,a)
b0 = 0.0197
B = 1.0000    1.5066    1.0000
    1.0000    0.9268    1.0000
    1.0000   -0.9268    1.0000
    1.0000   -1.5066    1.0000
A = 1.0000    0.5963    0.9399
    1.0000    0.2774    0.7929
    1.0000   -0.2774    0.7929
    1.0000   -0.5963    0.9399
```

Note that the designed filter is a tenth-order filter. The frequency-domain plots
are shown in Figure 8.33.   □

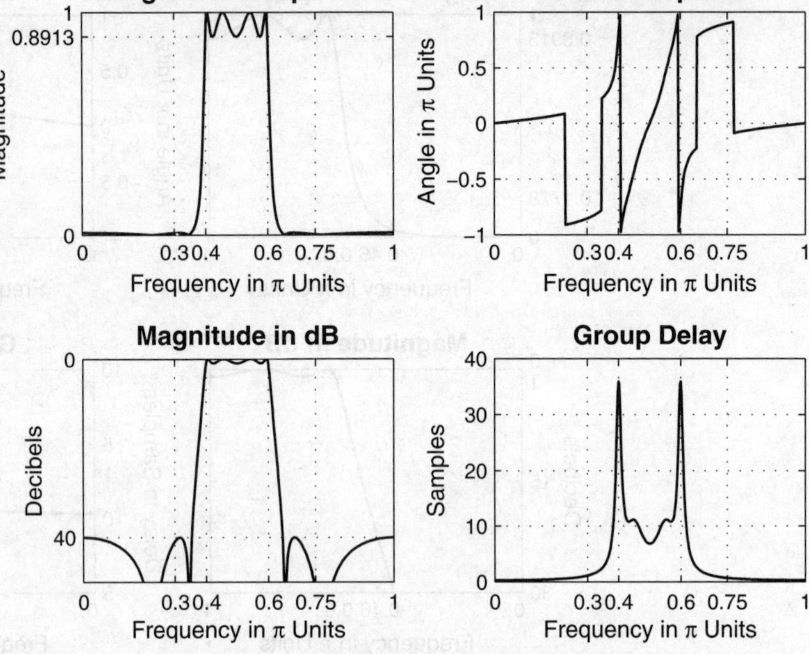

FIGURE 8.33 *Digital elliptic bandpass filter in Example 8.29*

☐ **EXAMPLE 8.30** Finally, we will design a Chebyshev-II bandstop filter whose specifications are given in the following MATLAB script.

```
>> % Digital filter specifications:      % Type: Chebyshev-II bandstop
>> ws = [0.4*pi 0.7*pi];                 % Dig. stopband-edge frequency
>> wp = [0.25*pi 0.8*pi];                % Dig. passband-edge frequency
>> Rp = 1;                               % Passband ripple in dB
>> As = 40;                              % Stopband attenuation in dB

>> % Calculations of Chebyshev-II filter parameters:
>> [N,wn] = cheb2ord(wp/pi,ws/pi,Rp,As);

>> % Digital Chebyshev-II bandstop filter design:
>> [b,a] = cheby2(N,As,ws/pi,'stop');

>> % Cascade form realization:
>> [b0,B,A] = dir2cas(b,a)
b0 = 0.1558
B = 1.0000      1.1456      1.0000
    1.0000      0.8879      1.0000
    1.0000      0.3511      1.0000
    1.0000     -0.2434      1.0000
    1.0000     -0.5768      1.0000
```

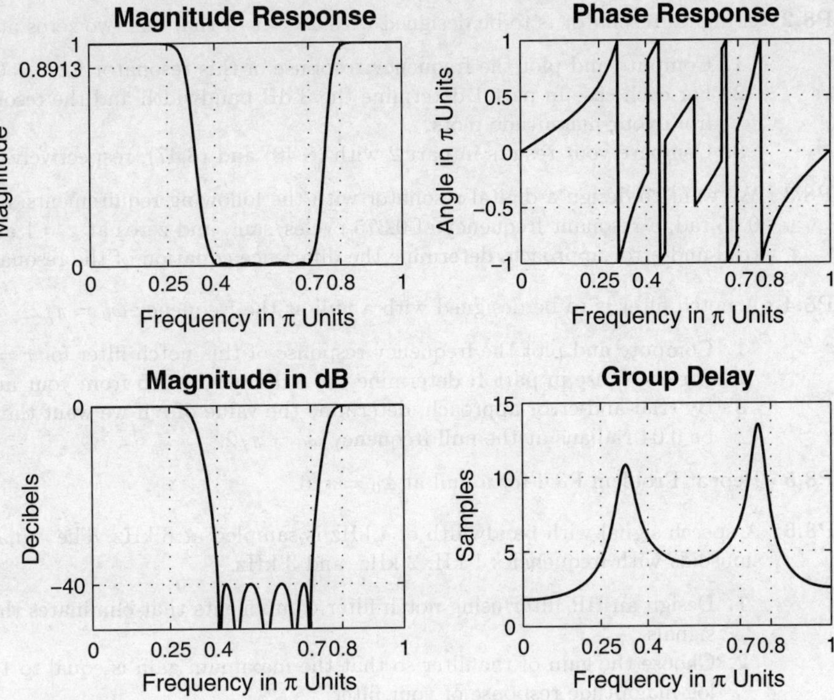

FIGURE 8.34 *Digital Chebyshev-II bandstop filter in Example 8.30*

```
A = 1.0000    1.3041    0.8031
    1.0000    0.8901    0.4614
    1.0000    0.2132    0.2145
    1.0000   -0.4713    0.3916
    1.0000   -0.8936    0.7602
```

This is also a tenth-order filter. The frequency domain plots are shown in Figure 8.34. □

8.7 PROBLEMS

P8.1 A digital resonator is to be designed with $\omega_0 = \pi/4$ that has two zeros at $z = 0$.

1. Compute and plot the frequency response of this resonator for $r = 0.8$, 0.9, and 0.99.
2. For each case in part 1, determine the 3 dB bandwidth and the resonant frequency ω_r from your magnitude plots.
3. Check if your results in part 2 are in agreement with the theoretical results.

P8.2   A digital resonator is to be designed with $\omega_0 = \pi/4$ that has two zeros at $z = 1$ and $z = -1$.

1. Compute and plot the frequency response of this resonator for $r = 0.8$, 0.9, and 0.99.
2. For each case in part 1 determine the 3 dB bandwidth and the resonant frequency ω_r from your magnitude plots.
3. Compare your results in part 2 with (8.48) and (8.47), respectively.

P8.3   We want to design a digital resonator with the following requirements: a 3 dB bandwidth of 0.05 rad, a resonant frequency of 0.375 cycles/sam, and zeros at $z = 1$ and $z = -1$. Using trial-and-error approach, determine the difference equation of the resonator.

P8.4   A notch filter is to be designed with a null at the frequency $\omega_0 = \pi/2$.

1. Compute and plot the frequency response of this notch filter for $r = 0.7$, 0.9, and 0.99.
2. For each case in part 1, determine the 3 dB bandwidth from your magnitude plots.
3. By trial-and-error approach, determine the value of r if we want the 3 dB bandwidth to be 0.04 radians at the null frequency $\omega_0 = \pi/2$.

P8.5   Repeat Problem P8.4 for a null at $\omega_0 = \pi/6$.

P8.6   A speech signal with bandwidth of 4 kHz is sampled at 8 kHz. The signal is corrupted by sinusoids with frequencies 1 kH, 2 kHz, and 3 kHz.

1. Design an IIR filter using notch filter components that eliminates these sinusoidal signals.
2. Choose the gain of the filter so that the maximum gain is equal to 1, and plot the log-magnitude response of your filter.
3. Load the `handel` sound file in MATLAB, and add the preceding three sinusoidal signals to create a corrupted sound signal. Now filter the corrupted sound signal using your filter and comment on its performance.

P8.7   Consider the system function of an IIR lowpass filter

$$H(z) = K \frac{1 + z^{-1}}{1 - 0.9z^{-1}} \tag{8.72}$$

where K is a constant that can be adjusted to make the maximum gain response equal to 1. We obtain the system function of an Lth-order comb filter $H_L(z)$ using $H_L(z) = H\big(z^L\big)$.

1. Determine the value of K for the system function in (8.72).
2. Using the K value from part 1, determine and plot the log-magnitude response of the comb filter for $L = 6$.
3. Describe the shape of your plot in part 2.

P8.8   Consider the system function of an IIR highpass filter

$$H(z) = K \frac{1 - z^{-1}}{1 - 0.9z^{-1}} \tag{8.73}$$

where K is a constant that can be adjusted to make the maximum gain response equal to 1. We obtain the system function of an Lth-order comb filter $H_L(z)$ using $H_L(z) = H\big(z^L\big)$.

1. Determine the value of K for the system function in (8.73).
2. Using the K value from part 1, determine and plot the log-magnitude response of the comb filter for $L = 6$.
3. Describe the shape of your plot in part 2.

P8.9 (Adapted from [72]) As discussed in Chapter 1, echos and reverberations of a signal $x(n)$ can be obtained by scaling and delaying, that is,

$$y(n) = \sum_{k=0}^{\infty} \alpha_k x(n - kD) \tag{8.74}$$

where D is a positive integer for minimum delay and $\alpha_k > \alpha_{k-1} > 0$.

1. Consider the IIR comb filter given by

$$H(z) = \frac{1}{1 - az^{-D}} \tag{8.75}$$

Determine its impulse response. Explain why this filter can be used as a reverberator.
2. Consider the cascade of three allpass comb filters

$$H(z) = \frac{z^{D_1} - a_1}{1 - a_1 z^{-D_1}} \times \frac{z^{D_2} - a_2}{1 - a_2 z^{-D_2}} \times \frac{z^{D_3} - a_3}{1 - a_3 z^{-D_3}} \tag{8.76}$$

which can be used as a practical digital reverberator. Compute and plot the impulse response of this reverberator for $D_1 = 50$, $a_1 = 0.7$; $D_2 = 41$, $a_2 = 0.665$; and $D_3 = 32$, $a_3 = 0.63175$.
3. Repeat part 2 for $D_1 = 53$, $a_1 = 0.7$; $D_2 = 40$, $a_2 = 0.665$; and $D_3 = 31$, $a_3 = 0.63175$. How does the shape of this reverberator differ from the one in part 2? Which is a good reverberator?

P8.10 Consider the first-order allpass system function given by

$$H(z) = \frac{a + z^{-1}}{1 + az^{-1}}, \qquad 0 < a < 1 \tag{8.77}$$

The phase-delay of a system is defined as $\Phi(\omega) \underset{=}{\triangle} -\angle H\left(e^{j\omega}\right)/\omega$ and is measured in samples.

1. Show that the phase-delay of the system in (8.77) at low frequencies is given by

$$\Phi(\omega) \approx \frac{1 - a}{1 + a} \quad \text{for } a \approx 1 \tag{8.78}$$

2. Plot the phase-delay over $-\pi/2 \leq \omega \leq \pi/2$ for $a = 0.9$, 0.95, and 0.99 to verify Problem P8.10. Comment on the accuracy of the results.
3. Design a first-order allpass system that has phase delay of 0.01 samples. Plot its magnitude and phase-delay responses.

P8.11 Consider the second-order allpass system function given by

$$H(z) = \frac{a_2 + a_1 z^{-1} + z^{-2}}{1 + a_1 z^{-1} + a_2 z^{-2}} \tag{8.79}$$

The phase-delay of a system is defined as $\Phi(\omega) \underset{=}{\triangle} -\angle H\left(e^{j\omega}\right)/\omega$ and is measured in samples.
It can be shown that if we choose

$$a_1 = 1\left(\frac{2-d}{1+d}\right), \qquad a_2 = \frac{(2-d)(1-d)}{(2+d)(1+d)} \tag{8.80}$$

then phase-delay $\Phi(\omega)$ at low frequencies is approximated by d in samples. Verify this result by plotting $\Phi(\omega)$ over $-\pi/2 \leq \omega \leq \pi/2$ for $d = 0.1$, $d = 0.05$, and $d = 0.01$.

P8.12 Design an analog Butterworth lowpass filter that has a 0.25 dB or better ripple at 500 rad/sec and at least 50 dB of attenuation at 2000 rad/sec. Determine the system function in a rational function form. Plot the magnitude response, the log-magnitude response in dB, the phase response, and the impulse response of the filter.

P8.13 Design an analog Butterworth lowpass filter that has a 0.5 dB or better ripple at 10 kHz and at least 45 dB of attenuation at 20 kHz. Determine the system function in a cascade form. Plot the magnitude response, the log-magnitude response in dB, the group-delay, and the impulse response of the filter.

P8.14 Design a lowpass analog Chebyshev-I filter with an acceptable ripple of 1 dB for $|\Omega| \leq 10$ and an attenuation of 50 dB or greater beyond $|\Omega| = 15$ rad/sec. Determine the system function in a rational function form. Plot the magnitude response, the log-magnitude response in dB, the group-delay, and the impulse response of the filter.

P8.15 Design a lowpass analog Chebyshev-I filter with the following characteristics:

- a passband ripple of 0.5 dB,
- passband cutoff frequency of 4 kHz, and
- stopband attenuation of 45 dB or greater beyond 20 kHz.

Determine the system function in a cascade form. Plot the magnitude response, the log-magnitude response in dB, the phase response, and the impulse response of the filter.

P8.16 A signal $x_a(t)$ contains two frequencies, 10 kHz and 15 kHz. We want to suppress the 15 kHz component to 50 dB attenuation while passing the 10 kHz component with less than 0.25 dB attenuation. Design a minimum-order Chebyshev-II analog filter to perform this filtering operation. Plot the log-magnitude response, and verify the design.

P8.17 Design an analog Chebyshev-II lowpass filter that has a 0.25 dB or better ripple at 250 Hz and at least 40 dB of attenuation at 400 Hz. Plot the magnitude response, the log-magnitude response in dB, the group-delay, and the impulse response of the filter.

P8.18 A signal $x_a(t)$ contains two frequencies, 10 kHz and 15 kHz. We want to suppress the 15 kHz component to 50 dB attenuation while passing the 10 kHz component with less than 0.25 dB attenuation. Design a minimum-order elliptic analog filter to perform this filtering operation. Plot the log-magnitude response and verify the design. Compare your design with the Chebyshev-II design in Problem P8.16.

P8.19 Design an analog elliptic lowpass filter that has a 0.25 dB or better ripple at 500 rad/sec and at least 50 dB of attenuation at 2000 rad/sec. Determine the system function in a rational function form. Plot the magnitude response, the log-magnitude response in dB, the phase response, and the impulse response of the filter. Compare your design with the Butterworth design in Problem P8.12.

P8.20 Write a MATLAB function to design analog lowpass filters. The format of this function should be

```
function [b,a] =afd(type,Fp,Fs,Rp,As)
%
% function [b,a] =afd(type,Fp,Fs,Rp,As)
%    Designs analog lowpass filters
% type = 'butter' or 'cheby1' or 'cheby2' or 'ellip'
%    Fp = passband cutoff in Hz
%    Fs = stopband cutoff in Hz
%    Rp = passband ripple in dB
%    As = stopband attenuation in dB
```

Use the `afd_butt`, `afd_chb1`, `afd_chb2`, and `afd_elip` functions developed in this chapter. Check your function using specifications given in Problems P8.12 through P8.17.

P8.21 We want to design a Chebyshev-I prototype lowpass digital filter operating at a sampling rate of 8 kHz with a passband edge of 3.2 kHz, a passband ripple of 0.5 dB, and a minimum stopband attenuation of 45 dB at 3.8 kHz.

1. Using the impulse invariance transformation with $T = 1$ sec, design the digital filter. Plot the magnitude and the log-magnitude responses as functions of analog frequency in kHz.
2. Repeat part 1 using $T = 1/8000$ sec.
3. Compare the above two designs in parts 1 and 2 in terms of their frequency responses. Comment on the effect of T on the impulse invariance design.

P8.22 Design a Butterworth digital lowpass filter to satisfy the following specifications.

$$\text{passband edge:} \quad 0.4\pi, \quad R_p = 0.5 \text{ dB}$$

$$\text{stopband edge:} \quad 0.6\pi, \quad A_s = 50 \text{ dB}$$

Use the impulse invariance method with $T = 2$. Determine the system function in the rational form, and plot the log-magnitude response in dB. Plot the impulse response $h(n)$ and the impulse response $h_a(t)$ of the analog prototype and compare their shapes.

P8.23 Write a MATLAB function to design digital lowpass filters based on the impulse invariance transformation. The format of this function should be

```
function [b,a] =dlpfd_ii(type,wp,ws,Rp,As,T)
%
% function [b,a] =dlpfd_ii(type,wp,ws,Rp,As,T)
%    Designs digital lowpass filters using impulse invariance
% type = 'butter' or 'cheby1'
%    wp = passband cutoff in Hz
%    ws = stopband cutoff in Hz
%    Rp = passband ripple in dB
%    As = stopband attenuation in dB
%     T = sampling interval
```

Use the `afd` function developed in Problem P8.20. Check your function on specifications given in Problems P8.21 and P8.22.

P8.24 In this problem, we will develop a technique called the *step invariance* transformation. In this technique, the step response of an analog prototype filter is preserved in the resulting digital filter; that is, if $v_a(t)$ is the step response of the prototype and if $v(n)$ is the step response of the digital filter, then

$$v(n) = v_a(t)|_{t=nT}, \quad T : \text{sampling interval}$$

Note that the frequency-domain quantities are related by

$$V_a(s) \triangleq \mathcal{L}[v_a(t)] = H_a(s)/s$$

and

$$V(z) \triangleq \mathcal{Z}[v(n)] = H(z)\frac{1}{1 - z^{-1}}$$

Hence the step invariance transformation steps are as follows. Given $H_a(s)$,

- divide $H_a(s)$ by s to obtain $V_a(s)$,
- find residues $\{R_k\}$ and poles $\{p_k\}$ of $V_a(s)$,
- transform analog poles $\{p_k\}$ into digital poles $\left\{e^{p_k T}\right\}$ where T is arbitrary,
- determine $V(z)$ from residues $\{R_k\}$ and poles $\left\{e^{p_k T}\right\}$, and finally
- determine $H(z)$ by multiplying $V(z)$ by $\left(1 - z^{-1}\right)$.

Use the above procedure to develop a MATLAB function to implement the step invariance transformation. The format of this function should be

```
function [b,a] =stp_invr(c,d,T)
% Step invariance transformation from analog to digital filter
% [b,a] =stp_invr(c,d,T)
%  b = numerator polynomial in z^(-1) of the digital filter
%  a = denominator polynomial in z^(-1) of the digital filter
%  c = numerator polynomial in s of the analog filter
%  d = denominator polynomial in s of the analog filter
%  T = sampling (transformation) parameter
```

P8.25 Design the lowpass Butterworth digital filter of Problem P8.22 using the step invariance method. Plot the log-magnitude response in dB and compare it with that in Problem P8.22. Plot the step response $v(n)$ and the impulse response $v_a(t)$ of the analog prototype and compare their shapes.

P8.26 In this chapter, we discussed a filter transformation technique called the matched-z transformation. Using (8.69), write a MATLAB function called **mzt** that maps the analog system function $H_a(s)$ into the digital system function $H(z)$. The format of the function should be

```
function [b,a] = mzt(c,d,T)
% Matched-z transformation from analog to digital filter
% [b,a] = MZT(c,d,T)
%   b = numerator polynomial in z^(-1) of the digital filter
%   a = denominator polynomial in z^(-1) of the digital filter
%   c = numerator polynomial in s of the analog filter
%   d = denominator polynomial in s of the analog filter
%   T = sampling interval (transformation parameter)
```

Using this function, transform

$$H_a(s) = \frac{s+1}{s^2 + 5s + 6}$$

into a digital filter $H(z)$ for the sampling intervals (in seconds) $T = 0.05$, $T = 0.1$, and $T = 0.2$. In each case, obtain a plot similar to that in Figure 8.20 and comment on the performance of this technique.

P8.27 Consider an analog Butterworth lowpass filter that has a 1 dB or better ripple at 100 Hz and at least 30 dB of attenuation at 150 Hz. Transform this filter into a digital filter using the matched-z transformation technique in which $F_s = 1000$ Hz. Plot the magnitude and phase response of the resulting digital filter and determine the exact band-edge frequencies for the given dB specifications. Comment on the results.

P8.28 Consider an analog Chebyshev-I lowpass filter that has a 0.5 dB or better ripple at 500 Hz and at least 40 dB of attenuation at 700 Hz. Transform this filter into a digital filter using the matched-z transformation technique in which $F_s = 2000$ Hz. Plot the magnitude and phase response of the resulting digital filter and determine the exact band-edge frequencies for the given dB specifications. Comment on the results.

P8.29 Consider an analog Chebyshev-II lowpass filter that has a 0.25 dB or better ripple at 1500 Hz and at least 80 dB of attenuation at 2000 Hz. Transform this filter into a digital filter using the matched-z transformation technique in which $F_s = 8000$ Hz. Plot the magnitude and phase response of the resulting digital filter, and determine the exact band-edge frequencies for the given dB specifications. Comment on the results. Is this a satisfactory design?

P8.30 Consider the design of the lowpass Butterworth filter of Problem P8.22.

1. Use the bilinear transformation technique outlined in this chapter and the `bilinear` function. Plot the log-magnitude response in dB. Compare the impulse responses of the analog prototype and the digital filter.
2. Use the `butter` function and compare this design with the one in part 1.

P8.31 Consider the design of the digital Chebyshev-1 filter of Problem P8.21.

1. Use the bilinear transformation technique outlined in this chapter and the `bilinear` function. Plot the log-magnitude response in dB. Compare the impulse responses of the analog prototype and the digital filter.
2. Use the `cheby1` function and compare this design with the one above.

P8.32 Design a digital lowpass filter using elliptic prototype to satisfy the requirements

$$\text{passband edge: } 0.3\pi, \ R_p = 0.25 \text{ dB}$$

$$\text{stopband edge: } 0.4\pi, \ A_s = 50 \text{ dB}$$

Use the `bilinear` as well as the `ellip` function and compare your designs.

P8.33 Design a digital lowpass filter to satisfy the specifications

$$\text{passband edge: } 0.45\pi, \ R_p = 0.5 \text{ dB}$$

$$\text{stopband edge: } 0.5\pi, \ A_s = 60 \text{ dB}$$

1. Use the `butter` function and determine the order N and the actual minimum stopband attenuation in dB.
2. Use the `cheby1` function and determine the order N and the actual minimum stopband attenuation in dB.
3. Use the `cheby2` function and determine the order N and the actual minimum stopband attenuation in dB.
4. Use the `ellip` function and determine the order N and the actual minimum stopband attenuation in dB.
5. Compare the orders, the actual minimum stopband attenuations, and the group delays in each of the above designs.

P8.34 Write a MATLAB function to determine the lowpass prototype digital filter frequencies from an highpass digital filter specifications using the procedure outlined in this chapter. The format of this function should be

```
function [wpLP,wsLP,alpha] = hp2lpfre(wphp,wshp)
% Band-edge frequency conversion from highpass to lowpass digital filter
% [wpLP,wsLP,a] = hp2lpfre(wphp,wshp)
%  wpLP = passband edge for the lowpass prototype
%  wsLP = stopband edge for the lowpass prototype
% alpha = lowpass-to-highpass transformation parameter
%  wphp = passband edge for the highpass
%  wshp = stopband edge for the highpass
```

Using this function, develop a MATLAB function to design a highpass digital filter using the bilinear transformation. The format of this function should be

```
function [b,a] = dhpfd_bl(type,wp,ws,Rp,As)
% IIR highpass filter design using bilinear transformation
% [b,a] = dhpfd_bl(type,wp,ws,Rp,As)
% type = 'butter' or 'cheby1' or 'chevy2' or 'ellip'
%    b = numerator polynomial of the highpass filter
%    a = denominator polynomial of the highpass filter
%   wp = passband frequency in radians
%   ws = stopband frequency in radians (wp < ws)
%   Rp = passband ripple in dB
%   As = stopband attenuation in dB
```

Verify your function using the specifications in Example 8.27.

P8.35 Design a highpass filter to satisfy the specifications

$$\text{stopband edge: } 0.4\pi, \ A_s = 60 \text{ dB}$$
$$\text{passband edge: } 0.6\pi, \ R_p = 0.5 \text{ dB}$$

1. Use the `dhpfd_bl` function of Problem P8.34 and the Chebyshev-I prototype to design this filter. Plot the log-magnitude response in dB of the designed filter.
2. Use the `cheby1` function for design and plot the log-magnitude response in dB. Compare these two designs.

P8.36 Write a MATLAB function to determine the lowpass prototype digital filter frequencies from an arbitrary lowpass digital filter specifications using the functions given in Table 8.2 and the procedure outlined for highpass filters. The format of this function should be

```
function [wpLP,wsLP,alpha] = lp2lpfre(wplp,wslp)
% Band-edge frequency conversion from lowpass to lowpass digital filter
% [wpLP,wsLP,a] = lp2lpfre(wplp,wslp)
%  wpLP = passband edge for the lowpass prototype
%  wsLP = stopband edge for the lowpass prototype
% alpha = lowpass-to-highpass transformation parameter
%  wplp = passband edge for the given lowpass
%  wslp = passband edge for the given lowpass
```

Using this function, develop a MATLAB function to design a lowpass filter from a prototype lowpass digital filter using the bilinear transformation. The format of this function should be

```
function [b,a] = dlpfd_bl(type,wp,ws,Rp,As)
% IIR lowpass filter design using bilinear transformation
% [b,a] = dlpfd_bl(type,wp,ws,Rp,As)
% type = 'butter' or 'cheby1' or 'chevy2' or 'ellip'
%    b = numerator polynomial of the bandpass filter
%    a = denominator polynomial of the bandpass filter
%   wp = passband frequency in radians
%   ws = stopband frequency in radians
%   Rp = passband ripple in dB
%   As = stopband attenuation in dB
```

Verify your function using the designs in Problem P8.33.

P8.37 Design a bandpass digital filter using the `Cheby2` function. The specifications are

$$\begin{aligned}
\text{lower stopband edge: } & 0.3\pi \\
\text{upper stopband edge: } & 0.6\pi
\end{aligned} \quad A_s = 50 \text{ dB}$$
$$\begin{aligned}
\text{lower passband edge: } & 0.4\pi \\
\text{upper passband edge: } & 0.5\pi
\end{aligned} \quad R_p = 0.5 \text{ dB}$$

Plot the impulse response and the log-magnitude response in dB of the designed filter.

P8.38 Write a MATLAB function to determine the lowpass prototype digital filter frequencies from a bandpass digital filter specifications using the functions given in Table 8.2 and the procedure outlined for highpass filters. The format of this function should be

```
function [wpLP,wsLP,alpha] = bp2lpfre(wpbp,wsblp)
% Band-edge frequency conversion from bandpass to lowpass digital filter
% [wpLP,wsLP,a] = bp2lpfre(wpbp,wsbp)
%  wpLP = passband edge for the lowpass prototype
%  wsLP = stopband edge for the lowpass prototype
% alpha = lowpass-to-highpass transformation parameter
%  wpbp = passband-edge frequency array [wp_lower, wp_upper] for the bandpass
%  wsbp = passband-edge frequency array [ws_lower, ws_upper] for the bandpass
```

Using this function, develop a MATLAB function to design a bandpass filter from a
prototype lowpass digital filter using the bilinear transformation. The format of this
function should be

```
function [b,a] = dbpfd_bl(type,wp,ws,Rp,As)
% IIR bandpass filter design using bilinear transformation
% [b,a] = dbpfd_bl(type,wp,ws,Rp,As)
% type = 'butter' or 'cheby1' or 'chevy2' or 'ellip'
%    b = numerator polynomial of the bandpass filter
%    a = denominator polynomial of the bandpass filter
%   wp = passband frequency array [wp_lower, wp_upper] in radians
%   ws = stopband frequency array [wp_lower, wp_upper] in radians
%   Rp = passband ripple in dB
%   As = stopband attenuation in dB
```

Verify your function using the design in Problem P8.37.

P8.39 We wish to use the Chebyshev-I prototype to design a bandstop digital IIR filter that meets
the following specifications:

$$0.95 \leq |H(e^{j\omega})| \leq 1.05, \qquad 0 \leq |\omega| \leq 0.25\pi$$
$$0 \leq |H(e^{j\omega})| \leq 0.01, \; 0.35\pi \leq |\omega| \leq 0.65\pi$$
$$0.95 \leq |H(e^{j\omega})| \leq 1.05, \; 0.75\pi \leq |\omega| \leq \pi$$

Use the `cheby1` function and determine the system function $H(z)$ of such a filter. Provide a
plot containing subplots of the log-magnitude response in dB and the impulse response.

P8.40 Write a MATLAB function to determine the lowpass prototype digital filter frequencies
from a bandstop digital filter specifications using the functions given in Table 8.2 and the
procedure outlined for highpass filters. The format of this function should be

```
function [wpLP,wsLP,alpha] = bs2lpfre(wpbp,wsblp)
% Band-edge frequency conversion from bandstop to lowpass digital filter
% [wpLP,wsLP,a] = bs2lpfre(wpbp,wsbp)
%  wpLP = passband edge for the lowpass prototype
%  wsLP = stopband edge for the lowpass prototype
% alpha = lowpass-to-highpass transformation parameter
%  wpbp = passband-edge frequency array [wp_lower, wp_upper] for the bandstop
%  wsbp = passband-edge frequency array [ws_lower, ws_upper] for the bandstop
```

Using this function, develop a MATLAB function to design a bandstop filter from a prototype lowpass digital filter using the bilinear transformation. The format of this function should be

```
function [b,a] = dbsfd_bl(type,wp,ws,Rp,As)
% IIR bandstop filter design using bilinear transformation
% [b,a] = dbsfd_bl(type,wp,ws,Rp,As)
% type = 'butter' or 'cheby1' or 'chevy2' or 'ellip'
%    b = numerator polynomial of the bandstop filter
%    a = denominator polynomial of the bandstop filter
%   wp = passband frequency array [wp_lower, wp_upper] in radians
%   ws = stopband frequency array [wp_lower, wp_upper] in radians
%   Rp = passband ripple in dB
%   As = stopband attenuation in dB
```

Verify your function using the design in Problem P8.39.

P8.41 An analog signal

$$x_a(t) = 3\sin(40\pi t) + 3\cos(50\pi t)$$

is to be processed by a

$$x_a(t) \longrightarrow \boxed{\text{A/D}} \longrightarrow \boxed{H(z)} \longrightarrow \boxed{\text{D/A}} \longrightarrow y_a(t)$$

system in which the sampling frequency is 100 sam/sec.

1. Design a minimum-order IIR digital filter that will pass the first component of $x_a(t)$ with attenuation of less than 1 dB and suppress the second component to at least 50 dB. The filter should have a monotone passband and an equiripple stopband. Determine the system function in rational function form and plot the log-magnitude response.
2. Generate 500 samples (sampled at 100 sam/sec) of the signal $x_a(t)$ and process through the designed filter to obtain the output sequence. Interpolate this sequence (using any one of the interpolating techniques discussed in Chapter 3) to obtain $y_a(t)$. Plot the input and the output signals and comment on your results.

P8.42 Using the bilinear transformation method, design a tenth-order elliptic bandstop filter to remove the digital frequency $\omega = 0.44\pi$ with bandwidth of 0.08π. Choose a reasonable value for the stopband attenuation. Plot the magnitude response. Generate 201 samples of the sequence

$$x(n) = \sin\left[0.44\pi n\right], \quad n = 0, \ldots, 200$$

and process thorough the bandstop filter. Comment on your results.

P8.43 Design a digital highpass filter $H(z)$ to be used in a

$$x_a(t) \longrightarrow \boxed{\text{A/D}} \longrightarrow \boxed{H(z)} \longrightarrow \boxed{\text{D/A}} \longrightarrow y_a(t)$$

structure to satisfy the following requirements:

- sampling rate of 10 Khz,
- stopband edge of 1.5 Khz with attenuation of 40 dB,
- passband edge of 2 Khz with ripple of 1 dB,
- equiripple passband and stopband, and
- bilinear transformation method.

1. Plot the magnitude response of the overall analog filter over the [0, 5 Khz] interval.
2. Plot the magnitude response of the digital lowpass prototype.
3. What limitations must be placed on the input signals so that the preceding structure truly acts as a highpass filter to them?

P8.44 The filter specifications shown in Figure P8.1 can be considered a combination of a bandpass and a highpass specifications. Design a minimum-order IIR digital filter to satisfy these specifications. Provide a plot of the magnitude response with grid lines as shown in Figure P8.1. From your design and plot determine the order of the filter and the exact band-edge frequencies.

P8.45 The filter specifications shown in Figure P8.2 can be considered as a combination of a lowpass and a bandpass specifications. Design a minimum-order IIR digital filter to satisfy these specifications. Provide a plot of the magnitude response with grid lines as shown in Figure P8.2. From your design and plot determine the order of the filter and the exact band-edge frequencies.

P8.46 Design a minimum-order IIR digital filter to satisfy the following specifications:

- a passband over the $[0.35\pi, 0.5\pi]$ interval,
- stopbands over the $[0, 0.3\pi]$ and $[0.6\pi, \pi]$ intervals,
- passband ripple of 1 dB,

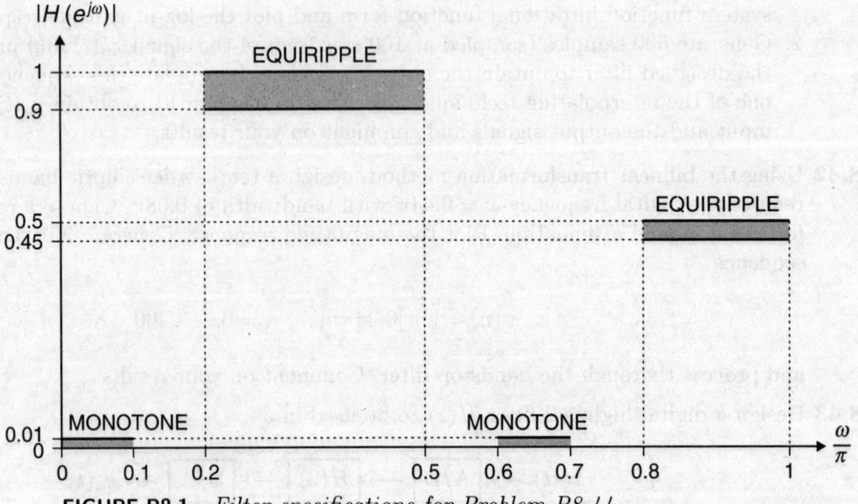

FIGURE P8.1 *Filter specifications for Problem P8.44*

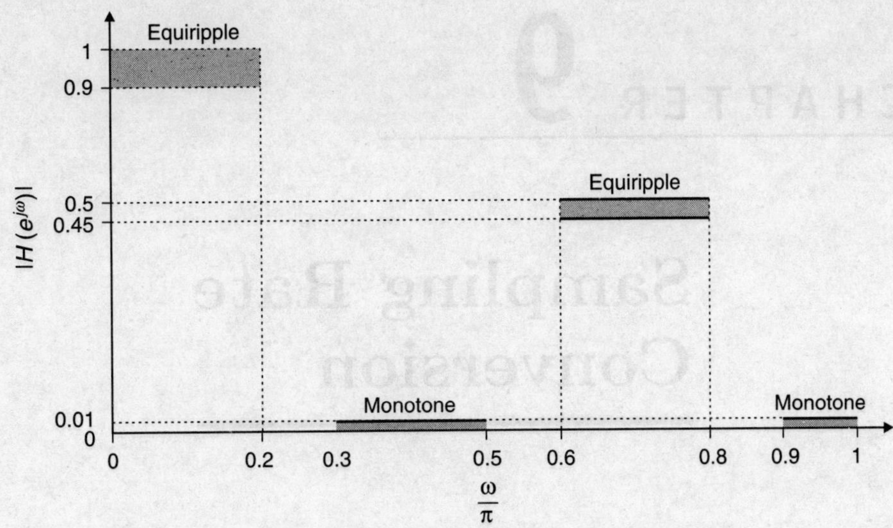

FIGURE P8.2 *Filter specifications for Problem P8.45*

- stopband attenuation of 40 dB, and
- equiripple passbands and stopband.

Determine the system function $H(z)$ of the designed filter in the rational function form. Provide a plot of the log-magnitude response in dB. From your design and plot, answer the following questions.

1. What is the order of the filter?
2. From your plot what are the exact band-edge frequencies for the given passband and stopband attenuations?
3. Why is there a discrepancy between the specification frequencies and the exact frequencies?

CHAPTER 9

Sampling Rate Conversion

In many practical applications of digital signal processing, one is faced with the problem of changing the sampling rate of a signal, either increasing it or decreasing it by some amount. The process of converting a signal from a given rate to a different rate is called *sampling rate conversion*. In turn, systems that employ multiple sampling rates in the processing of digital signals are called *multirate digital signal processing systems*. In this chapter, we describe sampling rate conversion and multirate signal processing in the digital domain.

As an example, consider the system shown in Figure 9.1, in which an analog signal $x_a(t)$ is sampled using the sampling rate of $F_s = \frac{1}{T}$ samples/second. The resulting digital signal $x(n)$ is subsequently filtered using a lowpass filter (LPF) with a cutoff frequency of ω_c.

Thus the output signal $y(n)$ has all its energy in the band $0 \leq \omega \leq \omega_c = 2\pi f_c$. According to the sampling theorem, such a signal may be represented by the rate of $2f_c/T$ samples/second instead of its existing rate of $F_s = 1/T$. Note that $|f_c| \leq 0.5$. However, if $f_c \ll 0.5$, then $2f_c/T \ll F_s$. Hence it would seem more advantageous to lower the sampling frequency to a value closer to $2f_c/T$ and perform signal processing operations at this lower rate.

Other applications include the need for an optimal interpolation in computer tomography and efficient multistage designs of narrowband lowpass filters.

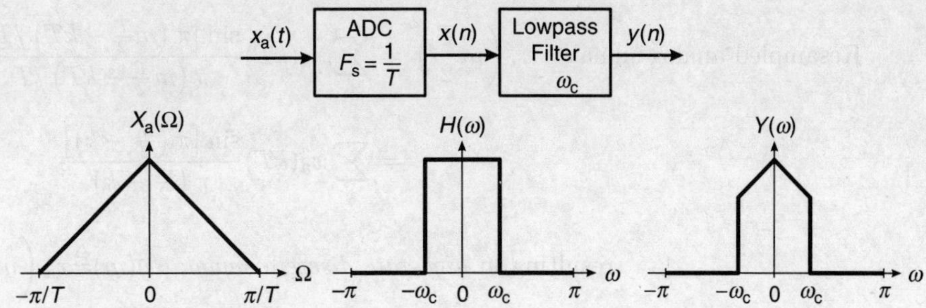

FIGURE 9.1 *A typical signal processing system*

9.1 INTRODUCTION

The idea of interpolation is a very familiar concept to most of us and has its origin in numerical analysis. Typically, interpolation is performed on a table of numbers representing a mathematical function. Such a table may be printed in a handbook or stored in a computer memory device. The interpolation, often simply a linear (or straight line) approximation, creates an error called the *interpolation error*. The main difference between interpolation in digital signal processing and interpolation in numerical analysis is that we will assume that the given data is bandlimited to some band of frequencies and develop schemes that are optimal on this basis, whereas a numerical analyst typically assumes that the data consists of samples of polynomials (or very nearly so) and develops schemes to minimize the resulting error.

To motivate this concept of interpolation in signal processing, it is helpful to think of an underlying (or original) analog signal $x_a(t)$ that was sampled to produce the given discrete signal $x(n)$. If the $x_a(t)$ was sampled at the minimum required rate, then, according to the sampling theorem, it can be recovered completely from the samples $x(n)$. If we now sample this recovered analog signal, at, say, twice the old rate, we have succeeded in doubling the sampling rate or interpolating by a factor of 2 with zero interpolation error. Specifically, we have the following.

$$\text{Original discrete signal:} \quad x(n) = x_a(nT) \tag{9.1}$$

$$\text{Reconstructed analog signal:} \quad x_a(t) = \sum_k x_a(kT)\frac{\sin[\pi(t - kT)/T]}{\pi(t - kT)/T} \tag{9.2}$$

$$\text{Resampled analog signal:} \quad x_\mathrm{a}\left(m\frac{T}{2}\right) = \sum_k x_\mathrm{a}(kT)\frac{\sin\left[\pi\left(m\frac{T}{2} - kT\right)/T\right]}{\pi\left(m\frac{T}{2} - kT\right)/T}$$

$$= \sum_k x_\mathrm{a}(kT)\frac{\sin\left[\pi\left(\frac{m}{2} - k\right)\right]}{\pi\left(\frac{m}{2} - k\right)} \tag{9.3}$$

$$\text{resulting in } \textit{high-rate discrete signal:} \quad y(m) \overset{\triangle}{=} x_\mathrm{a}\left(m\frac{T}{2}\right) \tag{9.4}$$

In this formulation of ideal interpolation, the discrete signal was converted to the analog signal and then back to the discrete signal at twice the rate. In the subsequent sections, we will study how to avoid this roundabout approach and perform sampling rate conversion completely in the digital domain.

The process of sampling rate conversion in the digital domain can be viewed as a linear filtering operation, as illustrated in Figure 9.2a. The input signal $x(n)$ is characterized by the sampling rate $F_x = 1/T_x$, and the output signal $y(m)$ is characterized by the sampling rate $F_y = 1/T_y$, where T_x and T_y are the corresponding sampling intervals. In our treatment, the ratio F_y/F_x is constrained to be rational

$$\frac{F_y}{F_x} = \frac{I}{D} \tag{9.5}$$

where D and I are relatively prime integers. We shall show that the linear filter is characterized by a time-variant impulse response, denoted

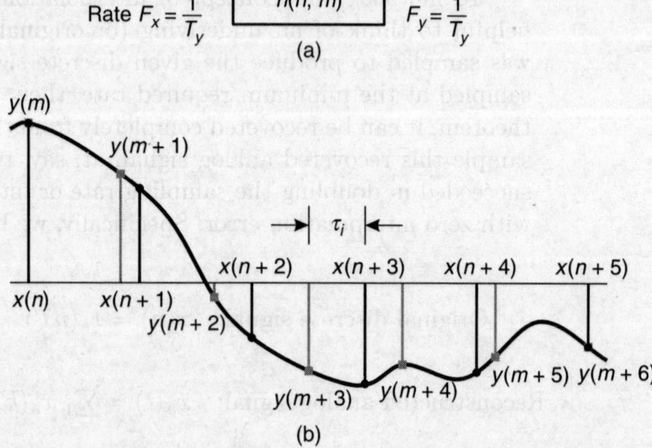

FIGURE 9.2   *Sampling rate conversion viewed as a linear filtering process*

as $h(n, m)$. Hence the input $x(n)$ and the output $y(m)$ are related by the superposition summation for time-variant systems.

The sampling rate conversion process can also be understood from the point of view of digital resampling of the same analog signal. Let $x_a(t)$ be the analog signal that is sampled at the first rate F_x to generate $x(n)$. The goal of rate conversion is to obtain another sequence $y(m)$ directly from $x(n)$, which is equal to the sampled values of $x_a(t)$ at a second rate F_y. As is depicted in Figure 9.2b, $y(m)$ is a time-shifted version of $x(n)$. Such a time shift can be realized by using a linear filter that has a flat magnitude response and a linear phase response (i.e., it has a frequency response of $e^{-j\omega \tau_i}$, where τ_i is the time delay generated by the filter). If the two sampling rates are not equal, the required amount of time shifting will vary from sample to sample, as shown in Figure 9.2b. Thus the rate converter can be implemented using a set of linear filters that have the same flat magnitude response but generate different time delays.

Before considering the general case of sampling rate conversion, we shall consider two special cases. One is the case of sampling rate reduction by an integer factor D, and the second is the case of a sampling rate increase by an integer factor I. The process of reducing the sampling rate by a factor D (downsampling by D) is called *decimation*. The process of increasing the sampling rate by an integer factor I (upsampling by I) is called *interpolation*.

9.2 DECIMATION BY A FACTOR D

The basic operation required in decimation is the downsampling of the *high-rate* signal $x(n)$ into a *low-rate* signal $y(m)$. We will develop the time- and frequency-domain relationships between these two signals to understand the frequency-domain aliasing in $y(m)$. We will then study the condition needed for error-free decimation and the system structure required for its implementation.

9.2.1 THE DOWNSAMPLER

Note that the downsampled signal $y(m)$ is obtained by selecting one out of D samples of $x(n)$ and throwing away the other $(D-1)$ samples out of every D samples—that is,

$$y(m) = x(n)|_{n=mD} = x(mD); \quad n, m, D \in \{\text{integers}\} \qquad (9.6)$$

The block diagram representation of (9.6) is shown in Figure 9.3. This downsampling element changes the rate of processing and thus is fundamentally different from other block diagram elements that we have used

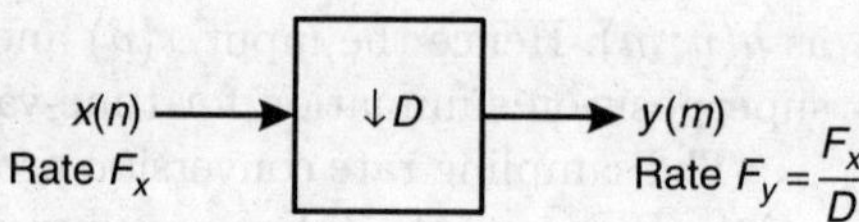

FIGURE 9.3 *A downsampling element*

previously. In fact, we can show that a system containing a downsampling element is shift varying. However, this fact does not prohibit the frequency-domain analysis of $y(m)$ in terms of $x(n)$, as we shall see later.

□ **EXAMPLE 9.1** Using $D = 2$ and $x(n) = \{1, 2, 3, 4, 3, 2, 1\}$, verify that the downsampler is time varying.

Solution The downsampled signal is $y(m) = \{1, 3, 3, 1\}$. If we now delay $x(n)$ by one sample, we get $x(n-1) = \{0, 1, 2, 3, 4, 3, 2, 1\}$. The corresponding downsampled signal is $y_1(m) = \{0, 2, 4, 2\}$, which is different from $y(m-1)$. □

MATLAB Implementation MATLAB provides the function `[y] = downsample(x,D)` that downsamples input array `x` into output array `y` by keeping every Dth sample starting with the first sample. An optional third parameter `"phase"` specifies the sample offset which must be an integer between 0 and (D-1). For example,

```
>> x = [1,2,3,4,3,2,1]; y = downsample(x,2)
y =
     1     3     3     1
```

downsamples by a factor of 2 starting with the first sample. However,

```
>> x = [1,2,3,4,3,2,1]; y = downsample(x,2,1)
y =
     2     4     2
```

produces an entirely different sequence by downsampling, starting with the second sample (i.e., offset by 1).

The frequency-domain representation of the downsampled signal $y(m)$ We now express $Y(\omega)$ in terms of $X(\omega)$ using z-transform relations. Toward this, we introduce a high-rate sequence $\bar{x}(n)$, which is given by

$$\bar{x}(n) \stackrel{\triangle}{=} \begin{cases} x(n), & n = 0, \pm D, \pm 2D, \ldots \\ 0, & \text{elsewhere} \end{cases} \tag{9.7}$$

Clearly, $\bar{x}(n)$ can be viewed as a sequence obtained by multiplying $x(n)$ with a periodic train of impulses $p(n)$, with period D, as illustrated in Figure 9.4. The discrete Fourier series representation of $p(n)$ is

$$p(n) \triangleq \begin{cases} 1, & n = 0, \pm D, \pm 2D, \ldots \\ 0, & \text{elsewhere} \end{cases} = \frac{1}{D} \sum_{\ell=0}^{D-1} e^{j\frac{2\pi}{D}\ell n} \qquad (9.8)$$

Hence we can write

$$\bar{x}(n) = x(n)p(n) \qquad (9.9)$$

and

$$y(m) = \bar{x}(mD) = x(mD)p(mD) = x(mD) \qquad (9.10)$$

as shown in (9.6). Figure 9.4 shows an example of sequences $x(n)$, $\bar{x}(n)$, and $y(m)$ defined in (9.7)–(9.10).

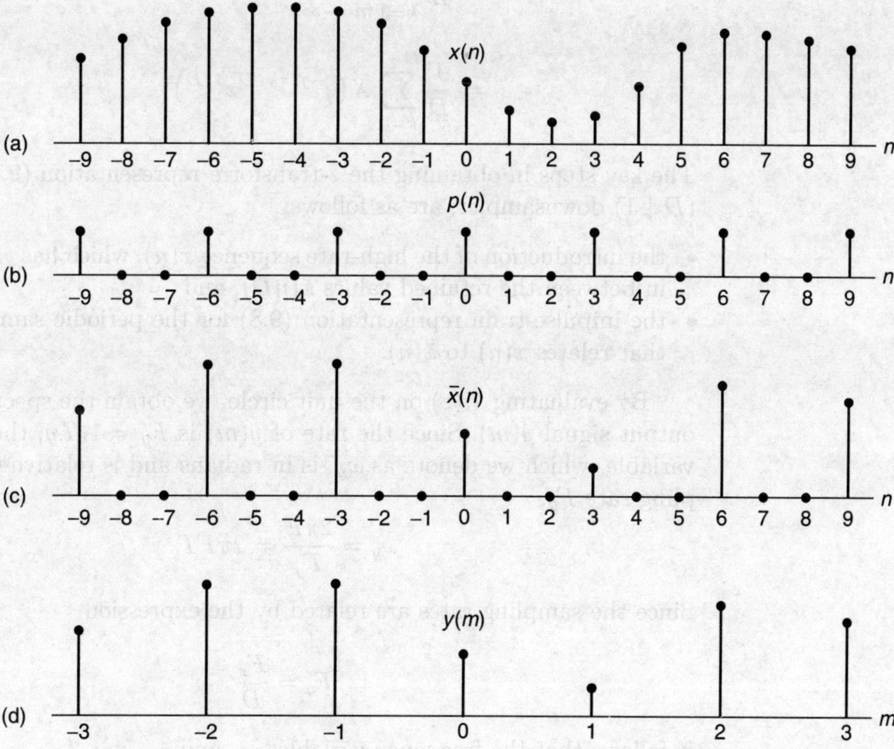

FIGURE 9.4 *Operation of downsampling: (a) original signal $x(n)$, (b) periodic impulse train $p(n)$ with period $D = 3$, (c) multiplication of $x(n)$ with $p(n)$, and (d) downsampled signal $y(m)$*

Now the z-transform of the output sequence $y(m)$ is

$$Y(z) = \sum_{m=-\infty}^{\infty} y(m)z^{-m} = \sum_{m=-\infty}^{\infty} \bar{x}(mD)z^{-m}$$

$$Y(z) = \sum_{m=-\infty}^{\infty} \bar{x}(m)z^{-m/D} \tag{9.11}$$

where the last step follows from the fact that $\bar{x}(m) = 0$, except at multiples of D. By making use of the relations in (9.7) and (9.8) in (9.11), we obtain

$$Y(z) = \sum_{m=-\infty}^{\infty} x(m)\left[\frac{1}{D}\sum_{k=0}^{D-1} e^{j2\pi mk/D}\right]z^{-m/D}$$

$$= \frac{1}{D}\sum_{k=0}^{D-1}\sum_{m=-\infty}^{\infty} x(m)\left(e^{-j2\pi k/D}z^{1/D}\right)^{-m}$$

$$= \frac{1}{D}\sum_{k=0}^{D-1} X\left(e^{-j2\pi k/D}z^{1/D}\right) \tag{9.12}$$

The key steps in obtaining the z-transform representation (9.12), for the $(D \downarrow 1)$ downsampler, are as follows:

- the introduction of the high-rate sequence $\bar{x}(n)$, which has $(D-1)$ zeros in between the retained values $x(nD)$, and
- the impulse-train representation (9.8) for the periodic sampling series that relates $x(n)$ to $\bar{x}(n)$.

By evaluating $Y(z)$ on the unit circle, we obtain the spectrum of the output signal $y(m)$. Since the rate of $y(m)$ is $F_y = 1/Ty$, the frequency variable, which we denote as ω_y, is in radians and is relative to the sampling rate F_y,

$$\omega_y = \frac{2\pi F}{F_y} = 2\pi F T_y \tag{9.13}$$

Since the sampling rates are related by the expression

$$F_y = \frac{F_x}{D} \tag{9.14}$$

it follows that the frequency variables ω_y and

$$\omega_x = \frac{2\pi F}{F_x}2\pi F T_x \tag{9.15}$$

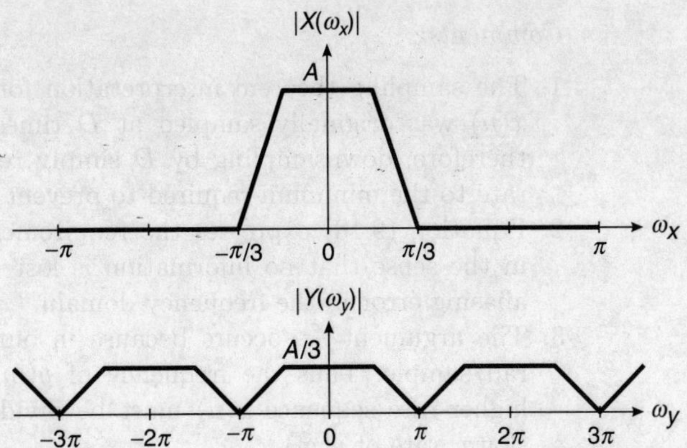

FIGURE 9.5 *Spectra of $x(n)$ and $y(m)$ in no-aliasing case*

are related by

$$\omega_y = D\omega_x \tag{9.16}$$

Thus, as expected, the frequency range $0 \leq |\omega_x| \leq \pi/D$ is stretched into the corresponding frequency range $0 \leq |\omega_y| \leq \pi$ by the downsampling process.

We conclude that the spectrum $Y(\omega_y)$, which is obtained by evaluating (9.12) on the unit circle, can be expressed as[1]

$$Y(\omega_y) = \frac{1}{D} \sum_{k=0}^{D-1} X\left(\frac{\omega_y - 2\pi k}{D}\right) \tag{9.17}$$

which is an aliased version of the spectrum $X(\omega_x)$ of $x(n)$. To avoid aliasing error, one needs the spectrum $X(\omega_x)$ to be less than full band or bandlimited (note that this bandlimitedness is in the digital frequency domain). In fact, we must have

$$X(\omega_x) = 0 \quad \text{for} \quad \frac{\pi}{D} \leq |\omega_x| \leq \pi \tag{9.18}$$

Then

$$Y(\omega_y) = \frac{1}{D} X\left(\frac{\omega_y}{D}\right), |\omega_y| \leq \pi \tag{9.19}$$

and no aliasing error is present. An example of this for $D = 3$ is shown in Figure 9.5.

---

[1] In this chapter, we will make a slight change in our notation for the DTFT. We will use $X(\omega)$ to denote the spectrum of $x(n)$ instead of the previously used notation $X(e^{j\omega})$. Although this change does conflict with the z-transform notation, the meaning should be clear from the context. This change is made for the sake of clarity and visibility of variables.

Comments:

1. The sampling theorem interpretation for (9.19) is that the sequence $x(n)$ was originally sampled at D times higher rate than required; therefore, downsampling by D simply reduces the effective sampling rate to the minimum required to prevent aliasing.

2. Equation (9.18) expresses the requirement for *zero decimation error* in the sense that no information is lost—i.e., there is no irreversible aliasing error in the frequency domain.

3. The argument $\frac{\omega_y}{D}$ occurs because in our notation ω is expressed in rad/sample. Thus the frequency of $y(m)$ expressed in terms of the higher-rate sequence $x(n)$ must be divided by D to account for the slower rate of $y(m)$.

4. Note that there is a factor $\frac{1}{D}$ in (9.19). This factor is required to make the inverse Fourier transform work out properly and is entirely consistent with the spectra of the sampled analog signals.

9.2.2 THE IDEAL DECIMATOR

In general, (9.18) will not be exactly true, and the $(D \downarrow 1)$ downsampler would cause irreversible aliasing error. To avoid aliasing, we must first reduce the bandwidth of $x(n)$ to $F_{x,\max} = F_x/2D$, or equivalently, to $\omega_{x,\max} = \pi/D$. Then we may downsample by D and thus avoid aliasing.

The decimation process is illustrated in Figure 9.6. The input sequence $x(n)$ is passed through a lowpass filter, characterized by the impulse response $h(n)$ and a frequency response $H_D(\omega_x)$, which ideally satisfies the condition

$$H_D(\omega_x) = \begin{cases} 1, & |\omega_x| \leq \pi/D \\ 0, & \text{otherwise} \end{cases} \qquad (9.20)$$

Thus the filter eliminates the spectrum of $X(\omega_x)$ in the range $\pi/D < \omega_x < \pi$. Of course, the implication is that only the frequency components of $x(n)$ in the range $|\omega_x| \leq \pi/D$ are of interest in further processing of the signal.

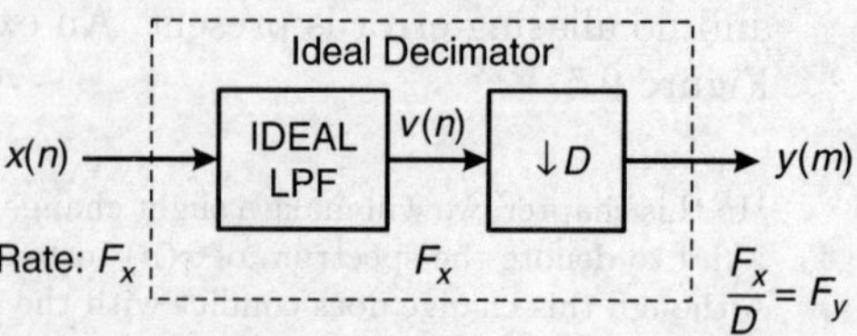

FIGURE 9.6   *Ideal decimation by a factor D*

The output of the filter is a sequence $v(n)$ given as

$$v(n) \triangleq \sum_{k=0}^{\infty} h(k)x(n-k) \qquad (9.21)$$

which is then downsampled by the factor D to produce $y(m)$. Thus

$$y(m) = v(mD) = \sum_{k=0}^{\infty} h(k)x(mD-k) \qquad (9.22)$$

Although the filtering operation on $x(n)$ is linear and time invariant, the downsampling operation in combination with the filtering results also in a time-variant system.

The frequency-domain characteristics of the output sequence $y(m)$ obtained through the filtered signal $v(n)$ can be determined by following the analysis steps given before—that is, by relating the spectrum of $y(m)$ to the spectrum of the input sequence $x(n)$. Using these steps, we can show that

$$Y(z) = \frac{1}{D} \sum_{k=0}^{D-1} H\left(e^{-j2\pi k/D} z^{1/D}\right) X\left(e^{-j2\pi k/D} z^{1/D}\right) \qquad (9.23)$$

or that

$$Y(\omega_y) = \frac{1}{D} \sum_{k=0}^{D-1} H\left(\frac{\omega_y - 2\pi k}{D}\right) X\left(\frac{\omega_y - 2\pi k}{D}\right) \qquad (9.24)$$

With a properly designed filter $H_D(\omega)$, the aliasing is eliminated and, consequently, all but the first term in (9.24) vanish. Hence

$$Y(\omega_y) = \frac{1}{D} H_D\left(\frac{\omega_y}{D}\right) X\left(\frac{\omega_y}{D}\right) = \frac{1}{D} X\left(\frac{\omega_y}{D}\right) \qquad (9.25)$$

for $0 \le |\omega_y| \le \pi$. The spectra for the sequences $x(n)$, $h(n)$, $v(n)$, and $y(m)$ are illustrated in Figure 9.7.

MATLAB Implementation MATLAB provides the function `y = decimate(x,D)` that resamples the sequence in array `x` at $1/D$ times the original sampling rate. The resulting resampled array `y` is D times shorter—that is, `length(y) = length(x)/D`. The ideal lowpass filter given in (9.20) is not possible in the MATLAB implementation; however, fairly accurate approximations are used. The default lowpass filter used in the function is an eighth-order Chebyshev type-I lowpass filter with the cutoff frequency of $0.8\pi/D$. Using additional optional arguments, the filter order can be changed or an FIR filter of specified order and cutoff frequency can be used.

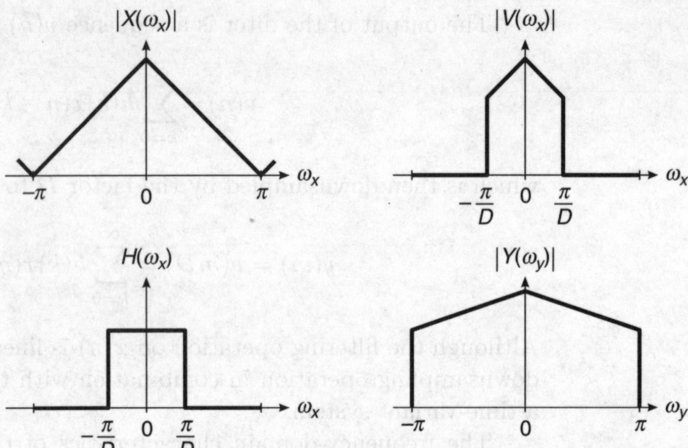

FIGURE 9.7 *Spectra of signals in the decimation of $x(n)$ by a factor D*

☐ **EXAMPLE 9.2**   Let $x(n) = \cos(0.125\pi n)$. Generate a large number of samples of $x(n)$ and decimate them using $D = 2$, 4, and 8 to show the results of decimation.

Solution   We will plot the middle segments of the signals to avoid end-effects due to the default lowpass filter in the `decimate` function. The following MATLAB script shows details of these operations, and Figure 9.7 shows the plots of the sequences.

```
n = 0:2048; k1 = 256; k2 = k1+32; m = 0:(k2-k1);
Hf1 = figure('units','inches','position',[1,1,6,4],...
    'paperunits','inches','paperposition',[0,0,6,4]);

% (a) Original signal
x = cos(0.125*pi*n); subplot(2,2,1);
Ha = stem(m,x(m+k1+1),'g','filled'); axis([-1,33,-1.1,1.1]);
set(Ha,'markersize',2); ylabel('Amplitude');
title('Original Sequence x(n)','fontsize',TF);
set(gca,'xtick',[0,16,32]); set(gca,'ytick',[-1,0,1]);

% (b) Decimation by D = 2
D = 2; y = decimate(x,D); subplot(2,2,2);
Hb = stem(m,y(m+k1/D+1),'c','filled');  axis([-1,33,-1.1,1.1]);
set(Hb,'markersize',2); ylabel('Amplitude');
title('Decimated by D = 2','fontsize',TF);
set(gca,'xtick',[0,16,32]); set(gca,'ytick',[-1,0,1]);
```

```
% (c) Decimation by D = 4
D = 4; y = decimate(x,D); subplot(2,2,3);
Hc = stem(m,y(m+k1/D+1),'r','filled');  axis([-1,33,-1.1,1.1]);
set(Hc,'markersize',2); ylabel('Amplitude');
title('Decimated by D = 4','fontsize',TF);
set(gca,'xtick',[0,16,32]); set(gca,'ytick',[-1,0,1]);
xlabel('n');

% (d) Decimation by D = 8
D = 8; y = decimate(x,D); subplot(2,2,4);
Hd = stem(m,y(m+k1/D+1),'m','filled');  axis([-1,33,-1.1,1.1]);
set(Hd,'markersize',2); ylabel('Amplitude');
title('Decimated by D = 8','fontsize',TF);
set(gca,'xtick',[0,16,32]); set(gca,'ytick',[-1,0,1]);
xlabel('n');
```

From Figure 9.8, we observe that the decimated sequences for $D = 2$ and $D = 4$ are correct and represent the original sinusoidal sequence $x(n)$ at lower sampling rates. However, the sequence for $D = 8$ is almost zero because the

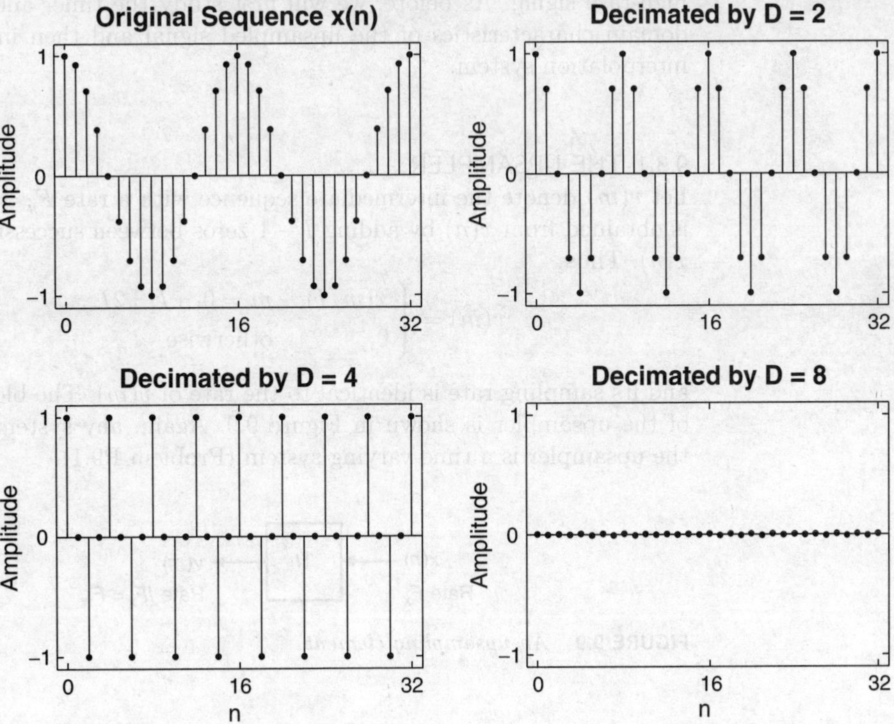

FIGURE 9.8 *Original and decimated signals in Example 9.2*

lowpass filter has attenuated $x(n)$ prior to downsampling. Recall that the cutoff frequency of the lowpass filter is set to $0.8\pi/D = 0.1\pi$, which eliminates $x(n)$. If we had used the downsampling operation on $x(n)$ instead of decimation, the resulting sequence would be $y(m) = 1$, which is an aliased signal. Thus the lowpass filtering is necessary. $\qquad\qquad\square$

9.3 INTERPOLATION BY A FACTOR I

An increase in the sampling rate by an integer factor of I—that is, $F_y = IF_x$—can be accomplished by interpolating $I - 1$ new samples between successive values of the signal. The interpolation process can be accomplished in a variety of ways. We shall describe a process that preserves the spectral shape of the signal sequence $x(n)$. This process can be accomplished in two steps. The first step creates an intermediate signal at the high rate F_y by interlacing zeros in between nonzero samples in an operation called *upsampling*. In the second step, the intermediate signal is filtered to "fill in" zero-interlaced samples to create the interpolated high-rate signal. As before, we will first study the time- and frequency-domain characteristics of the upsampled signal and then introduce the interpolation system.

9.3.1 THE UPSAMPLER

Let $v(m)$ denote the intermediate sequence with a rate $F_y = IF_x$, which is obtained from $x(n)$ by adding $I - 1$ zeros between successive values of $x(n)$. Thus

$$v(m) = \begin{cases} x(m/I), & m = 0, \pm I, \pm 2I, \ldots \\ 0, & \text{otherwise} \end{cases} \qquad (9.26)$$

and its sampling rate is identical to the rate of $v(m)$. The block diagram of the upsampler is shown in Figure 9.9. Again, any system containing the upsampler is a time-varying system (Problem P9.1).

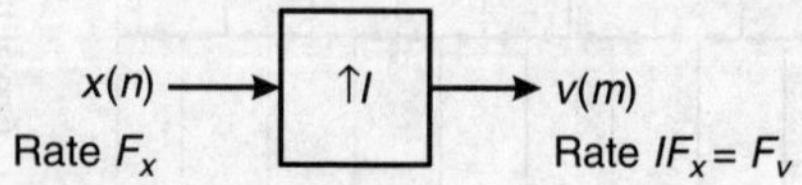

$x(n) \longrightarrow \boxed{\uparrow I} \longrightarrow v(m)$

Rate F_x Rate $IF_x = F_v$

FIGURE 9.9   *An upsampling element*

□   **EXAMPLE 9.3**   Let $I = 2$ and $x(n) = \{1, 2, 3, 4\}$. Verify that the upsampler is time varying.
                       ↑

Solution

The upsampled signal is $v(m) = \{1, 0, 2, 0, 3, 0, 4, 0\}$. If we now delay $x(n)$ by one sample, we get $x(n-1) = \{0, 1, 2, 3, 4\}$. The corresponding upsampled signal is $v_1(m) = \{0, 0, 1, 0, 2, 0, 3, 0, 4, 0\} = v(m-2)$ and not $v(m-1)$. $\square$

MATLAB Implementation MATLAB provides the function `[v] = upsample(x,I)` that upsamples input array `x` into output `v` by inserting (I-1) zeros between input samples. An optional third parameter, "phase," specifies the sample offset, which must be an integer between 0 and (I-1). For example,

```
>> x = [1,2,3,4]; v = upsample(x,3)
v =
    1    0    0    2    0    0    3    0    0    4    0    0
```

upsamples by a factor of 2 starting with the first sample. However,

```
>> v = upsample(x,3,1)
v =
    0    1    0    0    2    0    0    3    0    0    4    0
>> v = upsample(x,3,2)
v =
    0    0    1    0    0    2    0    0    3    0    0    4
```

produces two different signals by upsampling, starting with the second and the third sample (i.e., offset by 1), respectively. Note that the lengths of the upsampled signals are I times the length of the original signal.

The frequency-domain representation of the upsampled signal ***$y(m)$*** The sequence $v(m)$ has a z-transform

$$V(z) = \sum_{m=-\infty}^{\infty} v(m)z^{-m} = \sum_{m=-\infty}^{\infty} v(m)z^{-mI} = X(z^I) \qquad \text{(9.27)}$$

The corresponding spectrum of $v(m)$ is obtained by evaluating (9.27) on the unit circle. Thus

$$V(\omega_y) = X(\omega_y I) \qquad \text{(9.28)}$$

where ω_y denotes the frequency variable relative to the new sampling rate F_y (i.e., $\omega_y = 2\pi F/F_y$). Now the relationship between sampling rates is $F_y = IF_x$, and hence the frequency variables ω_x and ω_y are related according to the formula

$$\omega_y = \frac{\omega_x}{I} \qquad \text{(9.29)}$$

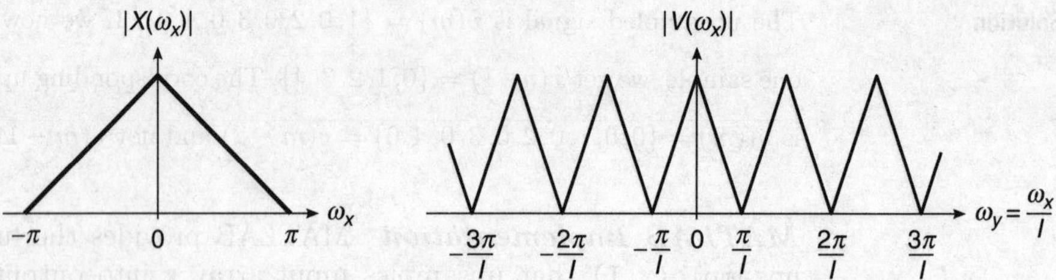

FIGURE 9.10 *Spectra of $x(n)$ and $v(m)$ where $V(\omega_y) = X(\omega_y I)$*

The spectra $X(\omega_x)$ and $V(\omega_y)$ are illustrated in Figure 9.10. We observe that the sampling rate increase, obtained by the addition of $I - 1$ zero samples between successive values of $x(n)$, results in a signal whose spectrum $V(\omega_y)$ is an I-fold periodic repetition of the input signal spectrum $X(\omega_x)$.

9.3.2 THE IDEAL INTERPOLATOR

Since only the frequency components of $x(n)$ in the range $0 \le \omega_y \le \pi/I$ are unique, the images of $X(\omega)$ above $\omega_y = \pi/I$ should be rejected by passing the sequence $v(m)$ through a lowpass filter with a frequency response $H_I(\omega_y)$ that ideally has the characteristic

$$H_I(\omega_y) = \begin{cases} C, \; 0 \le |\omega_y| \le \pi/I \\ 0, \; \text{otherwise} \end{cases} \tag{9.30}$$

where C is a scale factor required to properly normalize the output sequence $y(m)$. Consequently, the output spectrum is

$$Y(\omega_y) = \begin{cases} CX(\omega_y I), \; 0 \le |\omega_y| \le \pi/I \\ 0, \; \qquad\qquad \text{otherwise} \end{cases} \tag{9.31}$$

The scale factor C is selected so that the output $y(m) = x(m/I)$ for $m = 0, \pm I, \pm 2I, \ldots$. For mathematical convenience, we select the point $m = 0$. Thus

$$y(0) = \frac{1}{2\pi} \int_{-\pi}^{\pi} Y(\omega_y) d\omega_y = \frac{C}{2\pi} \int_{-\pi/I}^{\pi/I} X(\omega_y I) d\omega_y \tag{9.32}$$

Since $\omega_y = \omega_x/I$, (9.32) can be expressed as

$$y(0) = \frac{C}{I} \frac{1}{2\pi} \int_{-\pi}^{\pi} X(\omega_x) d\omega_x = \frac{C}{I} x(0) \tag{9.33}$$

therefore $C = I$ is the desired normalization factor.

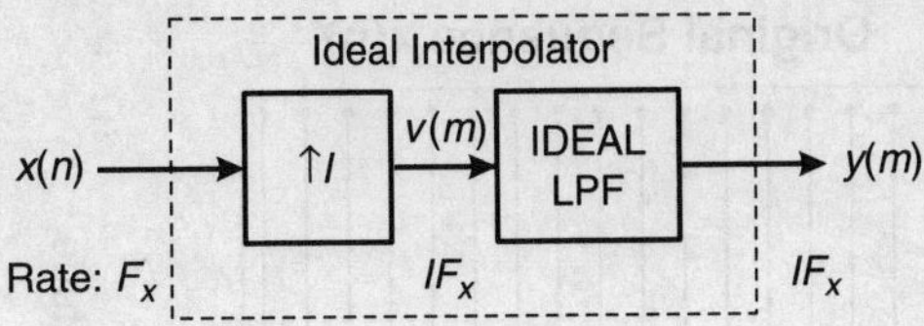

FIGURE 9.11   *Ideal interpolation by a factor I*

Finally, we indicate that the output sequence $y(m)$ can be expressed as a convolution of the sequence $v(n)$ with the unit sample response $h(n)$ of the lowpass filter. Thus

$$y(m) = \sum_{k=-\infty}^{\infty} h(m-k)v(k) \tag{9.34}$$

Since $v(k) = 0$ except at multiples of I, where $v(kI) = x(k)$, (9.34) becomes

$$y(m) = \sum_{k=-\infty}^{\infty} h(m-kI)x(k) \tag{9.35}$$

The ideal interpolator is shown in Figure 9.11.

MATLAB Implementation   MATLAB provides the function `[y,h] = interp(x,I)` that resamples the signal in array `x` at `I` times the original sampling rate. The resulting resampled array `y` is `I` times longer—that is, `length(y) = I*length(x)`. The ideal lowpass filter given in (9.30) is approximated by a symmetric filter impulse response, `h`, which is designed internally. It allows the original samples to pass through unchanged and interpolates between so that the mean square error between them and their ideal values is minimized. The third optional parameter, `L`, specifies the length of the symmetric filter as `2*L*I+1`, and the fourth optional parameter, `cutoff`, specifies the cutoff frequency of the input signal in π units. The default values are `L = 5` and `cutoff = 0.5`. Thus, if `I = 2`, then the length of the symmetric filter is 21 for the default `L = 5`.

☐   **EXAMPLE 9.4**   Let $x(n) = \cos(\pi n)$. Generate samples of $x(n)$ and interpolate them using $I = 2$, 4, and 8 to show the results of interpolation.

Solution   We will plot the middle segments of the signals to avoid end-effects due to the default lowpass filter in the `interp` function. The following MATLAB script shows details of these operations, and Figure 9.12 shows the plots of the sequences.

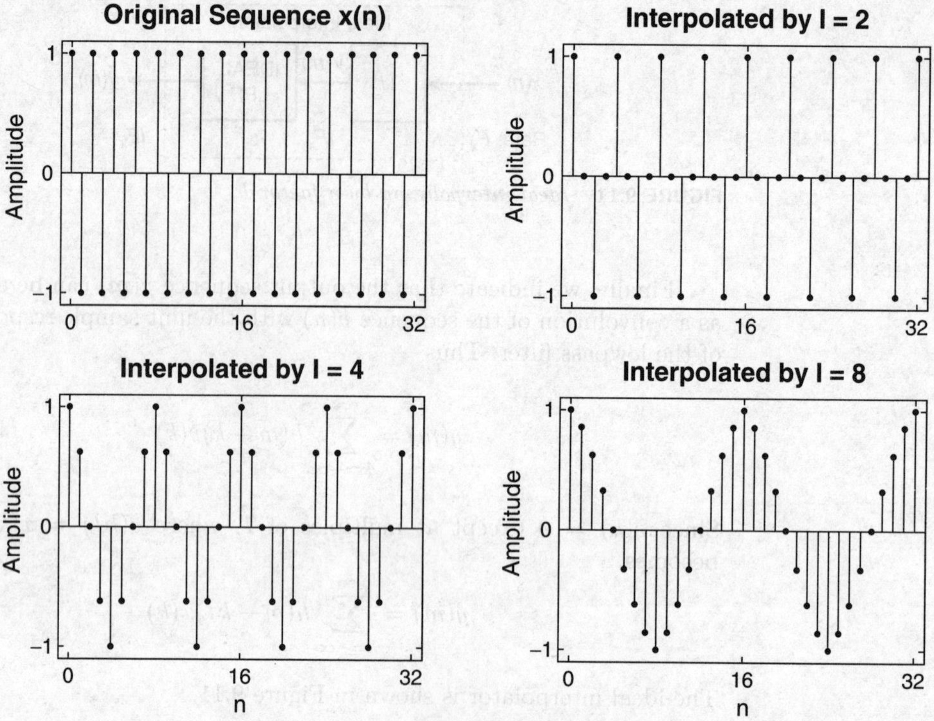

FIGURE 9.12   *Original and interpolated signals in Example 9.4*

```
n = 0:256; k1 = 64; k2 = k1+32; m = 0:(k2-k1);
Hf1 = figure('units','inches','position',[1,1,6,4],...
     'paperunits','inches','paperposition',[0,0,6,4]);

% (a) Original signal
x = cos(pi*n); subplot(2,2,1);
Ha = stem(m,x(m+k1+1),'g','filled'); axis([-1,33,-1.1,1.1]);
set(Ha,'markersize',2); ylabel('Amplitude');
title('Original Sequence x(n)','fontsize',TF);
set(gca,'xtick',[0,16,32]); set(gca,'ytick',[-1,0,1]);

% (b) Interpolation by I = 2
I = 2; y = interp(x,I); subplot(2,2,2);
Hb = stem(m,y(m+k1*I+1),'c','filled');  axis([-1,33,-1.1,1.1]);
set(Hb,'markersize',2); ylabel('Amplitude');
title('Interpolated by I = 2','fontsize',TF);
set(gca,'xtick',[0,16,32]); set(gca,'ytick',[-1,0,1]);
```

```
% (c) Interpolation by I = 4
I = 4; y = interp(x,I); subplot(2,2,3);
Hc = stem(m,y(m+k1*I+1),'r','filled');  axis([-1,33,-1.1,1.1]);
set(Hc,'markersize',2); ylabel('Amplitude');
title('Interpolated by I = 4','fontsize',TF);
set(gca,'xtick',[0,16,32]); set(gca,'ytick',[-1,0,1]);
xlabel('n');

% (d) Interpolation by I = 8
I = 8; y = interp(x,I); subplot(2,2,4);
Hd = stem(m,y(m+k1*I+1),'m','filled');  axis([-1,33,-1.1,1.1]);
set(Hd,'markersize',2); ylabel('Amplitude');
title('Interpolated by I = 8','fontsize',TF);
set(gca,'xtick',[0,16,32]); set(gca,'ytick',[-1,0,1]);
xlabel('n');
```

From Figure 9.11, we observe that the interpolated sequences for all three values of I are appropriate and represent the original sinusoidal signal $x(n)$ at higher sampling rates. In the case of $I = 8$, the resulting sequence does not appear to be perfectly sinusoidal in shape. This is due to the fact that the frequency response of the designed lowpass filter is not close to that of an ideal filter. $\square$

$\square$ **EXAMPLE 9.5** Examine the frequency response of the lowpass filter used in the interpolation of the signal in Example 10.4.

Solution The second optional argument in the `interp` function provides the impulse response from which we can compute the frequency response, as shown in the following MATLAB script.

```
n = 0:256; x = cos(pi*n); w = [0:100]*pi/100;
Hf1 = figure('units','inches','position',[1,1,6,4],...
    'paperunits','inches','paperposition',[0,0,6,4]);

% (a) Interpolation by I = 2, L = 5;
I = 2; [y,h] = interp(x,I); H = freqz(h,1,w); H = abs(H);
subplot(2,2,1);  plot(w/pi,H,'g'); axis([0,1,0,I+0.1]); ylabel('Magnitude');
title('I = 2, L = 5','fontsize',TF);
set(gca,'xtick',[0,0.5,1]); set(gca,'ytick',[0:1:I]);

% (b) Interpolation by I = 4, L = 5;
I = 4; [y,h] = interp(x,I); H = freqz(h,1,w); H = abs(H);
subplot(2,2,2);  plot(w/pi,H,'g'); axis([0,1,0,I+0.2]); ylabel('Magnitude');
title('I = 4, L = 5','fontsize',TF);
set(gca,'xtick',[0,0.25,1]); set(gca,'ytick',[0:1:I]);
```

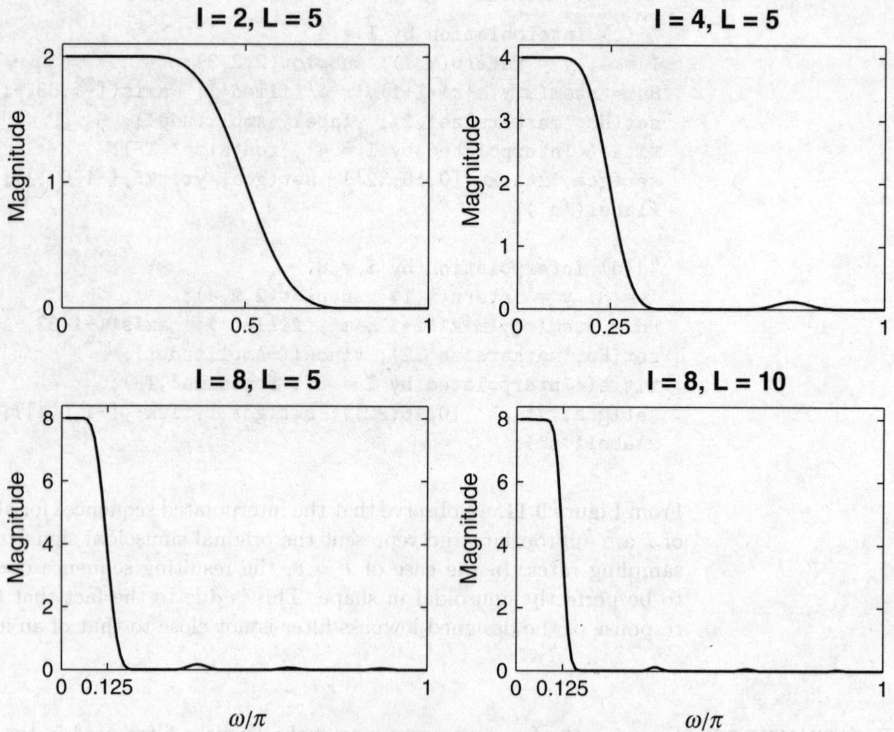

FIGURE 9.13   *Filter frequency responses in Example 9.5*

```
% (c) Interpolation by I = 8, L = 5;
I = 8; [y,h] = interp(x,I); H = freqz(h,1,w); H = abs(H);
subplot(2,2,3);  plot(w/pi,H,'g'); axis([0,1,0,I+0.4]); ylabel('Magnitude');
title('I = 8, L = 5','fontsize',TF); xlabel('\omega/\pi','fontsize',10)
set(gca,'xtick',[0,0.125,1]); set(gca,'ytick',[0:2:I]);

% (d) Interpolation by I = 8, L = 10;
I = 8; [y,h] = interp(x,I,10); H = freqz(h,1,w); H = abs(H);
subplot(2,2,4);  plot(w/pi,H,'g'); axis([0,1,0,I+0.4]); ylabel('Magnitude');
title('I = 8, L = 10','fontsize',TF); xlabel('\omega/\pi','fontsize',10)
set(gca,'xtick',[0,0.125,1]); set(gca,'ytick',[0:2:I]);
```

The frequency response plots are shown in Figure 9.13. The first three plots
are for L = 5, and, as expected, the filters are all lowpass with passband edges
approximately around π/I frequencies and the gain of I. Also note that the
filters do not have sharp transitions and thus are not good approximations to
the ideal filter. The last plot shows the response for L = 10, which indicates
a more sharp transition, which is to be expected. Any value beyond L = 10
results in an unstable filter design and hence should be avoided.   □

9.4 SAMPLING RATE CONVERSION BY A RATIONAL FACTOR I/D

Having discussed the special cases of decimation (downsampling by a factor D) and interpolation (upsampling by a factor I), we now consider the general case of sampling rate conversion by a rational factor I/D. Basically, we can achieve this sampling rate conversion by first performing interpolation by the factor I and then decimating the output of the interpolator by the factor D. In other words, a sampling rate conversion by the rational factor I/D is accomplished by cascading an interpolator with a decimator, as illustrated in Figure 9.14.

We emphasize that the importance of performing the interpolation first and the decimation second is to preserve the desired spectral characteristics of $x(n)$. Furthermore, with the cascade configuration illustrated in Figure 9.14, the two filters with impulse response $\{h_u(k)\}$ and $\{h_d(k)\}$ are operated at the same rate—namely, IF_x—and hence can be combined into a single lowpass filter with impulse response $h(k)$, as illustrated in Figure 9.15. The frequency response $H(\omega_v)$ of the combined filter must incorporate the filtering operations for both interpolation and decimation, and hence it should ideally possess the frequency-response characteristic

$$H(\omega_v) = \begin{cases} I, & 0 \leq |\omega_v| \leq \min(\pi/D, \pi/I) \\ 0, & \text{otherwise} \end{cases} \tag{9.36}$$

where $\omega_v = 2\pi F/F_v = 2\pi F/IF_x = \omega_x/I$.

Explanation of (9.36) Note that $V(\omega_v)$ and hence $W(\omega_v)$ in Figure 9.15 are periodic with period $2\pi/I$. Thus

- if $D < I$, then filter $H(\omega_v)$ allows a full period through and there is no net lowpass filtering;
- if $D > I$, then filter must first truncate the fundamental period of $W(\omega_v)$ to avoid aliasing error in the $(D\downarrow 1)$ decimation stage to follow.

Putting these two observations together, we can state that when $D/I < 1$, we have net interpolation and no smoothing is required by

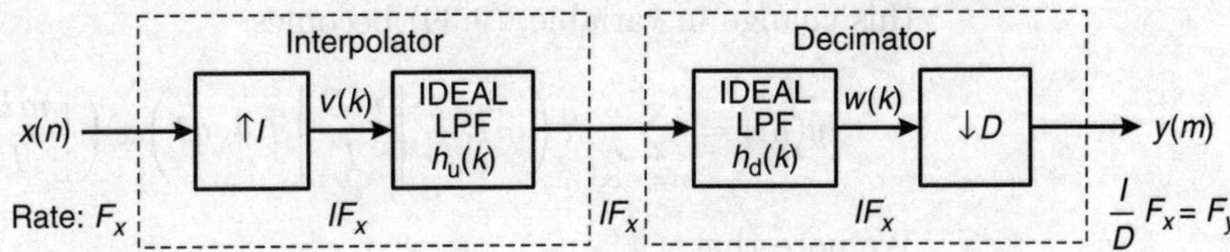

FIGURE 9.14 *Cascade of interpolator and decimator for sampling rate conversion by a factor I/D*

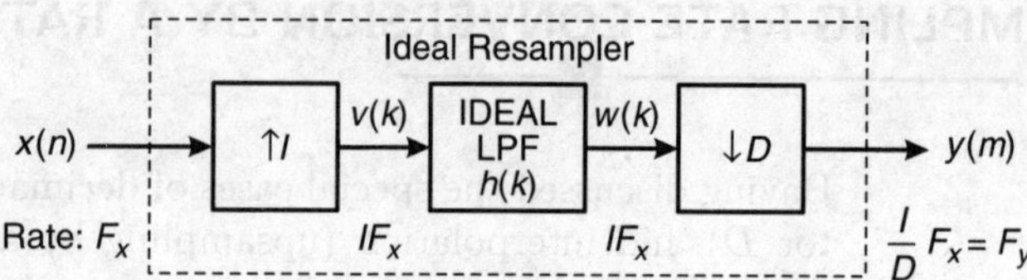

FIGURE 9.15 *Method for sampling rate conversion by a factor I/D*

$H(\omega_v)$ other than to extract the fundamental period of $W(\omega_v)$. In this respect, $H(\omega_v)$ acts as a lowpass filter as in the ideal interpolator. On the other hand, if $D/I > 1$, then we have net decimation. Hence it is necessary to first truncate even the fundamental period of $W(\omega_v)$ to get the frequency band down to $[-\pi/D, \pi/D]$ and to avoid aliasing in the decimation that follows. In this respect, $H(\omega_v)$ acts as a smoothing filter in the ideal decimator. When D or I is equal to 1, the general decimator/interpolator in Figure 9.15 along with (9.36) reduces to the ideal interpolator or decimator as a special case, respectively.

In the time domain, the output of the upsampler is the sequence

$$v(k) = \begin{cases} x(k/I), & k = 0, \pm I, \pm 2I, \ldots \\ 0, & \text{otherwise} \end{cases} \tag{9.37}$$

and the output of the linear time-invariant filter is

$$w(k) = \sum_{\ell=-\infty}^{\infty} h(k - \ell)v(\ell) = \sum_{\ell=-\infty}^{\infty} h(k - \ell I)x(\ell) \tag{9.38}$$

Finally, the output of the sampling rate converter is the sequence $\{y(m)\}$, which is obtained by downsampling the sequence $\{w(k)\}$ by a factor of D. Thus

$$y(m) = w(mD) = \sum_{\ell=-\infty}^{\infty} h(mD - \ell I)x(\ell) \tag{9.39}$$

It is illuminating to express (9.39) in a different form by making a change in variable. Let

$$\ell = \left\lfloor \frac{mD}{I} \right\rfloor - n \tag{9.40}$$

where the notation $\lfloor r \rfloor$ denotes the largest integer contained in r. With this change in variable, (9.39) becomes

$$y(m) = \sum_{n=-\infty}^{\infty} h\left(mD - \left\lfloor \frac{mD}{I} \right\rfloor I + nI\right) x\left(\left\lfloor \frac{mD}{I} \right\rfloor - n\right) \tag{9.41}$$

We note that

$$mD - \left\lfloor \frac{mD}{I} \right\rfloor I = (mD) \text{ modulo } I = ((mD))_I$$

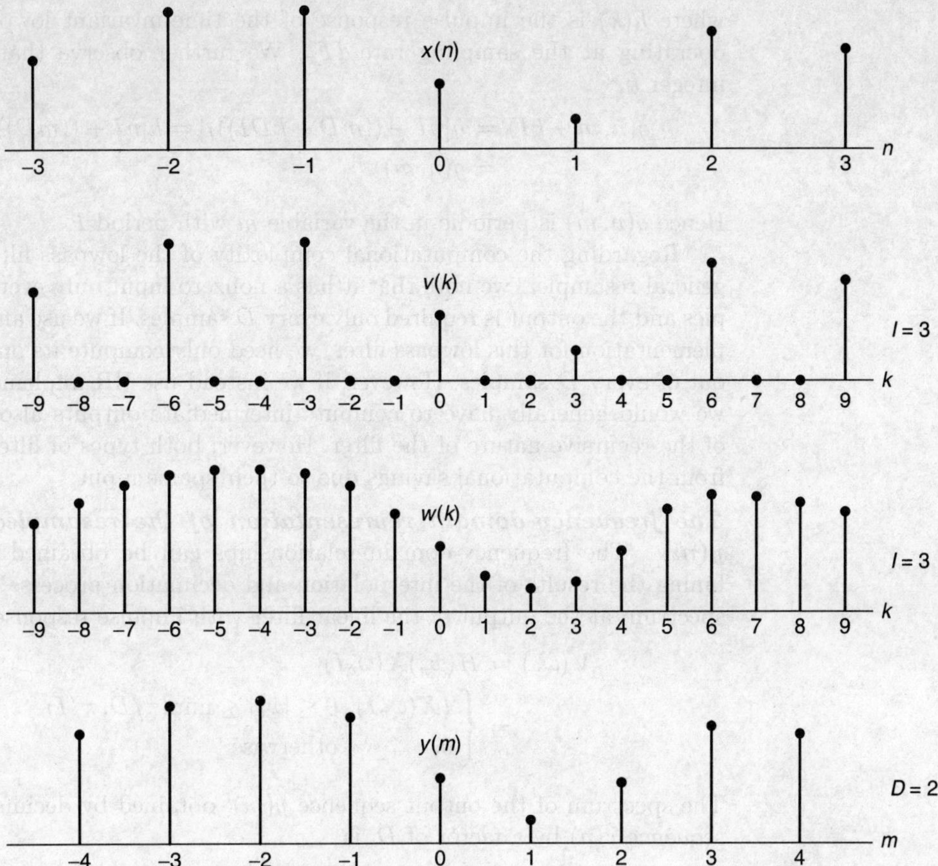

FIGURE 9.16 *Examples of signals $x(n)$, $v(k)$, $w(k)$, and $y(m)$ in the sampling rate converter of Figure 9.15 for $I = 3$ and $D = 2$*

Consequently, (9.41) can be expressed as

$$y(m) = \sum_{n=-\infty}^{\infty} h[nI + ((mD))_I]\, x\left(\left\lfloor \frac{mD}{I} \right\rfloor - n\right) \tag{9.42}$$

These operations are shown in Figure 9.16 for $I = 3$ and $D = 2$.

It is apparent from (9.41) and Figure 9.16 that the output $y(m)$ is obtained by passing the input sequence $x(n)$ through a time-variant filter with impulse response

$$g(n, m) = h[nI + ((mD))_I] \quad -\infty < m, n < \infty \tag{9.43}$$

where $h(k)$ is the impulse response of the time-invariant lowpass filter operating at the sampling rate IF_x. We further observe that for any integer k,

$$g(n, m + kI) = h[nI + ((mD + kDI))_I] = h[nI + ((mD))_I]$$
$$= g(n, m) \tag{9.44}$$

Hence $g(n, m)$ is periodic in the variable m with period I.

Regarding the computational complexity of the lowpass filter in the general resampler, we note that it has a nonzero input only every I samples and the output is required only every D samples. If we use an FIR implementation for this lowpass filter, we need only compute its output one out of every D samples. However, if we instead use IIR implementation, we would generally have to compute intermediate outputs also because of the recursive nature of the filter. However, both types of filter benefit from the computational savings due to their sparse input.

The frequency-domain representation of the resampled signal $y(m)$ The frequency-domain relationships can be obtained by combining the results of the interpolation and decimation process. Thus the spectrum at the output of the linear filter with impulse response $h(k)$ is

$$V(\omega_v) = H(\omega_v)X(\omega_v I)$$
$$= \begin{cases} IX(\omega_v I), & 0 \leq |\omega_v| \leq \min(\pi/D, \pi/I) \\ 0, & \text{otherwise} \end{cases} \tag{9.45}$$

The spectrum of the output sequence $y(m)$, obtained by decimating the sequence $v(n)$ by a factor of D, is

$$Y(\omega_y) = \frac{1}{D} \sum_{k=0}^{D-1} V\left(\frac{\omega_y - 2\pi k}{D}\right) \tag{9.46}$$

where $\omega_y = D\omega_v$. Since the linear filter prevents aliasing as implied by (9.45), the spectrum of the output sequence given by (9.46) reduces to

$$Y(\omega_y) = \begin{cases} \dfrac{I}{D} X\left(\dfrac{\omega_y}{D}\right), & 0 \leq |\omega_y| \leq \min\left(\pi, \frac{\pi D}{I}\right) \\ \\ 0, & \text{otherwise} \end{cases} \tag{9.47}$$

MATLAB Implementation   MATLAB provides the function `[y,h]=resample(x,I,D)` that resamples the signal in array `x` at I/D times the original sampling rate. The resulting resampled array `y` is I/D times longer (or the ceiling of it if the ratio is not an integer)—that is, `length(y) = ceil(I/D)*length(x)`. The function approximates the anti-aliasing (lowpass) filter given in (9.36) by an FIR filter, `h`, designed (internally) using the Kaiser window. It also compensates for the filter's delay.

The length of the FIR filter **h** that `resample` uses is proportional to the fourth (optional) parameter L that has the default value of 10. For L = 0, `resample` performs a nearest-neighbor interpolation. The fifth optional parameter `beta` (default value 5) can be used to specify the Kaiser window stopband attenuation parameter β. The filter characteristics can be studied using the impulse response **h**.

☐ **EXAMPLE 9.6**   Consider the sequence $x(n) = \cos(0.125\pi n)$ discussed in Example 9.2. Change its sampling rate by 3/2, 3/4, and 5/8.

Solution   The following MATLAB script shows the details.

```
n = 0:2048; k1 = 256; k2 = k1+32; m = 0:(k2-k1);
% (a) Original signal
x = cos(0.125*pi*n);
% (b) Sample rate conversion by 3/2: I= 3, D = 2
I = 3; D = 2; y = resample(x,I,D);
% (c) Sample rate conversion by 3/4: I= 3, D = 4
I = 3; D = 4; y = resample(x,I,D);
% (d) Sample rate conversion by 5/8: I= 5, D = 8
I = 5; D = 8; y = resample(x,I,D);
% Plotting commands follow
```

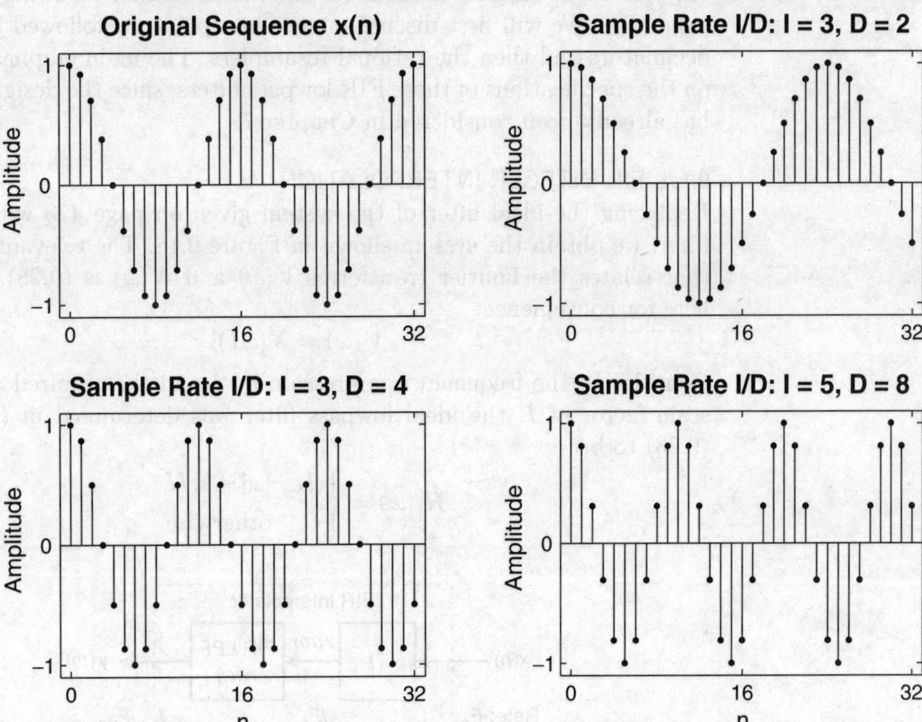

FIGURE 9.17   *Original and resampled signals in Example 9.6*

The resulting plots are shown in Figure 9.17. The original $x(n)$ signal has 16 samples in one period of the cosine waveform. Since the first sampling rate conversion by $3/2$ is greater than 1, the overall effect is to interpolate $x(n)$. The resulting signal has $16 \times 3/2 = 24$ samples in one period. The other two sampling rate conversion factors are less than 1; thus the overall effect is to decimate $x(n)$. The resulting signals have $16 \times 3/4 = 12$ and $16 \times 5/8 = 10$ samples per period, respectively.   □

9.5 FIR FILTER DESIGNS FOR SAMPLING RATE CONVERSION

In practical implementations of sampling rate converters, we must replace the ideal lowpass filters of equations (9.20), (9.30), and (9.36) by a practical finite-order filter. The lowpass filter can be designed to have linear phase, a specified passband ripple, and stopband attenuation. Any of the standard, well-known FIR filter design techniques (e.g., window method, frequency-sampling method) can be used to carry out this design. We consider linear-phase FIR filters for this purpose because of their ease of design and because they fit very nicely into a decimator stage where only one of D outputs is required [see the discussion following (9.44) on page 480]. We will first discuss integer interpolators, followed by integer decimators and then the rational resamplers. The main emphasis will be on the specifications of these FIR lowpass filters, since the design problem has already been considered in Chapter 7.

9.5.1 FIR INTEGER INTERPOLATION

Replacing the ideal filter of the system given on page 473 with an FIR filter, we obtain the system shown in Figure 9.18. The relevant equation that relates the Fourier transforms $V(\omega)$ and $X(\omega)$ is (9.28), repeated here for convenience:

$$V(\omega) = X(\omega I) \tag{9.48}$$

Considering the frequency compression by I and the required amplitude scale factor of I, the ideal lowpass filter was determined in (9.30) and (9.33) to be

$$H_{\mathrm{I}}(\omega) = \begin{cases} I, & |\omega| < \pi/I \\ 0, & \text{otherwise} \end{cases} \tag{9.49}$$

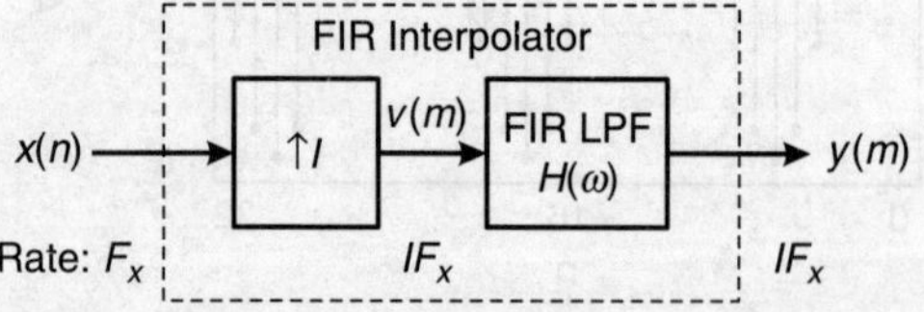

FIGURE 9.18   *An FIR integer interpolator*

MATLAB Implementation To design a linear-phase FIR filter for use in interpolation (and, as we shall see later, for decimation) operation, MATLAB provides the function `h = intfilt(I,L,alpha)`. When used on a sequence interspersed with `I-1` consecutive zeros between every `I` samples, the function performs ideal bandlimited interpolation using the nearest `2*L` nonzero samples. It assumes that the bandwidth of the signal $x(n)$ is `alpha` times π radians/sample—that is, `alpha=1` means the full signal bandwidth. The length of the filter impulse response array `h` is `2*I*L-1`. The designed filter is identical to that used by the `interp` function. Therefore, the parameter `L` should be chosen carefully to avoid numerical instability. It should be a smaller value for higher `I` value but no more than 10.

☐ **EXAMPLE 9.7** Design a linear-phase FIR interpolation filter to interpolate a signal by a factor of 4, using the bandlimited method.

Solution We will explore the `intfilt` function for the design using `L = 5` and study the effect of `alpha` on the filter design. The following MATLAB script provides the detail.

```
I = 4; L = 5;
% (a) Full signal bandwidth: alpha = 1
alpha = 1; h = intfilt(I,L,alpha);
[Hr,w,a,L] = Hr_Type1(h); Hr_min = min(Hr); w_min = find(Hr == Hr_min);
H = abs(freqz(h,1,w)); Hdb = 20*log10(H/max(H)); min_attn = Hdb(w_min);
% (b) Partial signal bandwidth: alpha = 0.75
alpha = 0.75; h = intfilt(I,L,alpha);
[Hr,w,a,L] = Hr_Type1(h); Hr_min = max(Hr(end/2:end)); w_min = find(Hr == Hr_min);
H = abs(freqz(h,1,w)); Hdb = 20*log10(H/max(H)); min_attn = Hdb(w_min);
% Plotting commands follow
```

The plots are shown in Figure 9.19. For the full bandwidth case of `alpha = 1`, the filter has more ripple in both the passband and the stopband with the minimum stopband attenuation of 22 dB. This is because the filter transition band is very narrow. For `alpha = 0.75`, the filter specifications are more lenient, and hence its response is well behaved with minimum stopband attenuation of 40 dB. Note that we do not have complete control over other design parameters. These issues are discussed in more detail further along in this section. ☐

In the following example, we design a linear-phase equiripple FIR interpolation filter using the Parks–McClellan algorithm.

☐ **EXAMPLE 9.8** Design an interpolator that increases the input sampling rate by a factor of $I = 5$. Use the `firpm` algorithm to determine the coefficients of the FIR filter that has 0.1 dB ripple in the passband and is down by at least 30 dB in the stopband. Choose reasonable values for band-edge frequencies.

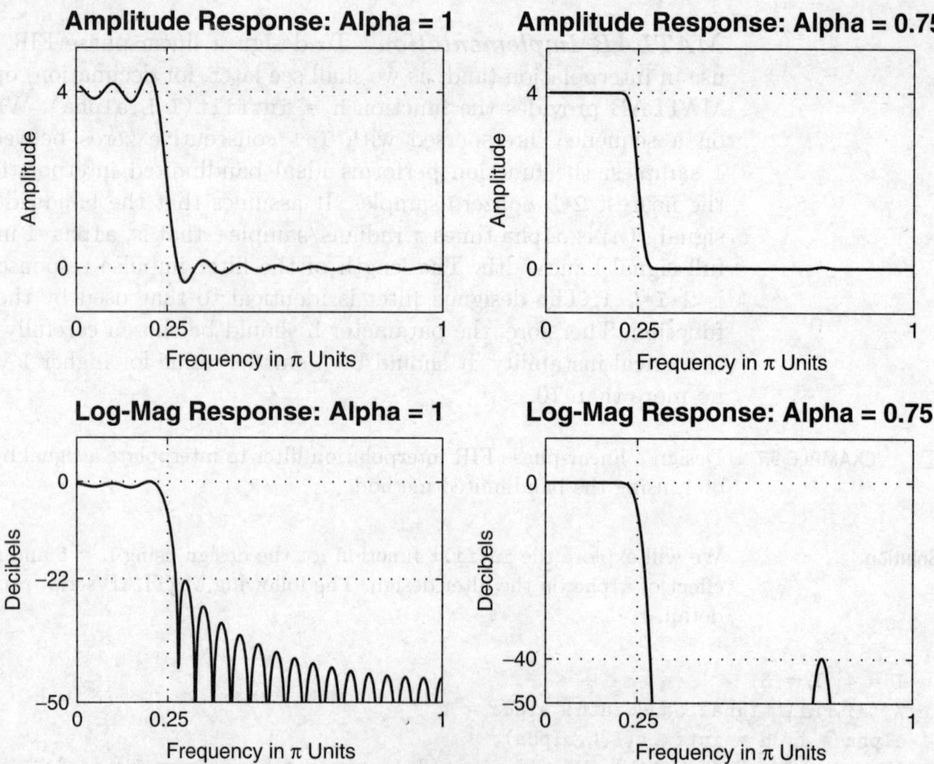

FIGURE 9.19 *FIR interpolation filter design plots for I = 4 and L = 5*

Solution

The passband cutoff frequency should be $\omega_\mathrm{p} = \pi/I = 0.2\pi$. To get a reasonable value for the filter length, we choose the transition width of 0.12π, which gives stopband cutoff frequency of $\omega_\mathrm{s} = 0.32\pi$. Note that the nominal gain of the filter in the passband should be equal to $I = 5$, which means that the ripple values computed using the decibel values are scaled by 5. A filter of length $M = 31$ achieves the design specifications given above. The details are given in the following MATLAB script.

```
I = 5; Rp = 0.1; As = 30; wp = pi/I; ws = wp+pi*0.12;
[delta1,delta2] = db2delta(Rp,As); weights = [delta2/delta1,1];
F = [0,wp,ws,pi]/pi; A = [I,I,0,0];
h = firpm(30,F,A,weights); n = [0:length(h)-1];
[Hr,w,a,L] = Hr_Type1(h); Hr_min = min(Hr); w_min = find(Hr == Hr_min);
H = abs(freqz(h,1,w)); Hdb = 20*log10(H/max(H)); min_attn = Hdb(w_min);
```

The responses of the designed FIR filter are given in Figure 9.20. Even though this filter passes the original signal, it is possible that some of the

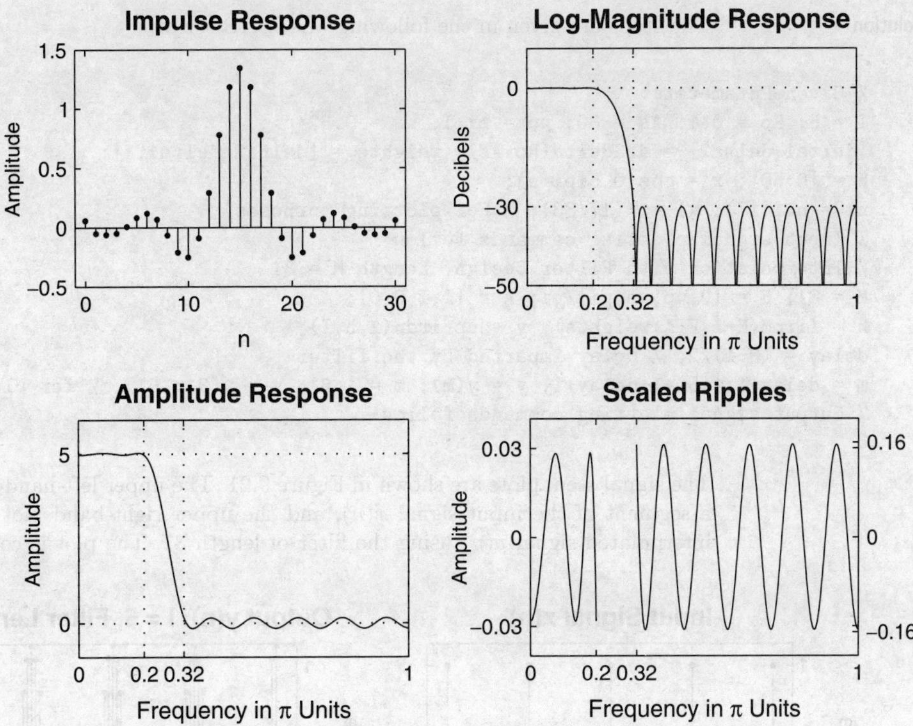

FIGURE 9.20 *Responses of the FIR interpolation filter in Example 9.8*

neighboring spectral energy may also leak through if the signal is of full bandwidth of π radians. Hence we need better design specifications, which are discussed further along in this section. □

MATLAB Implementation To use the FIR filter for interpolation purposes (such as the one designed in Example 9.8), MATLAB has provided a general function, `upfirdn`, that can be used for interpolation and decimation as well as for resampling purposes. Unlike other functions discussed in this chapter, `upfirdn` incorporates the user-defined FIR filter (which need not be linear phase) in the operation. When invoked as `y = upfirdn(x,h,I)`, the function upsamples the input data in the array `x` by a factor of the integer `I` and then filters the upsampled signal data with the impulse response sequence given in the array `h` to produce the output array `y`, thus implementing the system in Figure 9.18.

□ **EXAMPLE 9.9** Let $x(n) = \cos(0.5\pi n)$. Increase the input sampling rate by a factor of $I = 5$, using the filter designed in Example 9.8.

Solution   The steps are given in the following MATLAB script.

```
% Given Parameters:
I = 5; Rp = 0.1; As = 30; wp = pi/I; ws = 0.32*pi;
[delta1,delta2] = db2delta(Rp,As); weights = [delta2/delta1,1];
n = [0:50]; x = cos(0.5*pi*n);
n1 = n(1:17); x1 = x(17:33); % For plotting purposes
% Input signal plotting commands follow
% Interpolation with Filter Design: Length M = 31
M = 31; F = [0,wp,ws,pi]/pi; A = [I,I,0,0];
h = firpm(M-1,F,A,weights); y = upfirdn(x,h,I);
delay = (M-1)/2; % Delay imparted by the filter
m = delay+1:1:50*I+delay+1; y = y(m); m = 1:81; y = y(81:161); % for plotting
% Output signal plotting commands follow
```

The signal stem plots are shown in Figure 9.21. The upper left-hand plot shows
a segment of the input signal $x(n)$, and the upper right-hand plot shows the
interpolated signal $y(n)$ using the filter of length 31. The plot is corrected for

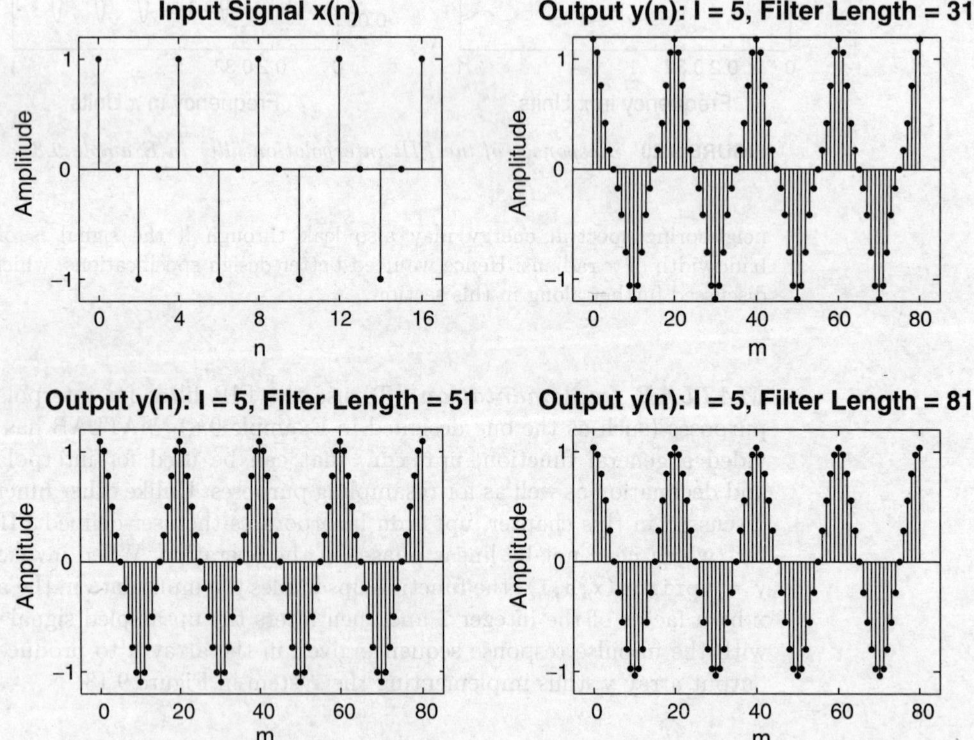

FIGURE 9.21 *Signal plots in Example 9.9*

filter delay and the effect of its transient response. It is somewhat surprising that the interpolated signal is not what it should be. The signal peak is more than 1, and the shape is distorted. A careful observation of the filter response plot in Figure 9.20 reveals that the broad transition width and a smaller attenuation has allowed some of the spectral energy to leak, creating a distortion.

To investigate this further, we designed filters with larger orders of 51 and 81, as detailed in the following MATLAB script.

```
% Interpolation with Filter Design: Length M = 51
M = 51; F = [0,wp,ws,pi]/pi; A = [I,I,0,0];
h = firpm(M-1,F,A,weights); y = upfirdn(x,h,I);
delay = (M-1)/2; % Delay imparted by the filter
m = delay+1:1:50*I+delay+1; y = y(m); m = 1:81; y = y(81:161);
% Plotting commands follow
% Interpolation with Filter Design: Length M = 81
M = 81; F = [0,wp,ws,pi]/pi; A = [I,I,0,0];
h = firpm(M-1,F,A,weights); y = upfirdn(x,h,I);
delay = (M-1)/2; % Delay imparted by the filter
m = delay+1:1:50*I+delay+1; y = y(m); m = 1:81; y = y(81:161);
% Plotting commands follow
```

The resulting signals are shown in lower plots in Figure 9.21. Clearly, for large orders, the filter has better lowpass characteristics. The signal peak value approaches 1, and its shape approaches the cosine waveform. Thus a good filter design is critical even in a simple signal case. $\qquad\square$

9.5.2 DESIGN SPECIFICATIONS

When we replace $H_\mathrm{I}(\omega)$ by a finite-order FIR filter $H(\omega)$, we must allow for a transition band; thus the filter cannot have a passband edge up to π/I. Toward this, we define

- $\omega_{x,\mathrm{p}}$ as the highest frequency of the signal $x(n)$ that we want to preserve, and
- $\omega_{x,\mathrm{s}}$ as the full signal bandwidth of $x(n)$,—that is, there is no energy in $x(n)$ above the frequency $\omega_{x,\mathrm{s}}$.

Thus we have $0 < \omega_{x,\mathrm{p}} < \omega_{x,\mathrm{s}} < \pi$. Note that the parameters $\omega_{x,\mathrm{p}}$ and $\omega_{x,\mathrm{s}}$, as defined, are *signal parameters*, not filter parameters; they are shown in Figure 9.22a. The filter parameters will be defined based on $\omega_{x,\mathrm{p}}$ and $\omega_{x,\mathrm{s}}$.

From equation (9.48), these signal parameter frequencies for $v(m)$ become $\omega_{x,\mathrm{p}}/I$ and $\omega_{x,\mathrm{s}}/I$, respectively, because the frequency scale is compressed by the factor I. This is shown in Figure 9.22b. A linear-phase

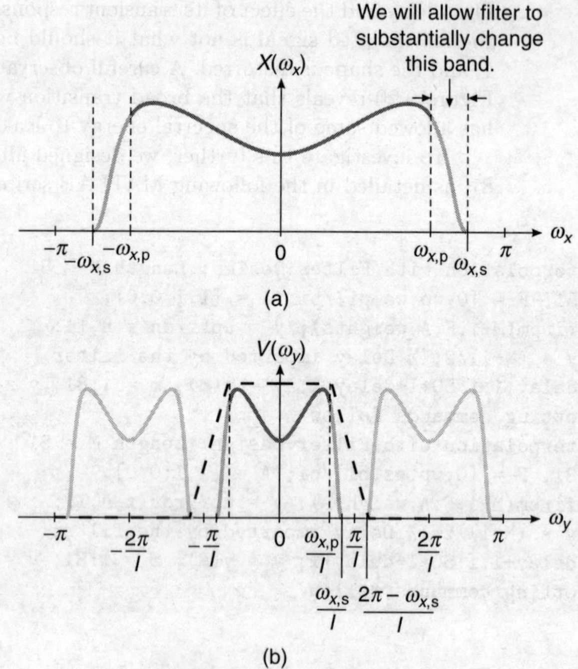

FIGURE 9.22　*Frequency parameters: (a) signal, (b) filter*

FIR filter can now be designed to pass frequencies up to $\omega_{x,p}/I$ and to suppress frequencies starting at $(2\pi - \omega_{x,s})/I$. Let

$$\omega_{\mathrm{p}} = \left(\frac{\omega_{x,p}}{I}\right) \quad \text{and} \quad \omega_{\mathrm{s}} = \left(\frac{2\pi - \omega_{x,s}}{I}\right) \tag{9.50}$$

be the passband and stopband edge frequencies, respectively, of the low-pass linear-phase FIR filter given by

$$H(\omega) = H_{\mathrm{r}}(\omega)e^{j\theta(\omega)} \tag{9.51}$$

where $H_{\mathrm{r}}(\omega)$ is the real-valued amplitude response and $\theta(\omega)$ is the un-wrapped phase response. Then we have the following filter design specifications:

$$\boxed{\begin{aligned}
\frac{1}{I}H_{\mathrm{r}}(\omega) &\leq 1 \pm \delta_1 \text{ for } |\omega| \in [0, \omega_{\mathrm{p}}] \\[2ex]
\frac{1}{I}H_{\mathrm{r}}(\omega) &\leq \pm \delta_2 \quad \text{for } |\omega| \in [\omega_{\mathrm{s}}, \pi]
\end{aligned}} \tag{9.52}$$

where ω_p and ω_s are as given in (9.50) and δ_1 and δ_2 are the passband and stopband ripple parameters, respectively, of the lowpass FIR filter.

Comment: Instead of beginning the stopband at π/I, we were able to shift it to $(2\pi - \omega_s)/I$. If $\omega_{x,s} \ll \pi$, then this will be an important consideration to lower filter order. However, in the worst-case scenario of $\omega_{x,s} = \pi$, the stopband will begin at $\frac{\pi}{I}$, which is the same as in the ideal lowpass filter of (9.49). Almost always, $\omega_{x,s} < \pi$, and we can then choose $\omega_{x,p}$ as close to $\omega_{x,s}$ as we want. However, this will reduce the size of the transition band, which means a higher filter order.

☐   **EXAMPLE 9.10**   Design a better FIR lowpass filter for sampling rate increase by a factor of $I = 5$ for the signal in Example 9.9.

Solution   Since $x(n) = \cos(0.5\pi n)$, the signal bandwidth and bandwidth to be preserved are the same—that is, $\omega_{x,p} = \omega_{x,s} = 0.5\pi$. Thus, from (9.50), $\omega_p = 0.5\pi/5 = 0.1\pi$ and $\omega_s = (2\pi - 0.5\pi)/5 = 0.3\pi$. We will design the filter for $R_p = 0.01$ and $A_s = 50$ dB. The resulting filter order is 32, which is 2 higher than the one in Example 9.9 but with much superior attenuation. The details are given below.

```
% Given Parameters:
n = [0:50]; wxp = 0.5*pi; x = cos(wxp*n);
n1 = n(1:9); x1 = x(9:17); % for plotting purposes
I = 5; I = 5; Rp = 0.01; As = 50; wp = wxp/I; ws = (2*pi-wxp)/I;
[delta1,delta2] = db2delta(Rp,As); weights = [delta2/delta1,1];
[N,Fo,Ao,weights] = firpmord([wp,ws]/pi,[1,0],[delta1,delta2],2);N = N+2;
% Input signal plotting commands follow
% Interpolation with Filter Design: Length M = 31
h = firpm(N,Fo,I*Ao,weights); y = upfirdn(x,h,I);
delay = (N)/2; % Delay imparted by the filter
m = delay+1:1:50*I+delay+1; y = y(m); m = 0:40; y = y(81:121);
% Output signal plotting commands follow
[Hr,w,a,L] = Hr_Type1(h); Hr_min = min(Hr); w_min = find(Hr == Hr_min);
H = abs(freqz(h,1,w)); Hdb = 20*log10(H/max(H)); min_attn = Hdb(w_min);
% Filter design plotting commands follow
```

The signal stem plots and filter design plots are shown in Figure 9.23. The designed filter has a minimum stopband attenuation of 53 dB, and the resulting interpolation is accurate even with the filter order of 32.   ☐

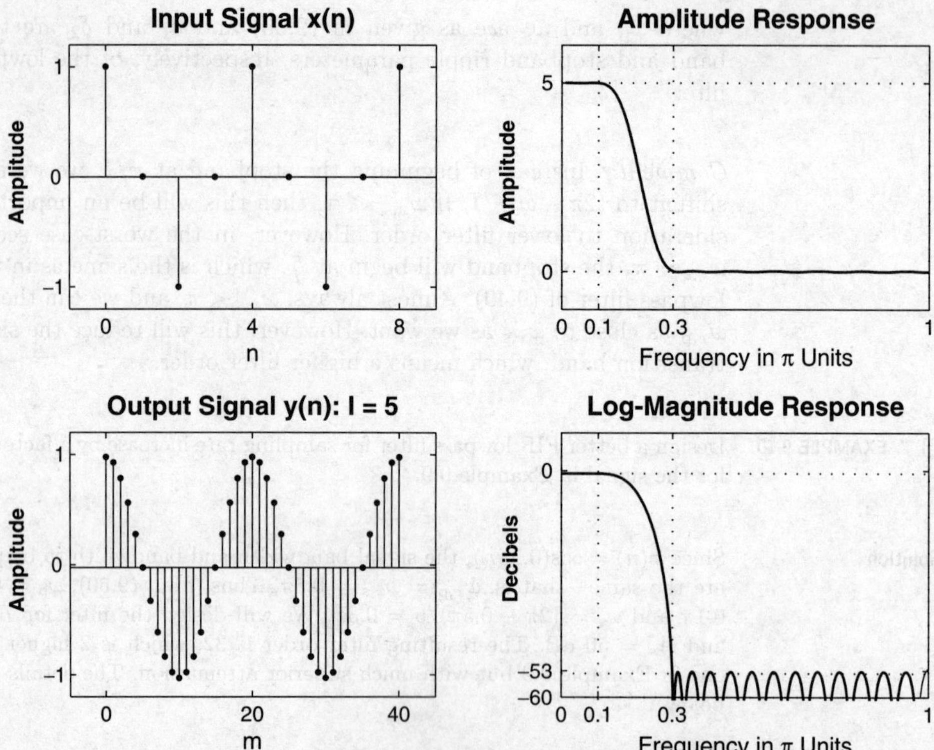

FIGURE 9.23 *Signal plots and filter design plots in Example 9.10*

9.5.3 FIR INTEGER DECIMATION

Consider the system in Figure 9.6 on page 466 in which the ideal lowpass filter is replaced by an FIR filter $H(\omega)$, which then results in the system shown in Figure 9.24. The relationship between $Y(\omega_y)$ and $X(\omega)$ is given by (9.24), which is repeated here for convenience:

$$Y(\omega_y) = \frac{1}{D} \sum_{k=0}^{D-1} H\left(\omega - \frac{2\pi k}{D}\right) X\left(\omega - \frac{2\pi k}{D}\right); \quad \omega = \frac{\omega_y}{D} \tag{9.53}$$

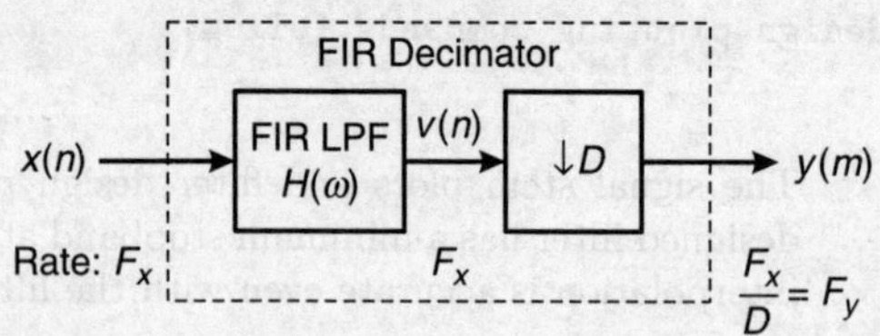

FIGURE 9.24 *An FIR integer decimator*

which is nothing but the aliased sum of the $H(\omega)X(\omega)$. Thus the condition necessary to avoid aliasing is

$$H(\omega)X(\omega) = 0 \quad \text{for} \quad \frac{\pi}{D} \le |\omega| \le \pi \qquad (9.54)$$

Then

$$Y(\omega_y) = \frac{1}{D}X(\omega)H(\omega) \qquad (9.55)$$

as in (9.25), where the ideal filtering was accomplished with $H_D(\omega)$ as given in (9.20).

☐ **EXAMPLE 9.11** Design a decimator that downsamples an input signal $x(n)$ by a factor $D = 2$. Use the `firpm` algorithm to determine the coefficients of the FIR filter that has a 0.1 dB ripple in the passband and is down by at least 30 dB in the stopband. Choose reasonable values for band-edge frequencies.

Solution The passband cutoff frequency should be $\omega_p = \pi/D = 0.5\pi$. To get a reasonable value for the filter length, we choose the transition width of 0.1π, which gives stopband a cutoff frequency of $\omega_s = 0.3\pi$. A filter of length $M = 37$ achieves the preceding design specifications. The details are given in the following MATLAB script.

```
% Filter Design
D = 2; Rp = 0.1; As = 30; wp = pi/D; ws = wp+0.1*pi;
[delta1,delta2] = db2delta(Rp,As);
[N,F,A,weights] = firpmord([wp,ws]/pi,[1,0],[delta1,delta2],2);
h = firpm(N,F,A,weights); n = [0:length(h)-1];
[Hr,w,a,L] = Hr_Type1(h); Hr_min = min(Hr); w_min = find(Hr == Hr_min);
H = abs(freqz(h,1,w)); Hdb = 20*log10(H/max(H)); min_attn = Hdb(w_min);
% Plotting commands follow
```

The responses of the designed FIR filter are given in Figure 9.25. This filter passes the signal spectrum over the passband $[0, \pi/2]$ without any distortion. However, since the transition width is not very narrow, it is possible that some of the signal over the transition band may alias into the band of interest. Also, the 30 db attenuation may allow a small fraction of the signal spectrum from the stopband into the passband after downsampling. Therefore, we need a better approach for filter specifications, as discussed further along in this section. ☐

MATLAB Implementation As discussed, the `upfirdn` function can also be used for implementing the user-designed FIR filter in the decimation operation. When invoked as `y = upfirdn(x,h,1,D)`, the function filters the signal data in the array x with the impulse response given in the array h and then downsamples the filtered data by the integer factor D to produce the output array y, thus implementing the system in Figure 9.24.

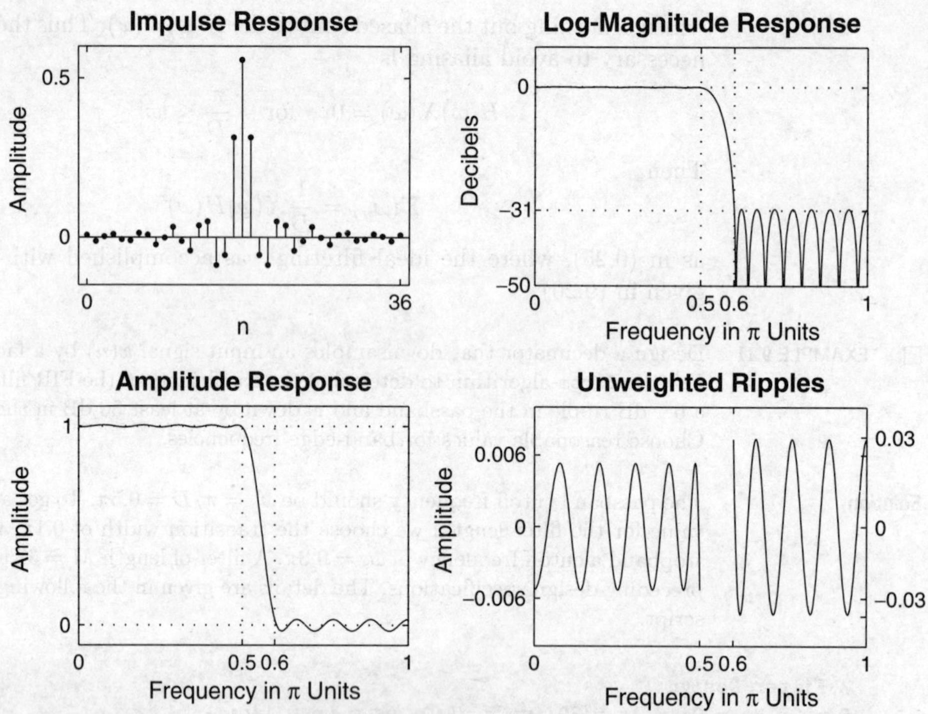

FIGURE 9.25 *Responses of the FIR decimation filter in Example 9.11*

☐ **EXAMPLE 9.12**   Using the filter designed in Example 9.11, decimate sinusoidal signals $x_1(n) = \cos(\pi n/8)$ and $x_2(n) = \cos(\pi n/2)$ with frequencies within the passband of the filter. Verify the performance of the FIR filter and the results of the decimation.

Solution   The following MATLAB script provides the details.

```
% Given Parameters:
D = 2; Rp = 0.1; As = 30; wp = pi/D; ws = wp+0.1*pi;
% Filter Design
[delta1,delta2] = db2delta(Rp,As);
[N,F,A,weights] = firpmord([wp,ws]/pi,[1,0],[delta1,delta2],2);
h = firpm(N,F,A,weights); delay = N/2; % Delay imparted by the filter
% Input signal x1(n) = cos(2*pi*n/16)
n = [0:256]; x = cos(pi*n/8);
n1 = n(1:33); x1 = x(33:65); % for plotting purposes
% Input signal plotting commands follow
% Decimation of x1(n): D = 2
y = upfirdn(x,h,1,D);
```

```
m = delay+1:1:128/D+delay+1; y = y(m); m = 0:16; y = y(16:32);
% Output signal plotting commands follow
% Input signal x2(n) = cos(8*pi*n/16)
n = [0:256]; x = cos(8*pi*n/(16));
n1 = n(1:33); x1 = x(33:65); % for plotting purposes
% Input signal plotting commands follow
% Decimation of x2(n): D = 2
y = upfirdn(x,[h],1,D); %y = downsample(conv(x,h),2);
m = delay+1:1:128/D+delay+1; y = y(m); m = 0:16; y = y(16:32);
% Output signal plotting commands follow
```

The signal stem plots are shown in Figure 9.26. The left-side plots show the signal $x_1(n)$ and the corresponding decimated signal $y_1(n)$, and the right-side plots show the same for $x_2(n)$ and $y_2(n)$. In both cases, the decimation appears to be correct. If we had chosen any frequency above $\pi/2$, then the filter would have attenuated or eliminated the signal. □

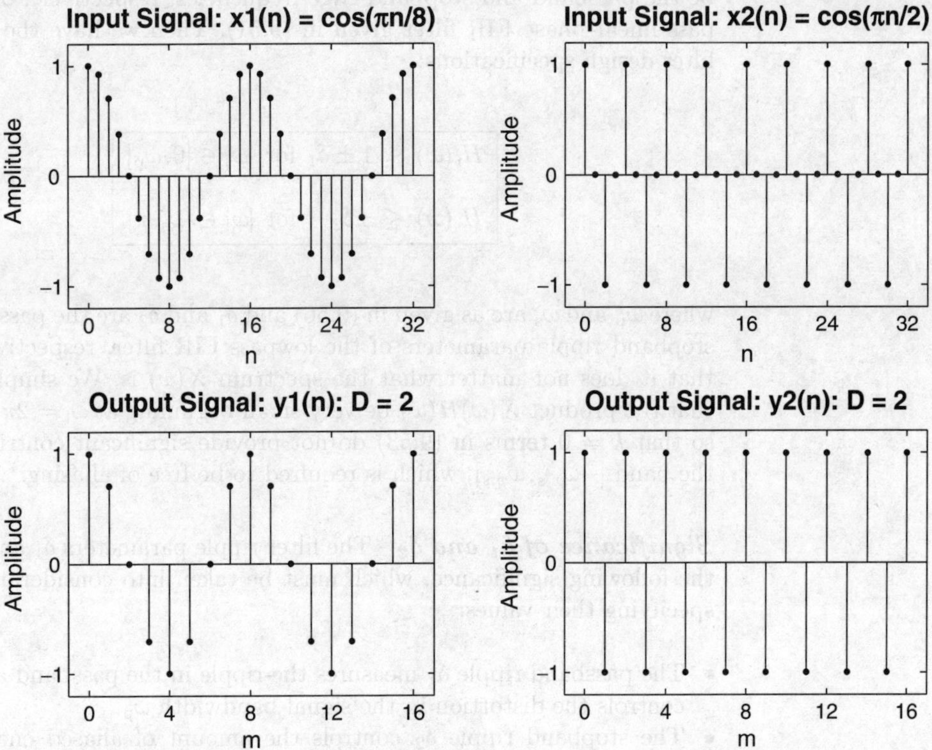

FIGURE 9.26 *Signal plots in Example 9.12*

9.5.4 DESIGN SPECIFICATIONS

When we replace the ideal lowpass filter $H_D(\omega)$ by a finite-order FIR filter $H(\omega)$, we must allow for a transition band. Again we define

- $\omega_{x,\mathrm{p}}$ as the signal bandwidth to be preserved, and
- $\omega_{x,\mathrm{s}}$ as the frequency above which aliasing error is tolerated.

Then we have $0 < \omega_{x,\mathrm{p}} \leq \omega_{x,\mathrm{s}} \leq \pi/D$. If we choose $\omega_{x,\mathrm{s}} = \pi/D$, then the decimator will give no aliasing error. If we choose $\omega_{x,\mathrm{s}} = \omega_{x,\mathrm{p}}$, then the band above the signal band will contain aliasing errors. With these definitions and observations, we can now specify the desired filter specifications. The filter must pass frequencies up to $\omega_{x,\mathrm{p}}$, and its stopband must begin at $\left(\frac{2\pi}{D} - \omega_{x,\mathrm{s}}\right)$ and continue up to π. Then none of the $k \neq 0$ terms in (9.53)—that is, the "aliases"—will cause appreciable distortion in the band up to $\omega_{x,\mathrm{s}}$. Let

$$\omega_{\mathrm{p}} = \omega_{x,\mathrm{p}} \quad \text{and} \quad \omega_{\mathrm{s}} = \left(\frac{2\pi}{D} - \omega_{x,\mathrm{s}}\right) \qquad (9.56)$$

be the passband and stopband edge frequencies, respectively, of the lowpass linear-phase FIR filter given in (9.51). Then we have the following filter design specifications:

$$\boxed{\begin{aligned} H_r(\omega) &\leq 1 \pm \delta_1 \text{ for } |\omega| \in [0, \omega_{\mathrm{p}}] \\[2mm] H_r(\omega) &\leq \pm \delta_2 \quad \text{for } |\omega| \in [\omega_{\mathrm{s}}, \pi] \end{aligned}} \qquad (9.57)$$

where ω_{p} and ω_{s} are as given in (9.56) and δ_1 and δ_2 are the passband and stopband ripple parameters of the lowpass FIR filter, respectively. Note that it does not matter what the spectrum $X(\omega)$ is. We simply require that the product $X(\omega)H(\omega)$ be very small beginning at $\omega_| = 2\pi/D - \omega_{x,\mathrm{s}}$ so that $k \neq 0$ terms in (9.53) do not provide significant contribution in the band $[-\omega_{x,\mathrm{s}}, \omega_{x,\mathrm{s}}]$, which is required to be free of aliasing.

Significance of δ_1 and δ_2 The filter ripple parameters δ_1 and δ_2 have the following significance, which must be taken into consideration while specifying their values:

- The passband ripple δ_1 measures the ripple in the passband and hence controls the distortion in the signal bandwidth ω_{p}.
- The stopband ripple δ_2 controls the amount of aliased energy (also called leakage) that gets into the band up to $\omega_{x,\mathrm{s}}$.

There are $(D-1)$ contributions due to $k \neq 0$ terms in (9.53). These are expected to add incoherently (i.e., have peaks at different locations), so the overall peak error should be about δ_2. The actual error depends on how $X(\omega)$ varies over the rest of the band $|\omega| > \omega_{x,\mathrm{p}}$. Clearly, the filter stopband ripple δ_2 controls the aliasing error in the signal passband. Therefore, *both δ_1 and δ_2 affect the decimated signal in its passband.*

Comment: Comparing the FIR decimator filter specifications (9.57) to those for the FIR interpolator in (9.52), we see a high degree of similarity. In fact, a filter designed to decimate by factor D can also be used to interpolate by the factor $I = D$, as we see from the following example. This means that the function `intfilt` can also be used to design FIR filters for decimation.

☐   **EXAMPLE 9.13**   To design a decimate by D stage, we need values for $\omega_{x,\mathrm{p}}$ and $\omega_{x,\mathrm{s}}$ (remember that these are signal parameters). Assume $\omega_{x,\mathrm{p}} = \pi/(2D)$, which satisfies the constraint $\omega_{x,\mathrm{p}} \leq \pi/D$ and is exactly half the decimated bandwidth. Let $\omega_{x,\mathrm{s}} = \omega_{x,\mathrm{p}}$. Then the FIR lowpass filter must pass frequencies up to $\omega_{\mathrm{p}} = \pi/(2D)$ and stop frequencies above $\omega_{\mathrm{s}} = 2\pi/D - \pi/(2D) = 3\pi/(2D)$.

Now consider the corresponding interpolation problem. We want to interpolate by I. We again choose $\omega_{x,\mathrm{s}} = \omega_{x,\mathrm{p}}$, but now the range is $\omega_{x,\mathrm{p}} < \pi$. If we take exactly half this band, we get $\omega_{x,\mathrm{p}} = \pi/2$. Then according to the specifications (9.52) for the interpolation, we want the filter to pass frequencies up to $\pi/2I$ and to stop above $3\pi/2I$. Thus for $I = D$, we have the same filter specifications, so the same filter could serve both the decimation and interpolation problems.   ☐

☐   **EXAMPLE 9.14**   Design a decimation FIR filter for the signal $x_1(n)$ in Example 9.12 that has a better stopband attenuation of $A_s = 50$ dB and a lower filter order.

Solution   The signal bandwidth is $\omega_{x,\mathrm{p}} = \pi/8$, and we will choose $\omega_{x,\mathrm{s}} = \pi/D = \pi/2$. Then $\omega_{\mathrm{p}} = \pi/8$ and $\omega_{\mathrm{s}} = (2\pi/D) - \omega_{x,\mathrm{s}} = \pi/2$. With these parameters the optimum FIR filter length is 13, which is much lower than the previous one of 37 with a higher attenuation.

MATLAB script:

```
% Given Parameters:
D = 2; Rp = 0.1; As = 50; wxp = pi/8; wxs = pi/D; wp = wxp; ws = (2*pi/D)-wxs;
% Filter Design
[delta1,delta2] = db2delta(Rp,As);
[N,F,A,weights] = firpmord([wp,ws]/pi,[1,0],[delta1,delta2],2); N = ceil(N/2)*2;
h = firpm(N,F,A,weights); delay = N/2; % Delay imparted by the filter
```

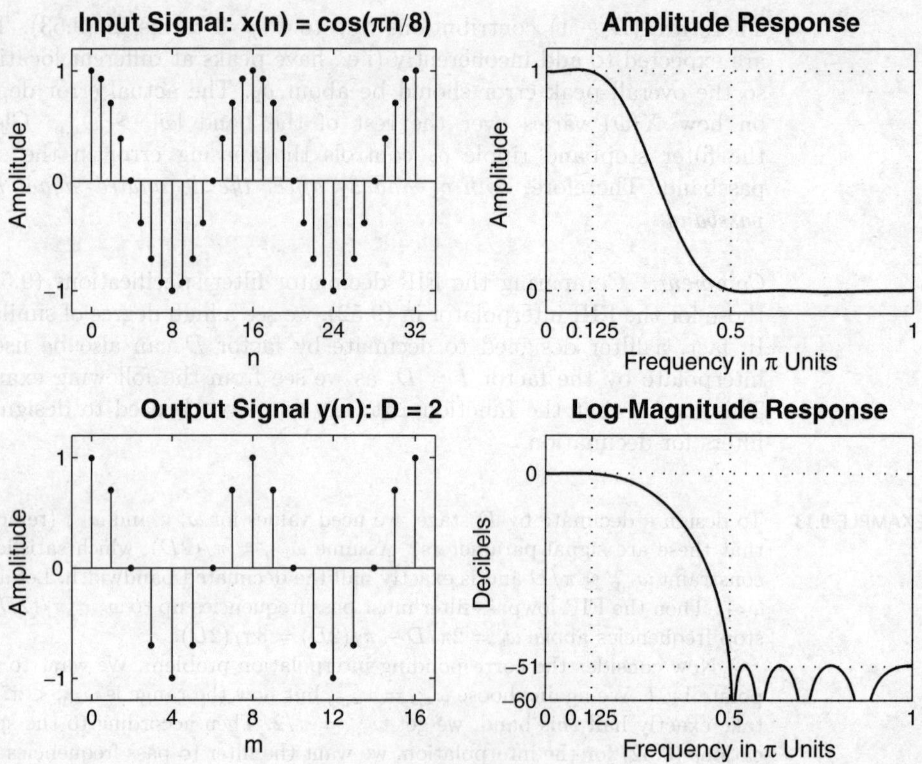

FIGURE 9.27   *Signal plots and filter design plots in Example 9.14*

```
% Input signal x(n) = cos(2*pi*n/16)
n = [0:256]; x = cos(pi*n/8);
n1 = n(1:33); x1 = x(33:65); % for plotting purposes
% Input signal plotting commands follow
% Decimation of x(n): D = 2
y = upfirdn(x,h,1,D);
m = delay+1:1:128/D+delay+1; y1 = y(m); m = 0:16; y1 = y1(14:30);
% Output signal plotting commands follow
% Filter Design Plots
[Hr,w,a,L] = Hr_Type1(h); Hr_min = min(Hr); w_min = find(Hr == Hr_min);
H = abs(freqz(h,1,w)); Hdb = 20*log10(H/max(H)); min_attn = Hdb(w_min);
% Filter design plotting commands follow
```

The signal stem plots and the filter responses are shown in Figure 9.27. The
designed filter achieves an attenuation of 51 dB, and the decimated signal is
correct.   □

9.5.5 FIR RATIONAL-FACTOR RATE CONVERSION

Replacing the ideal filter of the system given on page 478 with an FIR filter $H(\omega)$, we obtain the system shown in Figure 9.28. In this case, the relevant ideal lowpass filter is given by (9.36), which is repeated here for convenience:

$$H(\omega) = \begin{cases} I, \ 0 \leq |\omega| \leq \min(\pi/D, \pi/I) \\ 0, \ \text{otherwise} \end{cases} \tag{9.58}$$

For the signal $x(n)$, we define

- $\omega_{x,\mathrm{p}}$ as the signal bandwidth that should be preserved,
- ω_{x,s_1} as the overall signal bandwidth, and
- ω_{x,s_2} as the signal bandwidth that is required to be free of aliasing error after resampling.

Then we have

$$0 < \omega_{x,\mathrm{p}} \leq \omega_{x,\mathrm{s}_2} \leq \frac{I\pi}{D} \quad \text{and} \quad \omega_{x,\mathrm{s}_1} \leq \pi \tag{9.59}$$

Now, for the interpolation part, the lowpass filter must pass frequencies up to $\omega_{x,\mathrm{p}}/I$ and attenuate frequencies starting at $(2\pi/I - \omega_{x,\mathrm{s}_1}/I)$. The decimation part of the filter must again pass frequencies up to $\omega_{x,\mathrm{p}}/I$ but attenuate frequencies above $(2\pi/D - \omega_{x,\mathrm{s}_2}/I)$. Therefore, the stopband must start at the lower of these two values. Defining filter cutoff frequencies as

$$\omega_{\mathrm{p}} = \left(\frac{\omega_{x,\mathrm{p}}}{I}\right) \quad \text{and} \quad \omega_{\mathrm{s}} = \min\left[\frac{2\pi}{I} - \frac{\omega_{x,\mathrm{s}_1}}{I}, \frac{2\pi}{D} - \frac{\omega_{x,\mathrm{s}_2}}{I}\right] \tag{9.60}$$

and the corresponding ripple parameters as δ_1 and δ_2, we have the following filter specifications:

$$\boxed{\begin{aligned} &\frac{1}{I}H_{\mathrm{r}}(\omega) \leq 1 \pm \delta_1 \ \text{for } |\omega| \in [0, \omega_{\mathrm{p}}] \\[2ex] &\frac{1}{I}H_{\mathrm{r}}(\omega) \leq \pm\delta_2 \quad \text{for } |\omega| \in [\omega_{\mathrm{s}}, \pi] \end{aligned}} \tag{9.61}$$

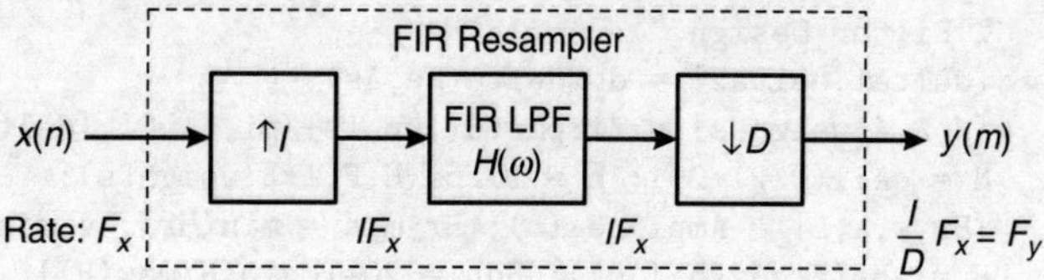

FIGURE 9.28 *An FIR rational-factor resampler*

where $H_r(\omega)$ is the amplitude response. Note that if we set $\omega_{x,s_1} = \pi$ and $\omega_{x,s_2} = I\pi/D$, which are their maximum values, then we get the ideal cutoff frequency $\max[\pi/I, \pi/D]$, as given before in (9.36).

MATLAB Implementation Clearly, the `upfirdn` function implements all the necessary operations needed in the rational sampling rate conversion system shown in Figure 9.28. When invoked as `y = upfirdn(x,h, I,D)`, it performs a cascade of three operations: upsampling the input data array `x` by a factor of the integer I, FIR filtering the upsampled signal data with the impulse response sequence given in the array `h`, and, finally, downsampling the result by a factor of the integer D. Using a well-designed filter, we have complete control over the sampling rate conversion operation.

☐ **EXAMPLE 9.15**   Design a sampling rate converter that increases the sampling rate by a factor of 2.5. Use the `firpm` algorithm to determine the coefficients of the FIR filter that has 0.1 dB ripple in the passband and is down by at least 30 dB in the stopband.

Solution   The FIR filter that meets the specifications of this problem is exactly the same as the filter designed in Example 9.8. Its bandwidth is $\pi/5$.   ☐

☐ **EXAMPLE 9.16**   A signal $x(n)$ has a total bandwidth of 0.9π. It is resampled by a factor of $4/3$ to obtain $y(m)$. We want to preserve the frequency band up to 0.8π and require that the band up to 0.7π be free of aliasing. Using the Parks–McClellan algorithm, determine the coefficients of the FIR filter that has 0.1 dB ripple in the passband and 40 dB attenuation in the stopband.

Solution   The overall signal bandwidth is $\omega_{x,s_1} = 0.9\pi$, the bandwidth to be preserved is $\omega_{x,p} = 0.8\pi$, and the bandwidth above which aliasing is tolerated is $\omega_{x,s_2} = 0.7\pi$. From (9.60) and using $I = 4$ and $D = 3$, the FIR filter design parameters are $\omega_p = 0.2\pi$ and $\omega_s = 0.275\pi$. With these parameters, along with the passband ripple of 0.1 dB and stopband attenuation of 40 dB, the optimum FIR filter length is 58. The details and computation of design plots follow.

```
% Given Parameters:
I = 4; D = 3; Rp = 0.1; As = 40;
wxp = 0.8*pi; wxs1 = 0.9*pi; wxs2 = 0.7*pi;
% Computed Filter Parameters
wp = wxp/I; ws = min((2*pi/I-wxs1/I),(2*pi/D-wxs2/I));
% Filter Design
[delta1,delta2] = db2delta(Rp,As);
[N,F,A,weights] = firpmord([wp,ws]/pi,[1,0],[delta1,delta2],2);
N = ceil(N/2)*2+1; h = firpm(N,F,I*A,weights);
[Hr,w,a,L] = Ampl_res(h); Hr_min = min(Hr); w_min = find(Hr == Hr_min);
H = abs(freqz(h,1,w)); Hdb = 20*log10(H/max(H)); min_attn = Hdb(w_min);
% Plotting commands follow
```

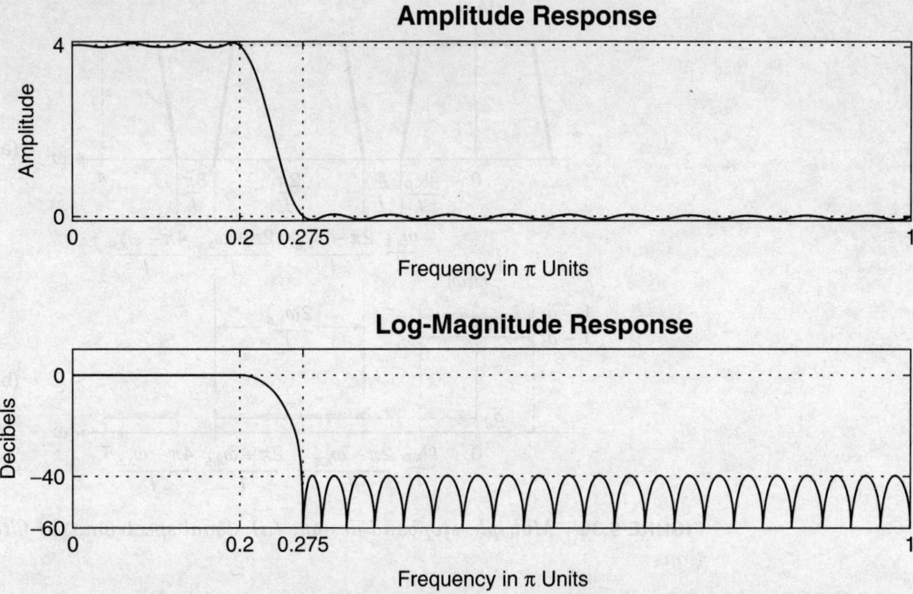

FIGURE 9.29   *The filter design plots in Example 9.16*

The filter responses are shown in Figure 9.29, which shows that the designed filter achieves the attenuation of 40 dB.   □

9.5.6 FIR FILTERS WITH MULTIPLE STOPBANDS

We now discuss the use of multiple stopbands in the design of FIR integer interpolators when the low sampling rate is more than two times that required. Let us refer back to the Figure 9.22b on page 488, which illustrates a typical spectrum $V(\omega)$ in integer interpolators. We could use a lowpass filter with multiple stopbands of bandwidth ω_s/I centered at $2\pi k/I$ for $k \neq 0$. For $I = 4$, such a spectrum is shown in Figure 9.30(a), and the corresponding filter specifications are shown in Figure 9.30b.

Clearly, these filter specifications differ from those given in (9.52) on page 488 in that the stopband is no longer one contiguous interval. Now, if $\omega_s < \pi/2$, then there is a practical advantage to using this multiband design because it results in a lower-order filter [9]. For $\pi \geq \omega_s > \pi/2$, the single-band lowpass filter specification (9.52) is easier and works as well.

Similar advantages can be obtained for FIR integer decimators. We again find that we can substitute a multiple-stopband lowpass filter for the single-stopband design given in (9.57). With reference to the

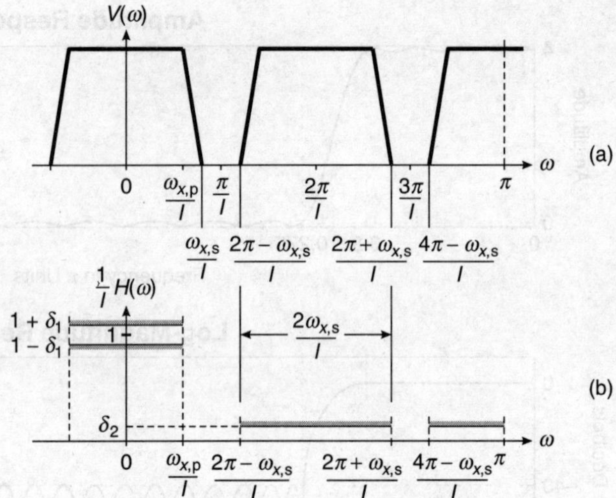

FIGURE 9.30 *Multiple-stopband design: (a) signal spectrum, (b) filter specifications*

signal specifications on page 494, we note that only part of the bands $[\pi/D, 3\pi/D]$, $[3\pi/D, 5\pi/D]$, ... and so on will get aliased into $[-\omega_s, +\omega_s]$. Therefore, the multiple stopbands are given by $[(2\pi/D)-\omega_s, (2\pi/D)+\omega_s]$, $[(4\pi/D)-\omega_s, (4\pi/D)+\omega_s]$, and so on, centered at $2\pi k/D$, $k \neq 0$. Once again, there are practical advantages when $\omega_s < \pi/2M$.

9.6 FIR FILTER STRUCTURES FOR SAMPLING RATE CONVERSION

As indicated in the discussion in Section 9.4, sampling rate conversion by a factor I/D can be achieved by first increasing the sampling rate by I, accomplished by inserting $I - 1$ zeros between successive values of the input signal $x(n)$, followed by linear filtering of the resulting sequence to eliminate the unwanted images of $X(\omega)$, and finally by downsampling the filtered signal by the factor D. In this section, we consider the design and implementation of the linear filter. We begin with the simplest structure, which is the direct form FIR filter structure, and develop its computationally efficient implementation. We then consider another computationally efficient structure called the *polyphase* structure, which is used in the implementation of the MATLAB functions `resample` and `upfirdn`. Finally, we close this section by discussing the time-variant filter structures for the general case of sampling rate conversion.

9.6.1 DIRECT FORM FIR FILTER STRUCTURES

In principle, the simplest realization of the filter is the direct form FIR structure with system function

$$H(z) = \sum_{k=0}^{M-1} h(k)z^{-k} \qquad (9.62)$$

where $h(k)$ is the unit sample response of the FIR filter. After designing the filter as discussed in the previous section, we will have the filter parameters $h(k)$, which allow us to implement the FIR filter directly, as shown in Figure 9.31.

Although the direct form FIR filter realization illustrated in Figure 9.31 is simple, it is also very inefficient. The inefficiency results from the fact that the upsampling process introduces $I-1$ zeros between successive points of the input signal. If I is large, most of the signal components in the FIR filter are zero. Consequently, most of the multiplications and additions result in zeros. Furthermore, the downsampling process at the output of the filter implies that only one out of every D output samples is required at the output of the filter. Consequently, only one out of every D possible values at the output of the filter should be computed.

To develop a more efficient filter structure, let us begin with a decimator that reduces the sampling rate by an integer factor D. From our previous discussion, the decimator is obtained by passing the input sequence

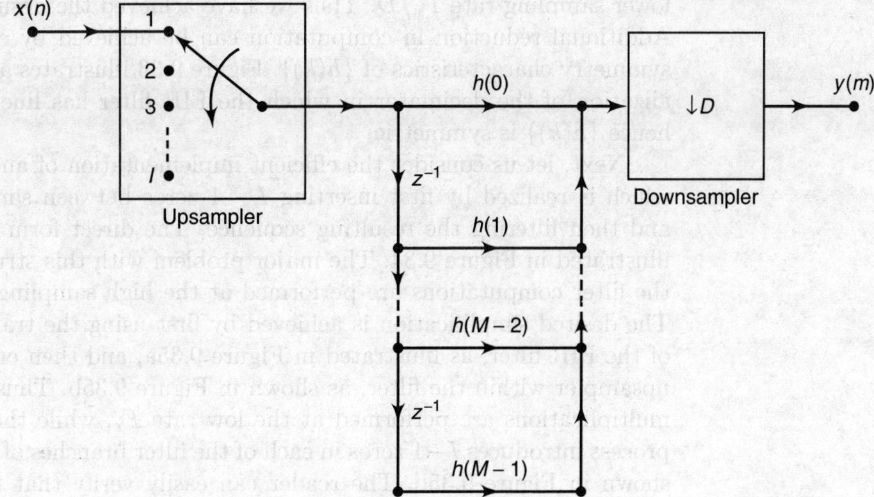

FIGURE 9.31 *Direct form realization of FIR filter in sampling rate conversion by a factor I/D*

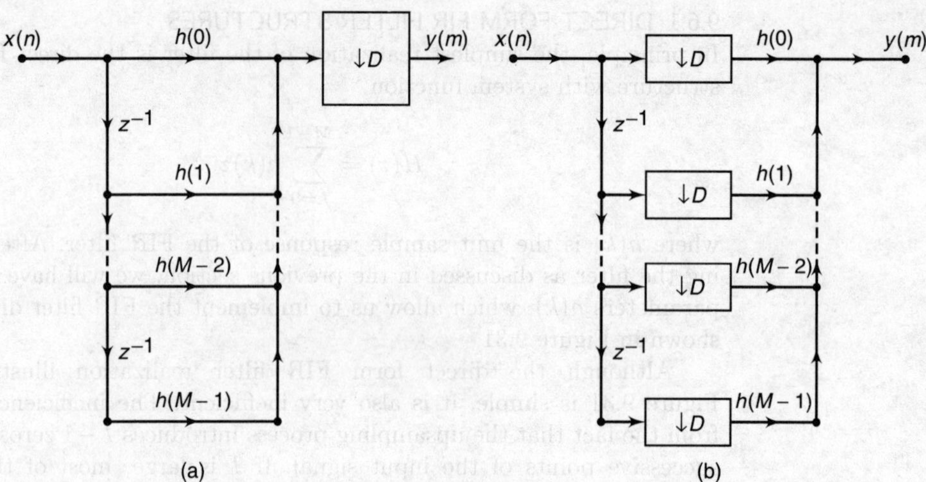

FIGURE 9.32 *Decimation by a factor D: (a) standard realization, (b) efficient realization*

$x(n)$ through an FIR filter and then downsampling the filter output by a factor D, as illustrated in Figure 9.32a. In this configuration, the filter is operating at the high sampling rate F_x, while only one out of every D output samples is actually needed. The logical solution to this inefficiency problem is to embed the downsampling operation within the filter, as illustrated in the filter realization given in Figure 9.32b. In this filter structure, all the multiplications and additions are performed at the lower sampling rate F_x/D. Thus we have achieved the desired efficiency. Additional reduction in computation can be achieved by exploiting the symmetry characteristics of $\{h(k)\}$. Figure 9.33 illustrates an efficient realization of the decimator in which the FIR filter has linear phase and hence $\{h(k)\}$ is symmetric.

Next, let us consider the efficient implementation of an interpolator, which is realized by first inserting $I-1$ zeros between samples of $x(n)$ and then filtering the resulting sequence. The direct form realization is illustrated in Figure 9.34. The major problem with this structure is that the filter computations are performed at the high sampling rate of IF_x. The desired simplification is achieved by first using the transposed form of the FIR filter, as illustrated in Figure 9.35a, and then embedding the upsampler within the filter, as shown in Figure 9.35b. Thus all the filter multiplications are performed at the low rate F_x, while the upsampling process introduces $I-1$ zeros in each of the filter branches of the structure shown in Figure 9.35b. The reader can easily verify that the two filter structures in Figure 9.35 are equivalent.

It is interesting to note that the structure of the interpolator, shown in Figure 9.35b, can be obtained by transposing the structure of the

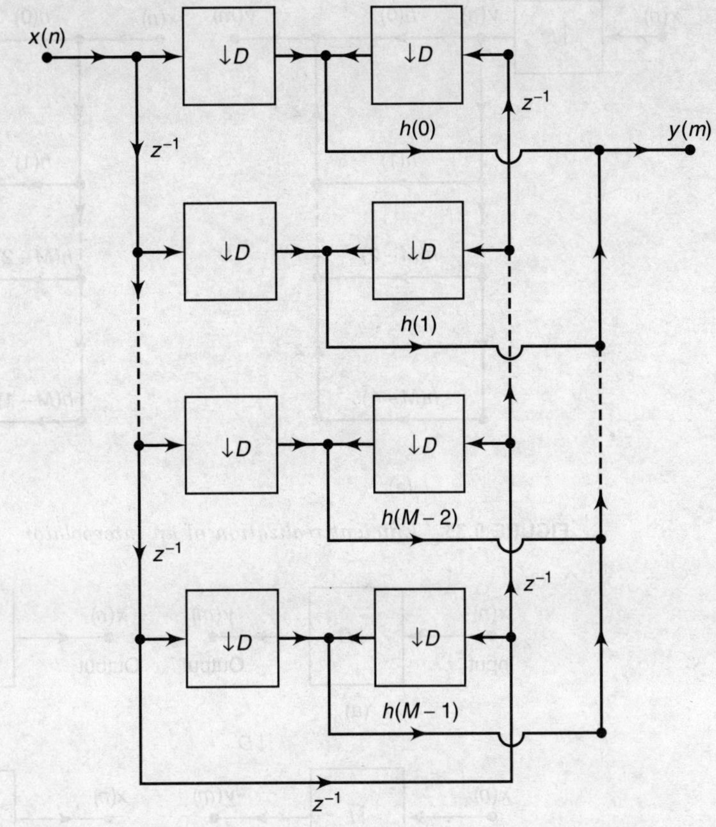

FIGURE 9.33 *Efficient realization of a decimator that exploits the symmetry in the FIR filter*

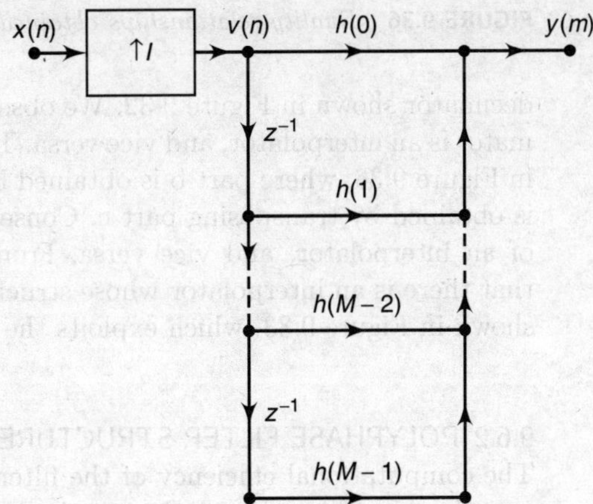

FIGURE 9.34 *Direct form realization of FIR filter in interpolation by a factor I*

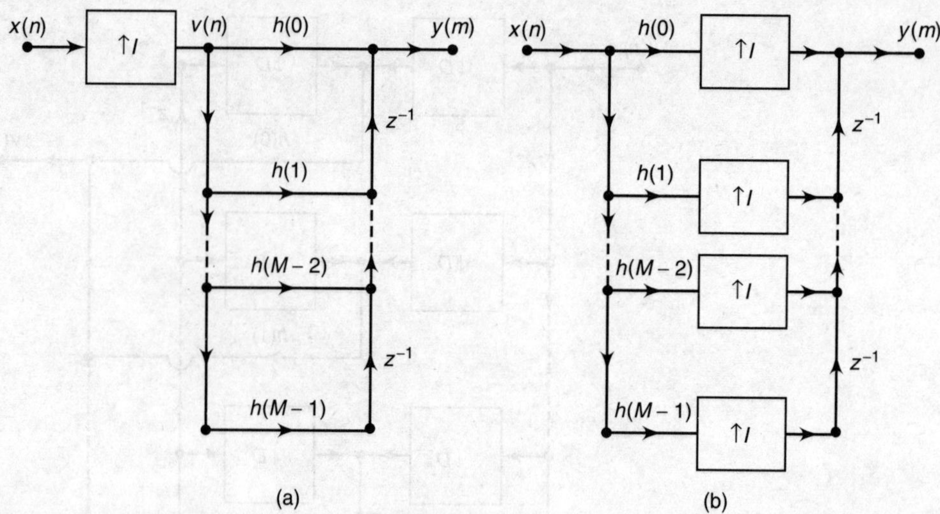

FIGURE 9.35 *Efficient realization of an interpolator*

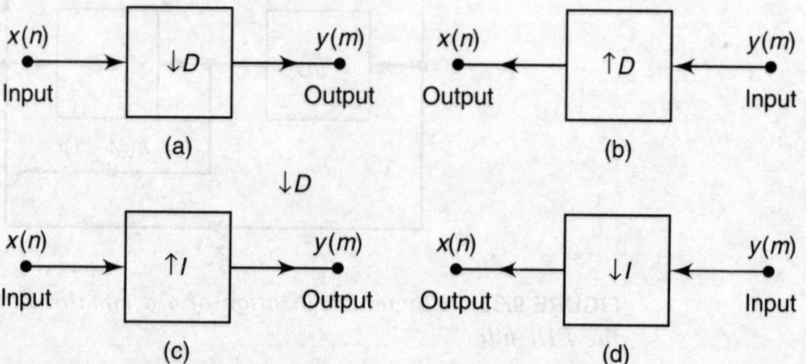

FIGURE 9.36 *Duality relationships obtained through transpositions*

decimator shown in Figure 9.32. We observe that the transpose of a decimator is an interpolator, and vice versa. These relationships are illustrated in Figure 9.36, where part b is obtained by transposing part a and part d is obtained by transposing part c. Consequently, a decimator is the dual of an interpolator, and vice versa. From these relationships, it follows that there is an interpolator whose structure is the dual of the decimator shown in Figure 9.33, which exploits the symmetry in $h(n)$.

9.6.2 POLYPHASE FILTER STRUCTURE

The computational efficiency of the filter structure shown in Figure 9.35 can also be achieved by reducing the large FIR filter of length M into a set of smaller filters of length $K = M/I$, where M is selected to be a multiple of I. To demonstrate this point, let us consider the interpolator given in Figure 9.34. Since the upsampling process inserts $I - 1$ zeros between successive values of $x(n)$, only K out of the M input values stored in the FIR filter at any one time are nonzero. At one time instant, these nonzero values coincide and are multiplied by the filter coefficients $h(0), h(I), h(2I), \ldots, h(M - I)$. In the following time instant, the nonzero values of the input sequence coincide and are multiplied by the filter coefficients $h(1), h(I + 1), h(2I + 1)$, and so on. This observation leads us to define a set of smaller filters, called polyphase filters, with unit sample responses

$$p_k(n) = h(k + nI); \quad k = 0, 1, \ldots, I - 1, \quad n = 0, 1, \ldots, K - 1 \quad \textbf{(9.63)}$$

where $K = M/I$ is an integer.

From this discussion, it follows that the set of I polyphase filters can be arranged as a parallel realization, and the output of each filter can be selected by a commutator, as illustrated in Figure 9.37. The rotation of the commutator is in the counterclockwise direction, beginning with the point at $m = 0$. Thus the polyphase filters perform the computations at the low sampling rate F_x, and the rate conversion results from the fact that I output samples are generated, one from each of the filters, for each input sample.

The decomposition of $\{h(k)\}$ into the set of I subfilters with impulse response $p_k(n), k = 0, 1, \ldots, I - 1$, is consistent with our previous observation that the input signal was being filtered by a periodically time-variant linear filter with impulse response

$$g(n, m) = h(nI + (mD)_I) \quad \textbf{(9.64)}$$

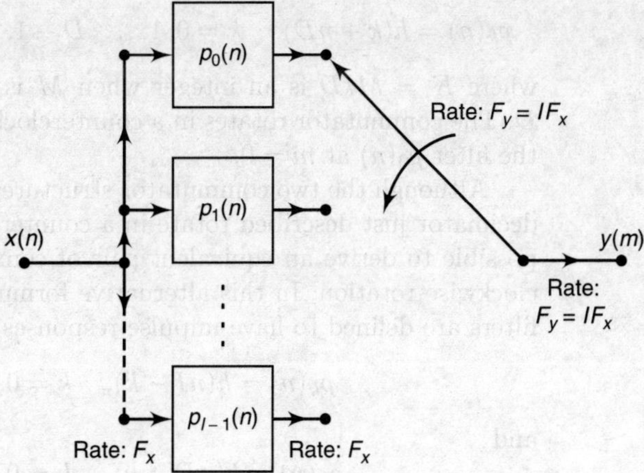

FIGURE 9.37 *Interpolation by use of polyphase filters*

where $D = 1$ in the case of the interpolator. We noted previously that $g(n, m)$ varies periodically with period I. Consequently, a different set of coefficients is used to generate the set of I output samples $y(m), m = 0, 1, \ldots, I - 1$.

Additional insight can be gained about the characteristics of the set of polyphase subfilters by noting that $p_k(n)$ is obtained from $h(n)$ by decimation with a factor I. Consequently, if the original filter frequency response $H(\omega)$ is flat over the range $0 \le |\omega| \le \omega/I$, each of the polyphase subfilters possesses a relatively flat response over the range $0 \le |\omega| \le \pi$ (i.e., the polyphase subfilters are basically allpass filters and differ primarily in their phase characteristics). This explains the reason for using the term *polyphase* in describing these filters.

The polyphase filter can also be viewed as a set of I subfilters connected to a common delay line. Ideally, the kth subfilter will generate a forward time shift of $(k/I)T_x$, for $k = 0, 1, 2, \ldots, I - 1$, relative to the zeroth subfilter. Therefore, if the zeroth filter generates zero delay, the frequency response of the kth subfilter is

$$p_k(\omega) = e^{j\omega k/I}$$

A time shift of an integer number of input sampling intervals (e.g., kT_x) can be generated by shifting the input data in the delay line by I samples and using the same subfilters. By combining these two methods, we can generate an output that is shifted forward by an amount $(k + i/I)T_x$ relative to the previous output.

By transposing the interpolator structure in Figure 9.37, we obtain a commutator structure for a decimator based on the parallel bank of polyphase filters, as illustrated in Figure 9.38. The unit sample responses of the polyphase filters are now defined as

$$p_k(n) = h(k + nD); \quad k = 0, 1, \ldots, D - 1, \quad n = 0, 1, \ldots, K - 1 \quad \textbf{(9.65)}$$

where $K = M/D$ is an integer when M is selected to be a multiple of D. The commutator rotates in a counterclockwise direction, starting with the filter $p_0(n)$ at $m = 0$.

Although the two commutator structures for the interpolator and the decimator just described rotate in a counterclockwise direction, it is also possible to derive an equivalent pair of commutator structures having a clockwise rotation. In this alternative formulation, the sets of polyphase filters are defined to have impulse responses

$$p_k(n) = h(nI - k), \quad k = 0, 1, \ldots, I - 1 \quad \textbf{(9.66)}$$

and

$$p_k(n) = h(nD - k), \quad k = 0, 1, \ldots, D - 1 \quad \textbf{(9.67)}$$

for the interpolator and decimator, respectively.

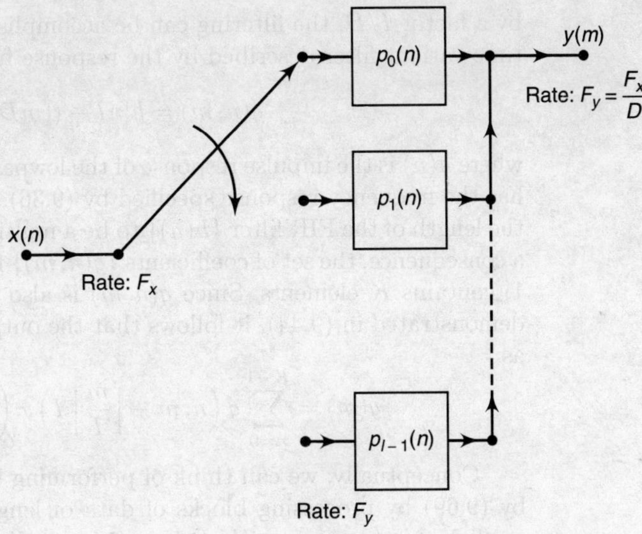

FIGURE 9.38 *Decimation by use of polyphase filters*

☐ **EXAMPLE 9.17**   For the decimation filter designed in Example 9.11, determine the polyphase filter coefficients $\{p_k(n)\}$ in terms of the FIR filter coefficients $\{h(n)\}$.

Solution   The polyphase filters obtained from $h(n)$ have impulse responses

$$p_k(n) = h(2n + k) \quad k = 0,1; \quad n = 0,1,\ldots,14$$

Note that $p_0(n) = h(2n)$ and $p_1(n) = h(2n + 1)$. Hence one filter consists of the even-numbered samples of $h(n)$, and the other filter consists of the odd-numbered samples of $h(n)$.   ☐

☐ **EXAMPLE 9.18**   For the interpolation filter designed in Example 9.8, determine the polyphase filter coefficients $\{p_k(n)\}$ in terms of the filter coefficients $\{h(n)\}$.

Solution   The polyphase filters obtained from $h(n)$ have impulse responses

$$p_k(n) = h(5n + k) \quad k = 0,1,2,3,4$$

Consequently, each filter has length 6.   ☐

9.6.3 TIME-VARIANT FILTER STRUCTURES

Having described the filter implementation for a decimator and an interpolator, let us now consider the general problem of sampling rate conversion by the factor I/D. In the general case of sampling rate conversion by a factor I/D, the filtering can be accomplished by means of the linear time-variant filter described by the response function

$$g(n, m) = h[nI - ((mD))_I] \tag{9.68}$$

where $h(n)$ is the impulse response of the lowpass FIR filter, which, ideally, has the frequency response specified by (9.36). For convenience, we select the length of the FIR filter $\{h(n)\}$ to be a multiple of I (i.e., $M = KI$). As a consequence, the set of coefficients $\{g(n, m)\}$ for each $m = 0, 1, 2, \ldots, I - 1$, contains K elements. Since $g(n, m)$ is also periodic with period I, as demonstrated in (9.44), it follows that the output $y(m)$ can be expressed as

$$y(m) = \sum_{n=0}^{K-1} g\left(n, m - \left\lfloor \frac{m}{I} \right\rfloor I\right) x\left(\left\lfloor \frac{mD}{I} \right\rfloor - n\right) \tag{9.69}$$

Conceptually, we can think of performing the computations specified by (9.69) by processing blocks of data of length K by a set of K filter coefficients $g(n, m - \lfloor m/I \rfloor I), n = 0, 1, \ldots, K - 1$. There are I such sets of coefficients, one set for each block of I output points of $y(m)$. For each block of I output points, there is a corresponding block of D input points of $x(n)$ that enter in the computation.

The block processing algorithm for computing (9.69) can be visualized as illustrated in Figure 9.39. A block of D input samples is buffered and shifted into a second buffer of length K, one sample at a time. The shifting from the input buffer to the second buffer occurs at a rate of one

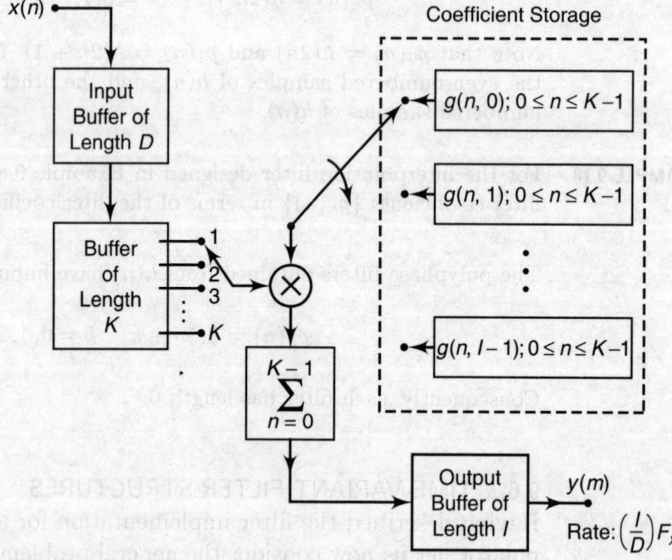

FIGURE 9.39 *Efficient implementation of sampling rate conversion by block processing*

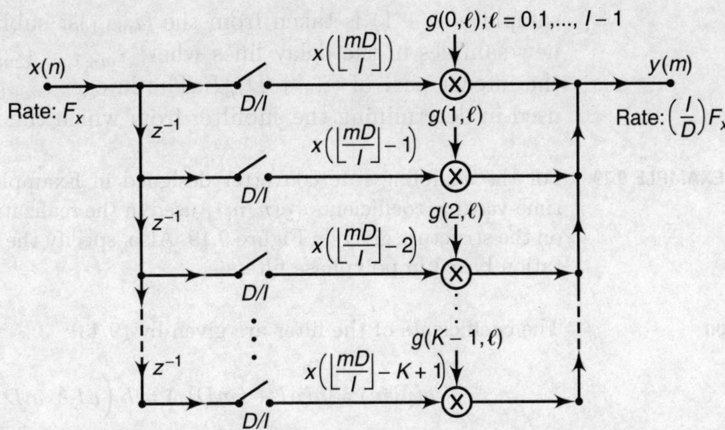

FIGURE 9.40 *Efficient realization of sampling rate conversion by a factor I/D*

sample each time the quantity $\lfloor mD/I \rfloor$ increases by 1. For each output sample $y(l)$, the samples from the second buffer are multiplied by the corresponding set of filter coefficients $g(n,l)$ for $n = 0, 1, \ldots, K-1$, and the K products are accumulated to give $y(l)$, for $l = 0, 1, \ldots, I-1$. Thus this computation produces I outputs. It is then repeated for a new set of D input samples, and so on.

An alternative method for computing the output of the sampling rate converter, specified by (9.69), is by means of an FIR filter structure with periodically varying filter coefficients. Such a structure is illustrated in Figure 9.40. The input samples $x(n)$ are passed into a shift register that operates at the sampling rate F_x and is of length $K = M/I$, where M is the length of the time-invariant FIR filter specified by the frequency response given by (9.36). Each stage of the register is connected to a hold-and-sample device that serves to couple the input sampling rate F_x to the output sampling rate $F_y = (I/D)F_x$. The sample at the input to each hold-and-sample device is held until the next input sample arrives and then is discarded. The output samples on the hold-and-sample device are taken at times $mD/I, m = 0, 1, 2, \ldots$. When both the input and output sampling times coincide (i.e., when mD/I is an integer), the input to the hold-and-sample is changed first; then the output samples the new input. The K outputs from the K hold-and-sample devices are multiplied by the periodically time-varying coefficients $g(n, m - \lfloor m/I \rfloor I)$, for $n = 0, 1, \ldots, K-1$, and the resulting products are summed to yield $y(m)$. The computations at the output of the hold-and-sample devices are repeated at the output sampling rate of $F_y = (I/D)F_x$.

Finally, rate conversion by a rational factor I/D can also be performed by use of a polyphase filter having I subfilters. If we assume that the mth sample $y(m)$ is computed by taking the output of the i_mth subfilter with input data $x(n), x(n-1), \ldots, x(n-K+1)$, in the delay line, the next sample $y(m+1)$ is taken from the (i_{m+1})st subfilter after shifting l_{m+1} new samples in the delay lines where $i_{m+1} = (i_m + D)_{\mathrm{mod}I}$ and l_{m+1} is the integer part of $(i_m + D)/I$. The integer i_{m+1} should be saved to be used in determining the subfilter from which the next sample is taken.

☐ **EXAMPLE 9.19**   For the sampling rate converter designed in Example 9.15, specify the set of time-varying coefficients $\{g(n, m)\}$ used in the realization of the converter based on the structure given in Figure 9.19. Also, specify the corresponding implementation based in polyphase filters.

Solution   The coefficients of the filter are given by (9.43):

$$g(n,m) = h(nI + (mD)_I) = h\left(nI + mD - \left\lfloor \frac{D}{I}m \right\rfloor I\right)$$

By substituting $I = 5$ and $D = 2$, we obtain

$$g(n,m) = h\left(5n + 2m - 5\left\lfloor \frac{2m}{5} \right\rfloor\right)$$

By evaluating $g(n, m)$ for $n = 0, 1, \ldots, 5$ and $m = 0, 1, \ldots, 4$, we obtain the following coefficients for the time-variant filter:

$$\begin{aligned}
g(0,m) &= \{h(0)\quad h(2)\quad h(4)\quad h(1)\quad h(3)\} \\
g(1,m) &= \{h(5)\quad h(7)\quad h(9)\quad h(6)\quad h(8)\} \\
g(2,m) &= \{h(10)\ h(12)\ h(14)\ h(11)\ h(13)\} \\
g(3,m) &= \{h(15)\ h(17)\ h(19)\ h(16)\ h(18)\} \\
g(4,m) &= \{h(20)\ h(22)\ h(24)\ h(21)\ h(23)\} \\
g(5,m) &= \{h(25)\ h(27)\ h(29)\ h(26)\ h(28)\}
\end{aligned}$$

A polyphase filter implementation would employ five subfilters, each of length 6. To decimate the output of the polyphase filters by a factor of $D = 2$ simply means that we take every other output from the polyphase filters. Thus the first output $y(0)$ is taken from $p_0(n)$, the second output $y(1)$ is taken from $p_2(n)$, the third output is taken from $p_4(n)$, the fourth output is taken from $p_1(n)$, the fifth output is taken from $p_3(n)$, and so on.   ☐

9.7 PROBLEMS

P9.1   Consider the upsampler with input $x(n)$ and output $v(m)$ given in (9.26). Show that the upsampler is a linear but time-varying system.

P9.2   Let $x(n) = 0.9^n u(n)$. The signal is applied to a downsampler that reduces the rate by a factor of 2 to obtain the signal $y(m)$.

1. Determine and plot the spectrum $X(\omega)$.
2. Determine and plot the spectrum $Y(\omega)$.
3. Show that the spectrum in part (2) is simply the DTFT of $x(2n)$.

P9.3   Consider a signal with spectrum

$$X(\omega) = \begin{cases} \text{nonzero,} & |\omega| \leq \omega_0 \\ 0, & \omega_0 < |\omega| \leq \pi \end{cases}$$

1. Show that the signal $x(n)$ can be recovered from its samples $x(mD)$ if the sampling frequency $\omega_{\mathrm{s}} \triangleq 2\pi/D \geq 2\omega_0$.
2. Sketch the spectra of $x(n)$ and $x(mD)$ for $D = 4$.
3. Show that $x(n)$ can reconstructed from the bandlimited interpolation

$$x(n) = \sum_{k=-\infty}^{\infty} x(kD)\,\text{sinc}[f_{\mathrm{c}}(n - kD)]; \quad \omega_0 < 2\pi f_{\mathrm{c}} < \omega_{\mathrm{s}} - \omega_0, f_{\mathrm{c}} = \frac{1}{D}$$

P9.4   Using the function `downsample`, study the operation of factor-of-4 downsampling on the following sequences. Use the `stem` function to plot the original and the downsampled sequences. Experiment using the default offset value of zero and the offset value equal to 2. Comment on any differences.

1. $x_1(n) = \cos(0.15\pi n)$, $0 \leq n \leq 100$
2. $x_2(n) = \sin(0.1\pi n) + \sin(0.4\pi n)$, $0 \leq n \leq 100$
3. $x_3(n) = 1 - \cos(0.25\pi n)$, $0 \leq n \leq 100$
4. $x_4(n) = 0.1\,n$, $0 \leq n \leq 100$
5. $x_5(n) = \{0,1,2,3,4,5,4,3,2,1\}_{\text{PERIODIC}}$, $0 \leq n \leq 100$

P9.5   Repeat Problem P9.4 using the factor-of-5 downsampler.

P9.6   Using the `fir2` function, generate a 101-length sequence $x(n)$ whose frequency-domain sampled-values are 0.5 at $\omega = 0$, 1 at $\omega = 0.1\pi$, 1 at $\omega = 0.2$, 0 at $\omega = 0.22\pi$, and 0 at $\omega = \pi$.

1. Compute and plot the DTFT magnitude of $x(n)$.
2. Downsample $x(n)$ by a factor of 2, and plot the DTFT of the resulting sequence.
3. Downsample $x(n)$ by a factor of 4, and plot the DTFT of the resulting sequence.
4. Downsample $x(n)$ by a factor of 5, and plot the DTFT of the resulting sequence.
5. Comment on your results.

P9.7   Using the function `decimate`, study the operation of factor-of-4 decimation on the following sequences. Use the `stem` function to plot the original and the decimated sequences. Experiment, using both the default IIR and FIR decimation filters. Comment on any differences.

1. $x_1(n) = \sin(0.15\pi n)$, $0 \leq n \leq 100$
2. $x_2(n) = \cos(0.1\pi n) + \cos(0.4\pi n)$, $0 \leq n \leq 100$
3. $x_3(n) = 1 - \cos(0.25\pi n)$, $0 \leq n \leq 100$
4. $x_4(n) = 0.1\,n$, $0 \leq n \leq 100$
5. $x_5(n) = \{0,1,2,3,4,5,4,3,2,1\}_{\text{PERIODIC}}$, $0 \leq n \leq 100$

P9.8   Repeat Problem P9.7 using the 4th-order IIR filter and the 15th-order FIR decimation filters. Comment on any performance differences.

P9.9   Repeat Problem P9.7 using the factor-of-5 decimation. Comment on any differences.

P9.10   Repeat Problem P9.9 using the the 4th-order IIR filter and the 15th-order FIR decimation filters. Comment on any differences.

P9.11 Using the `fir2` function, generate a 101-length sequence $x(n)$ whose frequency-domain sampled-values are 0.5 at $\omega = 0$, 1 at $\omega = 0.1\pi$, 1 at $\omega = 0.2$, 0 at $\omega = 0.22\pi$, and 0 at $\omega = \pi$.

  1. Compute and plot the DTFT of $x(n)$.
  2. Decimate $x(n)$ by a factor of 2, and plot the DTFT of the resulting sequence.
  3. Decimate $x(n)$ by a factor of 4, and plot the DTFT of the resulting sequence.
  4. Decimate $x(n)$ by a factor of 5, and plot the DTFT of the resulting sequence.
  5. Comment on your results.

P9.12 Using the function `upsample`, study the operation of factor-of-4 upsampling on the following sequences. Use the `stem` function to plot the original and the upsampled sequences. Experiment using the default offset value of zero and the offset value equal to 2.

  1. $x_1(n) = \sin(0.6\pi n)$, $0 \le n \le 100$
  2. $x_2(n) = \sin(0.8\pi n) + \cos(0.5\pi n)$, $0 \le n \le 100$
  3. $x_3(n) = 1 + \cos(\pi n)$, $0 \le n \le 100$
  4. $x_4(n) = 0.2\,n$, $0 \le n \le 100$
  5. $x_5(n) = \{1,1,1,1,0,0,0,0,0,0\}_{\text{PERIODIC}}$, $0 \le n \le 100$

P9.13 Using the `fir2` function, generate a 91-length sequence $x(n)$ whose frequency-domain sampled-values are 0 at $\omega = 0$, 0.5 at $\omega = 0.1\pi$, 1 at $\omega = 0.2$, 1 at $\omega = 0.7\pi$, 0.5 at $\omega = 0.75\pi$, 0 at $\omega = 0.8\pi$, and 0 at $\omega = \pi$.

  1. Compute and plot the DTFT magnitude of $x(n)$.
  2. Upsample $x(n)$ by a factor of 2, and plot the DTFT magnitude of the resulting sequence.
  3. Upsample $x(n)$ by a factor of 3, and plot the DTFT magnitude of the resulting sequence.
  4. Upsample $x(n)$ by a factor of 4, and plot the DTFT magnitude of the resulting sequence.
  5. Comment on your results.

P9.14 Using the function `interp`, study the operation of factor-of-4 interpolation on the sequences of Problem P9.12. Use the `stem` function to plot the original and the interpolated sequences. Experiment, using the filter length parameter values equal to 3 and 5. Comment on any differences in performance of the interpolation.

P9.15 Provide the frequency response plots of the lowpass filters used in the interpolators of Problem P9.14.

P9.16 Repeat Problem P9.14, using the factor-of-3 interpolation.

P9.17 Provide the frequency response plots of the lowpass filters used in the interpolators of Problem P9.16.

P9.18 Repeat Problem P9.14, using the factor-of-5 interpolation.

P9.19 Provide the frequency response plots of the lowpass filters used in the interpolators of Problem P9.18.

P9.20 Using the `fir2` function generate a 91-length sequence $x(n)$ whose frequency-domain sampled-values are 0 at $\omega = 0$, 0.5 at $\omega = 0.1\pi$, 1 at $\omega = 0.2$, 1 at $\omega = 0.7\pi$, 0.5 at $\omega = 0.75\pi$, 0 at $\omega = 0.8\pi$, and 0 at $\omega = \pi$.

1. Compute and plot the DTFT of $x(n)$.
2. Interpolate $x(n)$ by a factor of 2, and plot the DTFT of the resulting sequence.
3. Interpolate $x(n)$ by a factor of 3, and plot the DTFT of the resulting sequence.
4. Interpolate $x(n)$ by a factor of 4, and plot the DTFT of the resulting sequence.
5. Comment on your results.

P9.21 Consider two sequences $x_1(n)$ and $x_2(n)$, which appear to be related:

$$x_1(n) = \max\left(10 - |n|, 0\right) \quad \text{and} \quad x_2(n) = \min\left(|n|, 10\right)$$

Use the `resample` function with default parameters.

1. Resample the sequence $x_1(n)$ at 3/2 times the original rate to obtain $y_1(m)$, and provide the `stem` plots of both sequences.
2. Resample the sequence $x_2(n)$ at 3/2 times the original rate to obtain $y_2(m)$, and provide the `stem` plots of both sequences.
3. Explain why the resampled plot of $y_2(n)$ has inaccuracies near the boundaries that $y_1(n)$ does not have.
4. Plot the frequency response of the filter used in the resampling operation.

P9.22 Let $x(n) = \cos(0.1\pi n) + 0.5\sin(0.2\pi n) + 0.25\cos(0.4\pi n)$. Use the `resample` function with default parameters.

1. Resample the sequence $x(n)$ at 4/5 times the original rate to obtain $y_1(m)$, and provide the `stem` plots of both sequences.
2. Resample the sequence $x(n)$ at 5/4 times the original rate to obtain $y_2(m)$, and provide the `stem` plots of both sequences.
3. Resample the sequence $x(n)$ at 2/3 times the original rate to obtain $y_3(m)$, and provide the `stem` plots of both sequences.
4. Explain which of the three output sequences retain the "shape" of the original sequence $x(n)$.

P9.23 Let $x(n) = \{0, 0, 0, 1, 1, 1, 1, 0, 0, 0\}_{\text{PERIODIC}}$ be a periodic sequence with period 10. Use the `resample` function for the following parts to resample the sequence $x(n)$ at 3/5 times the original rate. Consider the length of the input sequence to be 80.

1. Use the filter length parameter L equal to zero to obtain $y_1(m)$, and provide the `stem` plots of $x(n)$ and $y_1(m)$ sequences.
2. Use the default value of the filter length parameter L to obtain $y_2(m)$, and provide the `stem` plots of $x(n)$ and $y_2(m)$ sequences.
3. Use the filter length parameter L equal to 15 to obtain $y_3(m)$, and provide the `stem` plots of $x(n)$ and $y_3(m)$ sequences.

P9.24 Using the `fir2` function, generate a 101-length sequence $x(n)$ whose frequency-domain sampled-values are 0 at $\omega = 0$, 0.5 at $\omega = 0.1\pi$, 1 at $\omega = 0.2\pi$, 1 at $\omega = 0.5\pi$, 0.5 at $\omega = 0.55\pi$, 0 at $\omega = 0.6\pi$, and 0 at $\omega = \pi$.

1. Compute and plot the DTFT of $x(n)$.
2. Resample $x(n)$ by a factor of 4/3, and plot the DTFT of the resulting sequence.
3. Resample $x(n)$ by a factor of 3/4, and plot the DTFT of the resulting sequence.
4. Resample $x(n)$ by a factor of 4/5, and plot the DTFT of the resulting sequence.
5. Comment on your results.

P9.25 We want to design a linear-phase FIR filter to increase the input sampling rate by a factor
of 3 using the `intfilt` function.

1. Assuming full bandwidth of the signal to be interpolated, determine the impulse
   response of the required FIR filter. Plot its amplitude response and the log-magnitude
   response in dB. Experiment with the length parameter L to obtain a reasonable
   stopband attenuation.
2. Assuming that bandwidth of the signal to be interpolated is $\pi/2$, determine the
   impulse response of the required FIR filter. Plot its amplitude response and the
   log-magnitude response in decibels. Again, experiment with the length parameter L to
   obtain a reasonable stopband attenuation.

P9.26 We want to design a linear-phase FIR filter to increase the input sampling rate by a factor
of 5 using the `intfilt` function.

1. Assuming full bandwidth of the signal to be interpolated, determine the impulse
   response of the required FIR filter. Plot its amplitude response and the log-magnitude
   response in decibels. Experiment with the length parameter L to obtain a reasonable
   stopband attenuation.
2. Assuming that bandwidth of the signal to be interpolated is $4\pi/5$, determine the
   impulse response of the required FIR filter. Plot its amplitude response and the
   log-magnitude response in decibels. Again, experiment with the length parameter L to
   obtain a reasonable stopband attenuation.

P9.27 Using the Parks–McClellan algorithm, design an interpolator that increases the input
sampling rate by a factor of $I = 2$.

1. Determine the coefficients of the FIR filter that has 0.5 dB ripple in the passband and
   50 dB attenuation in the stopband. Choose reasonable values for the band-edge
   frequencies.
2. Provide plots of the impulse and the log-magnitude responses.
3. Determine the corresponding polyphase structure for implementing the filter.
4. Let $x(n) = \cos(0.4\pi n)$. Generate 100 samples of $x(n)$, and process it using this filter to
   interpolate by $I = 2$ to obtain $y(m)$. Provide the `stem` plots of the both sequences.

P9.28 Using the Parks–McClellan algorithm, design an interpolator that increases the input
sampling rate by a factor of $I = 3$.

1. Determine the coefficients of the FIR filter that has 0.1 dB ripple in the passband and
   40 dB attenuation in the stopband. Choose reasonable values for the band-edge
   frequencies.
2. Provide plots of the impulse and the log-magnitude responses.
3. Determine the corresponding polyphase structure for implementing the filter.
4. Let $x(n) = \cos(0.3\pi n)$. Generate 100 samples of $x(n)$ and process it using this filter to
   interpolate by $I = 3$ to obtain $y(m)$. Provide the `stem` plots of both sequences.

P9.29 A signal $x(n)$ is to be interpolated by a factor of 3. It has a bandwidth of 0.4π, but we
want to preserve frequency band up to 0.3π in the interpolated signal. Using the
Parks–McClellan algorithm, we want to design such an interpolator.

1. Determine the coefficients of the FIR filter that has 0.1 dB ripple in the passband and
   40 dB attenuation in the stopband.
2. Provide plots of the impulse and the log-magnitude responses.

3. Let $x(n) = \cos(0.3\pi n) + 0.5\sin(0.4\pi n)$. Generate 100 samples of $x(n)$, and process it using this filter to interpolate by $I = 3$ to obtain $y(m)$. Provide the **stem** plots of both sequences.

P9.30 A signal $x(n)$ is to be interpolated by a factor of 4. It has a bandwidth of 0.7π, but we want to preserve frequency band up to 0.6π in the interpolated signal. Using the Parks–McClellan algorithm, we want to design such an interpolator.

1. Determine the coefficients of the FIR filter that has 0.5 dB ripple in the passband and 50 dB attenuation in the stopband.
2. Provide plots of the impulse and the log-magnitude responses.
3. Let $x(n) = \sin(0.5\pi n) + \cos(0.7\pi n)$. Generate 100 samples of $x(n)$ and process it using this filter to interpolate by $I = 4$ to obtain $y(m)$. Provide the **stem** plots of both sequences.

P9.31 Using the Parks–McClellan algorithm, design a decimator that downsamples an input signal $x(n)$ by a factor of $D = 5$.

1. Determine the coefficients of the FIR filter that has 0.1 dB ripple in the passband and 30 dB attenuation in the stopband. Choose reasonable values for the band-edge frequencies.
2. Provide plots of the impulse and the log-magnitude responses.
3. Determine the corresponding polyphase structure for implementing the filter.
4. Using the **fir2** function, generate a 131-length sequence $x(n)$ whose frequency-domain sampled-values are 1 at $\omega = 0$, 0.9 at $\omega = 0.1\pi$, 1 at $\omega = 0.2\pi$, 1 at $\omega = 0.5\pi$, 0.5 at $\omega = 0.55\pi$, 0 at $\omega = 0.6\pi$, and 0 at $\omega = \pi$. Process $x(n)$ using this filter to decimate it by a factor of 5 to obtain $y(m)$. Provide the spectral plots of both sequences.

P9.32 Using the Parks–McClellan algorithm, design a decimator that downsamples an input signal $x(n)$ by a factor of $D = 3$.

1. Determine the coefficients of the FIR filter that has 0.5 dB ripple in the passband and 30 dB attenuation in the stopband. Choose reasonable values for the band-edge frequencies.
2. Provide plots of the impulse and the log-magnitude responses.
3. Let $x_1(n) = \sin(0.2\pi n) + 0.2\cos(0.5\pi n)$. Generate 500 samples of $x_1(n)$, and process it using this to decimate by $D = 3$ to obtain $y_1(m)$. Provide the **stem** plots of both sequences.
4. Using the **fir2** function, generate a 131-length sequence $x_2(n)$ whose frequency-domain sampled-values are 1 at $\omega = 0$, 0.8 at $\omega = 0.15\pi$, 1 at $\omega = 0.3\pi$, 1 at $\omega = 0.4\pi$, 0.5 at $\omega = 0.45\pi$, 0 at $\omega = 0.5\pi$, and 0 at $\omega = \pi$. Process $x_2(n)$, using this filter to decimate it by a factor of 3 to obtain $y_2(m)$. Provide the spectral plots of both sequences.

P9.33 A signal $x(n)$ is to be decimated by a factor of $D = 2$. It has a bandwidth of 0.4π, and we will tolerate aliasing this frequency 0.45π in the decimated signal. Using the Parks–McClellan algorithm, we want to design such a decimator.

1. Determine the coefficients of the FIR filter that has 0.1 dB ripple in the passband and 45 dB attenuation in the stopband.
2. Provide plots of the impulse and the log-magnitude responses.
3. Let $x_1(n) = \cos(0.4\pi n) + 2\sin(0.45\pi n)$. Generate 200 samples of $x_1(n)$, and process it using this filter to decimate by $D = 2$ to obtain $y_1(m)$. Provide the **stem** plots of both sequences.

4. Using the `fir2` function, generate a 151-length sequence $x_2(n)$ whose frequency-domain sampled-values are 1 at $\omega = 0$, 0.9 at $\omega = 0.2\pi$, 1 at $\omega = 0.4\pi$, 0.5 at $\omega = 0.45\pi$, 0 at $\omega = 0.5\pi$, and 0 at $\omega = \pi$. Process $x_2(n)$, using this filter to decimate it by a factor of 2 to obtain $y_2(m)$. Provide the spectral plots of both sequences.

P9.34 A signal $x(n)$ is to be decimated by a factor of $D = 3$. It has a bandwidth of 0.25π, and we will tolerate aliasing this frequency 0.3π in the decimated signal. Using the Parks–McClellan algorithm, we want to design such a decimator.

1. Determine the coefficients of the FIR filter that has 0.1 dB ripple in the passband and 40 dB attenuation in the stopband.
2. Provide plots of the impulse and the log-magnitude responses.
3. Let $x_1(n) = \cos(0.2\pi n) + 2\sin(0.3\pi n)$. Generate 300 samples of $x_1(n)$, and process it using this filter to decimate by $D = 3$ to obtain $y_1(m)$. Provide the **stem** plots of both sequences.
4. Using the `fir2` function, generate a 151-length sequence $x_2(n)$ whose frequency-domain sampled-values are 1 at $\omega = 0$, 1 at $\omega = 0.1\pi$, 1 at $\omega = 0.25\pi$, 0.5 at $\omega = 0.3\pi$, 0 at $\omega = 0.35\pi$, and 0 at $\omega = \pi$. Process $x_2(n)$, using this filter to decimate it by a factor of 3 to obtain $y_2(m)$. Provide the spectral plots of both sequences.

P9.35 Design a sampling rate converter that reduces the sampling rate by a factor of 2/5.

1. Using the Parks–McClellan algorithm, determine the coefficients of the FIR filter that has 0.1 dB ripple in the passband and 30 dB attenuation in the stopband. Choose reasonable values for the band-edge frequencies.
2. Provide plots of the impulse and the log-magnitude responses.
3. Specify the sets of the time-varying coefficients $g(m, n)$ and the corresponding coefficients in the polyphase filter realization.
4. Let $x(n) = \sin(0.35\pi n) + 2\cos(0.45\pi n)$. Generate 500 samples of $x(n)$ and process it using this filter to resample by 2/5 to obtain $y(m)$. Provide the **stem** plots of both sequences.

P9.36 Design a sampling rate converter that increases the sampling rate by a factor of 7/4.

1. Using the Parks–McClellan algorithm, determine the coefficients of the FIR filter that has 0.1 dB ripple in the passband and 40 dB attenuation in the stopband. Choose reasonable values for the band-edge frequencies.
2. Provide plots of the impulse and the log-magnitude responses.
3. Specify the sets of the time-varying coefficients $g(m, n)$ and the corresponding coefficients in the polyphase filter realization.
4. Let $x(n) = 2\sin(0.35\pi n) + \cos(0.95\pi n)$. Generate 500 samples of $x(n)$ and process it, using this filter to resample by 7/4 to obtain $y(m)$. Provide the **stem** plots of both sequences.

P9.37 A signal $x(n)$ is to be resampled by a factor of 3/2. It has a total bandwidth of 0.8π, but we want to preserve frequencies only up to 0.6π and require that the band up to 0.75π be free of aliasing in the resampled signal.

1. Using the Parks–McClellan algorithm, determine the coefficients of the FIR filter that has 0.5 dB ripple in the passband and 50 dB attenuation in the stopband.
2. Provide plots of the impulse and the log-magnitude responses.

3. Using the `fir2` function, generate a 101-length sequence $x(n)$ whose frequency-domain sampled-values are 0.7 at $\omega = 0$, 1 at $\omega = 0.3\pi$, 1 at $\omega = 0.7\pi$, 0.5 at $\omega = 0.75\pi$, 0 at $\omega = 0.8\pi$, and 0 at $\omega = \pi$. Process $x(n)$ using this filter to resample it by 3/2 to obtain $y(m)$. Provide the spectral plots of both sequences.

P9.38 A signal $x(n)$ is to be resampled by a factor of 4/5. It has a total bandwidth of 0.8π, but we want to preserve frequencies only up to 0.5π and require that the band up to 0.75π be free of aliasing in the resampled signal.

1. Using the Parks–McClellan algorithm, determine the coefficients of the FIR filter that has 0.1 dB ripple in the passband and 40 dB attenuation in the stopband.
2. Provide plots of the impulse and the log-magnitude responses.
3. Using the `fir2` function, generate a 101-length sequence $x(n)$ whose frequency-domain sampled-values are 0.7 at $\omega = 0$, 1 at $\omega = 0.3\pi$, 1 at $\omega = 0.7\pi$, 0.5 at $\omega = 0.75\pi$, 0 at $\omega = 0.8\pi$, and 0 at $\omega = \pi$. Process $x(n)$, using this filter to resample it by 4/5 to obtain $y(m)$. Provide the spectral plots of both sequences.

P9.39 A signal $x(n)$ is to be resampled by a factor of 5/2. It has a total bandwidth of 0.8π, but we want to preserve frequencies only up to 0.7π and require that the band up to 0.75π be free of aliasing in the resampled signal.

1. Using the Parks–McClellan algorithm, determine the coefficients of the FIR filter that has 0.5 dB ripple in the passband and 50 dB attenuation in the stopband.
2. Provide plots of the impulse and the log-magnitude responses.
3. Using the `fir2` function, generate a 101-length sequence $x(n)$ whose frequency-domain sampled-values are 0.7 at $\omega = 0$, 1 at $\omega = 0.3\pi$, 1 at $\omega = 0.7\pi$, 0.5 at $\omega = 0.75\pi$, 0 at $\omega = 0.8\pi$, and 0 at $\omega = \pi$. Process $x(n)$ using this filter to resample it by a 5/2 to obtain $y(m)$. Provide the spectral plots of both sequences.

P9.40 A signal $x(n)$ is to be resampled by a factor of 3/8. It has a total bandwidth of 0.5π, but we want to preserve frequencies only up to 0.3π and require that the band up to 0.35π be free of aliasing in the resampled signal.

1. Using the Parks–McClellan algorithm, determine the coefficients of the FIR filter that has 0.1 dB ripple in the passband and 40 dB attenuation in the stopband.
2. Provide plots of the impulse and the log-magnitude responses.
3. Using the `fir2` function, generate a 101-length sequence $x(n)$ whose frequency-domain sampled-values are 1 at $\omega = 0$, 1 at $\omega = 0.25\pi$, 1 at $\omega = 0.5\pi$, 0.5 at $\omega = 0.55\pi$, 0 at $\omega = 0.6\pi$, and 0 at $\omega = \pi$. Process $x(n)$ using this filter to resample it by 3/8 to obtain $y(m)$. Provide the spectral plots of both sequences.

CHAPTER 10

Round-Off Effects in Digital Filters

In the latter part of Chapter 6, we discussed the finite-precision number representations for the purpose of implementing filtering operations on digital hardware. In particular, we focused on the process of number quantization, the resulting error characterizations, and the effects of filter coefficient quantization on filter specifications and responses. In this chapter, we further extend the effects of finite-precision numerical effects to the filtering aspects in signal processing.

We begin by discussing analog-to-digital (A/D) conversion noise using the number representations and quantization error characteristics developed in Chapter 6. We then analyze the multiplication and addition quantization (collectively known as arithmetic round-off error) models. The effects of these errors on filter output are discussed as two topics: correlated errors called *limit cycles* and uncorrelated *round-off noise*.

10.1 ANALYSIS OF A/D QUANTIZATION NOISE

From the quantizer characteristics obtained in Chapter 6, it is obvious that the quantized value $Q[x]$ is a nonlinear operation on the value x. Hence the exact analysis of the finite word-length effects in digital filters is generally difficult and one has to consider less ideal analysis techniques that work well in practice.

One such technique is the statistical modeling technique. It converts the nonlinear analysis problem into a linear one and allows us to examine

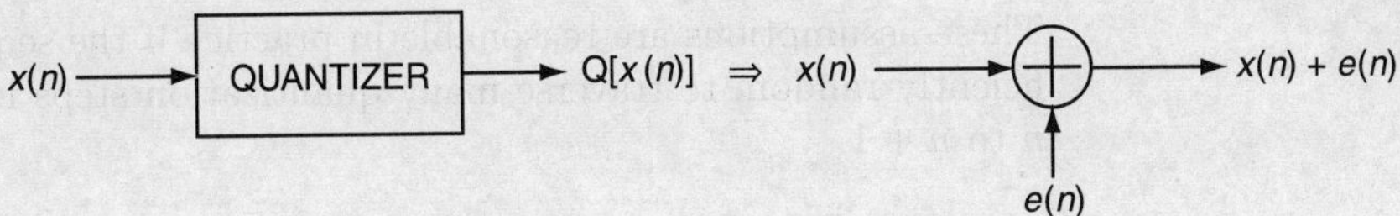

FIGURE 10.1 *Statistical model of a quantizer*

output-error characteristics. In this technique, we assume that the quantized value $\mathcal{Q}[x]$ is a sum of the exact value x and the quantization error e, which is assumed to be a random variable. When $x(n)$ is applied as an input sequence to the quantizer, the error $e(n)$ is assumed to be a random sequence. We then develop a statistical model for this random sequence to analyze its effects through a digital filter.

For the purpose of analysis, we assume that the quantizer employs fixed-point two's-complement number format representation. Using the results given previously, we can extend this analysis to other formats as well.

10.1.1 STATISTICAL MODEL

We model the quantizer block on the input as a signal-plus-noise operation—that is, from (6.46),

$$\mathcal{Q}[x(n)] = x(n) + e(n) \tag{10.1}$$

where $e(n)$ is a random sequence that describes the quantization error sequence and is termed the *quantization noise*. This is shown in Figure 10.1.

Model assumptions For the model in (10.1) to be mathematically convenient and hence practically useful, we have to assume *reasonable* statistical properties for the sequences involved. That these assumptions are practically reasonable can be ascertained using simple MATLAB examples, as we shall see. We assume that the error sequence, $e(n)$ has the following characteristics:[1]

1. The sequence $e(n)$ is a sample sequence from a stationary random process $\{e(n)\}$.
2. This random process $\{e(n)\}$ is *uncorrelated* with sequence $x(n)$.
3. The process $\{e(n)\}$ is an independent process (i.e., the samples are independent of each other).
4. The probability density function (pdf), $f_E(e)$, of sample $e(n)$ for each n is uniformly distributed over the interval of width $\Delta = 2^{-B}$, which is the quantizer resolution.

---

[1]The review of random variables, processes, and the associated terminology is given in Chapter 13.

These assumptions are reasonable in practice if the sequence $x(n)$ is sufficiently random to traverse many quantization steps in going from time n to $n+1$.

10.1.2 ANALYSIS USING MATLAB

To investigate the statistical properties of the error samples, we will have to generate a large number of these samples and plot their distribution using a histogram (or a probability bar graph). Furthermore, we have to design the sequence $x(n)$ so that its samples do not repeat; otherwise, the error samples will also repeat, which will result in an inaccurate analysis. This can be guaranteed either by choosing a well-defined aperiodic sequence or a random sequence.

We will quantize $x(n)$ using B-bit *rounding* operation. A similar implementation can be developed for the truncation operation. Since all three error characteristics are exactly the same under the rounding operation, we will choose the sign-magnitude format for ease in implementation. After quantization, the resulting error samples $e(n)$ are uniformly distributed over the $[-\frac{\Delta}{2}, \frac{\Delta}{2}]$ interval. Let $e_1(n)$ be the normalized error given by

$$e_1(n) \triangleq \frac{e(n)}{\Delta} = e(n)\,2^B \quad \Rightarrow \quad e_1(n) \in [-1/2, 1/2] \tag{10.2}$$

Then $e_1(n)$ is uniform over the interval $[-\frac{1}{2}, +\frac{1}{2}]$, as shown in Figure 10.2a. Thus the histogram interval will be uniform across all B-bit values, which will make its computation and plotting easier. This interval will be divided into 128 bins for the purpose of plotting.

To determine the sample independence, we consider the histogram of the sequence

$$e_2(n) \triangleq \frac{e_1(n) + e_1(n-1)}{2} \tag{10.3}$$

which is the average of two consecutive normalized error samples. If $e_1(n)$ is uniformly distributed between $[-1/2, 1/2]$, then, for sample independence, $e_2(n)$ must have a triangle-shaped distribution between $[-1/2, 1/2]$, as shown in Figure 10.2b. We will again generate a 128-bin histogram for $e_2(n)$. These steps are implemented in the following MATLAB function.

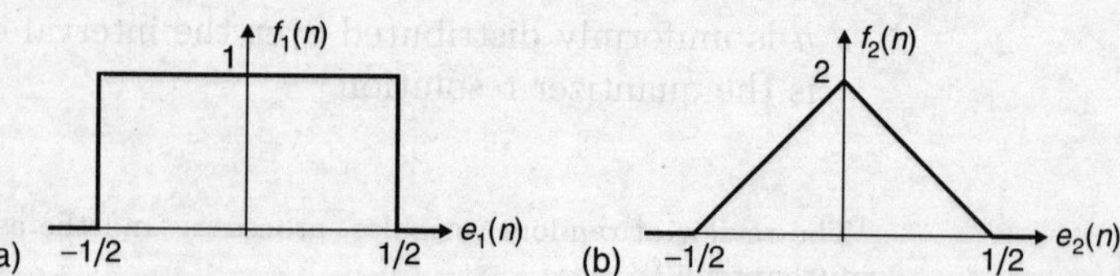

FIGURE 10.2   *Probability distributions of the normalized errors $e_1(n)$ and $e_2(n)$*

```matlab
function [H1,H2,Q, estat] = StatModelR(xn,B,N);
% Statistical Model (Rounding) for A/D Quantization error and its Distribution
% ------------    ------------------------------------------------------------
% [H1,H2,Q] = StatModelR(xn,B,N);
%   OUT: H1 = normalized histogram of e1
%        H2 = normalized histogram of e2
%         Q = normalized histogram bins
%      estat = row vector: [[e1avg,e1std,e2avg,e2std]
%     IN:  B = bits to quantize
%          N = number of samples of x(n)
%         xn = samples of the sequence
% Plot variables
   bM = 7; DbM = 2^bM;                      % Bin parameter
    M = round((DbM)/2);                     % Half number of bins
 bins = [-M+0.5:1:M-0.5];                   % Bin values from -M to M
    Q = bins/(DbM);                         % Normalized bins
% Quantization error analysis
     xq = (round(xn*(2^B)))/(2^B);          % Quantized to B bits
     e1 = xq-xn; clear xn xq;               % Quantization error
     e2 = 0.5*(e1(1:N-1)+e1(2:N));          % Average of two adj errors
  e1avg = mean(e1); e1std = std(e1);        % Mean & std dev of the error e1
  e2avg = mean(e2); e2std = std(e2);        % Mean & std dev of the error e2
  estat = [e1avg,e1std,e2avg,e2std];
% Probability distribution of e1
e1 = floor(e1*(2^(B+bM)));                  % Normalized e1 (int between -M & M)
e1 = sort([e1,-M-1:1:M]);                   %
H1 = diff(find(diff(e1)))-1; clear e1;      % Error histogram
if length(H1) == DbM+1
   H1(DbM) = H1(DbM)+H1(DbM+1);
   H1 = H1(1:DbM);
 end
H1 = H1/N;                                  % Normalized histogram
% Probability distribution of e2
e2 = floor(e2*(2^(B+bM)));                  % Normalized e2 (int between -M & M)
e2 = sort([e2,-M-1:1:M]);                   %
H2 = diff(find(diff(e2)))-1; clear e2;      % Error histogram
if length(H2) == DbM+1
   H2(DbM) = H2(DbM)+H2(DbM+1);
   H2 = H2(1:DbM);
 end
H2 = H2/N;                                  % Normalized histogram
```

To validate the model assumptions, we consider the following two examples. In the first example, an aperiodic sinusoidal sequence is quantized to B bits, and in the second example, a random sequence is quantized to B bits. The resulting quantization errors are analyzed for their distribution properties and for their sample independence for various values of B.

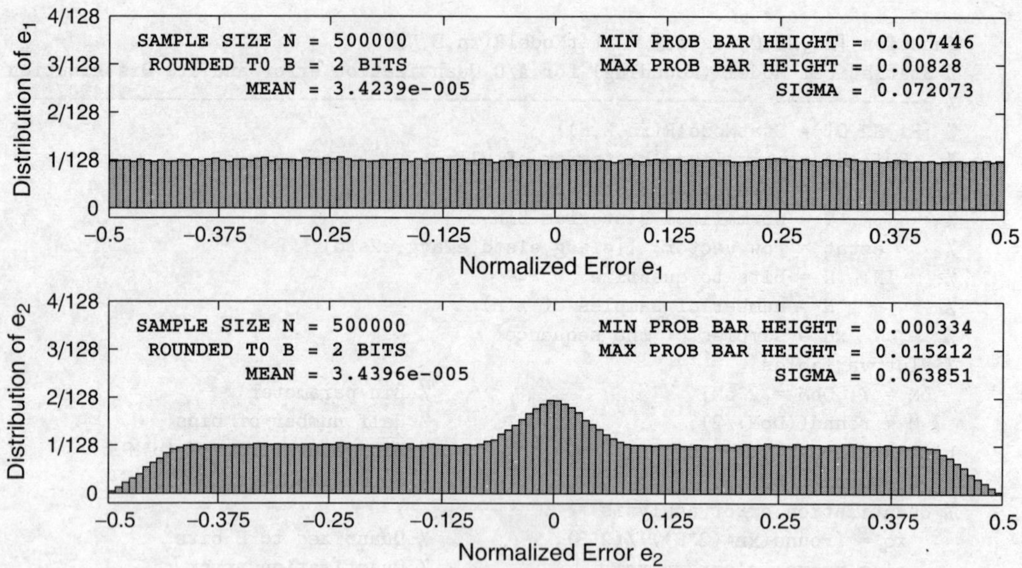

FIGURE 10.3 *A/D quantization error distribution for the sinusoidal signal in Example 10.1, B = 2 bits*

Through these examples, we hope to learn how small error e must be (or equivalently, how large B must be) for the above assumptions to be valid.

☐ **EXAMPLE 10.1**   Let $x(n) = \frac{1}{3}\{\sin(n/11) + \sin(n/31) + \cos(n/67)\}$. This sequence is not periodic, and hence its samples never repeat using infinite-precision representation. However, since the sequence is of sinusoidal nature, its continuous envelope is periodic and the samples are continuously distributed over the fundamental period of this envelope. Determine the error distributions for B = 2 and 6 bits.

Solution   To minimize statistical variations, the sample size must be large. We choose 500,000 samples. The following MATLAB script computes the distributions for $B = 2$ bits.

```
clear; close all;
% Example parameters
B = 2; N = 500000; n = [1:N];
xn = (1/3)*(sin(n/11)+sin(n/31)+cos(n/67)); clear n;
% Quantization error analysis
[H1,H2,Q, estat]] = StatModelR(xn,B,N);     % Compute histograms
H1max = max(H1); H1min = min(H1);  % Max and Min of H1
H2max = max(H2); H2min = min(H2);  % Max and Min of H2
```

The plots of the resulting histogram are shown in Figure 10.3. Clearly, even though the error samples appear to be uniformly distributed, the samples are not independent. The corresponding plots for $B = 6$ bits are shown in

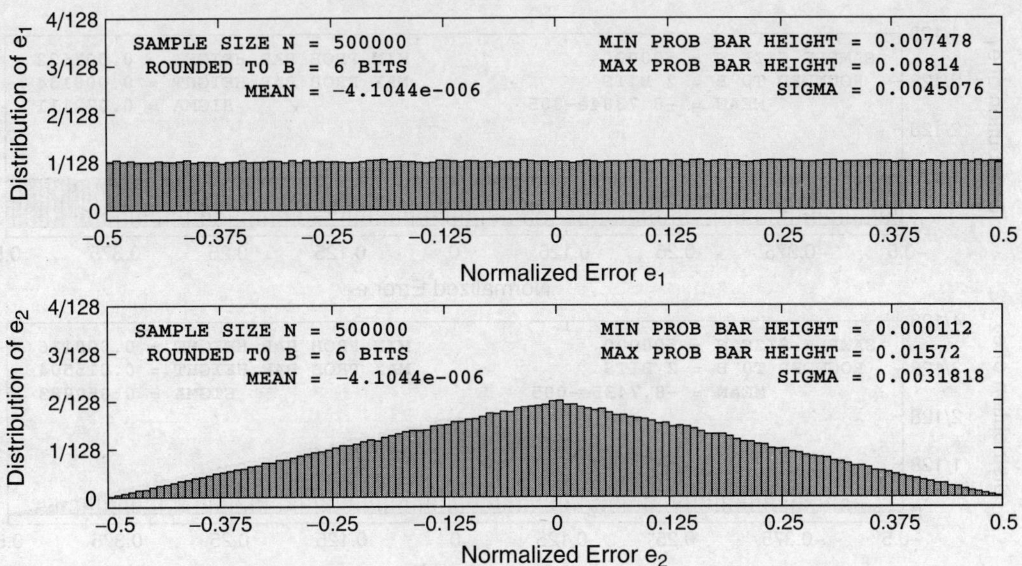

FIGURE 10.4 *Quantization error distribution for the sinusoidal signal in Example 10.1, $B = 6$ bits*

Figure 10.4, from which we observe that the quantization error sequence appears to satisfy the model assumptions for $B \geq 6$ bits. □

EXAMPLE 10.2 Let $x(n)$ be an independent and identically distributed random sequence whose samples are uniformly distributed over the $[-1, 1]$ interval. Determine the error distributions for B = 2 and 6 bits.

Solution We again choose 500,000 samples to minimize any statistical variations. The following MATLAB fragment computes the distributions for $B = 2$ bits.

```
clear; close all;
% Example parameters
B = 2; N = 500000; xn = (2*rand(1,N)-1);
% Quantization error analysis
[H1,H2,Q, estat]] = StatModelR(xn,B,N);     % Compute histograms
H1max = max(H1); H1min = min(H1);  % Max and Min of H1
H2max = max(H2); H2min = min(H2);  % Max and Min of H2
```

The plots of the resulting histogram are shown in Figure 10.5. The corresponding plots for $B = 6$ bits are shown in Figure 10.6. From these plots, we observe that even for $B = 2$ bits the quantization error samples are independent and uniformly distributed. □

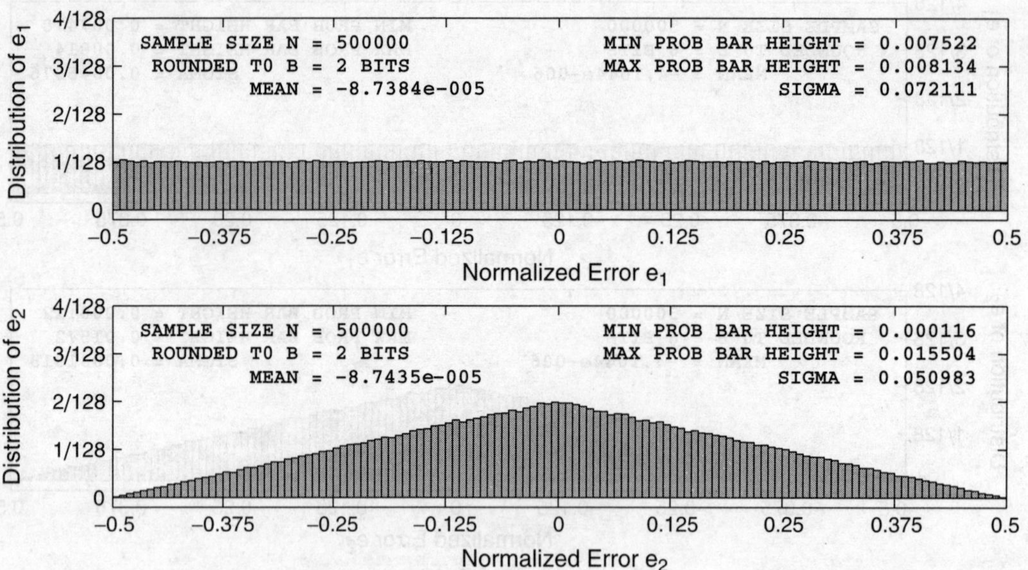

FIGURE 10.5 *A/D quantization error distribution for the random signal in Example 10.2, $B = 2$ bits*

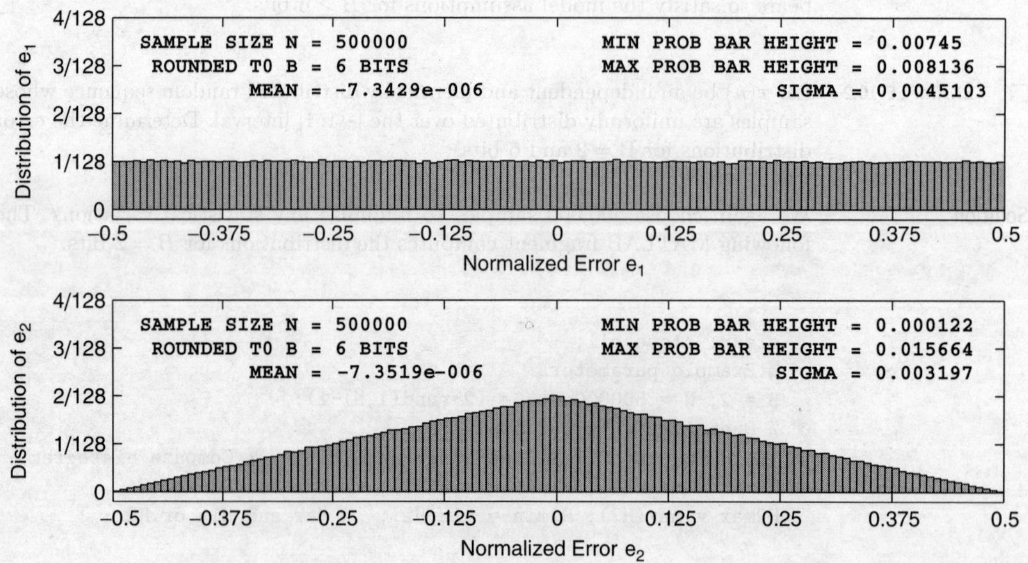

FIGURE 10.6 *Quantization error distribution for the random signal in Example 10.2, $B = 6$ bits*

Since practical signals processed using a DSP chip are typically random in nature (or can be modeled as such), we conclude from these two examples that the statistical model, with its stated assumptions, is a very good model.

10.1.3 STATISTICS OF A/D QUANTIZATION NOISE

We now develop a second-order statistical description of the error sequence $e(n)$ for both the truncation and rounding operations.

10.1.4 TRUNCATION

From (6.57), the pdf $f_{E_T}(e)$ of $e_T(n)$ is uniform over $[-\Delta, 0]$, as shown in Figure 10.7a. Then the average of $e_T(n)$ is given by

$$m_{e_T} \triangleq \mathrm{E}[e_T(n)] = -\Delta/2 \tag{10.4}$$

and the variance is

$$\sigma_{e_T}^2 \triangleq \mathrm{E}\left[(e_T(n) - m_{e_T})^2\right] = \int_{-\Delta}^{0} (e - \Delta/2)^2\, f_{E_T}(e)\, de$$

$$= \int_{-\Delta/2}^{\Delta/2} e^2 \left(\frac{1}{\Delta}\right) de = \frac{\Delta^2}{12} \tag{10.5}$$

Using $\Delta = 2^{-B}$, we obtain

$$\sigma_{e_T}^2 = \frac{2^{-2B}}{12} \quad \text{or} \quad \sigma_{e_T} = \frac{2^{-B}}{2\sqrt{3}} \tag{10.6}$$

Rounding From (6.59), the pdf $f_{E_R}(e)$ of $e_R(n)$ is uniform over $[-\Delta/2, \Delta/2]$, as shown in Figure 10.7b. Then the average of $e_R(n)$ is given by

$$m_{e_R} \triangleq [\mathrm{E}e_R] = 0 \tag{10.7}$$

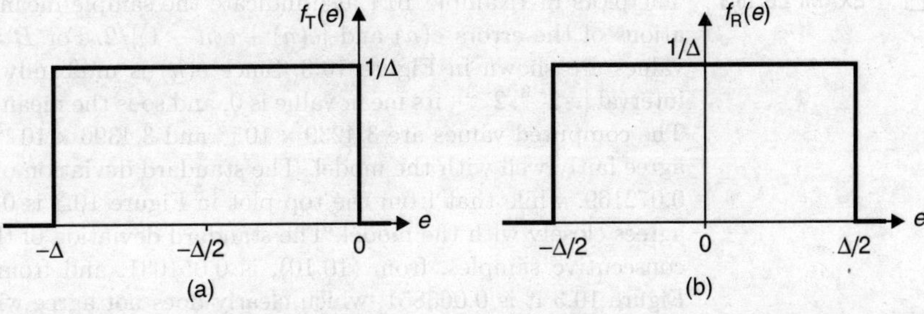

FIGURE 10.7 *Probability density functions: (a) truncation and (b) rounding*

and the variance is

$$\sigma_{e_R}^2 \triangleq \mathrm{E}\left[(e_R(n) - m_{e_R})^2\right] = \int_{-\Delta/2}^{\Delta/2} e^2 f_{E_R}(e)\, de = \int_{-\Delta/2}^{\Delta/2} e^2 \left(\frac{1}{\Delta}\right) de$$

$$= \frac{\Delta^2}{12} \qquad (10.8)$$

Using (6.45), we obtain

$$\sigma_{e_R}^2 = \frac{2^{-2B}}{12} \quad \text{or} \quad \sigma_{e_R} = \frac{2^{-B}}{2\sqrt{3}} \qquad (10.9)$$

Since the samples of the sequence $e_R(n)$ are assumed to be independent of each other, the variance of $[e_R(n) + e_R(n-1)]/2$ is given by

$$\mathrm{var}\left[\frac{e_R(n) + e_R(n-1)}{2}\right] = \frac{1}{4}\left(\frac{2^{-2B}}{12} + \frac{2^{-2B}}{12}\right) = \frac{2^{-2B}}{24} = \frac{1}{2}\sigma_{e_R}^2 \qquad (10.10)$$

or the standard deviation is $\sigma_{e_R}/\sqrt{2}$.

From the model assumptions and (10.6) or (10.9), the covariance of the error sequence (which is an independent sequence) is given by

$$\mathrm{E}[e(m)e(n)] \triangleq C_e(m-n) \triangleq C_e(\ell) = \frac{2^{-2B}}{12}\delta(\ell) \qquad (10.11)$$

where $\ell \triangleq m - n$ is called the lag variable. Such an error sequence is also known as a white noise sequence.

10.1.5 MATLAB IMPLEMENTATION

In MATLAB, the sample mean and standard deviation are computed using the functions **mean** and **std**, respectively. The last argument of the function **StatModelR** is a vector containing sample means and standard deviations of unnormalized errors $e(n)$ and $[e(n)+e(n-1)]/2$. Thus these values can be compared with the theoretical values obtained from the statistical model.

□ **EXAMPLE 10.3**   The plots in Example 10.1 also indicate the sample means and standard deviations of the errors $e(n)$ and $[e(n) + e(n-1)]/2$. For $B = 2$, these computed values are shown in Figure 10.3. Since $e(n)$ is uniformly distributed over the interval $[-2^{-3}, 2^{-3}]$, its mean value is 0, and so is the mean of $[e(n)+e(n-1)]/2$. The computed values are 3.4239×10^{-5} and 3.4396×10^{-5}, respectively, which agree fairly well with the model. The standard deviation of $e(n)$, from (10.9), is 0.072169, while that from the top plot in Figure 10.3 is 0.072073, which again agrees closely with the model. The standard deviation of the average of the two consecutive samples, from (10.10), is 0.051031, and from the bottom plot in Figure 10.3 it is 0.063851, which clearly does not agree with the model. Hence the samples of $e(n)$ for $B = 2$ are not independent. This was confirmed by the bottom plot in Figure 10.3.

Similarly, for $B = 6$ computed statistical values are shown in Figure 10.4. The computed values of the two means are -4.1044×10^{-6}, which agree very well with the model. The standard deviation of $e(n)$, from (10.9), is 0.0045105, while that from the top plot in Figure 10.4 is 0.0045076, which again agrees closely with the model. The standard deviation of the average of the two consecutive samples, from (10.10), is 0.0031894, while from the bottom plot in Figure 10.4 it is 0.00318181, which clearly agrees with the model. Hence the samples of $e(n)$ for $B = 6$ are independent. This was also confirmed by the bottom plot in Figure 10.4. $\qquad\square$

Similar calculations can be carried out for the signal in Example 10.2. The details are left to the reader.

10.1.6 A/D QUANTIZATION NOISE THROUGH DIGITAL FILTERS

Let a digital filter be described by the impulse response, $h(n)$, or the frequency response, $H(e^{\jmath\omega})$. When a quantized input, $\mathcal{Q}[x(n)] = x(n) + e(n)$, is applied to this system, we can determine the effects of the error sequence $e(n)$ on the filter output as it propagates through the filter, assuming infinite-precision arithmetic implementation in the filter. We are generally interested in the mean and variance of this output-noise sequence, which we can obtain using linear system theory concepts. Details of these results are given in Section 13.5.

Referring to Figure 10.8, let the output of the filter be $\hat{y}(n)$. Using LTI properties and the statistical independence between $x(n)$ and $e(n)$, the output $\hat{y}(n)$ can be expressed as the sum of two components. Let $y(n)$ be the (true) output due to $x(n)$ and let $q(n)$ be the response due to $e(n)$. Then we can show that $q(n)$ is also a random sequence with mean

$$m_q \triangleq \mathrm{E}[q(n)] = m_e \sum_{-\infty}^{\infty} h(n) = m_e\, H(e^{\jmath 0}) \qquad (10.12)$$

where the term $H(e^{\jmath 0})$ is termed the *DC gain* of the filter. For truncation, $m_{e_{\mathrm{T}}} = -\Delta/2$, which gives

$$m_{q_{\mathrm{T}}} = -\frac{\Delta}{2} H(e^{\jmath 0}) \qquad (10.13)$$

For rounding, $m_{e_{\mathrm{R}}} = 0$ or

$$m_{q_{\mathrm{R}}} = 0 \qquad (10.14)$$

$$\hat{x}(n) = x(n) + e(n) \longrightarrow \boxed{h(n),\ H(e^{j\omega})} \longrightarrow \hat{y}(n) = y(n) + q(n)$$

FIGURE 10.8 *Noise through digital filter*

We can also show that the variance of $q(n)$, for both the truncation and rounding, is given by

$$\sigma_q^2 = \sigma_e^2 \sum_{-\infty}^{\infty} |h(n)|^2 = \frac{\sigma_e^2}{2\pi} \int_{-\pi}^{\pi} |H(e^{j\omega})|^2 \, d\omega \qquad (10.15)$$

The *variance gain* from the input to the output (also known as the *normalized output variance*) is the ratio

$$\frac{\sigma_q^2}{\sigma_e^2} = \sum_{-\infty}^{\infty} |h(n)|^2 = \frac{1}{2\pi} \int_{-\pi}^{\pi} |H(e^{j\omega})|^2 \, d\omega \qquad (10.16)$$

For a real and stable filter, using the substitution $z = e^{j\omega}$, the integral in (10.16) can be further expressed as a complex contour integral

$$\frac{1}{2\pi} \int_{-\pi}^{\pi} |H(e^{j\omega})|^2 \, d\omega = \frac{1}{2\pi j} \oint_{\text{UC}} H(z)H(z^{-1})z^{-1} dz \qquad (10.17)$$

where UC is the unit circle and can be computed using residues (or the inverse $\mathcal{Z}$-transform) as

$$\frac{1}{2\pi} \int_{-\pi}^{\pi} |H(e^{j\omega})|^2 \, d\omega = \sum [\text{Res of } H(z)H(z^{-1})z^{-1} \text{ inside UC}] \quad (10.18a)$$

$$= \mathcal{Z}^{-1} \left[H(z)H(z^{-1}) \right]\Big|_{n=0} \qquad (10.18b)$$

10.1.7 MATLAB IMPLEMENTATION

Computation of the variance-gain for the A/D quantization noise can be carried out in MATLAB using (10.16) and (10.18). For FIR filters, we can perform exact calculations using the time-domain expression in (10.16). In the case of IIR filters, exact calculations can only be done using (10.18) in special cases, as we shall see (fortunately, this works for most practical filters). The approximate computations can always be done using the time-domain expression.

Let the FIR filter be given by the coefficients $\{b_k\}_0^{M-1}$. Then using the time-domain expression in (10.16), the variance-gain is given by

$$\frac{\sigma_q^2}{\sigma_e^2} = \sum_{k=0}^{M-1} |b_k|^2 \qquad (10.19)$$

Let an IIR filter be given by the system function

$$H(z) = \frac{\sum_{\ell=0}^{N-1} b_\ell z^{-\ell}}{1 + \sum_{k=1}^{N-1} a_k z^{-k}} \qquad (10.20)$$

with impulse response $h(n)$. If we assume that the filter is real, causal, and stable and has only simple poles, then using the partial fraction expansion, we can write

$$H(z) = R_0 + \sum_{k=1}^{N-1} \frac{R_k}{z - p_k} \qquad (10.21)$$

where R_0 is the constant term and R_k's are the residues at the pole locations p_k. This expansion can be computed using the **residue** function. Note that both poles and the corresponding residues are either real-valued or occur in complex-conjugate pairs. Then using (10.18a), we can show that (see [68] and also Problem P10.3)

$$\frac{\sigma_q^2}{\sigma_e^2} = R_0^2 + \sum_{k=1}^{N-1} \sum_{\ell=1}^{N-1} \frac{R_k R_\ell^*}{1 - p_k p_\ell^*} \tag{10.22}$$

The variance-gain expression in (10.22) is applicable for most practical filters since rarely do they have multiple poles. The approximate value of the variance-gain for IIR filters is given by

$$\frac{\sigma_q^2}{\sigma_e^2} \simeq \sum_{k=0}^{K-1} |h(n)|^2, \quad K \gg 1 \tag{10.23}$$

where K is chosen so that the impulse response values (magnitudewise) are almost zero beyond K samples. The following MATLAB function, **VarGain**, computes variance-gain using (10.19) or (10.22).

```
function Gv = VarGain(b,a)
% Computation of variance-gain for the output noise process
% of digital filter described by b(z)/a(z)
%  Gv = VarGain(b,a)
a0 = a(1); a = a/a0; b = b/a0; M = length(b); N = length(a);
if N == 1                          % FIR Filter
    Gv = sum(b.*b);
    return
else                               % IIR Filter
    [R,p,P] = residue(b,a);
    if length(P) > 1
        error('*** Variance Gain Not computable ***');
    elseif length(P) == 1
        Gv = P*P;
    else
        Gv = 0;
    end
    Rnum = R*R'; pden = 1-p*p';
    H = Rnum./pden; Gv = Gv + real(sum(H(:)));
end
```

It should be noted that the actual output noise variance is obtained by multiplying the A/D quantization noise variance by the variance-gain.

◻   **EXAMPLE 10.4**   Consider an eighth-order IIR filter with poles at $p_k = r\,e^{j2\pi k/8}$, $k = 0, \ldots, 7$. If r is close to 1, then the filter has four narrowband peaks. Determine the variance-gain for this filter when $r = 0.9$ and $r = 0.99$.

Solution   The following MATLAB script illustrates calculations for $r = 0.9$, which implements exact as well as approximate approaches.

```
% Filter Parameters
N = 8; r = 0.9; b = 1; pl = r*exp(j*2*pi*[0:N-1]/N); a = real(poly(pl));

% Variance-gain (Exact)
Vg = VarGain(b,a)
Vg =
    1.02896272593178
% Variance-gain (approximate)
x = [1,zeros(1,10000)]; % Unit sample sequence
h = filter(b,a,x);         % Impulse response
VgCheck = sum(h.*h)
VgCheck =
    1.02896272593178
```

Clearly, both approaches give the same variance-gain, which for $r = 0.9$ is about 3% above unity. For $r = 0.99$ the calculations are

```
% Filter Parameters
N = 8; r = 0.99; b = 1; pl = r*exp(j*2*pi*[0:N-1]/N); a = real(poly(pl));
% Variance-gain (Exact)
Vg = VarGain(b,a)
Vg =
    6.73209233071894
```

The variance-gain is more than 673%, which means that when poles are close to the unit circle, the filter output can be very noisy.   □

10.2 ROUND-OFF EFFECTS IN IIR DIGITAL FILTERS

■

With our insight into the quantizer operation and its simpler statistical model, we are now ready to delve into the analysis of finite word-length effects in both IIR and FIR digital filters. We have already studied the effects of input signal quantization and filter coefficient quantization on filter behavior. We will now turn our attention to the effects of arithmetic operation quantization on filter output responses (in terms of signal-to-noise ratios). For this study, we will consider both fixed-point and floating-point arithmetic. We first consider the effects on IIR filters since, due to feedback paths, the results are more complicated—yet more interesting—than those in FIR filters. The effects on FIR filters are studied in the next section.

We will restrict ourselves to the rounding operation of the quantizer due to its superior statistical qualities (no bias or average value). From (6.59), we know that, for the rounding operation, the quantizer error, e_R, has the same characteristics across all three number representation formats. Hence for MATLAB simulation purposes, we will consider the sign-magnitude format because it is easy to program and simulate for arithmetic operation. However, in practice, two's-complement format number representation has advantages over the others in terms of hardware implementation.

Digital filter implementation requires arithmetic operations of multiplication and addition. If two B-bit fractional numbers are multiplied, the result is a $2B$-bit fractional number that must be quantized to B bits. Similarly, if two B-bit fractional numbers are added, the sum could be more than 1, which results in an *overflow* (which in itself is a nonlinear characteristic), or the sum must be corrected using a *saturation* strategy, which is also nonlinear. Thus a finite word-length implementation of the filter is a highly nonlinear filter and must be analyzed carefully for any meaningful results.

In this section, we will consider two approaches to deal with errors due to finite word-length representation. The first type of error can occur when error samples become *correlated* with each other due to the nonlinearity of the quantizer. This is called *limit-cycle behavior*, and it can exist only in IIR filters. We will analyze this problem using the nonlinear quantizer model rather than the statistical model of the quantizer. In the second type of error, we assume that more nonlinear effects in the quantizer have been suppressed. Then, using the statistical model of the quantizer, we develop a quantization noise model for IIR filters that is more useful in predicting the finite word-length effects.

10.2.1 LIMIT CYCLES

Digital filters are linear systems, but when quantizers are incorporated in their implementation, they become nonlinear systems. For nonlinear systems, it is possible to have an output sequence even when there is no input. Limit cycles is one such behavior that creates an oscillatory periodic output that is highly undesirable.

■ DEFINITION 1 *Limit cycle*

A zero-input limit cycle is a nonzero periodic output sequence produced by nonlinear elements or quantizers in the feedback loop of a digital filter. □

There are two types of limit cycles. The *granular* limit cycles are due
to nonlinearities in multiplication quantization and are of low amplitude.
The *overflow* limit cycles are a result of overflow in addition and can have
large amplitudes.

10.2.2 GRANULAR LIMIT CYCLES

This type of limit cycle can easily be demonstrated with a simple rounding quantizer following a multiplication. We illustrate with the following
example.

☐   **EXAMPLE 10.5**   Consider a simple first-order IIR filter given by

$$y(n) = \alpha\, y(n-1) + x(n); \quad y(-1) = 0, \quad n \geq 0 \tag{10.24}$$

Let $\alpha = -\frac{1}{2}$; then this is a highpass filter, since its pole is near $z = -1$.
Determine the output $y(n)$ when $x(n) = \frac{7}{8}\delta(n)$, assuming a 3-bit quantizer in
the multiplier.

Solution   After multiplication by α, we have to quantize the result. Let the output due
to this quantization be $\hat{y}(n)$. Then the actual implementable digital filter is

$$\hat{y}(n) = \mathcal{Q}\left[-\frac{1}{2}\hat{y}(n-1)\right] + x(n); \quad \hat{y}(-1) = 0, \quad n \geq 0 \tag{10.25}$$

We assume that the input in (10.24) is quantized and that there is no overflow
due to addition. Let $B = 3$ (i.e., we have 3 fraction bits and 1 sign bit), and
let $x(n) = \frac{7}{8}\delta(n)$. Now $\alpha = -\frac{1}{2}$ is represented by $1{\scriptstyle\blacktriangle}110$ in two's-complement
format. Hence the output sequence is obtained as

$$\hat{y}(0) = x(0) \qquad\qquad\qquad\qquad\qquad = +\frac{7}{8} : 0{\scriptstyle\blacktriangle}111$$

$$\hat{y}(1) = \mathcal{Q}\left[\alpha\,\hat{y}(0)\right] = \mathcal{Q}\left[-\frac{1}{2}\left(+\frac{7}{8}\right)\right] = \mathcal{Q}\left[-\frac{7}{16}\right] = -\frac{1}{2} : 1{\scriptstyle\blacktriangle}100$$

$$\hat{y}(2) = \mathcal{Q}\left[\alpha\,\hat{y}(1)\right] = \mathcal{Q}\left[-\frac{1}{2}\left(-\frac{1}{2}\right)\right] = \mathcal{Q}\left[+\frac{1}{4}\right] = +\frac{1}{4} : 0{\scriptstyle\blacktriangle}010$$

$$\hat{y}(3) = \mathcal{Q}\left[\alpha\,\hat{y}(2)\right] = \mathcal{Q}\left[-\frac{1}{2}\left(+\frac{1}{4}\right)\right] = \mathcal{Q}\left[-\frac{1}{8}\right] = -\frac{1}{8} : 1{\scriptstyle\blacktriangle}111 \tag{10.26}$$

$$\hat{y}(4) = \mathcal{Q}\left[\alpha\,\hat{y}(3)\right] = \mathcal{Q}\left[-\frac{1}{2}\left(-\frac{1}{8}\right)\right] = \mathcal{Q}\left[+\frac{1}{16}\right] = +\frac{1}{8} : 0{\scriptstyle\blacktriangle}001$$

$$\hat{y}(5) = \mathcal{Q}\left[\alpha\,\hat{y}(4)\right] = \mathcal{Q}\left[-\frac{1}{2}\left(+\frac{1}{8}\right)\right] = \mathcal{Q}\left[-\frac{1}{16}\right] = -\frac{1}{8} : 1{\scriptstyle\blacktriangle}111$$

$$\vdots \quad \vdots \qquad\qquad \vdots \qquad\qquad\qquad \vdots \qquad\qquad \vdots$$

Thus $\hat{y}(n) = \pm\frac{1}{8}$ for $n \geq 5$. The desired output $y(n)$ is

$$y(n) = \left\{\frac{7}{8}, -\frac{7}{16}, \frac{7}{32}, -\frac{7}{64}, \frac{7}{128}, \cdots, \rightarrow 0\right\} \tag{10.27}$$

Hence the error sequence is

$$e(n) = \hat{y}(n) - y(n) = \left\{0, -\frac{1}{16}, \frac{1}{32}, -\frac{1}{64}, \frac{9}{128}, \cdots, \rightarrow \pm\frac{1}{8}\right\} \tag{10.28}$$

This shows that the error $e(n)$ slowly builds up to $\pm\frac{1}{8}$. Hence the error is *asymptotically periodic* with period 2. $\square$

From Example 10.5, it is clear that, in the steady state, the system has poles on the unit circle and hence the nonlinear system has effectively become a linear system [37]. This implies that, effectively, for the system in (10.24)

$$Q\left[\alpha\hat{y}(n-1)\right] = \begin{cases} \hat{y}(n-1), & \alpha > 0 \\ -\hat{y}(n-1), & \alpha < 0 \end{cases} \tag{10.29}$$

Also due to the rounding operation, the quantization error is bounded by $\pm\Delta/2$, where $\Delta = 2^{-B}$ is the quantization step, or

$$\left|Q\left[\alpha\hat{y}(n-1)\right] - \alpha\hat{y}(n-1)\right| \leq \frac{\Delta}{2} \tag{10.30}$$

From (10.29) and (10.30), we conclude that

$$\left|\hat{y}(n-1)\right| \leq \frac{\Delta}{2(1 - |\alpha|)} \tag{10.31}$$

which is the amplitude range of limit-cycle oscillations and is called a *dead band*. For the system in Example 10.5, $B = 3$ and $\alpha = -\frac{1}{2}$. Hence the dead-band range is $\pm\frac{1}{8}$, which agrees with (10.31). If the output $\hat{y}(n-1)$ gets trapped in this band when the input is zero, the filter exhibits the granular limit cycle. From (10.29), the period of the oscillation is either 1 or 2.

Analysis using MATLAB   In our previous MATLAB simulations, we did not worry about the quantization in multiplication or addition operations because the emphasis was on either signal quantization or on filter coefficient quantization. The important operation that we have to consider is the arithmetic overflow characteristics. We assume that the represented numbers are in fractional two's-complement format. Then in practice, two overflow characteristics are used: a two's-complement overflow, which is a modulo (periodic) function, and a saturation, which is a limiting function. These characteristics are shown in Figure 10.9.

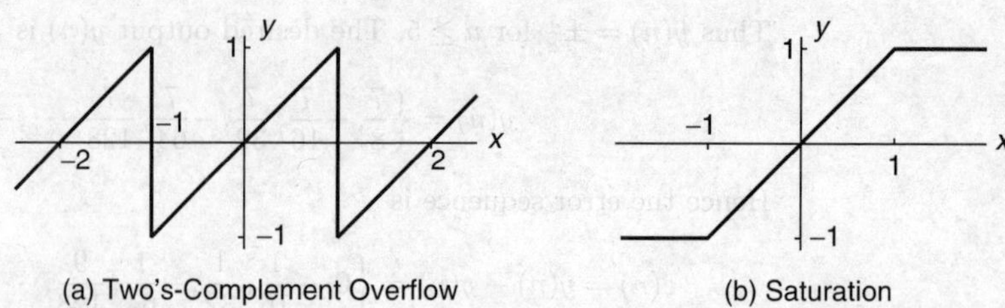

FIGURE 10.9 *Overflow characteristics used in* `Qfix`

To simulate these two effects, we provide the function `y = Qfix(x,B, 'Qmode','Omode')`. This function performs a fixed-point two's-complement format quantization using (B+1)-bit representation so that the resulting number y is between $-1 \leq y < 1$. The quantization mode, `Qmode`, is either a rounding or a truncation operation. The overflow characteristic is provided in `Omode`. Using this function, we can study both types of limit cycles.

```
function [y] = QFix(x,B,Qmode,Omode)
% Fixed-point Arithmetic using (B+1)-bit Representation
% -------------------------------------------------------
%    [y] = QFix(x,B,Qmode,Omode)
%       y: decimal equivalent of quantized x with values in [-1,1)
%       x: a real number array
%       B: Number of fractional bits
%   Qmode: quantizer mode
%          'round': Two's-complement rounding characteristics
%          'trunc': Two's complement truncation characteristics
%   Omode: overflow mode
%          'satur': Saturation limiter
%          'twosc': Two's-complement overflow
% Quantization operation
if strcmp(lower(Qmode), 'round');
    y = round(x.*(2^B));
elseif strcmp(lower(Qmode), 'trunc');
    y = floor(x.*(2^B));
else
    error('Use Qmode = "round" or "trunc"');
end;
y = y*(2^(-B)); % (B+1)-bit representation
% Overflow operation
if strcmp(lower(Omode), 'satur');
    y = min(y,1-2^(-B)); y = max(-1,y); % Saturation
elseif strcmp(lower(Omode), 'twosc');
    y = 2*(mod(y/2-0.5,1)-0.5);          % Overflow
else error('Use Omode = "satur" or "twosc"');
end;
```

☐ **EXAMPLE 10.6**   In this example, simulate the results for the system given in Example 10.5 using the `Qfix` function with $B = 3$ bits. In addition, also examine limit-cycle behavior for the truncation operation in the multiplier and for the case when the system is a lowpass filter with coefficient $\alpha = 0.5$.

Solution   MATLAB script:

```
% Highpass filter, rounding operation in multiplier
a = -0.5; yn1 = 0; m = 0:10; y = [yn1, zeros(1,length(m))];
x = 0.875*impseq(m(1),m(1)-1,m(end));
for n = m+2
    yn1 = y(n-1);
    y(n) = QFix(a*yn1,3,'round','satur') + x(n);
end
% Plotting commands follow
% Lowpass filter, rounding operation in multiplier
a = 0.5; yn1 = 0; m = 0:10; y = [yn1, zeros(1,length(m))];
x = 0.875*impseq(m(1),m(1)-1,m(end));
for n = m+2
    yn1 = y(n-1);
    y(n) = QFix(a*yn1,3,'round','satur') + x(n);
end
% Plotting commands follow
% Highpass filter, Truncation operation in multiplier
a = -0.5; yn1 = 0; m = 0:10; y = [yn1, zeros(1,length(m))];
x = 0.875*impseq(m(1),m(1)-1,m(end));
for n = m+2
    yn1 = y(n-1);
    y(n) = QFix(a*yn1,3,'trunc','satur') + x(n);
end
% Plotting commands follow
```

The resulting plots are shown in Figure 10.10. The output signal in the left plot agrees with that in Example 10.5 and has an asymptotic period of two samples. The middle plot for $\alpha = 0.5$ (lowpass filter) shows that the limit cycle has a period of one sample with amplitude of $\frac{1}{8}$. Finally, the right plot shows that the limit cycles vanish for the truncation operation. This behavior for the truncation operation is also exhibited for lowpass filters.   ☐

In the case of second-order and higher-order digital filters, granular limit cycles not only exist but also are of various types. These cycles in second-order filters can be analyzed, and dead-band as well as frequency of oscillations can be estimated. For example, if the recursive all-pole filter is implemented with rounding quantizers in the multipliers as

$$\hat{y}(n) = \mathcal{Q}[a_1\hat{y}(n-1)] + \mathcal{Q}[a_2\hat{y}(n-2)] + x(n) \qquad (10.32)$$

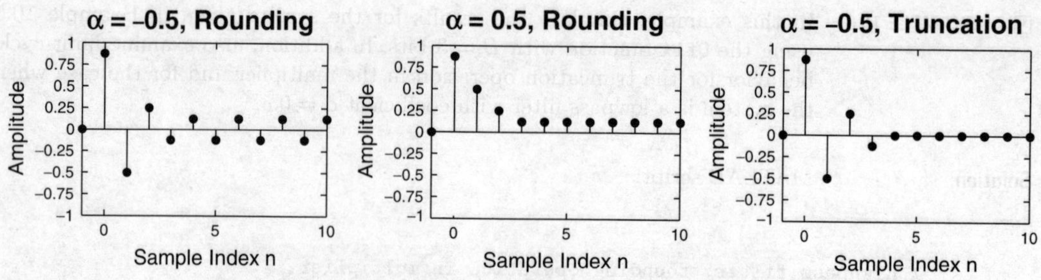

FIGURE 10.10　*Granular limit cycles in Example 10.6*

where $\hat{y}(n)$ is the quantized output, then using the analysis similar to that of the 1-order case, the dead-band region is given by

$$\hat{y}(n-2) \leq \frac{\Delta}{2(1-|a_2|)} \tag{10.33}$$

with a_1 determining the frequency of oscillations. For more details, see Proakis and Manolakis [79]. We provide the following example to illustrate granular limit cycles in second-order filters using 3-bit quantizers.

☐　**EXAMPLE 10.7**　Consider the second-order recursive filter

$$y(n) = 0.875y(n-1) - 0.75y(n-2) + x(n) \tag{10.34}$$

with zero initial conditions. This filter has two complex-conjugate poles and hence is a bandpass filter. Let the input be $x(n) = 0.375\delta(n)$. Analyze the limit cycle behavior using a 3-bit quantizer.

Solution　In the filter implementation, the coefficient products are quantized, which results in

$$\hat{y}(n) = \mathcal{Q}[0.875\hat{y}(n-1)] - \mathcal{Q}[0.75\hat{y}(n-2)] + x(n) \tag{10.35}$$

where $\hat{y}(n)$ is the quantized output. We simulate (10.35) in MATLAB using both the rounding and truncation operations.

```
% Bandpass filter
a1 = 0.875; a2 = -0.75;
% Rounding operation in multipliers
yn1 = 0; yn2 = 0;
m = 0:20; y = [yn2,yn1,zeros(1,length(m))];
x = 0.375*impseq(m(1),m(1)-2,m(end));
for n = m+3
    yn1 = y(n-1); yn2 = y(n-2);
    y(n) = QFix(a1*yn1,3,'round','satur')+QF1x(a2*yn2,3,'round','satur')+x(n);
end
% Plotting commands follow
% Truncation operation in multipliers
```

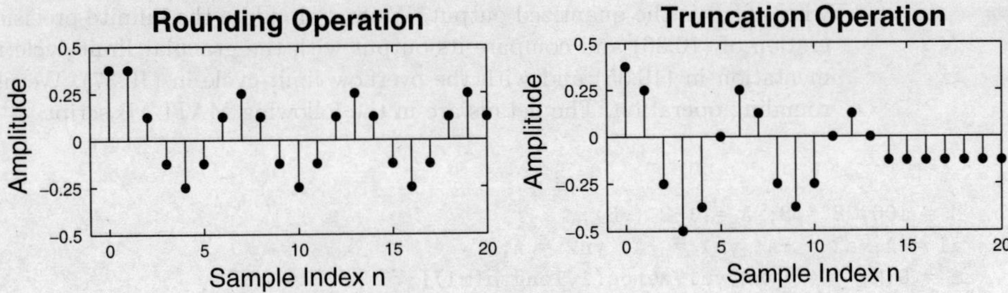

FIGURE 10.11 *Granular limit cycles in Example 10.7*

```
yn1 = 0; yn2 = 0;
m = 0:20; y = [yn2,yn1,zeros(1,length(m))];
x = 0.375*impseq(m(1),m(1)-2,m(end));
for n = m+3
    yn1 = y(n-1); yn2 = y(n-2);
    y(n) = QFix(a1*yn1,3,'trunc','satur')+QFix(a2*yn2,3,'trunc','satur')+x(n);
end
% Plotting commands follow
```

The resulting plots are shown in Figure 10.11. The round-off limit cycles have a period of six samples and amplitude of 0.25, which agrees with (10.33). Unlike in the case of first-order filters, the limit cycles for the second-order exist even when truncation is used in the quantizer. $\qquad\square$

10.2.3 OVERFLOW LIMIT CYCLES

This type of limit cycle is also a zero-input behavior that gives an oscillatory output. It is due to overflow in the addition even if we ignore multiplication or product quantization in the filter implementation. This is a more serious limit cycle because the oscillations can cover the entire dynamic range of the quantizer. It can be avoided in practice by using the saturation characteristics instead of overflow in the quantizer. In the following example, we simulate both granular and overflow limit cycles in a second-order filter, in addition to infinite-precision implementation.

$\square$ **EXAMPLE 10.8**   To obtain overflow in addition, we will consider the second-order filter with large coefficient values and initial conditions (magnitude-wise) excited by a zero input:

$$y(n) = 0.875y(n-1) - 0.875y(n-1); \quad y(-1) = -0.875, \; y(-2) = 0.875$$

$$\textbf{(10.36)}$$

The overflow in the addition is obtained by placing the quantizer after the additions as

$$\hat{y}(n) = \mathcal{Q}[0.875\hat{y}(n-1) - 0.875\hat{y}(n-1)]; \quad \hat{y}(-1) = -0.875, \; \hat{y}(-2) = 0.875$$

$$\textbf{(10.37)}$$

where $\hat{y}(n)$ is the quantized output. We first simulate the infinite-precision operation of (10.36) and compare its output with the granular limit-cycle implementation in (10.35) and with the overflow limit-cycle in (10.37). We use the rounding operation. The details are in the following MATLAB script.

```
M = 100; B = 3; A = 1-2^(-B);
a1 = A; a2 = -A; yn1 = -A; yn2 = A;
m = 0:M; y = [yn2,yn1,zeros(1,length(m))];
% Infinite precision
for n = m+3
    yn1 = y(n-1); yn2 = y(n-2);
    y(n) = a1*yn1 + a2*yn2;
end
% Plotting commands follow
% Granular limit cycle
for n = m+3
    yn1 = y(n-1); yn2 = y(n-2);
    y(n) = QFix(a1*yn1,B,'round','satur')+QFix(a2*yn2,B,'round','satur');
    y(n) = QFix(y(n),B,'round','satur');
end
% Plotting commands follow
% Overflow limit cycle
for n = m+3
    yn1 = y(n-1); yn2 = y(n-2);
    y(n) = a1*yn1 + a2*yn2;
    y(n) = QFix(y(n),B,'round','twosc');
end
% Plotting commands follow
```

The resulting plots are shown in Figure 10.12. As expected, the infinite-precision implementation has no limit cycles. The granular limit cycles are of smaller amplitudes. Clearly, the overflow limit cycles have large amplitudes spanning the -1 to 1 range of the quantizers.   □

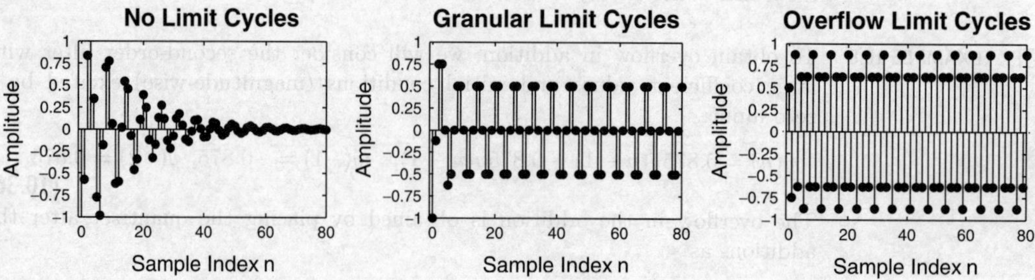

FIGURE 10.12   *Comparison of limit cycles in Example 10.8*

As shown in these examples, the limit-cycle behaviors of many different filters can be studied for different quantizer characteristics using the MATLAB function `QFix`.

10.2.4 MULTIPLICATION QUANTIZATION ERROR

A multiplier element in the filter implementation can introduce additional quantization errors since multiplication of two B-bit fractional numbers results in a $2B$-bit fraction and must be quantized to a B-bit fraction. Consider a multiplier in fixed-point arithmetic with $B = 8$. The number $\frac{1}{\sqrt{3}}$ is represented as 0.578125 in decimal. The square of 0.578125 rounded to 8 bits is 0.3359375 (which should not be confused with 1/3 rounded to 8 bits, which is 0.33203125). The additional error in the squaring operation is

$$0.3359375 - (0.578125)^2 = 0.001708984375$$

This additional error is termed as the *multiplication quantization error*. Its statistically equivalent model is similar to that of the A/D quantization error model, as shown in Figure 10.13.

Statistical model   Consider the B-bit quantizer block following the multiplier element shown in Figure 10.13a. The sequence $x(n)$ and the constant c are quantized to B fractional bits prior to multiplication (as would be the case in a typical implementation). The multiplied sequence $\{c\,x(n)\}$ is quantized to obtain $y(n)$. We want to replace the quantizer by a simpler linear system model shown in Figure 10.13b, in which $y(n) = c\,x(n)+e(n)$, where $e(n)$ is a multiplication quantization error. For analysis purposes we assume that the conditions on $e(n)$ are similar to those for the A/D quantization error:

1. The random signal $e(n)$ is *uncorrelated* with the sequence $x(n)$ for rounding operation (or two's-complement truncation operation) in the quantizer.
2. The signal $e(n)$ is an independent process (i.e., the samples are independent of each other).
3. The probability density function (pdf) $f_E(e)$ of $e(n)$ for each n is uniformly distributed over the interval of width $\Delta = 2^{-B}$, which is the quantizer resolution.

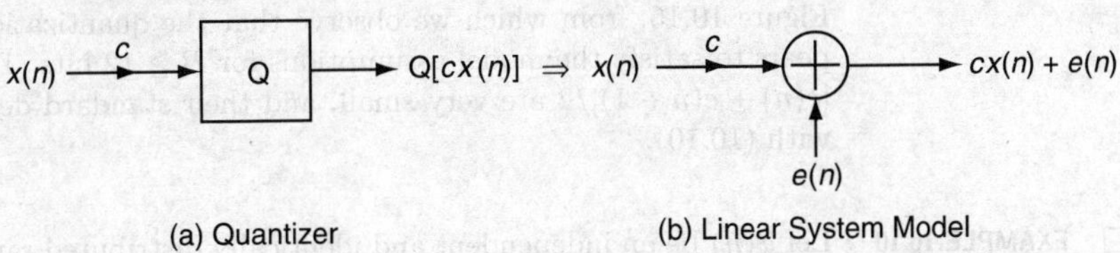

FIGURE 10.13   *Linear system model for multiplication quantization error*

We will emphasize the rounding operation for the rest of this section. Based on the above model assumptions, the results given in (10.7), (10.9), and (10.10) are also applicable for the multiplication quantization error $e(n)$.

We offer the following two MATLAB examples to illustrate this model. A more thorough investigation of this error can be found in Rabiner and Gold [83].

☐ **EXAMPLE 10.9**   Consider the sequence given in Example 10.1, which is repeated here:

$$x(n) = \frac{1}{3}\left[\sin(n/11) + \sin(n/31) + \cos(n/67)\right]$$

This signal is multiplied by $c = 1/\sqrt{2}$, quantized to B bits, and the resulting multiplication is quantized to B bits with rounding. Using the `StatModelR` function and 500,000 samples, compute and analyze normalized errors $e_1(n)$ and $e_2(n)$, defined in (10.2) and (10.3), respectively.

Solution   The following MATLAB script computes error distribution, for $B = 6$ bits.

```
clear; close all;
% Example parameters
B = 6; N = 500000; n = [1:N]; bM = 7;
xn = (1/3)*(sin(n/11)+sin(n/31)+cos(n/67)); clear n;
c = 1/sqrt(2);
% Signal and coefficient quantization
xq = (round(xn*(2^B)))/(2^B); c = (round(c*(2^B)))/(2^B);
cxq = c*xq;                          % Multiplication of constant and signal
% Quantization error analysis
[H1,H2,Q, estat] = StatModelR(cxq,B,N);
H1max = max(H1); H1min = min(H1);    % Max and min of H1
H2max = max(H2); H2min = min(H2);    % Max and min of H2
```

The plots of the resulting histogram are shown in Figure 10.14. For the sinusoidal signal, when $B = 6$ bits, the error samples are not uniformly distributed and the samples are not independent. The means of $e(n)$ and $[e(n)+e(n-1)]/2$ are small. Their standard deviations are 0.0045105 and 0.0031059, which do not agree with (10.10). The corresponding plots for $B = 12$ bits are shown in Figure 10.15, from which we observe that the quantization error sequence appears to satisfy the model assumptions for $B \geq 12$ bits. The means of $e(n)$ and $[e(n) + e(n - 1)]/2$ are very small, and their standard deviations agree closely with (10.10).   ☐

☐ **EXAMPLE 10.10**   Let $x(n)$ be an independent and identically distributed random sequence whose samples are uniformly distributed over the $[-1, 1]$ interval. Using 500,000 samples to minimize any statistical variations, analyze normalized errors.

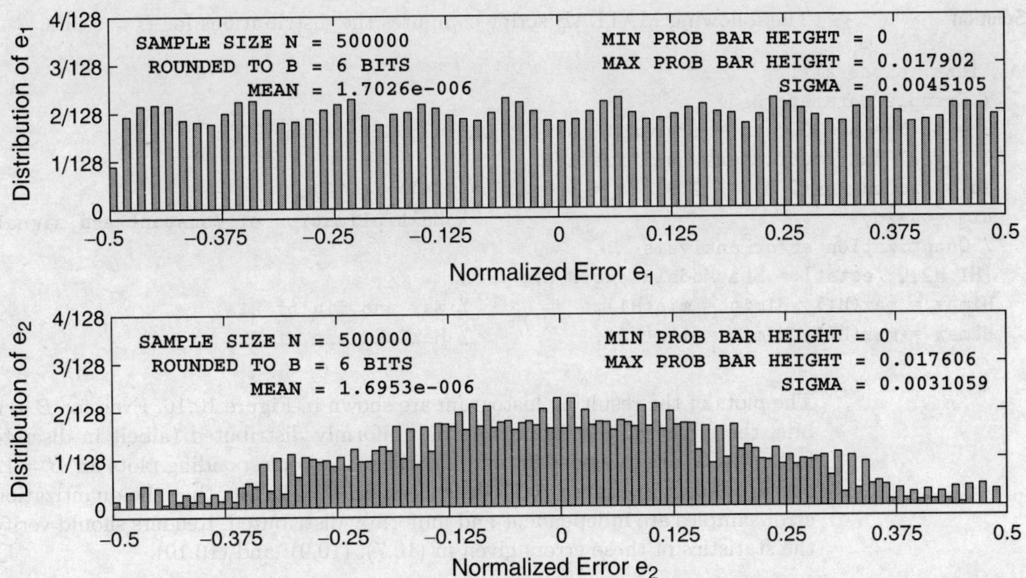

FIGURE 10.14 *Multiplication quantization error distribution for the sinusoidal signal in Example 10.9, B = 6 bits*

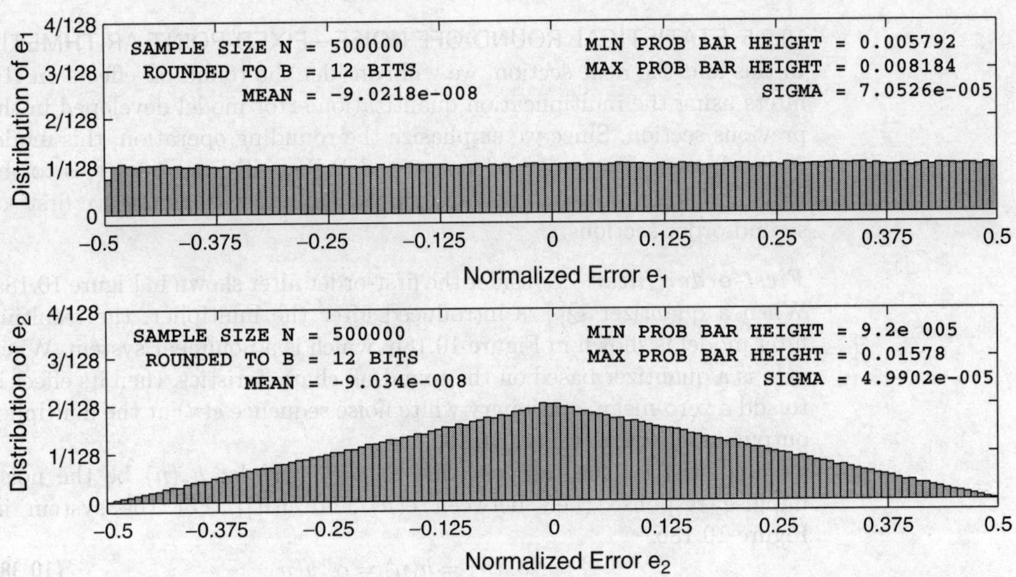

FIGURE 10.15 *Multiplication quantization error distribution for the sinusoidal signal in Example 10.9, B = 12 bits*

Solution   The following MATLAB script computes the distributions for $B = 6$ bits.

```
clear; close all;
% Example parameters
B = 6; N = 500000; xn = (2*rand(1,N)-1); bM = 7;  c = 1/sqrt(2);
% Signal and coefficient quantization
xq = (round(xn*(2^B)))/(2^B); c = (round(c*(2^B)))/(2^B);
cxq = c*xq;                               % Multiplication of constant and signal
% Quantization error analysis
[H1,H2,Q, estat] = StatModelR(cxq,B,N);
H1max = max(H1); H1min = min(H1);         % Max and min of H1
H2max = max(H2); H2min = min(H2);         % Max and min of H2
```

The plots of the resulting histogram are shown in Figure 10.16. Even for $B = 6$ bits, the error samples appear to be uniformly distributed (albeit in discrete fashion) and are independent of each other. The corresponding plots for $B = 12$ bits are shown in Figure 10.17. It is clear for $B = 12$ bits that the quantization error samples are independent and uniformly distributed. Readers should verify the statistics of these errors given in (10.7), (10.9), and (10.10).   □

From these two examples, we conclude that the statistical model for the multiplication quantization error, with its stated assumptions, is a very good model for random signals when the number of bits in the quantizer is large enough.

10.2.5 STATISTICAL ROUND-OFF NOISE—FIXED-POINT ARITHMETIC

In this and the next section, we will consider the round-off effects on IIR filters using the multiplication quantization error model developed in the previous section. Since we emphasize the rounding operation, this model is also known as a round-off noise model. We will limit ourselves to the first- and second-order filters since practical realizations involve first- or second-order sections.

First-order filter   Consider the first-order filter shown in Figure 10.18a. When a quantizer $\mathcal{Q}[\cdot]$ is introduced after the multiplier, the resulting filter model is shown in Figure 10.18b, which is a nonlinear system. When $\mathcal{Q}[\cdot]$ is a quantizer based on the round-off characteristics, then its effect is to add a zero-mean, stationary white noise sequence $e(n)$ at the multiplier output as shown in Figure 10.18c.

Let $q(n)$ be the response due to $e(n)$, and let $h_e(n)$ be the noise impulse response (i.e., between $e(n)$ and $q(n)$). For the system in Figure 10.18c,

$$h_e(n) = h(n) = \alpha^n u(n) \tag{10.38}$$

Using (10.12) and (10.7), the mean of $q(n)$ is

$$m_q = m_e \sum_{0}^{\infty} h_e(n) = 0 \tag{10.39}$$

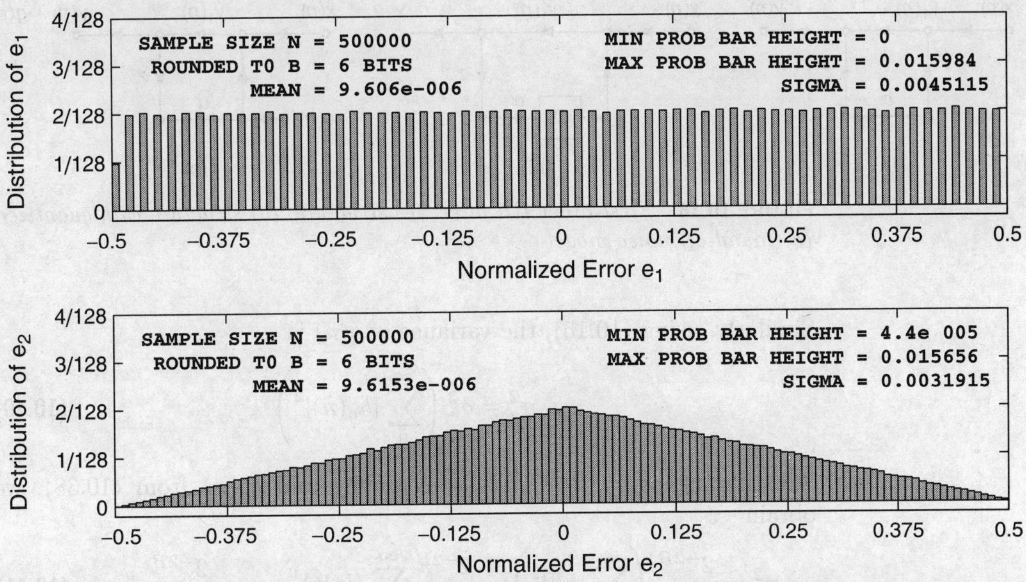

FIGURE 10.16 *Multiplication quantization error distribution for the random signal in Example 10.10, B = 6 bits*

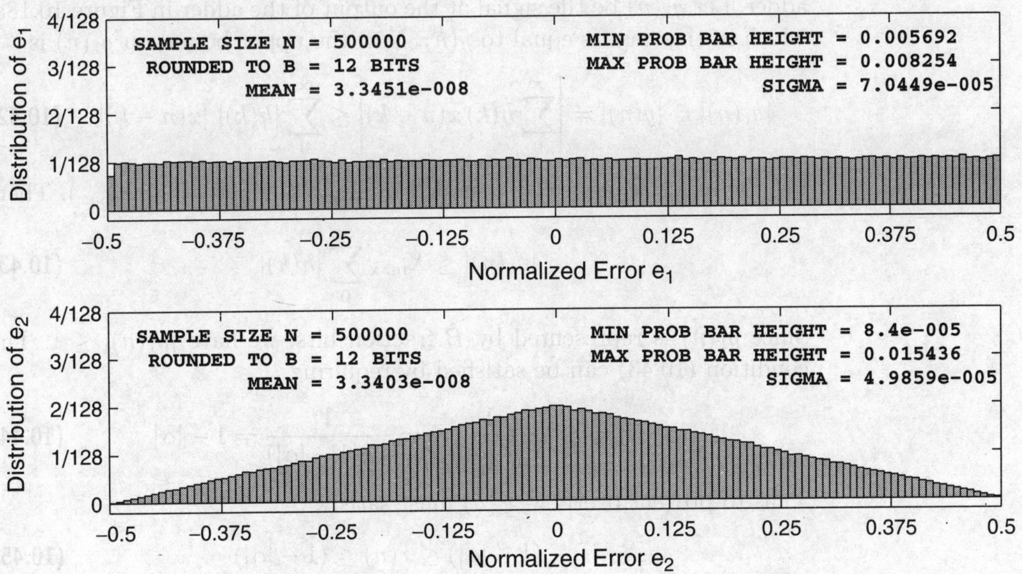

FIGURE 10.17 *Multiplication quantization error distribution for the random signal in Example 10.10, B = 12 bits*

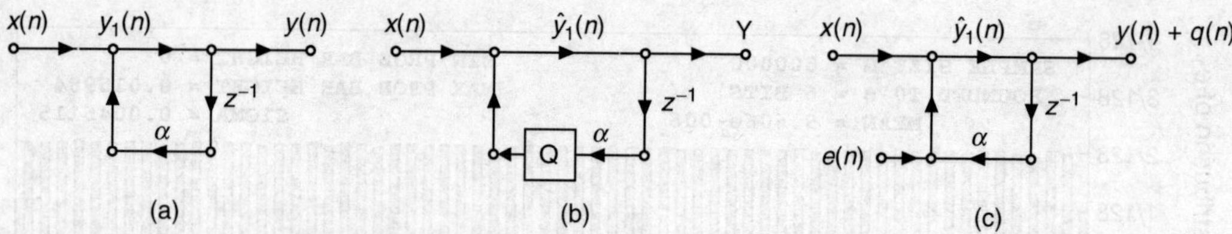

FIGURE 10.18 *First-order IIR filter: (a) structure, (b) structure with quantizer, (c) round-off noise model*

Similarly, using (10.15), the variance of $q(n)$ is

$$\sigma_q^2 = \sigma_e^2 \left(\sum_0^\infty |h_e(n)|^2 \right) \tag{10.40}$$

Substituting $\sigma_e^2 = 2^{-2B}/12$ for rounding and $h_e(n)$ from (10.38), we obtain

$$\sigma_q^2 = \frac{2^{-2B}}{12} \left(\sum_0^\infty |\alpha^n|^2 \right) = \frac{2^{-2B}}{12} \sum_0^\infty \left(|\alpha|^2 \right)^n = \frac{2^{-2B}}{12 \left(1 - |\alpha|^2 \right)} \tag{10.41}$$

which is the output noise power due to rounding following the multiplication.

However, we also have to prevent a possible overflow following the adder. Let $y_1(n)$ be the signal at the output of the adder in Figure 10.18a, which in this case is equal to $y(n)$. Now the upper bound on $y_1(n)$ is

$$|y_1(n)| = |y(n)| = \left| \sum_0^\infty h(k)\, x(n-k) \right| \leq \sum_0^\infty |h(k)|\, |x(n-k)| \tag{10.42}$$

Let the input sequence be bounded by $X_{\max}$ (i.e., $|x(n)| \leq X_{\max}$). Then

$$|y_1(n)| \leq X_{\max} \sum_0^\infty |h(k)| \tag{10.43}$$

Since $y_1(n)$ is represented by B fraction bits, we have $|y_1(n)| \leq 1$. The condition (10.43) can be satisfied by requiring

$$X_{\max} = \frac{1}{\sum_0^\infty |h(k)|} = \frac{1}{1/(1-|\alpha|)} = 1 - |\alpha| \tag{10.44}$$

Thus to prevent overflow, $x(n)$ must satisfy

$$-(1 - |\alpha|) \leq x(n) \leq (1 - |\alpha|) \tag{10.45}$$

Thus the input must be scaled before it is applied to the filter as shown in Figure 10.19.

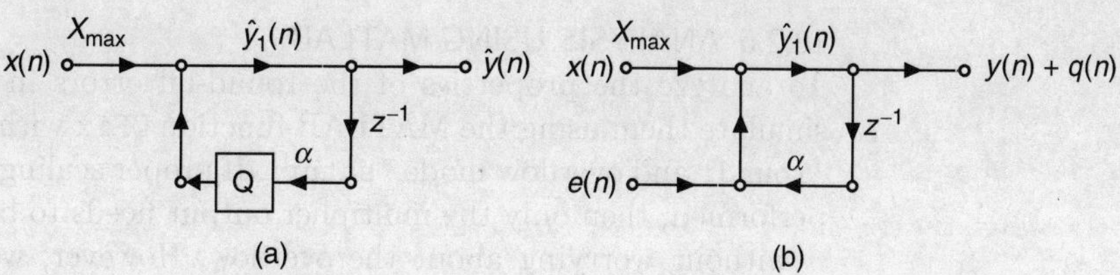

FIGURE 10.19 *Scaled first-order IIR filter: (a) structure with quantizer, (b) round-off noise model*

Signal-to-noise ratio We will now compute the finite word-length effect in terms of the output signal-to-noise ratio (SNR). We assume that there is no overflow at the output by properly scaling $x(n)$. Let $x(n)$ be a stationary white sequence, uniformly distributed between $[-(1-|\alpha|),(1-|\alpha|)]$. Then

$$m_x = 0 \quad \text{and} \quad \sigma_x^2 = \frac{(1-|\alpha|)^2}{3} \tag{10.46}$$

Therefore, $y(n)$ is also a stationary random sequence with mean $m_y = 0$ and

$$\sigma_y^2 = \sigma_x^2 \sum_0^\infty |h(n)|^2 = \frac{(1-|\alpha|)^2}{3} \frac{1}{1-|\alpha|^2} = \frac{(1-|\alpha|)^2}{3(1-|\alpha|^2)} \tag{10.47}$$

Using (10.41) and (10.47), the output SNR is

$$\text{SNR} \triangleq \frac{\sigma_y^2}{\sigma_q^2} = \frac{(1-|\alpha|)^2}{3(1-|\alpha|^2)} \frac{12(1-|\alpha|^2)}{2^{-2B}}$$
$$= 4\left(2^{2B}\right)(1-|\alpha|)^2 = 2^{2(B+1)}(1-|\alpha|)^2 \tag{10.48}$$

or the SNR in dB is

$$\text{SNR}_{\text{dB}} \triangleq 10\log_{10}(\text{SNR}) = 6.02 + 6.02B + 20\log_{10}(1-|\alpha|) \tag{10.49}$$

Let $\delta = 1 - |\alpha|$, which is the distance of the pole from the unit circle. Then

$$\text{SNR}_{\text{dB}} = 6.02 + 6.02B + 20\log_{10}(\delta) \tag{10.50}$$

which is a very informative result. First, it shows that the SNR is directly proportional to B and increases by about 6 dB for each additional bit added to the word length. Second, the SNR is also directly proportional to the distance δ. The smaller the δ (or nearer the pole to the unit circle), the smaller is the SNR, which is a consequence of the filter characteristics. As an example, if $B = 6$ and $\delta = 0.05$, then SNR $= 16.12$ dB, and if $B = 12$ and $\delta = 0.1$, then SNR $= 58.26$ dB.

10.2.6 ANALYSIS USING MATLAB

To analyze the properties of the round-off errors in IIR filters, we will simulate them using the MATLAB function QFix with quantization mode 'round' and overflow mode 'satur'. If proper scaling to avoid overflow is performed, then only the multiplier output needs to be quantized at each n without worrying about the overflow. However, we will still saturate the final sum to avoid any unforeseen problems. In previous simulations, we could perform the quantization operations on vectors (i.e., perform parallel processing). Since IIR filters are recursive filters and since each error is fed back into the system, vector operation is generally not possible. Hence the filter output will be computed sequentially from the first to the last sample. For a large number of samples, this implementation will slow the execution speed in MATLAB since MATLAB is optimized for vector calculations. However, for newer fast processors, the execution time is within a few seconds. These simulation steps are detailed in the following example.

☐ **EXAMPLE 10.11**   Consider the model given in Figure 10.19b. We will simulate this model in MATLAB and investigate its output error characteristics. Let $a = 0.9$, which will be quantized to B bits. The input signal is uniformly distributed over the $[-1, +1]$ interval and is also quantized to B bits prior to filtering. The scaling factor $X_{\max}$ is computed from (10.44). Using 100,000 signal samples and $B = 6$ bits, the following MATLAB script computes the true output $y(n)$, the quantized output $\hat{y}(n)$, the output error $q(n)$, and the output SNR.

```
close all; clc;

% Example Parameters
B = 6;                    % # of fractional bits
N = 100000;               % # of samples
xn = (2*rand(1,N)-1);     % Input sequence - uniform distribution
a = 0.9;                  % Filter parameter
Xm = 1-abs(a);            % Scaling factor

% Local variables
  bM = 7; DbM = 2^bM;     % Bin parameter
  BB = 2^B;               % Useful factor in quantization
   M = round(DbM/2);      % Half number of bins
bins = [-M+0.5:1:M-0.5];  % Bin values from -M to M
   Q = bins/DbM;          % Normalized bins
 YTN = 2^(-bM);           % Ytick marks interval
 YLM = 4*YTN;             % Yaxis limit

% Quantize the input and the filter coefficients
  xn = QFix(Xm*xn,B,'round','satur'); % Scaled input quant to B bits
   a = QFix(a,B,'round','satur');      % a quantized to B bits
```

```
% Filter output without multiplication quantization
  yn = filter(1,[1,-a],xn);  % Output using filter routine

% Filter output with multiplication quantization
   yq = zeros(1,N);                     % Initialize quantized output array
yq(1) = xn(1);                          % Calculation of the first sample yq(1)
for I = 2:N;
    A1Y = QFix(a*yq(I-1),B,'round','satur'); % Quantization of a*y(n-1)
  yq(I) = QFix(A1Y+xn(I),B,'round','satur'); % I-th sample yq(I)
end

% Output Error Analysis
   en = yn-yq;                          % Output error sequence
varyn = var(yn); varen = var(en);       % Signal and noise power
eemax = max(en); eemin = min(en);       % Maximum and minimum of the error
enmax = max(abs([eemax,eemin]));        % Absolute maximum range of the error
enavg = mean(en); enstd = std(en);      % Mean and std dev of the error
   en = round(en*(2^bM)/(2*enmax)+0.5); % Normalized en (integer between -M & M)
   en = sort([en,-M:1:(M+1)]);          %
    H = diff(find(diff(en)))-1;         % Error histogram
    H = H/N;                            % Normalized histogram
 Hmax = max(H); Hmin = min(H);          % Max and min of the normalized histogram

% Output SNRs
SNR_C = 10*log10(varyn/varen); % Computed SNR
SNR_T = 6.02 + 6.02*B + 20*log10(Xm); % Theoretical SNR
```

The part of the script not shown above also computes and plots the normalized histogram of the output error and prints the statistical values in the plot, as shown in Figure 10.20. The error appears to have a Gaussian distribution, which is to be expected. The exact value of the output SNR is 22.14 dB, which agrees with the computed value of 22.21 dB. Similar results done for $B = 12$ bits are shown in Figure 10.21. Again, the simulation results agree with the model results. $\square$

Second-order filter   Similar analysis can be done for second-order filters with poles near the unit circle. Let the two poles be at complex locations $re^{j\theta}$ and $re^{-j\theta}$. Then the system function of the filter is given by

$$H(z) = \frac{1}{(1 - re^{j\theta}z^{-1})(1 - re^{-j\theta}z^{-1})} = \frac{1}{1 - 2r\cos(\theta)\,z^{-1} + r^2 z^{-2}}$$

(10.51)

with impulse response

$$h(n) = \frac{r^n \sin\{(n+1)\theta\}}{\sin(\theta)} u(n)$$

(10.52)

The difference equation from (10.51) is given by

$$y(n) = x(n) - a_1 y(n-1) - a_2 y(n-2); \quad a_1 = -2r\cos(\theta),\ a_2 = r^2$$

(10.53)

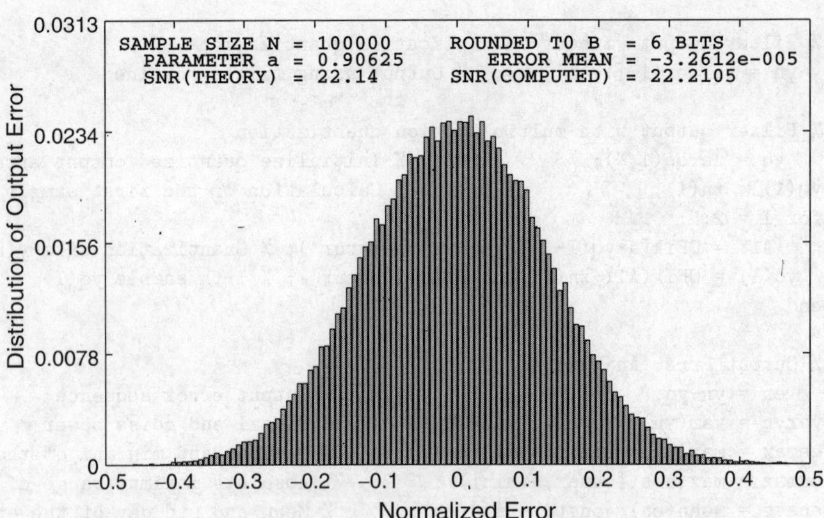

FIGURE 10.20 *Multiplication quantization effects in the first-order IIR filter in Example 10.11, $B = 6$ bits*

which requires two multiplications and two additions, as shown in Figure 10.22a. Thus there are two noise sources and two possible locations for overflow. The round-off noise model for quantization following

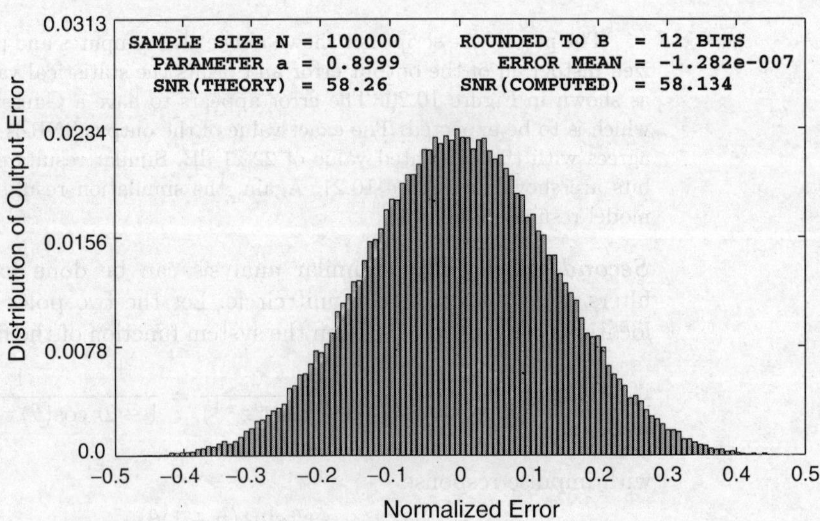

FIGURE 10.21 *Multiplication quantization effects in the first-order IIR filter in Example 10.11, $B = 12$ bits*

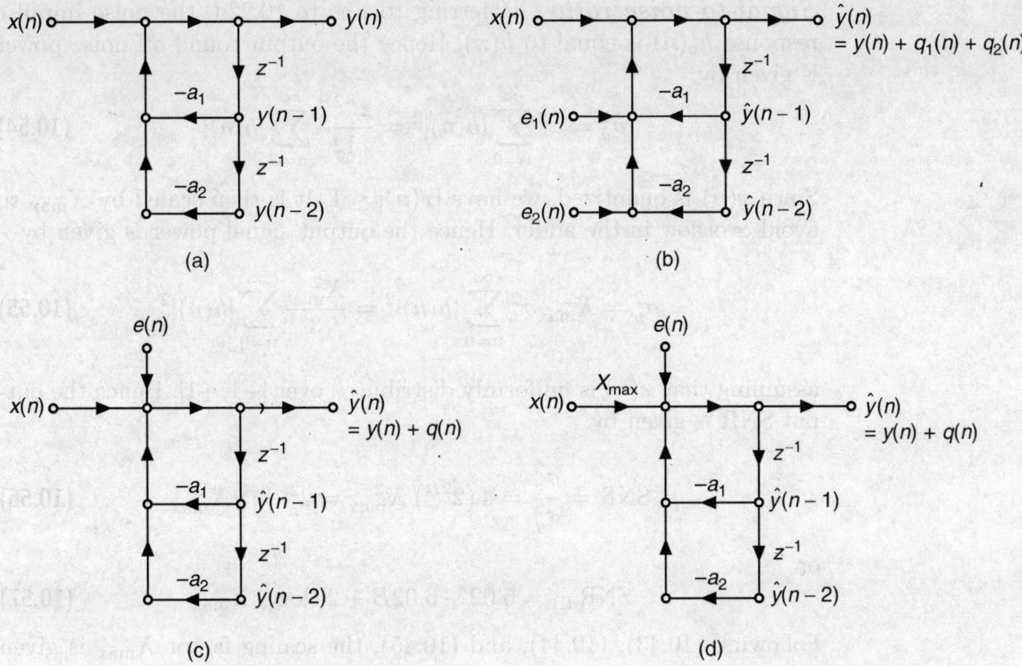

FIGURE 10.22 *Second-order IIR filter: (a) structure, (b) round-off noise model, (c) simplified model, (d) scaled simplified model*

the two multipliers is shown in Figure 10.22b, where the responses $q_1(n)$ and $q_2(n)$ are due to noise sources $e_1(n)$ and $e_2(n)$, respectively. We can combine two noise sources into one. However, to avoid overflow, we have to scale signals at the input of each adder, which can complicate this consolidation of sources.

In modern DSP chips, the intermediate results of multiply-add operations are stored in a multiply-accumulate (MAC) unit that has a double-precision register to accumulate sums. The final sum (which for Figure 10.22b is at the output of the top adder) is quantized to obtain $\hat{y}(n)$. This implementation not only reduces the total multiplication quantization noise but also makes the resulting analysis easier. Assuming this modern implementation, the resulting simplified model is shown in Figure 10.22c, where $e(n)$ is the single noise source that is uniformly distributed between $[-2^{-(B+1)}, 2^{-(B+1)}]$ and $q(n)$ is the response due to $e(n)$. Note that $e(n) \neq e_1(n) + e_2(n)$ and that $q(n) \neq q_1(n) + q_2(n)$. The only overflow that we have to worry about is at the output of the top adder, which can be controlled by scaling the input sequence $x(n)$ as shown in Figure 10.22d. Now the round-off noise analysis can be carried out in a fashion similar to that of the first-order filter. The details, however, are more involved due to the impulse response in (10.52).

Signal-to-noise ratio   Referring to Figure 10.22d, the noise impulse response $h_e(n)$ is equal to $h(n)$. Hence the output round-off noise power is given by

$$\sigma_q^2 = \sigma_e^2 \sum_{n=0}^{\infty} |h(n)|^2 = \frac{2^{-2B}}{12} \sum_{n=0}^{\infty} |h(n)|^2 \tag{10.54}$$

Since $x(n)$ is quantized, we have $|x(n)| \leq 1$. It is then scaled by $X_{\max}$ to avoid overflow in the adder. Hence the output signal power is given by

$$\sigma_y^2 = X_{\max}^2 \sigma_x^2 \sum_{n=0}^{\infty} |h(n)|^2 = \frac{X_{\max}^2}{3} \sum_{n=0}^{\infty} |h(n)|^2 \tag{10.55}$$

assuming that $x(n)$ is uniformly distributed over $[-1, +1]$. Hence the output SNR is given by

$$\text{SNR} = \frac{\sigma_y^2}{\sigma_q^2} = 4 \left(2^{2B}\right) X_{\max}^2 = 2^{2(B+1)} X_{\max}^2 \tag{10.56}$$

or

$$\text{SNR}_{\text{dB}} = 6.02 + 6.02B + 20 \log_{10} X_{\max} \tag{10.57}$$

Following (10.43), (10.44), and (10.45), the scaling factor $X_{\max}$ is given by

$$X_{\max} = \frac{1}{\sum_{n=0}^{\infty} |h(n)|} \tag{10.58}$$

which is not easy to compute. However, lower and upper bounds on $X_{\max}$ are easy to obtain. From (10.52), the upper bound on the denominator of (10.58) is given by

$$\sum_{n=0}^{\infty} |h(n)| = \frac{1}{\sin\theta} \sum_{n=0}^{\infty} r^n |\sin[(n+1)\theta]| \leq \frac{1}{\sin\theta} \sum_{n=0}^{\infty} r^n = \frac{1}{(1-r)\sin\theta} \tag{10.59}$$

or the lower bound on $X_{\max}$ is given by

$$X_{\max} \geq (1-r)\sin\theta \tag{10.60}$$

The lower bound on the denominator of (10.58) is obtained by noting that

$$|H(e^{j\omega})| = \left| \sum_{n=0}^{\infty} h(n) e^{-j\omega} \right| \leq \sum_{n=0}^{\infty} |h(n)|$$

Now from (10.51), the magnitude $|H(e^{j\omega})|$ is given by

$$|H(e^{j\omega})| = \left| \frac{1}{1 - 2r\cos(\theta)e^{-j\omega} + r^2 e^{-j2\omega}} \right|$$

which has the maximum value at the resonant frequency $\omega = \theta$, which can be easily obtained. Hence

$$\sum_{n=0}^{\infty} |h(n)| \geq \left| H(e^{j\theta}) \right| = \frac{1}{(1-r)\sqrt{1+r^2-2r\cos(2\theta)}} \qquad (10.61)$$

or the upper bound on $X_{\max}$ is given by

$$X_{\max} \leq (1-r)\sqrt{1+r^2-2r\cos(2\theta)} \qquad (10.62)$$

Substituting (10.60) and (10.62) in (10.56), the output SNR is upper and lower bounded by

$$2^{2(B+1)}(1-r)^2 \sin^2\theta \leq \text{SNR} \leq 2^{2(B+1)}(1-r)^2(1+r^2-2r\cos 2\theta) \qquad (10.63)$$

Substituting $1 - r = \delta \ll 1$ and after some simplification, we obtain

$$2^{2(B+1)}\delta^2 \sin^2\theta \leq \text{SNR} \leq 4\left(2^{2(B+1)}\right)\delta^2 \sin^2\theta \qquad (10.64)$$

or the difference between the upper and lower SNR bounds is about 6 dB. Once again, the output SNR is directly proportional to B and δ. Furthermore, it also depends on the angle θ. Some of these observations are investigated in Example 10.12.

10.2.7 ANALYSIS USING MATLAB

We will again simulate round-off errors using the MATLAB function `QFix` with quantization mode `'round'` and overflow mode `'satur'`. Since a MAC architecture is assumed, we do not have to quantize the intermediate results and worry about overflow. Only the final sum needs to be quantized with saturation. These operations are also simulated in sequential fashion, which has an impact on execution speed. The simulation steps for the second-order filter are detailed in the following example.

☐   **EXAMPLE 10.12**   Consider the model given in Figure 10.22d. We will simulate this model in MATLAB and investigate its output error characteristics. Let $r = 0.9$ and $\theta = \pi/3$, from which filter parameters are computed and quantized to B bits. The input signal is uniformly distributed over the $[-1, +1]$ interval and is also quantized to B bits prior to filtering. The scaling factor $X_{\max}$ is determined using (10.58), which can be obtained in MATLAB by computing the impulse response for a sufficiently large number of samples. Using 100,000 signal samples and $B = 6$ bits, the following MATLAB script computes the true output SNR, the computed SNR, and the lower and upper bounds of the SNR.

```matlab
close all; clc;

% Example Parameters
 B = 12;                 % # of fractional bits
 N = 100000;             % # of samples
xn = (2*rand(1,N)-1); % Input sequence - Uniform
 r = 0.9; theta = pi/3;% Pole locations

% Computed Parameters
p1 = r*exp(j*theta);  % Poles
p2 = conj(p1);        %
 a = poly([p1,p2]);   % Filter parameters
hn = filter(1,a,[1,zeros(1,1000)]); % Imp res
Xm = 1/sum(abs(hn));  % Scaling factor
Xm_L = (1-r)*sin(theta); % Lower bound
Xm_U = (1-r)*sqrt(1+r*r-2*r*cos(2*theta)); % Upper bound

% Local variables
  bM = 7; DbM = 2^bM;    % Bin parameter
  BB = 2^B;              % Useful factor in quantization
   M = round(DbM/2);     % Half number of bins
bins = [-M+0.5:1:M-0.5]; % Bin values from -M to M
   Q = bins/DbM;         % Normalized bins
 YTN = 2^(-bM);          % Ytick marks interval
 YLM = 4*YTN;            % Yaxis limit

% Quantize the input and the filter coefficients
  xn = QFix(Xm*xn,B,'round','satur'); % Scaled input quant B bits
   a = QFix(a,B,'round','satur');     % a quantized to B bits
  a1 = a(2); a2 = a(3);

% Filter output without multiplication quantization
  yn = filter(1,a,xn);  % output using filter routine

% Filter output with multiplication quantization
   yq = zeros(1,N); % Initialize quantized output array
yq(1) = xn(1);        % sample yq(1)
yq(2) = QFix((xn(2)-a1*yq(1)),B,'round','satur'); % sample yq(2)
for I = 3:N;
    yq(I) = xn(I)-a1*yq(I-1)-a2*yq(I-2); % Unquantized sample
    yq(I) = QFix(yq(I),B,'round','satur'); % Quantized sample
end

% Output Error Analysis
   en = yn-yq;                          % Output error sequence
varyn = var(yn); varen = var(en);       % Signal and noise power
eemax = max(en); eemin = min(en);       % Maximum and minimum of the error
```

```
enmax = max(abs([eemax,eemin]));       % Absolute maximum range of the error
enavg = mean(en); enstd = std(en);     % Mean and std dev of the error
   en = round(en*(2^bM)/(2*enmax)+0.5); % Normalized en (integer between -M & M)
   en = sort([en,-M:1:(M+1)]);         %
    H = diff(find(diff(en)))-1;        % Error histogram
    H = H/N;                           % Normalized histogram
 Hmax = max(H); Hmin = min(H);         % Max and Min of the normalized histogram

% Output SNRs
SNR_C = 10*log10(varyn/varen);         % Computed SNR
SNR_T = 6.02 + 6.02*B + 20*log10(Xm);  % Theoretical SNR
SNR_L = 6.02 + 6.02*B + 20*log10(Xm_L); % Lower SNR bound
SNR_U = 6.02 + 6.02*B + 20*log10(Xm_U); % Upper SNR bound
```

The part of the script not shown above also computes and plots the normalized histogram of the output error and prints the statistical values in the plot, as shown in Figure 10.23. The error again has a Gaussian distribution. The exact value of the output SNR is 25.22 dB, which agrees with the computed value of 25.11 dB and lies between the lower bound of 20.89 dB and the upper bound of 26.47 dB. Similar results done for $B = 12$ bits are shown in Figure 10.24. Again, the simulation results agree with the model results. □

10.2.8 HIGHER-ORDER FILTERS

The analysis of the quantization effects in a second-order filter can be applied directly to higher-order filters based on a parallel realization.

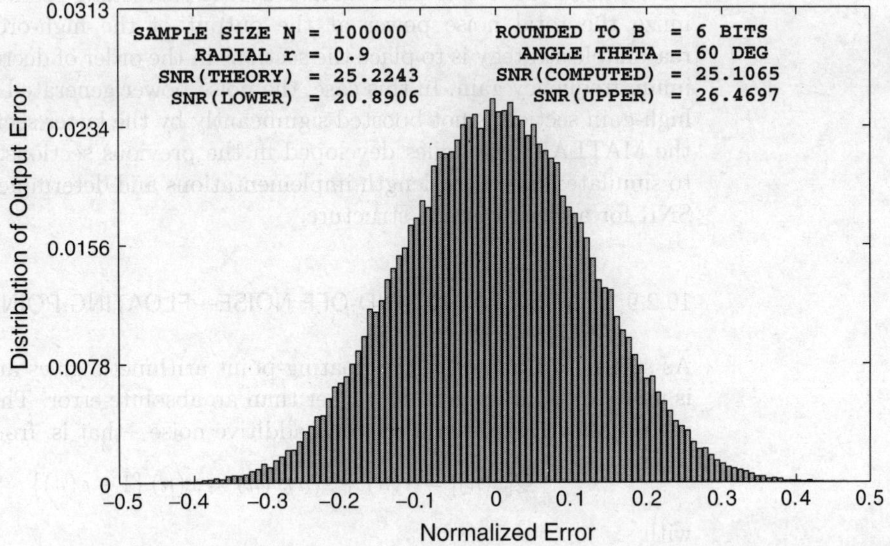

FIGURE 10.23 *Multiplication quantization effects in the first-order IIR filter in Example 10.12, $B = 6$ bits*

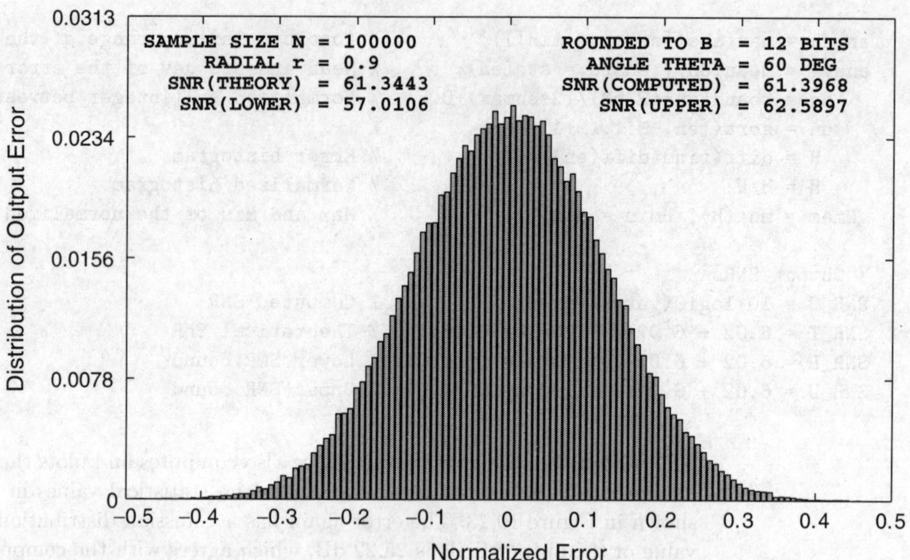

FIGURE 10.24 *Multiplication quantization effects in the first-order IIR filter in
Example 10.12, B = 12 bits*

In this case, each second-order filter section is independent of all the other
sections, and therefore the total quantization noise power at the output
of the parallel structure is simply the linear sum of the quantization noise
powers of each of the individual sections. On the other hand, the cascade
realization is more difficult to analyze because the noise generated in any
second-order filter section is filtered by the succeeding sections. To minimize the total noise power at the output of the high-order filter, a
reasonable strategy is to place the sections in the order of decreasing maximum frequency gain. In this case, the noise power generated in the early
high-gain section is not boosted significantly by the latter sections. Using
the MATLAB techniques developed in the previous sections, it is easier
to simulate finite word-length implementations and determine the output
SNR for a given cascade structure.

10.2.9 STATISTICAL ROUND-OFF NOISE—FLOATING-POINT ARITHMETIC

As stated in Chapter 6, the floating-point arithmetic gives an error that
is relative to the magnitude rather than an absolute error. This results in
a multiplicative noise rather than additive noise—that is, from (6.61),

$$\mathcal{Q}[x(n)] = x(n) + \varepsilon(n)x(n) = x(n)\left\{1 + \varepsilon(n)\right\} \qquad \textbf{(10.65)}$$

with

$$-2^{-B} < \varepsilon(n) \leq 2^{-B} \qquad \textbf{(10.66)}$$

for a $(B+1)$-bit mantissa. Hence the mean of the relative error is $m_\varepsilon = 0$ and its variance is

$$\sigma_\varepsilon^2 = \frac{2^{-2B}}{3} \qquad (10.67)$$

Since MATLAB is implemented in IEEE-754 floating-point arithmetic, all simulations that we perform are IEEE-754 floating-point calculations. It is difficult (if not impossible) to simulate arbitrary floating-point arithmetic in MATLAB. Therefore, we give theoretical results only.

First-order filter Consider a first-order filter as before and shown in Figure 10.25a. For the finite word-length analysis with floating-point arithmetic we need quantizers after both multiplication and addition to account for rounding off in the mantissa, as shown in Figure 10.25b. Hence there are two noise sources in the the statistical model, as shown in Figure 10.25c, where $e_1(n)$ is the noise source in the multiplier, $e_2(n)$ is the noise source in the adder, $\hat{g}(n)$ is an adder sequence prior to quantization, and $\hat{y}(n)$ is the quantized output. Now

$$e_1(n) = \varepsilon_1(n)\,\alpha\,\hat{y}(n-1) \qquad (10.68a)$$

$$e_2(n) = \varepsilon_2(n)\,\hat{g}(n) \qquad (10.68b)$$

where $\varepsilon_1(n)$ and $\varepsilon_2(n)$ are the relative errors in the corresponding quantizers. The exact analysis even for the first-order case is tedious; hence we make a few practically reasonable approximations. If the absolute values of the errors are small, then we have $\hat{y}(n-1) \approx y(n-1)$ and $\hat{g}(n) \approx y(n)$; hence from (10.68a) we obtain

$$e_1(n) \approx \alpha\,\varepsilon_1(n)\,y(n-1) \qquad (10.69a)$$

$$e_2(n) \approx \varepsilon_2(n)\,y(n) \qquad (10.69b)$$

Furthermore, we make the following assumption about the noise sources:

1. $\varepsilon_1(n)$ and $\varepsilon_2(n)$ are white noise sources.
2. $\varepsilon_1(n)$ and $\varepsilon_2(n)$ are uncorrelated with each other.

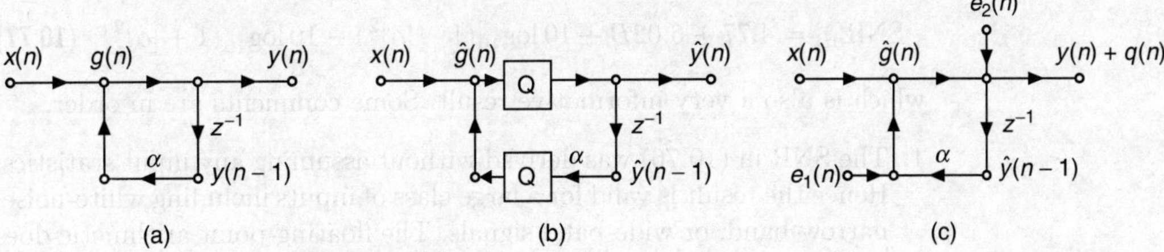

FIGURE 10.25 *First-order IIR filter: (a) structure, (b) finite word-length model for floating-point arithmetic, (c) statistical model for floating-point arithmetic*

3. $\varepsilon_1(n)$ and $\varepsilon_2(n)$ are uncorrelated with the input $x(n)$.

4. $\varepsilon_1(n)$ and $\varepsilon_2(n)$ are uniformly distributed between -2^{-B} and 2^{-B}.

Let $x(n)$ be a zero-mean, stationary random sequence. Then $y(n)$ is also a zero-mean, stationary sequence. Hence from (10.69),

$$\sigma_{e_1}^2 = |\alpha|^2 \sigma_{\varepsilon_1}^2 \sigma_y^2 \tag{10.70a}$$

$$\sigma_{e_2}^2 = \sigma_{\varepsilon_2}^2 \sigma_y^2 \tag{10.70b}$$

Let the error in the output due to $e_1(n)$ be $q_1(n)$, and let that due to $e_2(n)$ be $q_2(n)$. Let $h_1(n)$ and $h_2(n)$ be the corresponding noise impulse responses. Note that $h_1(n) = h_2(n) = h(n) = \alpha^n u(n)$. Then the total error $q(n)$ is

$$q(n) = q_1(n) + q_2(n) \tag{10.71}$$

with

$$\sigma_q^2 = \sigma_{q_1}^2 + \sigma_{q_2}^2 \tag{10.72}$$

where

$$\sigma_{q_1}^2 = \sigma_{e_1}^2 \sum_0^\infty |h_1(n)|^2 \quad \text{and} \quad \sigma_{q_2}^2 = \sigma_{e_2}^2 \sum_0^\infty |h_2(n)|^2 \tag{10.73}$$

Hence using (10.72), (10.73), and (10.70),

$$\sigma_q^2 = \left(\sigma_{e_1}^2 + \sigma_{e_2}^2\right)\left(\frac{1}{1 - |\alpha|^2}\right) = \sigma_y^2 \left(\frac{1}{1 - |\alpha|^2}\right)\left(|\alpha|^2 \sigma_{\varepsilon_1}^2 + \sigma_{\varepsilon_2}^2\right) \tag{10.74}$$

Using $\sigma_{\varepsilon_1}^2 = \sigma_{\varepsilon_2}^2 = 2^{-2B}/3$, we obtain

$$\sigma_q^2 = \sigma_y^2 \left(\frac{2^{-2B}}{3}\right)\left(\frac{1 + |\alpha|^2}{1 - |\alpha|^2}\right) \tag{10.75}$$

Therefore,

$$\text{SNR} = \frac{\sigma_y^2}{\sigma_q^2} = 3\left(2^{2B}\right)\left(\frac{1 - |\alpha|^2}{1 + |\alpha|^2}\right) \tag{10.76}$$

or

$$\text{SNR}_{\text{dB}} = 4.77 + 6.02B + 10\log_{10}(1 - |\alpha|^2) - 10\log_{10}(1 + |\alpha|^2) \tag{10.77}$$

which is also a very informative result. Some comments are in order.

1. The SNR in (10.76) was derived without assuming any input statistics, Hence the result is valid for a large class of inputs including white-noise, narrow-band, or wide-band signals. The floating-point arithmetic does not have to worry about the scaling or limiting input values, since it can handle a large dynamic range.

2. Using $0 < \delta = 1 - |\alpha| \ll 1$, the SNR in (10.77) can be put in the form

$$\text{SNR}_{\text{dB}} \approx 4.77 + 6.02B + 10\log_{10}(\delta) = \text{O}(\delta) \qquad \textbf{(10.78)}$$

This is to be compared with the fixed-point result (10.50), where $\text{SNR} \approx \text{O}(\delta^2)$. Thus the floating-point result is less sensitive to the distance of the pole to the unit circle.

3. In floating-point arithmetic, the output noise variance, σ_q^2, in (10.75) is proportional to σ_y^2. Thus, if the input signal is scaled up, so is the noise variance since σ_y^2 is also scaled up. Hence the SNR remains constant. This again should be compared with the fixed-point case (10.41), in which σ_q^2 is independent of the input signal. Hence if the signal level increases, then σ_y^2 increases, which increases the SNR.

Second-order filter   Similar analysis can be done for the second-order filter with poles close to the unit circle. If the poles are given by $re^{\pm j\theta}$, then we can show that (see [71])

$$\text{SNR} = \frac{\sigma_y^2}{\sigma_q^2} \approx 3\left(2^{2B}\right)\frac{4\delta\sin^{2\theta}}{3 + 4\cos\theta} \approx \text{O}\left(\delta\right) \qquad \textbf{(10.79)}$$

where $\delta = 1 - r$. This again is an approximate result that works very well in practice. In this case again, the SNR depends on δ rather than on δ^2 as in the fixed-point case.

10.3 ROUND-OFF EFFECTS IN FIR DIGITAL FILTERS

We will now turn our attention to the finite word-length effects in FIR digital filters. As before, we will consider the fixed-point and floating-point cases separately. We will then conclude this section with some representative examples.

10.3.1 FIXED-POINT ARITHMETIC

We will consider the effects on two realizations: direct form and cascade form. There is no parallel form realization for FIR filters, since we do not have a partial fraction expansion, except for the frequency-sampling realization, which can be analyzed using IIR filter techniques. The analysis of FIR filters is much simpler than that for IIR because there are no feedback paths. One consequence of this is the absence of limit cycles.

Direct-form realization Consider an FIR filter of length M (i.e., there are M samples in the impulse response), which is realized using the direct form as shown in Figure 10.26a. The filter coefficients are the samples of the impulse response $h(n)$. We have to introduce quantizers in the vertical branches. If we use the implementation in which each multiplier output is quantized, then we obtain the model shown in Figure 10.26b. On the other hand, if we implement the filter in a typical DSP chip, then the final sum is quantized, as shown in Figure 10.26c. We will separately consider the effects of round-off noise and scaling (to avoid overflow).

Round-off noise Let the output of the filter in Figure 10.26b due to round-off errors be $\hat{y}(n) = y(n) + q(n)$. Then

$$q(n) = \sum_{k=0}^{M-1} e_k(n) \tag{10.80}$$

where $e_k(n)$ are the noise sources introduced in each vertical branch to account for the rounding operations. Since these noise sources are all independent and identical, the noise power in $q(n)$ is given by

$$\sigma_q^2 = \sum_0^{M-1} \sigma_{e_k}^2 = M \sigma_e^2 = M \left(\frac{2^{-2B}}{12} \right) = \frac{M}{3} 2^{-2(B+1)} \tag{10.81}$$

In Figure 10.26c, the output due to the rounding operation is $\hat{y}(n) = y(n) + e(n)$. Hence the noise power in this case is given by

$$\sigma_q^2 = \sigma_e^2 = \frac{1}{3} 2^{-2(B+1)} \tag{10.82}$$

which is smaller by a factor of M compared to (10.81), as expected.

Scaling to avoid overflow We assume that the fixed-point numbers have the two's-complement form representation, which is a reasonable assumption. Then we will have to check only the overflow of the total sum. Thus this analysis is the same for both implementations in Figure 10.26 and is similar to that for the IIR filter in (10.42)–(10.44). The upper-bound on $y(n)$ is obtained as

$$|y(n)| = \left| \sum h(k)\, x(n-k) \right| \le X_{\max} \sum |h(n)| \tag{10.83}$$

where $X_{\max}$ is the upper-bound on $x(n)$. To guarantee that $|y(n)| \le 1$, we need the scaling factor $X_{\max}$ on $x(n)$ as

$$X_{\max} \le \frac{1}{\sum |h(n)|} \tag{10.84}$$

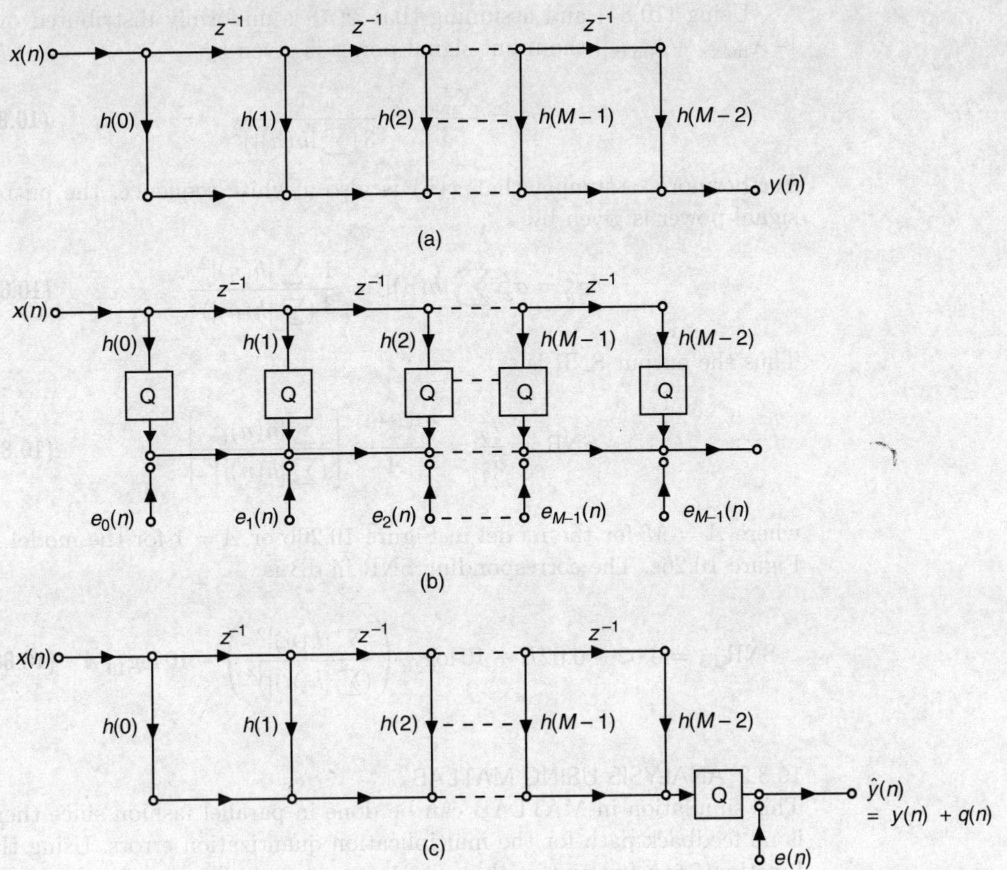

FIGURE 10.26 *Direct form FIR filter: (a) structure, (b) round-off noise model with quantizers after each multiplier, (c) round-off noise mode with one quantizer after the final sum*

which is the most conservative scaling factor. There are other scaling factors, depending on the applications—for example, the narrowband signals use

$$X_{\max} \leq \frac{1}{\max |H(e^{j\omega})|}$$

and wideband random signals use

$$X_{\max} \leq \frac{1}{4\sigma_x \sqrt{\sum |h(n)|^2}}$$

Using (10.84) and assuming that $x(n)$ is uniformly distributed over $[-X_{\max}, +X_{\max}]$, the input signal power is given by

$$\sigma_x^2 = \frac{X_{\max}^2}{3} = \frac{1}{3\left(\sum |h(n)|\right)^2} \tag{10.85}$$

Furthermore, assuming that $x(n)$ is also a white sequence, the output signal power is given by

$$\sigma_y^2 = \sigma_x^2 \sum |h(n)|^2 = \frac{1}{3} \frac{\sum |h(n)|^2}{\left(\sum |h(n)|\right)^2} \tag{10.86}$$

Thus the output SNR is

$$\text{SNR} = \frac{\sigma_y^2}{\sigma_q^2} = \frac{2^{2(B+1)}}{A} \left[\frac{\sum |h(n)|^2}{\left(\sum |h(n)|\right)^2} \right] \tag{10.87}$$

where $A = M$ for the model in Figure 10.26b or $A = 1$ for the model in Figure 10.26c. The corresponding SNR in dB is

$$\text{SNR}_{\text{dB}} = 6.02 + 6.02B + 10\log_{10}\left(\frac{\sum |h(n)|^2}{\left(\sum |h(n)|\right)^2}\right) - 10\log_{10} A \quad \textbf{(10.88)}$$

10.3.2 ANALYSIS USING MATLAB

This simulation in MATLAB can be done in parallel fashion since there is no feedback path for the multiplication quantization errors. Using the function `Qfix` function with `'round'` mode, we will compute the quantized multiplier output. In the case of M quantizers, assuming two's-complement format, we will use the `'twosc'` mode for each quantizer. Only the final sum will be quantized and saturated. In the case of one quantizer, we need the `'satur'` mode. These simulation steps are detailed in the following example.

☐ **EXAMPLE 10.13**   Let a fourth-order ($M = 5$) FIR filter be given by

$$H(z) = 0.1 + 0.2z^{-1} + 0.4z^{-2} + 0.2z^{-3} + 0.1z^{-4} \tag{10.89}$$

which is implemented as a direct form with $B = 12$ fractional bit quantizers. Compute SNRs for models in Figure 10.26b and 10.26c and verify them using MATLAB. simulations.

Solution   We will need the quantities $\sum |h(n)|^2$ and $\left(\sum |h(n)|\right)^2$. These quantities should be computed using 12-bit quantization of the filter coefficients. These values using the quantized numbers are $\sum |h(n)|^2 = 0.2599$ and $(\sum |h(n)|)^2 = 1$. Using (10.88), the output SNR is 65.42 dB for five multipliers and is 72.41 dB for one multiplier. The following MATLAB script evaluates these and other quantities.

```
% Example Parameters
B = 12;                         % # of fractional bits
N = 100000;                     % # of samples
xn = (2*rand(1,N)-1);           % Input sequence - uniform distribution
h = [0.1,0.2,0.4,0.2,0.1]; % Filter parameters
M = length(h);

% Local variables
  bM = 7; DbM = 2^bM;        % Bin parameter
  BB = 2^B;                  % Useful factor in quantization
   K = round(DbM/2);         % Half number of bins
bins = [-K+0.5:1:K-0.5];    % Bin values from -K to K
   Q = bins/DbM;             % Normalized bins
 YTN = 2^(-bM);              % Ytick marks interval
 YLM = 4*YTN;                % Yaxis limit

% Quantize the input and the filter coefficients
 h = QFix(h,B,'round','satur'); % h quantized to B bits
Xm = 1/sum(abs(h));             % Scaling factor
xn = QFix(Xm*xn,B,'round','satur');% Scaled Input quant to B bits

% Filter output without multiplication quantization
yn = filter(h,1,xn);       % output using filter routine

% Filter output with multi quant (5 multipliers)
x1 = [zeros(1,1),xn(1:N-1)]; x2 = [zeros(1,2),xn(1:N-2)];
x3 = [zeros(1,3),xn(1:N-3)]; x4 = [zeros(1,4),xn(1:N-4)];
h0x0 = QFix(h(1)*xn,B,'round','twosc');
h1x1 = QFix(h(2)*x1,B,'round','twosc');
h2x2 = QFix(h(3)*x2,B,'round','twosc');
h3x3 = QFix(h(4)*x3,B,'round','twosc');
h4x4 = QFix(h(5)*x4,B,'round','twosc');
yq = h0x0+h1x1+h2x2+h3x3+h4x4;
yq = QFix(yq,B,'round','satur');

% Output Error Analysis
   qn = yn-yq;                          % Outout error sequence
varyn = var(yn); varqn = var(qn);       % Signal and noise power
qqmax = max(qn); qqmin = min(qn);       % Maximun and minimum of the error
qnmax = max(abs([qqmax,qqmin]));        % Absolute maximum range of the error
qnavg = mean(qn); qnstd = std(qn);      % Mean and std dev of the error
```

```
    qn = round(qn*(2^bM)/(2*qnmax)+0.5); % Normalized en (integer between -K & K)
    qn = sort([qn,-K:1:(K+1)]);          %
     H = diff(find(diff(qn)))-1;         % Error histogram
     H = H/N;                            % Normalized histogram
  Hmax = max(H); Hmin = min(H);          % Max and Min of the normalized histogram

% Output SNRs
SNR_C = 10*log10(varyn/varqn); % Computed SNR
SNR_T = 6.02 + 6.02*B + 10*log10(sum(h.*h)/Xm^2) - 10*log10(M); % Theoretical SNR

% Filter output with multi quant (1 multiplier)
yq = QFix(yn,B,'round','satur');

% Output Error Analysis
    qn = yn-yq;                          % Outout error sequence
 varyn = var(yn); varqn = var(qn);       % Signal and noise power
 qqmax = max(qn); qqmin = min(qn);       % Maximun and minimum of the error
 qnmax = max(abs([qqmax,qqmin]));        % Absolute maximum range of the error
 qnavg = mean(qn); qnstd = std(qn);      % Mean and std dev of the error
    qn = round(qn*(2^bM)/(2*qnmax)+0.5); % Normalized en (integer between -K & K)
    qn = sort([qn,-K:1:(K+1)]);          %
     H = diff(find(diff(qn)))-1;         % Error histogram
     H = H/N;                            % Normalized histogram
  Hmax = max(H); Hmin = min(H);          % Max and min of the normalized histogram

% Output SNRs
SNR_C = 10*log10(varyn/varqn); % Computed SNR
SNR_T = 6.02 + 6.02*B + 10*log10(sum(h.*h)/Xm^2); % Theoretical SNR
```

The computed and theoretical SNRs as well as output error histograms for the two models are shown in Figure 10.27. The top plot shows the histogram when five multipliers are used. The output error has Gaussian-like distribution with SNR equal to 65.42 dB, which agrees with the theoretical value. The bottom plot show the histogram when one multiplier is used. As expected, the error is uniformly distributed with SNR equal to 72.43 dB, which also agrees with the theoretical one.   □

Cascade-form realization   Let the filter be realized by a cascade of K, second-order ($M = 3$) sections given by

$$H(z) = \sum_{i=1}^{K} H_i(z) \quad \text{where } H_i(z) = \beta_{0i} + \beta_{1i}\, z^{-1} + \beta_{2i}\, z^{-2} \qquad \textbf{(10.90)}$$

as shown in Figure 10.28. The overall length of the filter is $M = 2K + 1$. Figure 10.28 also shows the finite word-length model for the cascade form,

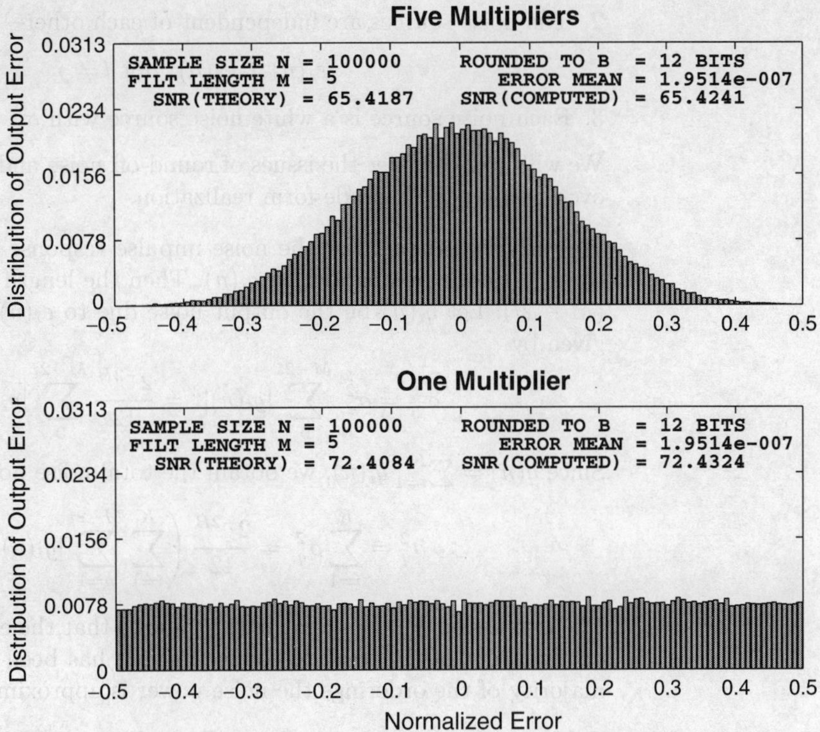

FIGURE 10.27 *Multiplication quantization effects for the direct form FIR filter in Example 10.13*

in which quantization noise sources, $e_i(n)$ $1 \leq i \leq K$, at each section's output are incorporated. Let $y(n)$ be the output due to input $x(n)$, and let $q(n)$ be the output due to all noise sources. We make the following reasonable assumptions:

1. The sections are implemented using the MAC (multiply-accumulate) architecture so that there is only one independent noise source in each section that contributes to $e_i(n)$. The other possibility of three multipliers in each section is straightforward.

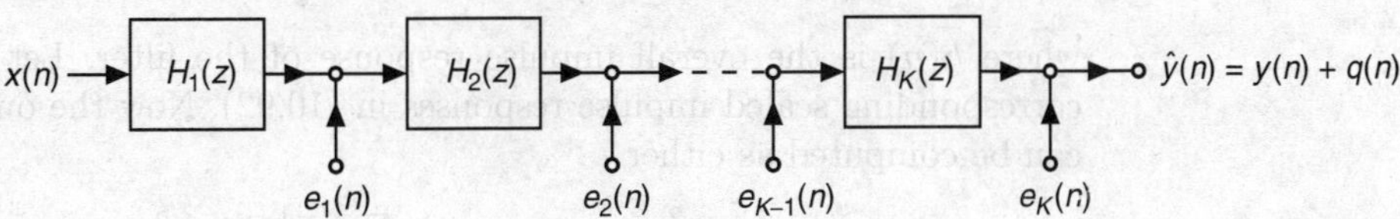

FIGURE 10.28 *Cascade form FIR filter structure with noise sources inserted for multiplication quantization*

2. The noise sources are independent of each other—that is,

$$e_i(n) \perp e_j(n) \quad \text{for } i \neq j$$

3. Each noise source is a white-noise source with $\sigma_{e_i}^2 = 2^{-2B}/12$.

We will now consider the issues of round-off noise and scaling (to prevent overflow) for the cascade form realization.

Round-off noise   Let the noise impulse response at the output from the $e_i(n)$ node be denoted by $g_i(n)$. Then the length of $g_i(n)$ is equal to $(M - 2i)$. Let $q_i(n)$ be the output noise due to $e_i(n)$. Then its power is given by

$$\sigma_{q_i}^2 = \sigma_{e_i}^2 \sum_{0}^{M-2i} |g_i(n)|^2 = \frac{2^{-2B}}{12} \sum_{0}^{M-2i} |g_i(n)|^2 \qquad \textbf{(10.91)}$$

Since $q(n) = \sum_{i=1}^{K} q_i(n)$, we obtain the total noise power as

$$\sigma_q^2 = \sum_{i=1}^{K} \sigma_{q_i}^2 = \frac{2^{-2B}}{12} \left(\sum_{i=1}^{K} \sum_{n=1}^{M-2i} |g_i(n)|^2 \right) \qquad \textbf{(10.92)}$$

The expression $\sum_{i=1}^{K} \sum_{n=1}^{M-2i} |g_i(n)|^2$ shows that the error power depends on the order of the cascade connections. It has been shown that for the majority of the orderings the noise power is approximately the same.

Scaling to prevent overflow   From Figure 10.28, we note that one must prevent overflow at each node. Let $h_k(n)$ be the impulse response at each node k; then we need a scaling constant $X_{\max}$ as

$$X_{\max} = \frac{1}{\max_k \sum |h_k(n)|}$$

so that $|y(n)| \leq 1$. Clearly, this is a very conservative value. A better approach is to scale the impulse responses of every section $\{h_i(n)\}$ so that $\sum |h_i| = 1$ for each i. Hence the output of every section is limited between -1 and $+1$ if the input $x(n)$ is distributed over the same interval. Assuming that $x(n)$ is uniformly distributed over $[-1, +1]$ and is white, the output signal power is

$$\sigma_y^2 = \sigma_x^2 \sum_{0}^{M-1} |h(n)|^2 = \frac{1}{3} \sum_{0}^{M-1} |h(n)|^2 \qquad \textbf{(10.93)}$$

where $h(n)$ is the overall impulse response of the filter. Let $\hat{g}_i$ be the corresponding scaled impulse responses in (10.92). Now the output SNR can be computed as either

$$\text{SNR} = \frac{\sigma_y^2}{\sigma_q^2} = 2^{2(B+1)} \frac{\sum_{0}^{M-1} |h(n)|^2}{\left(\sum_{i=1}^{K} \sum_{n=1}^{M-2i} |\hat{g}_i(n)|^2 \right)} \qquad \textbf{(10.94)}$$

or

$$\text{SNR}_{\text{dB}} = 6.02(B+1) + 10\log_{10}\left(\sum_{0}^{M-1}|h(n)|^2\right) - 10\log_{10}\left(\sum_{i=1}^{K}\sum_{n=1}^{M-2i}|\hat{g}_i(n)|^2\right)$$

$$(10.95)$$

10.3.3 ANALYSIS USING MATLAB

Using the `casfiltr` function, we can compute the output of the infinite-precision cascade structure. Using the scaling approach outlined above, each second-order section can be scaled and used in the simulation of quantized outputs. Again, all calculations can be done in vector fashion, which improves the execution speed. These and other simulation steps are detailed in the following example.

☐ **EXAMPLE 10.14** Consider the fourth-order FIR filter given in Example 10.13. Its cascade form realization has two sections along with a gain constant b_0, which can be obtained using the `dir2cas` function:

$$H_1(z) = 1 + 1.4859z^{-1} + 2.8901z^{-2}, \quad H_2(z) = 1 + 0.5141z^{-1} + 0.3460z^{-2}, \text{ and } b_0 = 0.1$$

$$(10.96)$$

Note that some of these coefficients are greater than 1, which will cause problems with coefficient quantization when only B fractional bits are used. Hence we need to scale each section as explained. The scaled values are

$$\hat{H}_1(z) = 0.1860 + 0.2764z^{-1} + 0.5376z^{-2}, \quad \hat{H}_2(z) = 0.5376 + 0.2764z^{-1} + 0.1860z^{-2}$$

$$(10.97)$$

and $\hat{b}_0 = 1$. Thus we do not need to scale the input. Now $\hat{g}_1(n) = \hat{h}_2(n)$ and $\hat{g}_2(n) = 1$ in (10.94). Thus from (10.95), the output SNR is 70.96 dB, which compares well with the one-multiplier direct form implementation (72.41 dB). These calculations and error histogram plotting are illustrated in the following MATLAB script.

```
% Example Parameters
B = 12;                         % # of fractional bits
N = 100000;                     % # of samples
xn = (2*rand(1,N)-1);           % Input sequence - uniform distribution
h = [0.1,0.2,0.4,0.2,0.1];      % Filter parameters
M = length(h);                  % Filter length
[b0,Bh,Ah] = dir2cas(h,1);      % Cascade sections
h1 = Bh(1,:);                   % Section-1
h2 = Bh(2,:);                   % Section-2
h1 = h1/sum(h1);                % Scaled so Gain=1
h2 = h2/sum(h2);                % Scaled so Gain=1
```

```matlab
% Local variables
  bM = 7; DbM = 2^bM;     % Bin parameter
  BB = 2^B;               % Useful factor in quantization
   K = round(DbM/2);      % Half number of bins
bins = [-K+0.5:1:K-0.5]; % Bin values from -K to K
   Q = bins/DbM;          % Normalized bins
 YTN = 2^(-bM);           % Ytick marks interval
 YLM = 20*YTN;            % Yaxis limit
% Quantize the input and the filter coefficients
h1 = QFix(h1,B,'round','satur'); % h1 quantized to B bits
h2 = QFix(h2,B,'round','satur'); % h1 quantized to B bits
xn = QFix(xn,B,'round','satur'); % Input quantized to B bits
% Filter output without multiplication quantization
yn = casfiltr(b0,Bh,Ah,xn); % output using Casfiltr routine
% Filter output with multi quant (1 multiplier/section)
xq = QFix(xn,B,'round','satur'); % Section-1 scaled input
wn = filter(h1,1,xq);           % Sec-1 unquantized output
wq = QFix(wn,B,'round','satur'); % Sec-1 quantized output
wq = QFix(wq,B,'round','satur'); % Section-2 scaled input
yq = filter(h2,1,wq);           % Sec-2 unquantized output
yq = QFix(yq,B,'round','satur'); % Sec-2 quantized output
% Output Error Analysis
  qn = yn-yq;                            % Outout error sequence
varyn = var(yn); varqn = var(qn);        % Signal and noise power
qqmax = max(qn); qqmin = min(qn);        % Maximun and minimum of the error
qnmax = max(abs([qqmax,qqmin]));         % Absolute maximum range of the error
qnavg = mean(qn); qnstd = std(qn);       % Mean and std dev of the error
  qn = round(qn*(2^bM)/(2*qnmax)+0.5); % Normalized en (integer between -K & K)
  qn = sort([qn,-K:1:(K+1)]);            %
   H = diff(find(diff(qn)))-1;           % Error histogram
   H = H/N;                              % Normalized histogram
 Hmax = max(H); Hmin = min(H);           % Max and min of the normalized histogram
% Output SNRs
SNR_C = 10*log10(varyn/varqn); % Computed SNR
SNR_T = 6.02*(B+1) + 10*log10(sum(h.*h)) ...
      - 10*log10(1+sum(h2.*h2)); % Theoretical SNR
```

The plot is shown in Figure 10.29. The error distribution appears to have a Gaussian envelope, but the error is not continuously distributed. This behavior indicates that the output error takes only a fixed set of values, which is due to a particular set of coefficient values. The computed SNR is 70.85 dB, which agrees with the above theoretical value. Thus our assumptions are reasonable.☐

10.3.4 FLOATING-POINT ARITHMETIC

Analysis for the floating-point arithmetic is more complicated and tedious. Hence we will consider only the direct form realization with simplified

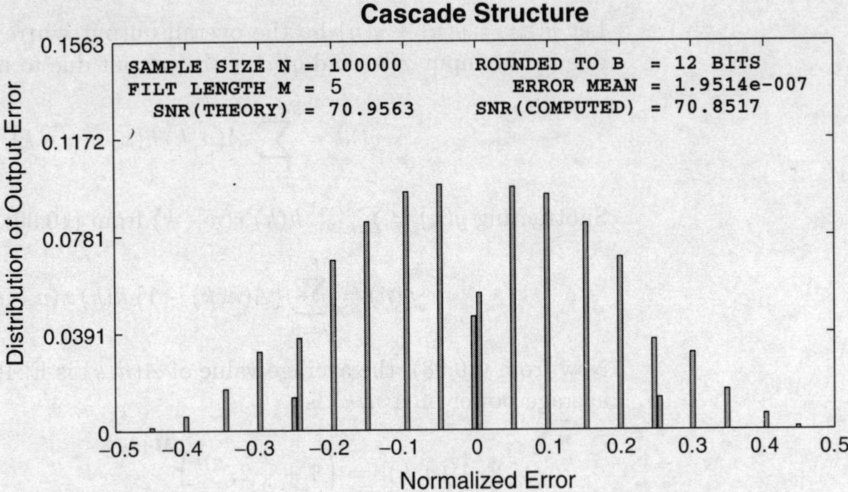

FIGURE 10.29 *Multiplication quantization effects for the cascade form FIR filter in Example 10.14*

assumptions. Figure 10.30 shows a direct form realization with a floating-point arithmetic model. In this realization, $\{\eta_i(n)\}$, $1 \le i \le M-1$ are the relative errors in adders and $\{\varepsilon_i(n)\}$, $0 \le i \le M-1$ are the relative errors in multipliers, with $|\eta_i| \le 2^{-2B}$ and $|\varepsilon_i| \le 2^{-2B}$.

Let $A(n,k)$ be the gain from the kth multiplier to the output node, which is given by

$$A(n,k) = \begin{cases} (1 + \varepsilon_k(n)) \prod_{r=k}^{M-1} (1 + \eta_r(n)), \ k \neq 0 \\ (1 + \varepsilon_0(n)) \prod_{r=k}^{M-1} (1 + \eta_r(n)), \ k = 0 \end{cases} \tag{10.98}$$

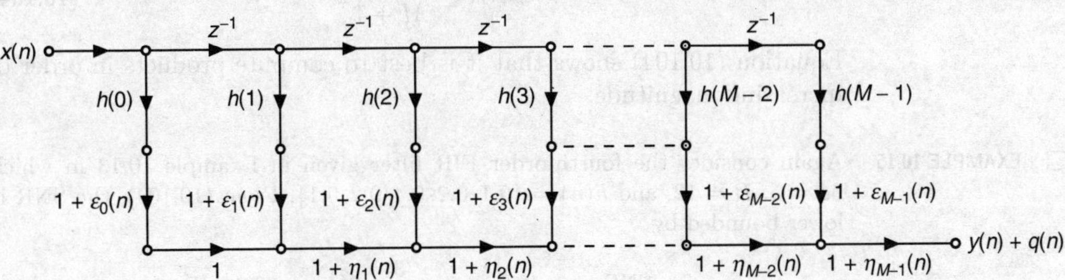

FIGURE 10.30 *Multiplication quantization model for direct form floating-point implementation of an FIR filter*

Let $\hat{y}(n) \triangleq y(n) + q(n)$ be the overall output where $y(n)$ is the output due to the input $x(n)$ and $q(n)$ is the output due to noise sources. Then

$$\hat{y}(n) = \sum_{k=0}^{M-1} A(n, k)\, h(k)\, x(n - k) \tag{10.99}$$

Subtracting $y(n) = \sum_{k=0}^{M-1} h(k)\, x(n - k)$ from (10.99), we obtain

$$q(n) = \sum_{k=0}^{M-1} \{A(n, k) - 1\}\, h(k)\, x(n - k) \tag{10.100}$$

Now from (10.98), the average value of $A(n, k)$ is $\mathrm{E}[A(n, k)] = 1$, and the average power of $A(n, k)$ is

$$\mathrm{E}[A^2(n, k)] = \left(1 + \frac{1}{3}\, 2^{-2B}\right)^{M+1-k}$$

$$\approx 1 + (M + 1 - k)\frac{2^{-2B}}{3} \quad \text{for small } 2^{-2B} \tag{10.101}$$

Assuming that the input signal $x(n)$ is also a white sequence with variance σ_x^2, then from (10.101) the noise power is given by

$$\sigma_q^2 = \frac{(M + 1)2^{-2B}}{3}\, \sigma_x^2 \sum_{k=0}^{M-1} |h(k)|^2 \left(1 - \frac{k}{M + 1}\right) \tag{10.102}$$

Since $\left(1 - \frac{k}{M+1}\right) \leq 1$ and using $\sigma_y^2 = \sigma_x^2 \sum_{k=0}^{M-1} |h(k)|^2$, the noise power σ_q^2 is upper bounded by

$$\sigma_q^2 \leq (M + 1)\frac{2^{-2B}}{3}\, \sigma_y^2 \tag{10.103}$$

or the SNR is lower bounded by

$$\mathrm{SNR} \geq \frac{3}{M + 1}\, 2^{2B} \tag{10.104}$$

Equation (10.104) shows that it is best to compute products in order of increasing magnitude.

☐   **EXAMPLE 10.15**   Again consider the fourth-order FIR filter given in Example 10.13 in which $M = 5$, $B = 12$, and $h(n) = \{0.1, 0.2, 0.4, 0.2, 0.1\}$. From (10.104), the SNR is lower bounded by

$$\mathrm{SNR}_{dB} \geq 10 \log_{10}\left(\frac{3}{M + 1}\, 2^{24}\right) = 69.24 \text{ dB}$$

and the approximate value from (10.102) is 71 dB, which is comparable to the fixed-point value of 72 dB. Note that the fixed-point results would degrade with less than optimum scaling (e.g., if signal amplitude were 10 dB down), whereas the floating-point SNR would remain the same. To counter this, one could put a variable scaling factor A on the fixed-point system, which is then getting close to the full floating-point system. In fact, floating-point is nothing but fixed-point with variable scaling—that is, a scaling by a power of two (or shifting) at each multiplication and addition. $\qquad\square$

10.4 PROBLEMS

P10.1 Let $x(n) = 0.5[\cos(n/17) + \sin(n/23)]$. For the following parts, use 500,000 samples of $x(n)$ and the `StatModelR` function.

1. Quantize $x(n)$ to $B = 2$ bits, and plot the resulting distributions for the error signals $e_1(n)$ and $e_2(n)$. Comment on these plots.
2. Quantize $x(n)$ to $B = 4$ bits, and plot the resulting distributions for the error signals $e_1(n)$ and $e_2(n)$. Comment on these plots.
3. Quantize $x(n)$ to $B = 6$ bits, and plot the resulting distributions for the error signals $e_1(n)$ and $e_2(n)$. Comment on these plots.

P10.2 Let $x(n) = \frac{1}{3}[\cos(0.1\pi n) + \sin(0.2\pi n) + \sin(0.4\pi n)]$. For the following parts, use 500,000 samples of $x(n)$ and the `StatModelR` function.

1. Quantize $x(n)$ to $B = 2$ bits, and plot the resulting distributions for the error signals $e_1(n)$ and $e_2(n)$. Comment on these plots.
2. Quantize $x(n)$ to $B = 4$ bits, and plot the resulting distributions for the error signals $e_1(n)$ and $e_2(n)$. Comment on these plots.
3. Quantize $x(n)$ to $B = 6$ bits, and plot the resulting distributions for the error signals $e_1(n)$ and $e_2(n)$. Comment on these plots.

P10.3 Let a real, causal, and stable IIR filter be given by

$$H(z) = R_0 + \sum_{k=1}^{N-1} \frac{R_k}{z - p_k} \qquad (10.105)$$

where all poles are distinct. Using (10.16), (10.18a), and (10.105), show that

$$\frac{\sigma_q^2}{\sigma_e^2} = R_0^2 + \sum_{k=1}^{N-1}\sum_{\ell=1}^{N-1} \frac{R_k R_\ell^*}{1 - p_k p_\ell^*}$$

P10.4 Consider the lowpass digital filter designed in Problem P6.39. The input to this filter is an independent and identically distributed Gaussian sequence with zero-mean and variance equal to 0.1.

1. Determine the variance of the filter output process using the `VarGain` function.
2. Determine numerically the variance of the output process by generating 500,000 samples of the input sequence. Comment on your results.

P10.5 Design an elliptic bandpass digital filter that has a lower stopband of 0.3π, a lower passband of 0.4π, an upper passband of 0.5π, and an upper stopband of 0.65π.

The passband ripple is 0.1 dB and the stopband attenuation is 50 dB. The input signal is a random sequence whose components are independent and uniformly distributed between -1 and 1.

1. Determine the variance of the filter output process using the `VarGain` function.
2. Determine numerically the variance of the output process by generating 500,000 samples of the input sequence. Comment on your results.

P10.6   Consider the first-order recursive system $y(n) = 0.75\,y(n-1) + 0.125\delta(n)$ with zero initial conditions. The filter is implemented in 4-bit (including sign) fixed-point two's-complement fractional arithmetic. Products are rounded to 3 bits.

1. Determine and plot the first 20 samples of the output using saturation limiter for the addition. Does the filter go into a limit cycle?
2. Determine and plot the first 20 samples of the output using two's-complement overflow for the addition. Does the filter go into a limit cycle?

P10.7   Repeat Problem P10.6 when products are truncated to 3 bits.

P10.8   Consider the second-order recursive system $y(n) = 0.125\delta(n) - 0.875\,y(n-2)$ with zero initial conditions. The filter is implemented in 5-bit (including sign) fixed-point two's-complement fractional arithmetic. Products are rounded to 4 bits.

1. Determine and plot the first 30 samples of the output using a saturation limiter for the addition. Does the filter go into a limit cycle?
2. Determine and plot the first 30 samples of the output using two's-complement overflow for the addition. Does the filter go into a limit cycle?

P10.9   Repeat Problem P10.8 when products are truncated to 4 bits.

P10.10   Let $x(n) = \frac{1}{4}[\sin(n/11) + \cos(n/13) + \sin(n/17) + \cos(n/19)]$ and $c = 0.7777$. For the following parts, use 500,000 samples of $x(n)$ and the `StatModelR` function.

1. Quantize $cx(n)$ to $B = 4$ bits, and plot the resulting distributions for the error signals $e_1(n)$ and $e_2(n)$. Comment on these plots.
2. Quantize $cx(n)$ to $B = 8$ bits, and plot the resulting distributions for the error signals $e_1(n)$ and $e_2(n)$. Comment on these plots.
3. Quantize $cx(n)$ to $B = 12$ bits, and plot the resulting distributions for the error signals $e_1(n)$ and $e_2(n)$. Comment on these plots.

P10.11   Let $x(n) =$ be a random sequence uniformly distributed between -1 and 1, and let $c = 0.7777$. For the following parts, use 500,000 samples of $x(n)$ and the `StatModelR` function.

1. Quantize $cx(n)$ to $B = 4$ bits, and plot the resulting distributions for the error signals $e_1(n)$ and $e_2(n)$. Comment on these plots.
2. Quantize $cx(n)$ to $B = 8$ bits, and plot the resulting distributions for the error signals $e_1(n)$ and $e_2(n)$. Comment on these plots.
3. Quantize $cx(n)$ to $B = 12$ bits, and plot the resulting distributions for the error signals $e_1(n)$ and $e_2(n)$. Comment on these plots.

P10.12   Consider an LTI system with the input $x(n)$ and output $y(n)$

$$y(n) = b_0x(n) + b_1x(n-1) + a_1y(n-1) \tag{10.106}$$

1. Draw the direct form I structure for the above system.
2. Let $e_{b_0}(n)$ denote the multiplication quantization error resulting from the product $b_0x(n)$, $e_{b_1}(n-1)$ from the product $b_1x(n-1)$, and $e_{a_1}(n-1)$ from the product

$a_1 y(n-1)$ in the direct form I realization. Draw an equivalent structure that contains only one noise source.

3. Draw an equivalent system that can be used to study multiplication quantization error for the system in (10.106). The input to this system should be the noise source in part 2, and the output should be the overall output error $q(n)$.

4. Using the model in part 3, determine an expression for the variance of the output error $e(n)$.

P10.13 Let the system be given by $y(n) = a\,y(n-1) + x(n)$. Let $a = 0.7$, which is quantized to B (fractional) bits in the filter realization. Let the input sequence be $x(n) = \sin(n/11)$, which is properly scaled to avoid overflow in the adder and quantized to B bits prior to filtering. The multiplications in the filtering operations are also quantized to B bits.

1. Let $B = 5$. Generate 100,000 samples of $x(n)$, and filter through the system with multiplication quantization. Compute the true output, the quantized output, the output error, and the output SNR. Plot the normalized histogram, and comment on the results.

2. Let $B = 10$. Generate 100,000 samples of $x(n)$ and filter through the system with multiplication quantization. Compute the true output, the quantized output, the output error, and the output SNR. Plot the normalized histogram, and comment on the results.

P10.14 Let the system be given by $y(n) = a\,y(n-1) + x(n)$. Let $a = 0.333$, which is quantized to B (fractional) bits in the filter realization. Let the input sequence be $x(n) = \sin(n/11)$, which is properly scaled to avoid overflow in the adder and quantized to B bits prior to filtering. The multiplications in the filtering operations are also quantized to B bits.

1. Let $B = 5$. Generate 100,000 samples of $x(n)$, and filter through the system with multiplication quantization. Compute the true output, the quantized output, the output error, and the output SNR. Plot the normalized histogram and comment on the results.

2. Let $B = 10$. Generate 100,000 samples of $x(n)$, and filter through the system with multiplication quantization. Compute the true output, the quantized output, the output error, and the output SNR. Plot the normalized histogram and comment on the results.

P10.15 Consider the second-order IIR filter given in (10.51) with $r = 0.8$ and $\theta = \pi/4$. The input to this filter is $x(n) = \sin(n/23)$.

1. Investigate the multiplication quantization error behavior of this filter for $B = 5$ bits. Determine the true output SNR, the computed output SNR, and the upper and lower bounds of the SNR. Plot the normalized histogram of the output error.

2. Investigate the multiplication quantization error behavior of this filter for $B = 10$ bits. Determine the true output SNR, the computed output SNR, and the upper and lower bounds of the SNR. Plot the normalized histogram of the output error.

P10.16 Consider the second-order IIR filter given in (10.51) with $r = 0. - 8$ and $\theta = 2\pi/3$. The input to this filter is $x(n) = \sin(n/23)$.

1. Investigate the multiplication quantization error behavior of this filter for $B = 5$ bits. Determine the true output SNR, the computed output SNR, and the upper and lower bounds of the SNR. Plot the normalized histogram of the output error.

2. Investigate the multiplication quantization error behavior of this filter for $B = 10$ bits. Determine the true output SNR, the computed output SNR, and the upper and lower bounds of the SNR. Plot the normalized histogram of the output error.

P10.17 Consider a fifth-order FIR system given by

$$H(z) = 0.1 + 0.2z^{-1} + 0.3z^{-2} + 0.3z^{-3} + 0.2z^{-4} + 0.1z^{-5}$$

which is implemented in a direct form using $B = 10$ bits. Input to the filter is a random sequence whose samples are independent and identically distributed over $[-1, 1]$.

1. Investigate the multiplication quantization errors when all six multipliers are used in the implementation. Plot the normalized histogram of the output error.
2. Investigate the multiplication quantization errors when one multiplier is used in the implementation. Plot the normalized histogram of the output error.

P10.18 Consider a fourth-order FIR system given by

$$H(z) = 0.1 + 0.2z^{-1} + 0.3z^{-2} + 0.2z^{-3} + 0.1z^{-4}$$

which is implemented in a cascade form containing second-order sections. Input to the filter is a random sequence whose samples are independent and identically distributed over $[-1, 1]$.

1. Investigate the multiplication quantization errors when $B = 6$ bits is used in the implementation. Plot the normalized histogram of the output error.
2. Investigate the multiplication quantization errors when $B = 12$ bits is used in the implementation. Plot the normalized histogram of the output error.

CHAPTER 11

Applications in Adaptive Filtering

In Chapters 7 and 8, we described methods for designing FIR and IIR digital filters to satisfy some desired specifications. Our goal was to determine the coefficients of the digital filter that met the desired specifications.

In contrast to the filter design techniques considered in those two chapters, there are many digital signal processing applications in which the filter coefficients cannot be specified a priori. For example, let us consider a high-speed modem that is designed to transmit data over telephone channels. Such a modem employs a filter called a channel equalizer to compensate for the channel distortion. The modem must effectively transmit data through communication channels that have different frequency response characteristics and hence result in different distortion effects. The only way in which this is possible is if the channel equalizer has *adjustable coefficients* that can be optimized to minimize some measure of the distortion, on the basis of measurements performed on the characteristics of the channel. Such a filter with adjustable parameters is called an *adaptive filter*—in this case, an *adaptive equalizer*.

Numerous applications of adaptive filters have been described in the literature. Some of the more noteworthy applications include (1) adaptive antenna systems, in which adaptive filters are used for beam steering and for providing nulls in the beam pattern to remove undesired interference [97], (2) digital communication receivers, in which adaptive filters are used to provide equalization of intersymbol interference and for channel identification [81], (3) adaptive noise canceling techniques, in which an adaptive filter is used to estimate and eliminate a noise component in some desired signal [96, 34, 15], and (4) system modeling, in which an adaptive filter is used as a model to estimate the characteristics of an unknown system. These are just a few of the best-known examples on the use of adaptive filters.

Although both IIR and FIR filters have been considered for adaptive filtering, the FIR filter is by far the most practical and widely used. The reason for this preference is quite simple. The FIR filter has only adjustable zeros, and hence it is free of stability problems associated with adaptive IIR filters that have adjustable poles as well as zeros. We should not conclude, however, that adaptive FIR filters are always stable. On the contrary, the stability of the filter depends critically on the algorithm for adjusting its coefficients.

Of the various FIR filter structures that we may use, the direct form and the lattice form are the ones often used in adaptive filtering applications. The direct form FIR filter structure with adjustable coefficients $h(0), h(1), \ldots, h(N-1)$ is illustrated in Figure 11.1. The FIR lattice structures are discussed in Chapter 14 and have adjustable parameters K_n, called reflection coefficients, shown in Figure 14.15.

An important consideration in the use of an adaptive filter is the criterion for optimizing the adjustable filter parameters. The criterion must not only provide a meaningful measure of filter performance, but it must also result in a practically realizable algorithm.

One criterion that provides a good measure of performance in adaptive filtering applications is the least-squares criterion, and its counterpart in a statistical formulation of the problem, namely, the mean-square-error (MSE) criterion. The least-squares (and MSE) criterion results in a quadratic performance index as a function of the filter coefficients, and hence it possesses a single minimum. The resulting algorithms for adjusting the coefficients of the filter are relatively easy to implement.

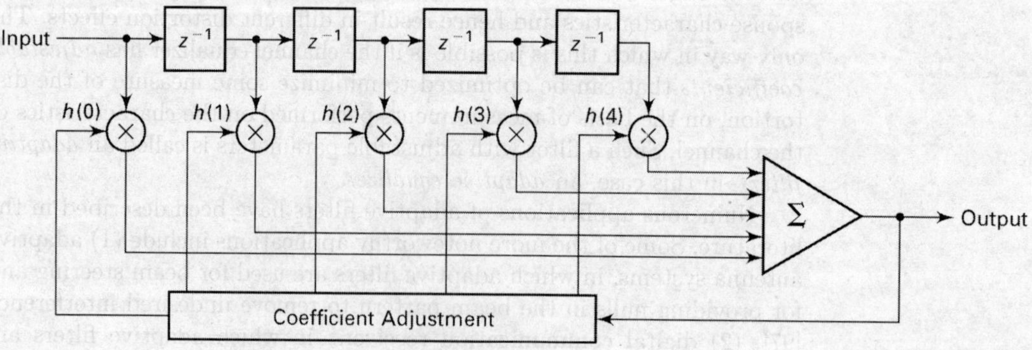

FIGURE 11.1   *Direct form adaptive FIR filter*

In this chapter, we describe a basic algorithm, called the *least-mean-square* (LMS) *algorithm*, to adaptively adjust the coefficients of an FIR filter. The adaptive filter structure that will be implemented is the direct form FIR filter structure with adjustable coefficients $h(0), h(1), \ldots, h(N-1)$, as illustrated in Figure 11.1. After we describe the LMS algorithm, we apply it to several practical systems in which adaptive filters are employed.

11.1 LMS ALGORITHM FOR COEFFICIENT ADJUSTMENT

Suppose we have an FIR filter with adjustable coefficients $\{h(k), 0 \le k \le N-1\}$. Let $\{x(n)\}$ denote the input sequence to the filter, and let the corresponding output be $\{y(n)\}$, where

$$y(n) = \sum_{k=0}^{N-1} h(k)x(n-k), \quad n = 0, \ldots, M \tag{11.1}$$

Suppose that we also have a desired sequence $\{d(n)\}$ with which we can compare the FIR filter output. Then we can form the error sequence $\{e(n)\}$ by taking the difference between $d(n)$ and $y(n)$, that is,

$$e(n) = d(n) - y(n), \quad n = 0, \ldots, M \tag{11.2}$$

The coefficients of the FIR filter will be selected to minimize the sum of squared errors. Thus we have

$$\mathcal{E} = \sum_{n=0}^{M} e^2(n) = \sum_{n=0}^{M} \left[d(n) - \sum_{k=0}^{N-1} h(k)x(n-k) \right]^2 \tag{11.3}$$

$$= \sum_{n=0}^{M} d^2(n) - 2\sum_{k=0}^{N-1} h(k)r_{dx}(k) + \sum_{k=0}^{N-1}\sum_{\ell=0}^{N-1} h(k)h(\ell)\,r_{xx}(k-\ell)$$

where, by definition,

$$r_{dx}(k) = \sum_{n=0}^{M} d(n)x(n-k), \quad 0 \le k \le N-1 \tag{11.4}$$

$$r_{xx}(k) = \sum_{n=0}^{M} x(n)x(n+k), \quad 0 \le k \le N-1 \tag{11.5}$$

We call $\{r_{dx}(k)\}$ the cross-correlation between the desired output sequence $\{d(n)\}$ and the input sequence $\{x(n)\}$, and $\{r_{xx}(k)\}$ is the autocorrelation sequence of $\{x(n)\}$.

The sum of squared errors $\mathcal{E}$ is a quadratic function of the FIR filter coefficients. Consequently, the minimization of $\mathcal{E}$ with respect to the filter coefficients $\{h(k)\}$ results in a set of linear equations. By differentiating $\mathcal{E}$ with respect to each of the filter coefficients, we obtain

$$\frac{\partial \mathcal{E}}{\partial h(m)} = 0, \quad 0 \leq m \leq N - 1 \tag{11.6}$$

and hence

$$\sum_{k=0}^{N-1} h(k) r_{xx}(k - m) = r_{dx}(m), \quad 0 \leq m \leq N - 1 \tag{11.7}$$

This is the set of linear equations that yield the optimum filter coefficients.

To solve the set of linear equations directly, we must first compute the autocorrelation sequence $\{r_{xx}(k)\}$ of the input signal and the cross-correlation sequence $\{r_{dx}(k)\}$ between the desired sequence $\{d(n)\}$ and the input sequence $\{x(n)\}$.

The LMS algorithm provides an alternative computational method for determining the optimum filter coefficients $\{h(k)\}$ without explicitly computing the correlation sequences $\{r_{xx}(k)\}$ and $\{r_{dx}(k)\}$. The algorithm is basically a recursive gradient (steepest-descent) method that finds the minimum of $\mathcal{E}$ and thus yields the set of optimum filter coefficients.

We begin with any arbitrary choice for the initial values of $\{h(k)\}$—say, $\{h_0(k)\}$. For example, we may begin with $h_0(k) = 0, \quad 0 \leq k \leq N-1$. Then after each new input sample $\{x(n)\}$ enters the adaptive FIR filter, we compute the corresponding output—say, $\{y(n)\}$—form the error signal $e(n) = d(n) - y(n)$, and update the filter coefficients according to the equation

$$h_n(k) = h_{n-1}(k) + \triangle \cdot e(n) \cdot x(n - k), \quad 0 \leq k \leq N - 1, \quad n = 0, 1, \ldots$$

$$\tag{11.8}$$

where $\triangle$ is called the step-size parameter, $x(n - k)$ is the sample of the input signal located at the kth tap of the filter at time n, and $e(n)x(n - k)$ is an approximation (estimate) of the negative of the gradient for the kth filter coefficient. This is the LMS recursive algorithm for adjusting the filter coefficients adaptively so as to minimize the sum of squared errors $\mathcal{E}$.

The step-size parameter $\triangle$ controls the rate of convergence of the algorithm to the optimum solution. A large value of $\triangle$ leads to large step-size adjustments and thus to rapid convergence, while a small value of $\triangle$ results in slower convergence. However, if $\triangle$ is made too large the algorithm becomes unstable. To ensure stability, $\triangle$ must be chosen [81] to be in the range

$$0 < \triangle < \frac{1}{10NP_x} \qquad (11.9)$$

where N is the length of the adaptive FIR filter and P_x is the power in the input signal, which can be approximated by

$$P_x \approx \frac{1}{1+M} \sum_{n=0}^{M} x^2(n) = \frac{r_{xx}(0)}{M+1} \qquad (11.10)$$

The mathematical justification of equations (11.9) and (11.10) and the proof that the LMS algorithm leads to the solution for the optimum filter coefficients is given in more advanced treatments of adaptive filters. The interested reader may refer to the books by Haykin [30] and Proakis and Manolakis [79].

11.1.1 MATLAB IMPLEMENTATION

The LMS algorithm (11.8) can easily be implemented in MATLAB. Given the input sequence $\{x(n)\}$, the desired sequence $\{d(n)\}$, step size $\triangle$, and the desired length of the adaptive FIR filter N, we can use (11.1), (11.2), and (11.8) to determine the adaptive filter coefficients $\{h(n), 0 \leq n \leq N-1\}$ recursively. This is shown in the following function, called lms.

```
function [h,y] = lms(x,d,delta,N)
% LMS Algorithm for Coefficient Adjustment
% ----------------------------------------
% [h,y] = lms(x,d,delta,N)
%       h = estimated FIR filter
%       y = output array y(n)
%       x = input array x(n)
%       d = desired array d(n), length must be same as x
% delta = step size
%       N = length of the FIR filter
%
M = length(x); y = zeros(1,M);
h = zeros(1,N);
for n = N:M
    x1 = x(n:-1:n-N+1);
    y = h * x1';
    e = d(n) - y;
    h = h + delta*e*x1;
end
```

In addition, the lms function provides the output $\{y(n)\}$ of the adaptive filter.

We will apply the LMS algorithm to several practical applications involving adaptive filtering.

11.2 SYSTEM IDENTIFICATION OR SYSTEM MODELING

To formulate the problem, let us refer to Figure 11.2. We have an unknown linear system that we wish to identify. The unknown system may be an all-zero (FIR) system or a pole-zero (IIR) system. The unknown system will be approximated (modeled) by an FIR filter of length N. Both the unknown system and the FIR model are connected in parallel and are excited by the same input sequence $\{x(n)\}$. If $\{y(n)\}$ denotes the output of the model and $\{d(n)\}$ denotes the output of the unknown system, the error sequence is $\{e(n) = d(n) - y(n)\}$. If we minimize the sum of squared errors, we obtain the same set of linear equations as in (11.7). Therefore, the LMS algorithm given by (11.8) may be used to adapt the coefficients of the FIR model so that its output approximates the output of the unknown system.

11.2.1 PROJECT 11.1: SYSTEM IDENTIFICATION
There are three basic modules that are needed to perform this project.

1. A noise signal generator that generates a sequence of random numbers with zero mean value. For example, we may generate a sequence of uniformly distributed random numbers over the interval $[-a, a]$. Such a sequence of uniformly distributed numbers has an average value of zero and a variance of $a^2/3$. This signal sequence, call it $\{x(n)\}$, will be used as the input to the unknown system and the adaptive FIR model. In this case, the input signal $\{x(n)\}$ has power $P_x = a^2/3$. In MATLAB this can be implemented using the **rand** function.

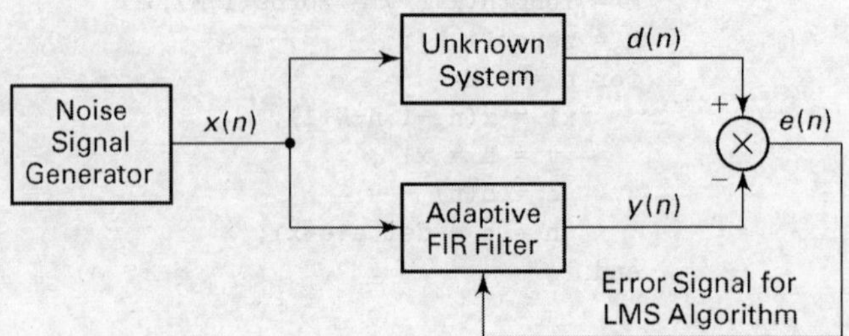

FIGURE 11.2 *Block diagram of system identification or system modeling problem*

2. An unknown system module that may be selected is an IIR filter and implemented by its difference equation. For example, we may select an IIR filter specified by the second-order difference equation

$$d(n) = a_1 d(n-1) + a_2 d(n-2) + x(n) + b_1 x(n-1) + b_2 x(n-2)$$

$$(11.11)$$

where the parameters $\{a_1, a_2\}$ determine the positions of the poles and $\{b_1, b_2\}$ determine the positions of the zeros of the filter. These parameters are input variables to the program. This can be implemented by the `filter` function.

3. An adaptive FIR filter module where the FIR filter has N tap coefficients that are adjusted by means of the LMS algorithm. The length N of the filter is an input variable to the program. This can be implemented using the `lms` function given in the previous section.

The three modules are configured as shown in Figure 11.2. From this project, we can determine how closely the impulse response of the FIR model approximates the impulse response of the unknown system after the LMS algorithm has converged.

To monitor the convergence rate of the LMS algorithm, we may compute a short-term average of the squared error $e^2(n)$ and plot it. That is, we may compute

$$\text{ASE}(m) = \frac{1}{K} \sum_{k=n+1}^{n+K} e^2(k) \qquad (11.12)$$

where $m = n/K = 1, 2, \ldots$. The averaging interval K may be selected to be (approximately) $K = 10N$. The effect of the choice of the step-size parameter Δ on the convergence rate of the LMS algorithm may be observed by monitoring the $\text{ASE}(m)$.

Besides the main part of the program, you should also include, as an aside, the computation of the impulse response of the unknown system, which can be obtained by exciting the system with a unit sample sequence $\delta(n)$. This actual impulse response can be compared with that of the FIR model after convergence of the LMS algorithm. The two impulse responses can be plotted for the purpose of comparison.

11.3 SUPPRESSION OF NARROWBAND INTERFERENCE IN A WIDEBAND SIGNAL

Let us assume that we have a signal sequence $\{x(n)\}$ that consists of a desired wideband signal sequence—say, $\{w(n)\}$—corrupted by an additive narrowband interference sequence $\{s(n)\}$. The two sequences are uncorrelated. This problem arises in digital communications and in signal detection, where the desired signal sequence $\{w(n)\}$ is a spread-spectrum signal, while the narrowband interference represents a signal from another user of the frequency band or some intentional interference from a jammer who is trying to disrupt the communication or detection system.

From a filtering point of view, our objective is to design a filter that suppresses the narrowband interference. In effect, such a filter should place a notch in the frequency band occupied by the interference. In practice, however, the frequency band of the interference might be unknown. Moreover, the frequency band of the interference may vary slowly in time.

The narrowband characteristics of the interference allow us to estimate $s(n)$ from past samples of the sequence $x(n) = s(n) + w(n)$ and to subtract the estimate from $x(n)$. Since the bandwidth of $\{s(n)\}$ is narrow compared to the bandwidth of $\{w(n)\}$, the samples of $\{s(n)\}$ are highly correlated. On the other hand, the wideband sequence $\{w(n)\}$ has a relatively narrow correlation.

The general configuration of the interference suppression system is shown in Figure 11.3. The signal $x(n)$ is delayed by D samples, where the delay D is chosen sufficiently large so that the wideband signal components $w(n)$ and $w(n - D)$, which are contained in $x(n)$ and $x(n - D)$, respectively, are uncorrelated. The output of the adaptive FIR filter is the estimate

$$\hat{s}(n) = \sum_{k=0}^{N-1} h(k)x(n - k - D) \qquad (11.13)$$

The error signal that is used in optimizing the FIR filter coefficients is $e(n) = x(n) - \hat{s}(n)$. The minimization of the sum of squared errors again leads to a set of linear equations for determining the optimum coefficients. Due to the delay D, the LMS algorithm for adjusting the coefficients recursively becomes

$$h_n(k) = h_{n-1}(k) + \Delta e(n)x(n - k - D), \qquad \begin{matrix} k = 0, 1, \ldots, N - 1 \\ n = 1, 2, \ldots \end{matrix} \qquad (11.14)$$

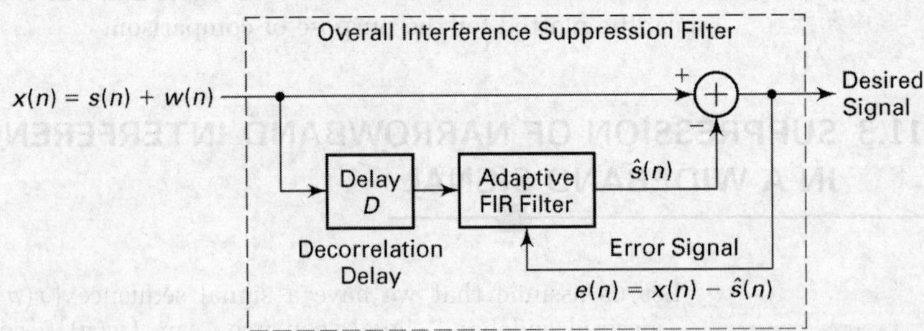

FIGURE 11.3 *Adaptive filter for estimating and suppressing a narrowband interference*

11.3.1 PROJECT 11.2: SUPPRESSION OF SINUSOIDAL INTERFERENCE
Three basic modules are required to perform this project.

1. A noise signal generator module that generates a wideband sequence $\{w(n)\}$ of random numbers with zero mean value. In particular, we may generate a sequence of uniformly distributed random numbers using the **rand** function as previously described in the project on system identification. The signal power is denoted as P_w.
2. A sinusoidal signal generator module that generates a sine wave sequence $s(n) = A \sin \omega_0 n$, where $0 < \omega_0 < \pi$ and A is the signal amplitude. The power of the sinusoidal sequence is denoted as P_s.
3. An adaptive FIR filter module using the **lms** function, where the FIR filter has N tap coefficients that are adjusted by the LMS algorithm. The length N of the filter is an input variable to the program.

The three modules are configured as shown in Figure 11.4. In this project, the delay $D = 1$ is sufficient, since the sequence $\{w(n)\}$ is a white noise (spectrally flat or uncorrelated) sequence. The objective is to adapt the FIR filter coefficients and then to investigate the characteristics of the adaptive filter.

It is interesting to select the interference signal to be much stronger than the desired signal $w(n)$, for example, $P_s = 10P_w$. Note that the power P_x required in selecting the step-size parameter in the LMS algorithm is $P_x = P_s + P_w$. The frequency response characteristic $H(e^{j\omega})$ of the adaptive FIR filter with coefficients $\{h(k)\}$ should exhibit a resonant peak at the frequency of the interference. The frequency response of the interference suppression filter is $H_s(e^{j\omega}) = 1 - H(e^{j\omega})$, which should then exhibit a notch at the frequency of the interference.

It is interesting to plot the sequences $\{w(n)\}$, $\{s(n)\}$, and $\{x(n)\}$. It is also interesting to plot the frequency responses $H(e^{j\omega})$ and $H_s(e^{j\omega})$ after the LMS algorithm has converged. The short-time average squared error $\mathrm{ASE}(m)$, defined by (11.12), may be used to monitor the convergence characteristics of the LMS algorithm. The effect of the length of the adaptive filter on the quality of the estimate should be investigated.

The project may be generalized by adding a second sinusoid of a different frequency. Then $H(e^{j\omega})$ should exhibit two resonant peaks, provided

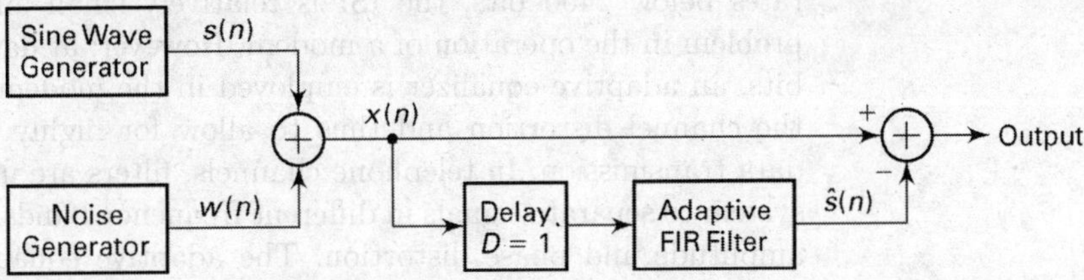

FIGURE 11.4　*Configuration of modules for experiment on interference suppression*

the frequencies are sufficiently separated. Investigate the effect of the filter length N on the resolution of two closely spaced sinusoids.

11.4 ADAPTIVE LINE ENHANCEMENT

In the preceding section, we described a method for suppressing a strong narrowband interference from a wideband signal. An adaptive line enhancer (ALE) has the same configuration as the interference suppression filter in Figure 11.3, except that the objective is different.

In the adaptive line enhancer, $\{s(n)\}$ is the desired signal and $\{w(n)\}$ represents a wideband noise component that masks $\{s(n)\}$. The desired signal $\{s(n)\}$ may be a spectral line (a pure sinusoid) or a relatively narrowband signal. Usually, the power in the wideband signal is greater than that in the narrowband signal—that is, $P_w > P_s$. It is apparent that the ALE is a self-tuning filter that has a peak in its frequency response at the frequency of the input sinusoid or in the frequency band occupied by the narrowband signal. By having a narrow bandwidth FIR filter, the noise outside the frequency band of the signal is suppressed, and thus the spectral line is enhanced in amplitude relative to the noise power in $\{w(n)\}$.

11.4.1 PROJECT 11.3: ADAPTIVE LINE ENHANCEMENT
This project requires the same software modules as those used in the project on interference suppression. Hence the description given in the preceding section applies directly. One change is that in the ALE, the condition is that $P_w > P_s$. Second, the output signal from the ALE is $\{s(n)\}$. Repeat the project described in the previous section under these conditions.

11.5 ADAPTIVE CHANNEL EQUALIZATION

The speed of data transmission over telephone channels is usually limited by channel distortion that causes intersymbol interference (ISI). At data rates below 2400 bits, the ISI is relatively small and is usually not a problem in the operation of a modem. However, at data rates above 2400 bits, an adaptive equalizer is employed in the modem to compensate for the channel distortion and thus to allow for highly reliable high-speed data transmission. In telephone channels, filters are used throughout the system to separate signals in different frequency bands. These filters cause amplitude and phase distortion. The adaptive equalizer is basically an adaptive FIR filter with coefficients that are adjusted by means of the LMS algorithm to correct for the channel distortion.

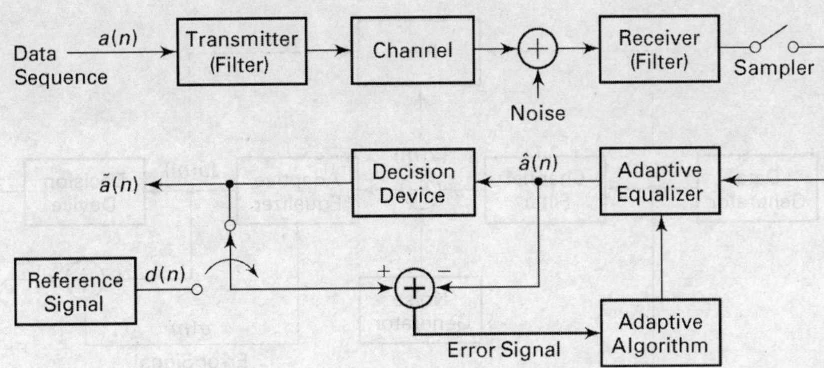

FIGURE 11.5 *Application of adaptive filtering to adaptive channel equalization*

A block diagram showing the basic elements of a modem transmitting data over a channel is given in Figure 11.5. Initially, the equalizer coefficients are adjusted by transmitting a short training sequence, usually less than 1 second in duration. After the short training period, the transmitter begins to transmit the data sequence $\{a(n)\}$. To track the possible slow time variations in the channel, the equalizer coefficients must continue to be adjusted in an adaptive manner while receiving data. This is usually accomplished, as illustrated in Figure 11.5, by treating the decisions at the output of the decision device as correct and by using the decisions in place of the reference $\{d(n)\}$ to generate the error signal. This approach works quite well when decision errors occur infrequently, such as less than one error in 100 data symbols. The occasional decision errors cause only a small misadjustment in the equalizer coefficients.

11.5.1 PROJECT 11.4: ADAPTIVE CHANNEL EQUALIZATION

The objective of this project is to investigate the performance of an adaptive equalizer for data transmission over a channel that causes inter-symbol interference. The basic configuration of the system to be simulated is shown in Figure 11.6. As we observe, five basic modules are required. Note that we have avoided carrier modulation and demodulation, which is required in a telephone channel modem. This is done to simplify the simulation program. However, all processing involves complex arithmetic operations.

The five modules are as follows.

1. The data generator module is used to generate a sequence of complex-valued information symbols $\{a(n)\}$. In particular, employ four equally probable symbols $s + js$, $s - js$, $-s + js$, and $-s - js$, where s is a scale factor that may be set to $s = 1$, or it can be an input parameter.

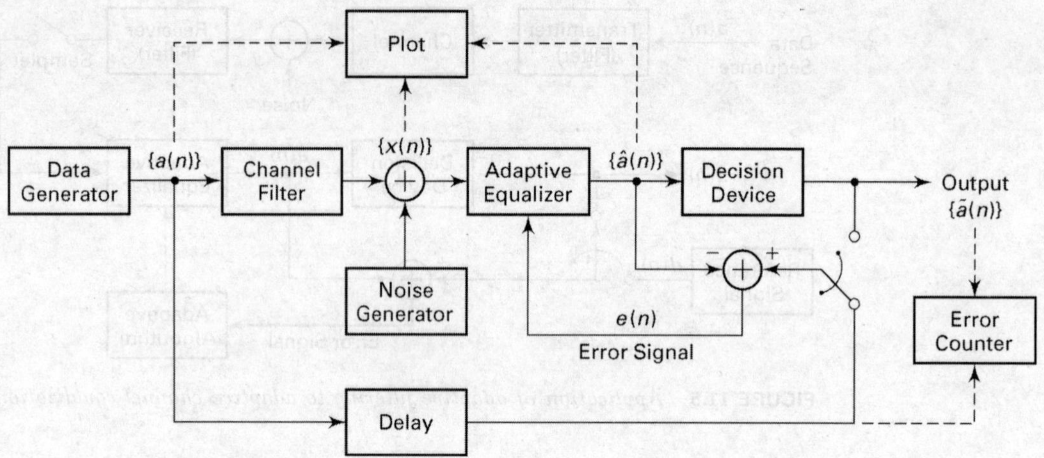

FIGURE 11.6 *Experiment for investigating the performance of an adaptive equalizer*

2. The channel filter module is an FIR filter with coefficients $\{c(n), 0 \le n \le K - 1\}$ that simulates the channel distortion. For distortionless transmission, set $c(0) = 1$ and $c(n) = 0$ for $1 \le n \le K - 1$. The length K of the filter is an input parameter.

3. The noise generator module is used to generate additive noise that is usually present in any digital communication system. If we are modeling noise that is generated by electronic devices, the noise distribution should be Gaussian with zero mean. Use the **randu** function.

4. The adaptive equalizer module is an FIR filter with tap coefficients $\{h(k), 0 < k < N - 1\}$, which are adjusted by the LMS algorithm. However, due to the use of complex arithmetic, the recursive equation in the LMS algorithm is slightly modified to

$$h_n(k) = h_{n-1}(k) + \triangle e(n)x^*(n - k) \tag{11.15}$$

where the asterisk denotes the complex conjugate.

5. The decision device module takes the estimate $\hat{a}(n)$ and quantizes it to one of the four possible signal points on the basis of the following decision rule:

$$\text{Re}\,[\hat{a}(n)] > 0 \text{ and } \text{Im}\,[\hat{a}(n)] > 0 \longrightarrow 1 + j$$
$$\text{Re}\,[\hat{a}(n)] > 0 \text{ and } \text{Im}\,[\hat{a}(n)] < 0 \longrightarrow 1 - j$$
$$\text{Re}\,[\hat{a}(n)] < 0 \text{ and } \text{Im}\,[\hat{a}(n)] > 0 \longrightarrow -1 + j$$
$$\text{Re}\,[\hat{a}(n)] < 0 \text{ and } \text{Im}\,[\hat{a}(n)] < 0 \longrightarrow -1 - j$$

The effectiveness of the equalizer in suppressing the ISI introduced by the channel filter may be seen by plotting the following relevant sequences in a two-dimensional (real–imaginary) display. The data generator output $\{a(n)\}$ should consist of four points with values $\pm 1 \pm j$. The effect of channel distortion and additive noise may be viewed by displaying the sequence $\{x(n)\}$ at the input to the equalizer. The effectiveness of the adaptive equalizer may be assessed by plotting its output $\{\hat{a}(n)\}$ after convergence of its coefficients. The short-time average squared error $\mathrm{ASE}(n)$ may also be used to monitor the convergence characteristics of the LMS algorithm. Note that a delay must be introduced into the output of the data generator to compensate for the delays that the signal encounters due to the channel filter and the adaptive equalizer. For example, this delay may be set to the largest integer closest to $(N+K)/2$. Finally, an error counter may be used to count the number of symbol errors in the received data sequence, and the ratio for the number of errors to the total number of symbols (error rate) may be displayed. The error rate may be varied by changing the level of the ISI and the level of the additive noise.

It is suggested that simulations be performed for the following three channel conditions.

a. No ISI: $c(0) = 1, c(n) = 0, 1 \leq n \leq K - 1$
b. Mild ISI: $c(0) = 1, c(1) = 0.2, c(2) = -0.2, c(n) = 0, 3 \leq n \leq K - 1$
c. Strong ISI: $c(0) = 1, c(1) = 0.5, c(2) = 0.5, c(n) = 0, 3 \leq n \leq K - 1$

The measured error rate may be plotted as a function of the signal-to-noise ratio (SNR) at the input to the equalizer, where SNR is defined as P_s/P_n, where P_s is the signal power, given as $P_s = s^2$, and P_n is the noise power of the sequence at the output of the noise generator.

CHAPTER 12

Applications in Communications

Today MATLAB finds widespread use in the simulation of a variety of communication systems. In this chapter, we shall focus on several applications dealing with waveform representation and coding, especially speech coding, and with digital communications. In particular, we shall describe several methods for digitizing analog waveforms, with specific application to speech coding and transmission. These methods are pulse-code modulation (PCM), differential PCM and adaptive differential PCM (ADPCM), delta modulation (DM) and adaptive delta modulation (ADM), and linear predictive coding (LPC). A project is formulated involving each of these waveform-encoding methods for simulation using MATLAB.

The last three topics treated in this chapter deal with signal-detection applications that are usually encountered in the implementation of a receiver in a digital communication system. For each of these topics, we describe a project that involves the implementations via simulation of the detection scheme in MATLAB.

12.1 PULSE-CODE MODULATION

Pulse-code modulation is a method for quantizing an analog signal for the purpose of transmitting or storing the signal in digital form. PCM is widely used for speech transmission in telephone communications and for telemetry systems that employ radio transmission. We shall concentrate our attention on the application of PCM to speech signal processing.

Speech signals transmitted over telephone channels are usually limited in bandwidth to the frequency range below 4 kHz. Hence the Nyquist rate for sampling such a signal is less than 8 kHz. In PCM, the analog speech signal is sampled at the nominal rate of 8 kHz (samples per second), and each sample is quantized to one of 2^b levels and represented digitally by a sequence of b bits. Thus the bit rate required to transmit the digitized speech signal is $8000\,b$ bits per second.

The quantization process may be modeled mathematically as

$$\tilde{s}(n) = s(n) + q(n) \tag{12.1}$$

where $\tilde{s}(n)$ represents the quantized value of $s(n)$ and $q(n)$ represents the quantization error, which we treat as an additive noise. Assuming that a uniform quantizer is used and the number of levels is sufficiently large, the quantization noise is well characterized statistically by the uniform probability density function

$$p(q) = \frac{1}{\Delta}, \quad -\frac{\Delta}{2} \le q \le \frac{\Delta}{2} \tag{12.2}$$

where the step size of the quantizer is $\Delta = 2^{-b}$. The mean square value of the quantization error is

$$E(q^2) = \frac{\Delta^2}{12} = \frac{2^{-2b}}{12} \tag{12.3}$$

Measured in decibels, the mean square value of the noise is

$$10 \log\left(\frac{\Delta^2}{12}\right) = 10 \log\left(\frac{2^{-2b}}{12}\right) = -6b - 10.8 \text{ dB} \tag{12.4}$$

We observe that the quantization noise decreases by 6 dB/bit used in the quantizer. High-quality speech requires a minimum of 12 bits per sample and hence a bit rate of 96,000 bits per second (bps) or 96 kbps.

Speech signals have the characteristic that small signal amplitudes occur more frequently than large signal amplitudes. However, a uniform quantizer provides the same spacing between successive levels throughout the entire dynamic range of the signal. A better approach is to use a nonuniform quantizer, which provides more closely spaced levels at the low signal amplitudes and more widely spaced levels at the large signal amplitudes. For a nonuniform quantizer with b bits, the resulting quantization error has a mean square value that is smaller than that given by (12.4). A nonuniform quantizer characteristic is usually obtained by passing the signal through a nonlinear device that compresses the signal amplitude, followed by a uniform quantizer. For example, a logarithmic compressor employed in United States and Canadian telecommunications systems, called a μ-law compressor, has an input-output magnitude characteristic of the form

$$y = \frac{\ln\left(1 + \mu|s|\right)}{\ln(1 + \mu)}\,\mathrm{sgn}(s); \quad |s| \le 1, |y| \le 1 \tag{12.5}$$

where s is the normalized input, y is the normalized output, $\mathrm{sgn}\left(\cdot\right)$ is the sign function, and μ is a parameter that is selected to give the desired compression characteristic.

In the encoding of speech waveforms, the value of $\mu = 255$ has been adopted as a standard in the United States and Canada. This value results in about a 24 dB reduction in the quantization noise power relative to uniform quantization. Consequently, an 8-bit quantizer used in conjunction with a $\mu = 255$ logarithmic compressor produces the same quality speech as a 12-bit uniform quantizer with no compression. Thus the compressed PCM speech signal has a bit rate of 64 kbps.

The logarithmic compressor standard used in European telecommunication systems is called A-law and is defined as

$$y = \begin{cases} \dfrac{1 + \ln(A|s|)}{1 + \ln A}\,\mathrm{sgn}(s), & \frac{1}{A} \le |s| \le 1 \\[2ex] \dfrac{A|s|}{1 + \ln A}\,\mathrm{sgn}(s), & 0 \le |s| \le \frac{1}{A} \end{cases} \tag{12.6}$$

where A is chosen as 87.56. Although (12.5) and (12.6) are different nonlinear functions, the two compression characteristics are very similar. Figure 12.1 illustrates these two compression functions. Note their strong similarity.

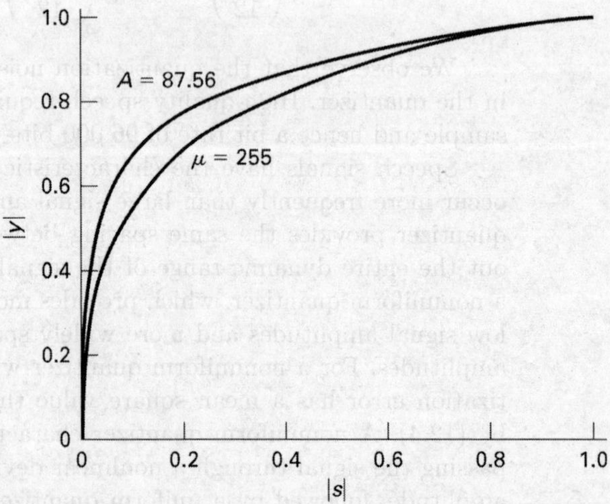

FIGURE 12.1   *Comparison of μ-law and A-law nonlinearities*

In the reconstruction of the signal from the quantized values, the decoder employs an inverse logarithmic relation to expand the signal amplitude. For example, in μ-law the inverse relation is given by

$$|s| = \frac{(1+\mu)^{|y|}-1}{\mu}; \quad |y| \leq 1, |s| \leq 1 \qquad (12.7)$$

The combined compressor-expander pair is termed a *compander*.

12.1.1 PROJECT 12.1: PCM

The purpose of this project is to gain an understanding of PCM compression (linear to logarithmic) and PCM expansion (logarithmic to linear). Write the following three MATLAB functions for this project:

1. a μ-law compressor function to implement (12.5) that accepts a zero-mean normalized ($|s| \leq 1$) signal and produces a compressed zero-mean signal with μ as a free parameter that can be specified,
2. a quantizer function that accepts a zero-mean input and produces an integer output after b-bit quantization that can be specified, and
3. a μ-law expander to implement (12.7) that accepts an integer input and produces a zero-mean output for a specified μ parameter.

For simulation purposes, generate a large number of samples (10,000 or more) of the following sequences: (a) a sawtooth sequence, (b) an exponential pulse train sequence, (c) a sinusoidal sequence, and (d) a random sequence with small variance. Care must be taken to generate nonperiodic sequences by choosing their normalized frequencies as irrational numbers (i.e., sample values should not repeat). For example, a sinusoidal sequence can be generated using

$$s(n) = 0.5\sin(n/33), \quad 0 \leq n \leq 10{,}000$$

From our discussions in Chapter 2, this sequence is nonperiodic, yet it has a periodic envelope. Other sequences can also be generated in a similar fashion. Process these signals through the above μ-law compressor, quantizer, and expander functions as shown in Figure 12.2, and compute

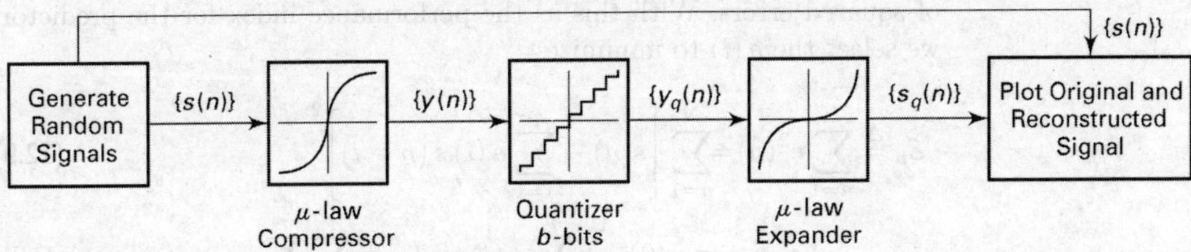

FIGURE 12.2 *PCM project*

the signal-to-quantization noise ratio (SQNR) in dB as

$$\text{SQNR} = 10 \log_{10} \left(\frac{\sum_{n=1}^{N} s^2(n)}{\sum_{n=1}^{N} \left(s(n) - s_q(n) \right)^2} \right)$$

For different b-bit quantizers, systematically determine the value of μ that maximizes the SQNR. Also plot the input and output waveforms, and comment on the results.

12.2 DIFFERENTIAL PCM (DPCM)

In PCM, each sample of the waveform is encoded independently of all the other samples. However, most signals, including speech, sampled at the Nyquist rate or faster exhibit significant correlation between successive samples. In other words, the average change in amplitude between successive samples is relatively small. Consequently, an encoding scheme that exploits the redundancy in the samples will result in a lower bit rate for the speech signal.

A relatively simple solution is to encode the differences between successive samples rather than the samples themselves. Since differences between samples are expected to be smaller than the actual sampled amplitudes, fewer bits are required to represent the differences. A refinement of this general approach is to predict the current sample based on the previous p samples. To be specific, let $s(n)$ denote the current sample of speech, and let $\hat{s}(n)$ denote the predicted value of $s(n)$, defined as

$$\hat{s}(n) = \sum_{i=1}^{p} a\,(i)\,s\,(n-i) \tag{12.8}$$

Thus $\hat{s}(n)$ is a weighted linear combination of the past p samples, and the $a\,(i)$ are the predictor (filter) coefficients. The $a\,(i)$ are selected to minimize some function of the error between $s(n)$ and $\hat{s}(n)$.

A mathematically and practically convenient error function is the sum of squared errors. With this as the performance index for the predictor, we select the $a\,(i)$ to minimize

$$\mathcal{E}_p \stackrel{\triangle}{=} \sum_{n=1}^{N} e^2(n) = \sum_{n=1}^{N} \left[s(n) - \sum_{i=1}^{p} a\,(i)\,s\,(n-i) \right]^2 \tag{12.9}$$

$$= r_{ss}\,(0) - 2 \sum_{i=1}^{p} a\,(i)\,r_{ss}\,(i) + \sum_{i=1}^{p} \sum_{j=1}^{p} a\,(i)\,a\,(j)\,r_{ss}\,(i-j)$$

where $r_{ss}(m)$ is the autocorrelation function of the sampled signal sequence $s(n)$, defined as

$$r_{ss}(m) = \sum_{i=1}^{N} s(i)\, s(i+m) \tag{12.10}$$

Minimization of $\mathcal{E}_p$ with respect to the predictor coefficients $\{a_i(n)\}$ results in the set of linear equations, called the normal equations,

$$\sum_{i=1}^{p} a(i)\, r_{ss}(i-j) = r_{ss}(j), \quad j = 1, 2, \ldots, p \tag{12.11}$$

or in the matrix form,

$$\mathbf{Ra} = \mathbf{r} \Longrightarrow \mathbf{a} = \mathbf{R}^{-1}\mathbf{r} \tag{12.12}$$

where $\mathbf{R}$ is the autocorrelation matrix, $\mathbf{a}$ is the coefficient vector, and $\mathbf{r}$ is the autocorrelation vector. Thus the values of the predictor coefficients are established.

Having described the method for determining the predictor coefficients, let us now consider the block diagram of a practical DPCM system, shown in Figure 12.3. In this configuration, the predictor is implemented with the feedback loop around the quantizer. The input to the predictor is denoted as $\tilde{s}(n)$, which represents the signal sample $s(n)$ modified by the quantization process, and the output of the predictor is

$$\widehat{\tilde{s}} = \sum_{i=1}^{p} a(i)\, \tilde{s}(n-i) \tag{12.13}$$

The difference

$$e(n) = s(n) - \widehat{\tilde{s}}(n) \tag{12.14}$$

is the input to the quantizer, and $\tilde{e}(n)$ denotes the output. Each value of the quantized prediction error $\tilde{e}(n)$ is encoded into a sequence of binary

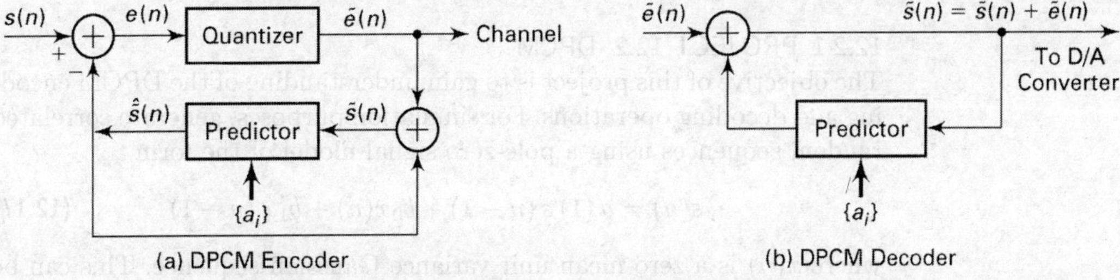

FIGURE 12.3 *Block diagram of a DPCM transcoder: (a) encoder, (b) decoder*

digits and transmitted over the channel to the receiver. The quantized error $\tilde{e}(n)$ is also added to the predicted value $\widehat{\tilde{s}}(n)$ to yield $\tilde{s}(n)$.

At the receiver, the same predictor that was used at the transmitting end is synthesized, and its output $\widehat{\tilde{s}}(n)$ is added to $\tilde{e}(n)$ to yield $\tilde{s}(n)$. The signal $\tilde{s}(n)$ is the desired excitation for the predictor and also the desired output sequence from which the reconstructed signal $\tilde{s}(t)$ is obtained by filtering, as shown in Figure 12.3b.

The use of feedback around the quantizer, as described, ensures that the error in $\tilde{s}(n)$ is simply the quantization error $q(n) = \tilde{e}(n) - e(n)$ and that there is no accumulation of previous quantization errors in the implementation of the decoder. That is,

$$q(n) = \tilde{e}(n) - e(n) = \tilde{e}(n) - s(n) + \widehat{\tilde{s}}(n) = \tilde{s}(n) - s(n) \qquad (12.15)$$

Hence $\tilde{s}(n) = s(n) + q(n)$. This means that the quantized sample $\tilde{s}(n)$ differs from the input $s(n)$ by the quantization error $q(n)$ independent of the predictor used. Therefore, the quantization errors do not accumulate.

In the DPCM system illustrated in Figure 12.3, the estimate or predicted value $\tilde{s}(n)$ of the signal sample $s(n)$ is obtained by taking a linear combination of past values $\tilde{s}(n-k)$, $k = 1, 2, \ldots, p$, as indicated by (12.13). An improvement in the quality of the estimate is obtained by including linearly filtered past values of the quantized error. Specifically, the estimate of $s(n)$ may be expressed as

$$\widehat{\tilde{s}}(n) = \sum_{i=1}^{p} a(i)\,\tilde{s}(n-i) + \sum_{i=1}^{m} b(i)\,\tilde{e}(n-i) \qquad (12.16)$$

where $b(i)$ are the coefficients of the filter for the quantized error sequence $\tilde{e}(n)$. The block diagram of the encoder at the transmitter and the decoder at the receiver are shown in Figure 12.4. The two sets of coefficients $a(i)$ and $b(i)$ are selected to minimize some function of the error $e(n) = \tilde{s}(n) - s(n)$, such as the sum of squared errors.

By using a logarithmic compressor and a 4-bit quantizer for the error sequence $e(n)$, DPCM results in high-quality speech at a rate of 32 kbps, which is a factor of 2 lower than logarithmic PCM.

12.2.1 PROJECT 12.2: DPCM

The objective of this project is to gain understanding of the DPCM encoding and decoding operations. For simulation purposes, generate correlated random sequences using a pole-zero signal model of the form

$$s(n) = a(1)\,s(n-1) + b_0 x(n) + b_1 x(n-1) \qquad (12.17)$$

where $x(n)$ is a zero-mean unit variance Gaussian sequence. This can be done using the `filter` function. The sequences developed in Project 12.1

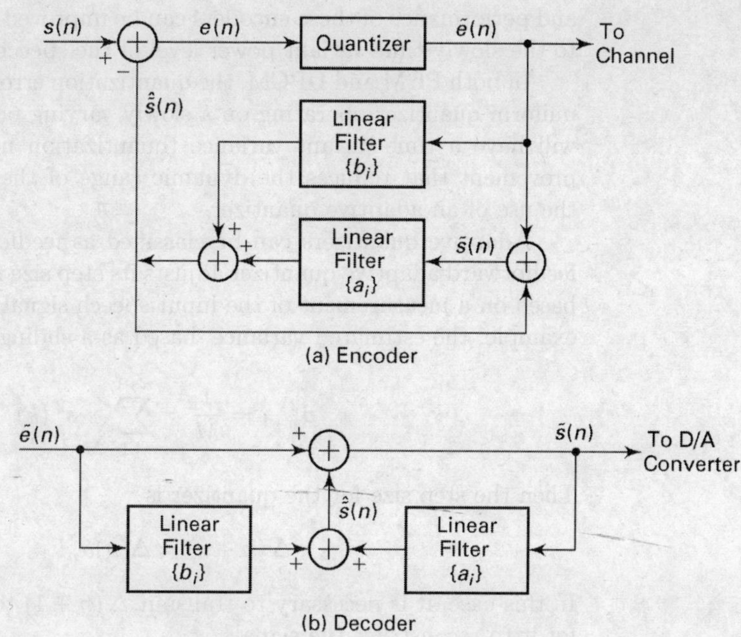

FIGURE 12.4   *DPCM modified by the linearly filtered error sequence*

can also be used for simulation. Develop the following three MATLAB modules for this project:

1. a model predictor function to implement (12.12), given the input signal $s(n)$;
2. a DPCM encoder function to implement the block diagram of Figure 12.3a, which accepts a zero-mean input sequence and produces a quantized b-bit integer error sequence, where b is a free parameter; and
3. a DPCM decoder function of Figure 12.3b, which reconstructs the signal from the quantized error sequence.

Experiment with several p-order prediction models for a given signal and determine the optimum order. Compare this DPCM implementation with the PCM system of Project 12.1 (at the end of the chapter) and comment on the results. Extend this implementation to include an mth-order moving average filter as indicated in (12.16).

12.3 ADAPTIVE PCM AND DPCM (ADPCM)

In general, the power in a speech signal varies slowly with time. PCM and DPCM encoders, however, are designed on the basis that the speech signal power is constant, and hence the quantizer is fixed. The efficiency and performance of these encoders can be improved by having them adapt to the slowly time-variant power level of the speech signal.

In both PCM and DPCM, the quantization error $q(n)$ resulting from a uniform quantizer operating on a slowly varying power level input signal will have a time-variant variance (quantization noise power). One improvement that reduces the dynamic range of the quantization noise is the use of an adaptive quantizer.

Adaptive quantizers can be classified as feedforward or feedback. A feedforward adaptive quantizer adjusts its step size for each signal sample, based on a measurement of the input speech signal variance (power). For example, the estimated variance, based as a sliding window estimator, is

$$\hat{\sigma}^2_{n+1} = \frac{1}{M} \sum_{k=n+1-M}^{n+1} s^2(k) \tag{12.18}$$

Then the step size for the quantizer is

$$\Delta(n+1) = \Delta(n)\hat{\sigma}_{n+1} \tag{12.19}$$

In this case, it is necessary to transmit $\Delta(n+1)$ to the decoder in order for it to reconstruct the signal.

A feedback-adaptive quantizer employs the output of the quantizer in the adjustment of the step size. In particular, we may set the step size as

$$\Delta(n+1) = \alpha(n)\Delta(n) \tag{12.20}$$

where the scale factor $\alpha(n)$ depends on the previous quantizer output. For example, if the previous quantizer output is small, we may select $\alpha(n) < 1$ in order to provide for finer quantization. On the other hand, if the quantizer output is large, then the step size should be increased to reduce the possibility of signal clipping. Such an algorithm has been successfully used in the encoding of speech signals. Figure 12.5 illustrates such a (3-bit) quantizer in which the step size is adjusted recursively according to the relation

$$\Delta(n+1) = \Delta(n) \cdot M(n)$$

where $M(n)$ is a multiplication factor whose value depends on the quantizer level for the sample $s(n)$ and $\Delta(n)$ is the step size of the quantizer for processing $s(n)$. Values of the multiplication factors optimized for speech encoding have been given by [39]. These values are displayed in Table 12.1 for 2-, 3-, and 4-bit quantization for PCM and DPCM.

In DPCM, the predictor can also be made adaptive. Thus in ADPCM, the coefficients of the predictor are changed periodically to reflect the changing signal statistics of the speech. The linear equations given by (12.11) still apply, but the short-term autocorrelation function of $s(n)$, $r_{ss}(m)$ changes with time.

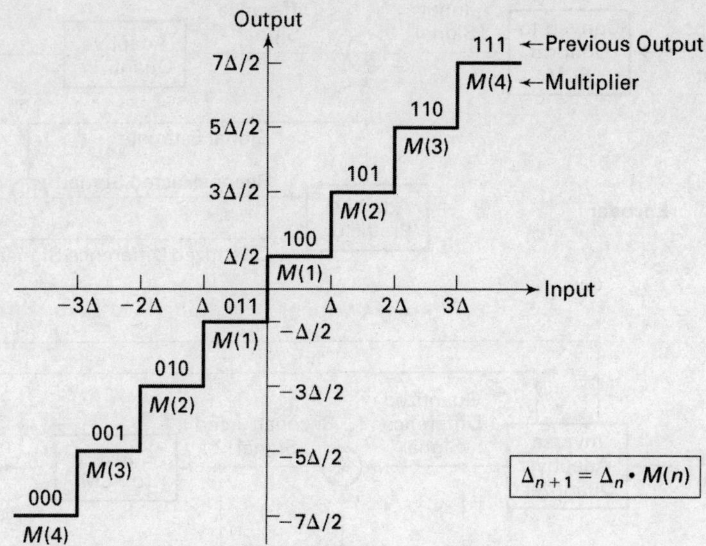

FIGURE 12.5 *Example of a quantizer with an adaptive step size ([39])*

TABLE 12.1 *Multiplication factors for adaptive step-size adjustment ([39])*

	PCM			DPCM		
	2	3	4	2	3	4
$M(1)$	0.60	0.85	0.80	0.80	0.90	0.90
$M(2)$	2.20	1.00	0.80	1.60	0.90	0.90
$M(3)$		1.00	0.80		1.25	0.90
$M(4)$		1.50	0.80		1.70	0.90
$M(5)$			0.80			1.20
$M(6)$			0.80			1.60
$M(7)$			0.80			2.00
$M(8)$			0.80			2.40

12.3.1 ADPCM STANDARD

Figure 12.6 illustrates, in block diagram form, a 32 kbps ADPCM encoder and decoder that has been adopted as an international (CCITT) standard for speech transmission over telephone channels. The ADPCM encoder is designed to accept 8-bit PCM compressed signal samples at 64 kbps, and by means of adaptive prediction and adaptive 4-bit quantization to reduce the bit rate over the channel to 32 kbps. The ADPCM decoder accepts the 32 kbps data stream and reconstructs the signal in the form of an 8-bit compressed PCM at 64 kbps. Thus we have a configuration shown in Figure 12.7, where the ADPCM encoder/decoder is embedded into a PCM system. Although the ADPCM encoder/decoder

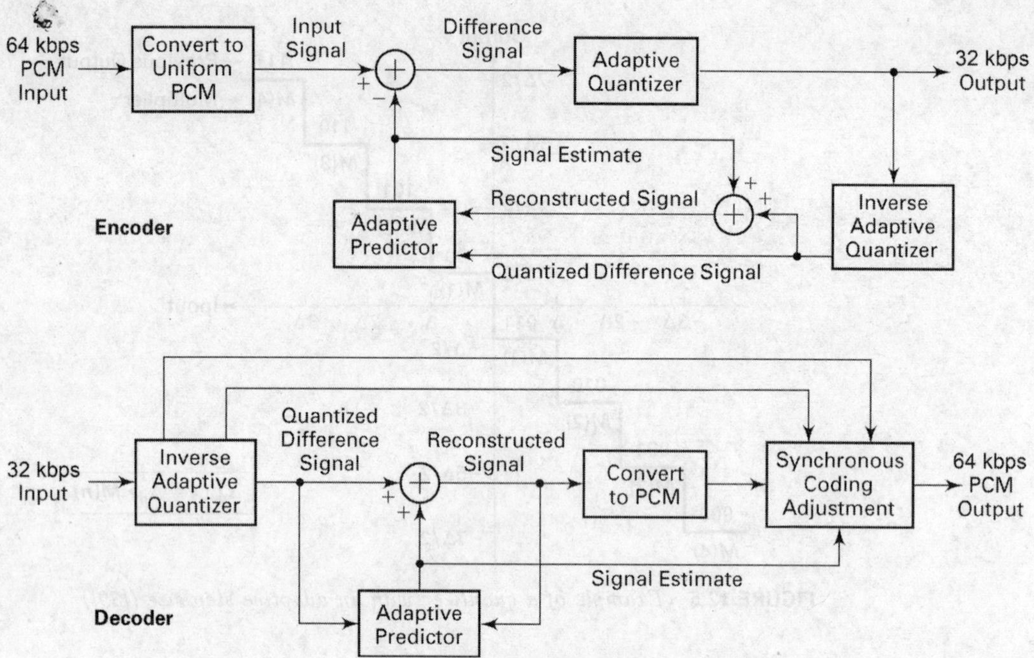

FIGURE 12.6   *ADPCM block diagram*

could be used directly on the speech signal, the interface to the PCM
system is necessary in practice in order to maintain compatibility with
existing PCM systems that are widely used in the telephone network.

The ADPCM encoder accepts the 8-bit PCM compressed signal and
expands it to a 14-bit-per-sample linear representation for processing. The
predicted value is subtracted from this 14-bit linear value to produce a
difference signal sample that is fed to the quantizer. Adaptive quantization is performed on the difference signal to produce a 4-bit output for
transmission over the channel.

Both the encoder and decoder update their internal variables, based
only on the ADPCM values that are generated. Consequently, an ADPCM

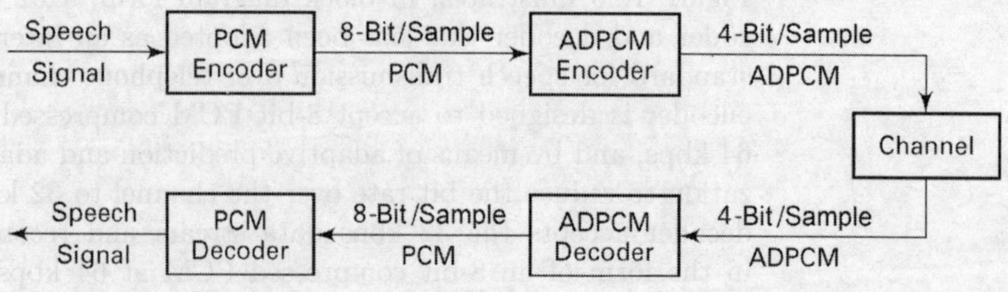

FIGURE 12.7   *ADPCM interface to PCM system*

decoder, including an inverse adaptive quantizer, is embedded in the encoder so that all internal variables are updated, based on the same data. This ensures that the encoder and decoder operate in synchronism without the need to transmit any information on the values of internal variables.

The adaptive predictor computes a weighted average of the last six dequantized difference values and the last two predicted values. Hence this predictor is basically a two-pole ($p = 2$) and six-zero ($m = 6$) filter governed by the difference equation given by (12.16). The filter coefficients are updated adaptively for every new input sample.

At the receiving decoder and at the decoder that is embedded in the encoder, the 4-bit transmitted ADPCM value is used to update the inverse adaptive quantizer, whose output is a dequantized version of the difference signal. This dequantized value is added to the value generated by the adaptive predictor to produce the reconstructed speech sample. This signal is the output of the decoder, which is converted to compressed PCM format at the receiver.

12.3.2 PROJECT 12.3: ADPCM

The objective of this project is to gain familiarity with, and understanding of, ADPCM and its interface with a PCM encoder/decoder (transcoder). As described, the ADPCM transcoder is inserted between the PCM compressor and the PCM expander as shown in Figure 12.7. Use the already developed MATLAB PCM and DPCM modules for this project.

The input to the PCM-ADPCM transcoder system can be supplied from internally generated waveform data files, just as in the case of the PCM project. The output of the transcoder can be plotted. Comparisons should be made between the output signal from the PCM-ADPCM transcoder with the signal from the PCM transcoder (PCM Project 12.1), and with the original input signal.

12.4 DELTA MODULATION (DM)

Delta modulation may be viewed as a simplified form of DPCM in which a two-level (1-bit) quantizer is used in conjunction with a fixed first-order predictor. The block diagram of a DM encoder-decoder is shown in Figure 12.8. We note that

$$\widehat{\tilde{s}}(n) = \tilde{s}(n-1) = \widehat{\tilde{s}}(n-1) + \tilde{e}(n-1) \qquad (12.21)$$

Since

$$q(n) = \tilde{e}(n) - e(n) = \tilde{e}(n) - \left[s(n) - \widehat{\tilde{s}}(n)\right]$$

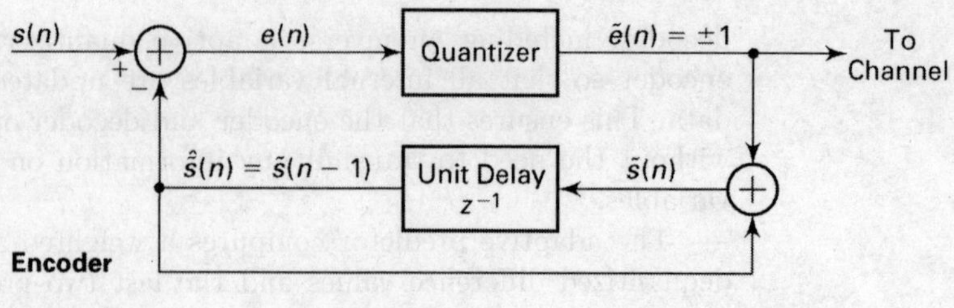

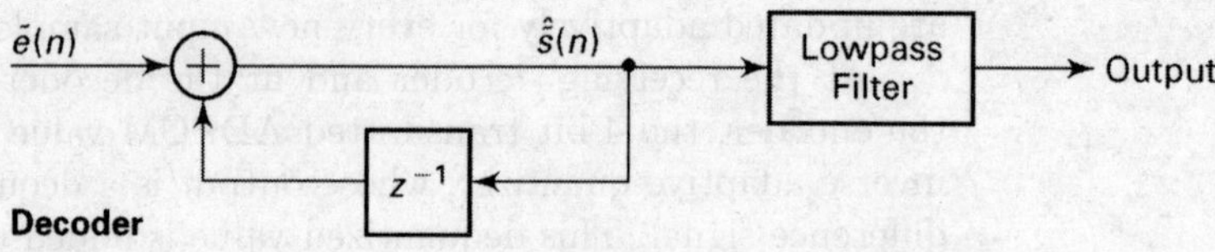

FIGURE 12.8   *Block diagram of a delta modulation system*

it follows that

$$\widehat{\tilde{s}}(n) = s(n-1) + q(n-1) \tag{12.22}$$

Thus the estimated (predicted) value of $s(n)$ is really the previous sample $s(n-1)$ modified by the quantization noise $q(n-1)$. We also note that the difference equation in (12.21) represents an integrator with an input $\tilde{e}(n)$. Hence an equivalent realization of the one-step predictor is an accumulator with an input equal to the quantized error signal $\tilde{e}(n)$. In general, the quantized error signal is scaled by some value—say, Δ_1—which is called the step size. This equivalent realization is illustrated in Figure 12.9. In effect, the encoder shown in Figure 12.9 approximates a waveform $s(t)$

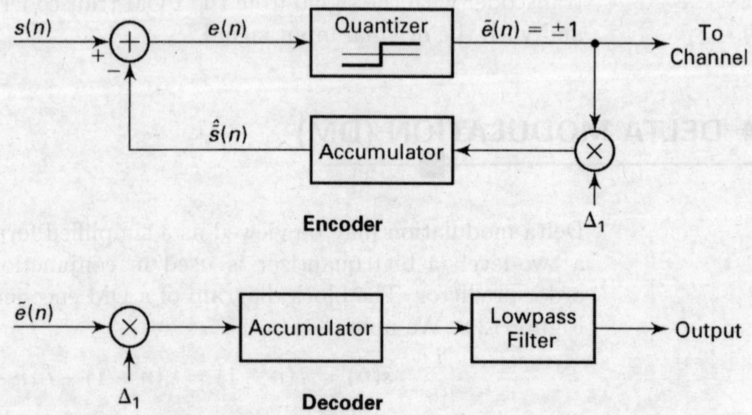

FIGURE 12.9   *An equivalent realization of a delta modulation system*

by a linear staircase function. In order for the approximation to be relatively good, the waveform $s(t)$ must change slowly relative to the sampling rate. This requirement implies that the sampling rate must be several (a factor of at least 5) times the Nyquist rate. A lowpass filter is usually incorporated into the decoder to smooth out discontinuities in the reconstructed signal.

12.4.1 ADAPTIVE DELTA MODULATION (ADM)

At any given sampling rate, the performance of the DM encoder is limited by two types of distortion, as shown in Figure 12.10. One is called slope-overload distortion. It is due to the use of a step size Δ_1 that is too small to follow portions of the waveform that have a steep slope. The second type of distortion, called granular noise, results from using a step size that is too large in parts of the waveform having a small slope. The need to minimize both of these two types of distortion results in conflicting requirements in the selection of the step size Δ_1.

An alternative solution is to employ a variable size that adapts itself to the short-term characteristics of the source signal. That is, the step size is increased when the waveform has a steep slope and decreased when the waveform has a relatively small slope.

A variety of methods can be used to set adaptively the step size in every iteration. The quantized error sequence $\tilde{e}(n)$ provides a good indication of the slope characteristics of the waveform being encoded. When the quantized error $\tilde{e}(n)$ is changing signs between successive iterations, this is an indication that the slope of the waveform in the locality is relatively small. On the other hand, when the waveform has a steep slope, successive values of the error $\tilde{e}(n)$ are expected to have identical signs. From these observations, it is possible to devise algorithms that decrease or increase the step size, depending on successive values of $\tilde{e}(n)$. A relatively simple rule devised by [38] is to vary adaptively the step size according to the relation

$$\Delta(n) = \Delta(n-1) K^{\tilde{e}(n)\tilde{e}(n-1)}, \quad n = 1, 2, \ldots \qquad \textbf{(12.23)}$$

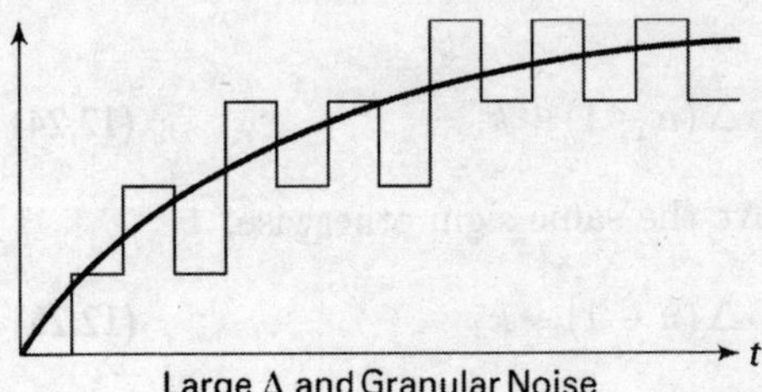

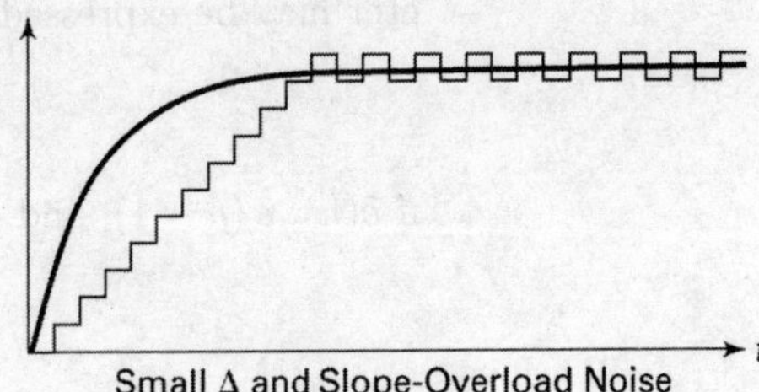

FIGURE 12.10 *Two types of distortion in the DM encoder*

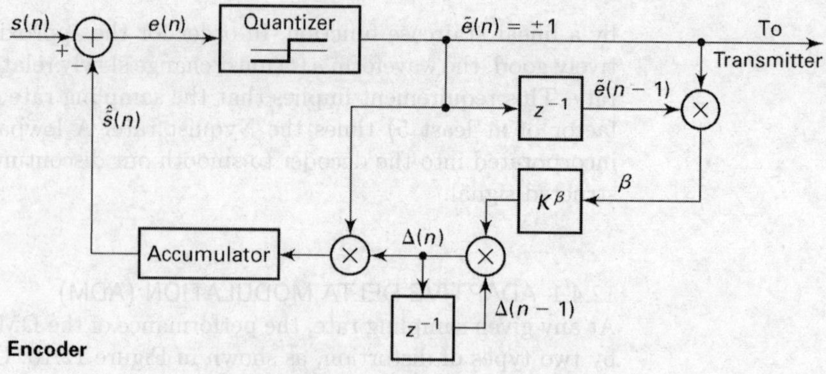

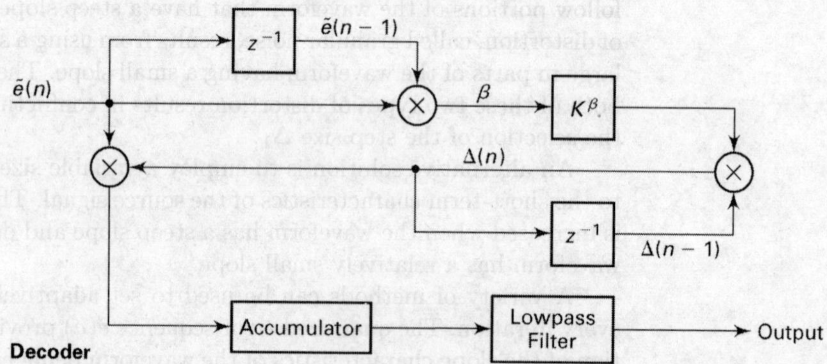

FIGURE 12.11 *An example of a delta modulation system with adaptive step size*

where $K \geq 1$ is a constant that is selected to minimize the total distortion. A block diagram of a DM encoder-decoder that incorporates this adaptive algorithm is illustrated in Figure 12.11.

Several other variations of adaptive DM encoding have been investigated and described in the technical literature. A particularly effective and popular technique first proposed by [27] is called *continuously variable slope delta modulation* (CVSD). In CVSD, the adaptive step-size parameter may be expressed as

$$\Delta(n) = \alpha\Delta(n-1) + k_1 \tag{12.24}$$

if $\tilde{e}(n)$, $\tilde{e}(n-1)$, and $\tilde{e}(n-2)$ have the same sign; otherwise,

$$\Delta(n) = \alpha\Delta(n-1) + k_2 \tag{12.25}$$

The parameters α, k_1, and k_2 are selected such that $0 < \alpha < 1$ and $k_1 > k_2 > 0$. For more discussion on this and other variations of adaptive

DM, the interested reader is referred to the papers by Jayant [39] and Flanagan et al. [15] and to the extensive references contained in these papers.

12.4.2 PROJECT 12.4: DM AND ADM

The purpose of this project is to gain an understanding of delta modulation and adaptive delta modulation for coding of waveforms. This project involves writing MATLAB functions for the DM encoder and decoder as shown in Figure 12.9, and for the ADM encoder and decoder shown in Figure 12.11. The lowpass filter at the decoder can be implemented as a linear-phase FIR filter. For example, a Hanning filter that has the impulse response

$$h(n) = \frac{1}{2}\left[1 - \cos\left(\frac{2\pi n}{N-1}\right)\right], \quad 0 \leq n \leq N-1 \tag{12.26}$$

may be used, where the length N may be selected in the range $5 \leq N \leq 15$.

The input to the DM and ADM systems can be supplied from the waveforms generated in Project 12.1 except that the sampling rate should be higher by a factor of 5 to 10. The output of the decoder can be plotted. Comparisons should be made between the output signal from the DM and ADM decoders and the original input signal.

12.5 LINEAR PREDICTIVE CODING (LPC) OF SPEECH

The linear predictive coding (LPC) method for speech analysis and synthesis is based on modeling the vocal tract as a linear all-pole (IIR) filter having the system function

$$H(z) = \frac{G}{1 + \displaystyle\sum_{k=1}^{p} a_p(k)\, z^{-k}} \tag{12.27}$$

where p is the number of poles, G is the filter gain, and $\{a_p(k)\}$ are the parameters that determine the poles. There are two mutually exclusive excitation functions to model voiced and unvoiced speech sounds. On a short-time basis, voiced speech is periodic with a fundamental frequency F_0, or a pitch period $1/F_0$, which depends on the speaker. Thus voiced speech is generated by exciting the all-pole filter model by a periodic impulse train with a period equal to the desired pitch period. Unvoiced speech sounds are generated by exciting the all-pole filter model by the output of a random-noise generator. This model is shown in Figure 12.12.

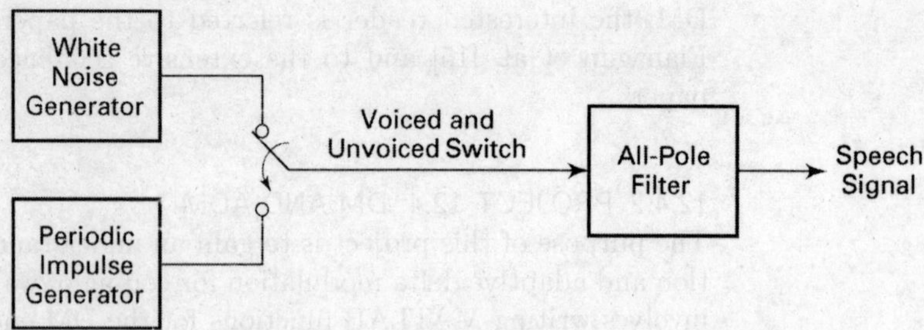

FIGURE 12.12 *Block diagram model for the generation of a speech signal*

Given a short-time segment of a speech signal, usually about 20 ms or 160 samples at an 8 kHz sampling rate, the speech encoder at the transmitter must determine the proper excitation function, the pitch period for voiced speech, the gain parameter G, and the coefficients $a_p(k)$. A block diagram that illustrates the speech encoding system is given in Figure 12.13. The parameters of the model are determined adaptively from the data and encoded into a binary sequence and transmitted to the receiver. At the receiver, the speech signal is synthesized from the model and the excitation signal.

The parameters of the all-pole filter model are easily determined from the speech samples by means of linear prediction. To be specific, the output of the FIR linear prediction filter is

$$\hat{s}(n) = -\sum_{k=1}^{p} a_p(k)\, s(n-k) \tag{12.28}$$

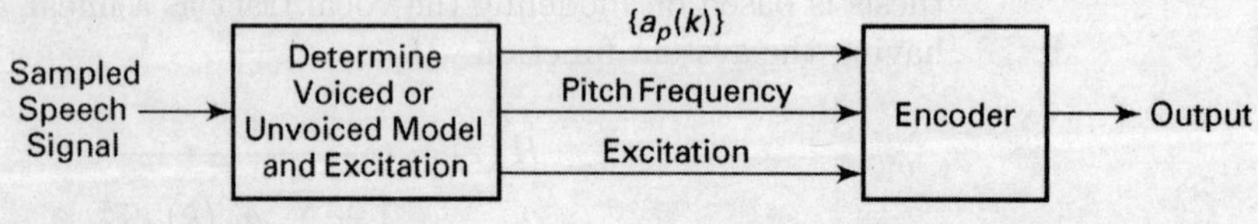

FIGURE 12.13 *Encoder and decoder for LPC*

and the corresponding error between the observed sample $s(n)$ and the predicted value $\hat{s}(n)$ is

$$e(n) = s(n) + \sum_{k=1}^{p} a_p(k)\, s(n-k) \tag{12.29}$$

By minimizing the sum of squared errors, that is,

$$\mathcal{E} = \sum_{n=0}^{N} e^2(n) = \sum_{n=0}^{N} \left[s(n) + \sum_{k=1}^{p} a_p(k)\, s(n-k) \right]^2 \tag{12.30}$$

we can determine the pole parameters $\{a_p(k)\}$ of the model. The result of differentiating $\mathcal{E}$ with respect to each of the parameters and equating the result to zero is a set of p linear equations

$$\sum_{k=1}^{p} a_p(k)\, r_{ss}(m-k) = -r_{ss}(m), \quad m = 1, 2, \ldots, p \tag{12.31}$$

where $r_{ss}(m)$ is the autocorrelation of the sequence $s(n)$ defined as

$$r_{ss}(m) = \sum_{n=0}^{N} s(n) s(n+m) \tag{12.32}$$

The linear equation (12.31) can be expressed in matrix form as

$$\mathbf{R}_{ss}\mathbf{a} = -\mathbf{r}_{ss} \tag{12.33}$$

where $\mathbf{R}_{ss}$ is a $p \times p$ autocorrelation matrix, $\mathbf{r}_{ss}$ is a $p \times 1$ autocorrelation vector, and $\mathbf{a}$ is a $p \times 1$ vector of model parameters. Hence

$$\mathbf{a} = -\mathbf{R}_{ss}^{-1}\mathbf{r}_{ss} \tag{12.34}$$

These equations can also be solved recursively and most efficiently, without resorting to matrix inversion, by using the Levinson–Durbin algorithm [54]. However, in MATLAB it is convenient to use the matrix inversion. The all-pole filter parameters $\{a_p(k)\}$ can be converted to the all-pole lattice parameters $\{K_i\}$ (called the reflection coefficients) using the MATLAB function `dir2latc` developed in Chapter 6.

The gain parameter of the filter can be obtained by noting that its input-output equation is

$$s(n) = -\sum_{k=1}^{p} a_p(k)\, s(n-k) + Gx(n) \tag{12.35}$$

where $x(n)$ is the input sequence. Clearly,

$$Gx(n) = s(n) + \sum_{k=1}^{p} a_p(k)\, s(n-k) = e(n)$$

Then

$$G^2 \sum_{n=0}^{N-1} x^2(n) = \sum_{n=0}^{N-1} e^2(n) \tag{12.36}$$

If the input excitation is normalized to unit energy by design, then

$$G^2 = \sum_{n=0}^{N-1} e^2(n) = r_{ss}(0) + \sum_{k=1}^{p} a_p(k) r_{ss}(k) \tag{12.37}$$

Thus G^2 is set equal to the residual energy resulting from the least-squares optimization.

Once the LPC coefficients are computed, we can determine whether the input speech frame is voiced, and if so, what the pitch is. This is accomplished by computing the sequence

$$r_e(n) = \sum_{k=1}^{p} r_a(k) r_{ss}(n-k) \tag{12.38}$$

where $r_a(k)$ is defined as

$$r_a(k) = \sum_{i=1}^{p} a_p(i) a_p(i+k) \tag{12.39}$$

which is the autocorrelation sequence of the prediction coefficients. The pitch is detected by finding the peak of the normalized sequence $r_e(n)/r_e(0)$ in the time interval that corresponds to 3 to 15 ms in the 20 ms sampling frame. If the value of this peak is at least 0.25, the frame of speech is considered voiced with a pitch period equal to the value of $n = N_p$, where $r_e(N_p)/r_e(0)$ is a maximum. If the peak value is less than 0.25, the frame of speech is considered unvoiced and the pitch is zero.

The values of the LPC coefficients, the pitch period, and the type of excitation are transmitted to the receiver, where the decoder synthesizes the speech signal by passing the proper excitation through the all-pole filter model of the vocal tract. Typically, the pitch period requires 6 bits, and the gain parameter may be represented by 5 bits after its dynamic range is compressed logarithmically. If the prediction coefficients were to be coded, they would require between 8 to 10 bits per coefficient for accurate representation. The reason for such high accuracy is that relatively small changes in the prediction coefficients result in a large change in the pole positions of the filter model. The accuracy requirements are lessened by transmitting the reflection coefficients $\{K_i\}$, which have a smaller dynamic range—that is, $|K_i| < 1$. These are adequately represented by 6 bits per coefficient. Thus for a tenth-order predictor, the total number of bits assigned to the model parameters per frame is 72. If the model parameters are changed every 20 μsec, the resulting bit rate is 3,600 bps. Since the reflection coefficients are usually transmitted to the receiver, the synthesis filter at the receiver is implemented as an all-pole lattice filter, described in Chapter 6.

12.5.1 PROJECT 12.5: LPC

The objective of this project is to analyze a speech signal through an LPC coder and then to synthesize it through the corresponding PLC decoder. Use several `.wav` sound files (sampled at 8000 sam/sec rate), which are available in MATLAB for this purpose. Divide speech signals into short-time segments (with lengths between 120 and 150 samples) and process each segment to determine the proper excitation function (voiced or unvoiced), the pitch period for voiced speech, the coefficients $\{a_p(k)\}$ ($p \leq 10$), and the gain G. The decoder that performs the synthesis is an all-pole lattice filter whose parameters are the reflection coefficients that can be determined from $\{a_p(k)\}$. The output of this project is a synthetic speech signal that can be compared with the original speech signal. The distortion effects due to LPC analysis/synthesis may be assessed qualitatively.

12.6 DUAL-TONE MULTIFREQUENCY (DTMF) SIGNALS

DTMF is the generic name for push-button telephone signaling that is equivalent to the Touch Tone system in use within the Bell System. DTMF also finds widespread use in electronic mail systems and telephone banking systems in which the user can select options from a menu by sending DTMF signals from a telephone.

In a DTMF signaling system, a combination of a high-frequency tone and a low-frequency tone represent a specific digit or the characters * and #. The eight frequencies are arranged as shown in Figure 12.14, to accommodate a total of 16 characters, 12 of which are assigned as shown, while the other four are reserved for future use.

DTMF signals are easily generated in software and detected by means of digital filters, also implemented in software, that are tuned to the eight frequency tones. Usually, DTMF signals are interfaced to the analog world via a *codec* (coder/decoder) chip or by linear A/D and D/A converters. Codec chips contain all the necessary A/D and D/A, sampling, and filtering circuitry for a bidirectional analog/digital interface.

The DTMF tones may be generated either mathematically or from a look-up table. In a hardware implementation (e.g., in a digital signal

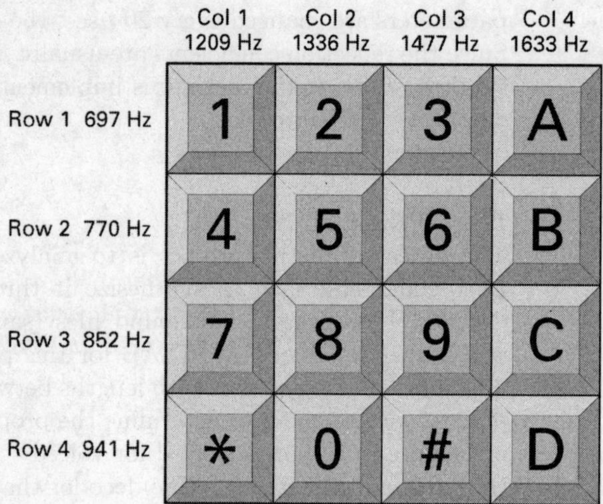

FIGURE 12.14 *DTMF digits*

processor), digital samples of two sine waves are generated mathematically, scaled, and added together. The sum is logarithmically compressed
and sent to the codec for conversion to an analog signal. At an 8 kHz
sampling rate, the hardware must output a sample every 125 ms. In this
case, a sine look-up table is not used, because the values of the sine wave
can be computed quickly without using the large amount of data memory that a table look-up would require. For simulation and investigation
purposes, the look-up table might be a good approach in MATLAB.

At the receiving end, the logarithmically compressed, 8-bit digital
data words from the codec are received and logarithmically expanded to
their 16-bit linear format. Then the tones are detected to decide on the
transmitted digit. The detection algorithm can be a DFT implementation using the FFT algorithm or a filter bank implementation. For the
relatively small number of tones to be detected, the filter bank implementation is more efficient. We now describe the use of the Goertzel algorithm
to implement the eight tuned filters.

Recall from the discussion in Chapter 5 that the DFT of an N-point
data sequence $\{x(n)\}$ is

$$X(k) = \sum_{n=0}^{N-1} x(n)W_N^{nk}, \quad k = 0, 1, \ldots, N-1 \tag{12.40}$$

If the FFT algorithm is used to perform the computation of the DFT,
the number of computations (complex multiplications and additions) is
$N \log_2 N$. In this case, we obtain all N values of the DFT at once.

However, if we desire to compute only M points of the DFT, where $M < \log_2 N$, then a direct computation of the DFT is more efficient. The Goertzel algorithm, which is now described, is basically a linear filtering approach to the computation of the DFT and provides an alternative to direct computation.

12.6.1 THE GOERTZEL ALGORITHM

The Goertzel algorithm exploits the periodicity of the phase factors $\{W_N^k\}$ and allows us to express the computation of the DFT as a linear filtering operation. Since $W_N^{-kN} = 1$, we can multiply the DFT by this factor. Thus

$$X(k) = W_N^{-kN} X(k) = \sum_{m=0}^{N-1} x(m) W_N^{-k(N-m)} \tag{12.41}$$

We note that (12.41) is in the form of a convolution. Indeed, if we define the sequence $y_k(n)$ as

$$y_k(n) = \sum_{m=0}^{N-1} x(m) W_N^{-k(n-m)} \tag{12.42}$$

then it is clear that $y_k(n)$ is the convolution of the finite-duration input sequence $x(n)$ of length N with a filter that has an impulse response

$$h_k(n) = W_N^{-kn} u(n) \tag{12.43}$$

The output of this filter at $n = N$ yields the value of the DFT at the frequency $\omega_k = 2\pi k/N$. That is,

$$X(k) = y_k(n)\big|_{n=N} \tag{12.44}$$

as can be verified by comparing (12.41) with (12.42).

The filter with impulse response $h_k(n)$ has the system function

$$H_k(z) = \frac{1}{1 - W_N^{-k} z^{-1}} \tag{12.45}$$

This filter has a pole on the unit circle at the frequency $\omega_k = 2\pi k/N$. Thus the entire DFT can be computed by passing the block of input data into a parallel bank of N single-pole filters (resonators), where each filter has a pole at the corresponding frequency of the DFT.

Instead of performing the computation of the DFT as in (12.42), via convolution, we can use the difference equation corresponding to the filter given by (12.45) to compute $y_k(n)$ recursively. Thus we have

$$y_k(n) = W_N^{-k} y_k(n-1) + x(n), \quad y_k(-1) = 0 \tag{12.46}$$

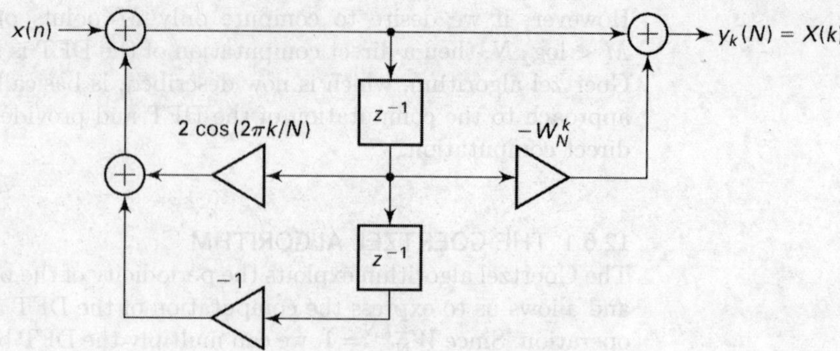

FIGURE 12.15 *Realization of two-pole resonator for computing the DFT*

The desired output is $X(k) = y_k(N)$. To perform this computation, we can compute once and store the phase factor W_N^{-k}.

The complex multiplications and additions inherent in (12.46) can be avoided by combining the pairs of resonators possessing complex conjugate poles. This leads to two-pole filters with system functions of the form

$$H_k(z) = \frac{1 - W_N^k z^{-1}}{1 - 2\cos(2\pi k/N)\, z^{-1} + z^{-2}} \tag{12.47}$$

The realization of the system illustrated in Figure 12.15 is described by the difference equations

$$v_k(n) = 2\cos\frac{2\pi k}{N} v_k(n-1) - v_k(n-2) + x(n) \tag{12.48}$$

$$y_k(n) = v_k(n) - W_N^k v_k(n-1) \tag{12.49}$$

with initial conditions $v_k(-1) = v_k(-2) = 0$. This is the Goertzel algorithm.

The recursive relation in (12.48) is iterated for $n = 0, 1, \ldots, N$, but the equation in (12.49) is computed only once, at time $n = N$. Each iteration requires one real multiplication and two additions. Consequently, for a real input sequence $x(n)$, this algorithm requires $N + 1$ real multiplications to yield not only $X(k)$ but also, due to symmetry, the value of $X(N - k)$.

We can now implement the DTMF decoder by use of the Goertzel algorithm. Since there are eight possible tones to be detected, we require eight filters of the type given by (12.47), with each filter tuned to one of the eight frequencies. In the DTMF detector, there is no need to compute the complex value $X(k)$; the magnitude $|X(k)|$ or the magnitude-squared value $|X(k)|^2$ will suffice. Consequently, the final step in the computation of the DFT value involving the numerator term (feedforward part of the filter computation) can be simplified. In particular, we have

$$|X(k)|^2 = |y_k(N)|^2 = \left| v_k(N) - W_N^k v_k\,(N-1) \right|^2 \tag{12.50}$$

$$= v_k^2(N) + v_k^2\,(N-1) - \left(2\cos\frac{2\pi k}{N} \right) v_k(N)v_k\,(N-1)$$

Thus complex-valued arithmetic operations are completely eliminated in the DTMF detector.

12.6.2 PROJECT 12.6: DTMF SIGNALING

The objective of this project is to gain an understanding of the DTMF tone generation software and the DTMF decoding algorithm (the Goertzel algorithm). Design the following MATLAB modules:

1. a tone generation function that accepts an array containing dialing digits and produces a signal containing appropriate tones (from Figure 12.14) of 0.5 sec duration for each digit at 8 kHz sampling frequency,
2. a dial-tone generator generating samples of $(350 + 440)$ Hz frequency at 8 kHz sampling interval for a specified amount of duration, and
3. a decoding function to implement (12.50) that accepts a DTMF signal and produces an array containing dialing digits.

Generate several dialing list arrays containing a mix of digits and dial tones. Experiment with the tone generation and detection modules and comment on your observations. Use MATLAB's sound generation capabilities to listen to the tones and to observe the frequency components of the generated tones.

12.7 BINARY DIGITAL COMMUNICATIONS

Digitized speech signals that have been encoded via PCM, ADPCM, DM, and LPC are usually transmitted to the decoder by means of digital modulation. A binary digital communications system employs two signal waveforms—say, $s_1(t) = s(t)$ and $s_2(t) = -s(t)$—to transmit the binary sequence representing the speech signal. The signal waveform $s(t)$, which is nonzero over the interval $0 \le t \le T$, is transmitted to the receiver if the data bit is a 1, and the signal waveform $-s(t)$, $0 \le t \le T$ is transmitted if the data bit is a 0. The time interval T is called the signal interval, and the bit rate over the channel is $R = 1/T$ bits per second. A typical signal waveform $s(t)$ is a rectangular pulse—that is, $s(t) = A, 0 \le t \le T$—which has energy $A^2 T$.

In practice, the signal waveforms transmitted over the channel are corrupted by additive noise and other types of channel distortions that ultimately limit the performance of the communications system. As a measure of performance, we normally use the average probability of error, which is often called the bit error rate.

12.7.1 PROJECT 12.7: BINARY DATA COMMUNICATIONS SYSTEM

The purpose of this project is to investigate the performance of a binary data communications system on an additive noise channel by means of simulation. The basic configuration of the system to be simulated is shown in Figure 12.16. Five MATLAB functions are required.

1. A binary data generator module that generates a sequence of independent binary digits with equal probability.
2. A modulator module that maps a binary digit 1 into a sequence of M consecutive $+1$'s, and maps a binary digit 0 into a sequence of M consecutive -1's. Thus the M consecutive $+1$'s represent a sampled version of the rectangular pulse.
3. A noise generator that generates a sequence of uniformly distributed numbers over the interval $(-a, a)$. Each noise sample is added to a corresponding signal sample.
4. A demodulator module that sums the M successive outputs of the noise corrupted sequence $+1$'s or -1's received from the channel. We assume that the demodulator is time synchronized so that it knows the beginning and end of each waveform.
5. A detector and error-counting module. The detector compares the output of the modulator with zero and decides in favor of 1 if the output is greater than zero and in favor of zero if the output is less than zero. If the output of the detector does not agree with the transmitted bit from the transmitter, an error is counted by the counter. The error rate depends on the ratio (called signal-to-noise ratio) of the size of M to the additive noise power, which is $P_n = a^2/3$.

The measured error rate can be plotted for different signal-to-noise ratios, either by changing M and keeping P_n fixed or vice versa.

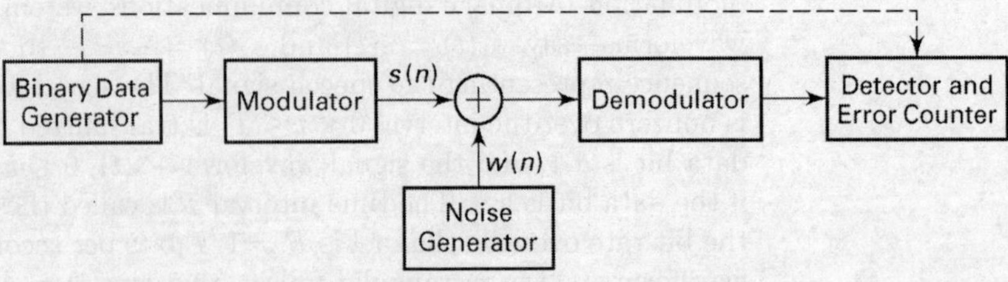

FIGURE 12.16 *Model of binary data communications system*

12.8 SPREAD-SPECTRUM COMMUNICATIONS

Spread-spectrum signals are often used in the transmission of digital data over communication channels that are corrupted by interference due to intentional jamming or from other users of the channel (e.g., cellular telephones and other wireless applications). In applications other than communications, spread-spectrum signals are used to obtain accurate range (time delay) and range rate (velocity) measurements in radar and navigation. For the sake of brevity, we shall limit our discussion to the use of spread spectrum for digital communications. Such signals have the characteristic that their bandwidth is much greater than the information rate in bits per second.

In combatting intentional interference (jamming), it is important to the communicators that the jammer who is trying to disrupt their communication does not have prior knowledge of the signal characteristics. To accomplish this, the transmitter introduces an element of unpredictability or randomness (pseudo-randomness) in each of the possible transmitted signal waveforms, which is known to the intended receiver, but not to the jammer. As a consequence, the jammer must transmit an interfering signal without knowledge of the pseudo-random characteristics of the desired signal.

Interference from other users arises in multiple-access communications systems in which a number of users share a common communications channel. At any given time, a subset of these users may transmit information simultaneously over a common channel to corresponding receivers. The transmitted signals in this common channel may be distinguished from one another by superimposing a different pseudo-random pattern, called a *multiple-access code*, in each transmitted signal. Thus a particular receiver can recover the transmitted data intended for it by knowing the pseudo-random pattern—that is, the key used by the corresponding transmitter. This type of communication technique, which allows multiple users to simultaneously use a common channel for data transmission, is called *code division multiple access* (CDMA).

The block diagram shown in Figure 12.17 illustrates the basic elements of a spread-spectrum digital communications system. It differs

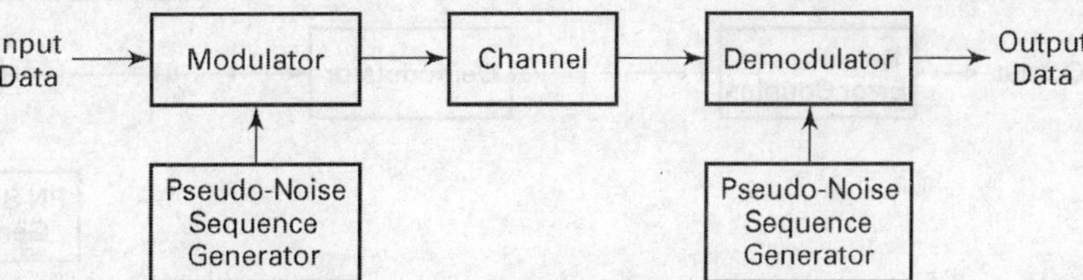

FIGURE 12.17 *Basic spread-spectrum digital communications system*

from a conventional digital communications system by the inclusion of two identical pseudo-random pattern generators, one that interfaces with the modulator at the transmitting end and a second that interfaces with the demodulator at the receiving end. The generators generate a pseudo-random or *pseudo-noise* (PN) binary-valued sequence ($\pm$1's), which is impressed on the transmitted signal at the modulator and removed from the received signal at the demodulator.

Synchronization of the PN sequence generated at the demodulator with the PN sequence contained in the incoming received signal is required in order to demodulate the received signal. Initially, prior to the transmission of data, synchronization is achieved by transmitting a short fixed PN sequence to the receiver for purposes of establishing synchronization. After time synchronization of the PN generators is established, the transmission of data commences.

12.8.1 PROJECT 12.8: BINARY SPREAD-SPECTRUM COMMUNICATIONS

The objective of this project is to demonstrate the effectiveness of a PN spread-spectrum signal in suppressing sinusoidal interference. Let us consider the binary communication system described in Project 12.7, and let us multiply the output of the modulator by a binary ($\pm$1) PN sequence. The same binary PN sequence is used to multiply the input to the demodulator and thus to remove the effect of the PN sequence in the desired signal. The channel corrupts the transmitted signal by the addition of a

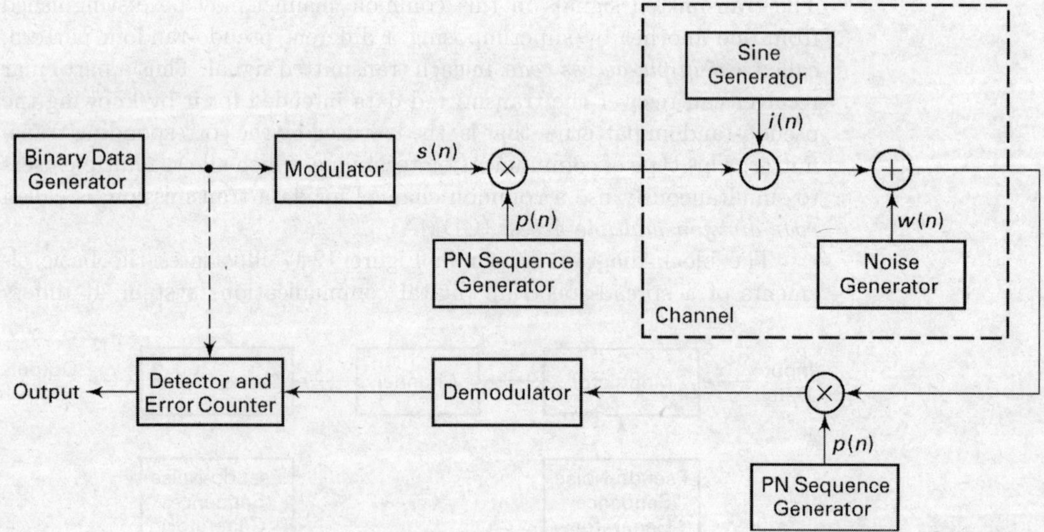

FIGURE 12.18 *Block diagram of binary PN spread-spectrum system for simulation experiment*

wideband noise sequence $\{w(n)\}$ and a sinusoidal interference sequence of the form $i(n) = A\sin\omega_0 n$, where $0 < \omega_0 < \pi$. We may assume that $A \geq M$, where M is the number of samples per bit from the modulator. The basic binary spread spectrum-system is shown in Figure 12.18. As can be observed, this is just the binary digital communication system shown in Figure 12.16, to which we have added the sinusoidal interference and the PN sequence generators. The PN sequence may be generated by using a random number generator to generate a sequence of equally probable ± 1's.

Execute the simulated system with and without the use of the PN sequence, and measure the error rate under the condition that $A \geq M$ for different values of M, such as $M = 50, 100, 500, 1000$. Explain the effect of the PN sequence on the sinusoidal interference signal. Thus explain why the PN spread-spectrum system outperforms the conventional binary communication system in the presence of the sinusoidal jamming signal.

BIBLIOGRAPHY

[1] F. S. Beckman. "The Solution of Linear Equations by the Conjugate Gradient Method," in *Mathematical Methods for Digital Computers*, A. Ralston and H. S. Wilf, eds., Wiley, New York, 1960.

[2] G. J. Bierman. *Factorization Methods for Discrete Sequential Estimation*, Academic Press, New York, 1977.

[3] R. C. Brown. *Introduction to Random Signal Analysis and Kalman Filtering*, Wiley, New York, 1983.

[4] C. Caraiscos and B. Liu. "A Roundoff Error Analysis of the LMS Adaptive Algorithm," *IEEE Trans. Acoustics, Speech, and Signal Processing*, vol. ASSP-32, pp. 34–41, January 1984.

[5] N. A. Carlson and A. F. Culmone. "Efficient Algorithms for On-Board Array Processing," *Record 1979 International Conference on Communications*, pp. 58.1.1–58.1.5, Boston, June 10–14, 1979.

[6] C. K. Chui and G. Chen. *Kalman Filtering*, Springer-Verlag, New York, 1987.

[7] J. M. Cioffi and T. Kailath. "Windowed Fast Transversal Filters Adaptive Algorithms with Normalization," *IEEE Trans. Acoustics, Speech, and Signal Processing*, vol. ASSP-33, pp. 607–625, June 1985.

[8] J. W. Cooley and J. W. Tukey. "An Algorithm for the Machine Computation of Complex Fourier Series," *Mathematical Computations*, vol. 19, pp. 297–301, April 1965.

[9] R. E. Crochiere and L. R. Rabiner. *Multirate Digital Signal Processing*, Prentice Hall, Englewood Cliffs, NJ, 1983.

[10] C. de Boor. *A Practical Guide to Splines*, Springer-Verlag, New York, 1978.

[11] J. R. Deller, J. H. L. Hansen, and J. G. Proakis. *Discrete-Time Processing of Speech Signals*, Wiley-IEEE Press, 2000.

[12] P. Delsarte and Y. Genin. "The Split Levinson Algorithm," *IEEE Trans. Acoustics, Speech, and Signal Processing*, vol. ASSP-34, pp. 470–478, June 1986.

[13] P. Delsarte, Y. Genin, and Y. Kamp. "Orthogonal Polynomial Matrices on the Unit Circle," *IEEE Trans. Circuits and Systems*, vol. CAS-25, pp. 149–160, January 1978.

[14] J. Durbin. "Efficient Estimation of Parameters in Moving-Average Models," *Biometrika*, vol. 46, pp. 306–316, 1959.

[15] J. L. Flanagan et al. "Speech Coding," *IEEE Transactions on Communications*, vol. COM-27, pp. 710–736, April 1979.

[16] R. Fletcher and M. J. D. Powell. "A Rapidly Convergent Descent Method for Minimization," *Comput. J.*, vol. 6, pp. 163–168, 1963.

[17] B. Friedlander. "Lattice Filters for Adaptive Processing," *Proc. IEEE*, vol. 70, pp. 829–867, August 1982.

[18] B. Friedlander. "Lattice Methods for Spectral Estimation," *Proc. IEEE*, vol. 70, pp. 990–1017, September 1982.

[19] F. R. Gantmacher. *The Theory of Matrices*, vol. I, Chelsea Publishing Company, Chelsea, NY, 1960.

[20] W. A. Gardner. "Learning Characteristics of Stochastic-Gradient-Descent Algorithms: A General Study, Analysis and Critique," *Signal Processing*, vol. 6, pp. 113–133, April 1984.

[21] D. A. George, R. R. Bowen, and J. R. Storey. "An Adaptive Decision-Feedback Equalizer," *IEEE Trans. Communication Technology*, vol. COM-19, pp. 281–293, June 1971.

[22] L. Y. Geronimus. *Orthogonal Polynomials* (in Russian) (English translation by Consultant's Bureau, New York, 1961), 1958.

[23] A. Gersho. "Adaptive Equalization of Highly Dispersive Channels for Data Transmission," *Bell Syst. Tech. J.*, vol. 48, pp. 55–70, January 1969.

[24] R. D. Gitlin and S. B. Weinstein. "On the Required Tap-Weight Precision for Digitally Implemented Mean-Squared Equalizers," *Bell Syst. Tech. J.*, vol. 58, pp. 301–321, February 1979.

[25] R. D. Gitlin, H. C. Meadors, and S. B. Weinstein. "The Tap-Leakage Algorithm: An Algorithm for the Stable Operation of a Digitally Implemented Fractionally Spaced, Adaptive Equalizer," *Bell Syst. Tech. J.*, vol. 61, pp. 1817–1839, October 1982.

[26] I. Gohberg, ed. *I. Schür Methods in Operator Theory and Signal Processing*, Birkhauser Verlag, Stuttgart, Germany, 1986.

[27] J. A. Greefties. "A Digitally Companded Delta Modulation Modem for Speech Transmission," In *Proceedings of IEEE International Conference on Communications*, pp. 7.33–7.48, June 1970.

[28] O. Grenander and G. Szegö. *Toeplitz Forms and Their Applications*, University of California Press, Berkeley, CA, 1958.

[29] D. Hanselman and B. Littlefield. *Mastering MATLAB 7*, Pearson/Prentice Hall, Englewood Cliffs, NJ, 2005.

[30] S. Haykin. *Adaptive Filter Theory*, 3rd ed., Prentice-Hall, Englewood Cliffs, NJ, 1996.

[31] A. S. Householder. "Unitary Triangularization of a Non-Symmetric Matrix," *J. Assoc. Comput. Math.*, vol. 5, pp. 204–243, 1958.

[32] A. S. Householder. *The Theory of Matrices in Numerical Analysis*, Blaisdell, Waltham, MA, 1964.

[33] F. M. Hsu. "Square-Root Kalman Filtering for High-Speed Data Received over Fading Dispersive HF Channels." *IEEE Trans. Information Theory*, vol. IT-28, pp. 753–763, September 1982.

[34] F. M. Hsu and A. A. Giordano. "Digital Whitening Techniques for Improving Spread Spectrum Communications Performance in the Presence of Narrowband Jamming and Interference," *IEEE Trans. Communications*, vol. COM-26, pp. 209–216, February 1978.

[35] B. R. Hunt, R. L. Lipsman, J. M. Rosenberg, and Kevin R. Coombes. *A Guide to MATLAB: For Beginners and Experienced Users*, Cambridge University Press, New York, NY, 2001.

[36] V. K. Ingle and J. G. Proakis. *Digital Signal Processing using the ADSP-2101*, Prentice Hall, Englewood Cliffs, NJ, 1991.

[37] L. B. Jackson. "An Analysis of Limit Cycles Due to Multiplicative Rounding in Recursive Digital Filters," *Proceedings of the 7th Allerton Conference on Circuits and System Theory*, pp. 69–78, 1969.

[38] N. S. Jayant. "Adaptive Delta Modulation with One-Bit Memory," *Bell System Technical Journal*, pp. 321–342, March 1970.

[39] N. S. Jayant. "Digital Coding of Speech Waveforms: PCM, DPCM, and DM Quantizers." *Proceedings of the IEEE*, vol. 62, pp. 611–632, May 1974.

[40] S. K. Jones, R. K. Cavin, and W. M. Reed. "Analysis of Error-Gradient Adaptive Linear Equalizers for a Class of Stationary-Dependent Processes," *IEEE Trans. Information Theory*, vol. IT-28, pp. 318–329, March 1982.

[41] T. Kailath. "A View of Three Decades of Linear Filter Theory," *IEEE Trans. Information Theory*, vol. IT-20, pp. 146–181, March 1974.

[42] T. Kailath. *Lectures on Wiener and Kalman Filtering*, Springer-Verlag, New York, 1981.

[43] T. Kailath. "Linear Estimation for Stationary and Near-Stationary Processes," in *Modern Signal Processing*, T. Kailath, ed., Hemisphere Publishing Corp., Washington, D.C., 1985.

[44] T. Kailath. "A Theorem of I. Schür and Its Impact on Modern Signal Processing," in [26].

[45] T. Kailath, A. C. G. Vieira, and M. Morf. "Inverses of Toeplitz Operators, Innovations, and Orthogonal Polynomials," *SIAM Rev.*, vol. 20, pp. 1006–1019, 1978.

[46] R. E. Kalman. "A New Approach to Linear Filtering and Prediction Problems,"

Trans. ASME, J. Basic Eng., vol. 82D, pp. 35–45, March 1960.

[47] R. E. Kalman and R. S. Bucy. "New Results in Linear Filtering Theory," *Trans. ASME, J. Basic Eng.*, vol. 83, pp. 95–108, 1961.

[48] S. M. Kay. *Modern Spectral Estimation*, Prentice-Hall, Englewood Cliffs, NJ, 1988.

[49] S. M. Kay and S. L. Marple, Jr. "Spectrum Analysis: A Modern Perspective," *Proc. IEEE*, vol. 69, pp. 1380–1419, November 1981.

[50] J. W. Ketchum and J. G. Proakis. "Adaptive Algorithms for Estimating and Suppressing Narrow-Band Interference in PN Spread-Spectrum Systems," *IEEE Trans. Communications*, vol. COM-30, pp. 913–923, May 1982.

[51] H. Krishna. "New Split Levinson, Schür, and Lattice Algorithms or Digital Signal Processing," *Proc. 1988 International Conference on Acoustics, Speech, and Signal Processing*, pp. 1640–1642, New York, April 1988.

[52] S. Y. Kung and Y. H. Hu. "A Highly Concurrent Algorithm and Pipelined Architecture for Solving Toeplitz Systems," *IEEE Trans. Acoustics, Speech, and Signal Processing*, vol. ASSP-31, pp. 66–76, January 1983.

[53] A. Leon-Garcia. *Probability, Statistics, and Random Processes for Electrical Engineering*, Pearson Prentice Hall, Upper Saddle River, NJ, third edition, 2008.

[54] N. Levinson. "The Wiener RMS Error Criterion in Filter Design and Prediction," *J. Math. Phys.*, vol. 25, pp. 261–278, 1947.

[55] R. W. Lucky. "Automatic Equalization for Digital Communications," *Bell Syst. Tech. J.*, vol. 44, pp. 547–588, April 1965.

[56] F. R. Magee and J. G. Proakis. "Adaptive Maximum-Likelihood Sequence Estimation for Digital Signaling in the Presence of Intersymbol Interference," *IEEE Trans. Information Theory*, vol. IT-19, pp. 120–124, January 1973.

[57] J. Makhoul. "Linear-Prediction: A Tutorial Review," *Proc. IEEE*, vol. 63, pp. 561–580, April 1975.

[58] J. Makhoul. "Stable and Efficient Lattice Methods for Linear Prediction," *IEEE Trans. Acoustics, Speech, and Signal Processing*, vol. ASSP-25, pp. 423–428, 1977.

[59] J. Makhoul. "A Class of All-Zero Lattice Digital Filters: Properties and Applications." *IEEE Trans. Acoustics, Speech, and Signal Processing*, vol. ASSP-26, pp. 304–314, August 1978.

[60] D. G. Manolakis and V. K. Ingle. *Applied Digital Signal Processing*, Cambridge University Press, Cambridge, UK, 2011.

[61] D. G. Manolakis, V. K. Ingle, and S. M. Kogon. *Statistical and Adaptive Signal Processing*, Artech House, Norwood, MA, 2005.

[62] D. G. Manolakis, F. Ling, and J. G. Proakis. "Efficient Time-Recursive Least-Squares Algorithms for Finite-Memory Adaptive Filtering," *IEEE Trans. Circuits and Systems*, vol. CAS-34, pp. 400–408, April 1987.

[63] J. D. Markel and A. H., Gray, Jr. *Linear Prediction of Speech*, Springer-Verlag, New York, 1976.

[64] S. L. Marple, Jr. *Digital Spectral Analysis with Applications*, Prentice-Hall, Englewood Cliffs, NJ, 1987.

[65] J. E. Mazo. "On the Independence Theory of Equalizer Convergence," *Bell Syst. Tech. J.*, vol. 58, pp. 963–993, May 1979.

[66] J. E. Meditch. *Stochastic Optimal Linear Estimation and Control*, McGraw-Hill, New York, 1969.

[67] S. L. Miller and D. G. Childers. *Probability and Random Processes*, Academic Press, Burlington, MA, second edition, 2012.

[68] S. K. Mitra. *Digital Signal Processing: A Computer-Based Approach*, McGraw-Hill, New York, NY, fourth edition, 2010.

[69] W. Murray, ed. *Numerical Methods of Unconstrained Minimization*, Academic Press, New York, 1972.

[70] H. E. Nichols, A. A. Giordano, and J. G. Proakis. "MLD and MSE Algorithms

for Adaptive Detection of Digital Signals in the Presence of Interchannel Interference," *IEEE Trans. Information Theory*, vol. IT-23, pp. 563–575, September 1977.

[71] A. V. Oppenheim and R. W. Schafer. *Discrete-Time Signal Processing*, Prentice Hall, Englewood Cliffs, NJ, third edition, 2010.

[72] S. J. Orfanidis. *Introduction to Signal Processing*, Prentice Hall, Englewood Cliffs, NJ, 1996, pp. 367–383.

[73] A. Papoulis and S. U. Pillai. *Probability, Random Variables, and Stochastic Processes*, McGraw-Hill, New York, NY, fourth edition, 2002.

[74] T. W. Parks and J. H. McClellan. "A Program for the Design of Linear-Phase Finite Impulse Response Digital Filters," *IEEE Transactions on Audio and Electroacoustics*, vol. AU-20, pp. 195–199, August 1972.

[75] B. Picinbono. "Adaptive Signal Processing for Detection and Communication," in *Communication Systems and Random Process Theory*, J. K. Skwirzynski, ed., Sijthoff en Noordhoff, Alphen aan den Rijn, The Netherlands, 1978.

[76] R. Pratap. *Getting Started with MAT-LAB7: A Quick Introduction for Scientists and Engineers*, Oxford University Press, USA, 2005.

[77] J. G. Proakis. "Adaptive Digital Filters for Equalization of Telephone Channels," *IEEE Trans. Audio and Electroacoustics*, vol. AU-18, pp. 195–200, June 1970.

[78] J. G. Proakis. "Advances in Equalization for Intersymbol Interference," in *Advances in Communication Systems*, vol. 4, A. J. Viterbi, ed., Academic Press, New York, 1975.

[79] J. G. Proakis and D. G. Manolakis. *Digital Signal Processing: Principles, Algorithms and Applications*, Prentice Hall, Upper Saddle River, NJ, third edition, 1996.

[80] J. G. Proakis and J. H. Miller. "Adaptive Receiver for Digital Signaling through Channels with Intersymbol Interference," *IEEE Trans. Information Theory*, vol. IT-15, pp. 484–497, July 1969.

[81] J. G. Proakis and M. Salehi. *Digital Communications*, McGraw-Hill, New York, NY, fifth edition, 2008.

[82] J. G. Proakis and M. Salehi. *Communication Systems Engineering*, Prentice Hall, Upper Saddle River, NJ, second edition, 2012.

[83] L. R. Rabiner and B. Gold. *Theory and Applications in Digital Signal Processing*, Prentice Hall, Englewood Cliffs, NJ, 1975.

[84] L. R. Rabiner and R. W. Schafer. *Digital Processing of Speech Signals*, Prentice Hall, Englewood Cliffs, NJ, 1978.

[85] L. R. Rabiner, R. W. Schafer, and C. A. McGonegal. "An Approach to the Approximation Problem for Nonrecursive Digital Filters," *IEEE Transactions on Audio and Electroacoustics*, vol. AU-18, pp. 83–106, June 1970.

[86] E. A. Robinson and S. Treitel. "Digital Signal Processing in Geophysics," in *Applications of Digital Signal Processing*, A. V. Oppenheim, ed., Prentice-Hall, Englewood Cliffs, NJ, 1978.

[87] E. A. Robinson and S. Treitel. *Geophysical Signal Analysis*, Prentice-Hall, Englewood Cliffs, NJ, 1980.

[88] Schur. "On Power Series Which Are Bounded in the Interior of the Unit Circle," (in German) *J. Reine Angew. Math.*, vol. 147, pp. 205–232, Berlin, 1917. (For an English translation of this paper, see [26]).

[89] M. Schetzen and V. K. Ingle. *Discrete Systems Laboratory Using MATLAB*, Brooks/Cole, Pacific Grove, CA, 2000.

[90] H. Stark and J. W. Woods. *Probability, Random Processes, and Estimation Theory for Engineers*, Prentice Hall, Upper Saddle River, NJ, fourth edition, 2012.

[91] G. Szegö. *Orthogonal Polynomials*, 3rd ed., Colloquium Publishers, no. 23, American Mathematical Society, Providence, RI, 1967.

[92] S. A. Tretter. *Introduction to Discrete-Time Signal Processing*, Wiley, New York, 1976.

[93] G. Ungerboeck. "Theory on the Speed of Convergence in Adaptive Equalizers for Digital Communication," *IBM J. Res. Devel.*, vol. 16, pp. 546–555, November 1972.

[94] A. C. G. Vieira. "Matrix Orthogonal Polynomials with Applications to Autoregressive Modeling and Ladder Forms," Ph.D. dissertation, Department of Electrical Engineering, Stanford University, Stanford, Calif., December 1977.

[95] B. Widrow and M. E. Hoff, Jr. "Adaptive Switching Circuits," *IRE WESCON Conv. Rec.*, pt. 4, pp. 96–104, 1960.

[96] B. Widrow et al. "Adaptive Noise Cancelling Principles and Applications,"

Proc. IEEE, vol. 63, pp. 1692–1716, December 1975.

[97] B. Widrow, P. Mantey, and L. J. Griffiths. "Adaptive Antenna Systems," *Proc. IEEE*, vol. 55, pp. 2143–2159, December 1967.

[98] N. Wiener. *Extrapolation, Interpolation and Smoothing of Stationary Time Series with Engineering Applications*, Wiley, New York, 1949.

[99] R. D. Yates and D. J. Goodman. *Probability and Stochastic Processes*, John Wiley & Sons, Hoboken, NJ, 2005.

[100] D. Youla and N. Kazanjian. "Bauer-Type Factorization of Positive Matrices and the Theory of Matrices Orthogonal on the Unit Circle," *IEEE Trans. Circuits and Systems*, vol. CAS-25, pp. 57–69, January 1978.

INDEX

' operator, 25
& operator, 26
(:) construct, 24
* operator, 27
.* operator, 10, 26
.^ operator, 10, 24
+ operator, 26
<= operator, 26
== operator, 26

A

Absolute specifications, FIR filter design, 292–293
Adaptive delta modulation (ADM), 599–600, 601
Adaptive differential PCM (ADPCM), 586
Adaptive direct-form FIR filters, *815–848*
  least-mean-square (LMS) algorithm, *820–824*
  MATLAB implementation of, *823–824*
  MATLAB scripts, *838*
  minimum mean-square-error criterion, *816–820*
  properties of the LMS algorithm, *824–841*
  recursive least-squares algorithms, *841–848*
Adaptive equalizers, 573
Adaptive filters, 573–585, *769–849*
  applications of, *769–815*
  arrays, *813–815*
  channel equalization, 582–585, *776–782*
  coefficient adjustment, 575–578
  echo cancellation, *783–788*
  least-mean-square (LMS) algorithm, 575, *815*
  line enhancement, 582, *795–801*
  MATLAB implementation, 577–578
  MATLAB scripts, *774, 781–782, 788, 797, 798, 799, 801, 804, 805, 806, 811–813*
  narrowband interference, suppression of, 579–582, *788–795*
  noise canceling, *801–807*
  sinusoidal interference, suppression of, 581–582
  speech signals, linear predictive coding of, *807–813*
  system identification (modeling), 578–579, *771–776*
  wideband signals, 579–582, *788–795*
Adaptive line enhancer (ALE), *795–801*
Adaptive PCM and DPCM (ADPCM), 593–597
Adders, 213

Addition, signal operation, 25
Adjustable coefficients, 573
A/D quantization noise, 518–530. *See also* Quantization
  statistics of, 525
  through digital filters, 527–530
afd_butt function, 392
afd_chb1 function, 398
afd_elip function, 405
Aliasing formula, 81
Allpass filters, 381–382
Allpass function, 506
All-pole systems, estimation of poles in, *811–813*
alpha function, 483
Amplitude response, 298
ampl-res function, 303
Analog filter design (AFD) tables, 370
Analog filters
  Butterworth lowpass, 371, 385–390
  Chebyshev lowpass, 371, 394–403
  design equations, 390–391
  elliptic lowpass, 403–406
  frequency response, 298–301
  IIR filter design, 370–457
  MATLAB implementation, 387–390, 392–394, 396–403, 427–432
  phase responses, 75–77
  prototype responses, 385–407
Analog signals, 3–5, 80–97
  aliasing formula, 81
  band-limited, 82
  cubic spine interpolation, 92
  digital signal processing (DSP) compared to, 1–2
  digital-to-analog (D/A) converters, 80–81
  discrete-time Fourier analysis of, 59–102
  first-order-hold (FOH) interpolation, 91–92, 94
  impulse train conversion, 87
  interpolation, 90–94
  MATLAB implementation, 84–87, 92–97
  reconstruction of, 87–92
  sampling, 81–84
  signal processing (ASP), 3–5
  sinusoidal, 75
  zero-order-hold (ZOH) interpolation, 90–91, 94
Analog-to-digital conversion (ADC), 80
  analysis of A/D quantization noise, 518–530

U

V

W